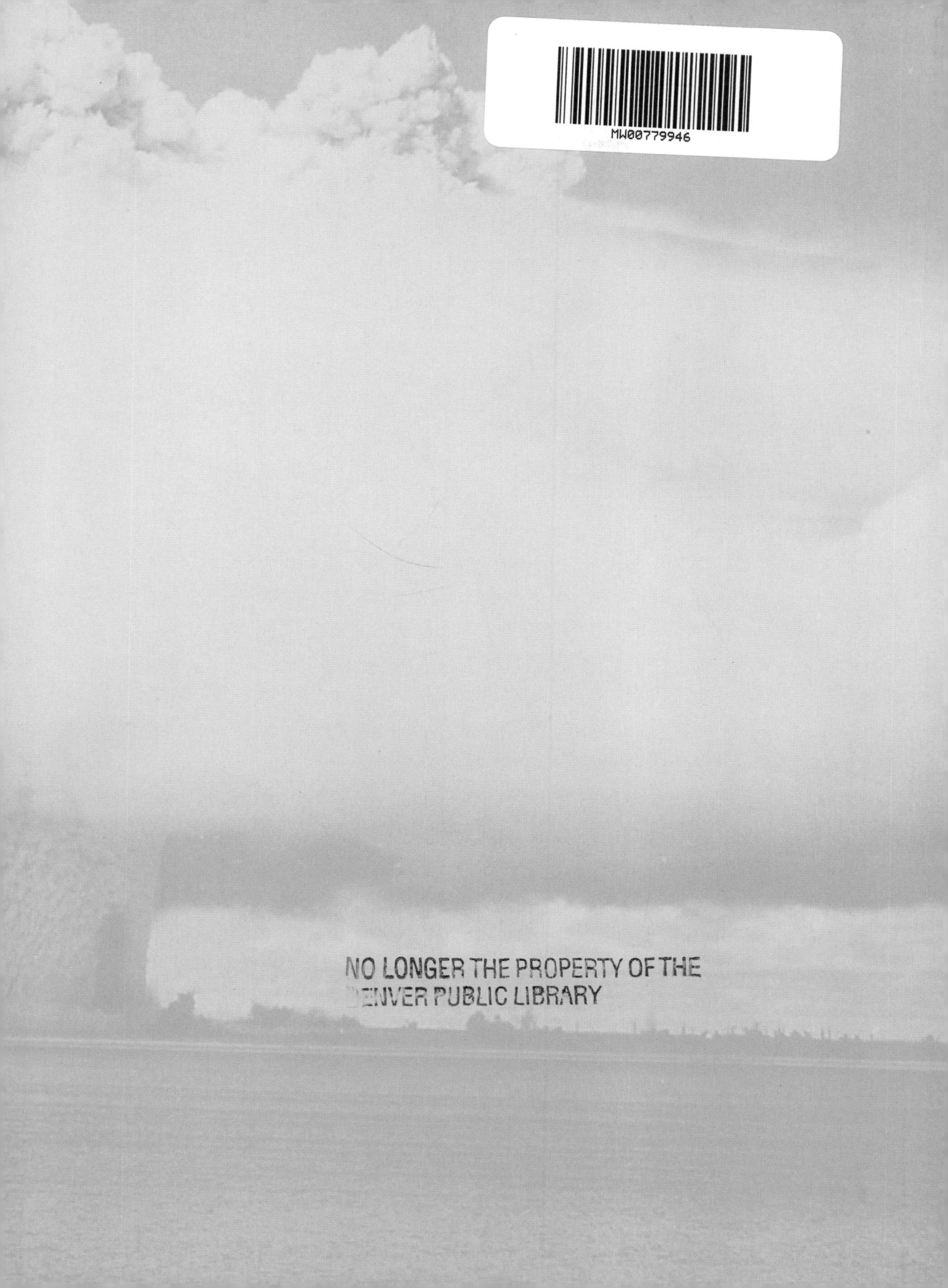

NUKE 'EM!

Classic Cold War Comics Celebrating the End of the World

Introduction by Arne R. Flaten

Hermes Press

Published by Hermes Press
Hermes Press is an imprint of Herman and Geer Communications, Inc.
2100 Wilmington Road
Neshannock, Pennsylvania 16105
www.HermesPress.com; info@hermespress.com
Daniel Herman, Publisher
Eileen Sabrina Herman, Managing Editor/Vice President
Troy Musguire, Production Manager
Alissa Fisher, Senior Graphic Designer
Kandice Hartner, Senior Editor
Benjamin Beers, Archivist

Cover and book design by Daniel Herman

First printing, 2019

From Dan, Louise, Sabrina, Jacob, Ruk'us, Noodle, and Ginger for D'Zur and Mellow

CREDITS: *Atomic War!* #1, "Sneak Attack," Ken Rice, pencils and inks; "Berlin Powderkeg," Lou Cameron, pencils and inks; and "Counterattck!," Bill Molno, pencils and inks. *Atomic War!* #2, "Operation Vengeance," Ken Rice, pencils and inks; "The Ice-Box Invasion," Jim McLaughlin, pencils and inks; and "Mission Demolition," Lou Cameron, pencils. *Atomic War!* #3, "Commando Crackerjack," Chic Stone pencils and inks; "Log of the Snorkel Wolf Pack," possibly, Sol Brodsky, pencils and inks; and "Slash by the Iron Greyhounds," Ken Rice, pencils and inks. *Atomic War!* #4, "Arctic Assault," Ken Rice, pencils and inks; "Old Timers Die Hard," Jim Mclaughlin, pencils and inks; "Operation Satellite," Lou Cameron, pencils and inks; and "Peril at Ploesti," possibly Bill Molno, pencils, Charles Nicholas, inks. *World War III* #1, Cover, Jim McLaughlin, pencils and inks; "World War III Unleashed," Robert Turner, script, Ken Rice, pencils and inks; "Operation Comeback," script, Robert Turner, Lou Cameron, pencils and inks; and "Last Stand for the Secret Missile," Robert Turner, script, Jim Mclaughlin, pencils and inks. *World War III* #2, Cover, possibly Jim McLaughlin, pencils and inks; "Jet Jammers' Jamboree," script, Robert Turner; "Commando in Mufti," script, Robert Turner, and "Devils in the Deep," script Robert Turner, Lou Cameron, pencils and inks.

LCCN applied for: 10 9 8 7 6 5 4 3 2 1
ISBN 978-1-61345-163-2

Acknowledgments: This book wouldn't be possible if not for the hard work of the design staff at Hermes Press who painstakingly reconstructed and enhanced these stories so that a new generation could enjoy them. Also a big "shout out" to Professor Arne Flaten for writing the informative essay which puts these comic book stories in proper historical and contemporary perspective.

Printed in China

NUKE 'EM!

Classic Cold War Comics Celebrating the End of the World

Contents

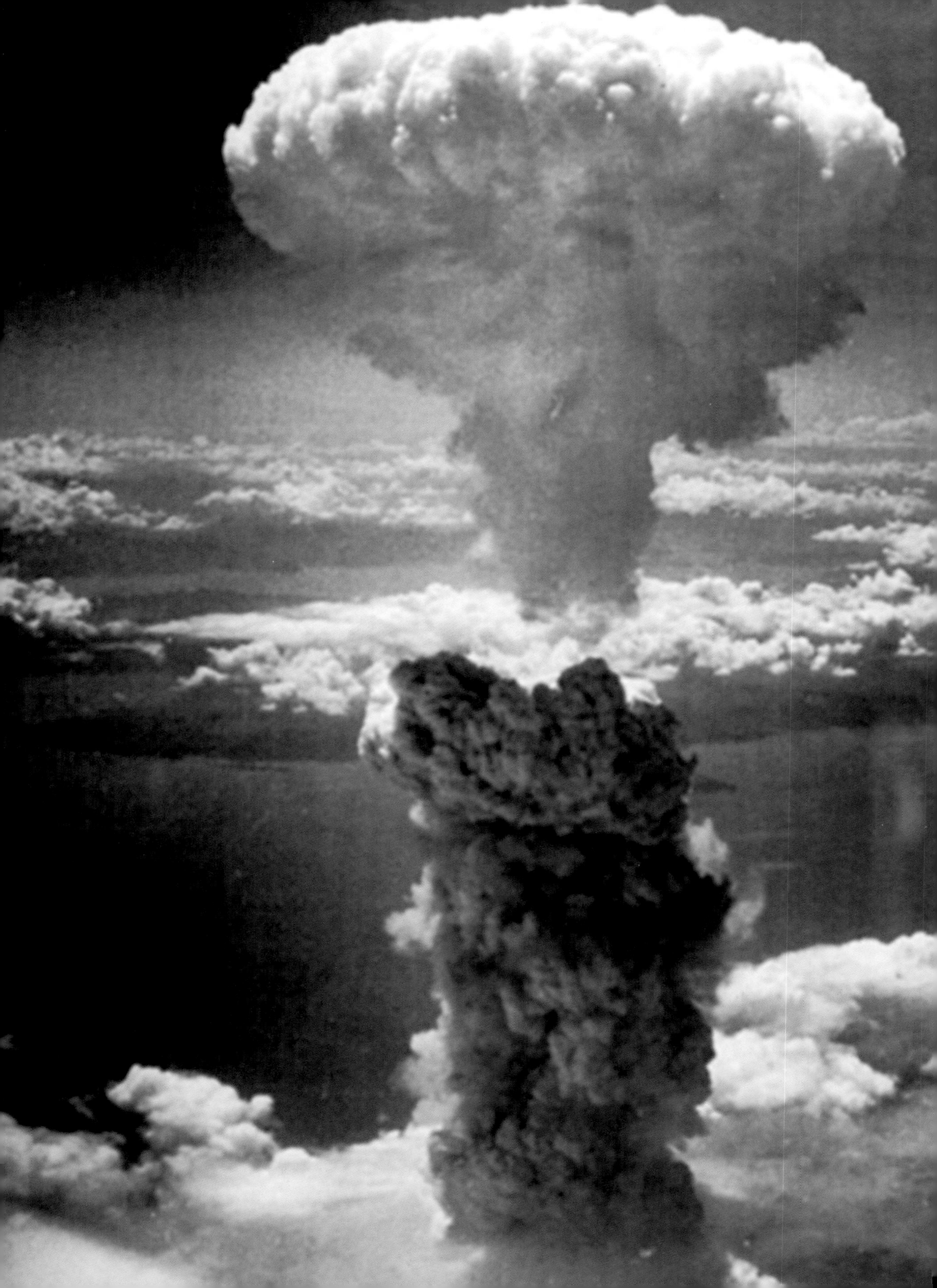

Introduction
Paranoia and Prognostications of Doom

"Let the reason for publishing this shocking account of World War III be completely clear. We want only to awaken America…and the world…to grim facts. The one way to prevent this mass destruction of humanity is to prepare NOW. Only a super-strong and fully enlightened America can stop this onrushing horror of the future!" (*World War III*, p. 1)

The contents of the present volume, collected and reproduced in their entirety here for the first time, include all four issues of *Atomic War!* and both issues of *WWIII* originally published by Ace Magazines in the early 1950s. They are not republished because of their superior artwork, prescient observations, existential musings or subtle narrative style. They are collected here because they present fascinating reflections of early Cold War America and its fears. And the message is earnest. They preach with pre-code, evangelical passion on the dangers of imminent atomic warfare. No one could accuse them of accuracy in their reductive projections of a nuclear apocalypse, but for all their sophomoric ineptness and excessive exclamation points, they echo that period's anxieties and are unnervingly relevant today.

All six comics were published between 1952 and 1954, bridging the Truman and Eisenhower presidencies, the Korean War, McCarthyism, and only seven years removed from the reduction of Hiroshima and Nagasaki to radioactive oblivion. The power and destructive force of Oppenheimer and his pals' theories had become reality: it was fresh, it

was overwhelming and it was scary. We were clearly in a different age, now. Mushroom clouds inevitably showed up on the covers of various comic books, from *Action Comics* #101 (1946) and *Atoman* #1 (1946) to *Weird Science* #18 (1953) and *Showcase* #23 (1959). Not surprisingly, the bomb became an essential backdrop to myriad stories across comic book genres. The broader view of this Atomic Age, with its dream of discovery, unlimited energy and interstellar travel, provided exceptional narrative opportunities; the comic books collected in this volume have nothing to do with those dreams.

The Nazis were defeated and the Japanese were decimated, so America turned her attention to those pesky Russians and the insidious threat of a Communist cancer. Once again, American sons and daughters were at war in a distant land as troops struggled to ward off the Reds and their infectious ideology from breaching the 38th parallel separating North from South Korea. Although concerns about a vast Russian infiltration of American democracy began much earlier, McCarthyism was firmly planted in our collective psyche by 1951 and was nurtured throughout much of the decade. It was a dark period when paranoia was high and neighbors turned

Left: Horrific image of the atomic bomb explosion over Nagasaki, Japan, detonated on August 9, 1945.

on one another in the glorious name of national security and patriotism. The bilateral stockpiling of nuclear weapons had begun and, simultaneously, the race between the USSR and the USA to put someone or something into orbit was all-consuming. Just as McCarthyism was beginning to ebb, Moscow shot a hunk of metal into the Exosphere in 1957: The Russians were winning, and America was afraid. Our fear of Russian satellites is clearly described in the third story of *Atomic War!* #4, published only three years before Sputnik.

These comic books and others like them are challenging to classify into traditional genres. At the risk of glossing over a spate of interesting and sometimes shocking details, most historians agree that the Golden Age of comic books ran from the first appearance of Superman in *Action Comics* #1, cover dated June 1938, to the implementation of the Comics Code in 1954. *Action* #1 was the not the first comic book, but it was the one that heralded a new age of adventure and profit: Heroes with amazing abilities and colorful tights quickly transformed the market from a small selection of tentative newspaper reprints with questionable financing and unpredictable sales into a billion-dollar industry. Companies such as National Allied Periodicals (DC), Timely (later Atlas, then Marvel), Quality, Fox, Fiction House, Avon, Harvey, Fawcett, MLJ, Nedor, Lev Gleason, St. John, Dell and a swarm of others fought for newsstand dominance. The end of WW2 brought most super characters to their knees, and by the early 1950s only Superman, Batman and Wonder Woman survived with any regularity. Yet the comic book business thrived, buoyed by the popularity of other genres: western, crime, romance, horror, funny animal, jungle and humor titles sold well. Indeed, by the late 1940s crime comics alone surpassed superheroes in sales and owned the largest slice of the colorful pulp-paper pie.

By 1951, romance comics outsold all other genres. During the period when *Atomic War!* and *WWIII* were published, some 150 horror comic titles were available monthly, another indicator of American fears in the early '50s. War comics continued as well, but now the sickle and hammer replaced swastikas as patent symbols of universal evil.

As their titles suggest, the books in the present collection seem to implicitly belong to the general category of war comics, but they were markedly different from the blood and glory competition. As a genre, war comics were unwaveringly, even romantically, patriotic. The only true exceptions to that mold were the brilliant, ahistorical anti-war comics published by EC: *Two-Fisted Tales* (1950-55) and *Frontline Combat* (1951-54). *Atomic War*! and *World War III* were overtly patriotic like so many war comics, but more than others they smack of hawkish, government sponsored propaganda, similar in tenor to short "educational" films such as Atomic Attack starring Phyllis Thaxter, Robert Keith and Walter Matthau (Motorola, 1954).

Atomic War! and *World War III* were not the only comic books to deal directly with nuclear war. *Atom-Age Combat* (#1-5, St. John publ., 1952-53), *Atom Age Combat* (#2-3, Fago) and *Atomic Attack!* (#5-8, Youthful Magazines, 1953) are similar in title to those in the present collection and they suggest similar content, but they are quite different. *Atom Age Combat* and *Atom-Age Combat* (it's complicated) are broader in scope than the stories collected here: they are more eclectic, more diverse in scope, often better drawn and plotted, and less unified in their anti-Russia, nuclear attack theme. As a group *Atomic Attack!* and *Atom-Age Combat* (particularly the two issues published by Fago) present as poorer cousins of various EC titles and stories, even down to typographic elements. More than war comics, *Atomic War!* and *World War III* function as apocalyptic science fiction and fantasy. Indeed, the basic plot lines might have appeared in EC titles, such as *Weird Science*, *Weird Fantasy* or *Weird Science-Fantasy* at any point during those titles' runs.

The stories in *Atomic War!* #1 are set in 1960, less than a decade after their publication dates (which suggests to readers that the horrific content is quite possible, even probable). They focus on the hours immediately before, during and after an unprovoked, well-orchestrated nuclear attack on Detroit, New York and Chicago by Russia and the subsequent response by an uncowed American spirit in spite of catastrophic losses. The intent of the comic books is clearly and unapologetically shouted across the top of every cover and opening splash page: "Only a Strong America can Avert World War III." The first story, "Sneak Attack," penciled and inked by Ken Rice, sets the stage for the series. The second story, "Berlin Powderkeg," with pencils and inks by Lou Cameron, views the same events by American soldiers stationed in Europe. "Counterattack!," by Bill Molno, finds American pilots launching their own attack from a secret airbase in Greenland. (The first issue also contains two full-page ads to buy U.S. Savings Bonds, a request for readers to write the company and win "valuable cash prizes" by telling them how successful the comic book was, and a full-page ad for a man's girdle to control the abdominal and groin areas. Subsequent issues 3 and 4 also call on Americans to buy Savings Bonds, reusing the same full-page ad several times…sometimes twice in the same book.) *Atomic War!* #2 picks up where the previous issue ended, with American retaliation and a hydrogen bomb attack on Moscow. The rest of the series follows that basic trend of offensives, counter-offensives, heroic bravery and minimal character development: The third issue finds American and U.N. forces driving the Reds back in Europe and along the New York coastline, while the final installment of the series focuses on atomic battles in the Arctic, sprinkled with not-so-subtle juxtapositions of ambient temperatures and homesickness for the South ("This oughta make southern fried chickens out 'em!"). All issues were illustrated with pencils and inks by Rice, Cameron, Jim McLaughlin, Chic Stone and perhaps Sol Brodsky. As if the reader were immune to the content, each issue reminds us on its opening splash page, "This book is designed to shock America into vigilance---and to help keep the horrors of atomic war from our shores. It CAN happen here, unless friend foe alike can be made to realize the awful devastation that another war will bring to all. So as you read these pages, pray that what you see here

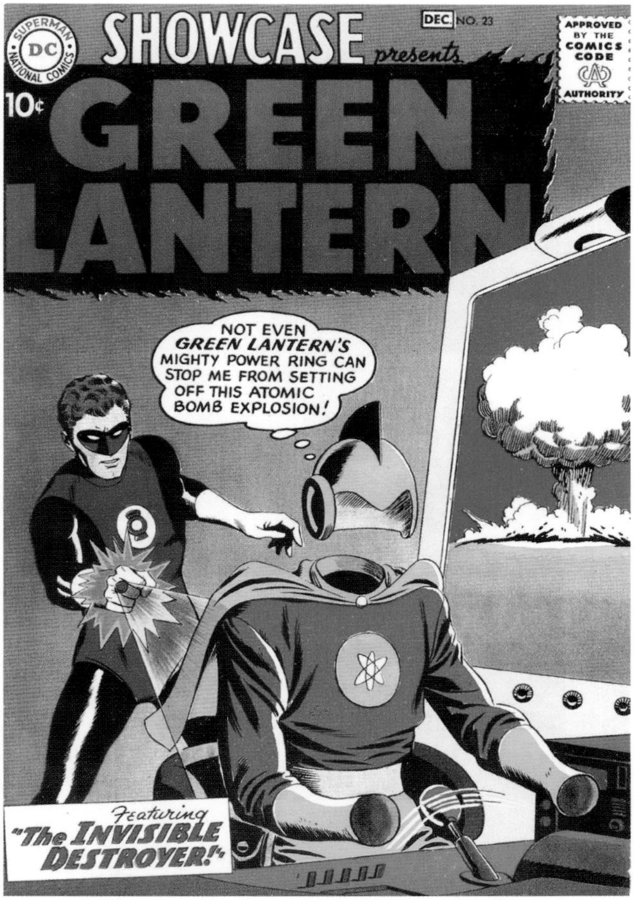
SHOWCASE presents
DEC NO. 23
10¢
APPROVED BY THE COMICS CODE AUTHORITY
GREEN LANTERN
NOT EVEN GREEN LANTERN'S MIGHTY POWER RING CAN STOP ME FROM SETTING OFF THIS ATOMIC BOMB EXPLOSION!
Featuring "The INVISIBLE DESTROYER!"

Above: Cover art from *Showcase* #23, December, 1959, Gil Kane, pencils, Joe Giella, inks, ©2019 DC Comics. Page 9: Cover art from *Weird Science* #18, March/April, 1953, Wally Wood, pencils and inks, ©2019 EC Comics.

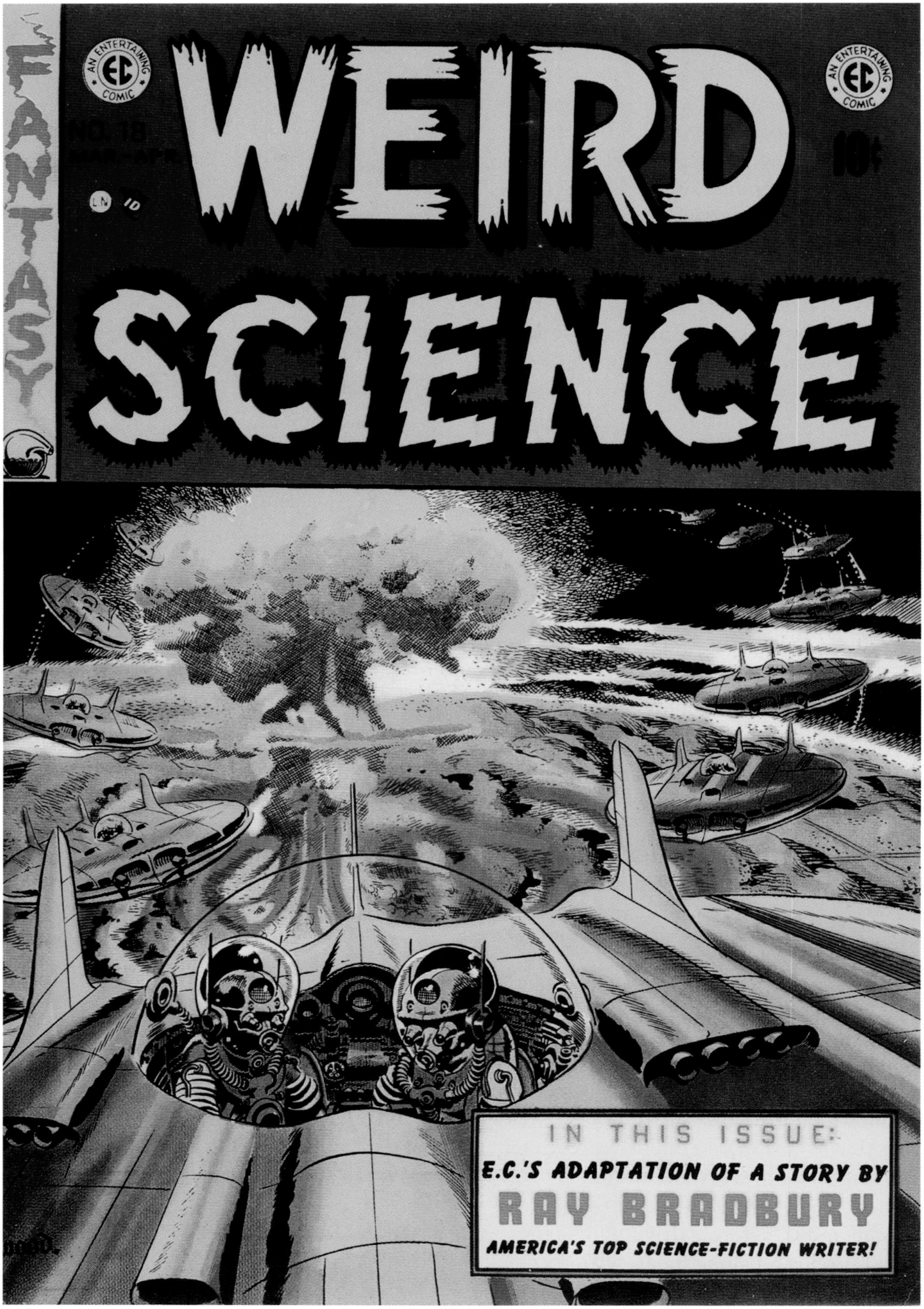
FANTASY
AN ENTERTAINING EC COMIC
WEIRD SCIENCE
10¢
IN THIS ISSUE:
E.C.'S ADAPTATION OF A STORY BY
RAY BRADBURY
AMERICA'S TOP SCIENCE-FICTION WRITER!

will never happen. And it won't---if we keep America strong!"

World War III, subtitled "The War that Will Never Happen if America Remains Strong and Alert," is bizarrely similar to *Atomic War!*, even following similar plot structures. The series starts with the nuclear destruction of Washington, D.C., followed by Manahatten and a counter-strike on Moscow. The scripts for both issues were written by Robert Turner, with pencils and inks by the same bullpen who delivered *Atomic War!* (although the artwork is somewhat improved from *Atomic War!* and there is disagreement about who worked on which stories). In both series, America's foes are painted as deceitful, ruthless, organized and fanatical devotees of mother Russia. "Americanskies" are selfless, intelligent, creative, hopeful, ethical, endlessly patriotic and sometimes gullible.

Part of the unsettling subtext to these books and others like them is their evident ignorance of or indifference to the devastating effects of nuclear radiation. Atomic explosions, as depicted in these comics, are little more than larger iterations of traditional explosions. Men run around firing atomic rifles and throwing nuclear grenades while surrounded by rampant nuclear artillery shelling and atomic Howitzers. And how can we ignore the imaginary weapons, such as Trintinium, Prometheum and Polytomic explosives, the jet-propelled ski tanks that move at two hundred miles per hour across the arctic tundra, or the devastating Jammaray? No one gets sick. No one dies from exposure. No one's skin burns off or suffers from internal organ failure. Awash in plenty of jingoist "win one for the Gipper" sentiment, there is sparse interest in horrifying medical realities, health concerns, ethical questions or scientific explanation. I suppose the same could be said for superhero comic books as well, but the latter don't purport to be true.

These books are among a subset of what might be called "Cold War comics," a proposed heading with the sole intention of providing the transition from the Golden Age to the Silver Age with slightly more nuance. Several authors in the past decade or so have started to think about this period with fresh and critical eyes. Studies of this particular period sometimes focus on how Marvel or DC superheroes in the Silver Age were created by science experiments: gamma rays, radioactive spiders, cosmic rays, lightning mixed with chemicals, etc. Other worlds, other galaxies, other universes, parallel universes, other religions and mythologies were being cranked out monthly in the late 1950s and through most of the 1960s. And while DC remained episodic and politically neutral throughout this period, Marvel introduced long plot trajectories and frequently cut its villains from Eastern Bloc cloth. Discussions of "cold war comics" also trade in conspiracy theories and governmental infiltration by T-men and operatives of a similar ilk. Of course, the Cold War was reflected in comic books in many ways beyond super heroes and spies, as William Savage and others have discussed. Collectively, putting these comic books under a lens of popular and political culture reveals a deep paranoia in the writers and publishers, and an anxiety was undoubtedly passed along to the readers. When Sputnik was launched, comic book readers knew it was coming. During the Cuban Missile Crisis, comic book readers feared the worst but they were not altogether surprised. They had read the four-color Cliff Notes on the Red Menace and nuclear war sold in drugstores and newsstands.

Are they shlock? Of course they are. So what.

—Arne R. Flaten
Purdue University

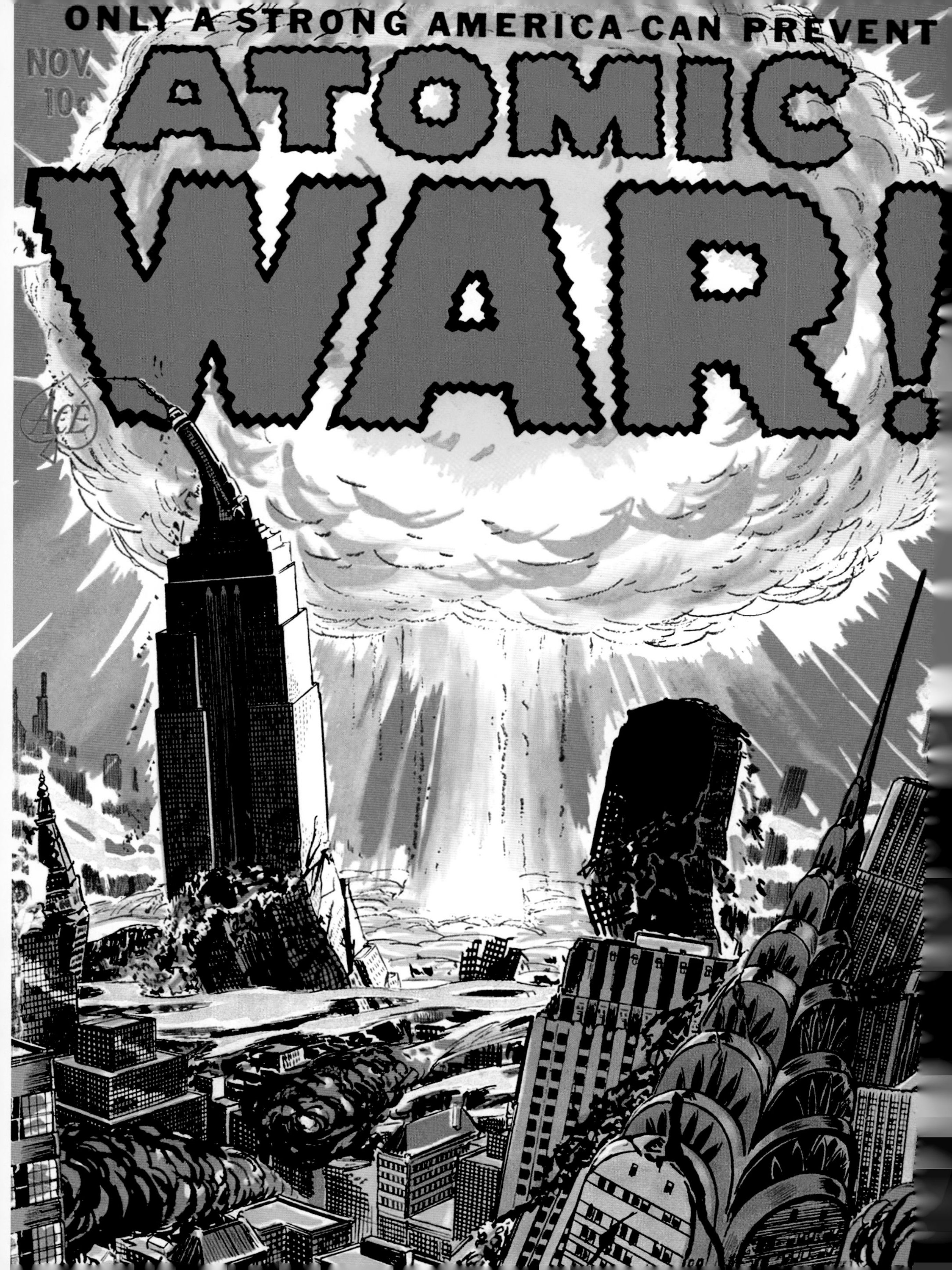
ONLY A STRONG AMERICA CAN PREVENT
NOV.
10¢
ATOMIC
WAR!
ACE

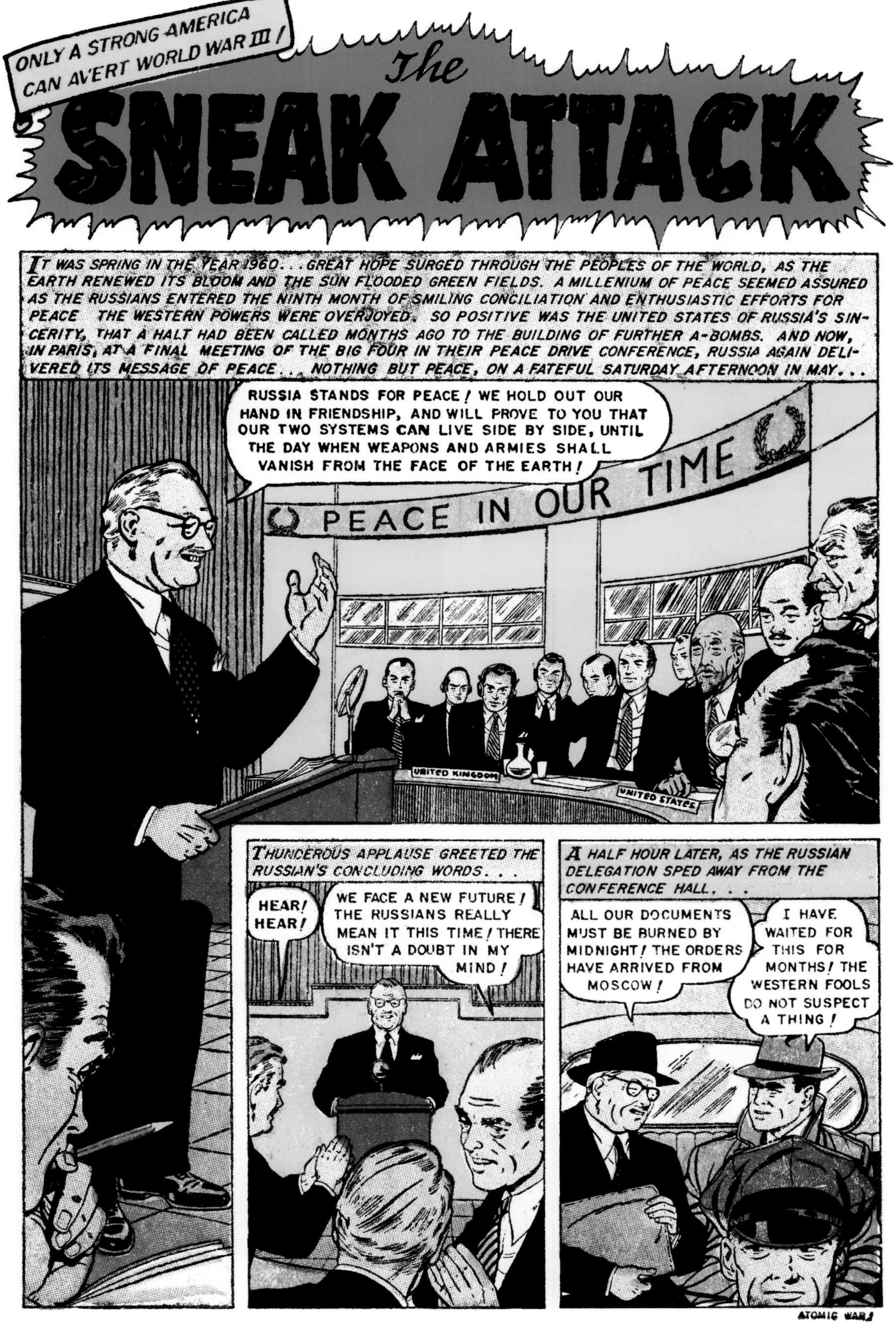
ONLY A STRONG AMERICA CAN AVERT WORLD WAR III!
The SNEAK ATTACK
IT WAS SPRING IN THE YEAR 1960... GREAT HOPE SURGED THROUGH THE PEOPLES OF THE WORLD, AS THE EARTH RENEWED ITS BLOOM AND THE SUN FLOODED GREEN FIELDS. A MILLENIUM OF PEACE SEEMED ASSURED AS THE RUSSIANS ENTERED THE NINTH MONTH OF SMILING CONCILIATION AND ENTHUSIASTIC EFFORTS FOR PEACE THE WESTERN POWERS WERE OVERJOYED. SO POSITIVE WAS THE UNITED STATES OF RUSSIA'S SINCERITY, THAT A HALT HAD BEEN CALLED MONTHS AGO TO THE BUILDING OF FURTHER A-BOMBS. AND NOW, IN PARIS, AT A FINAL MEETING OF THE BIG FOUR IN THEIR PEACE DRIVE CONFERENCE, RUSSIA AGAIN DELIVERED ITS MESSAGE OF PEACE... NOTHING BUT PEACE, ON A FATEFUL SATURDAY AFTERNOON IN MAY...
RUSSIA STANDS FOR PEACE! WE HOLD OUT OUR HAND IN FRIENDSHIP, AND WILL PROVE TO YOU THAT OUR TWO SYSTEMS CAN LIVE SIDE BY SIDE, UNTIL THE DAY WHEN WEAPONS AND ARMIES SHALL VANISH FROM THE FACE OF THE EARTH!
PEACE IN OUR TIME
UNITED KINGDOM
UNITED STATES
THUNDEROUS APPLAUSE GREETED THE RUSSIAN'S CONCLUDING WORDS...
HEAR! HEAR!
WE FACE A NEW FUTURE! THE RUSSIANS REALLY MEAN IT THIS TIME! THERE ISN'T A DOUBT IN MY MIND!
A HALF HOUR LATER, AS THE RUSSIAN DELEGATION SPED AWAY FROM THE CONFERENCE HALL...
ALL OUR DOCUMENTS MUST BE BURNED BY MIDNIGHT! THE ORDERS HAVE ARRIVED FROM MOSCOW!
I HAVE WAITED FOR THIS FOR MONTHS! THE WESTERN FOOLS DO NOT SUSPECT A THING!

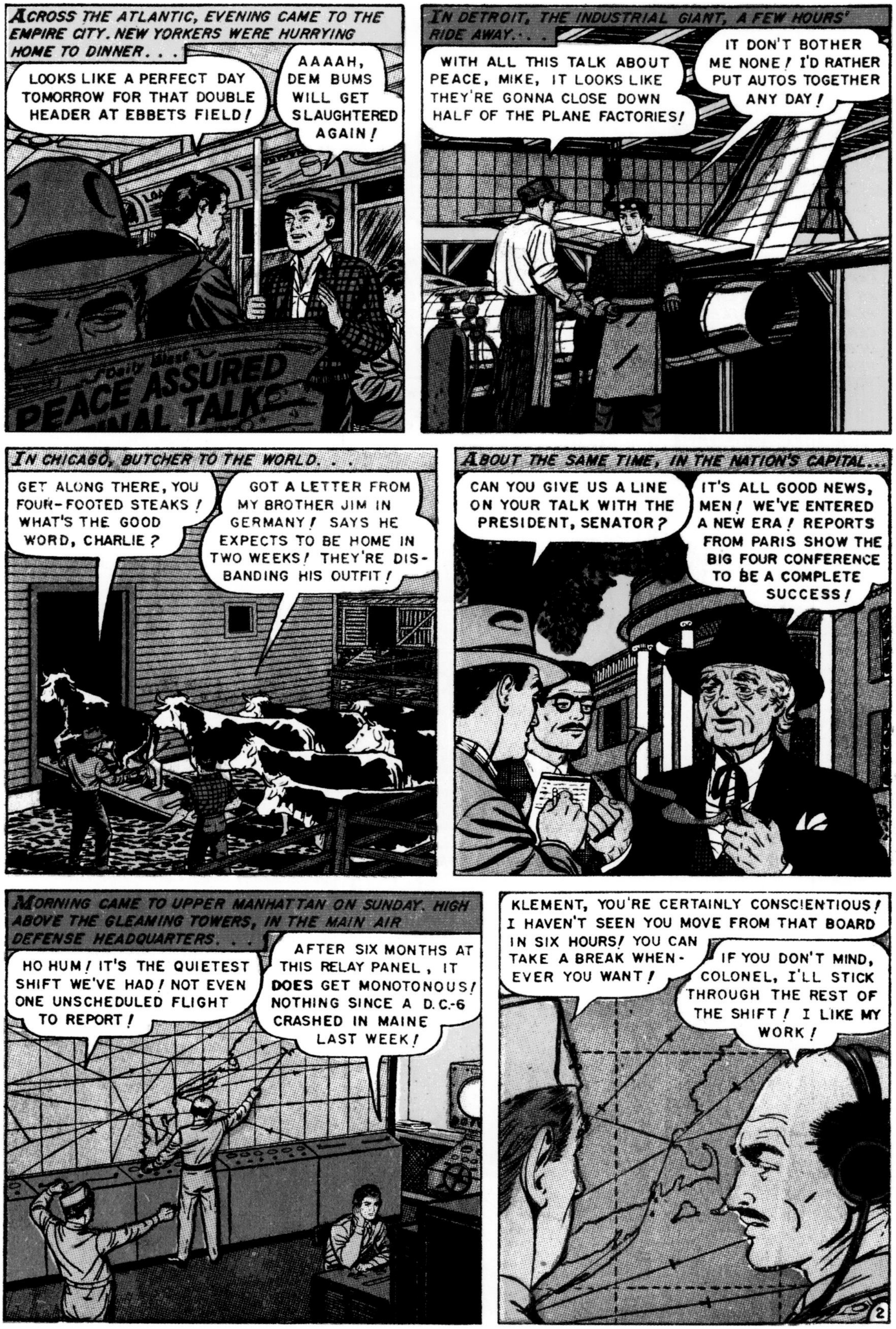
ACROSS THE ATLANTIC, EVENING CAME TO THE EMPIRE CITY. NEW YORKERS WERE HURRYING HOME TO DINNER . . .
LOOKS LIKE A PERFECT DAY TOMORROW FOR THAT DOUBLE HEADER AT EBBETS FIELD!
AAAAH, DEM BUMS WILL GET SLAUGHTERED AGAIN!
PEACE ASSURED
IN DETROIT, THE INDUSTRIAL GIANT, A FEW HOURS' RIDE AWAY . . .
WITH ALL THIS TALK ABOUT PEACE, MIKE, IT LOOKS LIKE THEY'RE GONNA CLOSE DOWN HALF OF THE PLANE FACTORIES!
IT DON'T BOTHER ME NONE! I'D RATHER PUT AUTOS TOGETHER ANY DAY!
IN CHICAGO, BUTCHER TO THE WORLD . . .
GET ALONG THERE, YOU FOUR-FOOTED STEAKS! WHAT'S THE GOOD WORD, CHARLIE?
GOT A LETTER FROM MY BROTHER JIM IN GERMANY! SAYS HE EXPECTS TO BE HOME IN TWO WEEKS! THEY'RE DISBANDING HIS OUTFIT!
ABOUT THE SAME TIME, IN THE NATION'S CAPITAL . . .
CAN YOU GIVE US A LINE ON YOUR TALK WITH THE PRESIDENT, SENATOR?
IT'S ALL GOOD NEWS, MEN! WE'VE ENTERED A NEW ERA! REPORTS FROM PARIS SHOW THE BIG FOUR CONFERENCE TO BE A COMPLETE SUCCESS!
MORNING CAME TO UPPER MANHATTAN ON SUNDAY. HIGH ABOVE THE GLEAMING TOWERS, IN THE MAIN AIR DEFENSE HEADQUARTERS . . .
HO HUM! IT'S THE QUIETEST SHIFT WE'VE HAD! NOT EVEN ONE UNSCHEDULED FLIGHT TO REPORT!
AFTER SIX MONTHS AT THIS RELAY PANEL, IT DOES GET MONOTONOUS! NOTHING SINCE A D.C.-6 CRASHED IN MAINE LAST WEEK!
KLEMENT, YOU'RE CERTAINLY CONSCIENTIOUS! I HAVEN'T SEEN YOU MOVE FROM THAT BOARD IN SIX HOURS! YOU CAN TAKE A BREAK WHENEVER YOU WANT!
IF YOU DON'T MIND, COLONEL, I'LL STICK THROUGH THE REST OF THE SHIFT! I LIKE MY WORK!
2

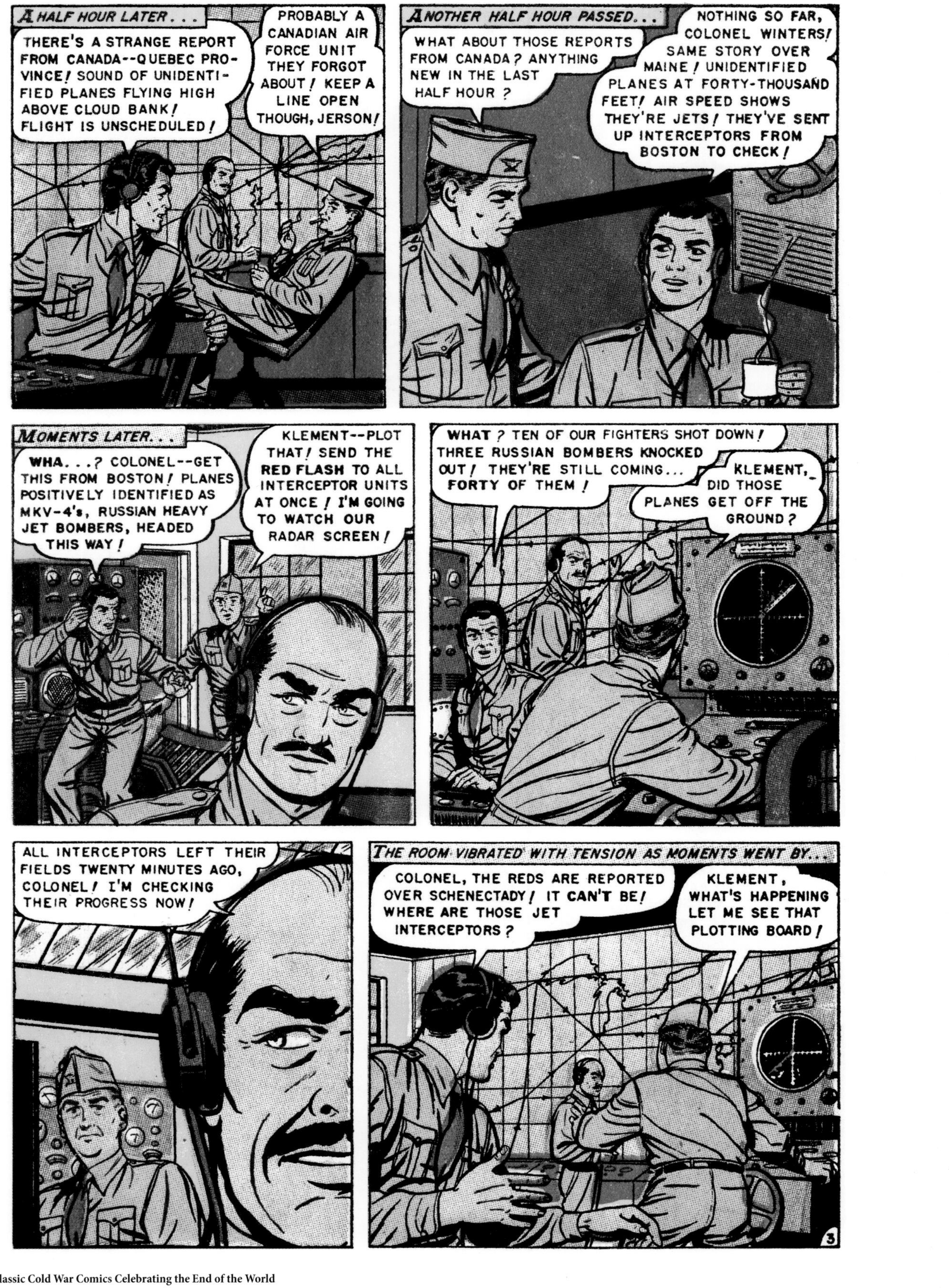
A HALF HOUR LATER . . .
THERE'S A STRANGE REPORT FROM CANADA--QUEBEC PROVINCE! SOUND OF UNIDENTIFIED PLANES FLYING HIGH ABOVE CLOUD BANK! FLIGHT IS UNSCHEDULED!
PROBABLY A CANADIAN AIR FORCE UNIT THEY FORGOT ABOUT! KEEP A LINE OPEN THOUGH, JERSON!
ANOTHER HALF HOUR PASSED. . .
WHAT ABOUT THOSE REPORTS FROM CANADA? ANYTHING NEW IN THE LAST HALF HOUR?
NOTHING SO FAR, COLONEL WINTERS! SAME STORY OVER MAINE! UNIDENTIFIED PLANES AT FORTY-THOUSAND FEET! AIR SPEED SHOWS THEY'RE JETS! THEY'VE SENT UP INTERCEPTORS FROM BOSTON TO CHECK!
MOMENTS LATER. . .
WHA. . .? COLONEL--GET THIS FROM BOSTON! PLANES POSITIVELY IDENTIFIED AS MKV-4's, RUSSIAN HEAVY JET BOMBERS, HEADED THIS WAY!
KLEMENT--PLOT THAT! SEND THE RED FLASH TO ALL INTERCEPTOR UNITS AT ONCE! I'M GOING TO WATCH OUR RADAR SCREEN!
WHAT? TEN OF OUR FIGHTERS SHOT DOWN! THREE RUSSIAN BOMBERS KNOCKED OUT! THEY'RE STILL COMING... FORTY OF THEM!
KLEMENT, DID THOSE PLANES GET OFF THE GROUND?
ALL INTERCEPTORS LEFT THEIR FIELDS TWENTY MINUTES AGO, COLONEL! I'M CHECKING THEIR PROGRESS NOW!
THE ROOM VIBRATED WITH TENSION AS MOMENTS WENT BY. . .
COLONEL, THE REDS ARE REPORTED OVER SCHENECTADY! IT CAN'T BE! WHERE ARE THOSE JET INTERCEPTORS?
KLEMENT, WHAT'S HAPPENING LET ME SEE THAT PLOTTING BOARD!
3

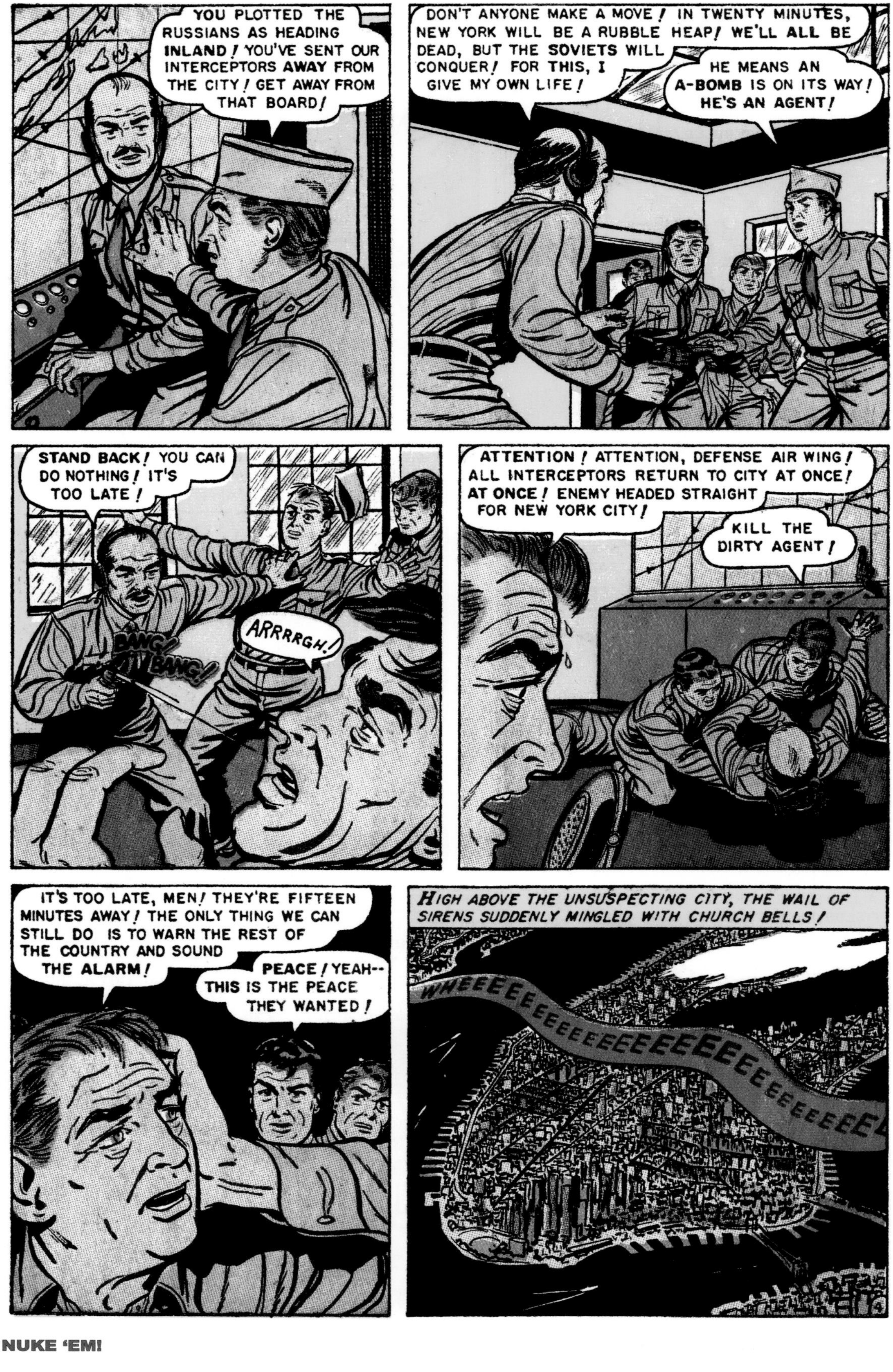
YOU PLOTTED THE RUSSIANS AS HEADING INLAND! YOU'VE SENT OUR INTERCEPTORS AWAY FROM THE CITY! GET AWAY FROM THAT BOARD!
DON'T ANYONE MAKE A MOVE! IN TWENTY MINUTES, NEW YORK WILL BE A RUBBLE HEAP! WE'LL ALL BE DEAD, BUT THE SOVIETS WILL CONQUER! FOR THIS, I GIVE MY OWN LIFE!
HE MEANS AN A-BOMB IS ON ITS WAY! HE'S AN AGENT!
STAND BACK! YOU CAN DO NOTHING! IT'S TOO LATE!
BANG! BANG!
ARRRRGH!
ATTENTION! ATTENTION, DEFENSE AIR WING! ALL INTERCEPTORS RETURN TO CITY AT ONCE! AT ONCE! ENEMY HEADED STRAIGHT FOR NEW YORK CITY!
KILL THE DIRTY AGENT!
IT'S TOO LATE, MEN! THEY'RE FIFTEEN MINUTES AWAY! THE ONLY THING WE CAN STILL DO IS TO WARN THE REST OF THE COUNTRY AND SOUND THE ALARM!
PEACE! YEAH-- THIS IS THE PEACE THEY WANTED!
HIGH ABOVE THE UNSUSPECTING CITY, THE WAIL OF SIRENS SUDDENLY MINGLED WITH CHURCH BELLS!
WHEEEEEEEEEEEEEEEEEEEEEEEEEEEEEEEEE

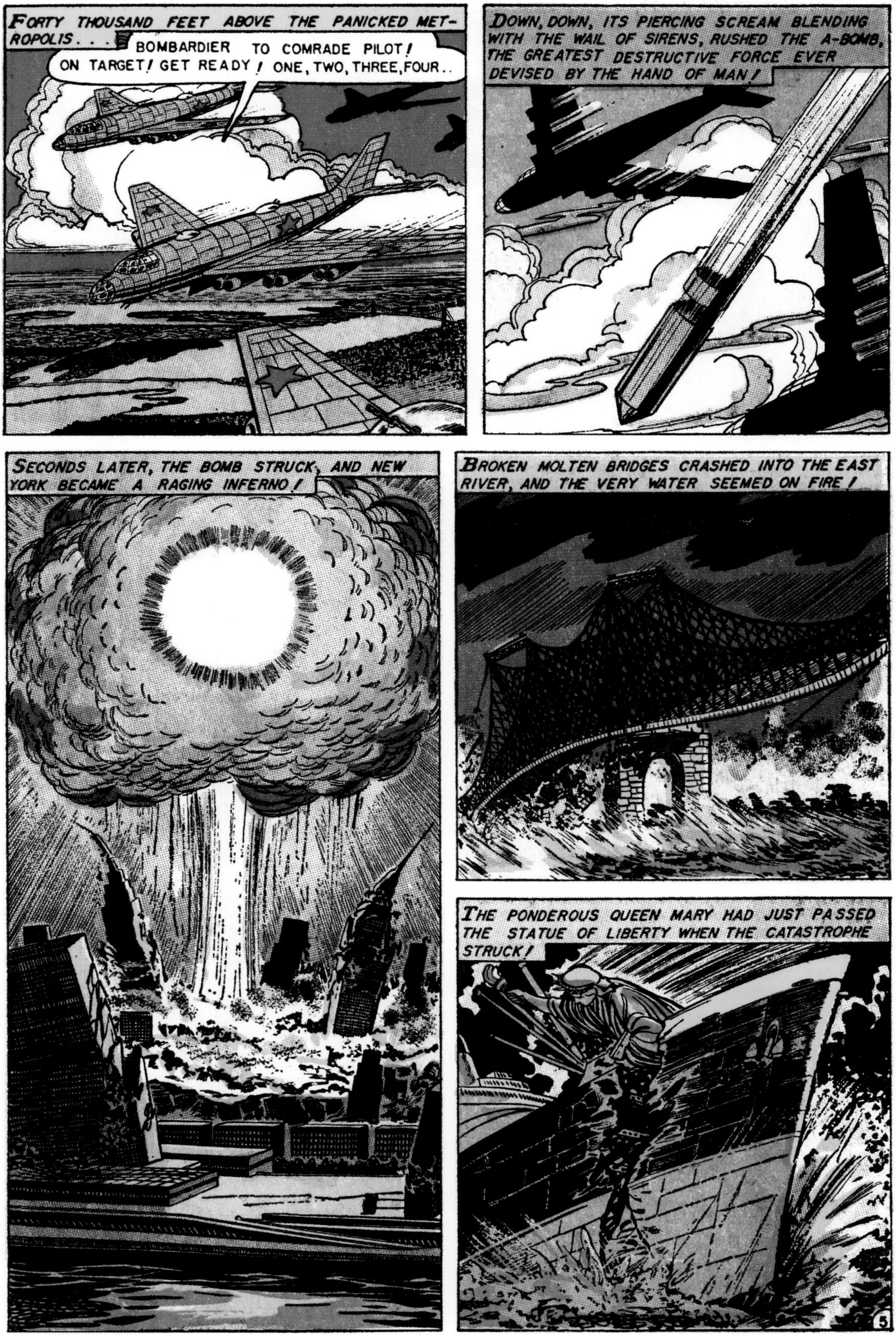
FORTY THOUSAND FEET ABOVE THE PANICKED METROPOLIS. . .
BOMBARDIER TO COMRADE PILOT! ON TARGET! GET READY! ONE, TWO, THREE, FOUR..
DOWN, DOWN, ITS PIERCING SCREAM BLENDING WITH THE WAIL OF SIRENS, RUSHED THE A-BOMB, THE GREATEST DESTRUCTIVE FORCE EVER DEVISED BY THE HAND OF MAN!
SECONDS LATER, THE BOMB STRUCK, AND NEW YORK BECAME A RAGING INFERNO!
BROKEN MOLTEN BRIDGES CRASHED INTO THE EAST RIVER, AND THE VERY WATER SEEMED ON FIRE!
THE PONDEROUS QUEEN MARY HAD JUST PASSED THE STATUE OF LIBERTY WHEN THE CATASTROPHE STRUCK!
5

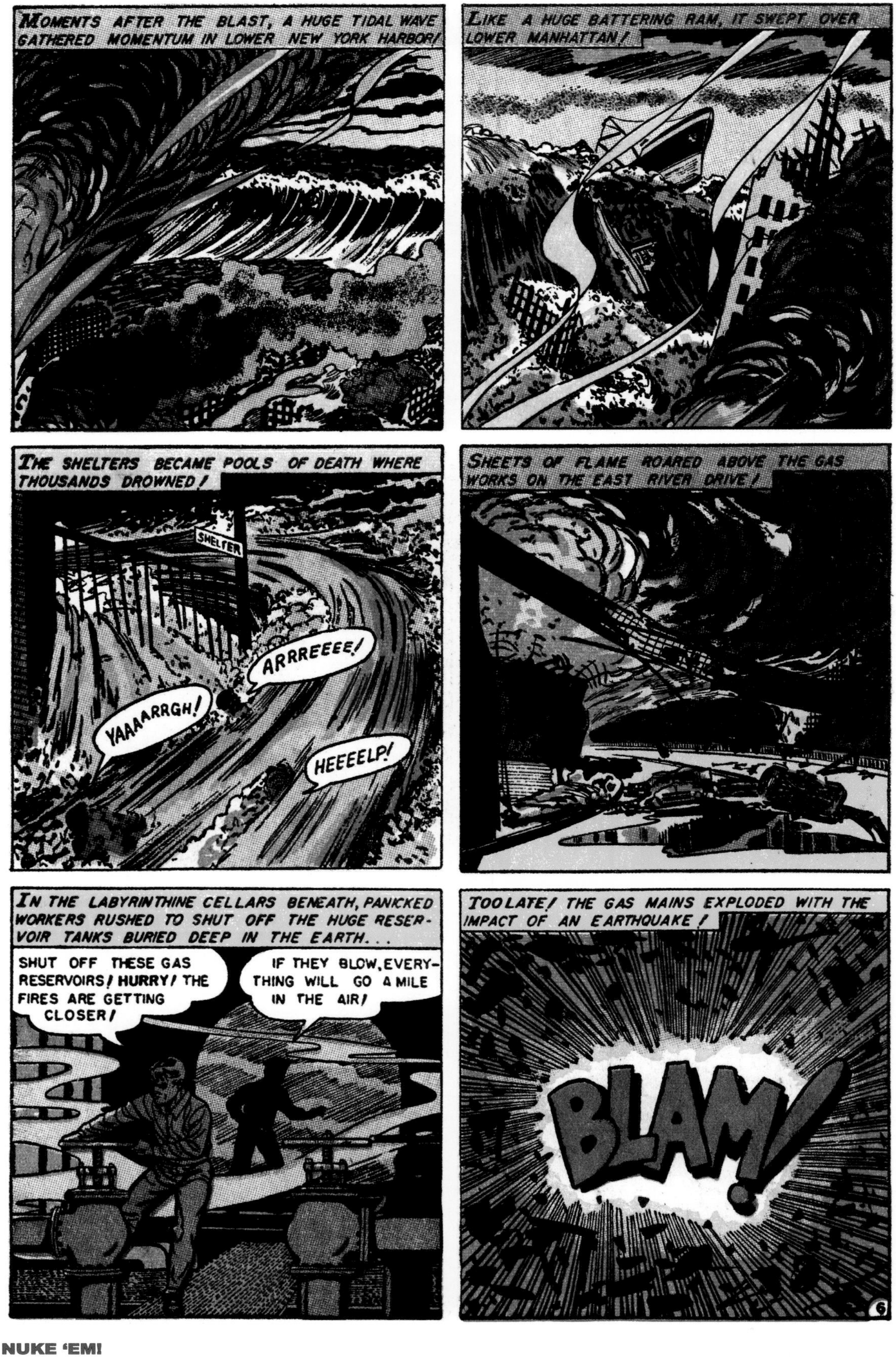
MOMENTS AFTER THE BLAST, A HUGE TIDAL WAVE GATHERED MOMENTUM IN LOWER NEW YORK HARBOR!
LIKE A HUGE BATTERING RAM, IT SWEPT OVER LOWER MANHATTAN!
THE SHELTERS BECAME POOLS OF DEATH WHERE THOUSANDS DROWNED!
SHELTER
ARRRREEEE!
YAAAARRGH!
HEEEELP!
SHEETS OF FLAME ROARED ABOVE THE GAS WORKS ON THE EAST RIVER DRIVE!
IN THE LABYRINTHINE CELLARS BENEATH, PANICKED WORKERS RUSHED TO SHUT OFF THE HUGE RESERVOIR TANKS BURIED DEEP IN THE EARTH...
SHUT OFF THESE GAS RESERVOIRS! HURRY! THE FIRES ARE GETTING CLOSER!
IF THEY BLOW, EVERYTHING WILL GO A MILE IN THE AIR!
TOO LATE! THE GAS MAINS EXPLODED WITH THE IMPACT OF AN EARTHQUAKE!
BLAM!
6

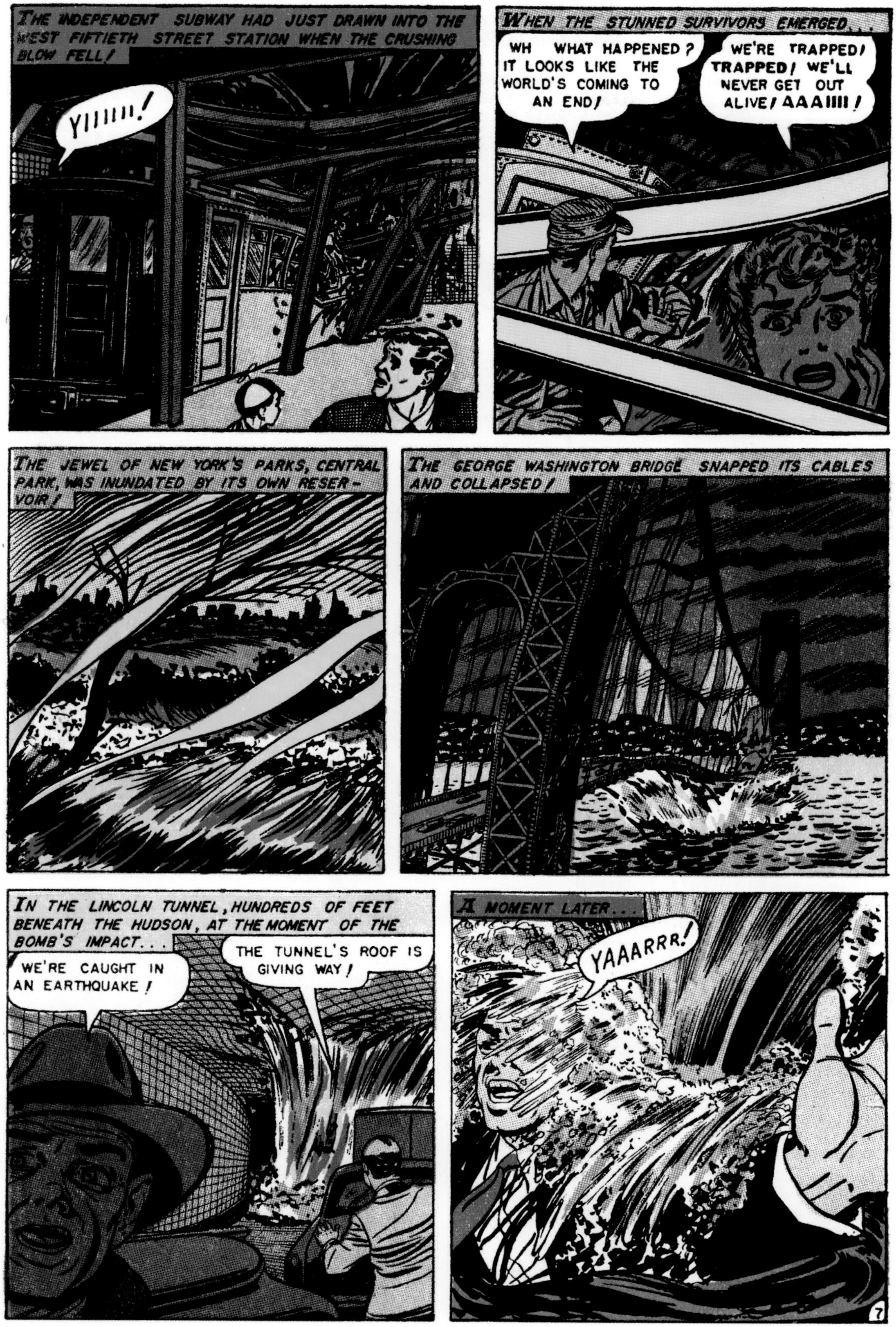
THE INDEPENDENT SUBWAY HAD JUST DRAWN INTO THE WEST FIFTIETH STREET STATION WHEN THE CRUSHING BLOW FELL!
YIIIIII!
WHEN THE STUNNED SURVIVORS EMERGED...
WH WHAT HAPPENED? IT LOOKS LIKE THE WORLD'S COMING TO AN END!
WE'RE TRAPPED! TRAPPED! WE'LL NEVER GET OUT ALIVE! AAAIIII!
THE JEWEL OF NEW YORK'S PARKS, CENTRAL PARK, WAS INUNDATED BY ITS OWN RESER-VOIR!
THE GEORGE WASHINGTON BRIDGE SNAPPED ITS CABLES AND COLLAPSED!
IN THE LINCOLN TUNNEL, HUNDREDS OF FEET BENEATH THE HUDSON, AT THE MOMENT OF THE BOMB'S IMPACT...
WE'RE CAUGHT IN AN EARTHQUAKE!
THE TUNNEL'S ROOF IS GIVING WAY!
A MOMENT LATER...
YAAARRR!
7

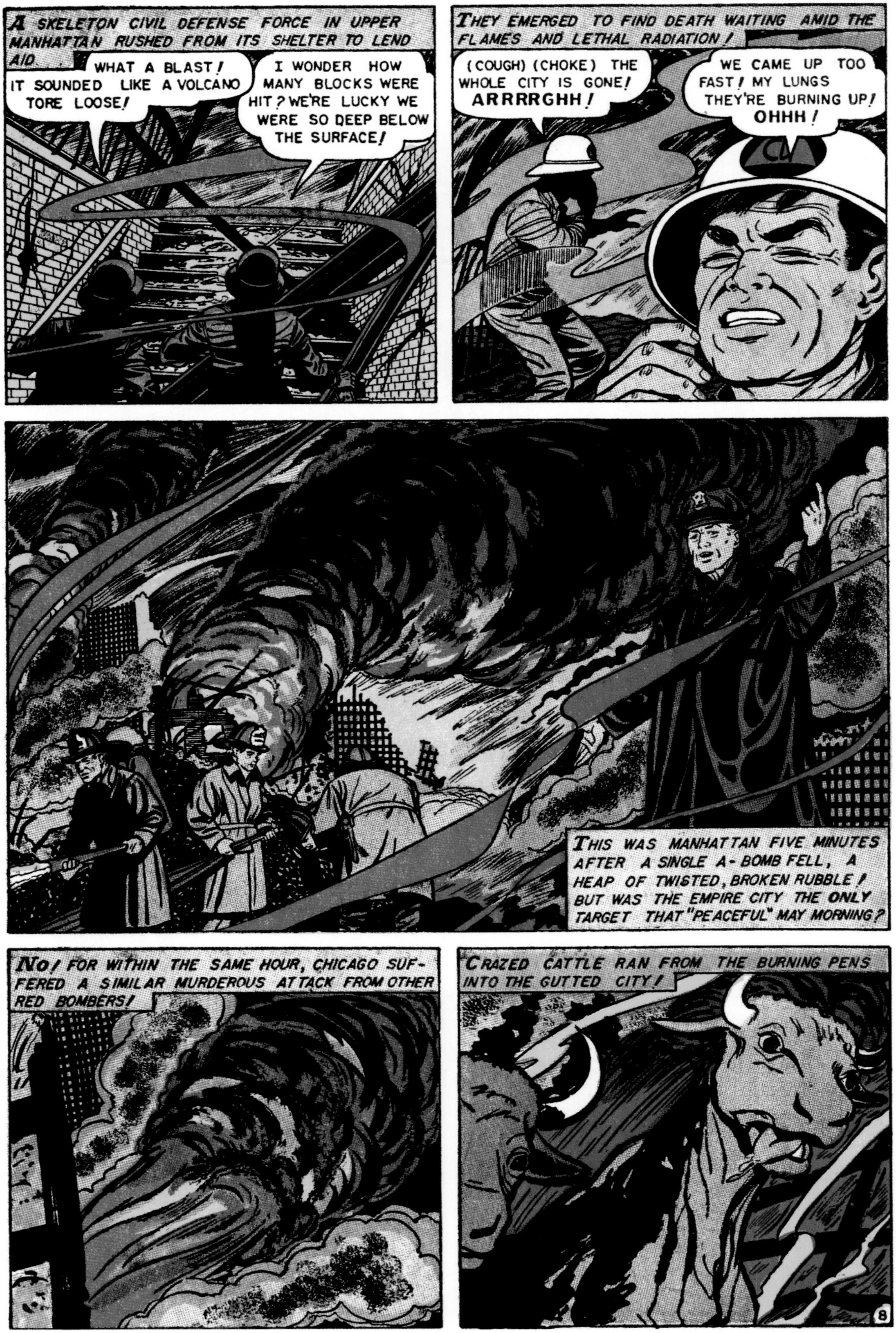

A SKELETON CIVIL DEFENSE FORCE IN UPPER MANHATTAN RUSHED FROM ITS SHELTER TO LEND AID.
WHAT A BLAST! IT SOUNDED LIKE A VOLCANO TORE LOOSE!
I WONDER HOW MANY BLOCKS WERE HIT? WE'RE LUCKY WE WERE SO DEEP BELOW THE SURFACE!
THEY EMERGED TO FIND DEATH WAITING AMID THE FLAMES AND LETHAL RADIATION!
(COUGH) (CHOKE) THE WHOLE CITY IS GONE! ARRRRGHH!
WE CAME UP TOO FAST! MY LUNGS THEY'RE BURNING UP! OHHH!
CD
THIS WAS MANHATTAN FIVE MINUTES AFTER A SINGLE A-BOMB FELL, A HEAP OF TWISTED, BROKEN RUBBLE! BUT WAS THE EMPIRE CITY THE ONLY TARGET THAT "PEACEFUL" MAY MORNING?
NO! FOR WITHIN THE SAME HOUR, CHICAGO SUFFERED A SIMILAR MURDEROUS ATTACK FROM OTHER RED BOMBERS!
CRAZED CATTLE RAN FROM THE BURNING PENS INTO THE GUTTED CITY!
8

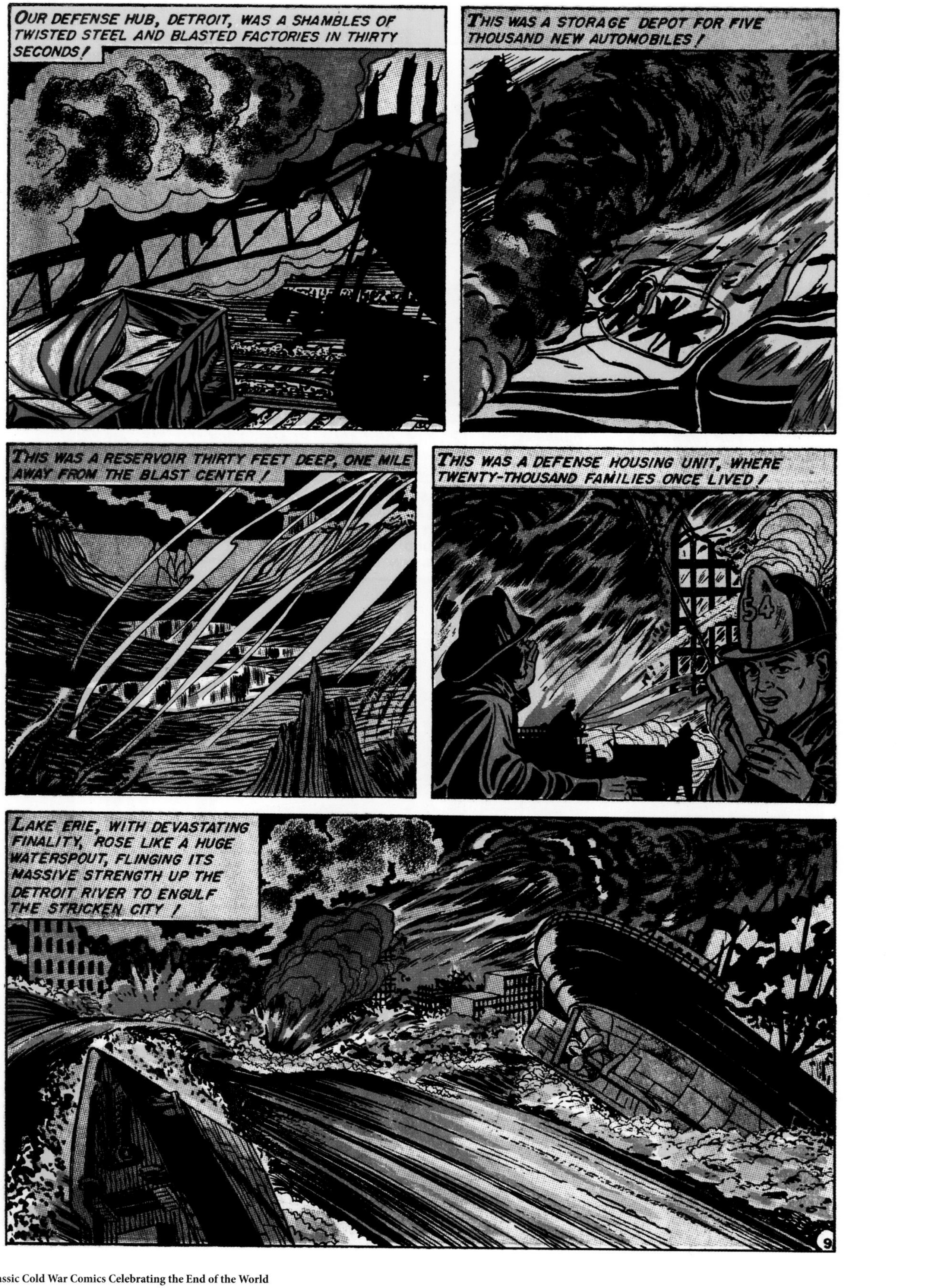
OUR DEFENSE HUB, DETROIT, WAS A SHAMBLES OF TWISTED STEEL AND BLASTED FACTORIES IN THIRTY SECONDS!
THIS WAS A STORAGE DEPOT FOR FIVE THOUSAND NEW AUTOMOBILES!
THIS WAS A RESERVOIR THIRTY FEET DEEP, ONE MILE AWAY FROM THE BLAST CENTER!
THIS WAS A DEFENSE HOUSING UNIT, WHERE TWENTY-THOUSAND FAMILIES ONCE LIVED!
54
LAKE ERIE, WITH DEVASTATING FINALITY, ROSE LIKE A HUGE WATERSPOUT, FLINGING ITS MASSIVE STRENGTH UP THE DETROIT RIVER TO ENGULF THE STRICKEN CITY!
9

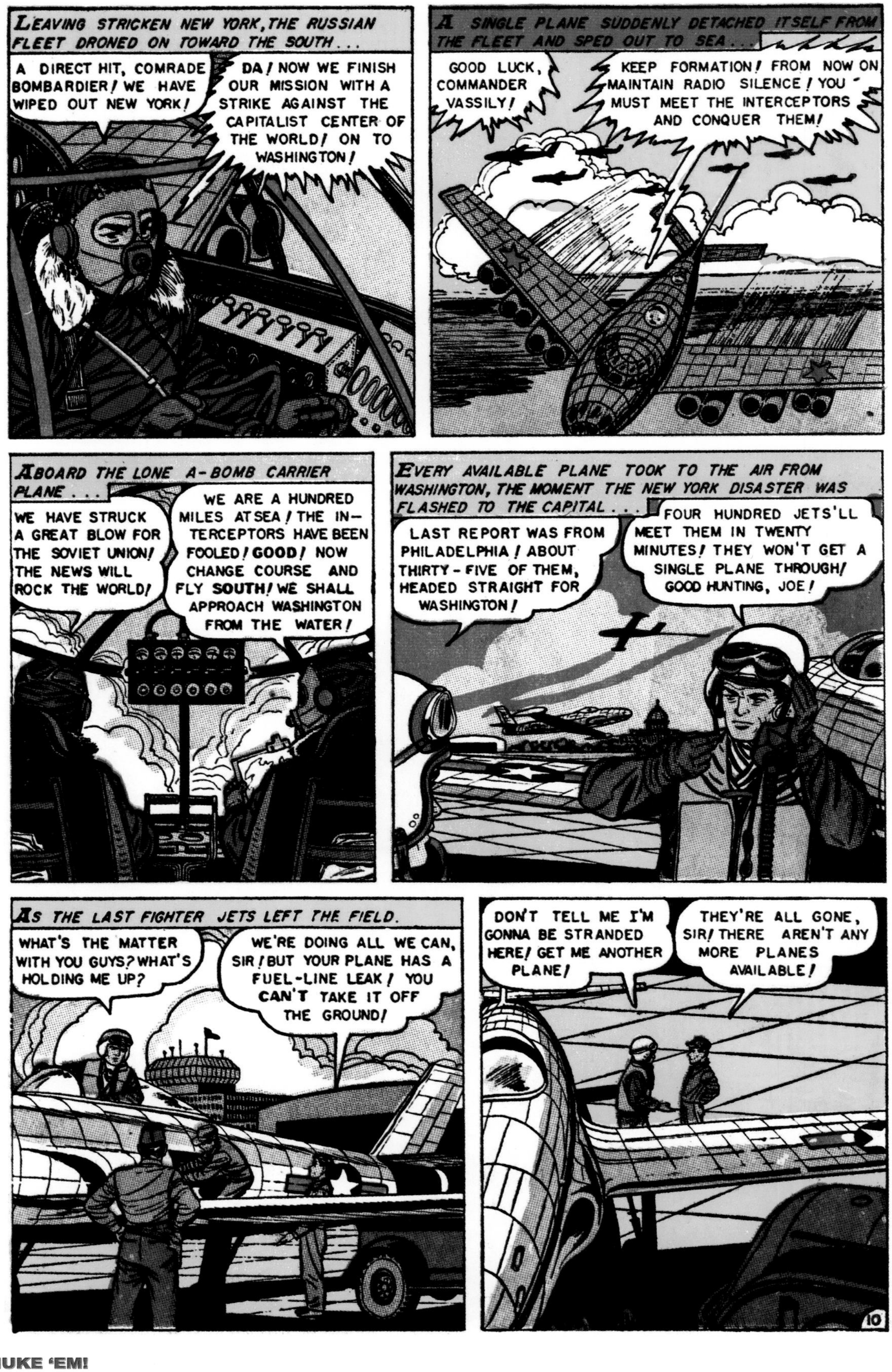
LEAVING STRICKEN NEW YORK, THE RUSSIAN FLEET DRONED ON TOWARD THE SOUTH . . .
A DIRECT HIT, COMRADE BOMBARDIER! WE HAVE WIPED OUT NEW YORK!
DA! NOW WE FINISH OUR MISSION WITH A STRIKE AGAINST THE CAPITALIST CENTER OF THE WORLD! ON TO WASHINGTON!
A SINGLE PLANE SUDDENLY DETACHED ITSELF FROM THE FLEET AND SPED OUT TO SEA . . .
GOOD LUCK, COMMANDER VASSILY!
KEEP FORMATION! FROM NOW ON MAINTAIN RADIO SILENCE! YOU MUST MEET THE INTERCEPTORS AND CONQUER THEM!
ABOARD THE LONE A-BOMB CARRIER PLANE . . .
WE HAVE STRUCK A GREAT BLOW FOR THE SOVIET UNION! THE NEWS WILL ROCK THE WORLD!
WE ARE A HUNDRED MILES AT SEA! THE INTERCEPTORS HAVE BEEN FOOLED! GOOD! NOW CHANGE COURSE AND FLY SOUTH! WE SHALL APPROACH WASHINGTON FROM THE WATER!
EVERY AVAILABLE PLANE TOOK TO THE AIR FROM WASHINGTON, THE MOMENT THE NEW YORK DISASTER WAS FLASHED TO THE CAPITAL . . .
LAST REPORT WAS FROM PHILADELPHIA! ABOUT THIRTY-FIVE OF THEM, HEADED STRAIGHT FOR WASHINGTON!
FOUR HUNDRED JETS'LL MEET THEM IN TWENTY MINUTES! THEY WON'T GET A SINGLE PLANE THROUGH! GOOD HUNTING, JOE!
AS THE LAST FIGHTER JETS LEFT THE FIELD.
WHAT'S THE MATTER WITH YOU GUYS? WHAT'S HOLDING ME UP?
WE'RE DOING ALL WE CAN, SIR! BUT YOUR PLANE HAS A FUEL-LINE LEAK! YOU CAN'T TAKE IT OFF THE GROUND!
DON'T TELL ME I'M GONNA BE STRANDED HERE! GET ME ANOTHER PLANE!
THEY'RE ALL GONE, SIR! THERE AREN'T ANY MORE PLANES AVAILABLE!
10

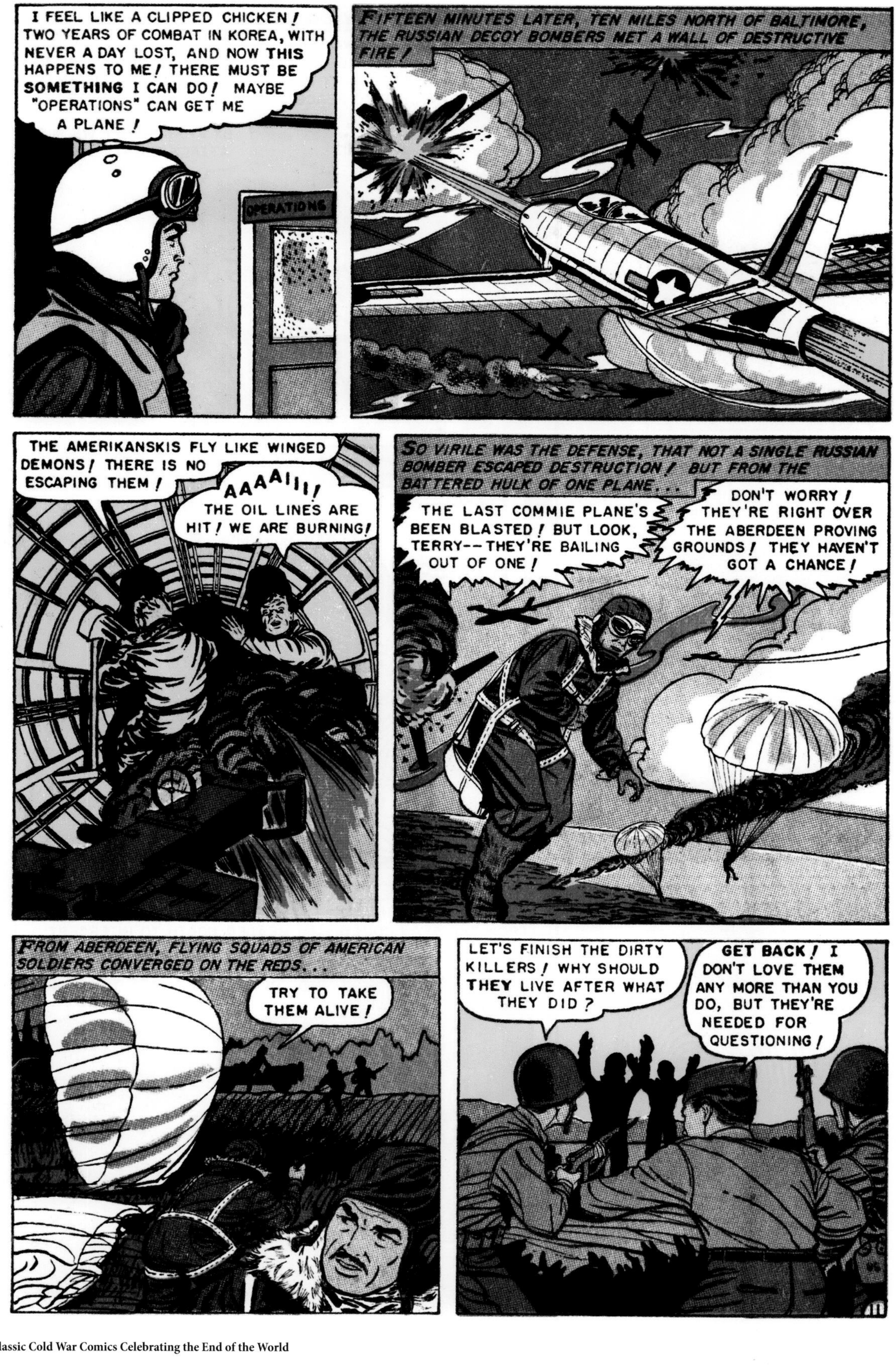
I FEEL LIKE A CLIPPED CHICKEN! TWO YEARS OF COMBAT IN KOREA, WITH NEVER A DAY LOST, AND NOW THIS HAPPENS TO ME! THERE MUST BE SOMETHING I CAN DO! MAYBE "OPERATIONS" CAN GET ME A PLANE!
OPERATIONS
FIFTEEN MINUTES LATER, TEN MILES NORTH OF BALTIMORE, THE RUSSIAN DECOY BOMBERS MET A WALL OF DESTRUCTIVE FIRE!
THE AMERIKANSKIS FLY LIKE WINGED DEMONS! THERE IS NO ESCAPING THEM!
AAAAIII! THE OIL LINES ARE HIT! WE ARE BURNING!
SO VIRILE WAS THE DEFENSE, THAT NOT A SINGLE RUSSIAN BOMBER ESCAPED DESTRUCTION! BUT FROM THE BATTERED HULK OF ONE PLANE...
THE LAST COMMIE PLANE'S BEEN BLASTED! BUT LOOK, TERRY--THEY'RE BAILING OUT OF ONE!
DON'T WORRY! THEY'RE RIGHT OVER THE ABERDEEN PROVING GROUNDS! THEY HAVEN'T GOT A CHANCE!
FROM ABERDEEN, FLYING SQUADS OF AMERICAN SOLDIERS CONVERGED ON THE REDS...
TRY TO TAKE THEM ALIVE!
LET'S FINISH THE DIRTY KILLERS! WHY SHOULD THEY LIVE AFTER WHAT THEY DID?
GET BACK! I DON'T LOVE THEM ANY MORE THAN YOU DO, BUT THEY'RE NEEDED FOR QUESTIONING!

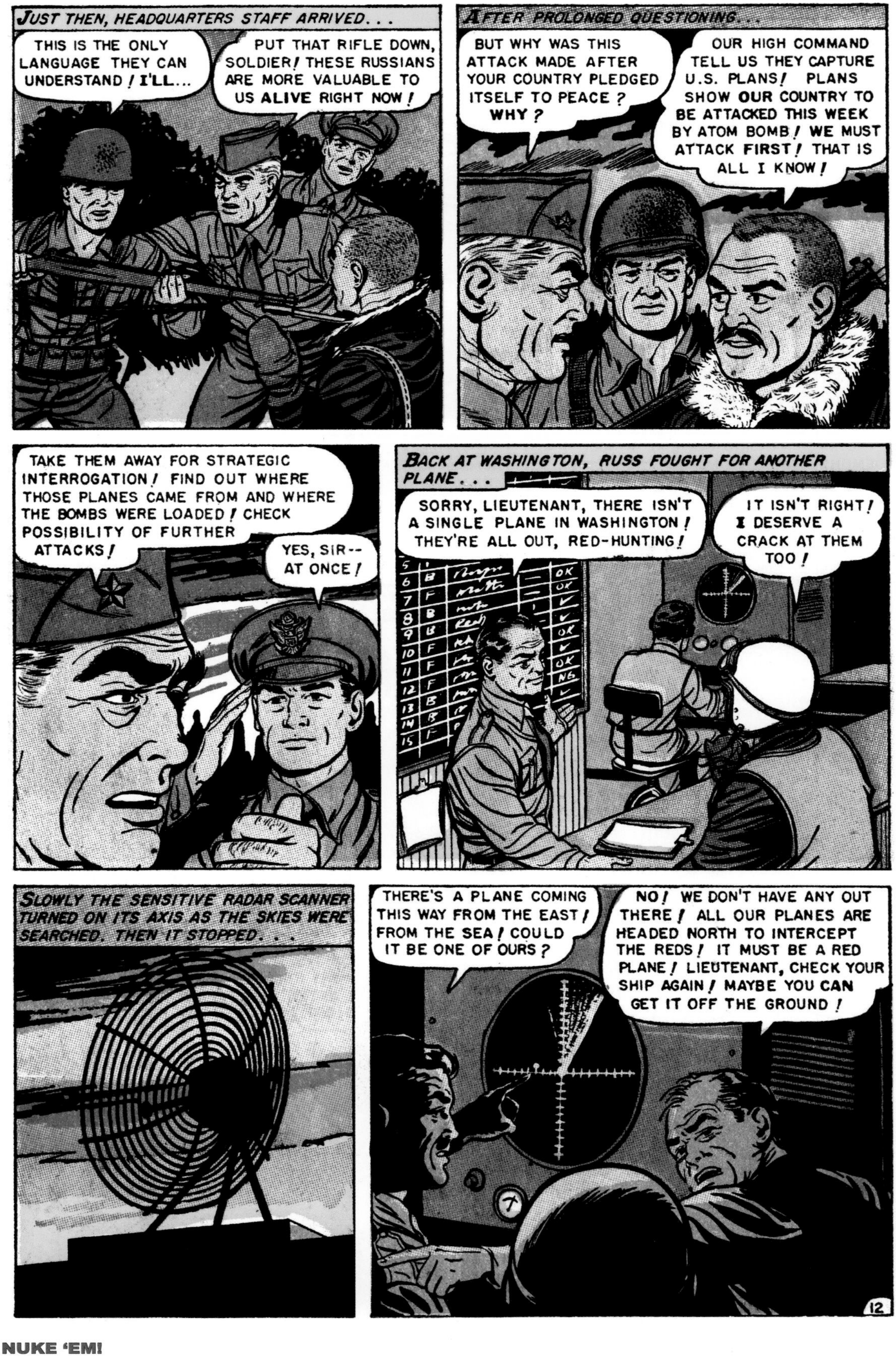

JUST THEN, HEADQUARTERS STAFF ARRIVED...
THIS IS THE ONLY LANGUAGE THEY CAN UNDERSTAND! I'LL...
PUT THAT RIFLE DOWN, SOLDIER! THESE RUSSIANS ARE MORE VALUABLE TO US ALIVE RIGHT NOW!
AFTER PROLONGED QUESTIONING...
BUT WHY WAS THIS ATTACK MADE AFTER YOUR COUNTRY PLEDGED ITSELF TO PEACE? WHY?
OUR HIGH COMMAND TELL US THEY CAPTURE U.S. PLANS! PLANS SHOW OUR COUNTRY TO BE ATTACKED THIS WEEK BY ATOM BOMB! WE MUST ATTACK FIRST! THAT IS ALL I KNOW!
TAKE THEM AWAY FOR STRATEGIC INTERROGATION! FIND OUT WHERE THOSE PLANES CAME FROM AND WHERE THE BOMBS WERE LOADED! CHECK POSSIBILITY OF FURTHER ATTACKS!
YES, SIR-- AT ONCE!
BACK AT WASHINGTON, RUSS FOUGHT FOR ANOTHER PLANE...
SORRY, LIEUTENANT, THERE ISN'T A SINGLE PLANE IN WASHINGTON! THEY'RE ALL OUT, RED-HUNTING!
IT ISN'T RIGHT! I DESERVE A CRACK AT THEM TOO!
SLOWLY THE SENSITIVE RADAR SCANNER TURNED ON ITS AXIS AS THE SKIES WERE SEARCHED. THEN IT STOPPED...
THERE'S A PLANE COMING THIS WAY FROM THE EAST! FROM THE SEA! COULD IT BE ONE OF OURS?
NO! WE DON'T HAVE ANY OUT THERE! ALL OUR PLANES ARE HEADED NORTH TO INTERCEPT THE REDS! IT MUST BE A RED PLANE! LIEUTENANT, CHECK YOUR SHIP AGAIN! MAYBE YOU CAN GET IT OFF THE GROUND!
12

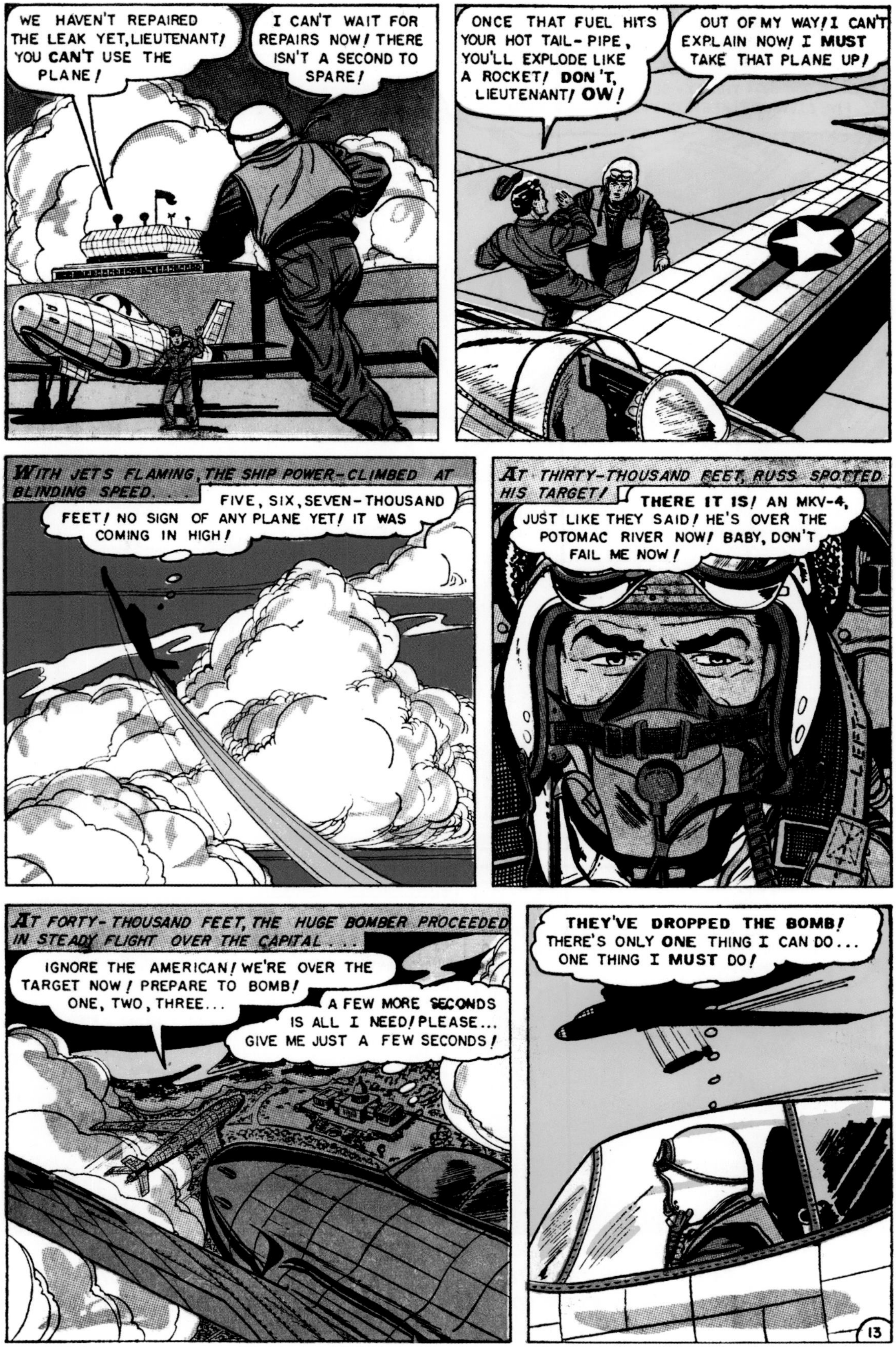

WE HAVEN'T REPAIRED THE LEAK YET, LIEUTENANT! YOU CAN'T USE THE PLANE!
I CAN'T WAIT FOR REPAIRS NOW! THERE ISN'T A SECOND TO SPARE!
ONCE THAT FUEL HITS YOUR HOT TAIL-PIPE, YOU'LL EXPLODE LIKE A ROCKET! DON'T, LIEUTENANT! OW!
OUT OF MY WAY! I CAN'T EXPLAIN NOW! I MUST TAKE THAT PLANE UP!
WITH JETS FLAMING, THE SHIP POWER-CLIMBED AT BLINDING SPEED.
FIVE, SIX, SEVEN-THOUSAND FEET! NO SIGN OF ANY PLANE YET! IT WAS COMING IN HIGH!
AT THIRTY-THOUSAND FEET, RUSS SPOTTED HIS TARGET!
THERE IT IS! AN MKV-4, JUST LIKE THEY SAID! HE'S OVER THE POTOMAC RIVER NOW! BABY, DON'T FAIL ME NOW!
LEFT
AT FORTY-THOUSAND FEET, THE HUGE BOMBER PROCEEDED IN STEADY FLIGHT OVER THE CAPITAL...
IGNORE THE AMERICAN! WE'RE OVER THE TARGET NOW! PREPARE TO BOMB! ONE, TWO, THREE...
A FEW MORE SECONDS IS ALL I NEED! PLEASE... GIVE ME JUST A FEW SECONDS!
THEY'VE DROPPED THE BOMB! THERE'S ONLY ONE THING I CAN DO... ONE THING I MUST DO!
13

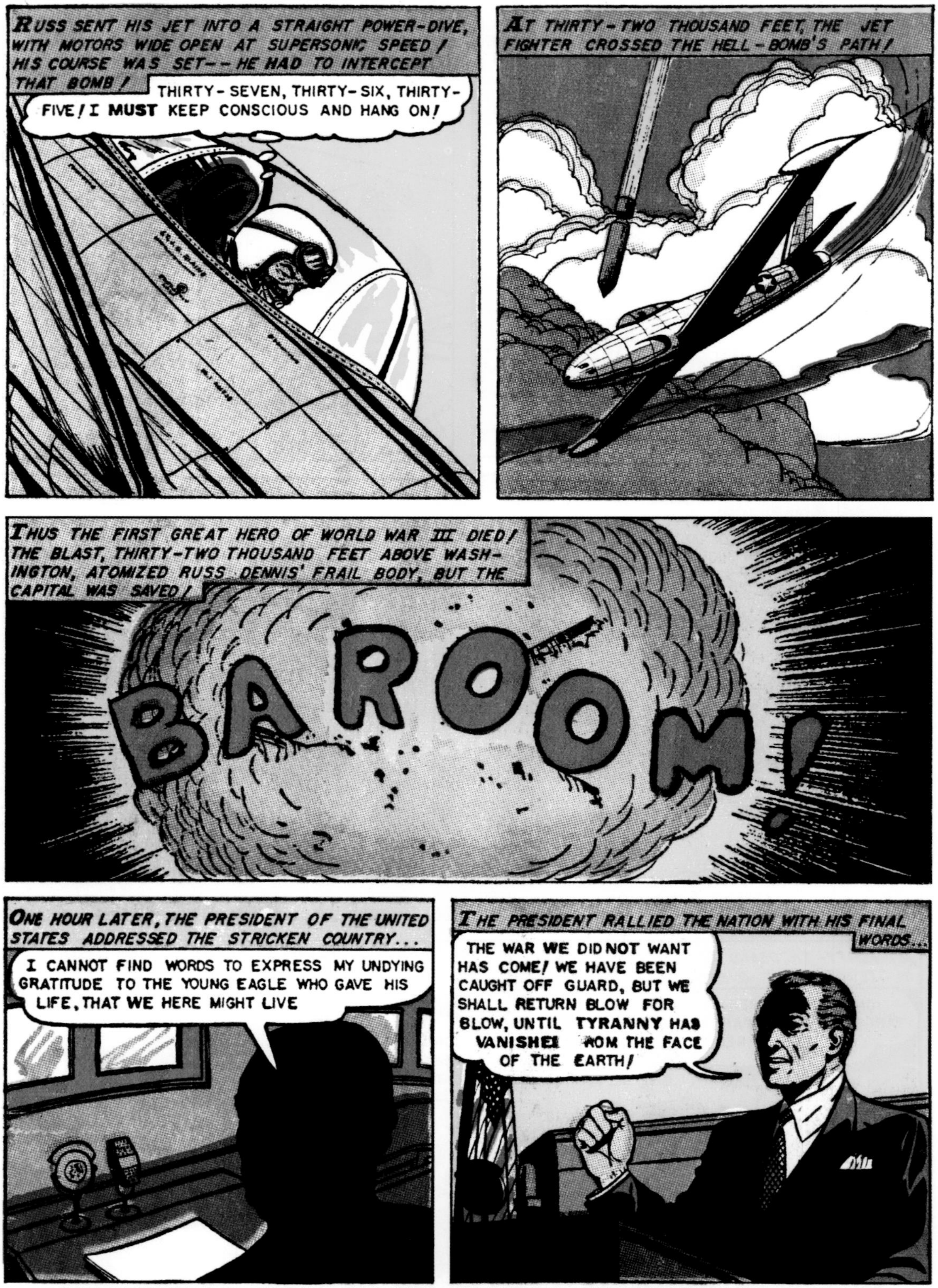
RUSS SENT HIS JET INTO A STRAIGHT POWER-DIVE, WITH MOTORS WIDE OPEN AT SUPERSONIC SPEED! HIS COURSE WAS SET-- HE HAD TO INTERCEPT THAT BOMB!
THIRTY-SEVEN, THIRTY-SIX, THIRTY-FIVE! I MUST KEEP CONSCIOUS AND HANG ON!
AT THIRTY-TWO THOUSAND FEET, THE JET FIGHTER CROSSED THE HELL-BOMB'S PATH!
THUS THE FIRST GREAT HERO OF WORLD WAR III DIED! THE BLAST, THIRTY-TWO THOUSAND FEET ABOVE WASHINGTON, ATOMIZED RUSS DENNIS' FRAIL BODY, BUT THE CAPITAL WAS SAVED!
BAROOM!
ONE HOUR LATER, THE PRESIDENT OF THE UNITED STATES ADDRESSED THE STRICKEN COUNTRY...
I CANNOT FIND WORDS TO EXPRESS MY UNDYING GRATITUDE TO THE YOUNG EAGLE WHO GAVE HIS LIFE, THAT WE HERE MIGHT LIVE
THE PRESIDENT RALLIED THE NATION WITH HIS FINAL WORDS...
THE WAR WE DID NOT WANT HAS COME! WE HAVE BEEN CAUGHT OFF GUARD, BUT WE SHALL RETURN BLOW FOR BLOW, UNTIL TYRANNY HAS VANISHED FROM THE FACE OF THE EARTH!

LOOK UPON THE PICTURES OF OUR GIANT CITIES HUNDREDS OF YEARS IN THE BUILDING, SMASHED BY THE ATOM-BOMB, AND SAY: THIS SHALL NOT COME TO PASS! MORE THAN EVER TODAY, ONLY A STRONG AMERICA CAN PREVENT THIS FROM BECOMING A REALITY!

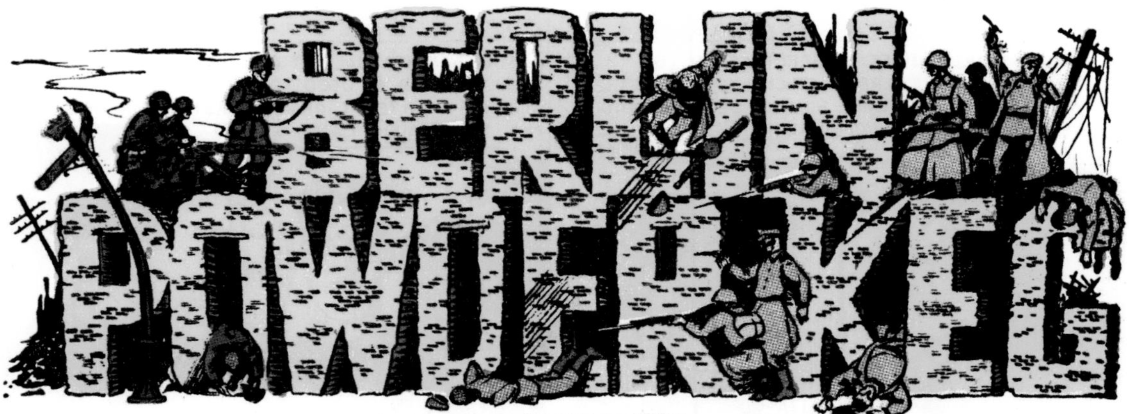
BERLIN POWDER KEG

A FEW HOURS BEFORE THE RAIN OF DEATH DESCENDED UPON THE AMERICAN CITIES, BERLIN LAY ASLEEP, LULLED IN A FALSE SECURITY, LIKE THE REST OF THE WORLD, MORE THAN WILLING TO BELIEVE THE GREAT PEACE MYTH WHICH THE MOSCOW SALESMEN WERE PEDDLING ON AN INTERNATIONAL SCALE. FOR BERLIN WAS A LIVING TESTAMENT, OF THE DESTRUCTION A MODERN CITY CAN EXPECT, TO THE SURVIVORS OF WORLD WAR II . THE DEBRIS OF THE TERRIBLE BLASTING IT HAD EXPERIENCED THEN HAD NOT YET BEEN CARTED AWAY. NOT EVERYBODY WAS ASLEEP. IN A SMALL CAFE, WELL ON THE OUTSKIRTS OF TOWN, SERGEANT JEFF RAINSFORD AND HIS SQUAD WERE CELEBRATING THEIR DEPARTURE FOR THE STATES ON THE FOLLOWING DAY...

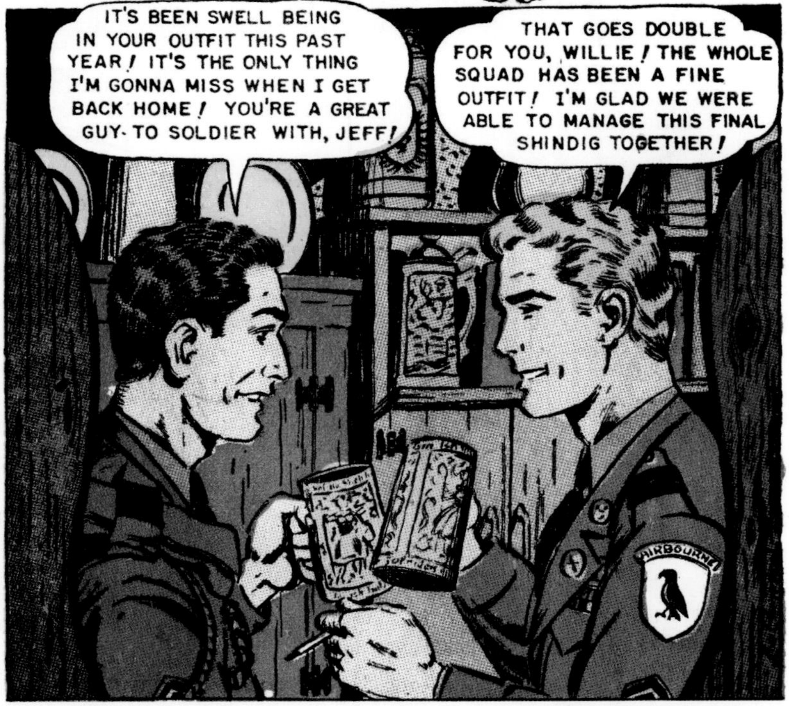
IT'S BEEN SWELL BEING IN YOUR OUTFIT THIS PAST YEAR! IT'S THE ONLY THING I'M GONNA MISS WHEN I GET BACK HOME! YOU'RE A GREAT GUY-TO SOLDIER WITH, JEFF!
THAT GOES DOUBLE FOR YOU, WILLIE! THE WHOLE SQUAD HAS BEEN A FINE OUTFIT! I'M GLAD WE WERE ABLE TO MANAGE THIS FINAL SHINDIG TOGETHER!

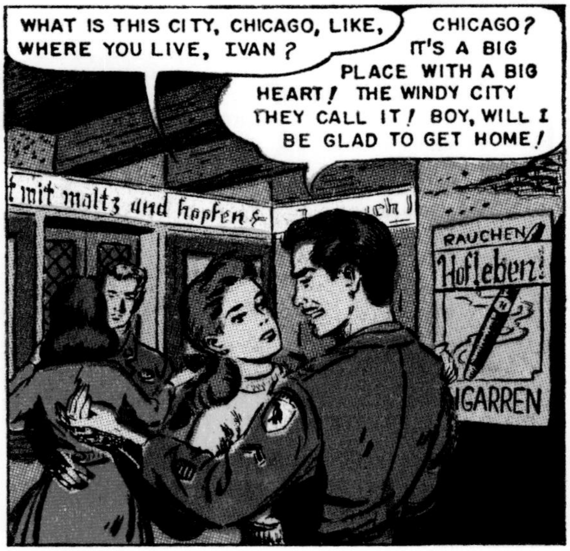
WHAT IS THIS CITY, CHICAGO, LIKE, WHERE YOU LIVE, IVAN?
CHICAGO? IT'S A BIG PLACE WITH A BIG HEART! THE WINDY CITY THEY CALL IT! BOY, WILL I BE GLAD TO GET HOME!
mit maltz und hopfen
RAUCHEN
Hofleben!
IGARREN

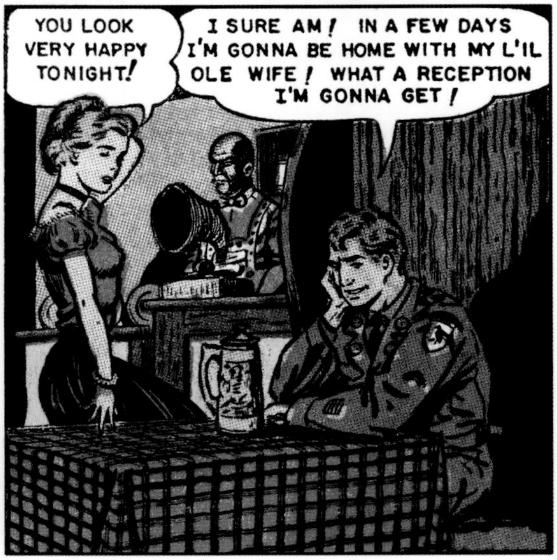
YOU LOOK VERY HAPPY TONIGHT!
I SURE AM! IN A FEW DAYS I'M GONNA BE HOME WITH MY L'IL OLE WIFE! WHAT A RECEPTION I'M GONNA GET!

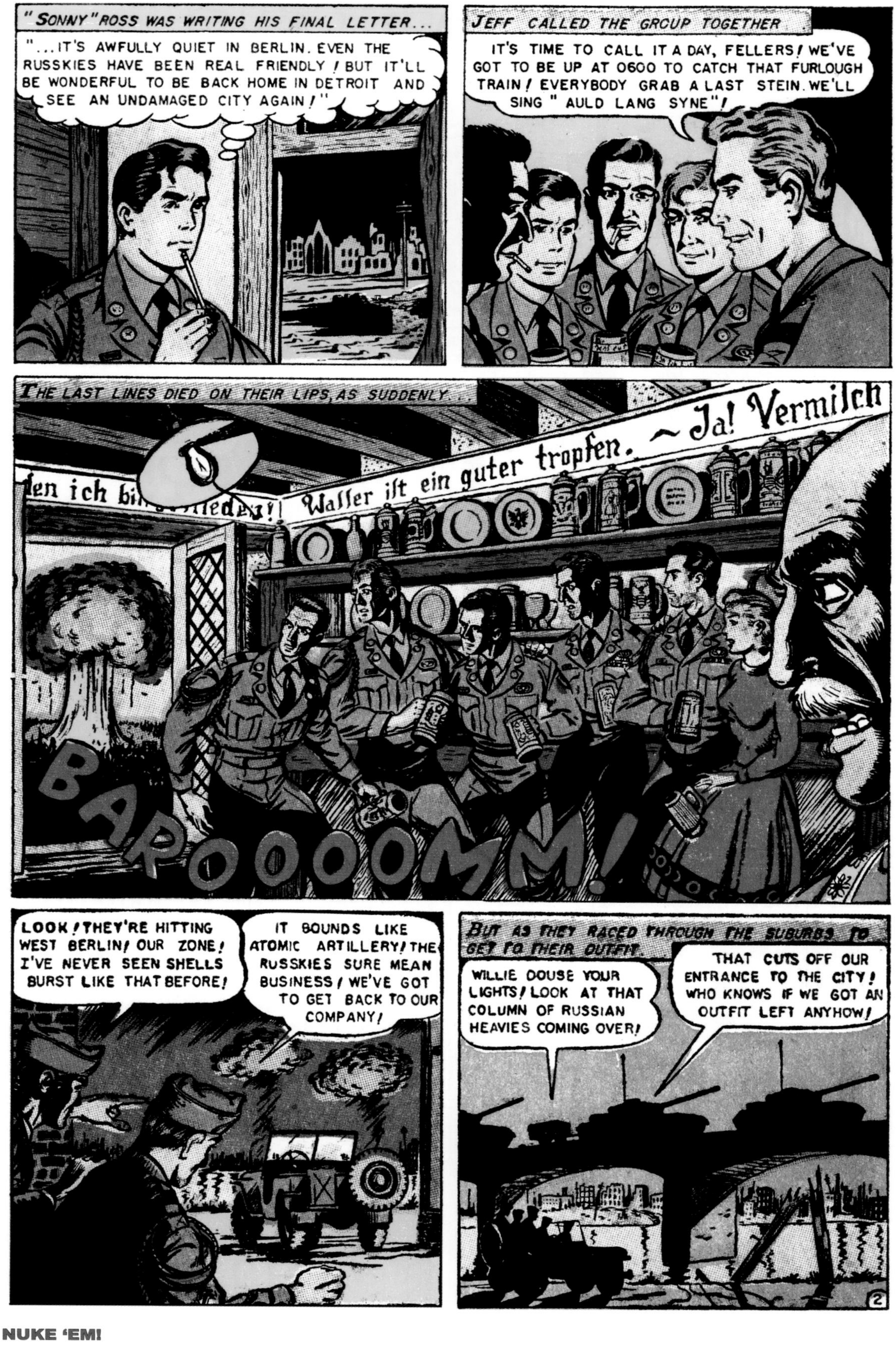
"SONNY" ROSS WAS WRITING HIS FINAL LETTER...
"...IT'S AWFULLY QUIET IN BERLIN. EVEN THE RUSSKIES HAVE BEEN REAL FRIENDLY! BUT IT'LL BE WONDERFUL TO BE BACK HOME IN DETROIT AND SEE AN UNDAMAGED CITY AGAIN!"
JEFF CALLED THE GROUP TOGETHER
IT'S TIME TO CALL IT A DAY, FELLERS! WE'VE GOT TO BE UP AT 0600 TO CATCH THAT FURLOUGH TRAIN! EVERYBODY GRAB A LAST STEIN. WE'LL SING "AULD LANG SYNE"!
THE LAST LINES DIED ON THEIR LIPS, AS SUDDENLY...
Waller ilt ein guter tropfen. ~ Ja! Vermilch
BAROOOOMM!
LOOK! THEY'RE HITTING WEST BERLIN! OUR ZONE! I'VE NEVER SEEN SHELLS BURST LIKE THAT BEFORE!
IT SOUNDS LIKE ATOMIC ARTILLERY! THE RUSSKIES SURE MEAN BUSINESS! WE'VE GOT TO GET BACK TO OUR COMPANY!
BUT AS THEY RACED THROUGH THE SUBURBS TO GET TO THEIR OUTFIT...
WILLIE DOUSE YOUR LIGHTS! LOOK AT THAT COLUMN OF RUSSIAN HEAVIES COMING OVER!
THAT CUTS OFF OUR ENTRANCE TO THE CITY! WHO KNOWS IF WE GOT AN OUTFIT LEFT ANYHOW!
2

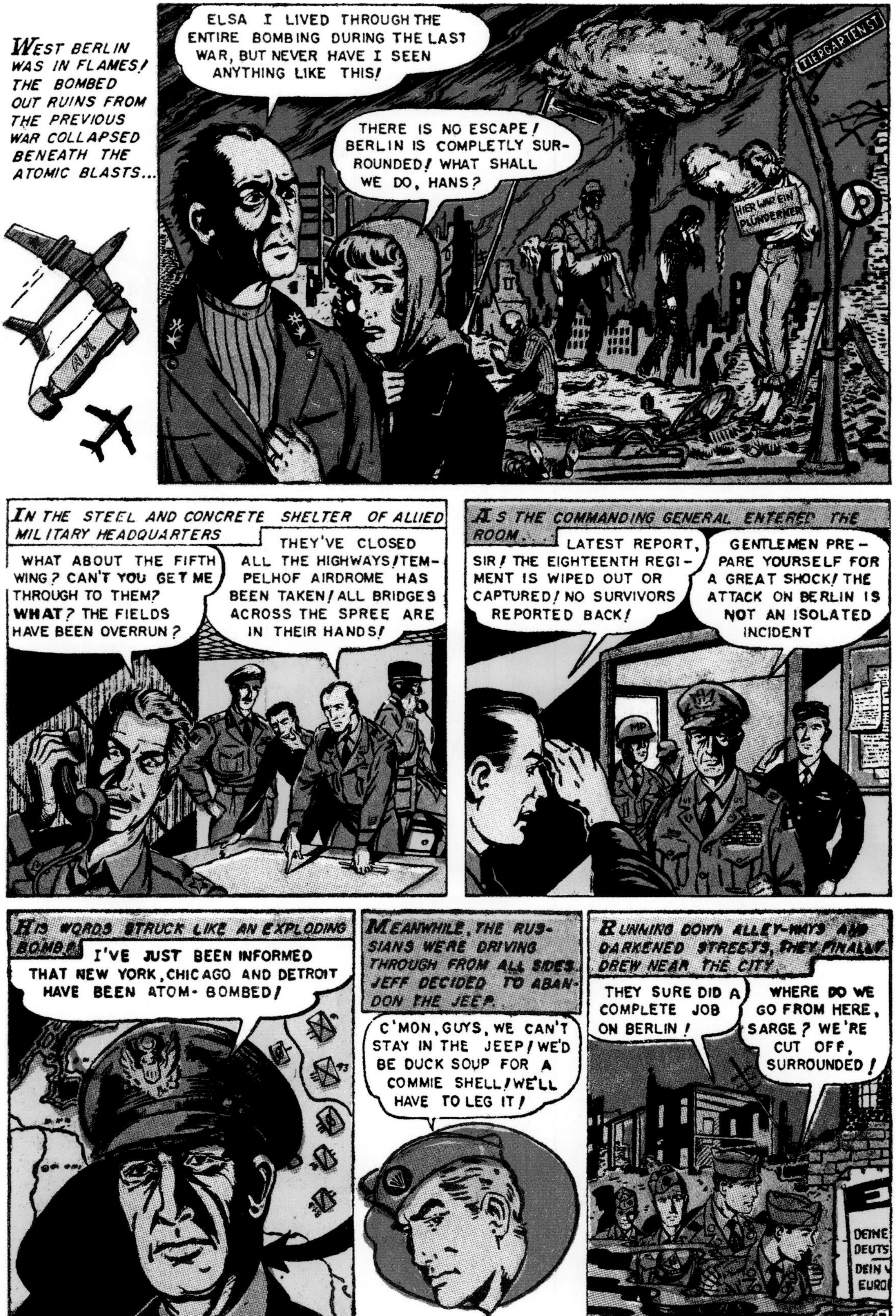
WEST BERLIN WAS IN FLAMES! THE BOMBED OUT RUINS FROM THE PREVIOUS WAR COLLAPSED BENEATH THE ATOMIC BLASTS...
ELSA I LIVED THROUGH THE ENTIRE BOMBING DURING THE LAST WAR, BUT NEVER HAVE I SEEN ANYTHING LIKE THIS!
THERE IS NO ESCAPE! BERLIN IS COMPLETLY SURROUNDED! WHAT SHALL WE DO, HANS?
TIERGARTEN ST
HIER WAR EIN PLÜNDERER
IN THE STEEL AND CONCRETE SHELTER OF ALLIED MILITARY HEADQUARTERS
WHAT ABOUT THE FIFTH WING? CAN'T YOU GET ME THROUGH TO THEM? WHAT? THE FIELDS HAVE BEEN OVERRUN?
THEY'VE CLOSED ALL THE HIGHWAYS! TEMPELHOF AIRDROME HAS BEEN TAKEN! ALL BRIDGES ACROSS THE SPREE ARE IN THEIR HANDS!
AS THE COMMANDING GENERAL ENTERED THE ROOM...
LATEST REPORT, SIR! THE EIGHTEENTH REGIMENT IS WIPED OUT OR CAPTURED! NO SURVIVORS REPORTED BACK!
GENTLEMEN PREPARE YOURSELF FOR A GREAT SHOCK! THE ATTACK ON BERLIN IS NOT AN ISOLATED INCIDENT
MP
HIS WORDS STRUCK LIKE AN EXPLODING BOMB!
I'VE JUST BEEN INFORMED THAT NEW YORK, CHICAGO AND DETROIT HAVE BEEN ATOM-BOMBED!
MEANWHILE, THE RUSSIANS WERE DRIVING THROUGH FROM ALL SIDES. JEFF DECIDED TO ABANDON THE JEEP.
C'MON, GUYS, WE CAN'T STAY IN THE JEEP! WE'D BE DUCK SOUP FOR A COMMIE SHELL! WE'LL HAVE TO LEG IT!
RUNNING DOWN ALLEY-WAYS AND DARKENED STREETS, THEY FINALLY DREW NEAR THE CITY
THEY SURE DID A COMPLETE JOB ON BERLIN!
WHERE DO WE GO FROM HERE, SARGE? WE'RE CUT OFF, SURROUNDED!
3

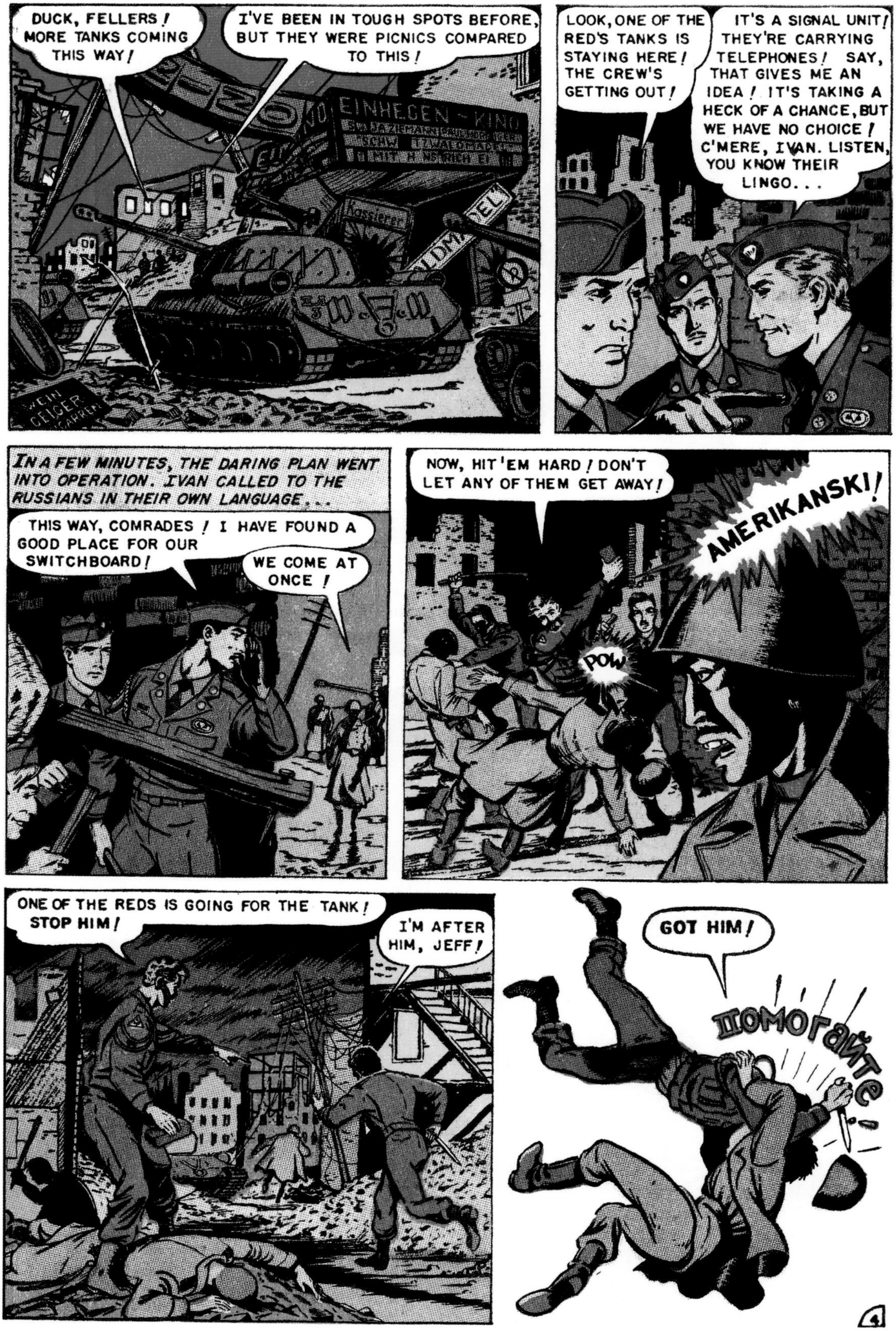

DUCK, FELLERS! MORE TANKS COMING THIS WAY!
I'VE BEEN IN TOUGH SPOTS BEFORE, BUT THEY WERE PICNICS COMPARED TO THIS!
EINHEGEN - KINO
Kassierer
LOOK, ONE OF THE RED'S TANKS IS STAYING HERE! THE CREW'S GETTING OUT!
IT'S A SIGNAL UNIT! THEY'RE CARRYING TELEPHONES! SAY, THAT GIVES ME AN IDEA! IT'S TAKING A HECK OF A CHANCE, BUT WE HAVE NO CHOICE! C'MERE, IVAN. LISTEN, YOU KNOW THEIR LINGO...
IN A FEW MINUTES, THE DARING PLAN WENT INTO OPERATION. IVAN CALLED TO THE RUSSIANS IN THEIR OWN LANGUAGE...
THIS WAY, COMRADES! I HAVE FOUND A GOOD PLACE FOR OUR SWITCHBOARD!
WE COME AT ONCE!
NOW, HIT 'EM HARD! DON'T LET ANY OF THEM GET AWAY!
AMERIKANSKI!
POW
ONE OF THE REDS IS GOING FOR THE TANK! STOP HIM!
I'M AFTER HIM, JEFF!
GOT HIM!
ПОМОГАЙТЕ!
4

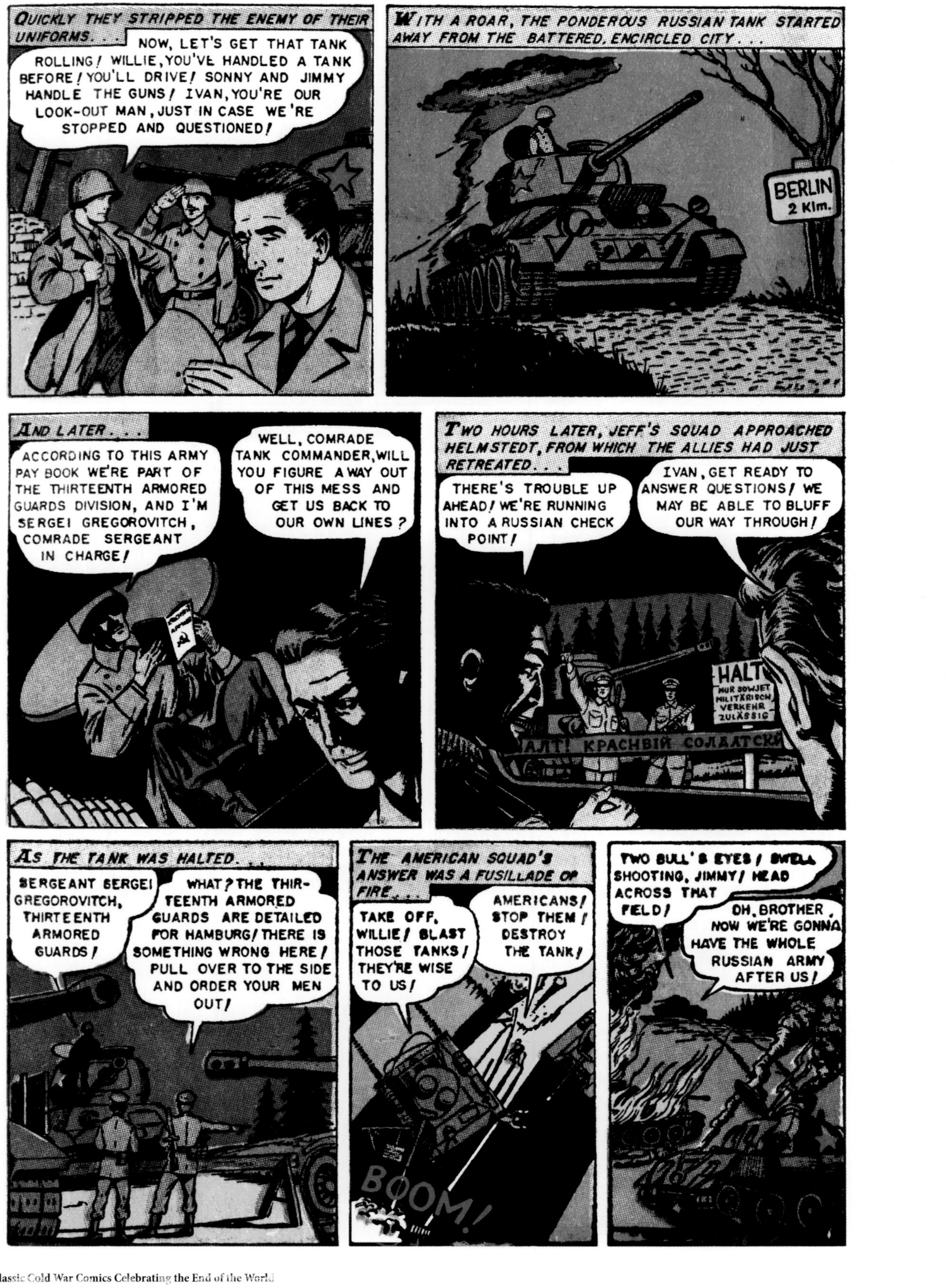

QUICKLY THEY STRIPPED THE ENEMY OF THEIR UNIFORMS. . .
NOW, LET'S GET THAT TANK ROLLING! WILLIE, YOU'VE HANDLED A TANK BEFORE! YOU'LL DRIVE! SONNY AND JIMMY HANDLE THE GUNS! IVAN, YOU'RE OUR LOOK-OUT MAN, JUST IN CASE WE'RE STOPPED AND QUESTIONED!
WITH A ROAR, THE PONDEROUS RUSSIAN TANK STARTED AWAY FROM THE BATTERED, ENCIRCLED CITY . . .
BERLIN 2 Klm.
AND LATER. . .
ACCORDING TO THIS ARMY PAY BOOK WE'RE PART OF THE THIRTEENTH ARMORED GUARDS DIVISION, AND I'M SERGEI GREGOROVITCH, COMRADE SERGEANT IN CHARGE!
WELL, COMRADE TANK COMMANDER, WILL YOU FIGURE A WAY OUT OF THIS MESS AND GET US BACK TO OUR OWN LINES?
TWO HOURS LATER, JEFF'S SQUAD APPROACHED HELMSTEDT, FROM WHICH THE ALLIES HAD JUST RETREATED. . .
THERE'S TROUBLE UP AHEAD! WE'RE RUNNING INTO A RUSSIAN CHECK POINT!
IVAN, GET READY TO ANSWER QUESTIONS! WE MAY BE ABLE TO BLUFF OUR WAY THROUGH!
HALT NUR SOWJET MILITÄRISCH VERKEHR ZULÄSSIG
AS THE TANK WAS HALTED. . .
SERGEANT SERGEI GREGOROVITCH, THIRTEENTH ARMORED GUARDS!
WHAT? THE THIRTEENTH ARMORED GUARDS ARE DETAILED FOR HAMBURG! THERE IS SOMETHING WRONG HERE! PULL OVER TO THE SIDE AND ORDER YOUR MEN OUT!
THE AMERICAN SQUAD'S ANSWER WAS A FUSILLADE OF FIRE. . .
TAKE OFF, WILLIE! BLAST THOSE TANKS! THEY'RE WISE TO US!
AMERICANS! STOP THEM! DESTROY THE TANK!
BOOM!
TWO BULL'S EYES! SWELL SHOOTING, JIMMY! HEAD ACROSS THAT FELD!
OH, BROTHER NOW WE'RE GONNA HAVE THE WHOLE RUSSIAN ARMY AFTER US!

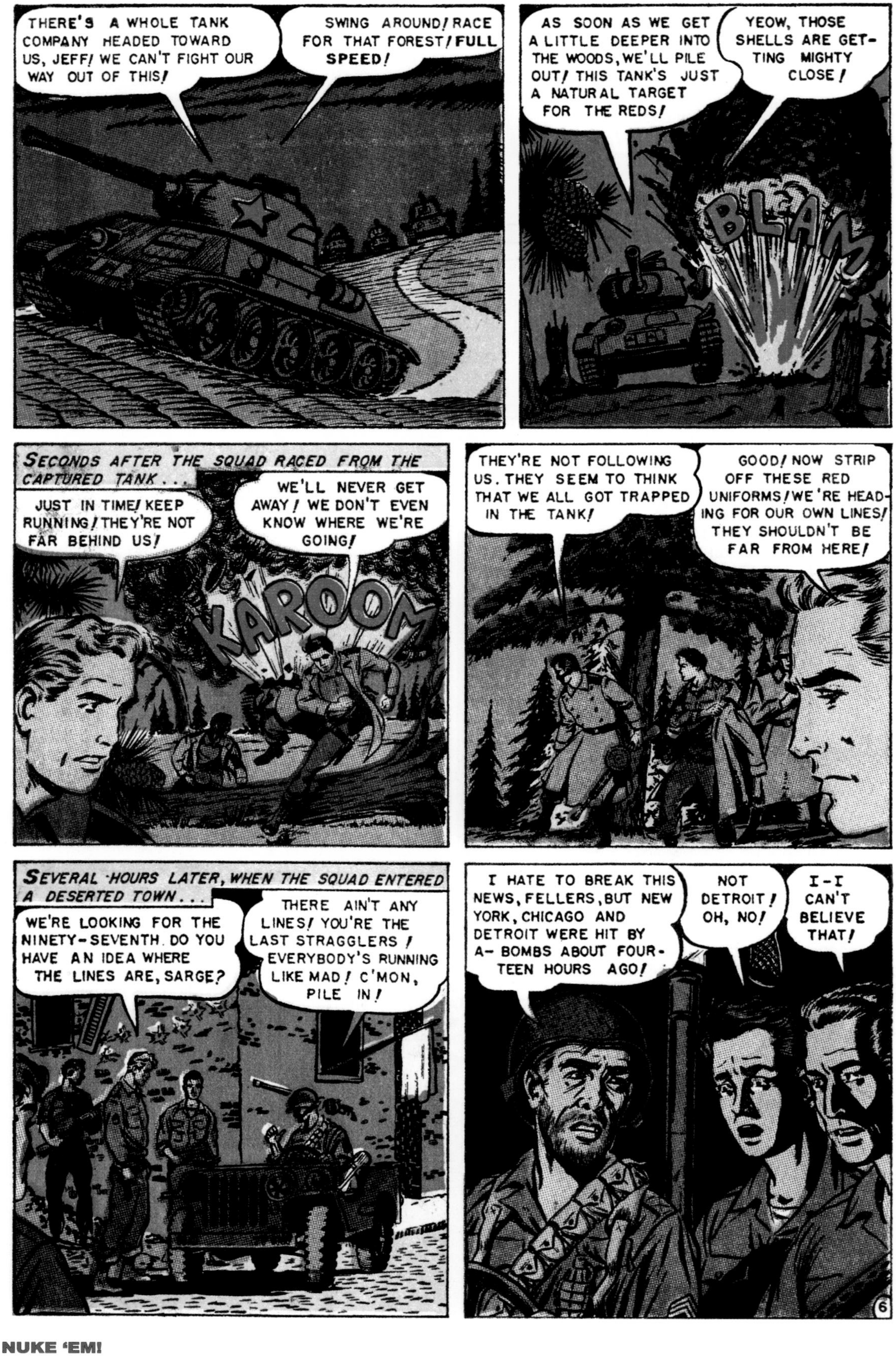
THERE'S A WHOLE TANK COMPANY HEADED TOWARD US, JEFF! WE CAN'T FIGHT OUR WAY OUT OF THIS!
SWING AROUND! RACE FOR THAT FOREST! FULL SPEED!
AS SOON AS WE GET A LITTLE DEEPER INTO THE WOODS, WE'LL PILE OUT! THIS TANK'S JUST A NATURAL TARGET FOR THE REDS!
YEOW, THOSE SHELLS ARE GETTING MIGHTY CLOSE!
BLAM
SECONDS AFTER THE SQUAD RACED FROM THE CAPTURED TANK . . .
JUST IN TIME! KEEP RUNNING! THEY'RE NOT FAR BEHIND US!
WE'LL NEVER GET AWAY! WE DON'T EVEN KNOW WHERE WE'RE GOING!
KAROOM
THEY'RE NOT FOLLOWING US. THEY SEEM TO THINK THAT WE ALL GOT TRAPPED IN THE TANK!
GOOD! NOW STRIP OFF THESE RED UNIFORMS! WE'RE HEADING FOR OUR OWN LINES! THEY SHOULDN'T BE FAR FROM HERE!
SEVERAL HOURS LATER, WHEN THE SQUAD ENTERED A DESERTED TOWN . . .
WE'RE LOOKING FOR THE NINETY-SEVENTH. DO YOU HAVE AN IDEA WHERE THE LINES ARE, SARGE?
THERE AIN'T ANY LINES! YOU'RE THE LAST STRAGGLERS! EVERYBODY'S RUNNING LIKE MAD! C'MON, PILE IN!
I HATE TO BREAK THIS NEWS, FELLERS, BUT NEW YORK, CHICAGO AND DETROIT WERE HIT BY A-BOMBS ABOUT FOURTEEN HOURS AGO!
NOT DETROIT! OH, NO!
I-I CAN'T BELIEVE THAT!
6

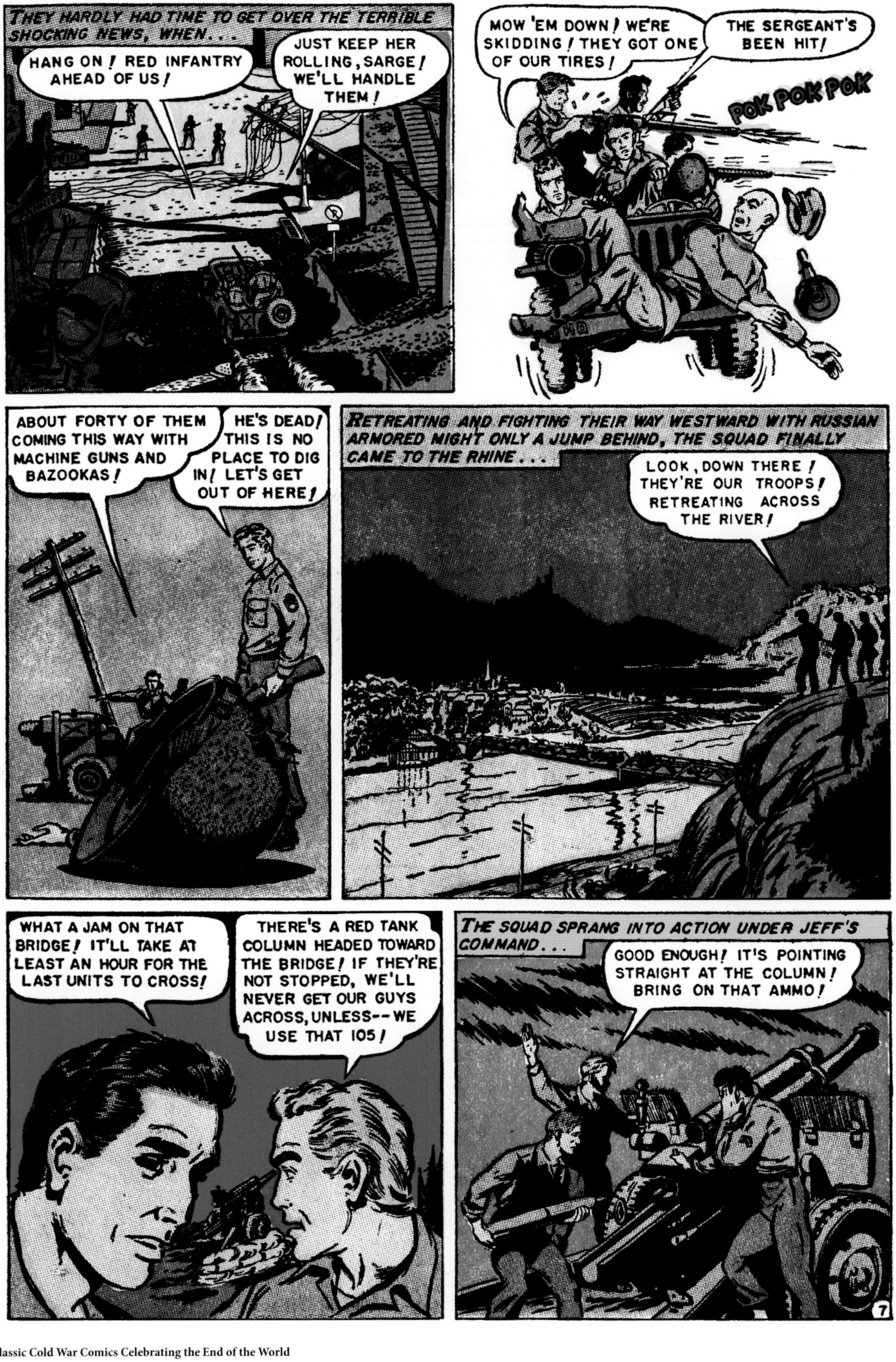

THEY HARDLY HAD TIME TO GET OVER THE TERRIBLE SHOCKING NEWS, WHEN...
HANG ON! RED INFANTRY AHEAD OF US!
JUST KEEP HER ROLLING, SARGE! WE'LL HANDLE THEM!
MOW 'EM DOWN! WE'RE SKIDDING! THEY GOT ONE OF OUR TIRES!
THE SERGEANT'S BEEN HIT!
POK POK POK
ABOUT FORTY OF THEM COMING THIS WAY WITH MACHINE GUNS AND BAZOOKAS!
HE'S DEAD! THIS IS NO PLACE TO DIG IN! LET'S GET OUT OF HERE!
RETREATING AND FIGHTING THEIR WAY WESTWARD WITH RUSSIAN ARMORED MIGHT ONLY A JUMP BEHIND, THE SQUAD FINALLY CAME TO THE RHINE...
LOOK, DOWN THERE! THEY'RE OUR TROOPS! RETREATING ACROSS THE RIVER!
WHAT A JAM ON THAT BRIDGE! IT'LL TAKE AT LEAST AN HOUR FOR THE LAST UNITS TO CROSS!
THERE'S A RED TANK COLUMN HEADED TOWARD THE BRIDGE! IF THEY'RE NOT STOPPED, WE'LL NEVER GET OUR GUYS ACROSS, UNLESS-- WE USE THAT 105!
THE SQUAD SPRANG INTO ACTION UNDER JEFF'S COMMAND...
GOOD ENOUGH! IT'S POINTING STRAIGHT AT THE COLUMN! BRING ON THAT AMMO!
7

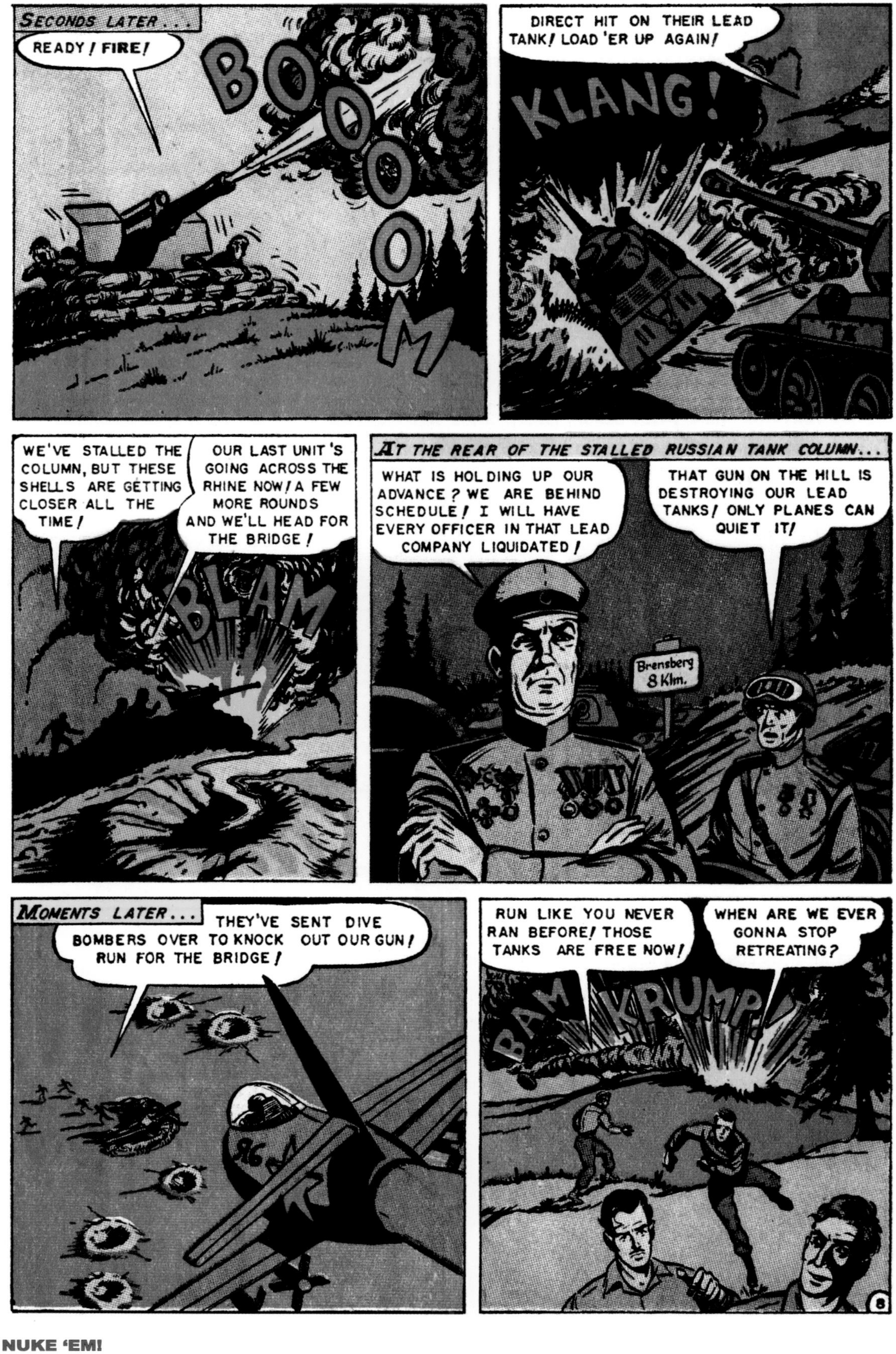
SECONDS LATER . . .
READY! FIRE!
BOOOOOM
DIRECT HIT ON THEIR LEAD TANK! LOAD 'ER UP AGAIN!
KLANG!
WE'VE STALLED THE COLUMN, BUT THESE SHELLS ARE GETTING CLOSER ALL THE TIME!
OUR LAST UNIT'S GOING ACROSS THE RHINE NOW! A FEW MORE ROUNDS AND WE'LL HEAD FOR THE BRIDGE!
BLAM
AT THE REAR OF THE STALLED RUSSIAN TANK COLUMN...
WHAT IS HOLDING UP OUR ADVANCE? WE ARE BEHIND SCHEDULE! I WILL HAVE EVERY OFFICER IN THAT LEAD COMPANY LIQUIDATED!
THAT GUN ON THE HILL IS DESTROYING OUR LEAD TANKS! ONLY PLANES CAN QUIET IT!
Brensberg 8 Klm.
MOMENTS LATER...
THEY'VE SENT DIVE BOMBERS OVER TO KNOCK OUT OUR GUN! RUN FOR THE BRIDGE!
RUN LIKE YOU NEVER RAN BEFORE! THOSE TANKS ARE FREE NOW!
WHEN ARE WE EVER GONNA STOP RETREATING?
BAM
KRUMP
8

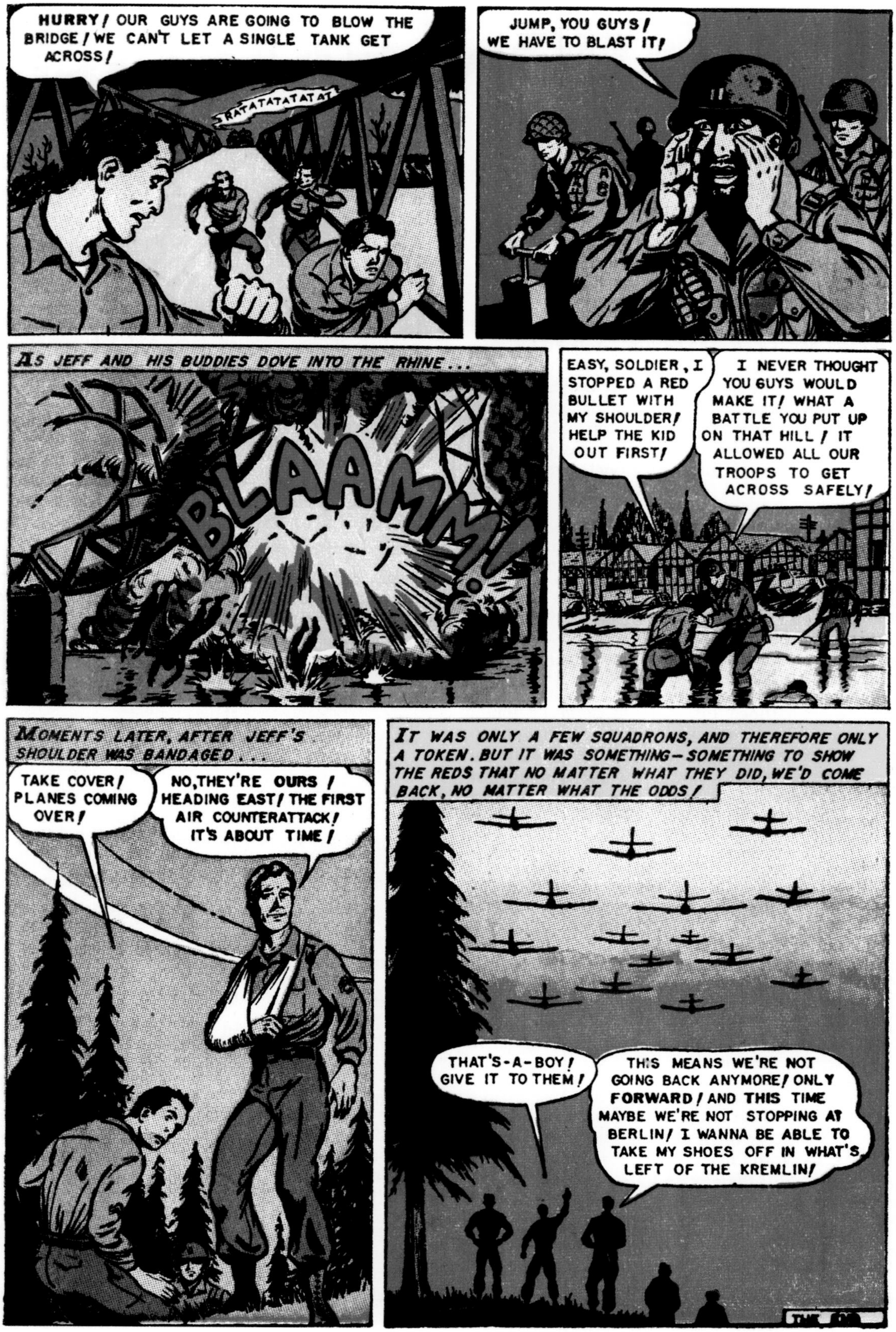
HURRY! OUR GUYS ARE GOING TO BLOW THE BRIDGE! WE CAN'T LET A SINGLE TANK GET ACROSS!
RATATATATATAT
JUMP, YOU GUYS! WE HAVE TO BLAST IT!
AS JEFF AND HIS BUDDIES DOVE INTO THE RHINE...
BLAAMM!
EASY, SOLDIER, I STOPPED A RED BULLET WITH MY SHOULDER! HELP THE KID OUT FIRST!
I NEVER THOUGHT YOU GUYS WOULD MAKE IT! WHAT A BATTLE YOU PUT UP ON THAT HILL! IT ALLOWED ALL OUR TROOPS TO GET ACROSS SAFELY!
MOMENTS LATER, AFTER JEFF'S SHOULDER WAS BANDAGED...
TAKE COVER! PLANES COMING OVER!
NO, THEY'RE OURS! HEADING EAST! THE FIRST AIR COUNTERATTACK! IT'S ABOUT TIME!
IT WAS ONLY A FEW SQUADRONS, AND THEREFORE ONLY A TOKEN. BUT IT WAS SOMETHING—SOMETHING TO SHOW THE REDS THAT NO MATTER WHAT THEY DID, WE'D COME BACK, NO MATTER WHAT THE ODDS!
THAT'S-A-BOY! GIVE IT TO THEM!
THIS MEANS WE'RE NOT GOING BACK ANYMORE! ONLY FORWARD! AND THIS TIME MAYBE WE'RE NOT STOPPING AT BERLIN! I WANNA BE ABLE TO TAKE MY SHOES OFF IN WHAT'S LEFT OF THE KREMLIN!

OPERATION HAYSTACK

Lieutenant Edwards led his patrol down the hot, dusty Italian road. It would be getting dark soon, and they were due back at First Army Field Headquarters. As far as he was concerned, it had been an uneventful foray. Except for a skirmish with some Russian soldiers who had wandered off to search for loot, they'd seen nothing to indicate the Russians considered this region of strategic importance.

There was a farmhouse up the road, and just to take precautions, Lieutenant Edwards ordered his men to scatter off the road. In a moment he realized they'd been lucky. Someone had come out of the farmhouse, and Edwards sighted him with his field glasses. Then a tremor of excitement ran through him as he handed the glasses to Sergeant Jones. Unless his eyes were mistaken, he'd seen a Russian colonel come out of the farmhouse.

As the sergeant confirmed his judgment, Edwards pondered the puzzle. What would a high-ranking officer be doing along this supposedly unimportant road? Something important must be brewing.

It didn't take long for Lieutenant Edwards to make up his mind. In another hour it would be dark. He knew he wasn't going to leave that farmhouse until he found out what was happening there.

Quickly he outlined his plans to Sergeant Jones. "If there's really something important going on up there," he explained, "the place will be well defended. Twenty men would be a handful against what we can expect. Best thing is for me to creep up and reconnoiter. If I'm not back in an hour, go on to field headquarters and report what we've seen."

As soon as darkness enveloped the countryside, Lieutenant Edwards took off. As he approached the farmhouse, he lay flat on the ground, squirming ahead on his stomach, and lifting his rifle slightly to keep it out of the mud. Ahead was only darkness and quiet It was still; there was something ominous about it, as if unseen eyes were watching his every move. He heard the whir of planes overhead. U. S. reconnaisance, he knew by the sound of the engines, out to try to locate that munitions dump intelligence knew was in the area.

There was just this hill to get over, and he'd be approaching the rear of the farmhouse. It was almost too simple. Down on his stomach, Edwards squirmed down the hill. Still there wasn't a sound. Was it possible that the Russians had left this side unguarded? There was no sound of life around the place. He began to wonder if his eyes had been playing tricks on him before.

He'd made it down the hill, and he paused for a moment, crouched in the shelter of the stacked hay near the barn. From this vantage point he could see a thin sliver of light seeping out from the shuttered back windows of the farmhouse.

The point of the bayonet at his back was sharp! He didn't dare turn around as a guttural voice rapped out what was obviously a command in Russian. Then the guard repeated it, and there was the sound of running feet as someone else came up. The second Russian soldier fronted him, and Edwards saw the blue color of the private's uniform. There was a wicked-looking Russian snub-nosed revolver in the other's hand.

For a moment Edwards wondered if they were going to shoot him right there. But then the soldier was motioning with his gun for Edwards to rise, and slowly he got to his feet, keeping his hands carefully above his head. He felt the bayonet still at his back as he stumbled toward the farmhouse.

After the darkness outside, the light of the room hit him like a shock. But then his surprise widened as he saw the place had been set up as a field office! It was humming with activity. The colonel he'd seen earlier was seated behind the desk, and suddenly Edwards was convinced he'd stumbled onto the location of the munitions dump First Army Field Headquarters had been searching for so desperately. But, Edwards thought, there was little he could do about it now!

He didn't have time to ponder it further. The guard who'd discovered him said something in Russian, and the colonel nodded. He eyed Edwards speculatively, and then he said in perfect English, "Sit down." He motioned toward the chair alongside him.

Edwards stumbled toward the chair after a final thrust from his guard. He warily watched the Russian colonel. The guard had emptied Edwards pockets, and now the colonel thumbed swiftly through the assortment on his desk. There was nothing there.

Suddenly the colonel spoke to him. "What are you doing here?" he rapped. "Who sent you? How many men are with you?" He fired the questions one after the other.

Edwards was silent. The colonel waited, and when he saw Edwards didn't intend to answer he said, "Bah! You intend to play the brave soldier, eh? We'll see how easily you'll break down!"

The questioning went on and on. Hour after hour the colonel hurled questions at him. The light hurt Edwards' eyes. The colonel looked disheveled, but somehow he didn't let up for a moment.

Edwards didn't remember when the first blow landed. It came suddenly from the huge, meaty Russian who had captured him and had stood motionless by his side throughout the interrogation. But now Edwards' head snapped back under the impact of the blow. He felt blood running down his split lip. He tried to rise, and he felt someone grip his arms from behind him. The blows continued, and in between each blow the questions were hurled at him. Crazily he thought that even if he had wanted to say something, the words would never come out from between his smashed lips.

Then dimly he heard the colonel say, "Take him away. Let him have time to think what it will be like to have to return to my questioning. Bring him back in two hours."

Edwards felt himself yanked to his feet. The soldier who had been smashing his mouth helped him out. Slowly they stumbled through the dark around the farmhouse. As Edwards' eyes became accustomed to the gloom, he made out the haystack. He became aware of the activity around him. Why, he realized, he was standing right in the middle of the munitions dump! The Russians had burrowed a huge cavern in the earth in back of the farmhouse. Since the top shrubbery hadn't been disturbed, there would be no evidence of the dump from the air. No wonder recon hadn't been able to spot it! But now men were running back and forth, wheeling out barrows stacked with rifles and cartridges. These were being loaded into a truck which stood camouflaged alongside the entrance.

He felt the guard nudge him, and he trudged along with the man. Finally they came to what had been the barn. Obviously no provision had been made for holding anyone captive here. The Russian guard shoved Edwards inside, and then Edwards heard the bolt being slid outside.

There was nothing in the barn that could be used as a weapon, Edwards saw quickly. The place had been stripped bare. There wasn't even a window. He'd hardly finished his examination when he heard the bolt being slipped back again. He tensed with alarm as the door creaked open slightly.

It was the second soldier that had helped capture him. The fellow came softly into the room. In one hand he was holding his cocked revolver, and in the other, Edwards saw with amazement, that the fellow carried the field glasses Edwards had dropped when the guard had apprehended him. The Russian soldier approached him with a crafty smile. When he came up close to Edwards, he motioned to the field glasses, waved the gun, and said something in Russian.

Gradually, Edwards came to realize what the soldier wanted. He'd found the glasses, and obviously he believed Edwards had hidden some of his possessions before he'd been captured. The Russian soldier motioned to his wrist significantly. Edwards hadn't been wearing a wristwatch. He'd broken it and it was back at headquarters awaiting a replacement. The soldier obviously wanted to know where Edwards had hidden the watch. These men in the Russian Army were ill-equipped, and they were starved for American luxuries. They'd do anything for a watch, Edwards realized incredulously, even endanger their army.

As if to ingratiate himself, the Russian offered him a cigarette. Edwards took it, lit it, and puffed slowly, stalling for time. What should he do next, he wondered. He looked longingly out the partially opened barn door. He'd like to run for it, he thought, but there was no chance of making it. His eyes lit on the haystack near where the Russian had found the field glasses. Overhead his ears picked up the delicate throb of U. S. recon planes approaching on their way back to base.

Suddenly, as if he'd come to a decision, Edwards made a motion to the ground as if he'd toss down the cigarette. But before he ground the heel of his shoe over the butt, he'd quickly snapped in two the stiff Russian cigarette. He shoved his hands into his pockets, palming the burning butt, and motioned to the Russian with his head.

Together they left the barn, and Edwards led the way back to the haystack. The sound of the approaching planes was louder now. His timing had to be right! Just as the recon swarmed overhead, Edwards tossed the lighted butt atop the dry hay.

The Russian uttered an oath. He came at Edwards, cocking his gun, and Edwards desperately plowed into him, deflecting his aim. He heard the crackle of burning hay. If only, he thought desperately, recon would know what it meant—if only the blaze would spread and outline the activity on the ground!

As he struggled with the Russian, he heard the sweetest sound of his career. The slow whine of the dive bombers, and then the crashing thunder as the released bombs hit their mark. Flaming debris fell, and suddenly he heard another sound—the high-pitched yell of Sergeant Jones. Gunfire rattled as Jones and the boys stormed in.

The Russian twisted free and tried to run. Edwards saw the gun in Jones' hand aimed, and the Russian toppled. Then Edwards felt Jones' pounding on his back.

Later he listened to Jones apologize for going against orders. When Edwards hadn't returned, the men had itched to go trouble-shooting. "Heck, Lieutenant," Jones drawled. "We ain't one of those sissy record-keeping patrols. The only kind of report we turn in is 'mission accomplished!'"

THE END

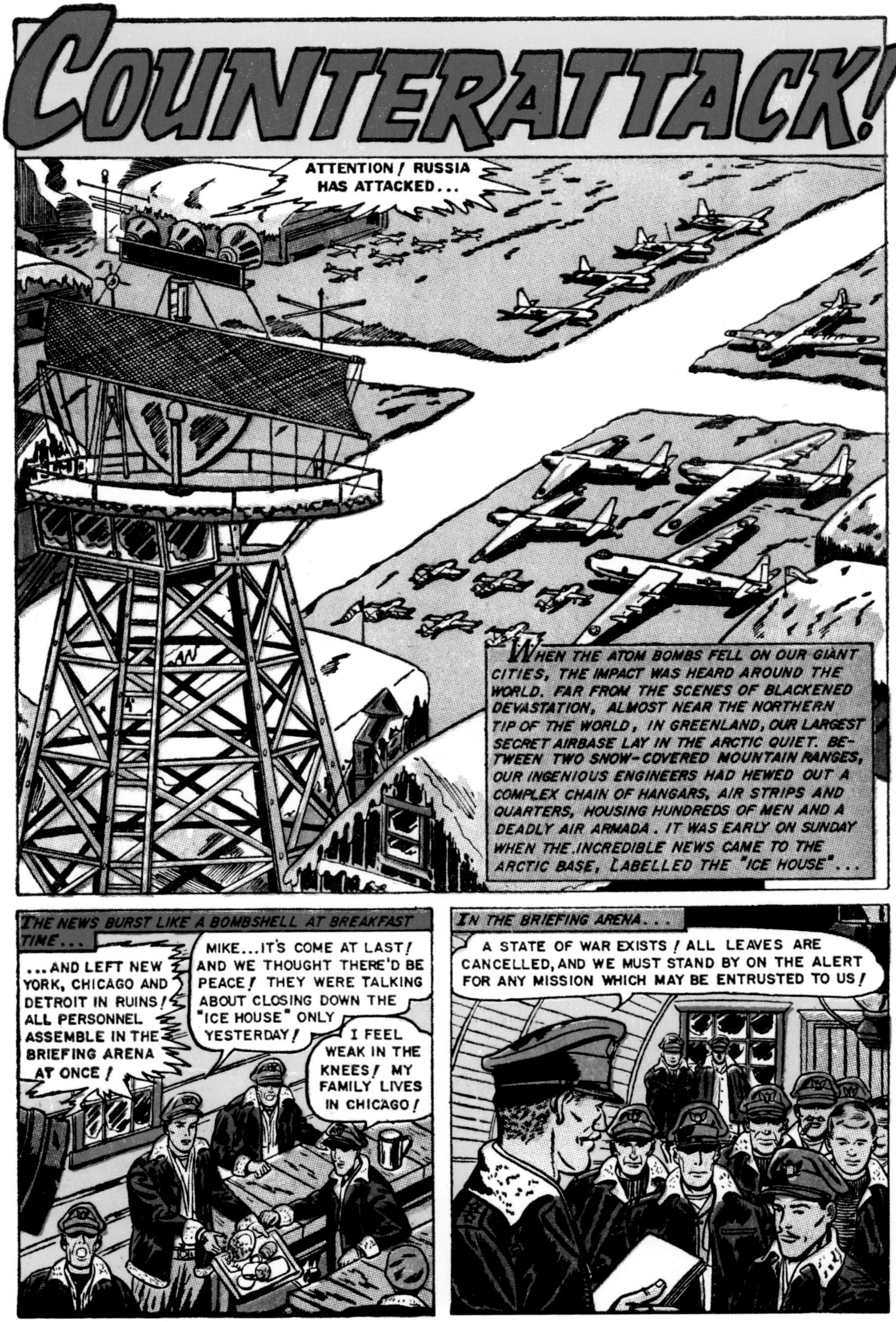
COUNTERATTACK!
ATTENTION! RUSSIA HAS ATTACKED...
WHEN THE ATOM BOMBS FELL ON OUR GIANT CITIES, THE IMPACT WAS HEARD AROUND THE WORLD. FAR FROM THE SCENES OF BLACKENED DEVASTATION, ALMOST NEAR THE NORTHERN TIP OF THE WORLD, IN GREENLAND, OUR LARGEST SECRET AIRBASE LAY IN THE ARCTIC QUIET. BETWEEN TWO SNOW-COVERED MOUNTAIN RANGES, OUR INGENIOUS ENGINEERS HAD HEWED OUT A COMPLEX CHAIN OF HANGARS, AIR STRIPS AND QUARTERS, HOUSING HUNDREDS OF MEN AND A DEADLY AIR ARMADA. IT WAS EARLY ON SUNDAY WHEN THE INCREDIBLE NEWS CAME TO THE ARCTIC BASE, LABELLED THE "ICE HOUSE"...
THE NEWS BURST LIKE A BOMBSHELL AT BREAKFAST TIME...
...AND LEFT NEW YORK, CHICAGO AND DETROIT IN RUINS! ALL PERSONNEL ASSEMBLE IN THE BRIEFING ARENA AT ONCE!
MIKE...IT'S COME AT LAST! AND WE THOUGHT THERE'D BE PEACE! THEY WERE TALKING ABOUT CLOSING DOWN THE "ICE HOUSE" ONLY YESTERDAY!
I FEEL WEAK IN THE KNEES! MY FAMILY LIVES IN CHICAGO!
IN THE BRIEFING ARENA...
A STATE OF WAR EXISTS! ALL LEAVES ARE CANCELLED, AND WE MUST STAND BY ON THE ALERT FOR ANY MISSION WHICH MAY BE ENTRUSTED TO US!

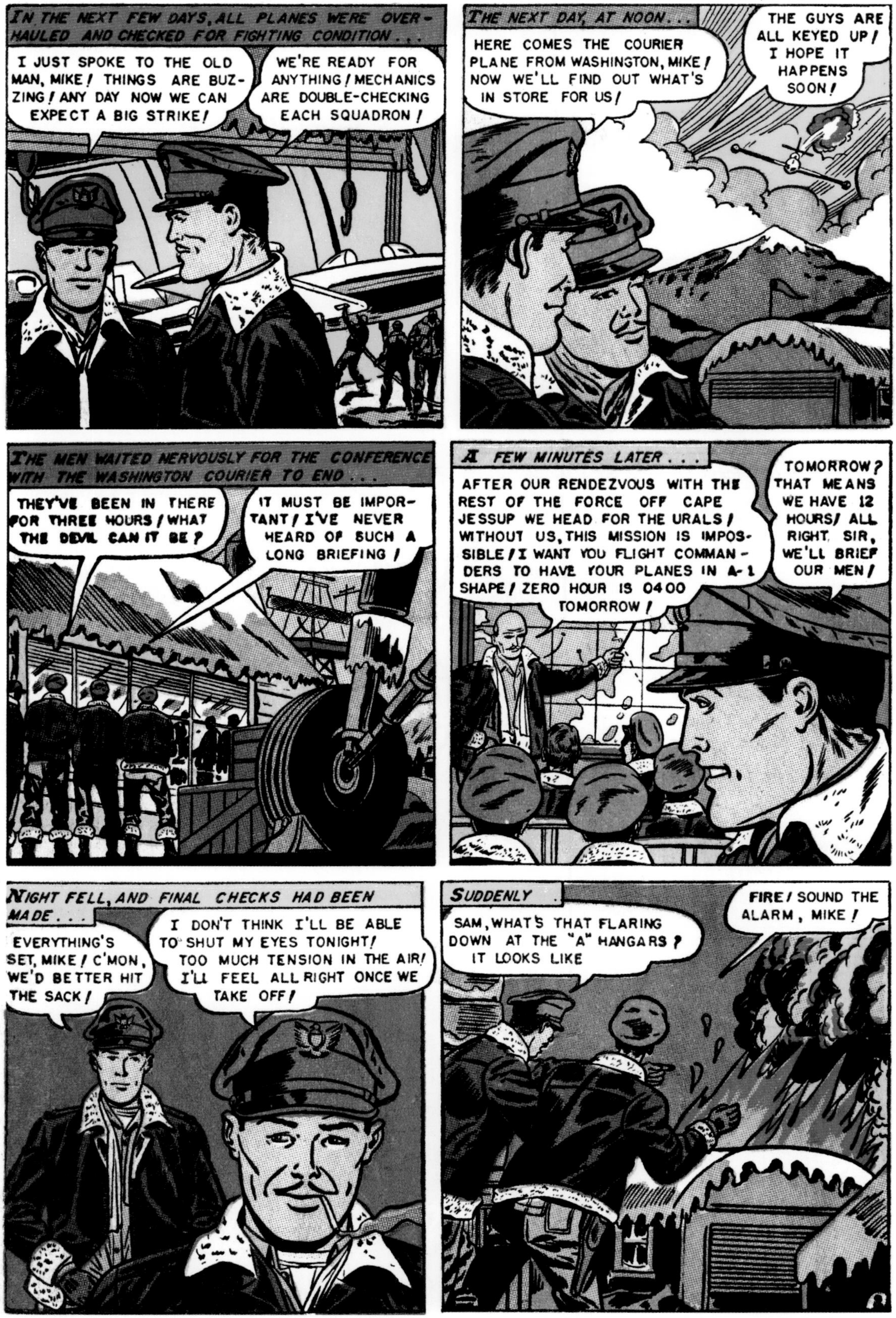

IN THE NEXT FEW DAYS, ALL PLANES WERE OVER-HAULED AND CHECKED FOR FIGHTING CONDITION...
I JUST SPOKE TO THE OLD MAN, MIKE! THINGS ARE BUZ-ZING! ANY DAY NOW WE CAN EXPECT A BIG STRIKE!
WE'RE READY FOR ANYTHING! MECHANICS ARE DOUBLE-CHECKING EACH SQUADRON!
THE NEXT DAY, AT NOON...
HERE COMES THE COURIER PLANE FROM WASHINGTON, MIKE! NOW WE'LL FIND OUT WHAT'S IN STORE FOR US!
THE GUYS ARE ALL KEYED UP! I HOPE IT HAPPENS SOON!
THE MEN WAITED NERVOUSLY FOR THE CONFERENCE WITH THE WASHINGTON COURIER TO END...
THEY'VE BEEN IN THERE FOR THREE HOURS! WHAT THE DEVIL CAN IT BE?
IT MUST BE IMPOR-TANT! I'VE NEVER HEARD OF SUCH A LONG BRIEFING!
A FEW MINUTES LATER...
AFTER OUR RENDEZVOUS WITH THE REST OF THE FORCE OFF CAPE JESSUP WE HEAD FOR THE URALS! WITHOUT US, THIS MISSION IS IMPOS-SIBLE! I WANT YOU FLIGHT COMMAN-DERS TO HAVE YOUR PLANES IN A-1 SHAPE! ZERO HOUR IS 0400 TOMORROW!
TOMORROW? THAT MEANS WE HAVE 12 HOURS! ALL RIGHT, SIR, WE'LL BRIEF OUR MEN!
NIGHT FELL, AND FINAL CHECKS HAD BEEN MADE...
EVERYTHING'S SET, MIKE! C'MON, WE'D BETTER HIT THE SACK!
I DON'T THINK I'LL BE ABLE TO SHUT MY EYES TONIGHT! TOO MUCH TENSION IN THE AIR! I'LL FEEL ALL RIGHT ONCE WE TAKE OFF!
SUDDENLY.
SAM, WHAT'S THAT FLARING DOWN AT THE "A" HANGARS? IT LOOKS LIKE
FIRE! SOUND THE ALARM, MIKE!

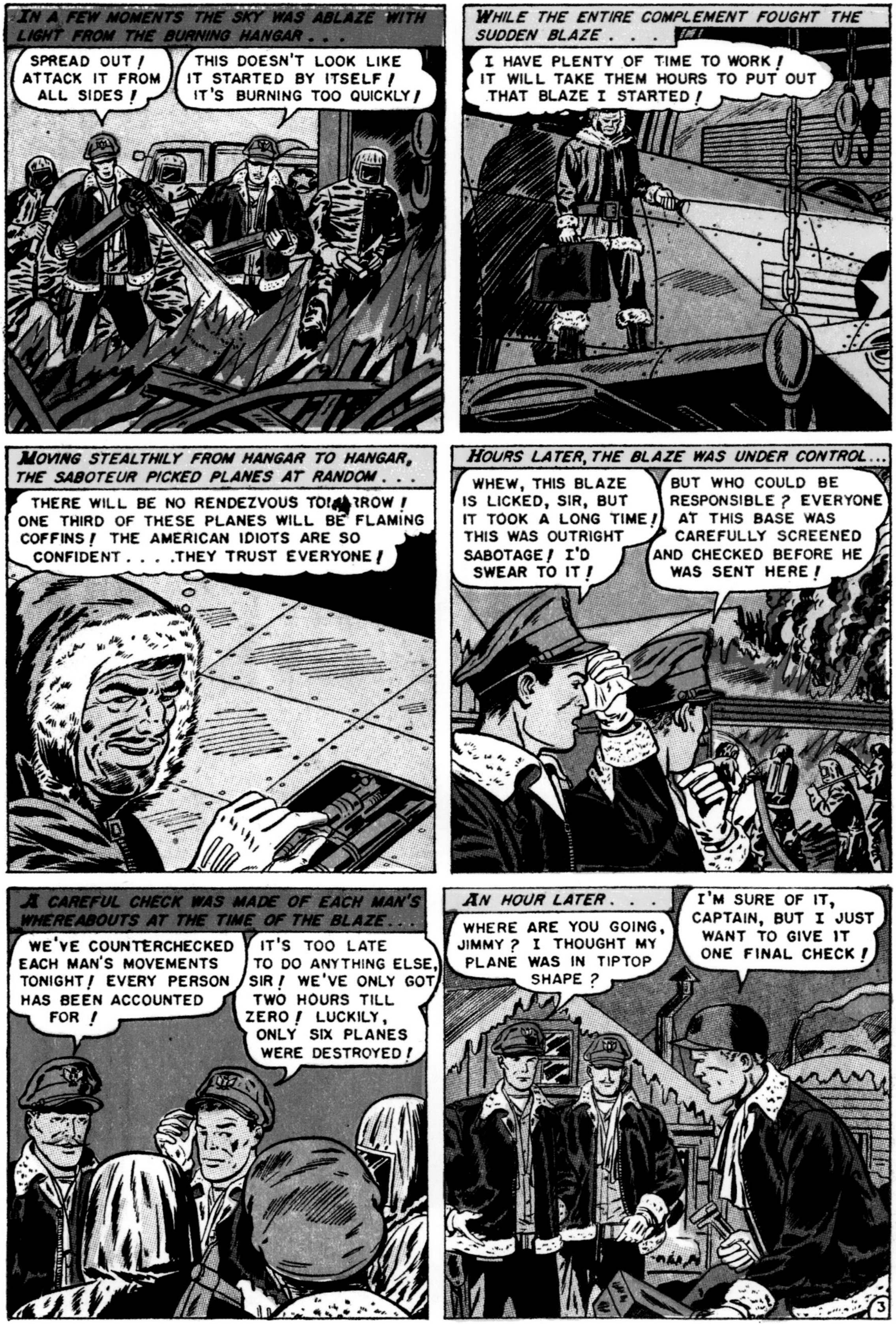
IN A FEW MOMENTS THE SKY WAS ABLAZE WITH LIGHT FROM THE BURNING HANGAR . . .
SPREAD OUT! ATTACK IT FROM ALL SIDES!
THIS DOESN'T LOOK LIKE IT STARTED BY ITSELF! IT'S BURNING TOO QUICKLY!
WHILE THE ENTIRE COMPLEMENT FOUGHT THE SUDDEN BLAZE . . .
I HAVE PLENTY OF TIME TO WORK! IT WILL TAKE THEM HOURS TO PUT OUT THAT BLAZE I STARTED!
MOVING STEALTHILY FROM HANGAR TO HANGAR, THE SABOTEUR PICKED PLANES AT RANDOM . . .
THERE WILL BE NO RENDEZVOUS TO RROW! ONE THIRD OF THESE PLANES WILL BE FLAMING COFFINS! THE AMERICAN IDIOTS ARE SO CONFIDENT . . . .THEY TRUST EVERYONE!
HOURS LATER, THE BLAZE WAS UNDER CONTROL...
WHEW, THIS BLAZE IS LICKED, SIR, BUT IT TOOK A LONG TIME! THIS WAS OUTRIGHT SABOTAGE! I'D SWEAR TO IT!
BUT WHO COULD BE RESPONSIBLE? EVERYONE AT THIS BASE WAS CAREFULLY SCREENED AND CHECKED BEFORE HE WAS SENT HERE!
A CAREFUL CHECK WAS MADE OF EACH MAN'S WHEREABOUTS AT THE TIME OF THE BLAZE...
WE'VE COUNTERCHECKED EACH MAN'S MOVEMENTS TONIGHT! EVERY PERSON HAS BEEN ACCOUNTED FOR!
IT'S TOO LATE TO DO ANYTHING ELSE, SIR! WE'VE ONLY GOT TWO HOURS TILL ZERO! LUCKILY, ONLY SIX PLANES WERE DESTROYED!
AN HOUR LATER . . .
WHERE ARE YOU GOING, JIMMY? I THOUGHT MY PLANE WAS IN TIPTOP SHAPE?
I'M SURE OF IT, CAPTAIN, BUT I JUST WANT TO GIVE IT ONE FINAL CHECK!
3

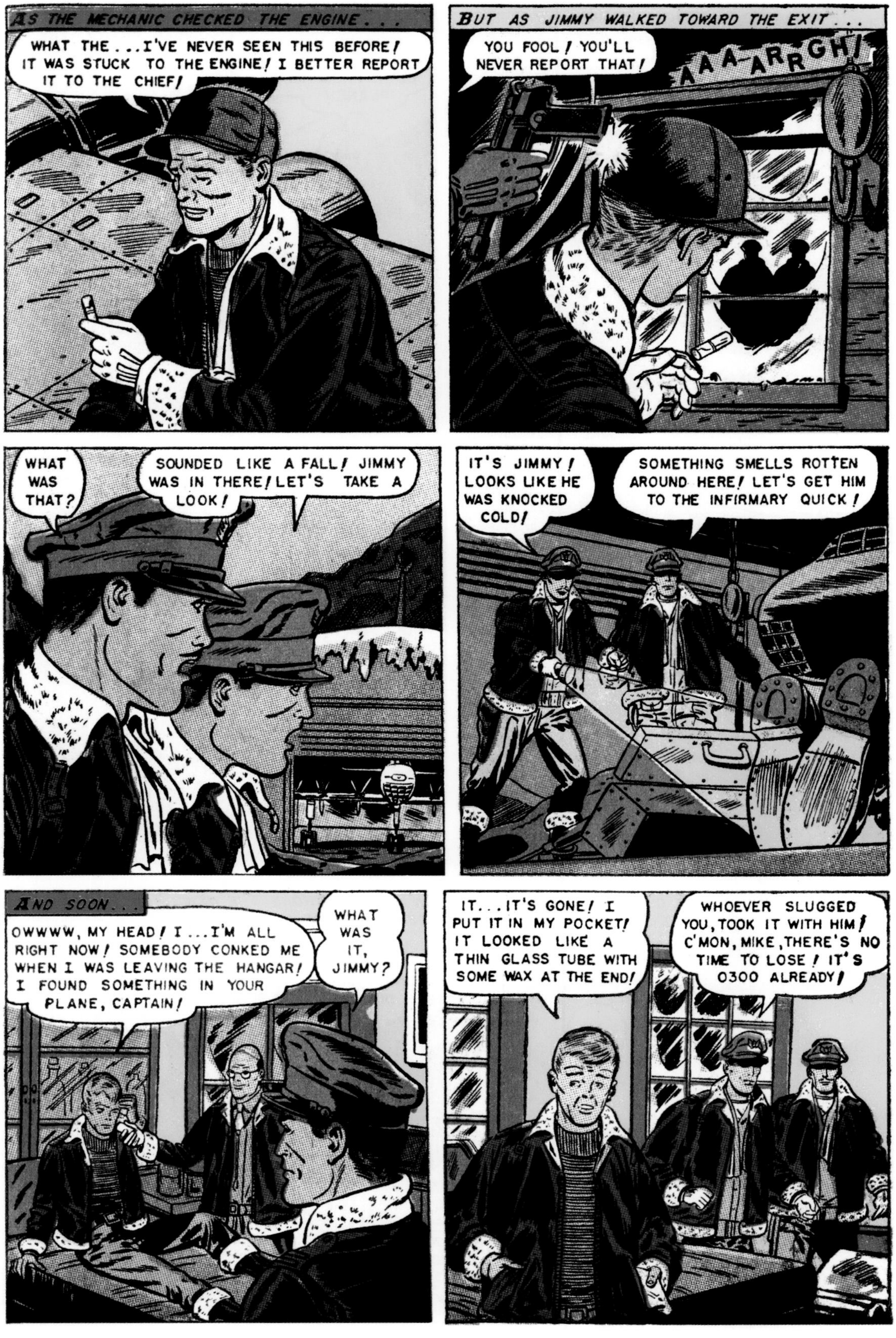
AS THE MECHANIC CHECKED THE ENGINE . . .
WHAT THE . . . I'VE NEVER SEEN THIS BEFORE! IT WAS STUCK TO THE ENGINE! I BETTER REPORT IT TO THE CHIEF!
BUT AS JIMMY WALKED TOWARD THE EXIT . . .
YOU FOOL! YOU'LL NEVER REPORT THAT!
AAAARRGH!
WHAT WAS THAT?
SOUNDED LIKE A FALL! JIMMY WAS IN THERE! LET'S TAKE A LOOK!
IT'S JIMMY! LOOKS LIKE HE WAS KNOCKED COLD!
SOMETHING SMELLS ROTTEN AROUND HERE! LET'S GET HIM TO THE INFIRMARY QUICK!
AND SOON . . .
OWWWW, MY HEAD! I . . . I'M ALL RIGHT NOW! SOMEBODY CONKED ME WHEN I WAS LEAVING THE HANGAR! I FOUND SOMETHING IN YOUR PLANE, CAPTAIN!
WHAT WAS IT, JIMMY?
IT . . . IT'S GONE! I PUT IT IN MY POCKET! IT LOOKED LIKE A THIN GLASS TUBE WITH SOME WAX AT THE END!
WHOEVER SLUGGED YOU, TOOK IT WITH HIM! C'MON, MIKE, THERE'S NO TIME TO LOSE! IT'S 0300 ALREADY!

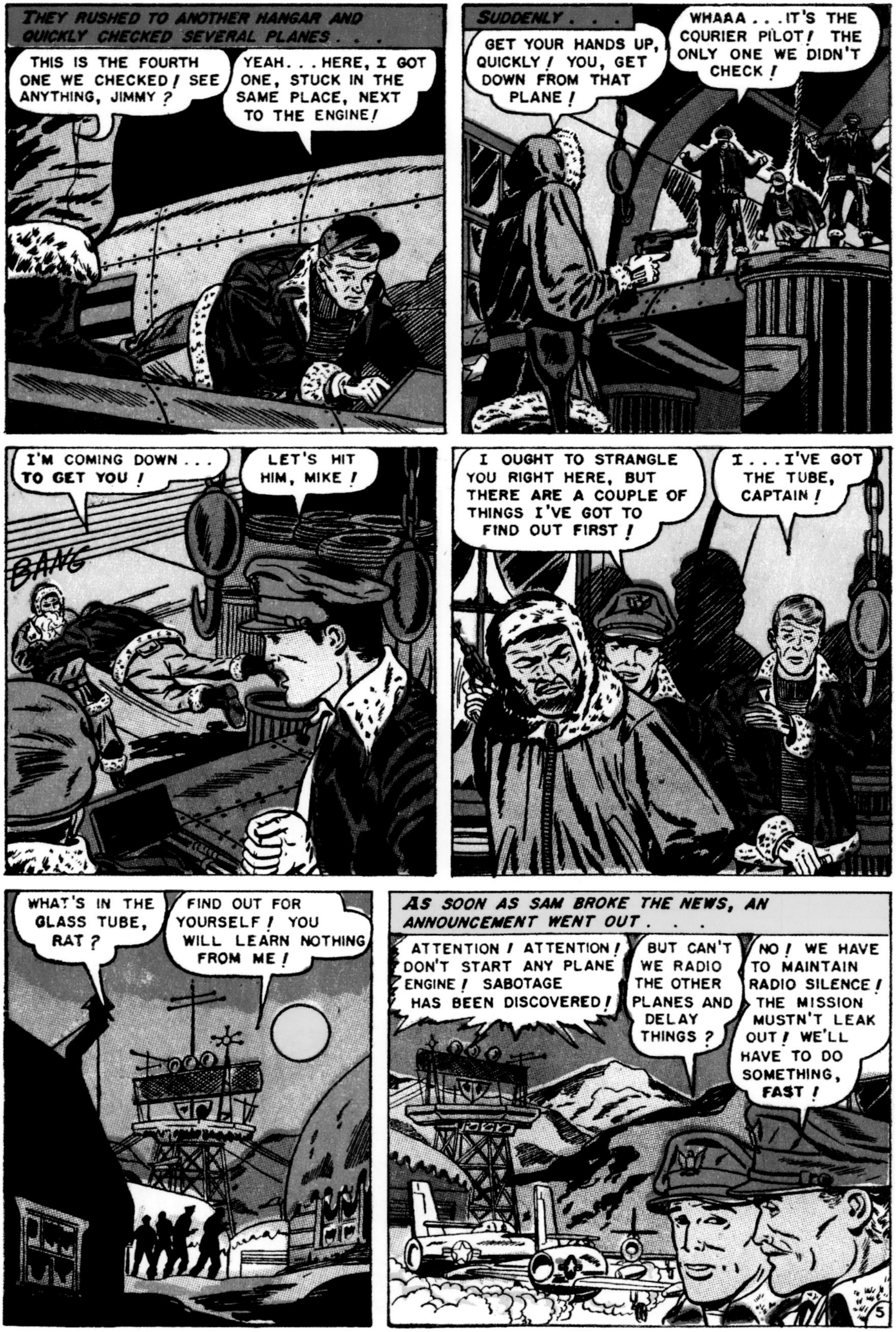

THEY RUSHED TO ANOTHER HANGAR AND QUICKLY CHECKED SEVERAL PLANES . . .
THIS IS THE FOURTH ONE WE CHECKED! SEE ANYTHING, JIMMY?
YEAH. . . HERE, I GOT ONE, STUCK IN THE SAME PLACE, NEXT TO THE ENGINE!
SUDDENLY . . .
GET YOUR HANDS UP, QUICKLY! YOU, GET DOWN FROM THAT PLANE!
WHAAA . . .IT'S THE COURIER PILOT! THE ONLY ONE WE DIDN'T CHECK!
I'M COMING DOWN . . . TO GET YOU!
LET'S HIT HIM, MIKE!
BANG
I OUGHT TO STRANGLE YOU RIGHT HERE, BUT THERE ARE A COUPLE OF THINGS I'VE GOT TO FIND OUT FIRST!
I . . . I'VE GOT THE TUBE, CAPTAIN!
WHAT'S IN THE GLASS TUBE, RAT?
FIND OUT FOR YOURSELF! YOU WILL LEARN NOTHING FROM ME!
AS SOON AS SAM BROKE THE NEWS, AN ANNOUNCEMENT WENT OUT . . .
ATTENTION! ATTENTION! DON'T START ANY PLANE ENGINE! SABOTAGE HAS BEEN DISCOVERED!
BUT CAN'T WE RADIO THE OTHER PLANES AND DELAY THINGS?
NO! WE HAVE TO MAINTAIN RADIO SILENCE! THE MISSION MUSTN'T LEAK OUT! WE'LL HAVE TO DO SOMETHING, FAST!
5

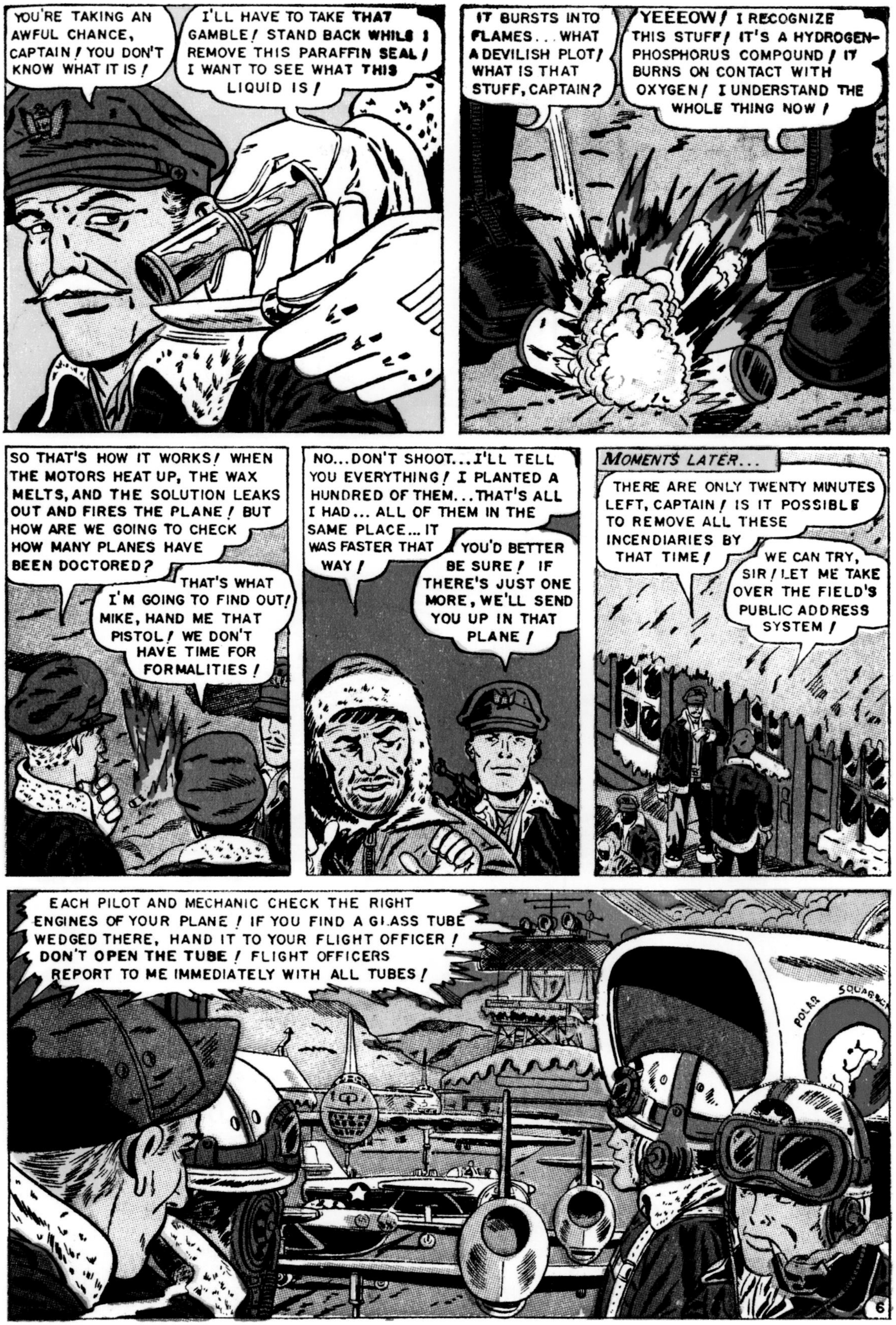
YOU'RE TAKING AN AWFUL CHANCE, CAPTAIN! YOU DON'T KNOW WHAT IT IS!
I'LL HAVE TO TAKE THAT GAMBLE! STAND BACK WHILE I REMOVE THIS PARAFFIN SEAL! I WANT TO SEE WHAT THIS LIQUID IS!
IT BURSTS INTO FLAMES... WHAT A DEVILISH PLOT! WHAT IS THAT STUFF, CAPTAIN?
YEEEOW! I RECOGNIZE THIS STUFF! IT'S A HYDROGEN-PHOSPHORUS COMPOUND! IT BURNS ON CONTACT WITH OXYGEN! I UNDERSTAND THE WHOLE THING NOW!
SO THAT'S HOW IT WORKS! WHEN THE MOTORS HEAT UP, THE WAX MELTS, AND THE SOLUTION LEAKS OUT AND FIRES THE PLANE! BUT HOW ARE WE GOING TO CHECK HOW MANY PLANES HAVE BEEN DOCTORED?
THAT'S WHAT I'M GOING TO FIND OUT! MIKE, HAND ME THAT PISTOL! WE DON'T HAVE TIME FOR FORMALITIES!
NO...DON'T SHOOT...I'LL TELL YOU EVERYTHING! I PLANTED A HUNDRED OF THEM...THAT'S ALL I HAD... ALL OF THEM IN THE SAME PLACE... IT WAS FASTER THAT WAY!
YOU'D BETTER BE SURE! IF THERE'S JUST ONE MORE, WE'LL SEND YOU UP IN THAT PLANE!
MOMENTS LATER...
THERE ARE ONLY TWENTY MINUTES LEFT, CAPTAIN! IS IT POSSIBLE TO REMOVE ALL THESE INCENDIARIES BY THAT TIME!
WE CAN TRY, SIR! LET ME TAKE OVER THE FIELD'S PUBLIC ADDRESS SYSTEM!
EACH PILOT AND MECHANIC CHECK THE RIGHT ENGINES OF YOUR PLANE! IF YOU FIND A GLASS TUBE WEDGED THERE, HAND IT TO YOUR FLIGHT OFFICER! DON'T OPEN THE TUBE! FLIGHT OFFICERS REPORT TO ME IMMEDIATELY WITH ALL TUBES!
POLAR SQUADRON
6

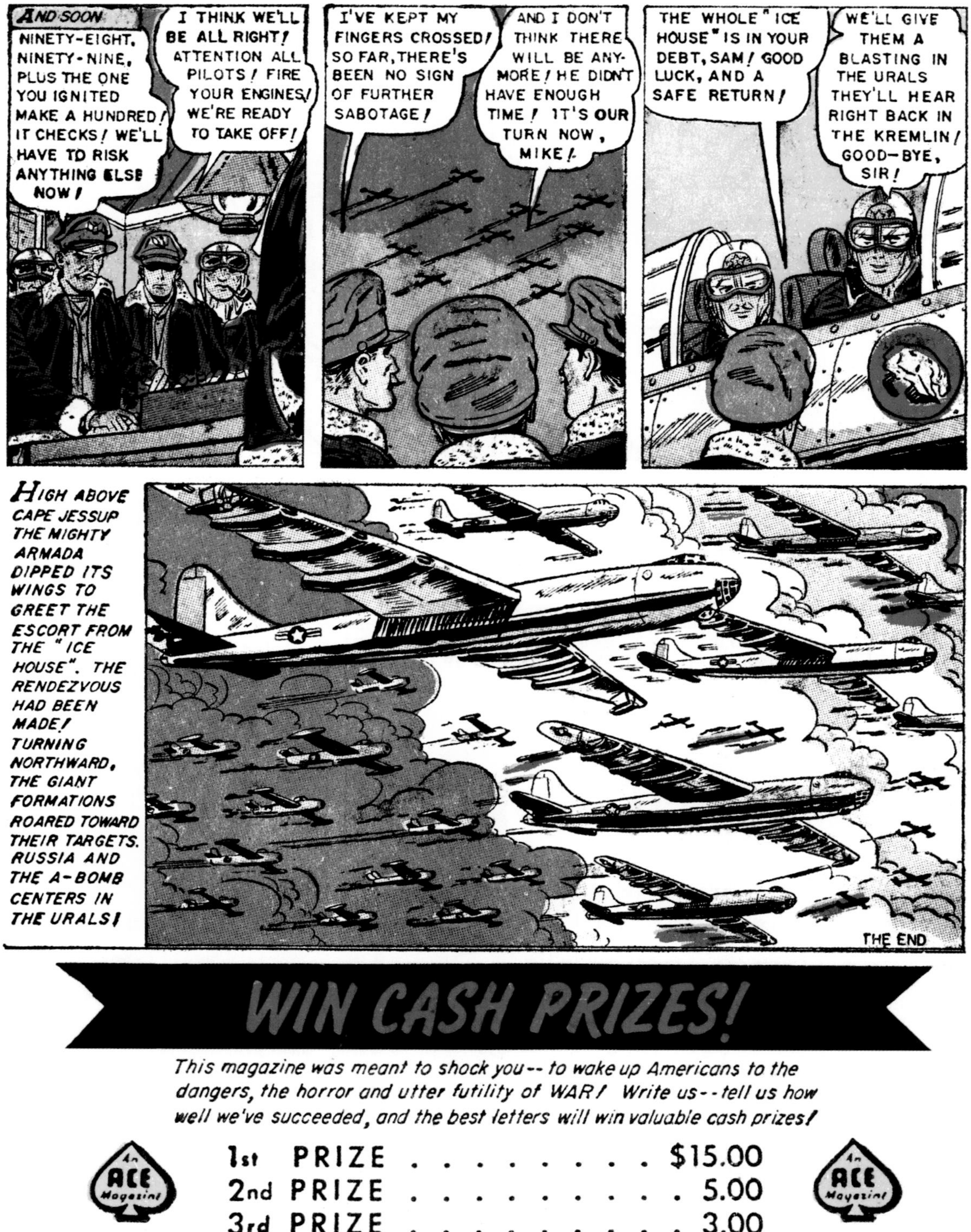
AND SOON
NINETY-EIGHT, NINETY-NINE, PLUS THE ONE YOU IGNITED MAKE A HUNDRED! IT CHECKS! WE'LL HAVE TO RISK ANYTHING ELSE NOW!
I THINK WE'LL BE ALL RIGHT! ATTENTION ALL PILOTS! FIRE YOUR ENGINES! WE'RE READY TO TAKE OFF!
I'VE KEPT MY FINGERS CROSSED! SO FAR, THERE'S BEEN NO SIGN OF FURTHER SABOTAGE!
AND I DON'T THINK THERE WILL BE ANY-MORE! HE DIDN'T HAVE ENOUGH TIME! IT'S OUR TURN NOW, MIKE!
THE WHOLE "ICE HOUSE" IS IN YOUR DEBT, SAM! GOOD LUCK, AND A SAFE RETURN!
WE'LL GIVE THEM A BLASTING IN THE URALS THEY'LL HEAR RIGHT BACK IN THE KREMLIN! GOOD-BYE, SIR!
HIGH ABOVE CAPE JESSUP THE MIGHTY ARMADA DIPPED ITS WINGS TO GREET THE ESCORT FROM THE "ICE HOUSE". THE RENDEZVOUS HAD BEEN MADE! TURNING NORTHWARD, THE GIANT FORMATIONS ROARED TOWARD THEIR TARGETS. RUSSIA AND THE A-BOMB CENTERS IN THE URALS!
THE END

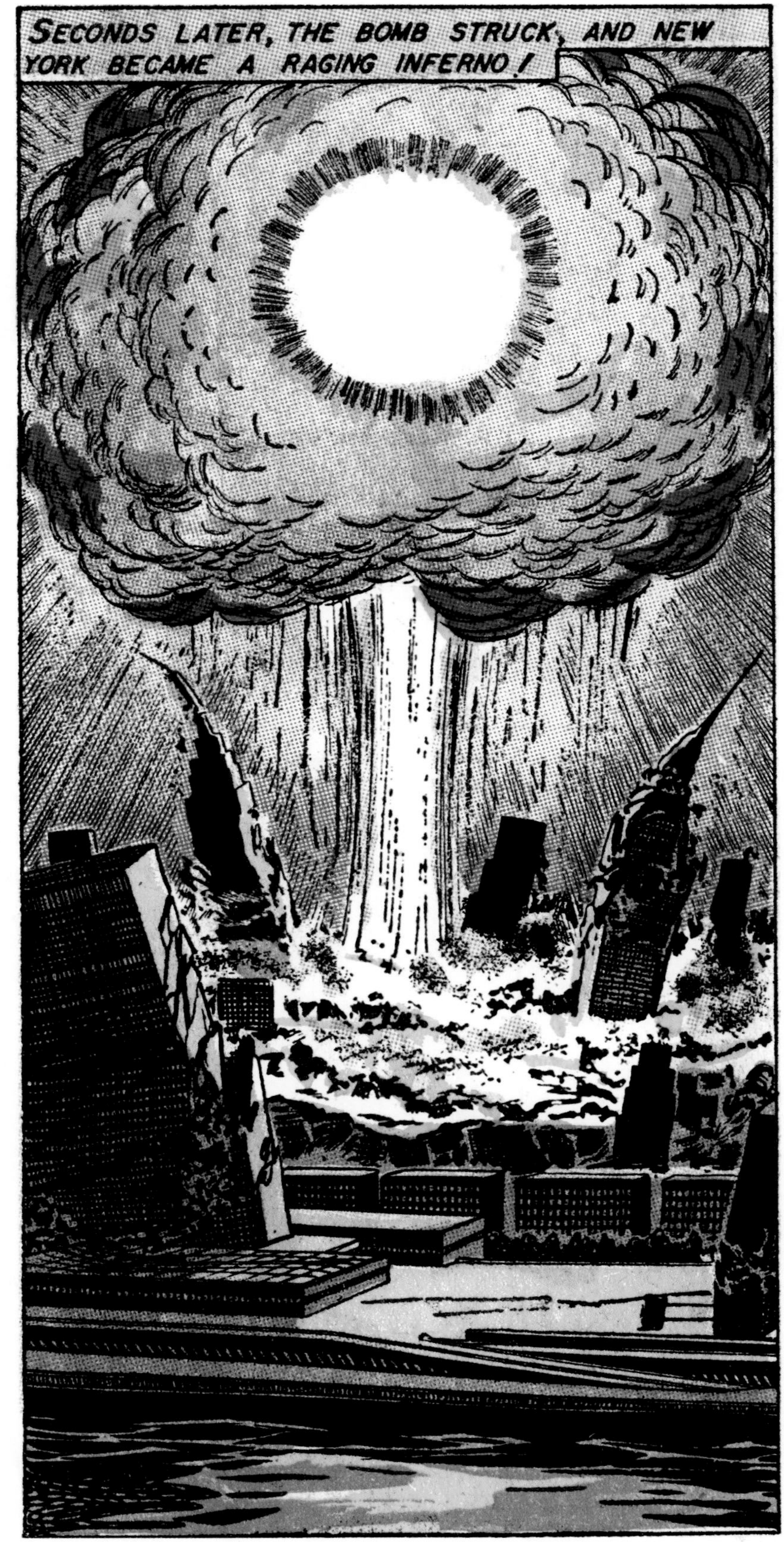
SECONDS LATER, THE BOMB STRUCK, AND NEW YORK BECAME A RAGING INFERNO!

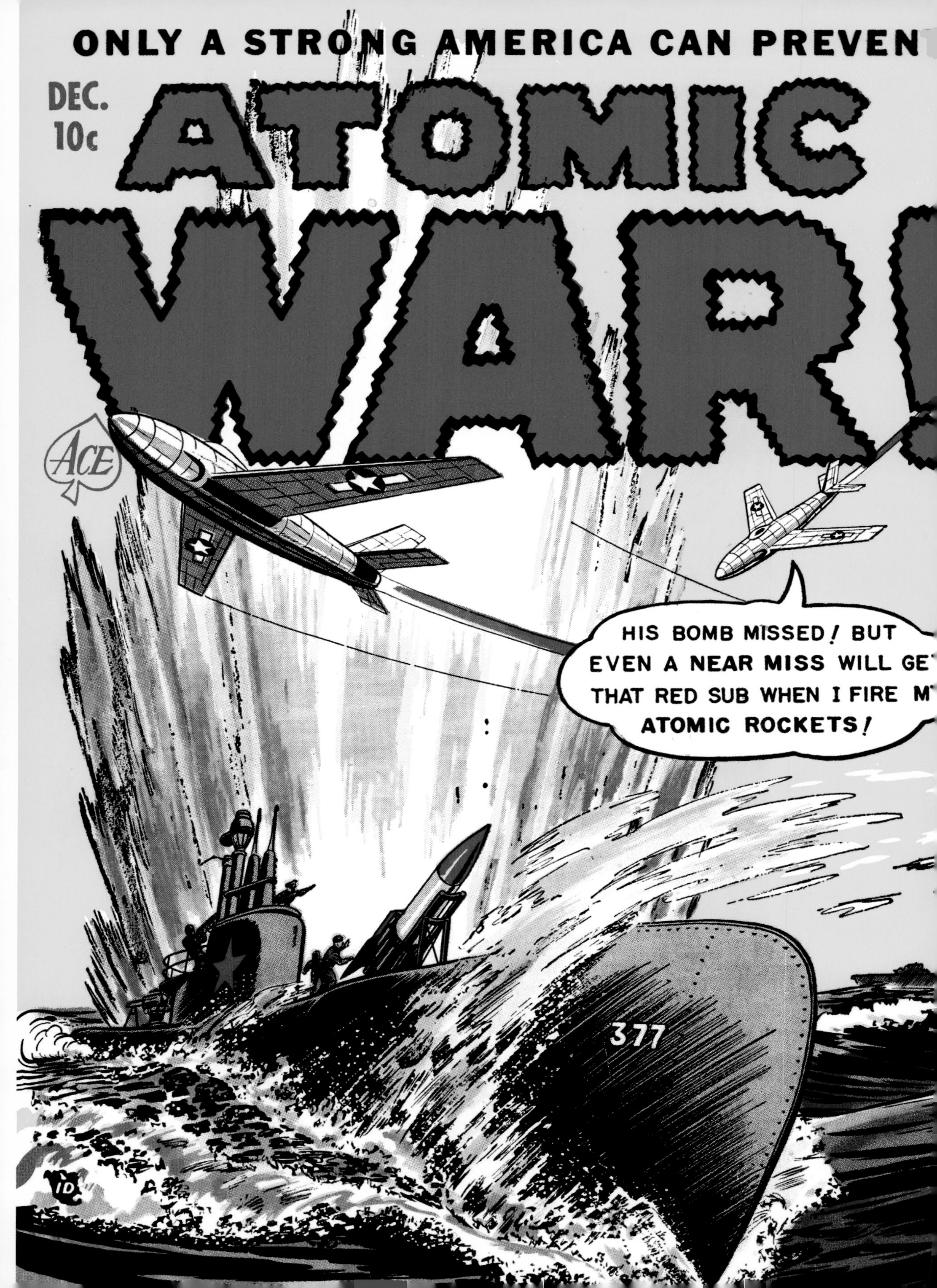
ONLY A STRONG AMERICA CAN PREVENT
DEC.
10¢
ATOMIC WAR!
ACE
HIS BOMB MISSED! BUT EVEN A NEAR MISS WILL GE THAT RED SUB WHEN I FIRE M ATOMIC ROCKETS!
377

THIS IS THE SECOND ISSUE OF ATOMIC WAR. *THE PURPOSE OF THIS BOOK IS CLEAR. WE WANT EVERYONE -- FRIEND AND FOE ALIKE -- TO KNOW THE UTTER DEVASTATION THAT ANOTHER WAR WILL BRING TO ALL, THE JUST AS WELL AS THE UNJUST. WE HOPE THAT ALL WHO READ THIS MAGAZINE WILL THINK ABOUT THIS -- AND PRAY THAT WHAT YOU SEE HERE WILL NEVER HAPPEN.*

THE EDITORS

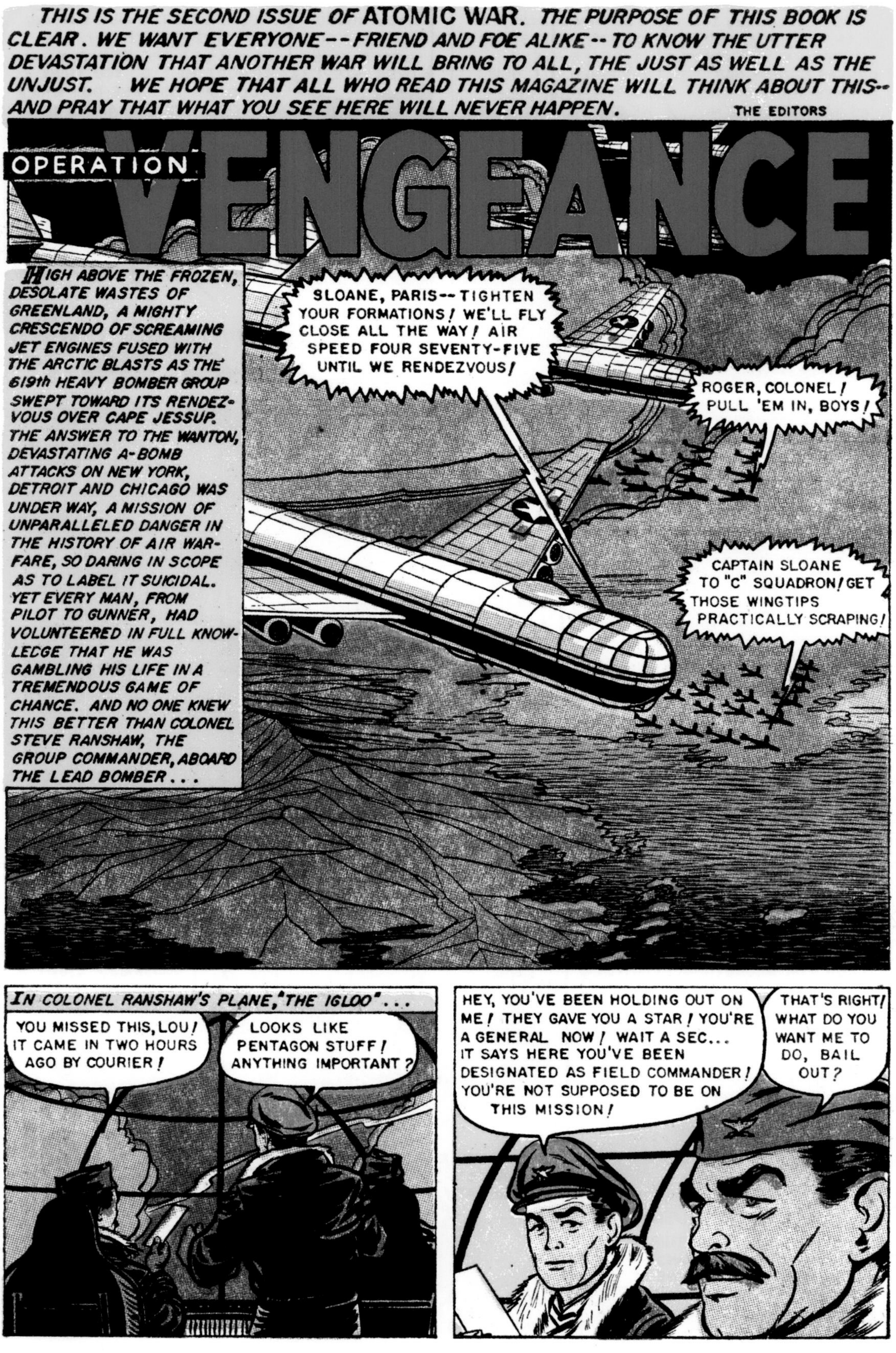
OPERATION VENGEANCE
HIGH ABOVE THE FROZEN, DESOLATE WASTES OF GREENLAND, A MIGHTY CRESCENDO OF SCREAMING JET ENGINES FUSED WITH THE ARCTIC BLASTS AS THE 619th HEAVY BOMBER GROUP SWEPT TOWARD ITS RENDEZVOUS OVER CAPE JESSUP. THE ANSWER TO THE WANTON, DEVASTATING A-BOMB ATTACKS ON NEW YORK, DETROIT AND CHICAGO WAS UNDER WAY, A MISSION OF UNPARALLELED DANGER IN THE HISTORY OF AIR WARFARE, SO DARING IN SCOPE AS TO LABEL IT SUICIDAL. YET EVERY MAN, FROM PILOT TO GUNNER, HAD VOLUNTEERED IN FULL KNOWLEDGE THAT HE WAS GAMBLING HIS LIFE IN A TREMENDOUS GAME OF CHANCE. AND NO ONE KNEW THIS BETTER THAN COLONEL STEVE RANSHAW, THE GROUP COMMANDER, ABOARD THE LEAD BOMBER...
SLOANE, PARIS -- TIGHTEN YOUR FORMATIONS! WE'LL FLY CLOSE ALL THE WAY! AIR SPEED FOUR SEVENTY-FIVE UNTIL WE RENDEZVOUS!
ROGER, COLONEL! PULL 'EM IN, BOYS!
CAPTAIN SLOANE TO "C" SQUADRON! GET THOSE WINGTIPS PRACTICALLY SCRAPING!
IN COLONEL RANSHAW'S PLANE, "THE IGLOO"...
YOU MISSED THIS, LOU! IT CAME IN TWO HOURS AGO BY COURIER!
LOOKS LIKE PENTAGON STUFF! ANYTHING IMPORTANT?
HEY, YOU'VE BEEN HOLDING OUT ON ME! THEY GAVE YOU A STAR! YOU'RE A GENERAL NOW! WAIT A SEC... IT SAYS HERE YOU'VE BEEN DESIGNATED AS FIELD COMMANDER! YOU'RE NOT SUPPOSED TO BE ON THIS MISSION!
THAT'S RIGHT! WHAT DO YOU WANT ME TO DO, BAIL OUT?

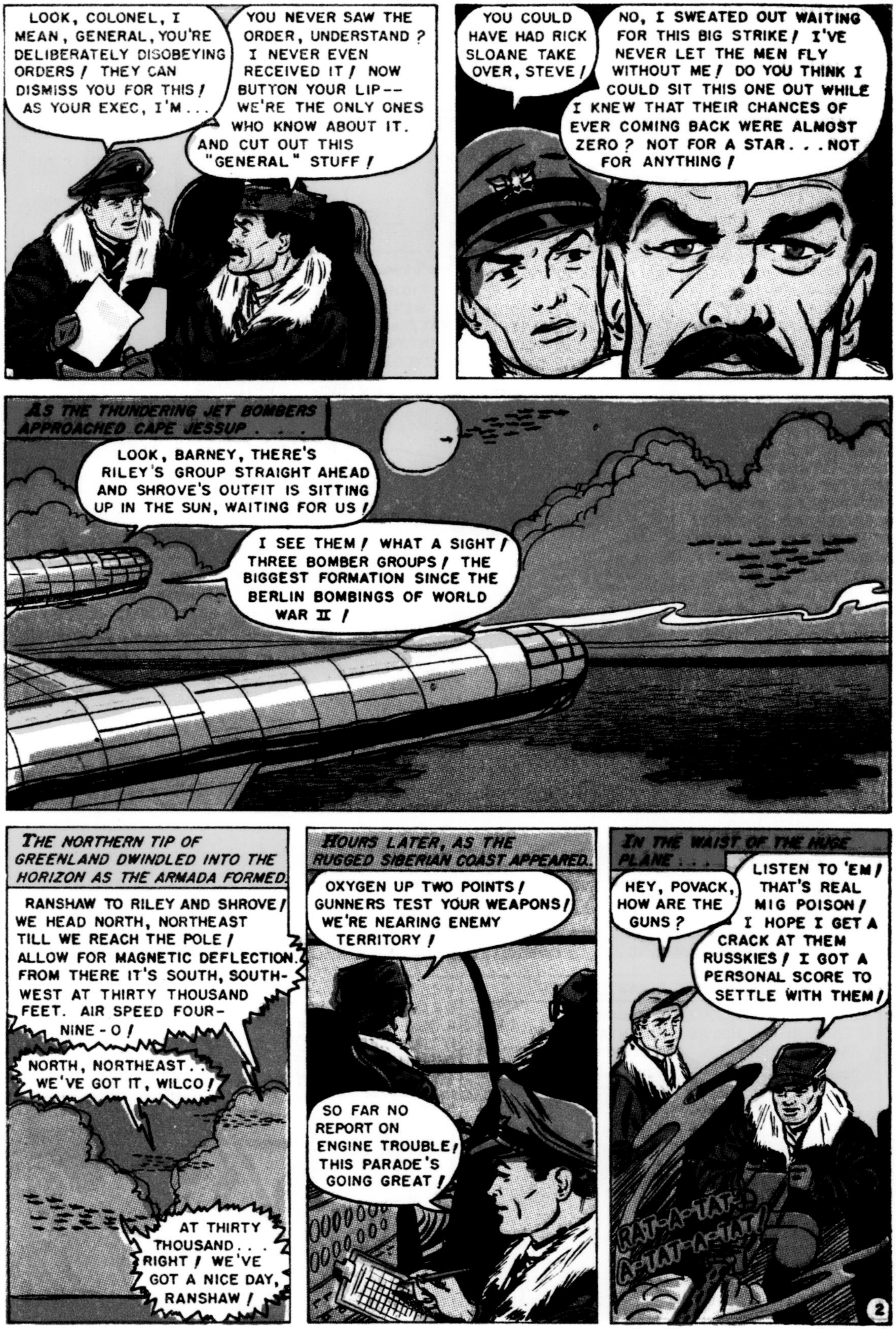
LOOK, COLONEL, I MEAN, GENERAL, YOU'RE DELIBERATELY DISOBEYING ORDERS! THEY CAN DISMISS YOU FOR THIS! AS YOUR EXEC, I'M . . .
YOU NEVER SAW THE ORDER, UNDERSTAND? I NEVER EVEN RECEIVED IT! NOW BUTTON YOUR LIP-- WE'RE THE ONLY ONES WHO KNOW ABOUT IT. AND CUT OUT THIS "GENERAL" STUFF!
YOU COULD HAVE HAD RICK SLOANE TAKE OVER, STEVE!
NO, I SWEATED OUT WAITING FOR THIS BIG STRIKE! I'VE NEVER LET THE MEN FLY WITHOUT ME! DO YOU THINK I COULD SIT THIS ONE OUT WHILE I KNEW THAT THEIR CHANCES OF EVER COMING BACK WERE ALMOST ZERO? NOT FOR A STAR . . . NOT FOR ANYTHING!
AS THE THUNDERING JET BOMBERS APPROACHED CAPE JESSUP . . .
LOOK, BARNEY, THERE'S RILEY'S GROUP STRAIGHT AHEAD AND SHROVE'S OUTFIT IS SITTING UP IN THE SUN, WAITING FOR US!
I SEE THEM! WHAT A SIGHT! THREE BOMBER GROUPS! THE BIGGEST FORMATION SINCE THE BERLIN BOMBINGS OF WORLD WAR II!
THE NORTHERN TIP OF GREENLAND DWINDLED INTO THE HORIZON AS THE ARMADA FORMED.
RANSHAW TO RILEY AND SHROVE! WE HEAD NORTH, NORTHEAST TILL WE REACH THE POLE! ALLOW FOR MAGNETIC DEFLECTION. FROM THERE IT'S SOUTH, SOUTH-WEST AT THIRTY THOUSAND FEET. AIR SPEED FOUR-NINE-O!
NORTH, NORTHEAST. . . WE'VE GOT IT, WILCO!
AT THIRTY THOUSAND. . . RIGHT! WE'VE GOT A NICE DAY, RANSHAW!
HOURS LATER, AS THE RUGGED SIBERIAN COAST APPEARED.
OXYGEN UP TWO POINTS! GUNNERS TEST YOUR WEAPONS! WE'RE NEARING ENEMY TERRITORY!
SO FAR NO REPORT ON ENGINE TROUBLE! THIS PARADE'S GOING GREAT!
IN THE WAIST OF THE HUGE PLANE . . .
HEY, POVACK, HOW ARE THE GUNS?
LISTEN TO 'EM! THAT'S REAL MIG POISON! I HOPE I GET A CRACK AT THEM RUSSKIES! I GOT A PERSONAL SCORE TO SETTLE WITH THEM!
RAT-A-TAT-A-TAT-A-TAT!
2

WHEN THE REDS OVERRAN POLAND IN 1945, THEY PUT MY WHOLE FAMILY AGAINST THE WALL AND KILLED 'EM. MY MOTHER AND I WERE THE ONLY ONES TO ESCAPE!

THEY STILL ARE KILLING PEOPLE, OR SENDING THEM TO CONCENTRATION CAMPS! DON'T WORRY, POVACK, YOU'LL GET YOUR CHANCE!

MOMENTS LATER, AS THE URALS CAME IN SIGHT...

ENEMY FIGHTERS COMING IN FAST AT TWELVE O'CLOCK!

ATTENTION ALL GROUPS! TIGHTEN YOUR FORMATIONS! WE'VE MADE CONTACT WITH THE ENEMY!

COLONEL YARASLAV TO SQUADRON! THE AMERICAN DOGS MUST BE DESTROYED! TO VICTORY, COMRADES!

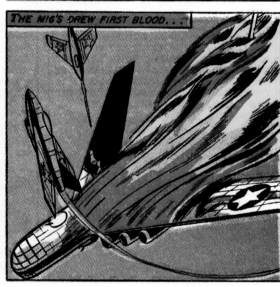

THE MIG'S DREW FIRST BLOOD...

GOOD WORK, PETROV! WE WILL TEACH THE SWINE A LESSON!

DA, NOW WE ATTACK THE SQUADRON LEADERS!

BOOM!

RANSHAW'S SHIP, THE IGLOO, WAS SAVAGELY ATTACKED...

WOW, THEY'RE GIVING US THE BUSINESS!

I'VE GOT ONE IN MY SIGHTS! HE'S HEADED RIGHT THIS WAY!

ZINNNGGG!

3

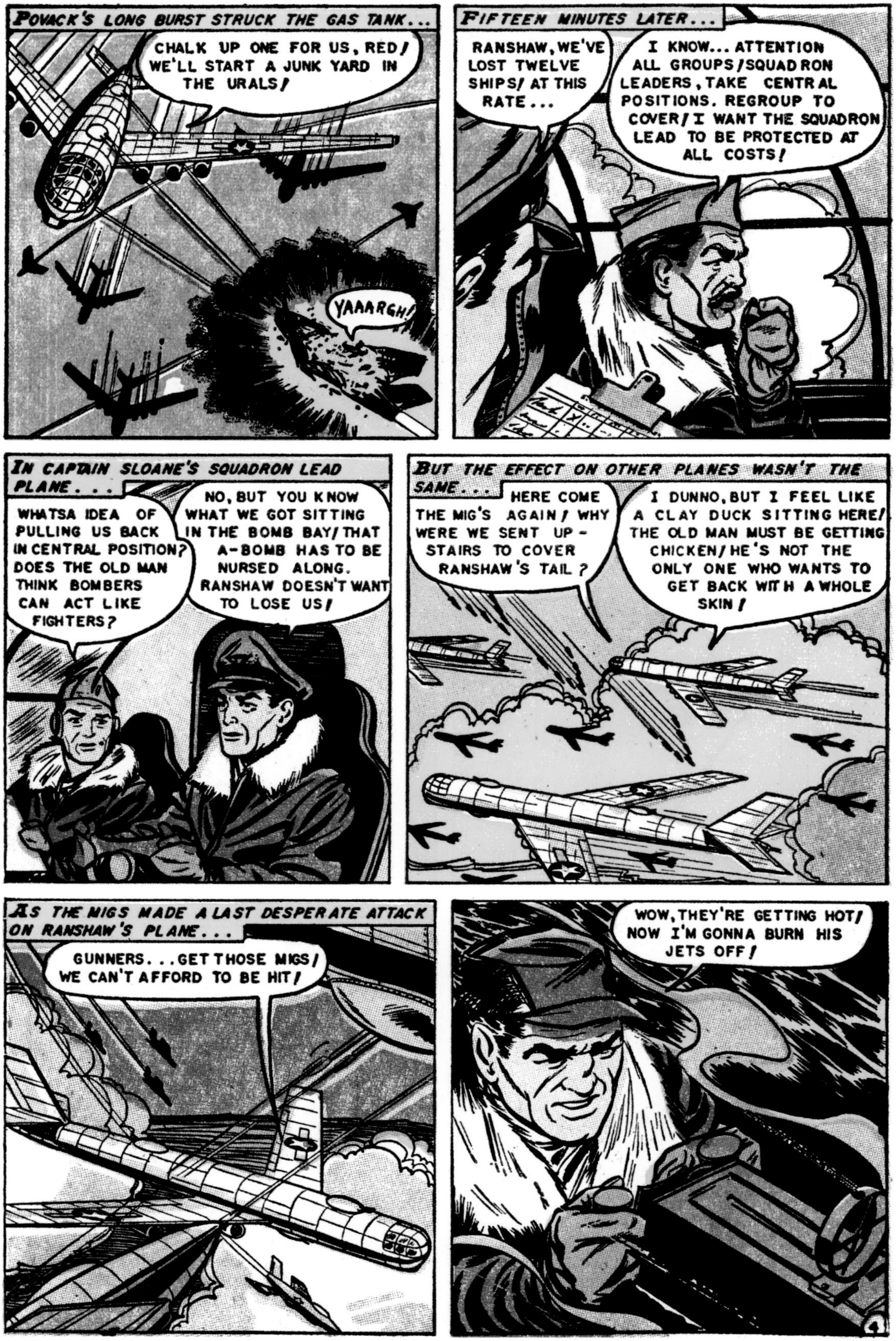
POVACK'S LONG BURST STRUCK THE GAS TANK...
CHALK UP ONE FOR US, RED! WE'LL START A JUNK YARD IN THE URALS!
YAAARGH!
FIFTEEN MINUTES LATER...
RANSHAW, WE'VE LOST TWELVE SHIPS! AT THIS RATE...
I KNOW... ATTENTION ALL GROUPS/SQUADRON LEADERS, TAKE CENTRAL POSITIONS. REGROUP TO COVER! I WANT THE SQUADRON LEAD TO BE PROTECTED AT ALL COSTS!
IN CAPTAIN SLOANE'S SQUADRON LEAD PLANE...
WHATSA IDEA OF PULLING US BACK IN CENTRAL POSITION? DOES THE OLD MAN THINK BOMBERS CAN ACT LIKE FIGHTERS?
NO, BUT YOU KNOW WHAT WE GOT SITTING IN THE BOMB BAY! THAT A-BOMB HAS TO BE NURSED ALONG. RANSHAW DOESN'T WANT TO LOSE US!
BUT THE EFFECT ON OTHER PLANES WASN'T THE SAME...
HERE COME THE MIG'S AGAIN! WHY WERE WE SENT UP-STAIRS TO COVER RANSHAW'S TAIL?
I DUNNO, BUT I FEEL LIKE A CLAY DUCK SITTING HERE! THE OLD MAN MUST BE GETTING CHICKEN! HE'S NOT THE ONLY ONE WHO WANTS TO GET BACK WITH A WHOLE SKIN!
AS THE MIGS MADE A LAST DESPERATE ATTACK ON RANSHAW'S PLANE...
GUNNERS...GET THOSE MIGS! WE CAN'T AFFORD TO BE HIT!
WOW, THEY'RE GETTING HOT! NOW I'M GONNA BURN HIS JETS OFF!
4

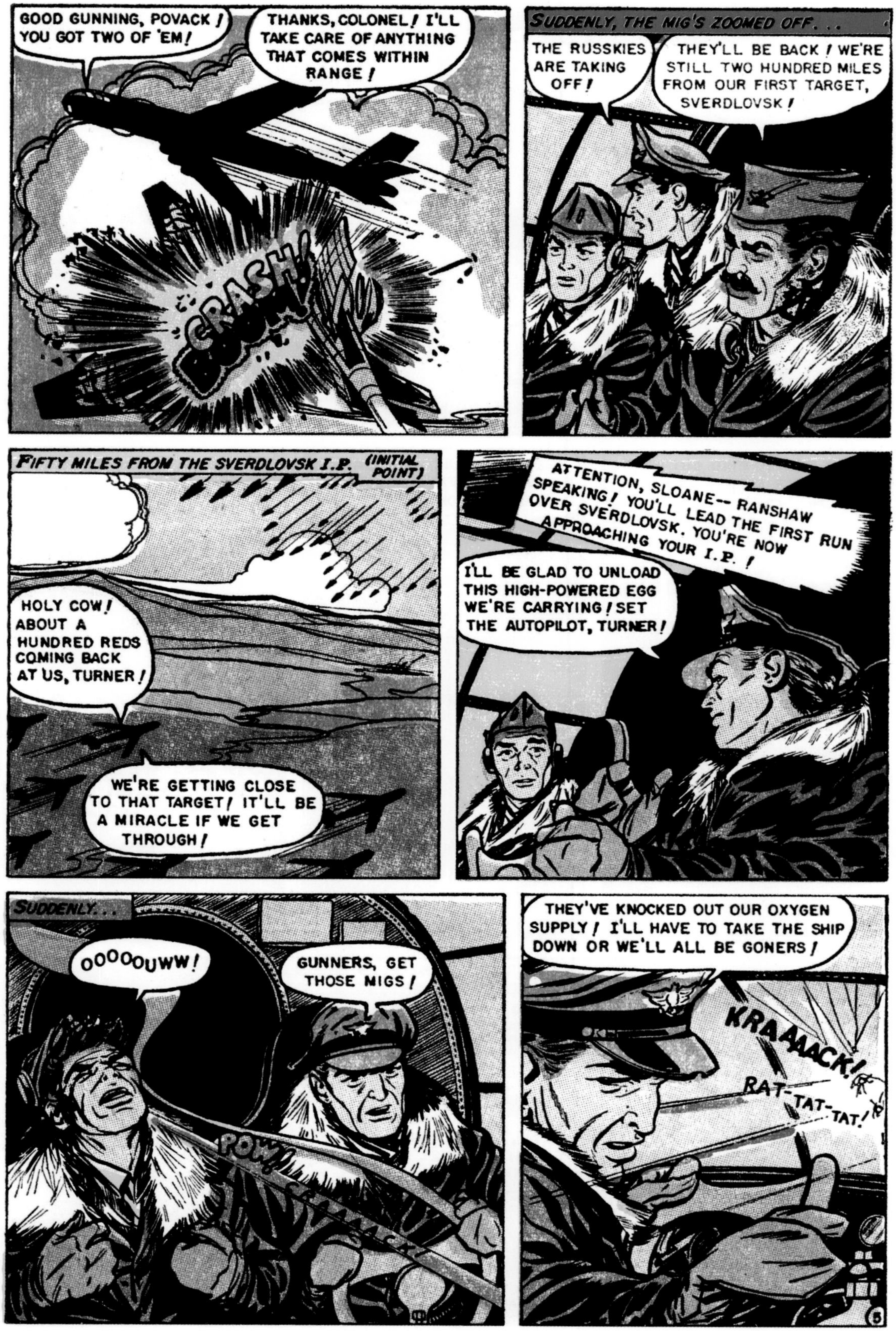
GOOD GUNNING, POVACK! YOU GOT TWO OF 'EM!
THANKS, COLONEL! I'LL TAKE CARE OF ANYTHING THAT COMES WITHIN RANGE!
CRASH!
BOOM!
SUDDENLY, THE MIG'S ZOOMED OFF...
THE RUSSKIES ARE TAKING OFF!
THEY'LL BE BACK! WE'RE STILL TWO HUNDRED MILES FROM OUR FIRST TARGET, SVERDLOVSK!
FIFTY MILES FROM THE SVERDLOVSK I.P. (INITIAL POINT)
HOLY COW! ABOUT A HUNDRED REDS COMING BACK AT US, TURNER!
WE'RE GETTING CLOSE TO THAT TARGET! IT'LL BE A MIRACLE IF WE GET THROUGH!
ATTENTION, SLOANE-- RANSHAW SPEAKING! YOU'LL LEAD THE FIRST RUN OVER SVERDLOVSK. YOU'RE NOW APPROACHING YOUR I.P.!
I'LL BE GLAD TO UNLOAD THIS HIGH-POWERED EGG WE'RE CARRYING! SET THE AUTOPILOT, TURNER!
SUDDENLY...
OOOOOUWW!
GUNNERS, GET THOSE MIGS!
POW!
THEY'VE KNOCKED OUT OUR OXYGEN SUPPLY! I'LL HAVE TO TAKE THE SHIP DOWN OR WE'LL ALL BE GONERS!
KRAAAACK!
RAT-TAT-TAT!
5

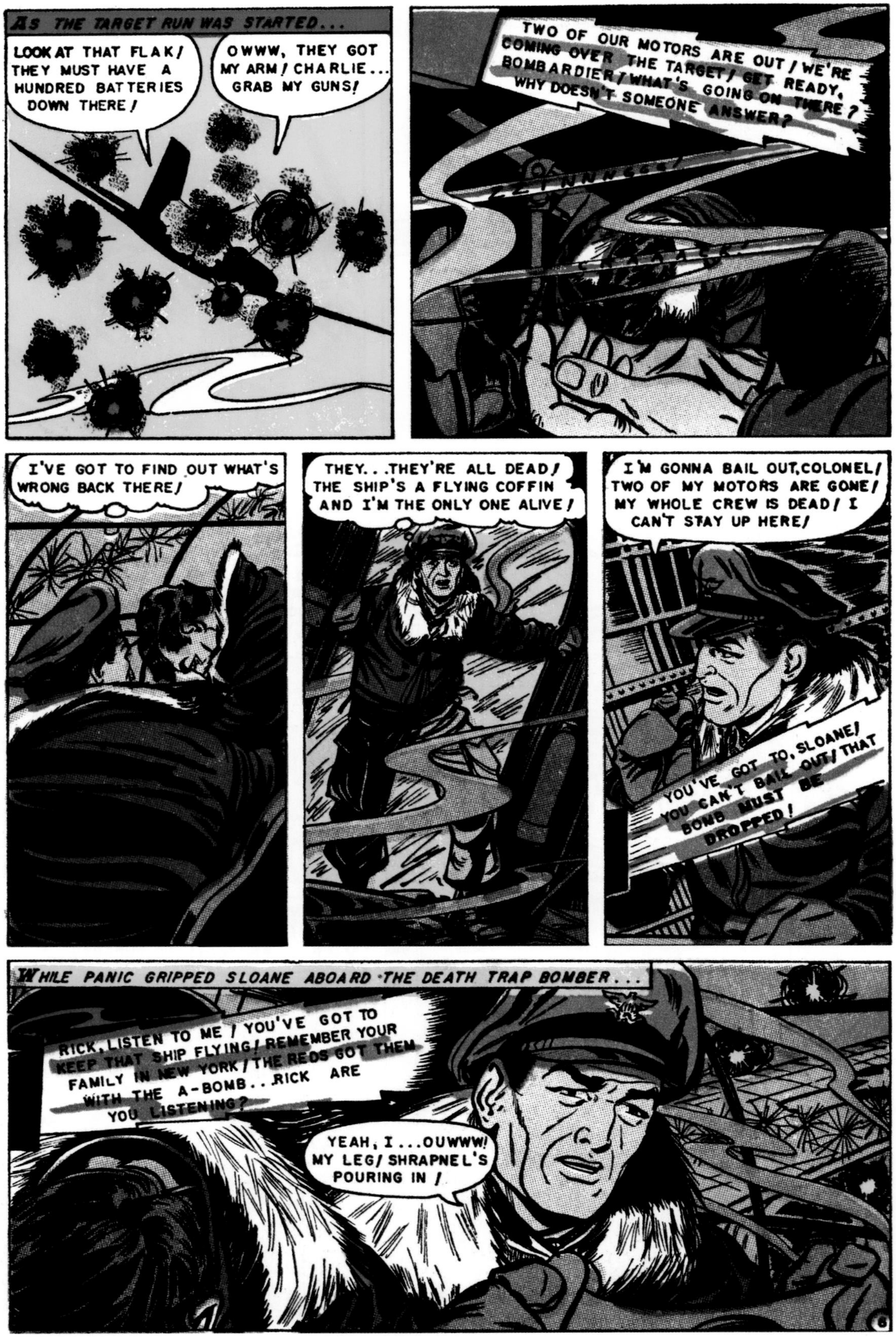
AS THE TARGET RUN WAS STARTED...
LOOK AT THAT FLAK! THEY MUST HAVE A HUNDRED BATTERIES DOWN THERE!
OWWW, THEY GOT MY ARM! CHARLIE... GRAB MY GUNS!
TWO OF OUR MOTORS ARE OUT! WE'RE COMING OVER THE TARGET! GET READY, BOMBARDIER! WHAT'S GOING ON THERE? WHY DOESN'T SOMEONE ANSWER?
I'VE GOT TO FIND OUT WHAT'S WRONG BACK THERE!
THEY...THEY'RE ALL DEAD! THE SHIP'S A FLYING COFFIN AND I'M THE ONLY ONE ALIVE!
I'M GONNA BAIL OUT, COLONEL! TWO OF MY MOTORS ARE GONE! MY WHOLE CREW IS DEAD! I CAN'T STAY UP HERE!
YOU'VE GOT TO, SLOANE! YOU CAN'T BAIL OUT! THAT BOMB MUST BE DROPPED!
WHILE PANIC GRIPPED SLOANE ABOARD THE DEATH TRAP BOMBER...
RICK, LISTEN TO ME! YOU'VE GOT TO KEEP THAT SHIP FLYING! REMEMBER YOUR FAMILY IN NEW YORK! THE REDS GOT THEM WITH THE A-BOMB.. RICK ARE YOU LISTENING?
YEAH, I...OUWWW! MY LEG! SHRAPNEL'S POURING IN!

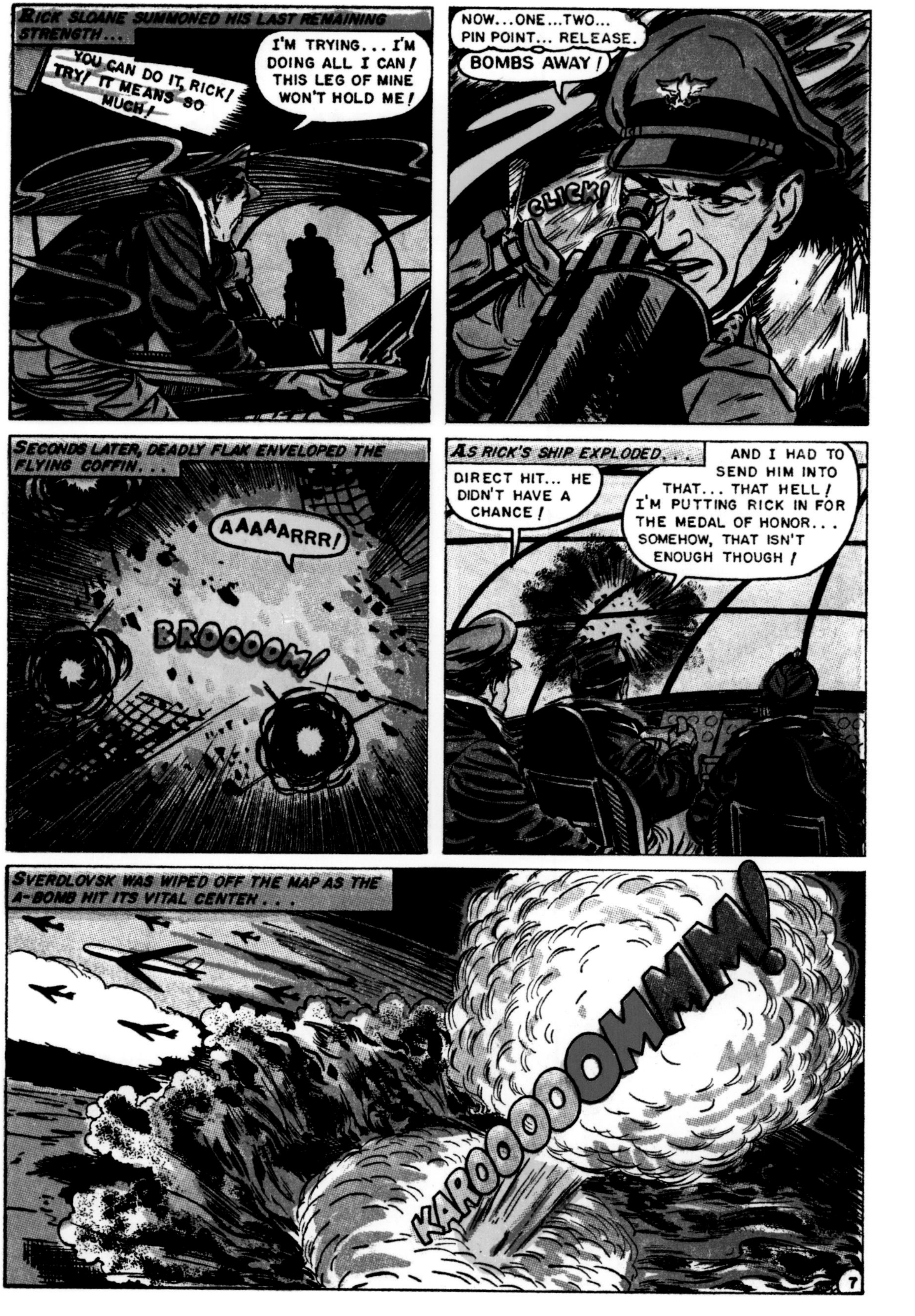
RICK SLOANE SUMMONED HIS LAST REMAINING STRENGTH...
YOU CAN DO IT, RICK! TRY! IT MEANS SO MUCH!
I'M TRYING... I'M DOING ALL I CAN! THIS LEG OF MINE WON'T HOLD ME!
NOW...ONE...TWO... PIN POINT... RELEASE.
BOMBS AWAY!
CLICK!
SECONDS LATER, DEADLY FLAK ENVELOPED THE FLYING COFFIN...
AAAAARRR!
BROOOOOM!
AS RICK'S SHIP EXPLODED...
DIRECT HIT... HE DIDN'T HAVE A CHANCE!
AND I HAD TO SEND HIM INTO THAT... THAT HELL! I'M PUTTING RICK IN FOR THE MEDAL OF HONOR... SOMEHOW, THAT ISN'T ENOUGH THOUGH!
SVERDLOVSK WAS WIPED OFF THE MAP AS THE A-BOMB HIT ITS VITAL CENTER...
KAROOOOOOOMMMM!
7

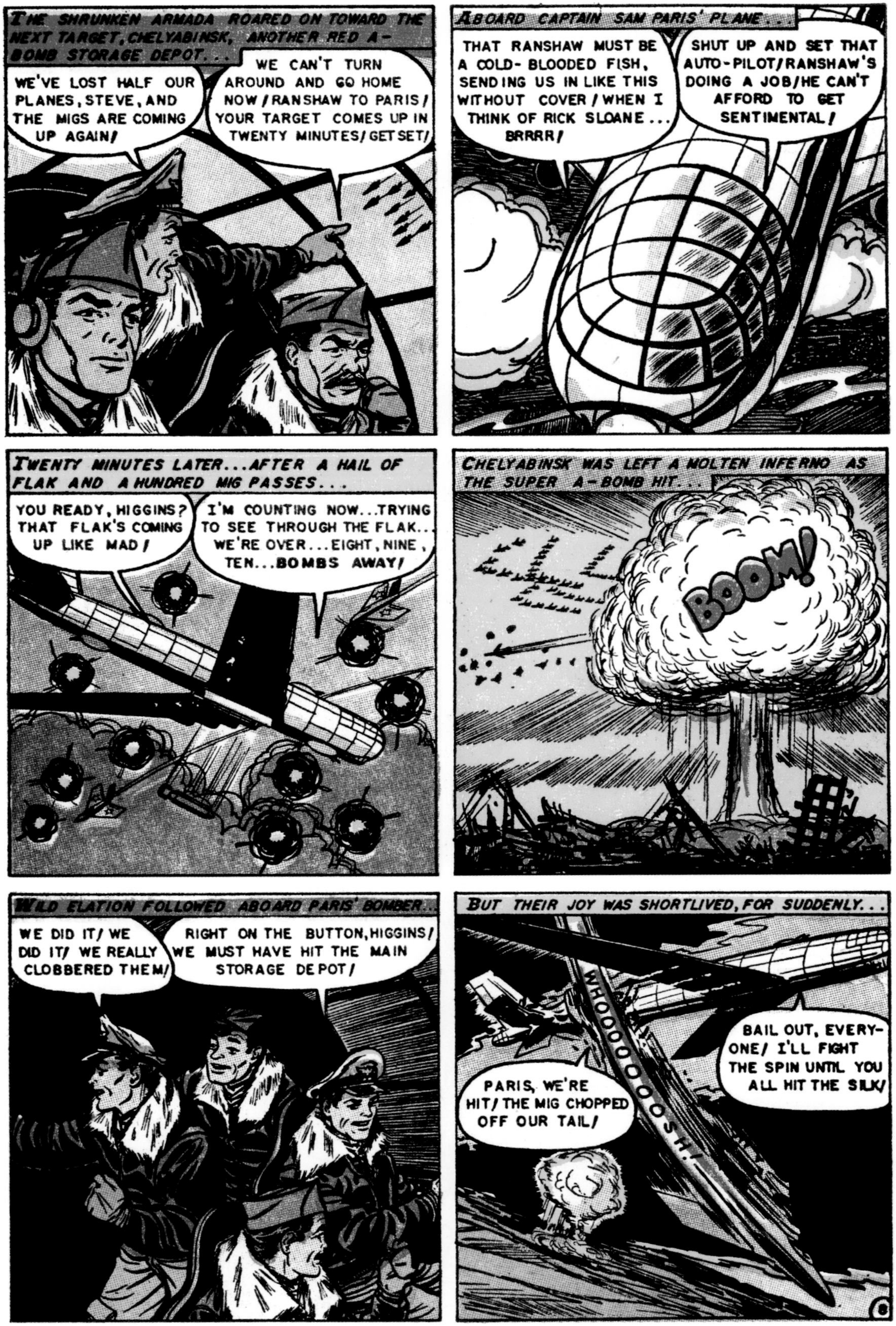
THE SHRUNKEN ARMADA ROARED ON TOWARD THE NEXT TARGET, CHELYABINSK, ANOTHER RED A-BOMB STORAGE DEPOT...
WE'VE LOST HALF OUR PLANES, STEVE, AND THE MIGS ARE COMING UP AGAIN!
WE CAN'T TURN AROUND AND GO HOME NOW! RANSHAW TO PARIS! YOUR TARGET COMES UP IN TWENTY MINUTES! GET SET!
ABOARD CAPTAIN SAM PARIS' PLANE...
THAT RANSHAW MUST BE A COLD-BLOODED FISH, SENDING US IN LIKE THIS WITHOUT COVER! WHEN I THINK OF RICK SLOANE... BRRRR!
SHUT UP AND SET THAT AUTO-PILOT! RANSHAW'S DOING A JOB! HE CAN'T AFFORD TO GET SENTIMENTAL!
TWENTY MINUTES LATER...AFTER A HAIL OF FLAK AND A HUNDRED MIG PASSES...
YOU READY, HIGGINS? THAT FLAK'S COMING UP LIKE MAD!
I'M COUNTING NOW...TRYING TO SEE THROUGH THE FLAK.. WE'RE OVER...EIGHT, NINE, TEN...BOMBS AWAY!
CHELYABINSK WAS LEFT A MOLTEN INFERNO AS THE SUPER A-BOMB HIT...
BOOM!
WILD ELATION FOLLOWED ABOARD PARIS' BOMBER...
WE DID IT! WE DID IT! WE REALLY CLOBBERED THEM!
RIGHT ON THE BUTTON, HIGGINS! WE MUST HAVE HIT THE MAIN STORAGE DEPOT!
BUT THEIR JOY WAS SHORTLIVED, FOR SUDDENLY...
WHOOOOOOOOOSH!
PARIS, WE'RE HIT! THE MIG CHOPPED OFF OUR TAIL!
BAIL OUT, EVERYONE! I'LL FIGHT THE SPIN UNTIL YOU ALL HIT THE SILK!
8

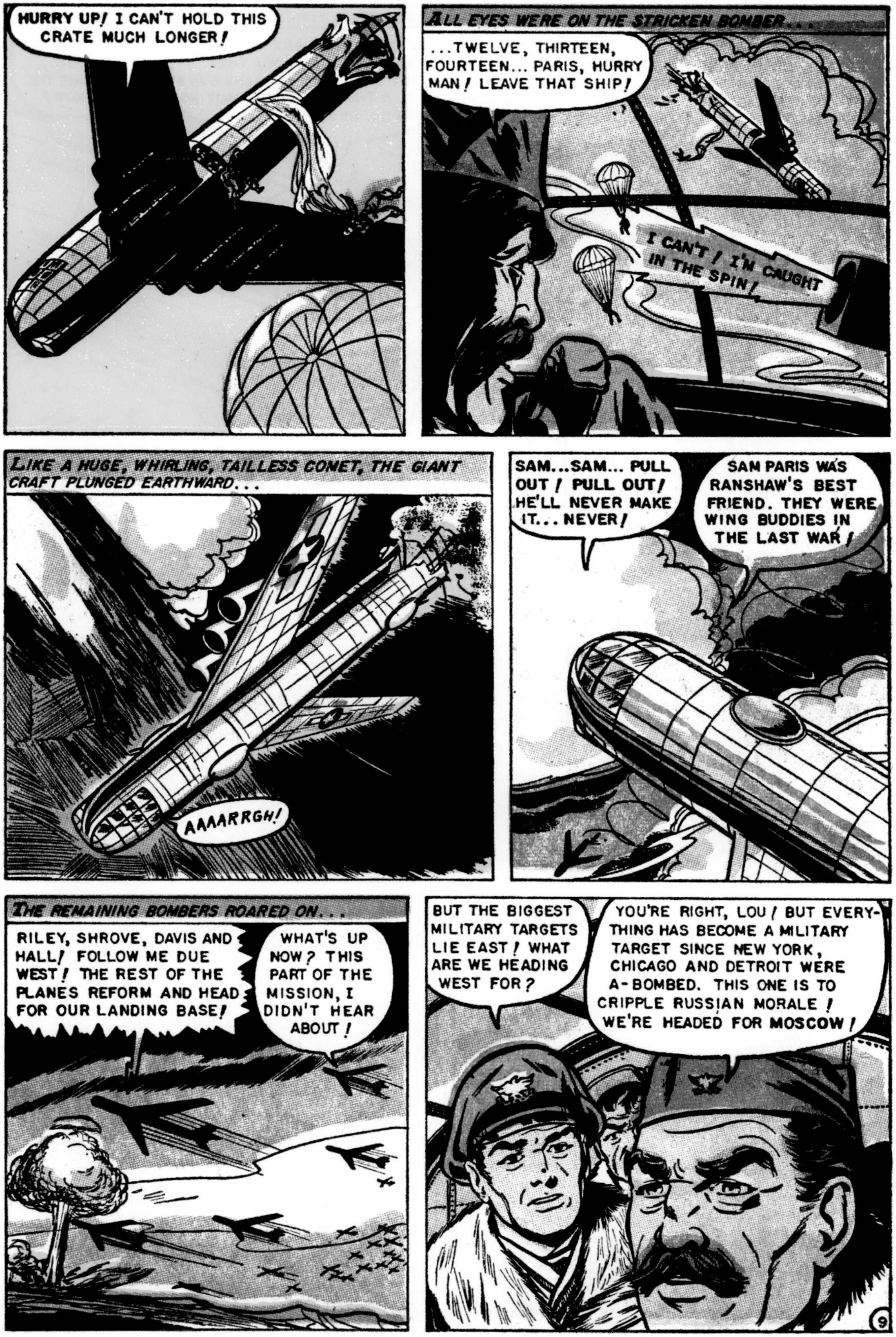
HURRY UP! I CAN'T HOLD THIS CRATE MUCH LONGER!
ALL EYES WERE ON THE STRICKEN BOMBER...
...TWELVE, THIRTEEN, FOURTEEN... PARIS, HURRY MAN! LEAVE THAT SHIP!
I CAN'T! I'M CAUGHT IN THE SPIN!
LIKE A HUGE, WHIRLING, TAILLESS COMET, THE GIANT CRAFT PLUNGED EARTHWARD...
AAAARRGH!
SAM...SAM... PULL OUT! PULL OUT! HE'LL NEVER MAKE IT... NEVER!
SAM PARIS WAS RANSHAW'S BEST FRIEND. THEY WERE WING BUDDIES IN THE LAST WAR!
THE REMAINING BOMBERS ROARED ON...
RILEY, SHROVE, DAVIS AND HALL! FOLLOW ME DUE WEST! THE REST OF THE PLANES REFORM AND HEAD FOR OUR LANDING BASE!
WHAT'S UP NOW? THIS PART OF THE MISSION, I DIDN'T HEAR ABOUT!
BUT THE BIGGEST MILITARY TARGETS LIE EAST! WHAT ARE WE HEADING WEST FOR?
YOU'RE RIGHT, LOU! BUT EVERYTHING HAS BECOME A MILITARY TARGET SINCE NEW YORK, CHICAGO AND DETROIT WERE A-BOMBED. THIS ONE IS TO CRIPPLE RUSSIAN MORALE! WE'RE HEADED FOR MOSCOW!
9

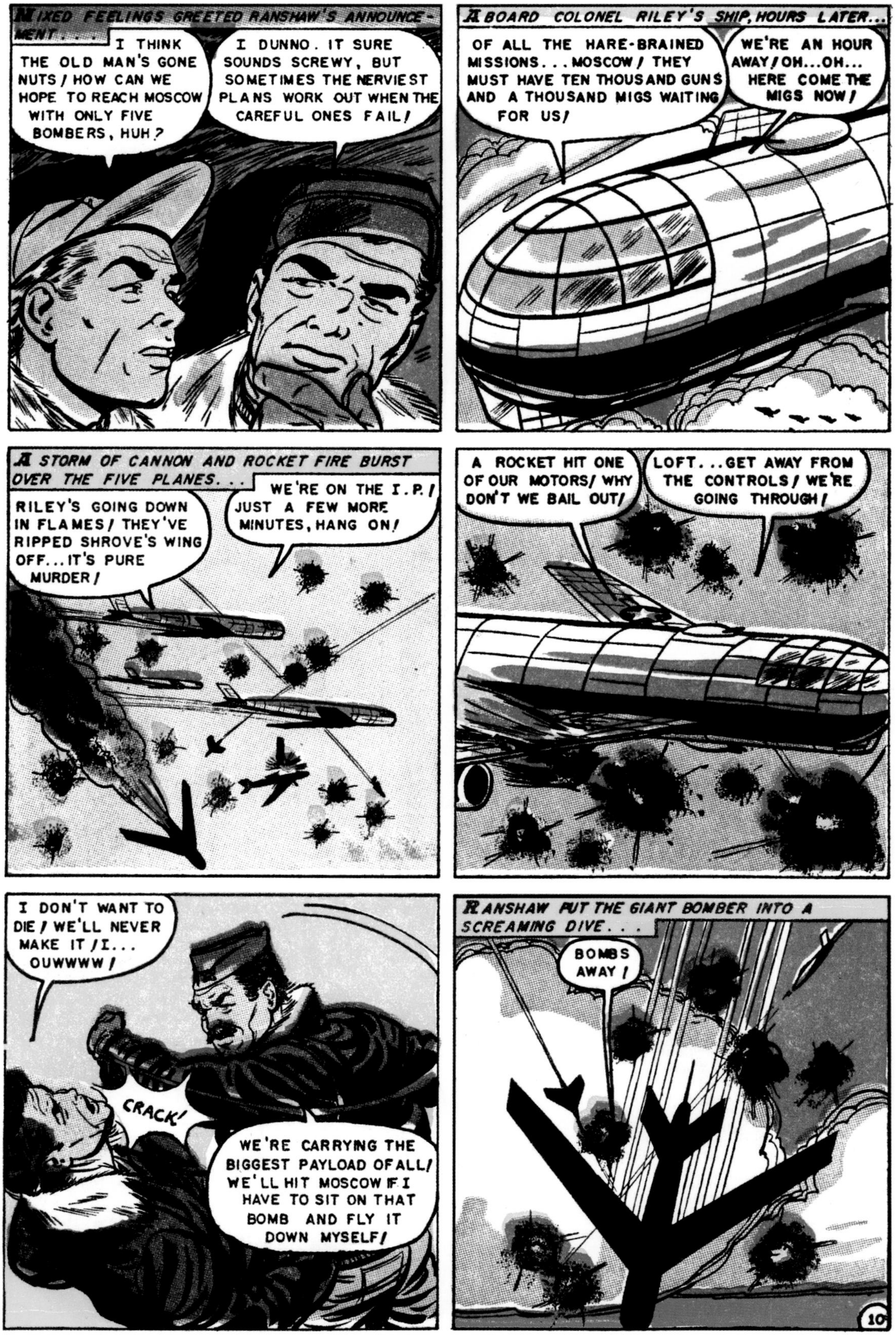
MIXED FEELINGS GREETED RANSHAW'S ANNOUNCEMENT . . .
I THINK THE OLD MAN'S GONE NUTS / HOW CAN WE HOPE TO REACH MOSCOW WITH ONLY FIVE BOMBERS, HUH ?
I DUNNO. IT SURE SOUNDS SCREWY, BUT SOMETIMES THE NERVIEST PLANS WORK OUT WHEN THE CAREFUL ONES FAIL /
ABOARD COLONEL RILEY'S SHIP, HOURS LATER...
OF ALL THE HARE-BRAINED MISSIONS... MOSCOW / THEY MUST HAVE TEN THOUSAND GUNS AND A THOUSAND MIGS WAITING FOR US /
WE'RE AN HOUR AWAY / OH...OH... HERE COME THE MIGS NOW /
A STORM OF CANNON AND ROCKET FIRE BURST OVER THE FIVE PLANES...
RILEY'S GOING DOWN IN FLAMES / THEY'VE RIPPED SHROVE'S WING OFF...IT'S PURE MURDER /
WE'RE ON THE I.P. / JUST A FEW MORE MINUTES, HANG ON /
A ROCKET HIT ONE OF OUR MOTORS / WHY DON'T WE BAIL OUT /
LOFT...GET AWAY FROM THE CONTROLS / WE'RE GOING THROUGH /
I DON'T WANT TO DIE / WE'LL NEVER MAKE IT / I... OUWWWW /
CRACK!
WE'RE CARRYING THE BIGGEST PAYLOAD OF ALL / WE'LL HIT MOSCOW IF I HAVE TO SIT ON THAT BOMB AND FLY IT DOWN MYSELF /
RANSHAW PUT THE GIANT BOMBER INTO A SCREAMING DIVE...
BOMBS AWAY /
10

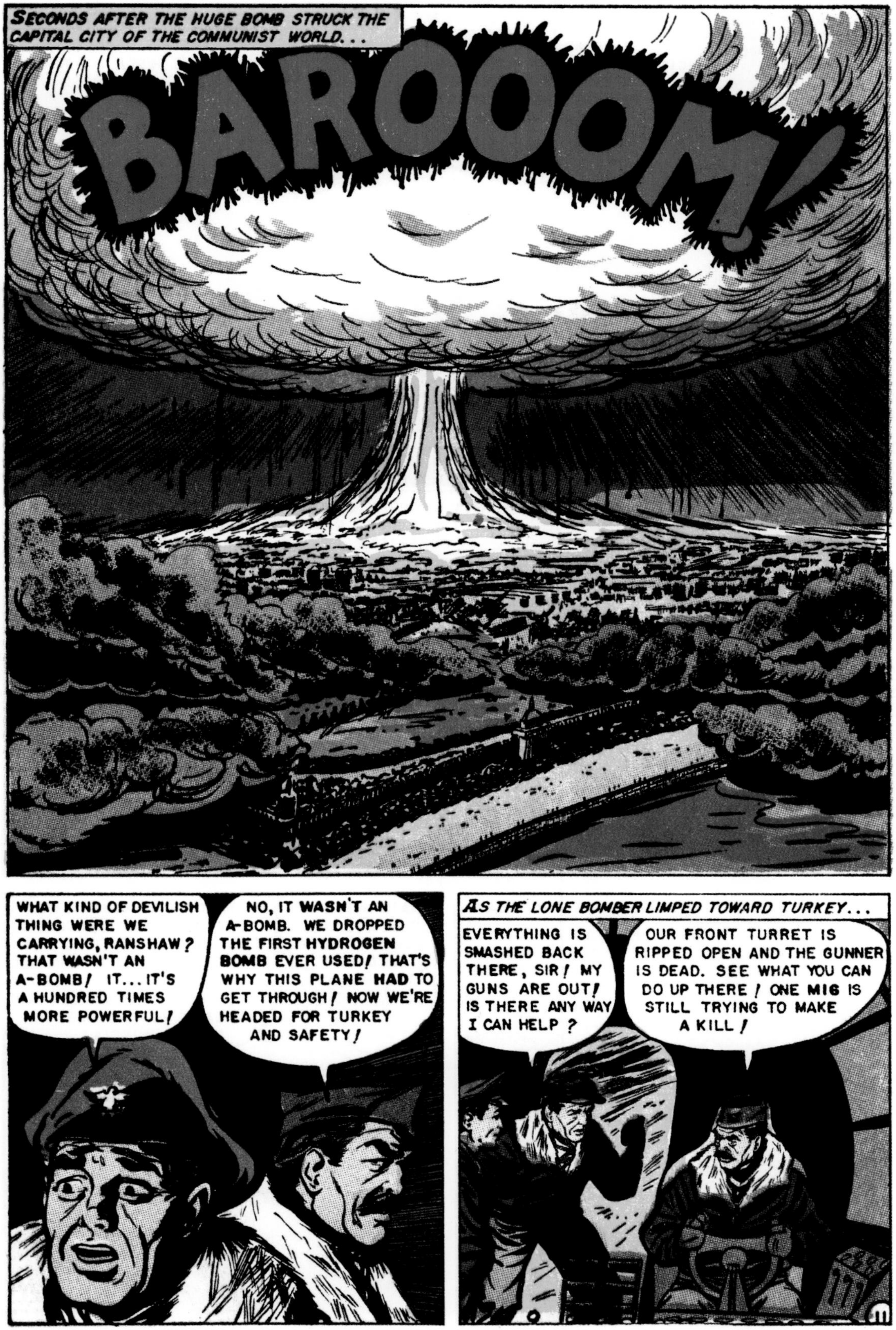
SECONDS AFTER THE HUGE BOMB STRUCK THE CAPITAL CITY OF THE COMMUNIST WORLD...
BAROOOM!
WHAT KIND OF DEVILISH THING WERE WE CARRYING, RANSHAW? THAT WASN'T AN A-BOMB! IT... IT'S A HUNDRED TIMES MORE POWERFUL!
NO, IT WASN'T AN A-BOMB. WE DROPPED THE FIRST HYDROGEN BOMB EVER USED! THAT'S WHY THIS PLANE HAD TO GET THROUGH! NOW WE'RE HEADED FOR TURKEY AND SAFETY!
AS THE LONE BOMBER LIMPED TOWARD TURKEY...
EVERYTHING IS SMASHED BACK THERE, SIR! MY GUNS ARE OUT! IS THERE ANY WAY I CAN HELP?
OUR FRONT TURRET IS RIPPED OPEN AND THE GUNNER IS DEAD. SEE WHAT YOU CAN DO UP THERE! ONE MIG IS STILL TRYING TO MAKE A KILL!
11

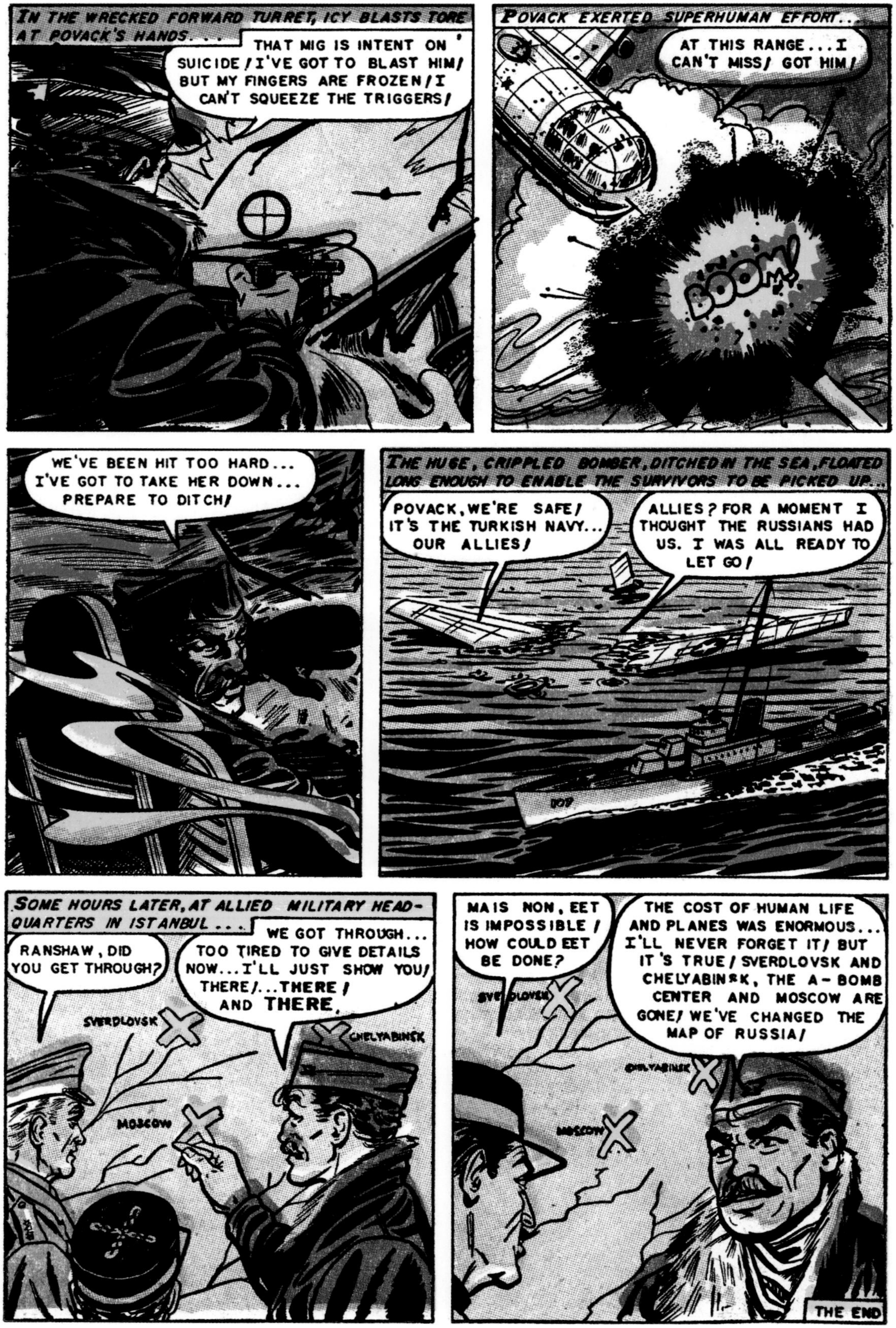
IN THE WRECKED FORWARD TURRET, ICY BLASTS TORE AT POVACK'S HANDS...
THAT MIG IS INTENT ON SUICIDE! I'VE GOT TO BLAST HIM! BUT MY FINGERS ARE FROZEN! I CAN'T SQUEEZE THE TRIGGERS!
POVACK EXERTED SUPERHUMAN EFFORT...
AT THIS RANGE... I CAN'T MISS! GOT HIM!
BOOM!
WE'VE BEEN HIT TOO HARD... I'VE GOT TO TAKE HER DOWN... PREPARE TO DITCH!
THE HUGE, CRIPPLED BOMBER, DITCHED IN THE SEA, FLOATED LONG ENOUGH TO ENABLE THE SURVIVORS TO BE PICKED UP...
POVACK, WE'RE SAFE! IT'S THE TURKISH NAVY... OUR ALLIES!
ALLIES? FOR A MOMENT I THOUGHT THE RUSSIANS HAD US. I WAS ALL READY TO LET GO!
SOME HOURS LATER, AT ALLIED MILITARY HEADQUARTERS IN ISTANBUL...
RANSHAW, DID YOU GET THROUGH?
WE GOT THROUGH... TOO TIRED TO GIVE DETAILS NOW... I'LL JUST SHOW YOU! THERE!... THERE! AND THERE.
SVERDLOVSK
CHELYABINSK
MOSCOW
MAIS NON, EET IS IMPOSSIBLE! HOW COULD EET BE DONE?
THE COST OF HUMAN LIFE AND PLANES WAS ENORMOUS... I'LL NEVER FORGET IT! BUT IT'S TRUE! SVERDLOVSK AND CHELYABINSK, THE A-BOMB CENTER AND MOSCOW ARE GONE! WE'VE CHANGED THE MAP OF RUSSIA!
THE END

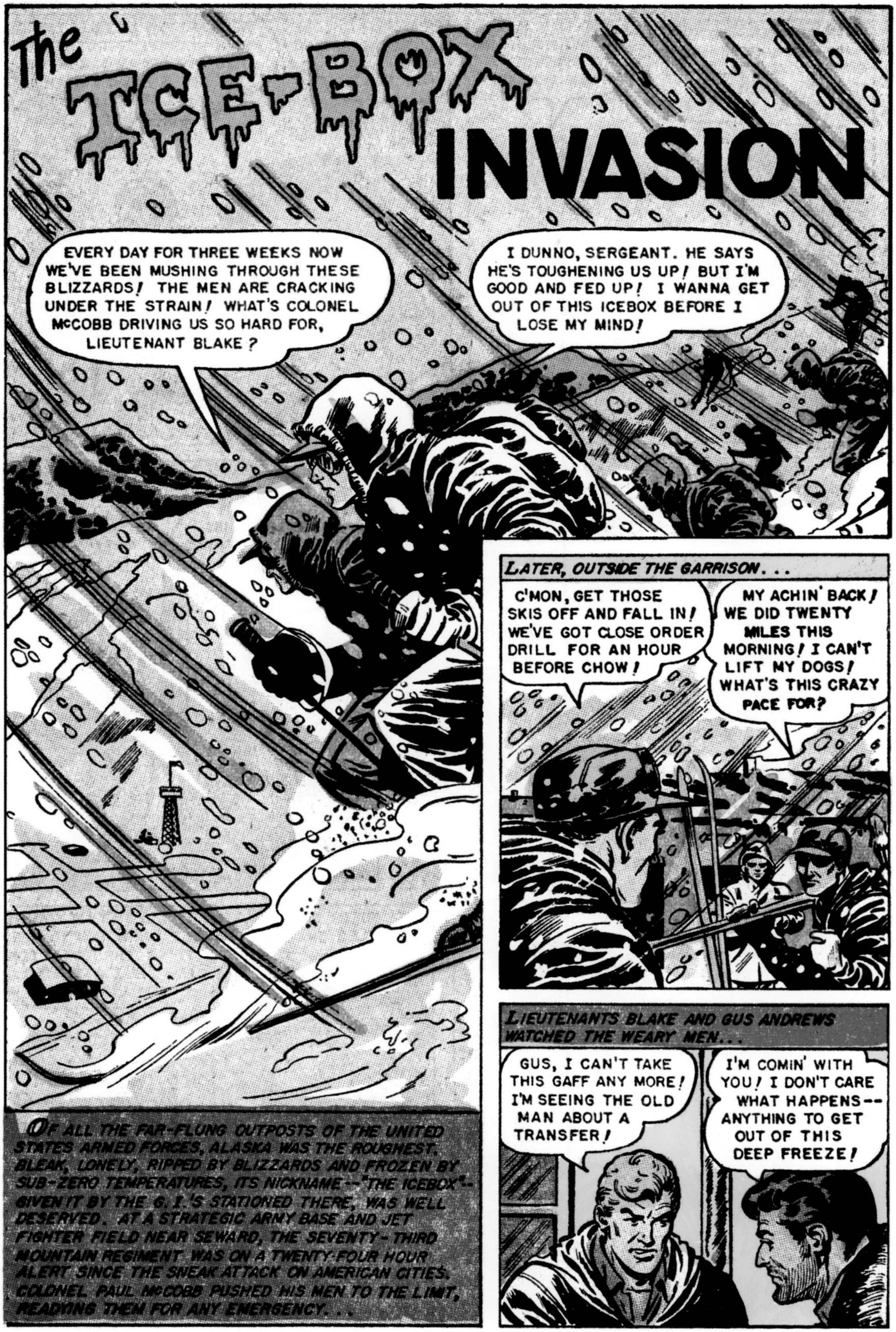

The ICE-BOX INVASION
EVERY DAY FOR THREE WEEKS NOW WE'VE BEEN MUSHING THROUGH THESE BLIZZARDS! THE MEN ARE CRACKING UNDER THE STRAIN! WHAT'S COLONEL McCOBB DRIVING US SO HARD FOR, LIEUTENANT BLAKE?
I DUNNO, SERGEANT. HE SAYS HE'S TOUGHENING US UP! BUT I'M GOOD AND FED UP! I WANNA GET OUT OF THIS ICEBOX BEFORE I LOSE MY MIND!
OF ALL THE FAR-FLUNG OUTPOSTS OF THE UNITED STATES ARMED FORCES, ALASKA WAS THE ROUGHEST. BLEAK, LONELY, RIPPED BY BLIZZARDS AND FROZEN BY SUB-ZERO TEMPERATURES, ITS NICKNAME--"THE ICEBOX"-- GIVEN IT BY THE G.I.'S STATIONED THERE, WAS WELL DESERVED. AT A STRATEGIC ARMY BASE AND JET FIGHTER FIELD NEAR SEWARD, THE SEVENTY-THIRD MOUNTAIN REGIMENT WAS ON A TWENTY-FOUR HOUR ALERT SINCE THE SNEAK ATTACK ON AMERICAN CITIES. COLONEL PAUL McCOBB PUSHED HIS MEN TO THE LIMIT, READYING THEM FOR ANY EMERGENCY. . .
LATER, OUTSIDE THE GARRISON. . .
C'MON, GET THOSE SKIS OFF AND FALL IN! WE'VE GOT CLOSE ORDER DRILL FOR AN HOUR BEFORE CHOW!
MY ACHIN' BACK! WE DID TWENTY MILES THIS MORNING! I CAN'T LIFT MY DOGS! WHAT'S THIS CRAZY PACE FOR?
LIEUTENANTS BLAKE AND GUS ANDREWS WATCHED THE WEARY MEN. . .
GUS, I CAN'T TAKE THIS GAFF ANY MORE! I'M SEEING THE OLD MAN ABOUT A TRANSFER!
I'M COMIN' WITH YOU! I DON'T CARE WHAT HAPPENS-- ANYTHING TO GET OUT OF THIS DEEP FREEZE!

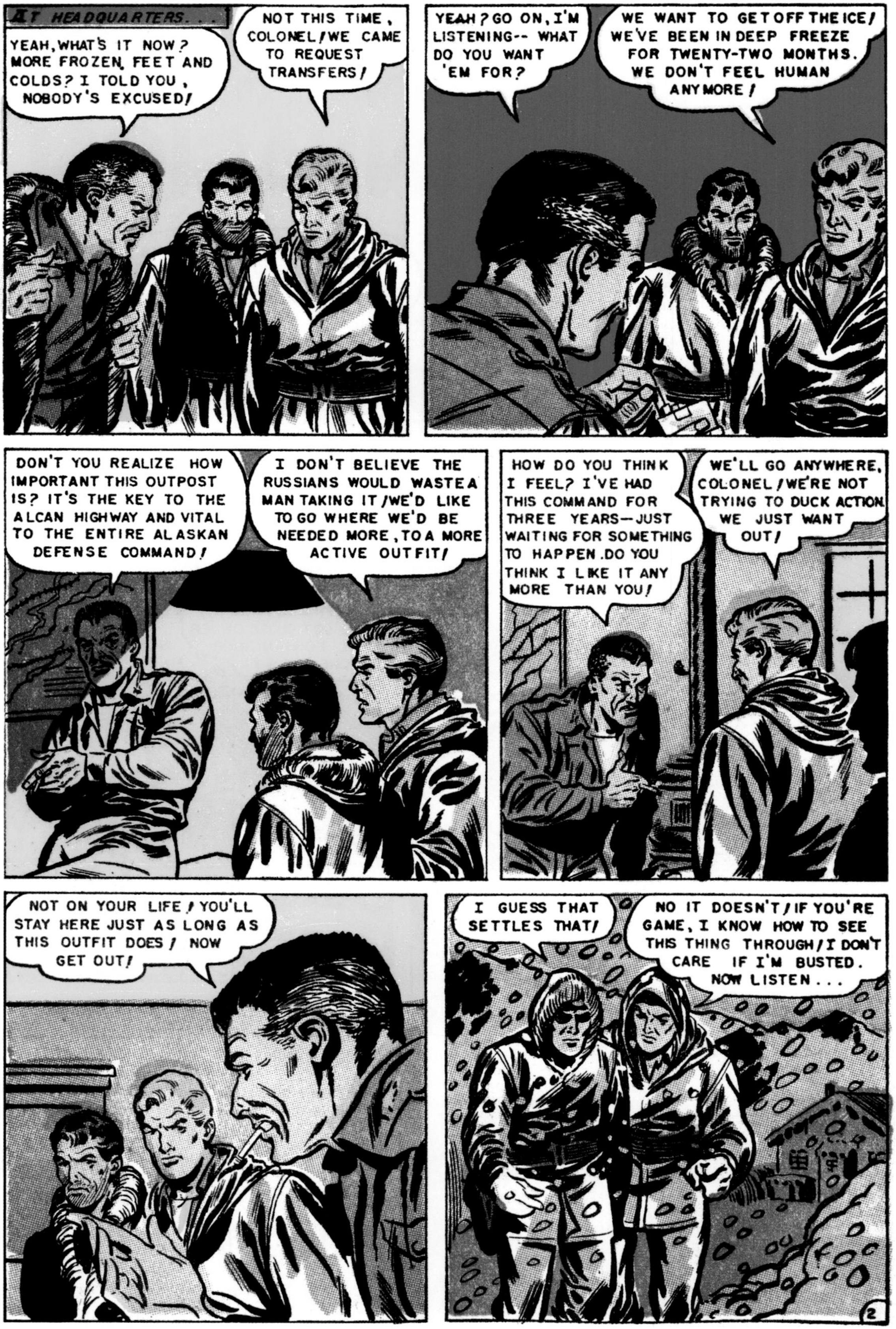
AT HEADQUARTERS...
YEAH, WHAT'S IT NOW? MORE FROZEN FEET AND COLDS? I TOLD YOU, NOBODY'S EXCUSED!
NOT THIS TIME, COLONEL! WE CAME TO REQUEST TRANSFERS!
YEAH? GO ON, I'M LISTENING-- WHAT DO YOU WANT 'EM FOR?
WE WANT TO GET OFF THE ICE! WE'VE BEEN IN DEEP FREEZE FOR TWENTY-TWO MONTHS. WE DON'T FEEL HUMAN ANYMORE!
DON'T YOU REALIZE HOW IMPORTANT THIS OUTPOST IS? IT'S THE KEY TO THE ALCAN HIGHWAY AND VITAL TO THE ENTIRE ALASKAN DEFENSE COMMAND!
I DON'T BELIEVE THE RUSSIANS WOULD WASTE A MAN TAKING IT! WE'D LIKE TO GO WHERE WE'D BE NEEDED MORE, TO A MORE ACTIVE OUTFIT!
HOW DO YOU THINK I FEEL? I'VE HAD THIS COMMAND FOR THREE YEARS—JUST WAITING FOR SOMETHING TO HAPPEN. DO YOU THINK I LIKE IT ANY MORE THAN YOU!
WE'LL GO ANYWHERE, COLONEL! WE'RE NOT TRYING TO DUCK ACTION. WE JUST WANT OUT!
NOT ON YOUR LIFE! YOU'LL STAY HERE JUST AS LONG AS THIS OUTFIT DOES! NOW GET OUT!
I GUESS THAT SETTLES THAT!
NO IT DOESN'T! IF YOU'RE GAME, I KNOW HOW TO SEE THIS THING THROUGH! I DON'T CARE IF I'M BUSTED. NOW LISTEN...
2

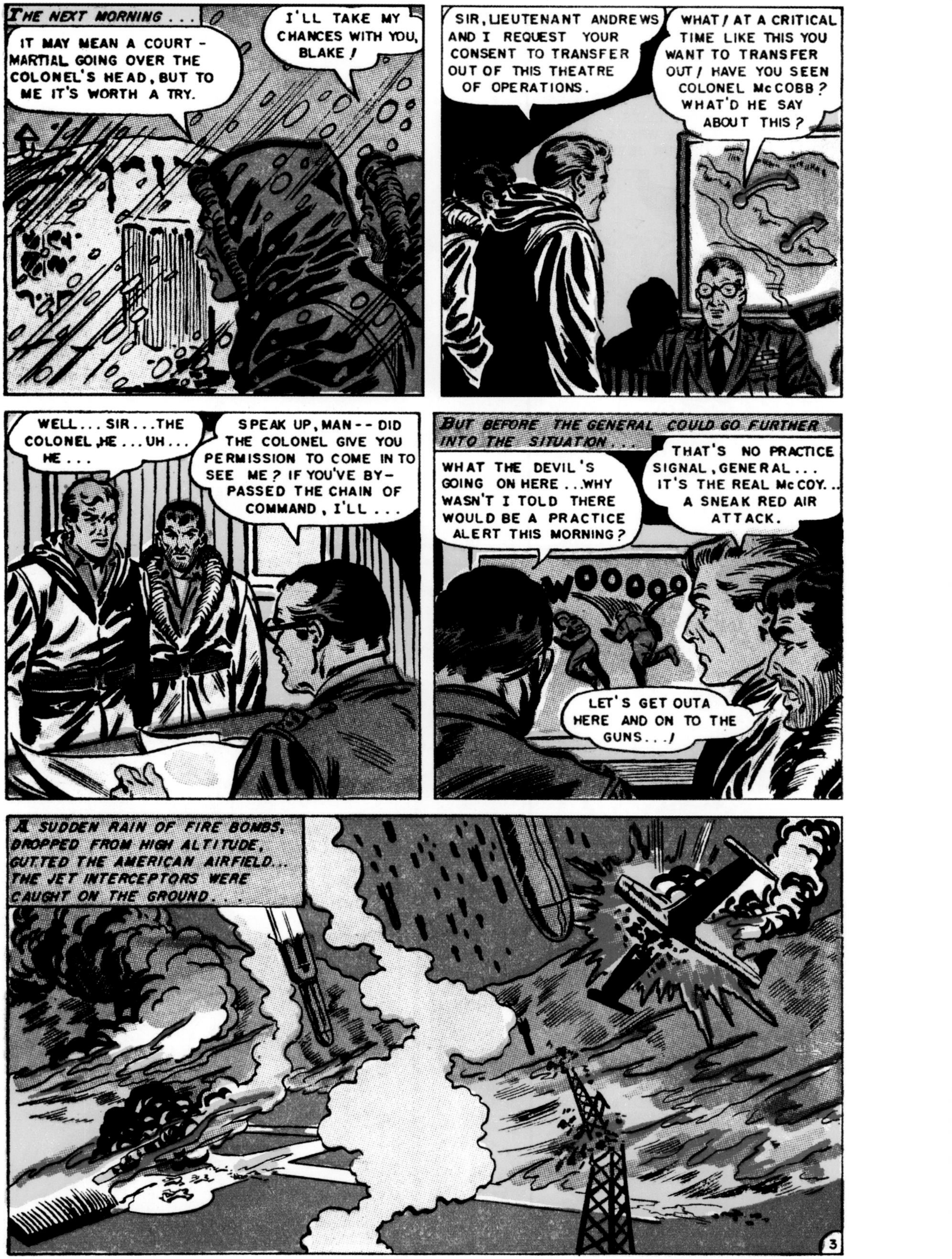
THE NEXT MORNING . . .
IT MAY MEAN A COURT - MARTIAL GOING OVER THE COLONEL'S HEAD, BUT TO ME IT'S WORTH A TRY.
I'LL TAKE MY CHANCES WITH YOU, BLAKE !
SIR, LIEUTENANT ANDREWS AND I REQUEST YOUR CONSENT TO TRANSFER OUT OF THIS THEATRE OF OPERATIONS.
WHAT / AT A CRITICAL TIME LIKE THIS YOU WANT TO TRANSFER OUT / HAVE YOU SEEN COLONEL McCOBB ? WHAT'D HE SAY ABOUT THIS ?
WELL... SIR... THE COLONEL, HE... UH... HE...
SPEAK UP, MAN-- DID THE COLONEL GIVE YOU PERMISSION TO COME IN TO SEE ME ? IF YOU'VE BY-PASSED THE CHAIN OF COMMAND, I'LL...
BUT BEFORE THE GENERAL COULD GO FURTHER INTO THE SITUATION...
WHAT THE DEVIL'S GOING ON HERE ...WHY WASN'T I TOLD THERE WOULD BE A PRACTICE ALERT THIS MORNING ?
THAT'S NO PRACTICE SIGNAL, GENERAL... IT'S THE REAL McCOY... A SNEAK RED AIR ATTACK.
WOOOOO
LET'S GET OUTA HERE AND ON TO THE GUNS... !
A SUDDEN RAIN OF FIRE BOMBS, DROPPED FROM HIGH ALTITUDE, GUTTED THE AMERICAN AIRFIELD... THE JET INTERCEPTORS WERE CAUGHT ON THE GROUND...
3

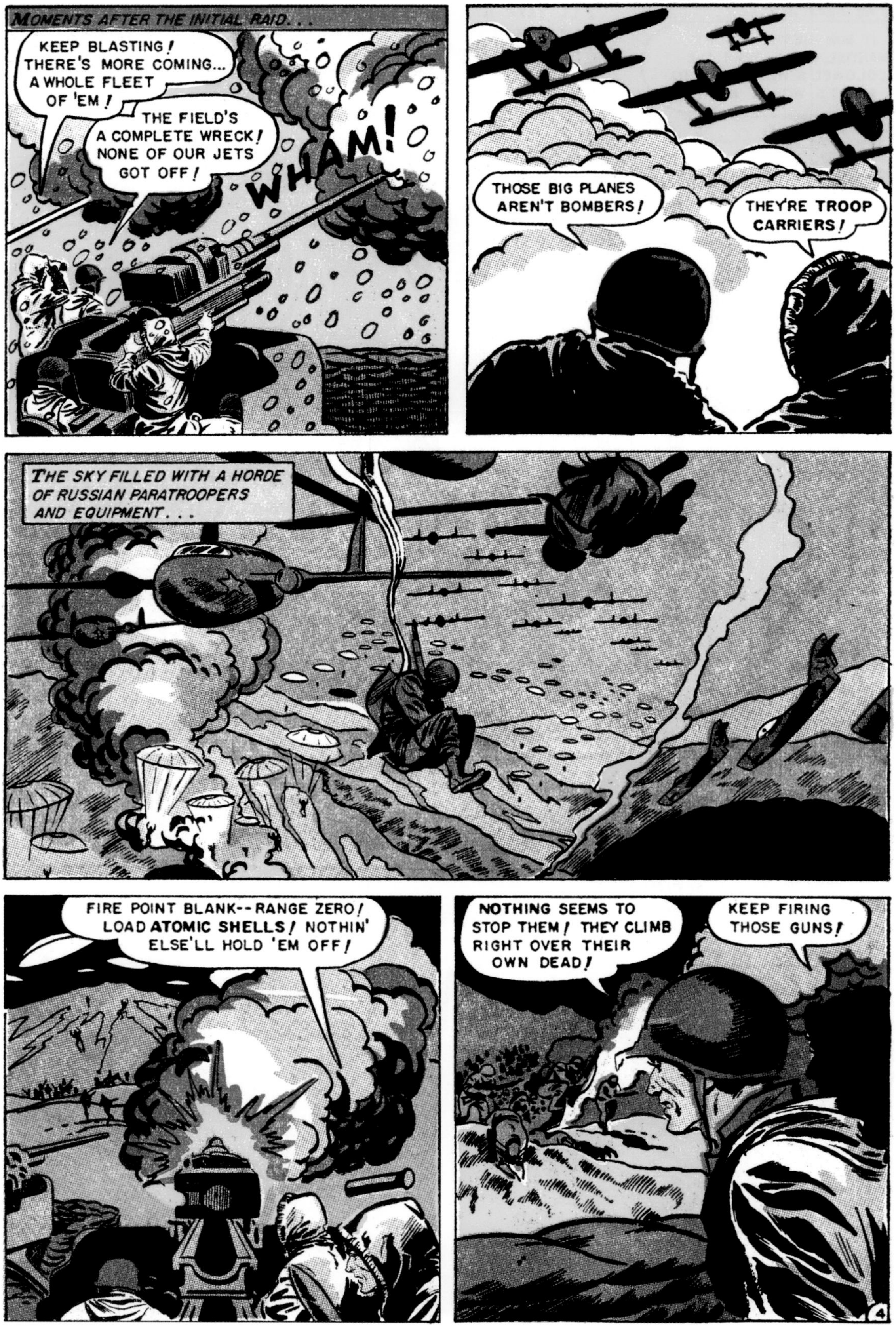

MOMENTS AFTER THE INITIAL RAID...
KEEP BLASTING! THERE'S MORE COMING... A WHOLE FLEET OF 'EM!
THE FIELD'S A COMPLETE WRECK! NONE OF OUR JETS GOT OFF!
WHAM!
THOSE BIG PLANES AREN'T BOMBERS!
THEY'RE TROOP CARRIERS!
THE SKY FILLED WITH A HORDE OF RUSSIAN PARATROOPERS AND EQUIPMENT...
FIRE POINT BLANK--RANGE ZERO! LOAD ATOMIC SHELLS! NOTHIN' ELSE'LL HOLD 'EM OFF!
NOTHING SEEMS TO STOP THEM! THEY CLIMB RIGHT OVER THEIR OWN DEAD!
KEEP FIRING THOSE GUNS!
4

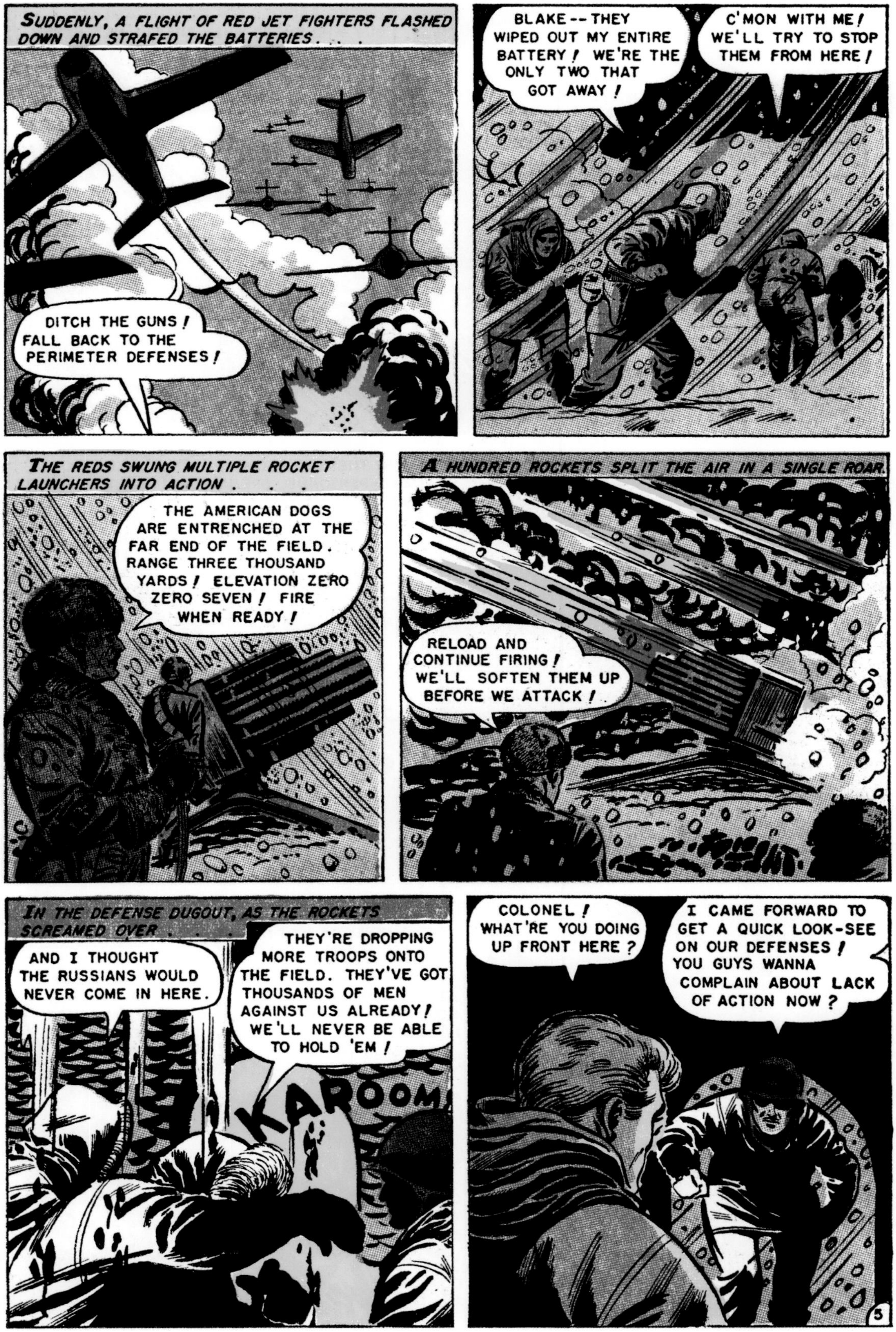
SUDDENLY, A FLIGHT OF RED JET FIGHTERS FLASHED DOWN AND STRAFED THE BATTERIES . . .
DITCH THE GUNS! FALL BACK TO THE PERIMETER DEFENSES!
BLAKE -- THEY WIPED OUT MY ENTIRE BATTERY! WE'RE THE ONLY TWO THAT GOT AWAY!
C'MON WITH ME! WE'LL TRY TO STOP THEM FROM HERE!
THE REDS SWUNG MULTIPLE ROCKET LAUNCHERS INTO ACTION . . .
THE AMERICAN DOGS ARE ENTRENCHED AT THE FAR END OF THE FIELD. RANGE THREE THOUSAND YARDS! ELEVATION ZERO ZERO SEVEN! FIRE WHEN READY!
A HUNDRED ROCKETS SPLIT THE AIR IN A SINGLE ROAR.
RELOAD AND CONTINUE FIRING! WE'LL SOFTEN THEM UP BEFORE WE ATTACK!
IN THE DEFENSE DUGOUT, AS THE ROCKETS SCREAMED OVER . . .
AND I THOUGHT THE RUSSIANS WOULD NEVER COME IN HERE.
THEY'RE DROPPING MORE TROOPS ONTO THE FIELD. THEY'VE GOT THOUSANDS OF MEN AGAINST US ALREADY! WE'LL NEVER BE ABLE TO HOLD 'EM!
KAROOM
COLONEL! WHAT'RE YOU DOING UP FRONT HERE?
I CAME FORWARD TO GET A QUICK LOOK-SEE ON OUR DEFENSES! YOU GUYS WANNA COMPLAIN ABOUT LACK OF ACTION NOW?
5

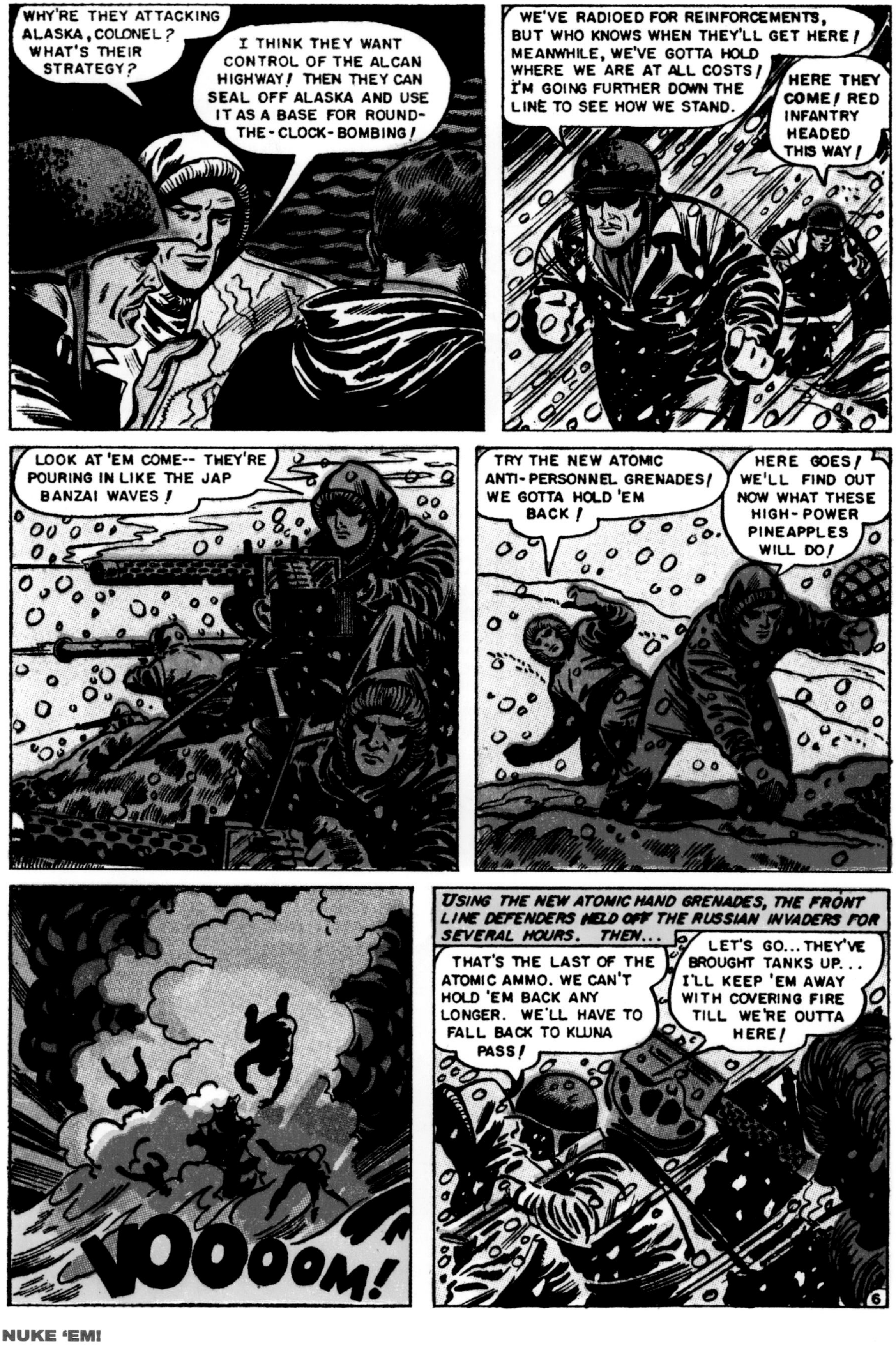
WHY'RE THEY ATTACKING ALASKA, COLONEL? WHAT'S THEIR STRATEGY?
I THINK THEY WANT CONTROL OF THE ALCAN HIGHWAY! THEN THEY CAN SEAL OFF ALASKA AND USE IT AS A BASE FOR ROUND-THE-CLOCK-BOMBING!
WE'VE RADIOED FOR REINFORCEMENTS, BUT WHO KNOWS WHEN THEY'LL GET HERE! MEANWHILE, WE'VE GOTTA HOLD WHERE WE ARE AT ALL COSTS! I'M GOING FURTHER DOWN THE LINE TO SEE HOW WE STAND.
HERE THEY COME! RED INFANTRY HEADED THIS WAY!
LOOK AT 'EM COME-- THEY'RE POURING IN LIKE THE JAP BANZAI WAVES!
TRY THE NEW ATOMIC ANTI-PERSONNEL GRENADES! WE GOTTA HOLD 'EM BACK!
HERE GOES! WE'LL FIND OUT NOW WHAT THESE HIGH-POWER PINEAPPLES WILL DO!
VOOOOOM!
USING THE NEW ATOMIC HAND GRENADES, THE FRONT LINE DEFENDERS HELD OFF THE RUSSIAN INVADERS FOR SEVERAL HOURS. THEN...
THAT'S THE LAST OF THE ATOMIC AMMO. WE CAN'T HOLD 'EM BACK ANY LONGER. WE'LL HAVE TO FALL BACK TO KLUNA PASS!
LET'S GO... THEY'VE BROUGHT TANKS UP... I'LL KEEP 'EM AWAY WITH COVERING FIRE TILL WE'RE OUTTA HERE!
6

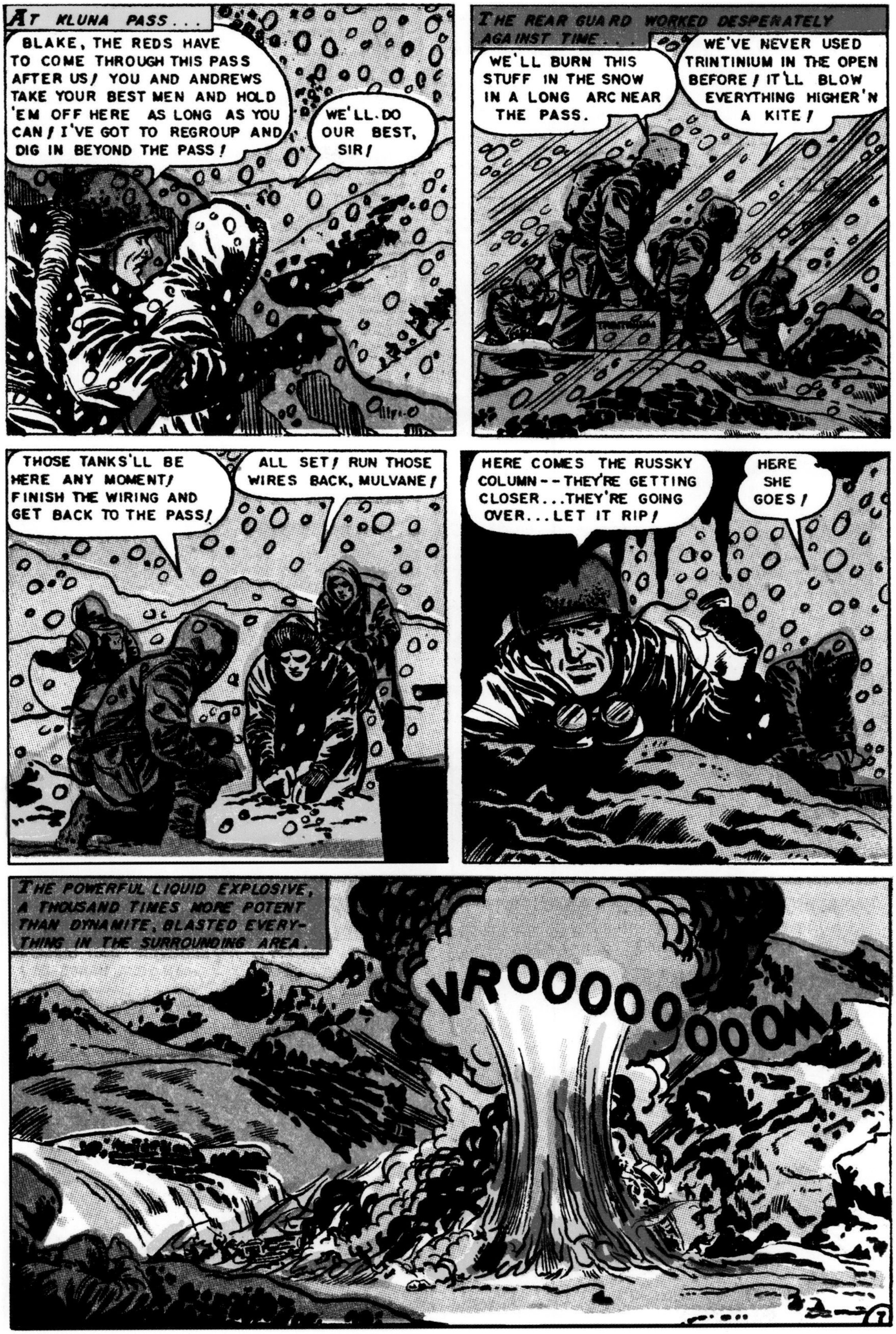
AT KLUNA PASS...
BLAKE, THE REDS HAVE TO COME THROUGH THIS PASS AFTER US! YOU AND ANDREWS TAKE YOUR BEST MEN AND HOLD 'EM OFF HERE AS LONG AS YOU CAN! I'VE GOT TO REGROUP AND DIG IN BEYOND THE PASS!
WE'LL DO OUR BEST, SIR!
THE REAR GUARD WORKED DESPERATELY AGAINST TIME...
WE'LL BURN THIS STUFF IN THE SNOW IN A LONG ARC NEAR THE PASS.
WE'VE NEVER USED TRINTINIUM IN THE OPEN BEFORE! IT'LL BLOW EVERYTHING HIGHER'N A KITE!
THOSE TANKS'LL BE HERE ANY MOMENT! FINISH THE WIRING AND GET BACK TO THE PASS!
ALL SET! RUN THOSE WIRES BACK, MULVANE!
HERE COMES THE RUSSKY COLUMN--THEY'RE GETTING CLOSER...THEY'RE GOING OVER...LET IT RIP!
HERE SHE GOES!
THE POWERFUL LIQUID EXPLOSIVE, A THOUSAND TIMES MORE POTENT THAN DYNAMITE, BLASTED EVERYTHING IN THE SURROUNDING AREA.
VROOOOOOOOOM!
7

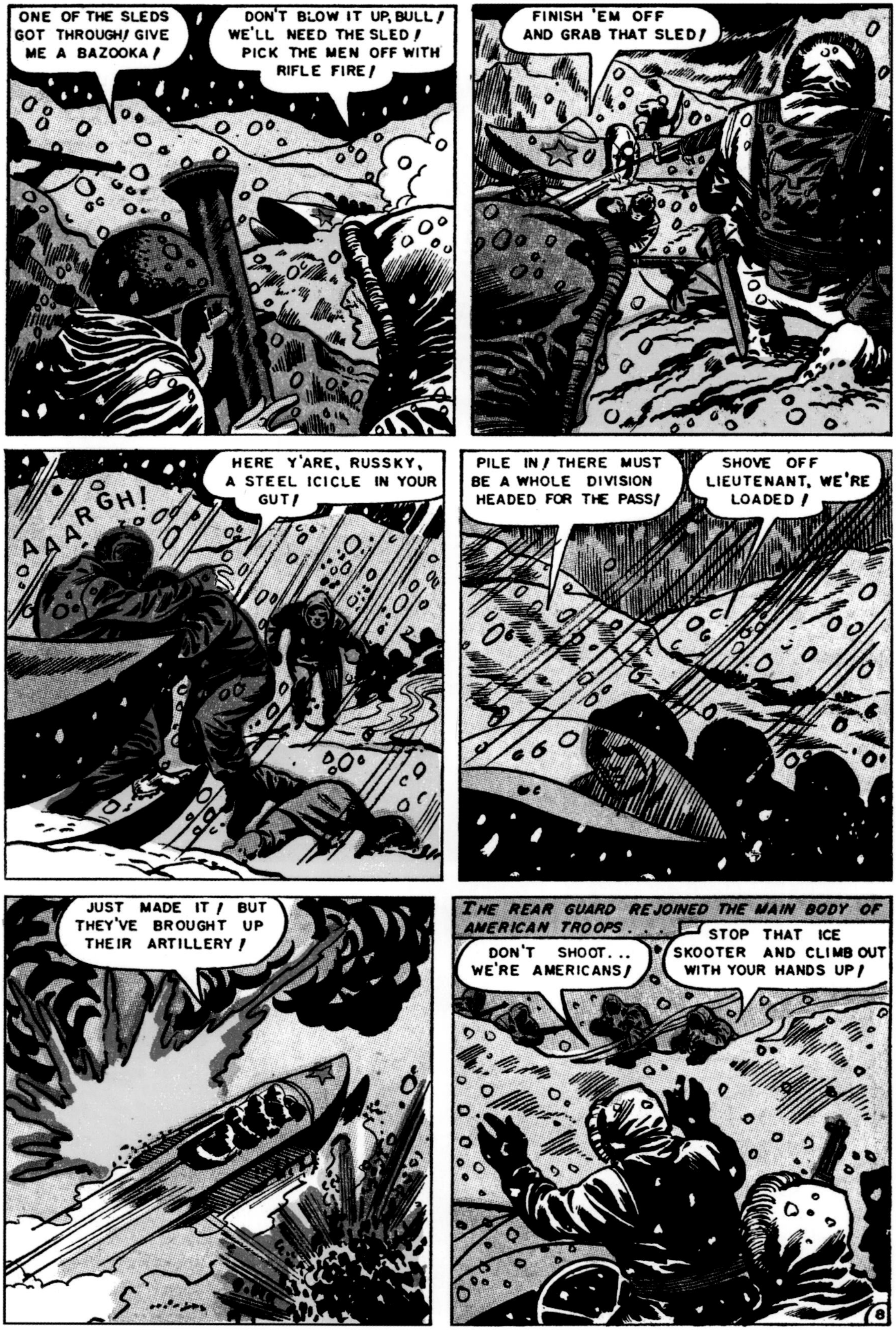
ONE OF THE SLEDS GOT THROUGH! GIVE ME A BAZOOKA!
DON'T BLOW IT UP, BULL! WE'LL NEED THE SLED! PICK THE MEN OFF WITH RIFLE FIRE!
FINISH 'EM OFF AND GRAB THAT SLED!
AAARGH!
HERE Y'ARE, RUSSKY, A STEEL ICICLE IN YOUR GUT!
PILE IN! THERE MUST BE A WHOLE DIVISION HEADED FOR THE PASS!
SHOVE OFF LIEUTENANT, WE'RE LOADED!
JUST MADE IT! BUT THEY'VE BROUGHT UP THEIR ARTILLERY!
THE REAR GUARD REJOINED THE MAIN BODY OF AMERICAN TROOPS...
DON'T SHOOT... WE'RE AMERICANS!
STOP THAT ICE SKOOTER AND CLIMB OUT WITH YOUR HANDS UP!
8

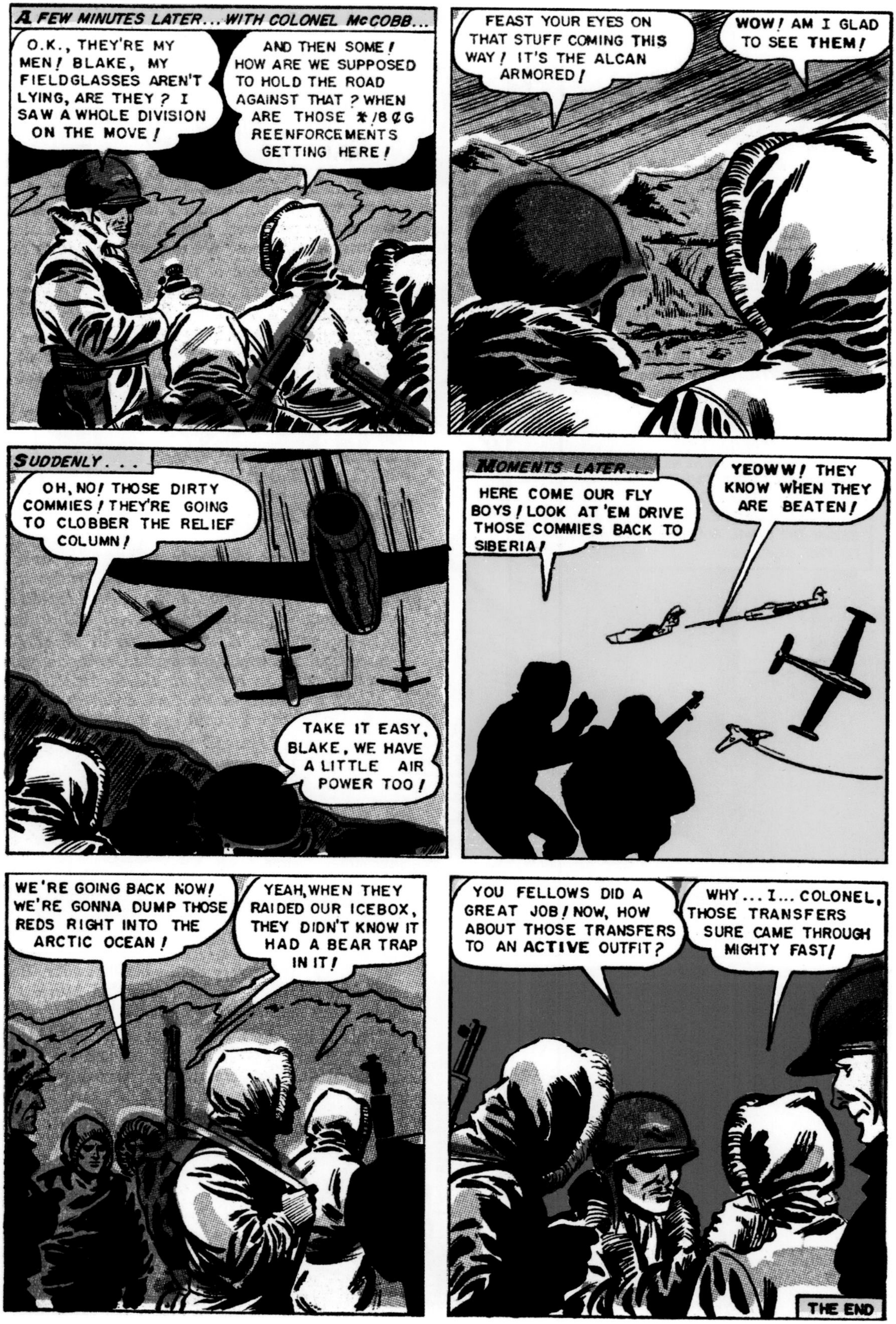
A FEW MINUTES LATER... WITH COLONEL McCOBB...
O.K., THEY'RE MY MEN! BLAKE, MY FIELDGLASSES AREN'T LYING, ARE THEY? I SAW A WHOLE DIVISION ON THE MOVE!
AND THEN SOME! HOW ARE WE SUPPOSED TO HOLD THE ROAD AGAINST THAT? WHEN ARE THOSE *!8¢G REENFORCEMENTS GETTING HERE!
FEAST YOUR EYES ON THAT STUFF COMING THIS WAY! IT'S THE ALCAN ARMORED!
WOW! AM I GLAD TO SEE THEM!
SUDDENLY...
OH, NO! THOSE DIRTY COMMIES! THEY'RE GOING TO CLOBBER THE RELIEF COLUMN!
TAKE IT EASY, BLAKE, WE HAVE A LITTLE AIR POWER TOO!
MOMENTS LATER...
HERE COME OUR FLY BOYS! LOOK AT 'EM DRIVE THOSE COMMIES BACK TO SIBERIA!
YEOWW! THEY KNOW WHEN THEY ARE BEATEN!
WE'RE GOING BACK NOW! WE'RE GONNA DUMP THOSE REDS RIGHT INTO THE ARCTIC OCEAN!
YEAH, WHEN THEY RAIDED OUR ICEBOX, THEY DIDN'T KNOW IT HAD A BEAR TRAP IN IT!
YOU FELLOWS DID A GREAT JOB! NOW, HOW ABOUT THOSE TRANSFERS TO AN ACTIVE OUTFIT?
WHY... I... COLONEL, THOSE TRANSFERS SURE CAME THROUGH MIGHTY FAST!
THE END

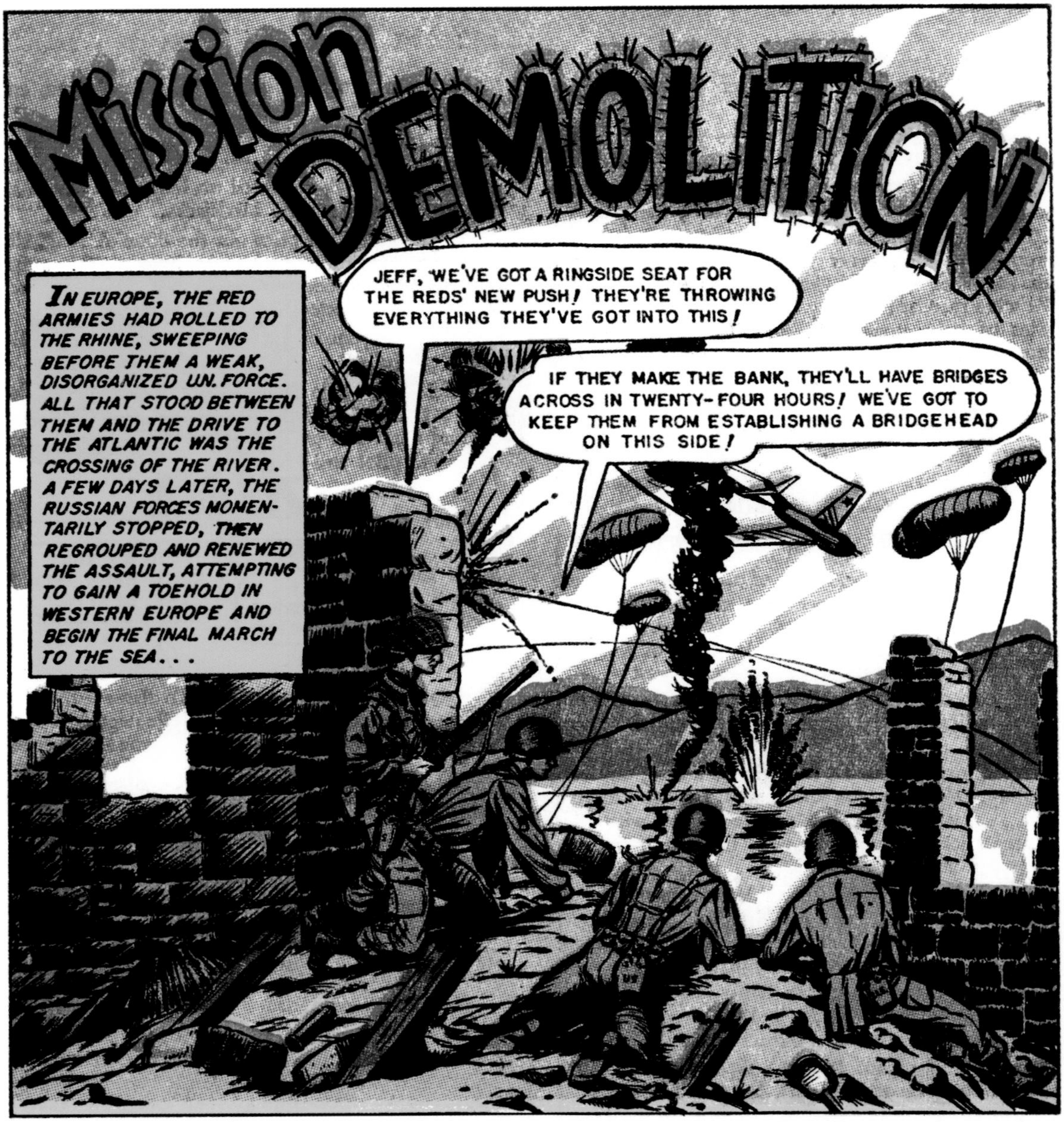
Mission DEMOLITION
IN EUROPE, THE RED ARMIES HAD ROLLED TO THE RHINE, SWEEPING BEFORE THEM A WEAK, DISORGANIZED U.N. FORCE. ALL THAT STOOD BETWEEN THEM AND THE DRIVE TO THE ATLANTIC WAS THE CROSSING OF THE RIVER. A FEW DAYS LATER, THE RUSSIAN FORCES MOMENTARILY STOPPED, THEN REGROUPED AND RENEWED THE ASSAULT, ATTEMPTING TO GAIN A TOEHOLD IN WESTERN EUROPE AND BEGIN THE FINAL MARCH TO THE SEA...
JEFF, WE'VE GOT A RINGSIDE SEAT FOR THE REDS' NEW PUSH! THEY'RE THROWING EVERYTHING THEY'VE GOT INTO THIS!
IF THEY MAKE THE BANK, THEY'LL HAVE BRIDGES ACROSS IN TWENTY-FOUR HOURS! WE'VE GOT TO KEEP THEM FROM ESTABLISHING A BRIDGEHEAD ON THIS SIDE!

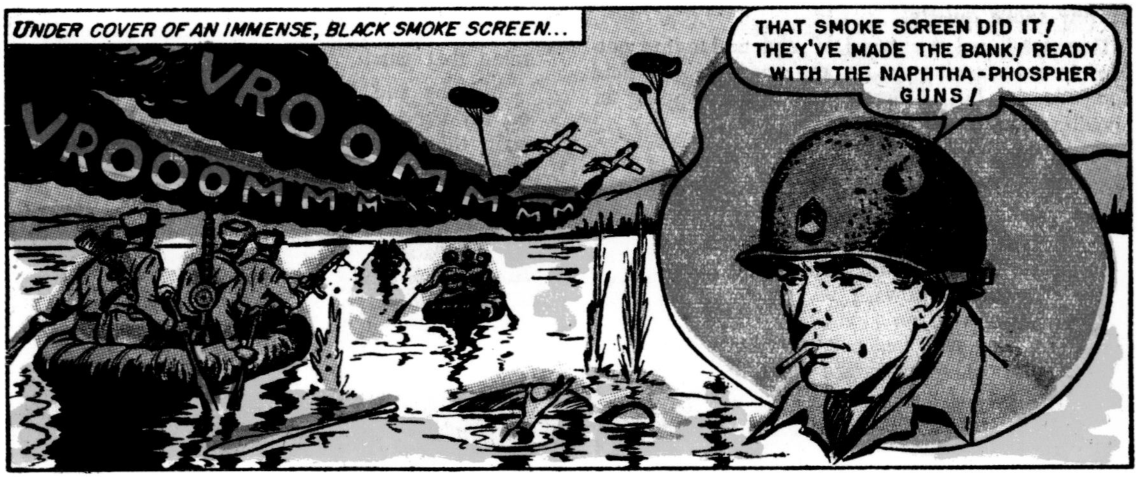
UNDER COVER OF AN IMMENSE, BLACK SMOKE SCREEN...
THAT SMOKE SCREEN DID IT! THEY'VE MADE THE BANK! READY WITH THE NAPHTHA-PHOSPHER GUNS!
VROOOM
VROOOOMMMMMMMM

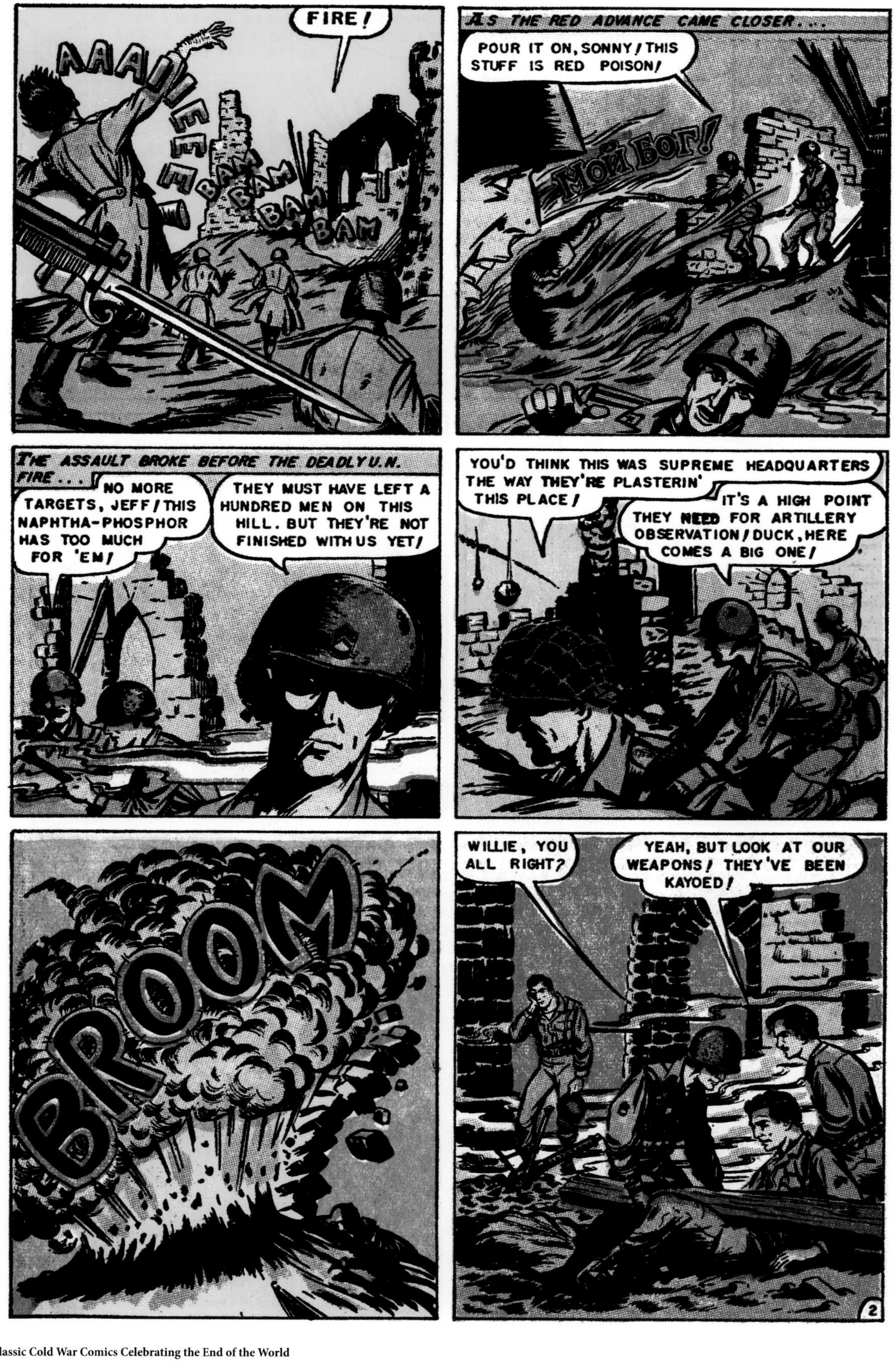
FIRE!
AAAIIIEEEE
BAM BAM BAM
AS THE RED ADVANCE CAME CLOSER...
POUR IT ON, SONNY! THIS STUFF IS RED POISON!
МОЙ БОГ!
THE ASSAULT BROKE BEFORE THE DEADLY U.N. FIRE...
NO MORE TARGETS, JEFF! THIS NAPHTHA-PHOSPHOR HAS TOO MUCH FOR 'EM!
THEY MUST HAVE LEFT A HUNDRED MEN ON THIS HILL. BUT THEY'RE NOT FINISHED WITH US YET!
YOU'D THINK THIS WAS SUPREME HEADQUARTERS THE WAY THEY'RE PLASTERIN' THIS PLACE!
IT'S A HIGH POINT THEY NEED FOR ARTILLERY OBSERVATION! DUCK, HERE COMES A BIG ONE!
BROOOM
WILLIE, YOU ALL RIGHT?
YEAH, BUT LOOK AT OUR WEAPONS! THEY'VE BEEN KAYOED!
2

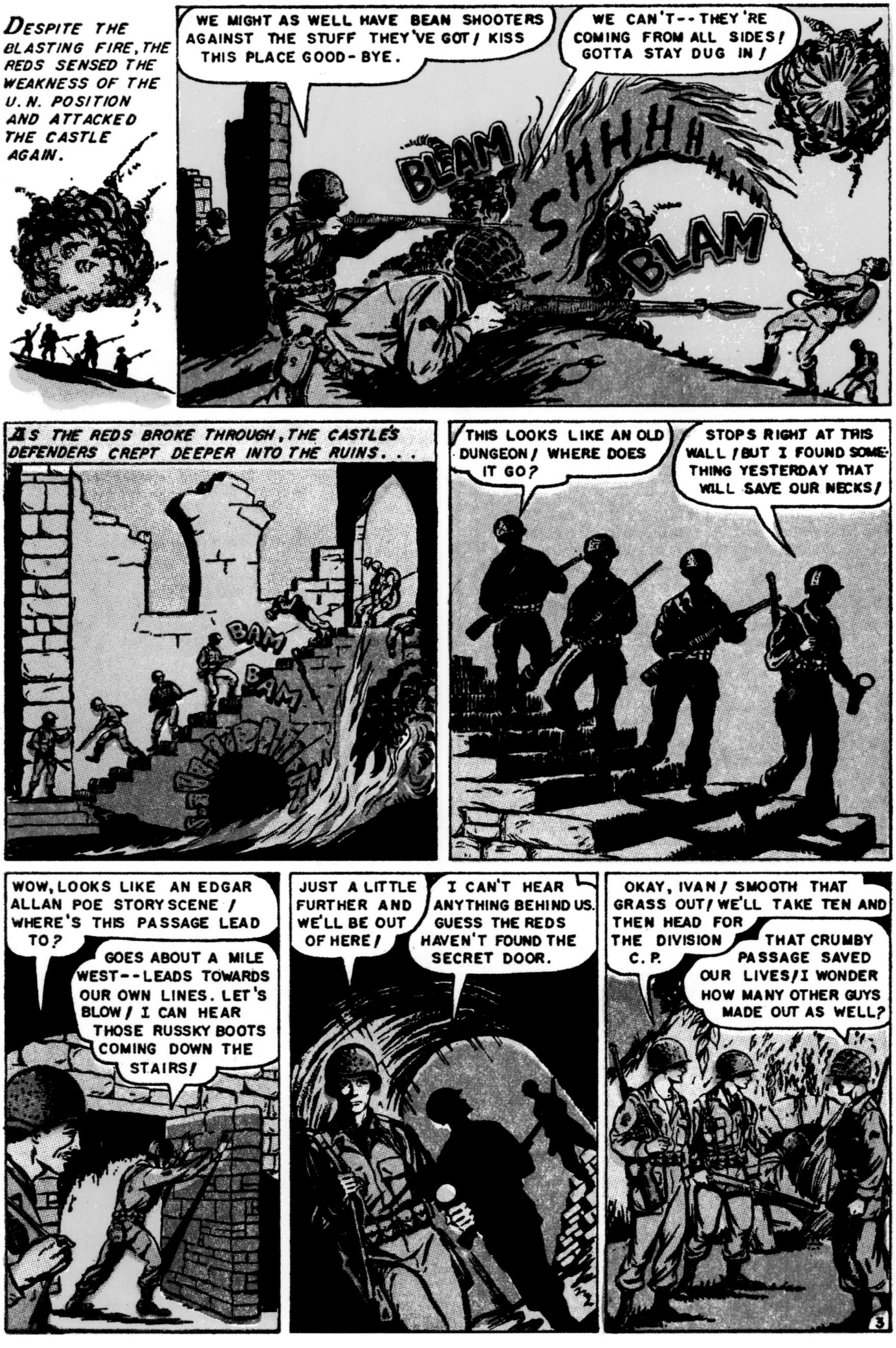
DESPITE THE BLASTING FIRE, THE REDS SENSED THE WEAKNESS OF THE U.N. POSITION AND ATTACKED THE CASTLE AGAIN.
WE MIGHT AS WELL HAVE BEAN SHOOTERS AGAINST THE STUFF THEY'VE GOT! KISS THIS PLACE GOOD-BYE.
WE CAN'T--THEY'RE COMING FROM ALL SIDES! GOTTA STAY DUG IN!
BLAM
SHHHHHHHH
BLAM
AS THE REDS BROKE THROUGH, THE CASTLE'S DEFENDERS CREPT DEEPER INTO THE RUINS...
BAM
BAM
THIS LOOKS LIKE AN OLD DUNGEON! WHERE DOES IT GO?
STOPS RIGHT AT THIS WALL! BUT I FOUND SOMETHING YESTERDAY THAT WILL SAVE OUR NECKS!
WOW, LOOKS LIKE AN EDGAR ALLAN POE STORY SCENE! WHERE'S THIS PASSAGE LEAD TO?
GOES ABOUT A MILE WEST--LEADS TOWARDS OUR OWN LINES. LET'S BLOW! I CAN HEAR THOSE RUSSKY BOOTS COMING DOWN THE STAIRS!
JUST A LITTLE FURTHER AND WE'LL BE OUT OF HERE!
I CAN'T HEAR ANYTHING BEHIND US. GUESS THE REDS HAVEN'T FOUND THE SECRET DOOR.
OKAY, IVAN! SMOOTH THAT GRASS OUT! WE'LL TAKE TEN AND THEN HEAD FOR THE DIVISION C.P.
THAT CRUMBY PASSAGE SAVED OUR LIVES! I WONDER HOW MANY OTHER GUYS MADE OUT AS WELL?
3

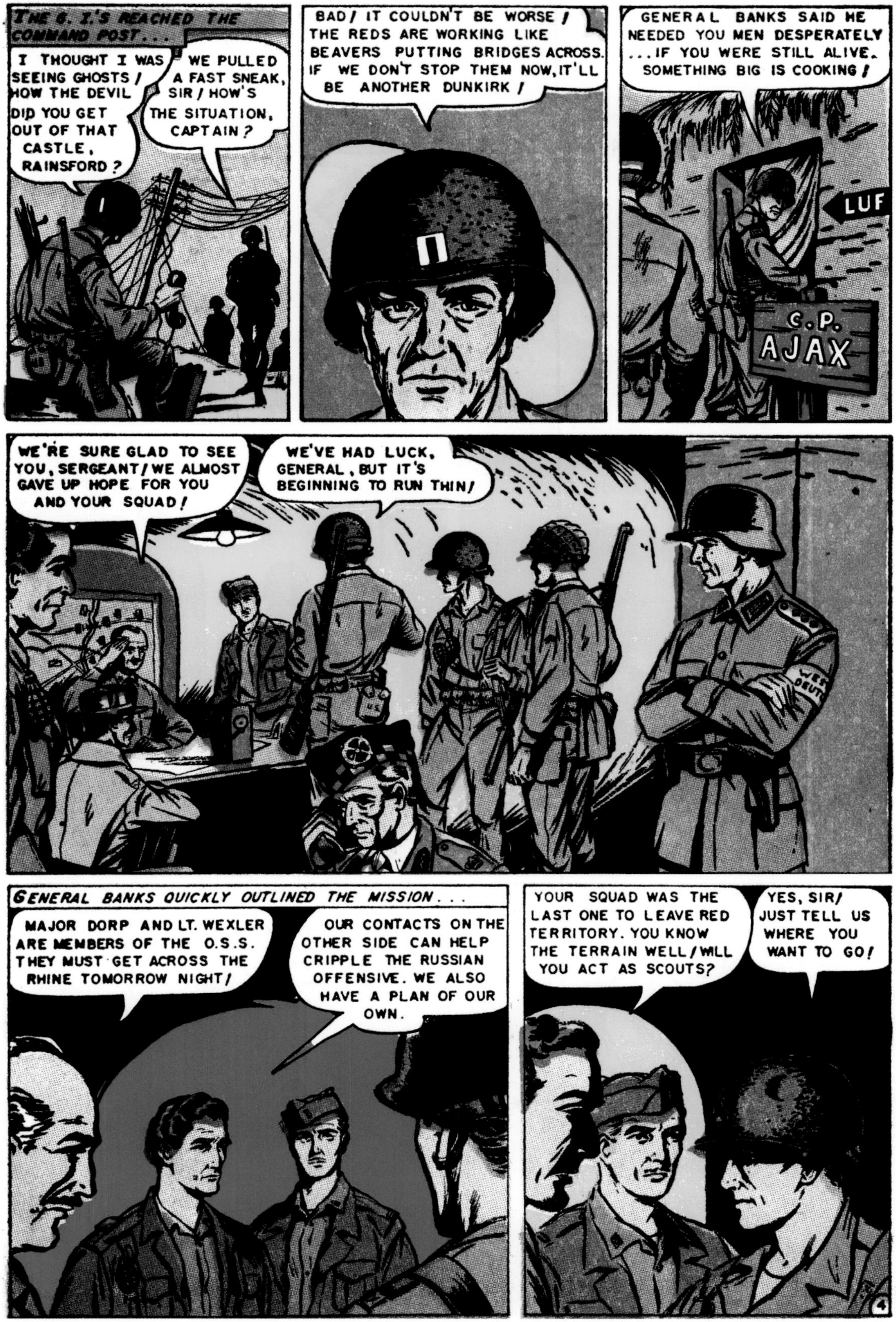
THE G. I.'S REACHED THE COMMAND POST...
I THOUGHT I WAS SEEING GHOSTS! HOW THE DEVIL DID YOU GET OUT OF THAT CASTLE, RAINSFORD?
WE PULLED A FAST SNEAK, SIR! HOW'S THE SITUATION, CAPTAIN?
BAD! IT COULDN'T BE WORSE! THE REDS ARE WORKING LIKE BEAVERS PUTTING BRIDGES ACROSS. IF WE DON'T STOP THEM NOW, IT'LL BE ANOTHER DUNKIRK!
GENERAL BANKS SAID HE NEEDED YOU MEN DESPERATELY ...IF YOU WERE STILL ALIVE. SOMETHING BIG IS COOKING!
LUF
C.P.
AJAX
WE'RE SURE GLAD TO SEE YOU, SERGEANT! WE ALMOST GAVE UP HOPE FOR YOU AND YOUR SQUAD!
WE'VE HAD LUCK, GENERAL, BUT IT'S BEGINNING TO RUN THIN!
GENERAL BANKS QUICKLY OUTLINED THE MISSION...
MAJOR DORP AND LT. WEXLER ARE MEMBERS OF THE O.S.S. THEY MUST GET ACROSS THE RHINE TOMORROW NIGHT!
OUR CONTACTS ON THE OTHER SIDE CAN HELP CRIPPLE THE RUSSIAN OFFENSIVE. WE ALSO HAVE A PLAN OF OUR OWN.
YOUR SQUAD WAS THE LAST ONE TO LEAVE RED TERRITORY. YOU KNOW THE TERRAIN WELL! WILL YOU ACT AS SCOUTS?
YES, SIR! JUST TELL US WHERE YOU WANT TO GO!
4

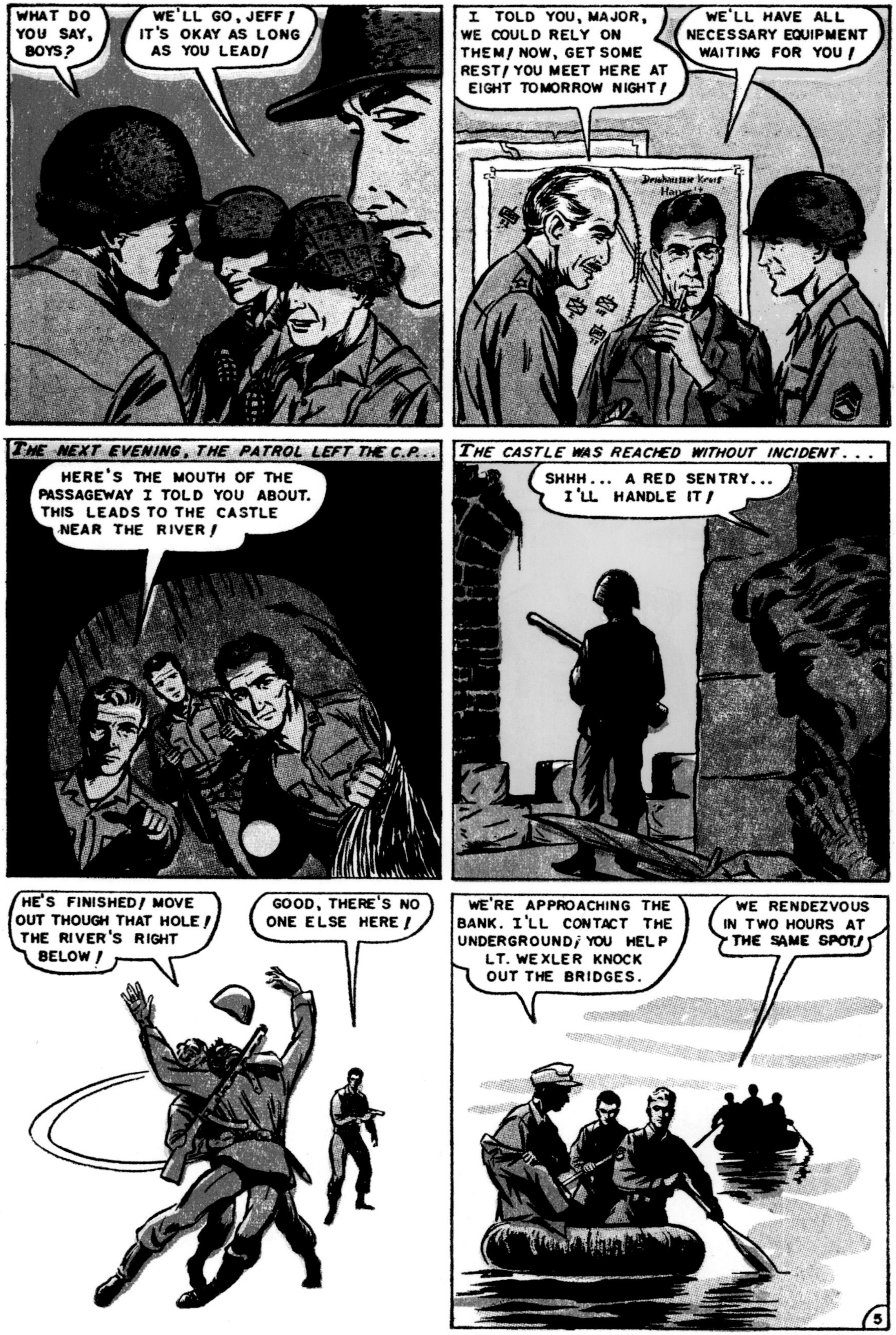
WHAT DO YOU SAY, BOYS?
WE'LL GO, JEFF! IT'S OKAY AS LONG AS YOU LEAD!
I TOLD YOU, MAJOR, WE COULD RELY ON THEM! NOW, GET SOME REST! YOU MEET HERE AT EIGHT TOMORROW NIGHT!
WE'LL HAVE ALL NECESSARY EQUIPMENT WAITING FOR YOU!
THE NEXT EVENING, THE PATROL LEFT THE C.P...
HERE'S THE MOUTH OF THE PASSAGEWAY I TOLD YOU ABOUT. THIS LEADS TO THE CASTLE NEAR THE RIVER!
THE CASTLE WAS REACHED WITHOUT INCIDENT...
SHHH... A RED SENTRY... I'LL HANDLE IT!
HE'S FINISHED! MOVE OUT THOUGH THAT HOLE! THE RIVER'S RIGHT BELOW!
GOOD, THERE'S NO ONE ELSE HERE!
WE'RE APPROACHING THE BANK. I'LL CONTACT THE UNDERGROUND; YOU HELP LT. WEXLER KNOCK OUT THE BRIDGES.
WE RENDEZVOUS IN TWO HOURS AT THE SAME SPOT!
5

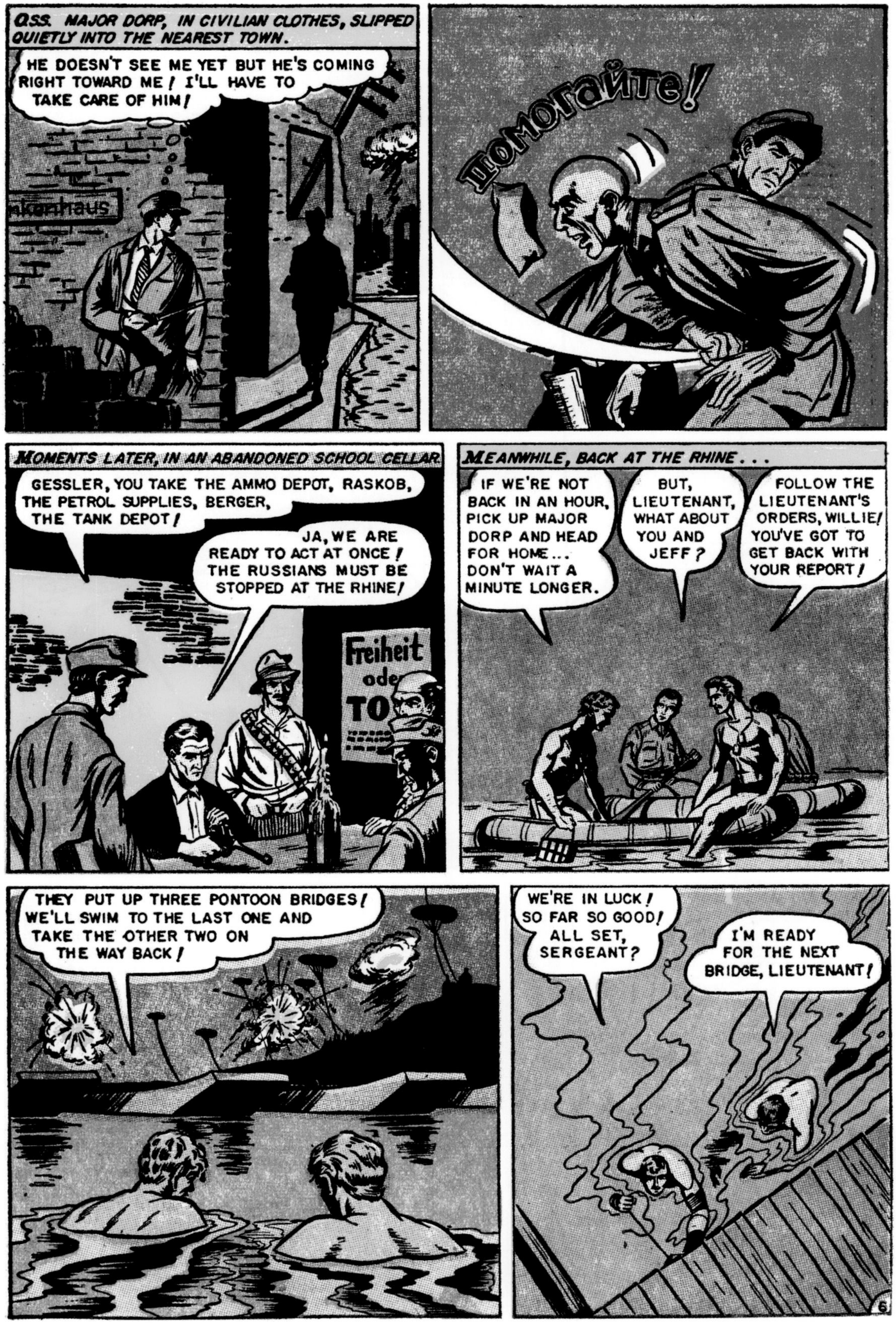
O.S.S. MAJOR DORP, IN CIVILIAN CLOTHES, SLIPPED QUIETLY INTO THE NEAREST TOWN.
HE DOESN'T SEE ME YET BUT HE'S COMING RIGHT TOWARD ME! I'LL HAVE TO TAKE CARE OF HIM!
nkenhaus
ПОМОГАЙТЕ!
MOMENTS LATER, IN AN ABANDONED SCHOOL CELLAR
GESSLER, YOU TAKE THE AMMO DEPOT, RASKOB, THE PETROL SUPPLIES, BERGER, THE TANK DEPOT!
JA, WE ARE READY TO ACT AT ONCE! THE RUSSIANS MUST BE STOPPED AT THE RHINE!
Freiheit ode TO
MEANWHILE, BACK AT THE RHINE . . .
IF WE'RE NOT BACK IN AN HOUR, PICK UP MAJOR DORP AND HEAD FOR HOME... DON'T WAIT A MINUTE LONGER.
BUT, LIEUTENANT, WHAT ABOUT YOU AND JEFF?
FOLLOW THE LIEUTENANT'S ORDERS, WILLIE! YOU'VE GOT TO GET BACK WITH YOUR REPORT!
THEY PUT UP THREE PONTOON BRIDGES! WE'LL SWIM TO THE LAST ONE AND TAKE THE OTHER TWO ON THE WAY BACK!
WE'RE IN LUCK! SO FAR SO GOOD! ALL SET, SERGEANT?
I'M READY FOR THE NEXT BRIDGE, LIEUTENANT!
6

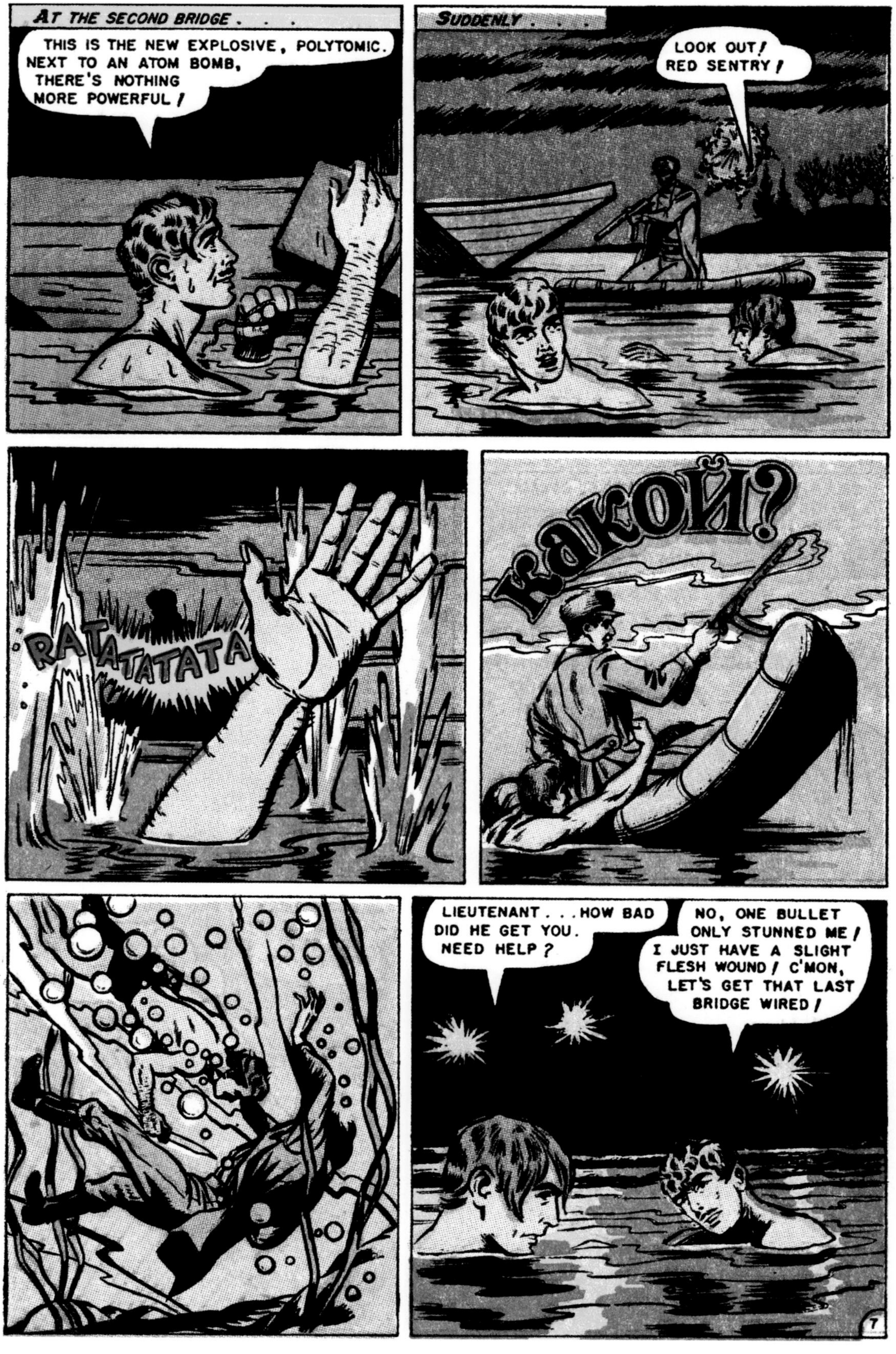
AT THE SECOND BRIDGE . . .
THIS IS THE NEW EXPLOSIVE, POLYTOMIC. NEXT TO AN ATOM BOMB, THERE'S NOTHING MORE POWERFUL!
SUDDENLY . . .
LOOK OUT! RED SENTRY!
RATATATATATA
КАКОЙ?
LIEUTENANT . . . HOW BAD DID HE GET YOU. NEED HELP?
NO, ONE BULLET ONLY STUNNED ME! I JUST HAVE A SLIGHT FLESH WOUND! C'MON, LET'S GET THAT LAST BRIDGE WIRED!
7

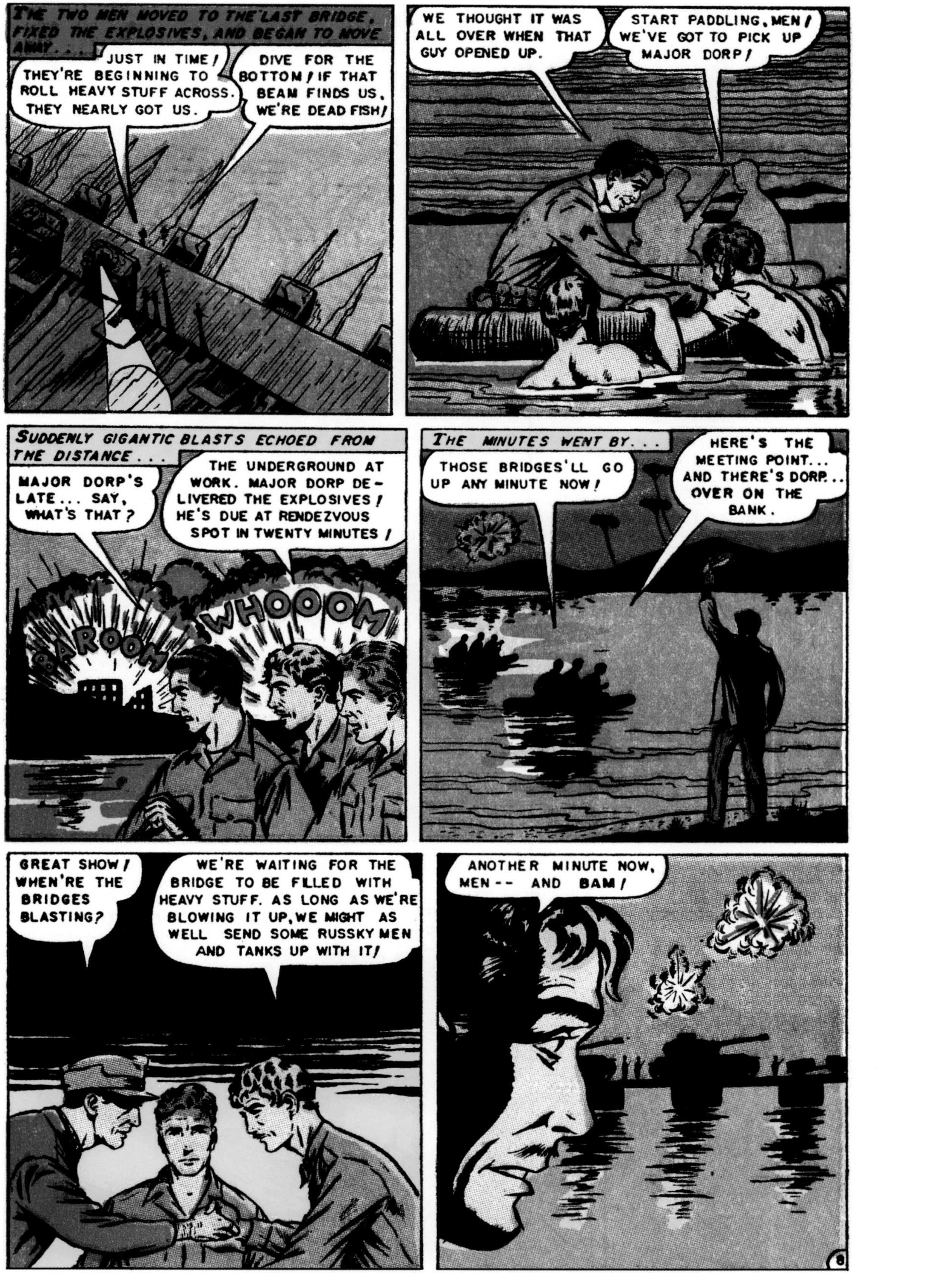
THE TWO MEN MOVED TO THE LAST BRIDGE, FIXED THE EXPLOSIVES, AND BEGAN TO MOVE AWAY...
JUST IN TIME! THEY'RE BEGINNING TO ROLL HEAVY STUFF ACROSS. THEY NEARLY GOT US.
DIVE FOR THE BOTTOM! IF THAT BEAM FINDS US, WE'RE DEAD FISH!
WE THOUGHT IT WAS ALL OVER WHEN THAT GUY OPENED UP.
START PADDLING, MEN! WE'VE GOT TO PICK UP MAJOR DORP!
SUDDENLY GIGANTIC BLASTS ECHOED FROM THE DISTANCE...
MAJOR DORP'S LATE... SAY, WHAT'S THAT?
THE UNDERGROUND AT WORK. MAJOR DORP DE-LIVERED THE EXPLOSIVES! HE'S DUE AT RENDEZVOUS SPOT IN TWENTY MINUTES!
BAROOM
WHOOOOM
THE MINUTES WENT BY...
THOSE BRIDGES'LL GO UP ANY MINUTE NOW!
HERE'S THE MEETING POINT... AND THERE'S DORP... OVER ON THE BANK.
GREAT SHOW! WHEN'RE THE BRIDGES BLASTING?
WE'RE WAITING FOR THE BRIDGE TO BE FILLED WITH HEAVY STUFF. AS LONG AS WE'RE BLOWING IT UP, WE MIGHT AS WELL SEND SOME RUSSKY MEN AND TANKS UP WITH IT!
ANOTHER MINUTE NOW, MEN-- AND BAM!
8

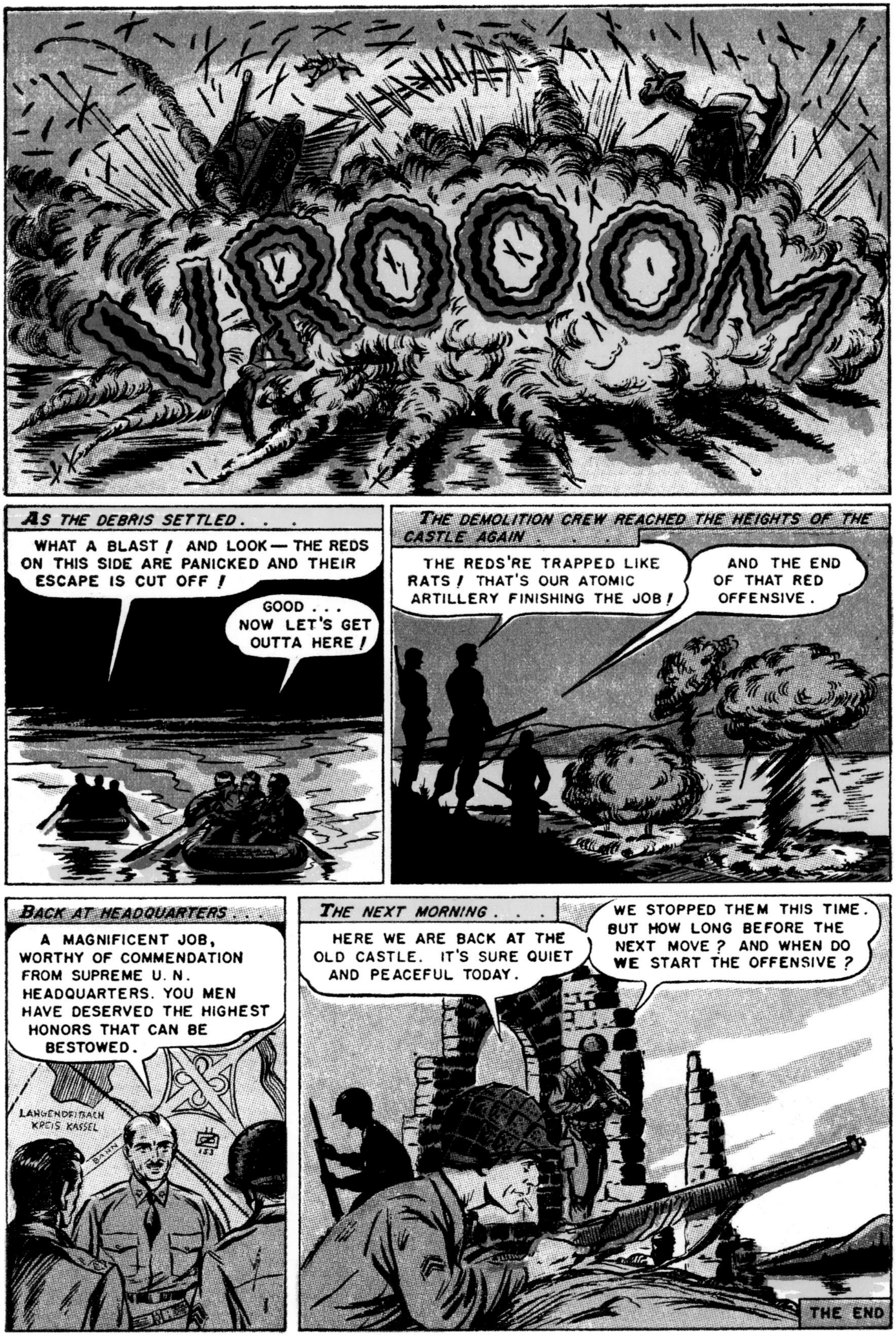
VROOOM
AS THE DEBRIS SETTLED . . .
WHAT A BLAST ! AND LOOK — THE REDS ON THIS SIDE ARE PANICKED AND THEIR ESCAPE IS CUT OFF !
GOOD . . . NOW LET'S GET OUTTA HERE !
THE DEMOLITION CREW REACHED THE HEIGHTS OF THE CASTLE AGAIN . . .
THE REDS'RE TRAPPED LIKE RATS ! THAT'S OUR ATOMIC ARTILLERY FINISHING THE JOB !
AND THE END OF THAT RED OFFENSIVE .
BACK AT HEADQUARTERS . . .
A MAGNIFICENT JOB, WORTHY OF COMMENDATION FROM SUPREME U. N. HEADQUARTERS. YOU MEN HAVE DESERVED THE HIGHEST HONORS THAT CAN BE BESTOWED.
THE NEXT MORNING . . .
HERE WE ARE BACK AT THE OLD CASTLE. IT'S SURE QUIET AND PEACEFUL TODAY.
WE STOPPED THEM THIS TIME. BUT HOW LONG BEFORE THE NEXT MOVE ? AND WHEN DO WE START THE OFFENSIVE ?
THE END

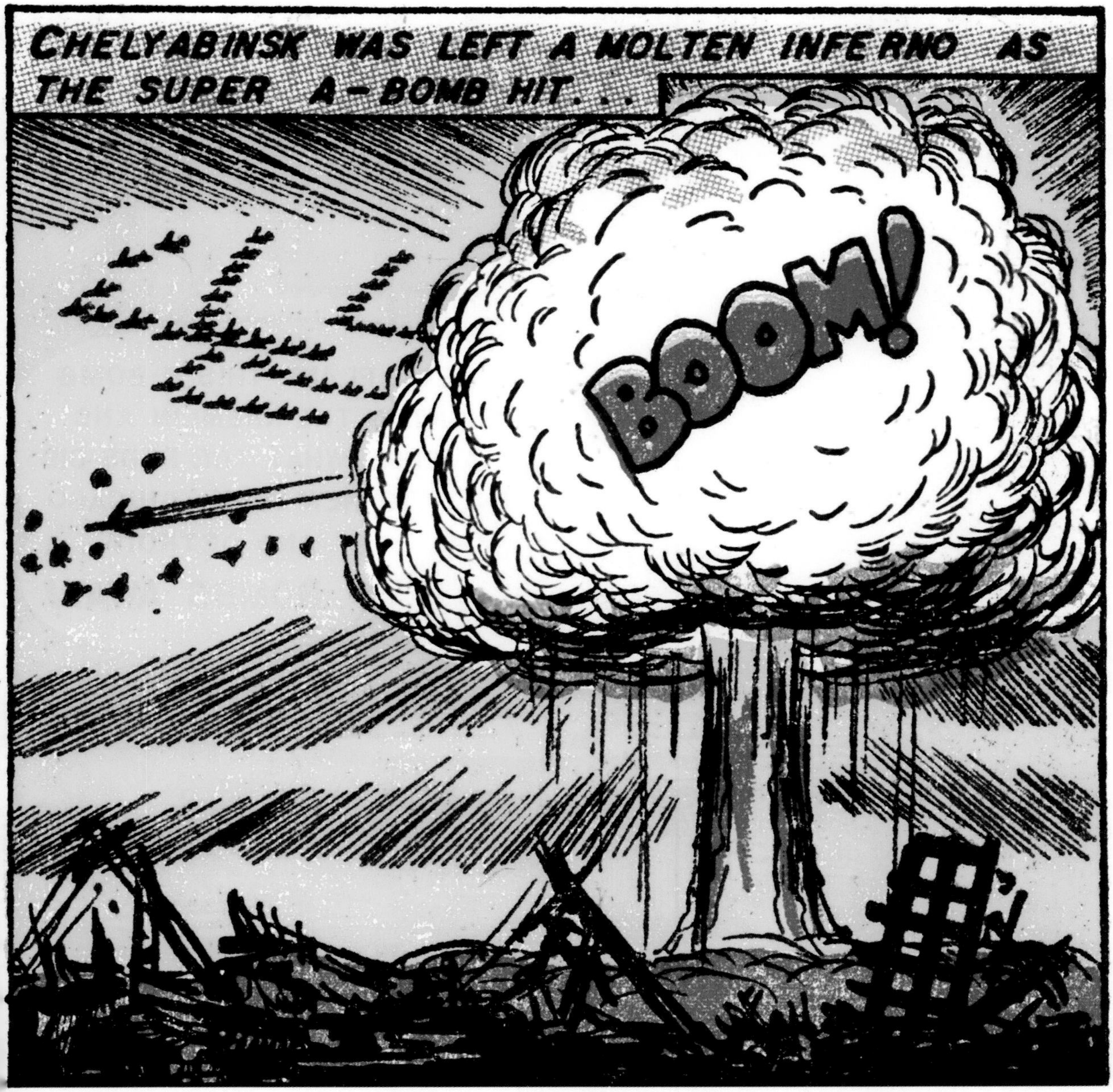
CHELYABINSK WAS LEFT A MOLTEN INFERNO AS THE SUPER A-BOMB HIT...
BOOM!

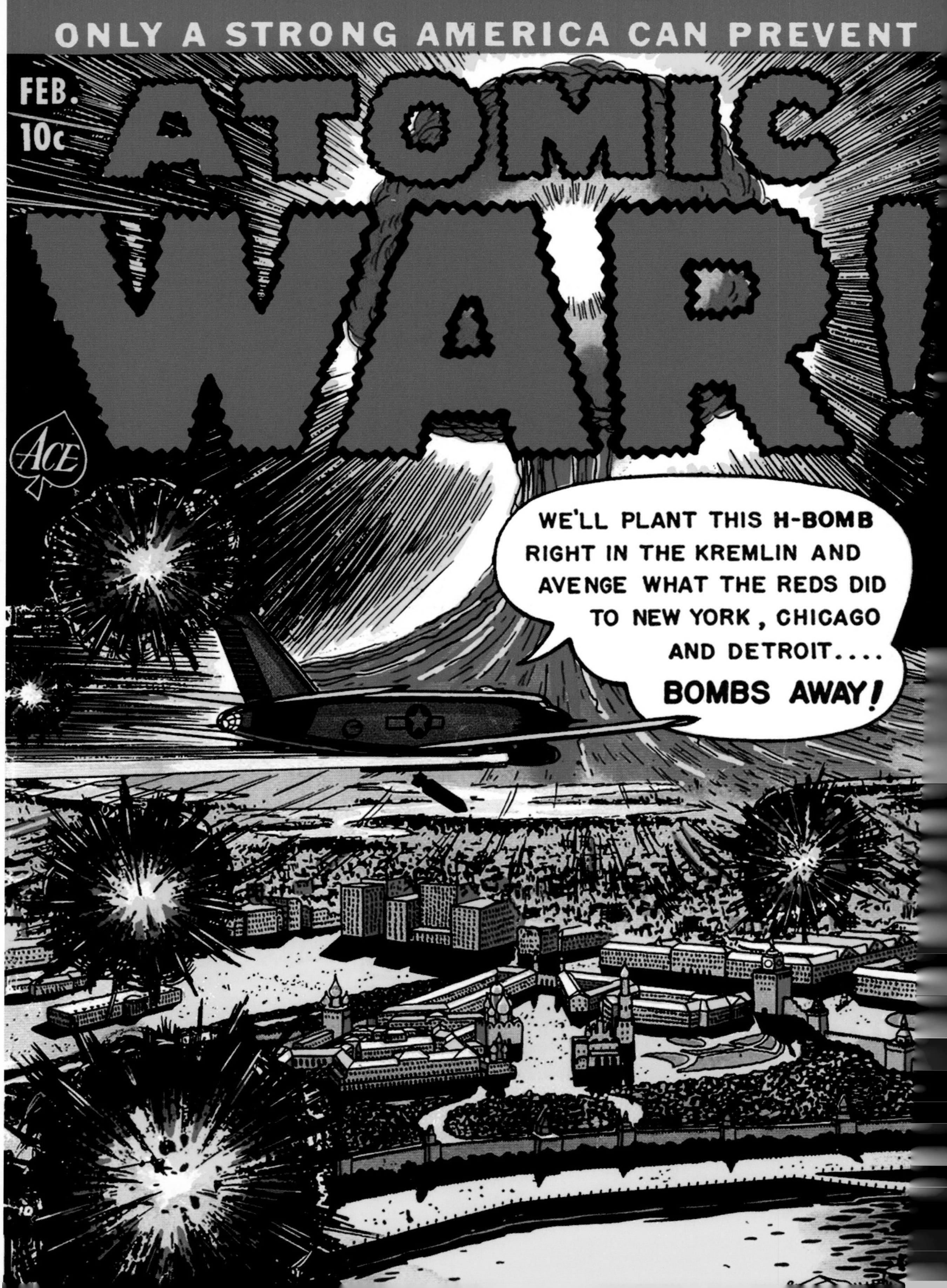
ONLY A STRONG AMERICA CAN PREVENT
FEB.
10c
ATOMIC WAR!
ACE
WE'LL PLANT THIS H-BOMB RIGHT IN THE KREMLIN AND AVENGE WHAT THE REDS DID TO NEW YORK, CHICAGO AND DETROIT.... BOMBS AWAY!

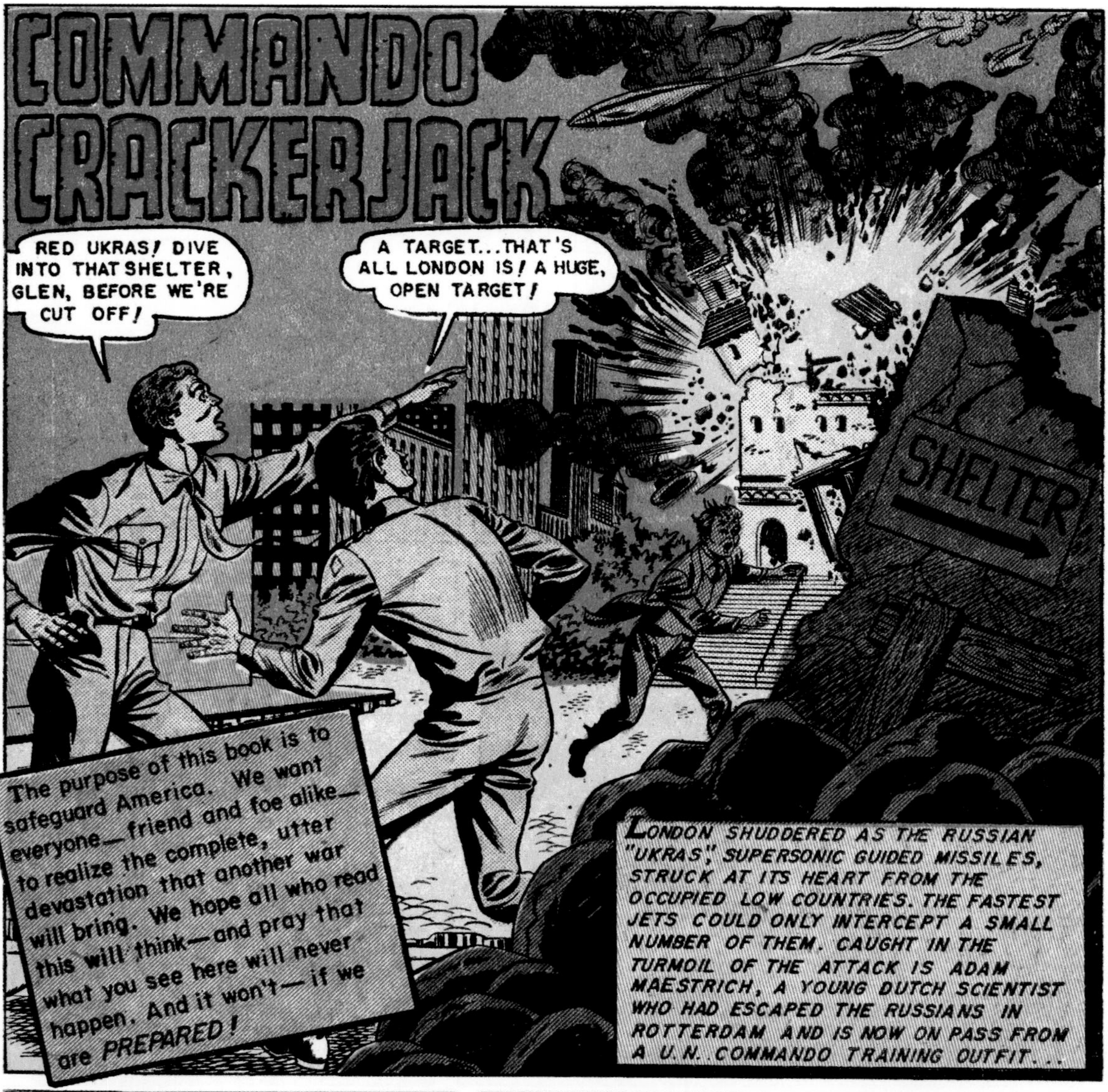
COMMANDO CRACKERJACK
RED UKRAS! DIVE INTO THAT SHELTER, GLEN, BEFORE WE'RE CUT OFF!
A TARGET...THAT'S ALL LONDON IS! A HUGE, OPEN TARGET!
SHELTER
The purpose of this book is to safeguard America. We want everyone—friend and foe alike—to realize the complete, utter devastation that another war will bring. We hope all who read this will think—and pray that what you see here will never happen. And it won't—if we are PREPARED!
LONDON SHUDDERED AS THE RUSSIAN "UKRAS", SUPERSONIC GUIDED MISSILES, STRUCK AT ITS HEART FROM THE OCCUPIED LOW COUNTRIES. THE FASTEST JETS COULD ONLY INTERCEPT A SMALL NUMBER OF THEM. CAUGHT IN THE TURMOIL OF THE ATTACK IS ADAM MAESTRICH, A YOUNG DUTCH SCIENTIST WHO HAD ESCAPED THE RUSSIANS IN ROTTERDAM AND IS NOW ON PASS FROM A U.N. COMMANDO TRAINING OUTFIT...

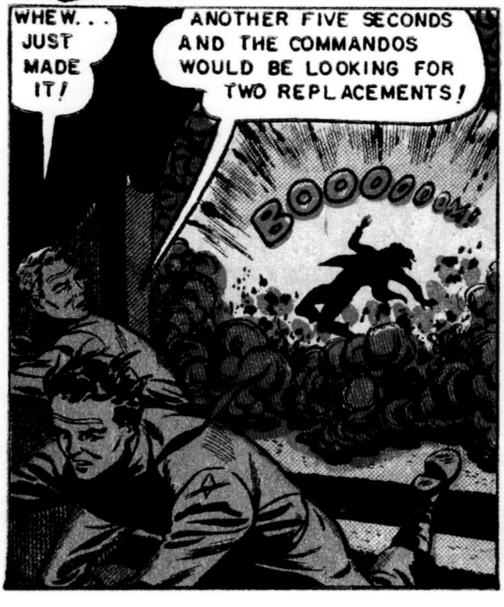
WHEW... JUST MADE IT!
ANOTHER FIVE SECONDS AND THE COMMANDOS WOULD BE LOOKING FOR TWO REPLACEMENTS!
BOOOOOOOM!

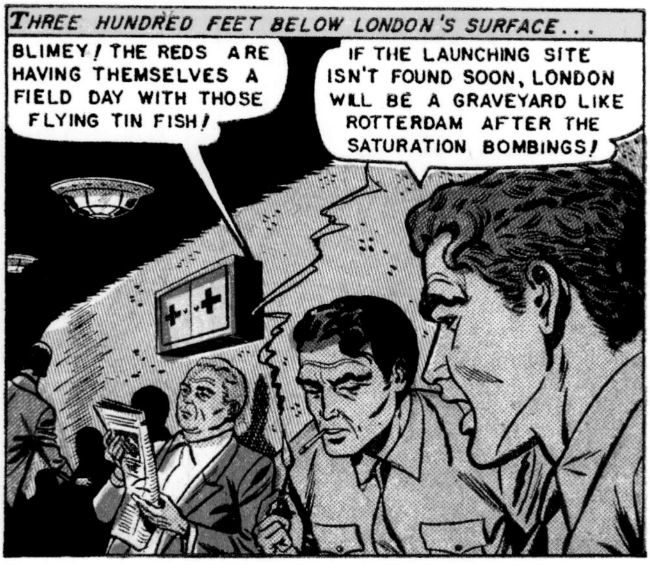
THREE HUNDRED FEET BELOW LONDON'S SURFACE...
BLIMEY! THE REDS ARE HAVING THEMSELVES A FIELD DAY WITH THOSE FLYING TIN FISH!
IF THE LAUNCHING SITE ISN'T FOUND SOON, LONDON WILL BE A GRAVEYARD LIKE ROTTERDAM AFTER THE SATURATION BOMBINGS!

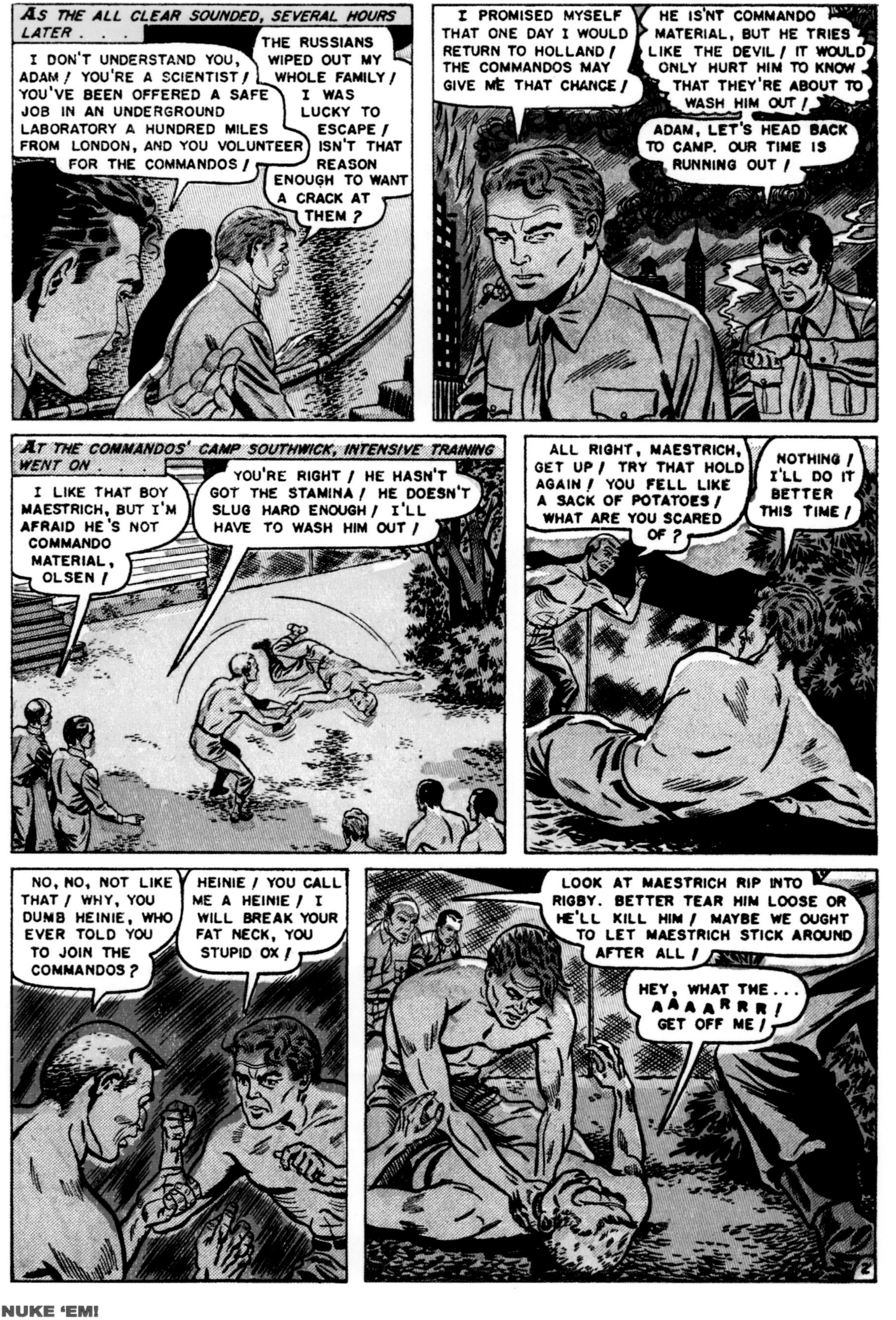
AS THE ALL CLEAR SOUNDED, SEVERAL HOURS LATER . . .
I DON'T UNDERSTAND YOU, ADAM / YOU'RE A SCIENTIST / YOU'VE BEEN OFFERED A SAFE JOB IN AN UNDERGROUND LABORATORY A HUNDRED MILES FROM LONDON, AND YOU VOLUNTEER FOR THE COMMANDOS /
THE RUSSIANS WIPED OUT MY WHOLE FAMILY / I WAS LUCKY TO ESCAPE / ISN'T THAT REASON ENOUGH TO WANT A CRACK AT THEM ?
I PROMISED MYSELF THAT ONE DAY I WOULD RETURN TO HOLLAND / THE COMMANDOS MAY GIVE ME THAT CHANCE /
HE IS'NT COMMANDO MATERIAL, BUT HE TRIES LIKE THE DEVIL / IT WOULD ONLY HURT HIM TO KNOW THAT THEY'RE ABOUT TO WASH HIM OUT /
ADAM, LET'S HEAD BACK TO CAMP. OUR TIME IS RUNNING OUT /
AT THE COMMANDOS' CAMP SOUTHWICK, INTENSIVE TRAINING WENT ON . . .
I LIKE THAT BOY MAESTRICH, BUT I'M AFRAID HE'S NOT COMMANDO MATERIAL, OLSEN /
YOU'RE RIGHT / HE HASN'T GOT THE STAMINA / HE DOESN'T SLUG HARD ENOUGH / I'LL HAVE TO WASH HIM OUT /
ALL RIGHT, MAESTRICH, GET UP / TRY THAT HOLD AGAIN / YOU FELL LIKE A SACK OF POTATOES / WHAT ARE YOU SCARED OF ?
NOTHING / I'LL DO IT BETTER THIS TIME /
NO, NO, NOT LIKE THAT / WHY, YOU DUMB HEINIE, WHO EVER TOLD YOU TO JOIN THE COMMANDOS ?
HEINIE / YOU CALL ME A HEINIE / I WILL BREAK YOUR FAT NECK, YOU STUPID OX /
LOOK AT MAESTRICH RIP INTO RIGBY. BETTER TEAR HIM LOOSE OR HE'LL KILL HIM / MAYBE WE OUGHT TO LET MAESTRICH STICK AROUND AFTER ALL /
HEY, WHAT THE . . . AAAARRR / GET OFF ME /
2

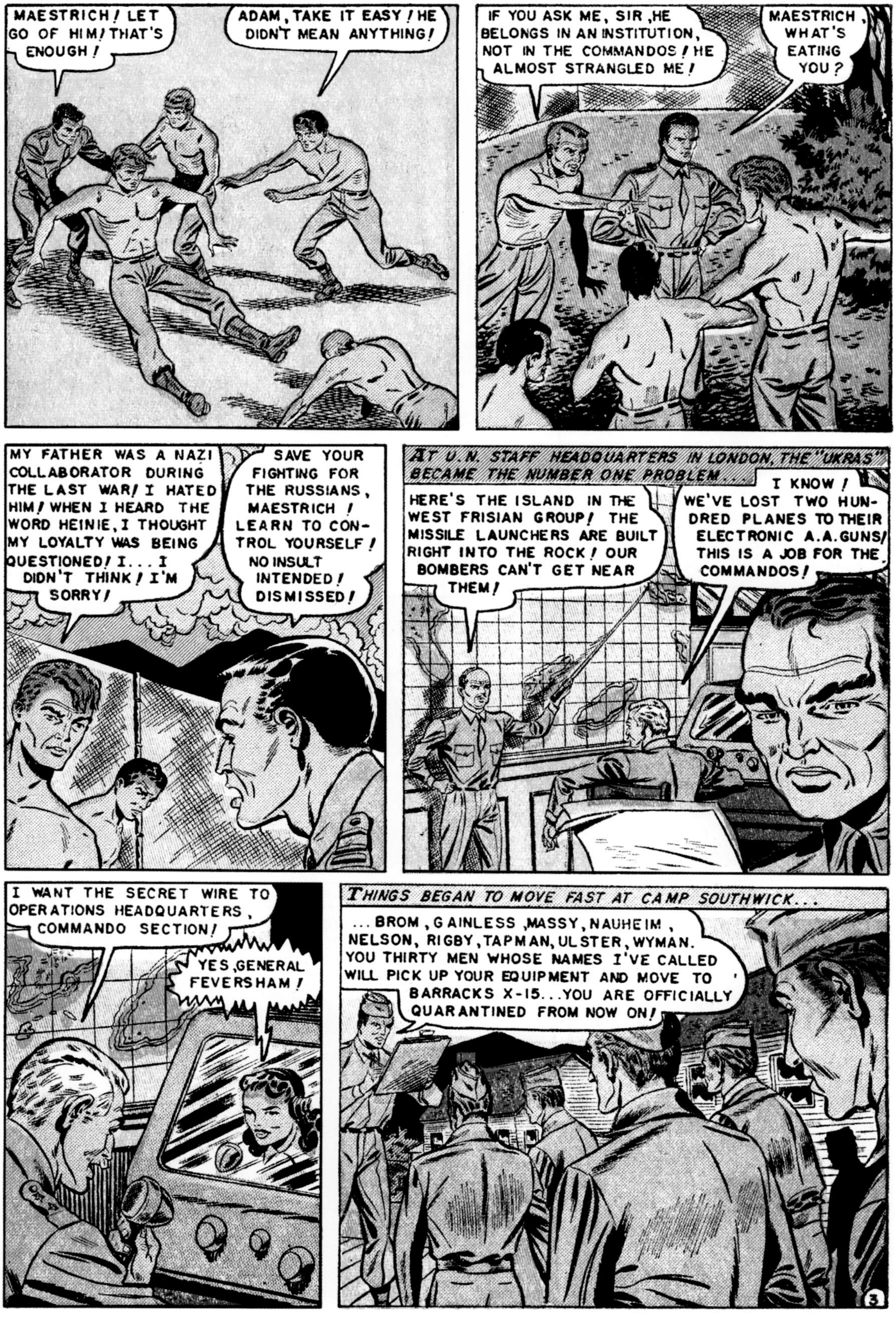
MAESTRICH! LET GO OF HIM! THAT'S ENOUGH!
ADAM, TAKE IT EASY! HE DIDN'T MEAN ANYTHING!
IF YOU ASK ME, SIR, HE BELONGS IN AN INSTITUTION, NOT IN THE COMMANDOS! HE ALMOST STRANGLED ME!
MAESTRICH, WHAT'S EATING YOU?
MY FATHER WAS A NAZI COLLABORATOR DURING THE LAST WAR! I HATED HIM! WHEN I HEARD THE WORD HEINIE, I THOUGHT MY LOYALTY WAS BEING QUESTIONED! I... I DIDN'T THINK! I'M SORRY!
SAVE YOUR FIGHTING FOR THE RUSSIANS, MAESTRICH! LEARN TO CONTROL YOURSELF! NO INSULT INTENDED! DISMISSED!
AT U.N. STAFF HEADQUARTERS IN LONDON, THE "UKRAS" BECAME THE NUMBER ONE PROBLEM...
HERE'S THE ISLAND IN THE WEST FRISIAN GROUP! THE MISSILE LAUNCHERS ARE BUILT RIGHT INTO THE ROCK! OUR BOMBERS CAN'T GET NEAR THEM!
I KNOW! WE'VE LOST TWO HUNDRED PLANES TO THEIR ELECTRONIC A.A. GUNS! THIS IS A JOB FOR THE COMMANDOS!
I WANT THE SECRET WIRE TO OPERATIONS HEADQUARTERS, COMMANDO SECTION!
YES, GENERAL FEVERSHAM!
THINGS BEGAN TO MOVE FAST AT CAMP SOUTHWICK...
... BROM, GAINLESS, MASSY, NAUHEIM, NELSON, RIGBY, TAPMAN, ULSTER, WYMAN. YOU THIRTY MEN WHOSE NAMES I'VE CALLED WILL PICK UP YOUR EQUIPMENT AND MOVE TO BARRACKS X-15... YOU ARE OFFICIALLY QUARANTINED FROM NOW ON!
3

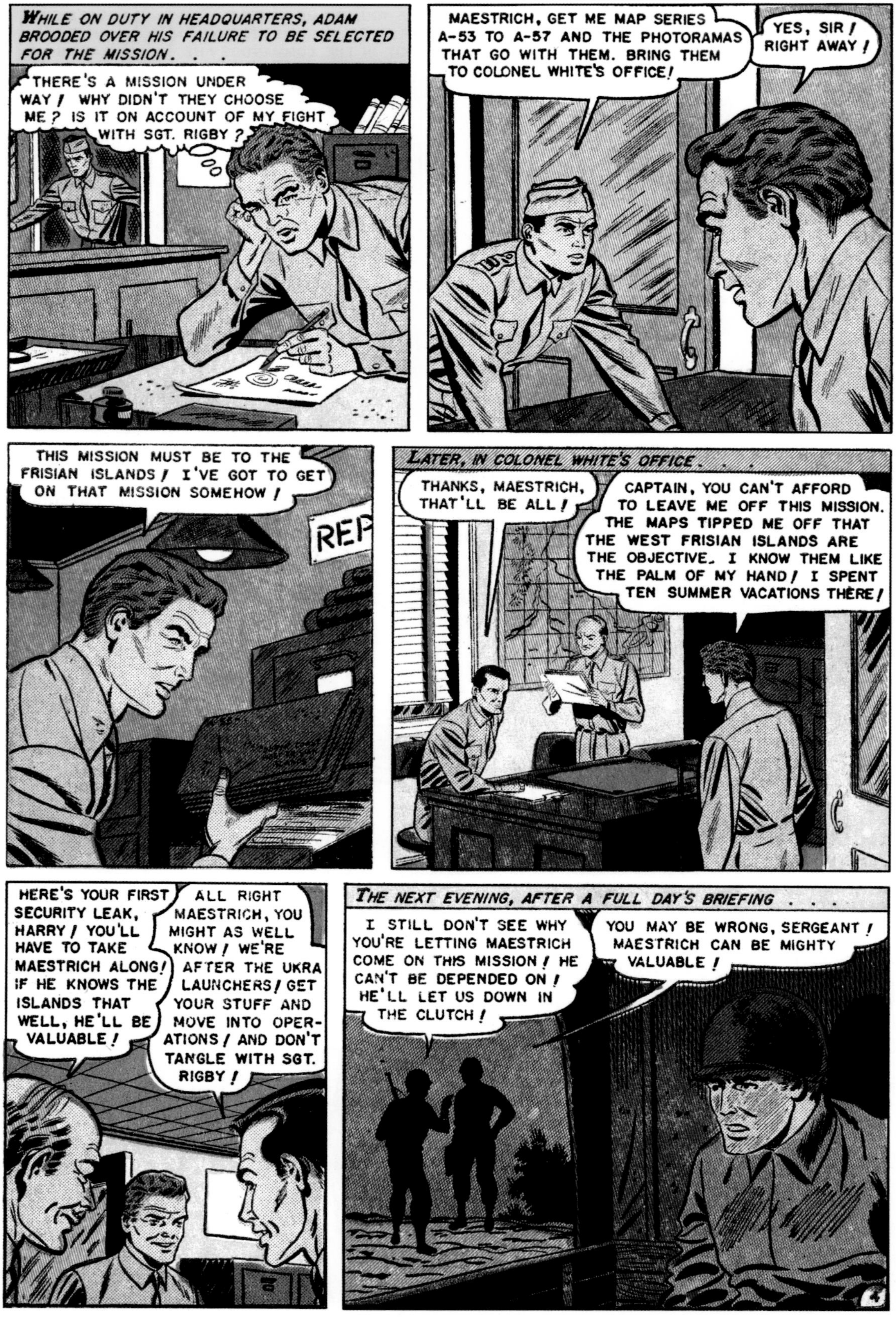
WHILE ON DUTY IN HEADQUARTERS, ADAM BROODED OVER HIS FAILURE TO BE SELECTED FOR THE MISSION . . .
THERE'S A MISSION UNDER WAY! WHY DIDN'T THEY CHOOSE ME? IS IT ON ACCOUNT OF MY FIGHT WITH SGT. RIGBY?
MAESTRICH, GET ME MAP SERIES A-53 TO A-57 AND THE PHOTORAMAS THAT GO WITH THEM. BRING THEM TO COLONEL WHITE'S OFFICE!
YES, SIR! RIGHT AWAY!
THIS MISSION MUST BE TO THE FRISIAN ISLANDS! I'VE GOT TO GET ON THAT MISSION SOMEHOW!
REP
LATER, IN COLONEL WHITE'S OFFICE . . .
THANKS, MAESTRICH, THAT'LL BE ALL!
CAPTAIN, YOU CAN'T AFFORD TO LEAVE ME OFF THIS MISSION. THE MAPS TIPPED ME OFF THAT THE WEST FRISIAN ISLANDS ARE THE OBJECTIVE. I KNOW THEM LIKE THE PALM OF MY HAND! I SPENT TEN SUMMER VACATIONS THERE!
HERE'S YOUR FIRST SECURITY LEAK, HARRY! YOU'LL HAVE TO TAKE MAESTRICH ALONG! IF HE KNOWS THE ISLANDS THAT WELL, HE'LL BE VALUABLE!
ALL RIGHT MAESTRICH, YOU MIGHT AS WELL KNOW! WE'RE AFTER THE UKRA LAUNCHERS! GET YOUR STUFF AND MOVE INTO OPERATIONS! AND DON'T TANGLE WITH SGT. RIGBY!
THE NEXT EVENING, AFTER A FULL DAY'S BRIEFING . . .
I STILL DON'T SEE WHY YOU'RE LETTING MAESTRICH COME ON THIS MISSION! HE CAN'T BE DEPENDED ON! HE'LL LET US DOWN IN THE CLUTCH!
YOU MAY BE WRONG, SERGEANT! MAESTRICH CAN BE MIGHTY VALUABLE!
4

AT MARGATE, ON THE EAST COAST OF ENGLAND, THREE JET-POWERED ASSAULT BOATS WERE READY...

EASY WITH THOSE DEMOL BLOCKS! GET THAT GEAR LOADED ON THE DOUBLE! PILE IN, MEN! START THOSE MOTORS!

C'MON, MAESTRICH, GET THE LEAD OUT OF YOUR BOOTS!

WITH A POWERFUL ROAR, THE JETS DROVE THE ASSAULT CRAFT ALONG AT A TREMENDOUS CLIP...

HOW LONG BEFORE WE HIT THE FRISIAN ISLANDS, SALWAY?

A LITTLE OVER AN HOUR, SIR, PROVIDED WE DON'T RUN INTO RED PATROL CRAFT!

TWENTY MINUTES LATER...

SALWAY, THIS SCREEN IS JUMPIN' WITH BLIPS! WHAT'S OUT THERE IN FRONT OF US?

LOOKS LIKE A RED PATROL FLEET! I DON'T THINK THEY'VE SPOTTED US YET! OUR ONLY CHANCE IS TO SUBMERGE!

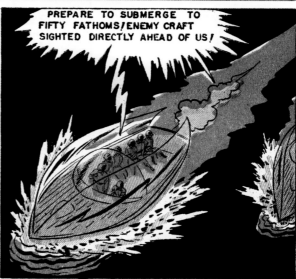

PREPARE TO SUBMERGE TO FIFTY FATHOMS! ENEMY CRAFT SIGHTED DIRECTLY AHEAD OF US!

AS THE JET CRAFT DOVE...

FIFTY FATHOMS BENEATH THE RUSSIAN FLEET...

ATTENTION! PROCEED SUBMERGED FOR FORTY MILES! CUT YOUR JETS! USE SILENT TURBO POWER!

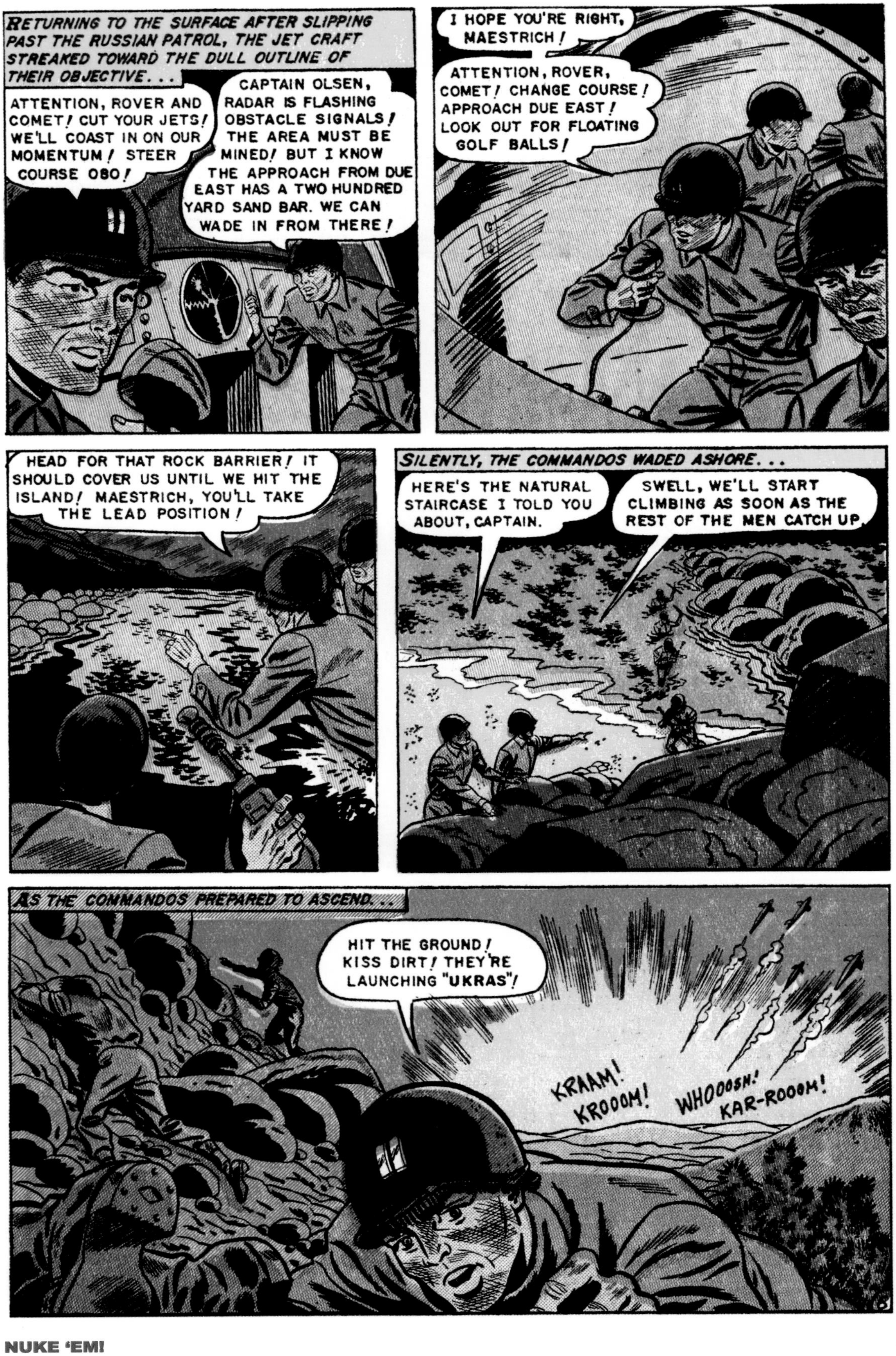

RETURNING TO THE SURFACE AFTER SLIPPING PAST THE RUSSIAN PATROL, THE JET CRAFT STREAKED TOWARD THE DULL OUTLINE OF THEIR OBJECTIVE...
ATTENTION, ROVER AND COMET! CUT YOUR JETS! WE'LL COAST IN ON OUR MOMENTUM! STEER COURSE 080!
CAPTAIN OLSEN, RADAR IS FLASHING OBSTACLE SIGNALS! THE AREA MUST BE MINED! BUT I KNOW THE APPROACH FROM DUE EAST HAS A TWO HUNDRED YARD SAND BAR. WE CAN WADE IN FROM THERE!
I HOPE YOU'RE RIGHT, MAESTRICH!
ATTENTION, ROVER, COMET! CHANGE COURSE! APPROACH DUE EAST! LOOK OUT FOR FLOATING GOLF BALLS!
HEAD FOR THAT ROCK BARRIER! IT SHOULD COVER US UNTIL WE HIT THE ISLAND! MAESTRICH, YOU'LL TAKE THE LEAD POSITION!
SILENTLY, THE COMMANDOS WADED ASHORE...
HERE'S THE NATURAL STAIRCASE I TOLD YOU ABOUT, CAPTAIN.
SWELL, WE'LL START CLIMBING AS SOON AS THE REST OF THE MEN CATCH UP.
AS THE COMMANDOS PREPARED TO ASCEND...
HIT THE GROUND! KISS DIRT! THEY'RE LAUNCHING "UKRAS"!
KRAAM! KROOOM!
WHOOOSH! KAR-ROOOM!

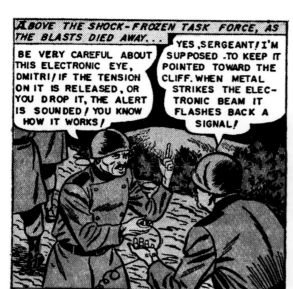

ABOVE THE SHOCK-FROZEN TASK FORCE, AS THE BLASTS DIED AWAY...

BE VERY CAREFUL ABOUT THIS ELECTRONIC EYE, DMITRI! IF THE TENSION ON IT IS RELEASED, OR YOU DROP IT, THE ALERT IS SOUNDED! YOU KNOW HOW IT WORKS!

YES, SERGEANT! I'M SUPPOSED TO KEEP IT POINTED TOWARD THE CLIFF. WHEN METAL STRIKES THE ELECTRONIC BEAM IT FLASHES BACK A SIGNAL!

THE COMMANDOS SCRAMBLED UP THE ROCKY LEDGE UNDER ADAM'S LEADERSHIP...

ONE OF THEM IS MINE!

CUT HIS THROAT, MAESTRICH! I'LL TAKE THE OTHER ONE!

I SAID I WOULD COME BACK! I'VE SETTLED MY FIRST SCORE!

STOP STRUGGLING, RUSSKY! JUST CLOSE YOUR EYES AND RELAX... FOREVER!

SUDDENLY...

WHAT HAPPENED? THE WHOLE ISLAND IS JUMPIN'!

AN ELECTRONIC EYE DID IT! THE MOMENT HE COLLAPSED, THE SIGNAL WAS RELEASED!

WHEEEEEEEEE

THE ELECTRONIC SIGNAL SOUNDED IN THE RED BARRACKS...

MAYBE THAT FOOL DMITRI DROPPED THE ELECTRONIC EYE!

OR COULD IT BE AN INVASION! LET'S GO, SERGEANT!

WHEEEEEEE

WE'RE OUTNUMBERED! THEY'LL KILL US ALL! LET'S GO BACK TO THE BOATS!

I'VE GOT TO STOP HIM OR HE'LL PANIC THE OTHERS!

GO AHEAD... RUN! I KNEW YOU'D CRACK THE MOMENT THINGS GOT TOUGH! G'WAN, BEAT IT! I KNEW YOU WERE A DIRTY, YELLOW HEINIE ALL ALONG!

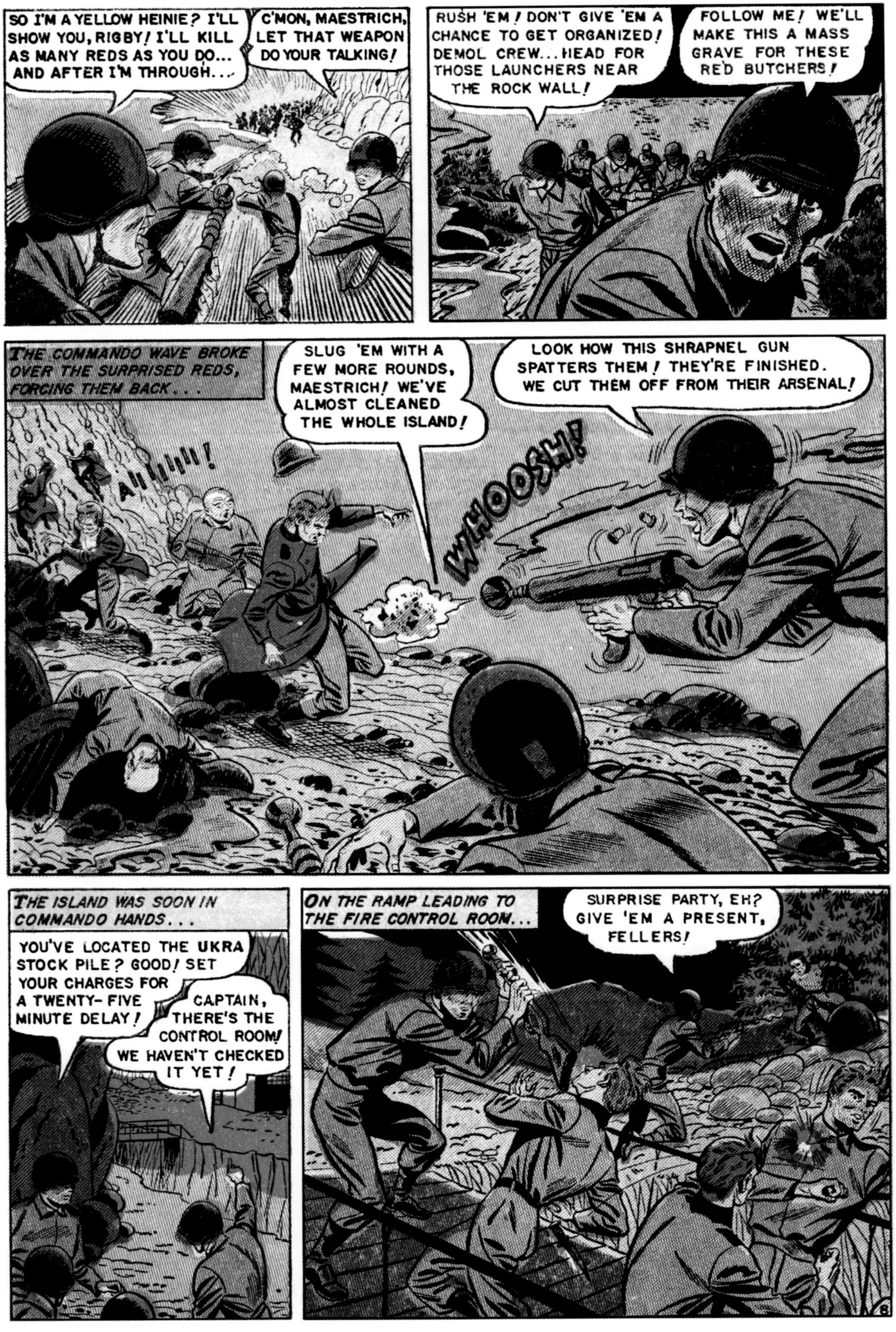
SO I'M A YELLOW HEINIE? I'LL SHOW YOU, RIGBY! I'LL KILL AS MANY REDS AS YOU DO... AND AFTER I'M THROUGH...
C'MON, MAESTRICH, LET THAT WEAPON DO YOUR TALKING!
RUSH 'EM! DON'T GIVE 'EM A CHANCE TO GET ORGANIZED! DEMOL CREW...HEAD FOR THOSE LAUNCHERS NEAR THE ROCK WALL!
FOLLOW ME! WE'LL MAKE THIS A MASS GRAVE FOR THESE RED BUTCHERS!
THE COMMANDO WAVE BROKE OVER THE SURPRISED REDS, FORCING THEM BACK...
SLUG 'EM WITH A FEW MORE ROUNDS, MAESTRICH! WE'VE ALMOST CLEANED THE WHOLE ISLAND!
LOOK HOW THIS SHRAPNEL GUN SPATTERS THEM! THEY'RE FINISHED. WE CUT THEM OFF FROM THEIR ARSENAL!
AIIIIIII!
WHOOSH!
THE ISLAND WAS SOON IN COMMANDO HANDS...
YOU'VE LOCATED THE UKRA STOCK PILE? GOOD! SET YOUR CHARGES FOR A TWENTY-FIVE MINUTE DELAY!
CAPTAIN, THERE'S THE CONTROL ROOM! WE HAVEN'T CHECKED IT YET!
ON THE RAMP LEADING TO THE FIRE CONTROL ROOM...
SURPRISE PARTY, EH? GIVE 'EM A PRESENT, FELLERS!

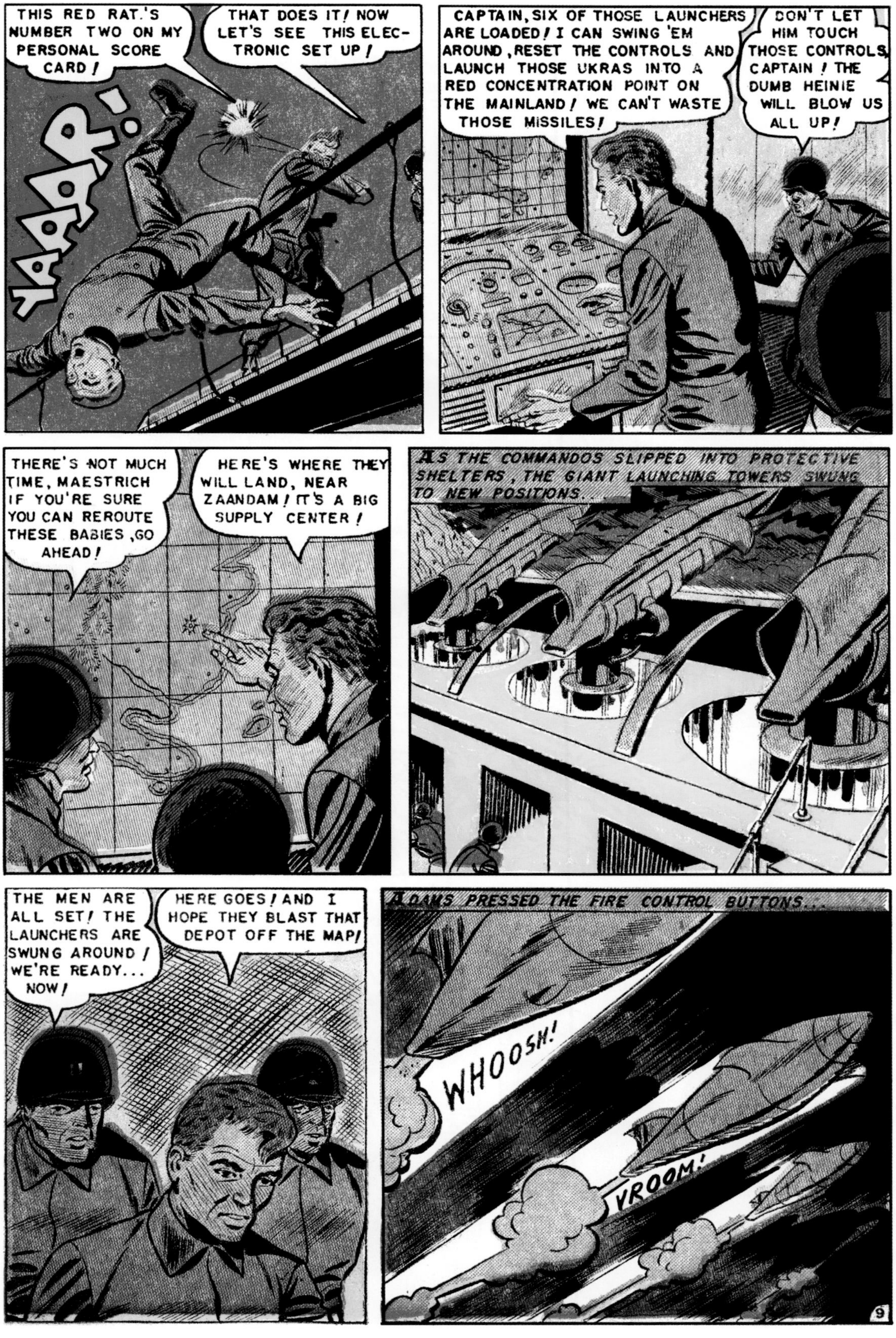
THIS RED RAT.'S NUMBER TWO ON MY PERSONAL SCORE CARD!
THAT DOES IT! NOW LET'S SEE THIS ELECTRONIC SET UP!
YAAAR!
CAPTAIN, SIX OF THOSE LAUNCHERS ARE LOADED! I CAN SWING 'EM AROUND, RESET THE CONTROLS AND LAUNCH THOSE UKRAS INTO A RED CONCENTRATION POINT ON THE MAINLAND! WE CAN'T WASTE THOSE MISSILES!
DON'T LET HIM TOUCH THOSE CONTROLS, CAPTAIN! THE DUMB HEINIE WILL BLOW US ALL UP!
THERE'S NOT MUCH TIME, MAESTRICH IF YOU'RE SURE YOU CAN REROUTE THESE BABIES, GO AHEAD!
HERE'S WHERE THEY WILL LAND, NEAR ZAANDAM! IT'S A BIG SUPPLY CENTER!
AS THE COMMANDOS SLIPPED INTO PROTECTIVE SHELTERS, THE GIANT LAUNCHING TOWERS SWUNG TO NEW POSITIONS...
THE MEN ARE ALL SET! THE LAUNCHERS ARE SWUNG AROUND! WE'RE READY... NOW!
HERE GOES! AND I HOPE THEY BLAST THAT DEPOT OFF THE MAP!
ADAMS PRESSED THE FIRE CONTROL BUTTONS...
WHOOSH!
VROOM!
9

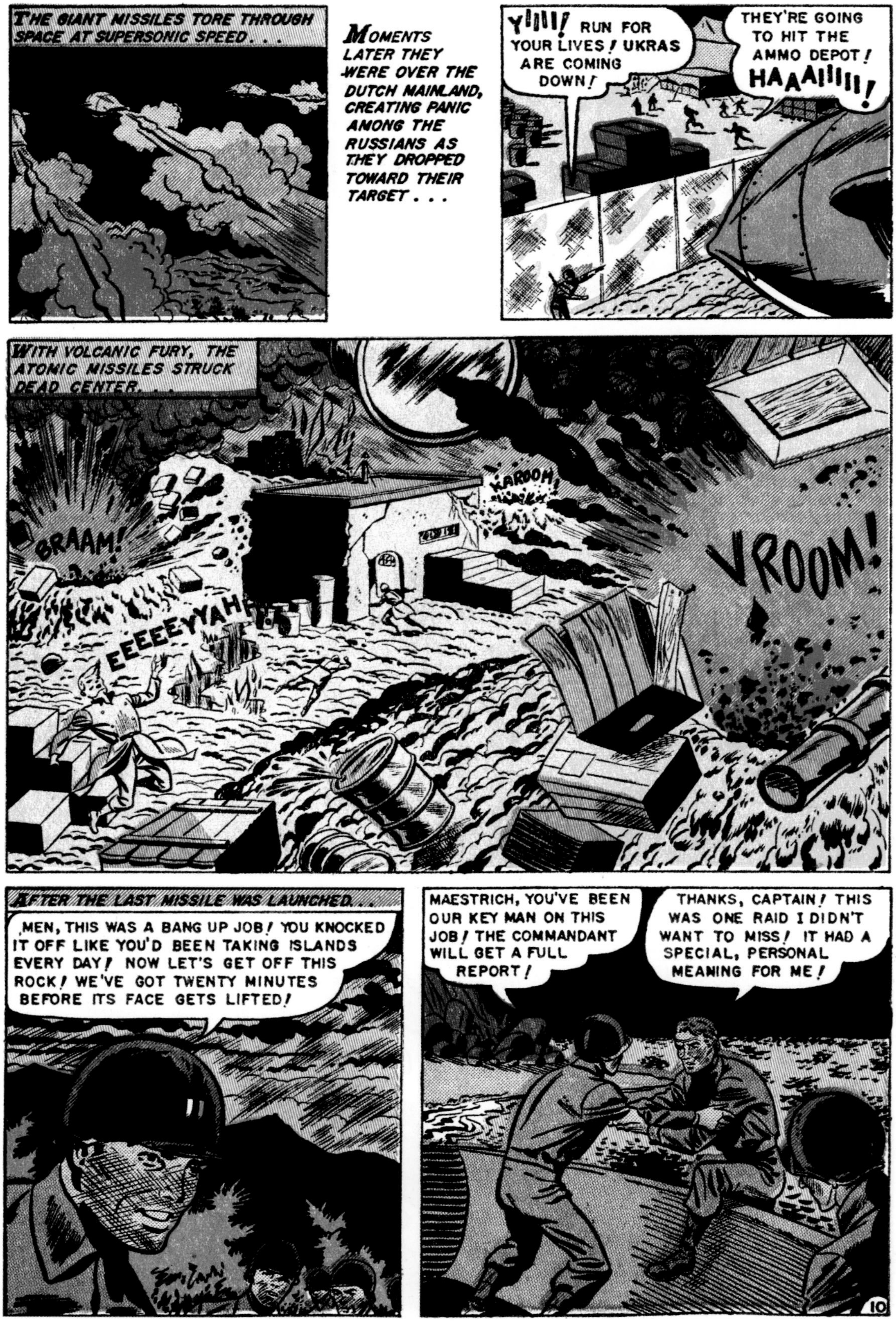
THE GIANT MISSILES TORE THROUGH SPACE AT SUPERSONIC SPEED . . .
MOMENTS LATER THEY WERE OVER THE DUTCH MAINLAND, CREATING PANIC AMONG THE RUSSIANS AS THEY DROPPED TOWARD THEIR TARGET . . .
YIIII! RUN FOR YOUR LIVES! UKRAS ARE COMING DOWN!
THEY'RE GOING TO HIT THE AMMO DEPOT! HAAAIIIII!
WITH VOLCANIC FURY, THE ATOMIC MISSILES STRUCK DEAD CENTER . . .
BRAAM!
KAROOM!
VROOM!
EEEEEYYAH
AFTER THE LAST MISSILE WAS LAUNCHED . . .
MEN, THIS WAS A BANG UP JOB! YOU KNOCKED IT OFF LIKE YOU'D BEEN TAKING ISLANDS EVERY DAY! NOW LET'S GET OFF THIS ROCK! WE'VE GOT TWENTY MINUTES BEFORE ITS FACE GETS LIFTED!
MAESTRICH, YOU'VE BEEN OUR KEY MAN ON THIS JOB! THE COMMANDANT WILL GET A FULL REPORT!
THANKS, CAPTAIN! THIS WAS ONE RAID I DIDN'T WANT TO MISS! IT HAD A SPECIAL, PERSONAL MEANING FOR ME!
10

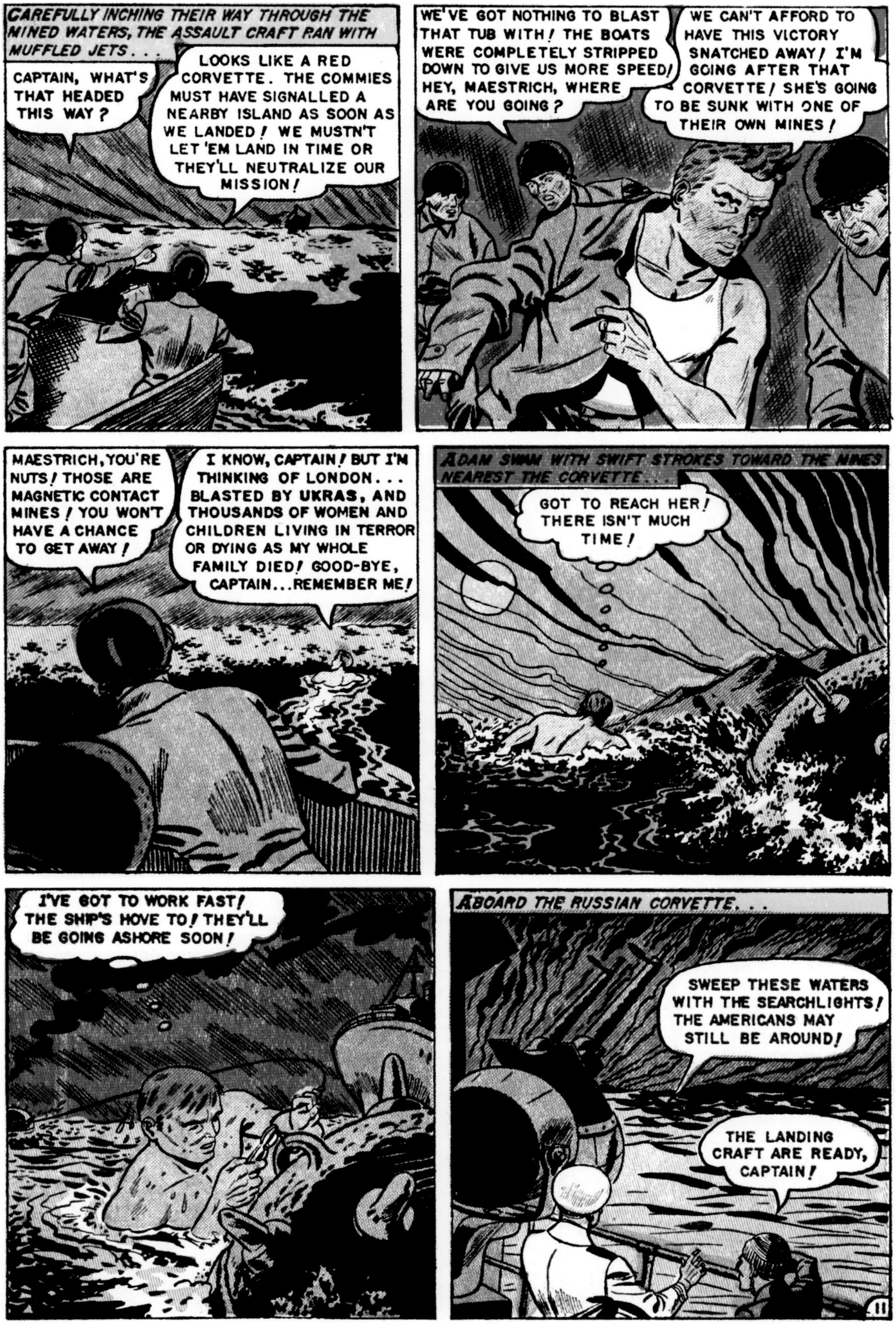
CAREFULLY INCHING THEIR WAY THROUGH THE MINED WATERS, THE ASSAULT CRAFT RAN WITH MUFFLED JETS . . .
CAPTAIN, WHAT'S THAT HEADED THIS WAY?
LOOKS LIKE A RED CORVETTE. THE COMMIES MUST HAVE SIGNALLED A NEARBY ISLAND AS SOON AS WE LANDED! WE MUSTN'T LET 'EM LAND IN TIME OR THEY'LL NEUTRALIZE OUR MISSION!
WE'VE GOT NOTHING TO BLAST THAT TUB WITH! THE BOATS WERE COMPLETELY STRIPPED DOWN TO GIVE US MORE SPEED! HEY, MAESTRICH, WHERE ARE YOU GOING?
WE CAN'T AFFORD TO HAVE THIS VICTORY SNATCHED AWAY! I'M GOING AFTER THAT CORVETTE! SHE'S GOING TO BE SUNK WITH ONE OF THEIR OWN MINES!
MAESTRICH, YOU'RE NUTS! THOSE ARE MAGNETIC CONTACT MINES! YOU WON'T HAVE A CHANCE TO GET AWAY!
I KNOW, CAPTAIN! BUT I'M THINKING OF LONDON... BLASTED BY UKRAS, AND THOUSANDS OF WOMEN AND CHILDREN LIVING IN TERROR OR DYING AS MY WHOLE FAMILY DIED! GOOD-BYE, CAPTAIN...REMEMBER ME!
ADAM SWAM WITH SWIFT STROKES TOWARD THE MINES NEAREST THE CORVETTE . . .
GOT TO REACH HER! THERE ISN'T MUCH TIME!
I'VE GOT TO WORK FAST! THE SHIP'S HOVE TO! THEY'LL BE GOING ASHORE SOON!
ABOARD THE RUSSIAN CORVETTE. . .
SWEEP THESE WATERS WITH THE SEARCHLIGHTS! THE AMERICANS MAY STILL BE AROUND!
THE LANDING CRAFT ARE READY, CAPTAIN!
11

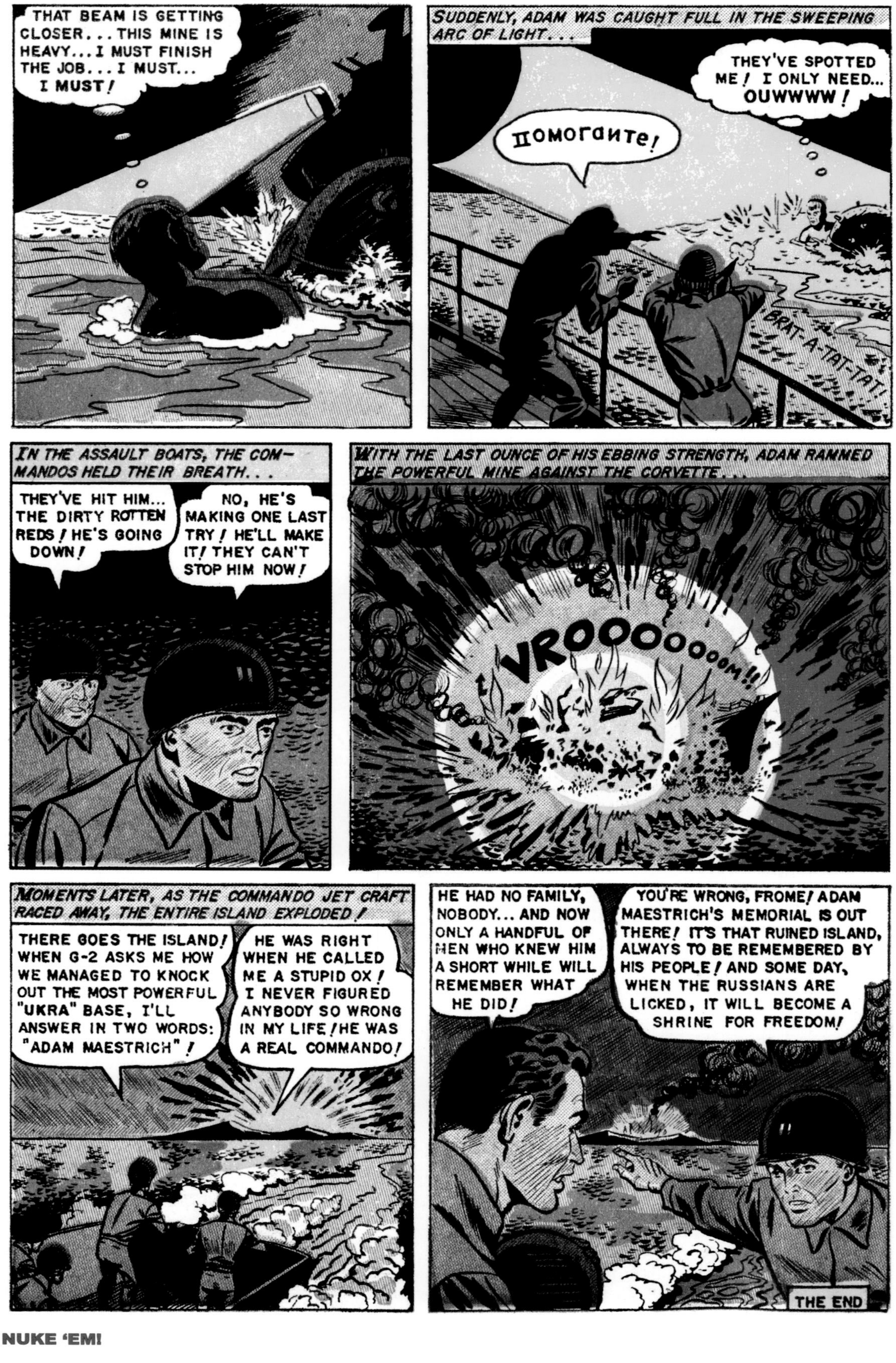
THAT BEAM IS GETTING CLOSER... THIS MINE IS HEAVY... I MUST FINISH THE JOB... I MUST... I MUST!
SUDDENLY, ADAM WAS CAUGHT FULL IN THE SWEEPING ARC OF LIGHT...
THEY'VE SPOTTED ME! I ONLY NEED... OUWWWW!
Помогите!
BRAT-A-TAT-TAT!
IN THE ASSAULT BOATS, THE COMMANDOS HELD THEIR BREATH...
THEY'VE HIT HIM... THE DIRTY ROTTEN REDS! HE'S GOING DOWN!
NO, HE'S MAKING ONE LAST TRY! HE'LL MAKE IT! THEY CAN'T STOP HIM NOW!
WITH THE LAST OUNCE OF HIS EBBING STRENGTH, ADAM RAMMED THE POWERFUL MINE AGAINST THE CORVETTE...
VROOOOoooom!!
MOMENTS LATER, AS THE COMMANDO JET CRAFT RACED AWAY, THE ENTIRE ISLAND EXPLODED!
THERE GOES THE ISLAND! WHEN G-2 ASKS ME HOW WE MANAGED TO KNOCK OUT THE MOST POWERFUL "UKRA" BASE, I'LL ANSWER IN TWO WORDS: "ADAM MAESTRICH"!
HE WAS RIGHT WHEN HE CALLED ME A STUPID OX! I NEVER FIGURED ANYBODY SO WRONG IN MY LIFE! HE WAS A REAL COMMANDO!
HE HAD NO FAMILY, NOBODY... AND NOW ONLY A HANDFUL OF MEN WHO KNEW HIM A SHORT WHILE WILL REMEMBER WHAT HE DID!
YOU'RE WRONG, FROME! ADAM MAESTRICH'S MEMORIAL IS OUT THERE! IT'S THAT RUINED ISLAND, ALWAYS TO BE REMEMBERED BY HIS PEOPLE! AND SOME DAY, WHEN THE RUSSIANS ARE LICKED, IT WILL BECOME A SHRINE FOR FREEDOM!
THE END

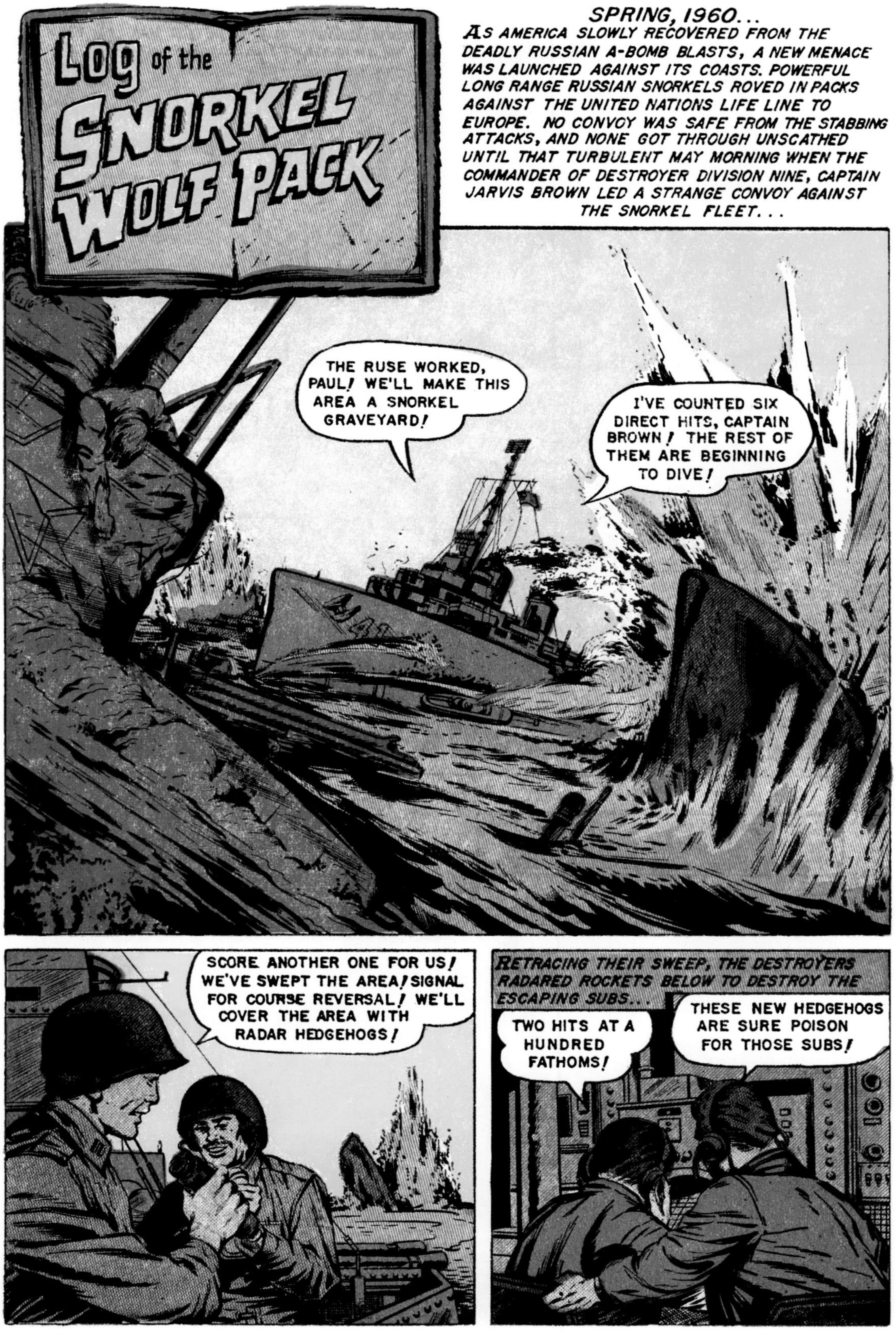

Log of the SNORKEL WOLF PACK
SPRING, 1960...
AS AMERICA SLOWLY RECOVERED FROM THE DEADLY RUSSIAN A-BOMB BLASTS, A NEW MENACE WAS LAUNCHED AGAINST ITS COASTS. POWERFUL LONG RANGE RUSSIAN SNORKELS ROVED IN PACKS AGAINST THE UNITED NATIONS LIFE LINE TO EUROPE. NO CONVOY WAS SAFE FROM THE STABBING ATTACKS, AND NONE GOT THROUGH UNSCATHED UNTIL THAT TURBULENT MAY MORNING WHEN THE COMMANDER OF DESTROYER DIVISION NINE, CAPTAIN JARVIS BROWN LED A STRANGE CONVOY AGAINST THE SNORKEL FLEET...
THE RUSE WORKED, PAUL! WE'LL MAKE THIS AREA A SNORKEL GRAVEYARD!
I'VE COUNTED SIX DIRECT HITS, CAPTAIN BROWN! THE REST OF THEM ARE BEGINNING TO DIVE!
SCORE ANOTHER ONE FOR US! WE'VE SWEPT THE AREA! SIGNAL FOR COURSE REVERSAL! WE'LL COVER THE AREA WITH RADAR HEDGEHOGS!
RETRACING THEIR SWEEP, THE DESTROYERS RADARED ROCKETS BELOW TO DESTROY THE ESCAPING SUBS...
TWO HITS AT A HUNDRED FATHOMS!
THESE NEW HEDGEHOGS ARE SURE POISON FOR THOSE SUBS!

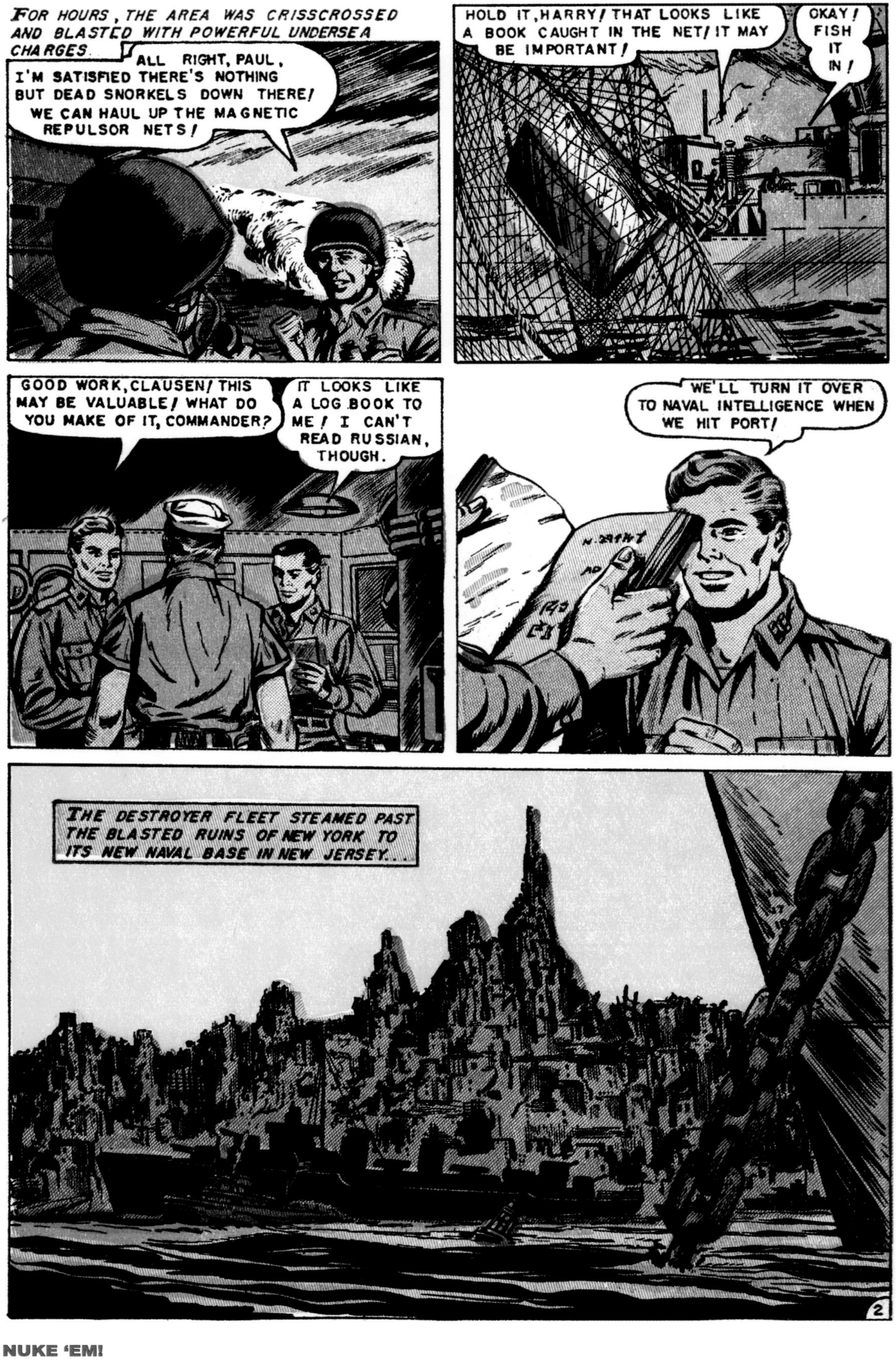
FOR HOURS, THE AREA WAS CRISSCROSSED AND BLASTED WITH POWERFUL UNDERSEA CHARGES.
ALL RIGHT, PAUL, I'M SATISFIED THERE'S NOTHING BUT DEAD SNORKELS DOWN THERE! WE CAN HAUL UP THE MAGNETIC REPULSOR NETS!
HOLD IT, HARRY! THAT LOOKS LIKE A BOOK CAUGHT IN THE NET! IT MAY BE IMPORTANT!
OKAY! FISH IT IN!
GOOD WORK, CLAUSEN! THIS MAY BE VALUABLE! WHAT DO YOU MAKE OF IT, COMMANDER?
IT LOOKS LIKE A LOG BOOK TO ME! I CAN'T READ RUSSIAN, THOUGH.
WE'LL TURN IT OVER TO NAVAL INTELLIGENCE WHEN WE HIT PORT!
THE DESTROYER FLEET STEAMED PAST THE BLASTED RUINS OF NEW YORK TO ITS NEW NAVAL BASE IN NEW JERSEY...
2

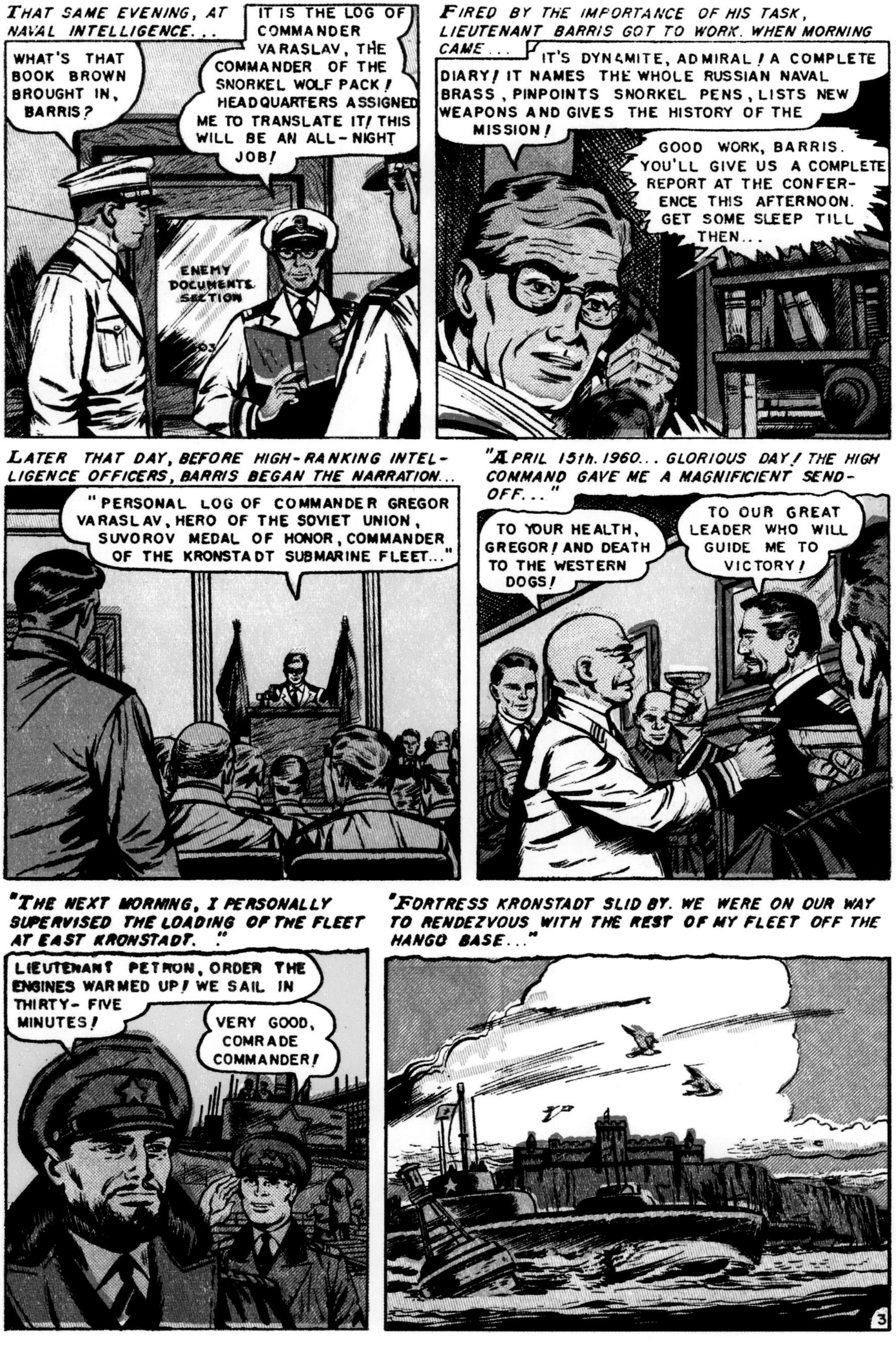
THAT SAME EVENING, AT NAVAL INTELLIGENCE...
WHAT'S THAT BOOK BROWN BROUGHT IN, BARRIS?
IT IS THE LOG OF COMMANDER VARASLAV, THE COMMANDER OF THE SNORKEL WOLF PACK! HEADQUARTERS ASSIGNED ME TO TRANSLATE IT! THIS WILL BE AN ALL-NIGHT JOB!
ENEMY DOCUMENTS SECTION
FIRED BY THE IMPORTANCE OF HIS TASK, LIEUTENANT BARRIS GOT TO WORK. WHEN MORNING CAME...
IT'S DYNAMITE, ADMIRAL! A COMPLETE DIARY! IT NAMES THE WHOLE RUSSIAN NAVAL BRASS, PINPOINTS SNORKEL PENS, LISTS NEW WEAPONS AND GIVES THE HISTORY OF THE MISSION!
GOOD WORK, BARRIS. YOU'LL GIVE US A COMPLETE REPORT AT THE CONFERENCE THIS AFTERNOON. GET SOME SLEEP TILL THEN...
LATER THAT DAY, BEFORE HIGH-RANKING INTELLIGENCE OFFICERS, BARRIS BEGAN THE NARRATION...
"PERSONAL LOG OF COMMANDER GREGOR VARASLAV, HERO OF THE SOVIET UNION, SUVOROV MEDAL OF HONOR, COMMANDER OF THE KRONSTADT SUBMARINE FLEET..."
"APRIL 15th. 1960... GLORIOUS DAY! THE HIGH COMMAND GAVE ME A MAGNIFICIENT SEND-OFF..."
TO YOUR HEALTH, GREGOR! AND DEATH TO THE WESTERN DOGS!
TO OUR GREAT LEADER WHO WILL GUIDE ME TO VICTORY!
"THE NEXT MORNING, I PERSONALLY SUPERVISED THE LOADING OF THE FLEET AT EAST KRONSTADT."
LIEUTENANT PETRON, ORDER THE ENGINES WARMED UP! WE SAIL IN THIRTY-FIVE MINUTES!
VERY GOOD, COMRADE COMMANDER!
"FORTRESS KRONSTADT SLID BY. WE WERE ON OUR WAY TO RENDEZVOUS WITH THE REST OF MY FLEET OFF THE HANGO BASE..."
3

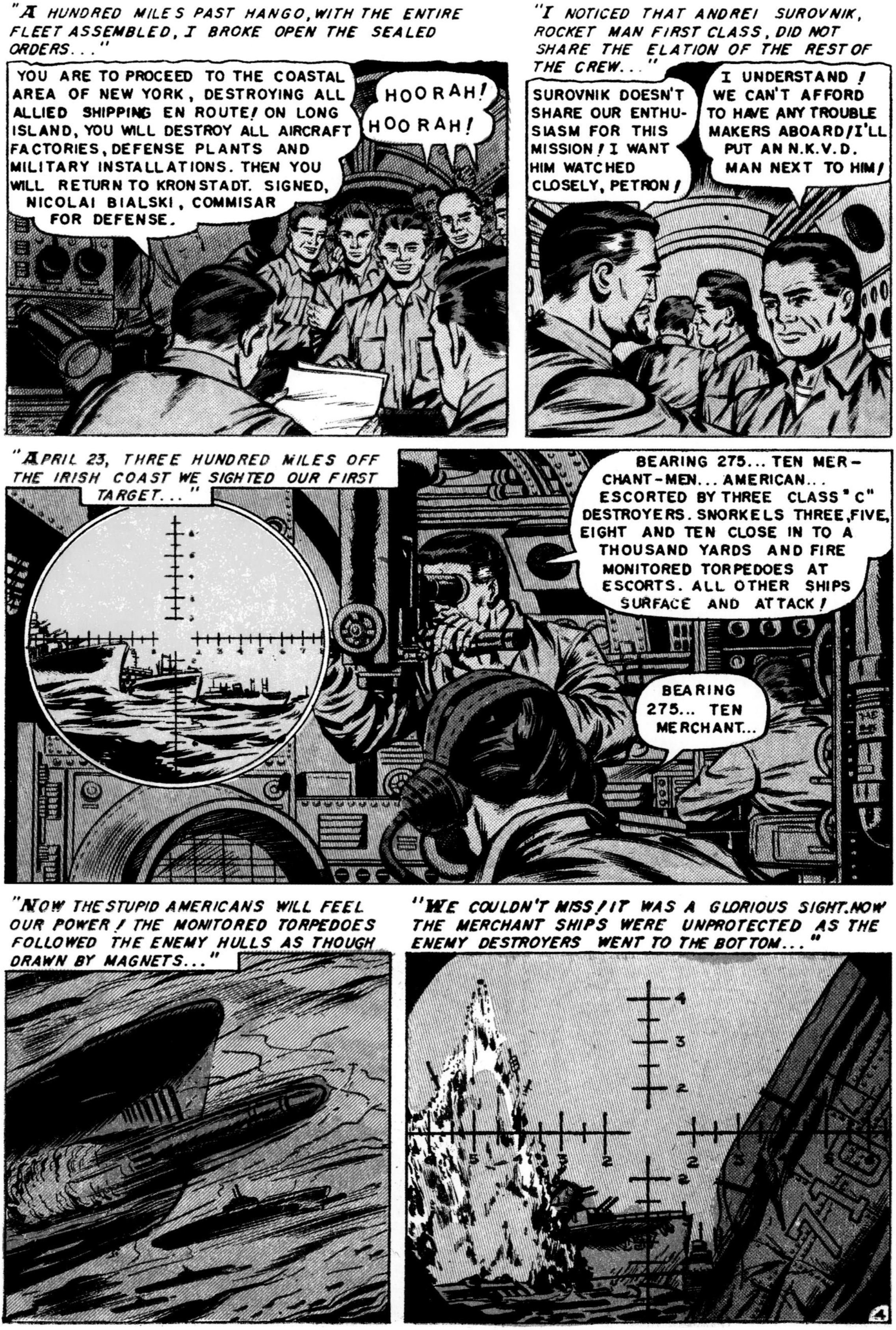
"A HUNDRED MILES PAST HANGO, WITH THE ENTIRE FLEET ASSEMBLED, I BROKE OPEN THE SEALED ORDERS..."
YOU ARE TO PROCEED TO THE COASTAL AREA OF NEW YORK, DESTROYING ALL ALLIED SHIPPING EN ROUTE! ON LONG ISLAND, YOU WILL DESTROY ALL AIRCRAFT FACTORIES, DEFENSE PLANTS AND MILITARY INSTALLATIONS. THEN YOU WILL RETURN TO KRONSTADT. SIGNED, NICOLAI BIALSKI, COMMISAR FOR DEFENSE.
HOORAH!
HOORAH!
"I NOTICED THAT ANDREI SUROVNIK, ROCKET MAN FIRST CLASS, DID NOT SHARE THE ELATION OF THE REST OF THE CREW..."
SUROVNIK DOESN'T SHARE OUR ENTHUSIASM FOR THIS MISSION! I WANT HIM WATCHED CLOSELY, PETRON!
I UNDERSTAND! WE CAN'T AFFORD TO HAVE ANY TROUBLE MAKERS ABOARD! I'LL PUT AN N.K.V.D. MAN NEXT TO HIM!
"APRIL 23, THREE HUNDRED MILES OFF THE IRISH COAST WE SIGHTED OUR FIRST TARGET..."
BEARING 275... TEN MERCHANT-MEN... AMERICAN... ESCORTED BY THREE CLASS "C" DESTROYERS. SNORKELS THREE, FIVE, EIGHT AND TEN CLOSE IN TO A THOUSAND YARDS AND FIRE MONITORED TORPEDOES AT ESCORTS. ALL OTHER SHIPS SURFACE AND ATTACK!
BEARING 275... TEN MERCHANT...
"NOW THE STUPID AMERICANS WILL FEEL OUR POWER! THE MONITORED TORPEDOES FOLLOWED THE ENEMY HULLS AS THOUGH DRAWN BY MAGNETS..."
"WE COULDN'T MISS! IT WAS A GLORIOUS SIGHT. NOW THE MERCHANT SHIPS WERE UNPROTECTED AS THE ENEMY DESTROYERS WENT TO THE BOTTOM..."
4

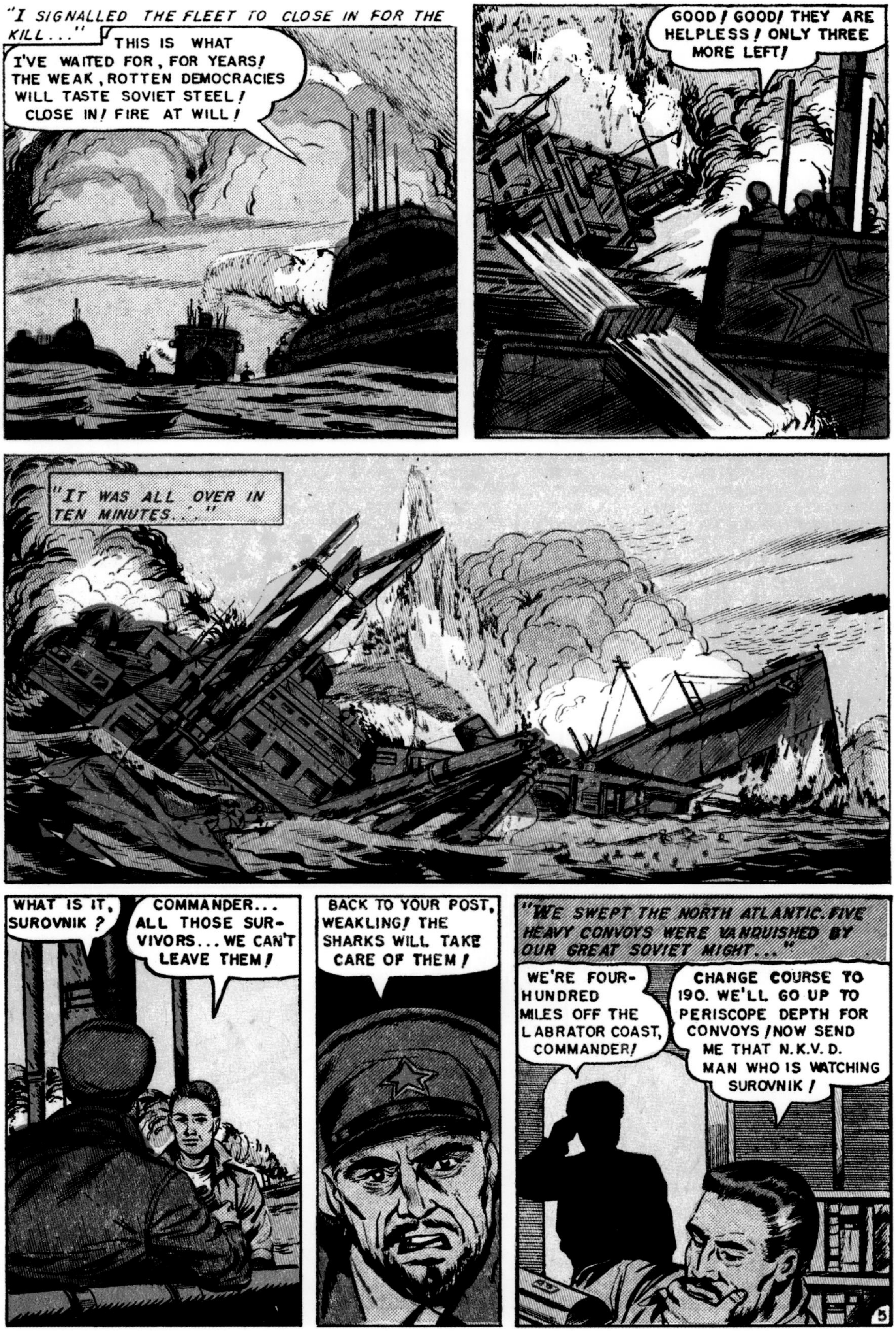
"I SIGNALLED THE FLEET TO CLOSE IN FOR THE KILL..."
THIS IS WHAT I'VE WAITED FOR, FOR YEARS! THE WEAK, ROTTEN DEMOCRACIES WILL TASTE SOVIET STEEL! CLOSE IN! FIRE AT WILL!
GOOD! GOOD! THEY ARE HELPLESS! ONLY THREE MORE LEFT!
"IT WAS ALL OVER IN TEN MINUTES..."
WHAT IS IT, SUROVNIK?
COMMANDER... ALL THOSE SURVIVORS... WE CAN'T LEAVE THEM!
BACK TO YOUR POST, WEAKLING! THE SHARKS WILL TAKE CARE OF THEM!
"WE SWEPT THE NORTH ATLANTIC. FIVE HEAVY CONVOYS WERE VANQUISHED BY OUR GREAT SOVIET MIGHT..."
WE'RE FOUR-HUNDRED MILES OFF THE LABRATOR COAST, COMMANDER!
CHANGE COURSE TO 190. WE'LL GO UP TO PERISCOPE DEPTH FOR CONVOYS! NOW SEND ME THAT N.K.V.D. MAN WHO IS WATCHING SUROVNIK!
5

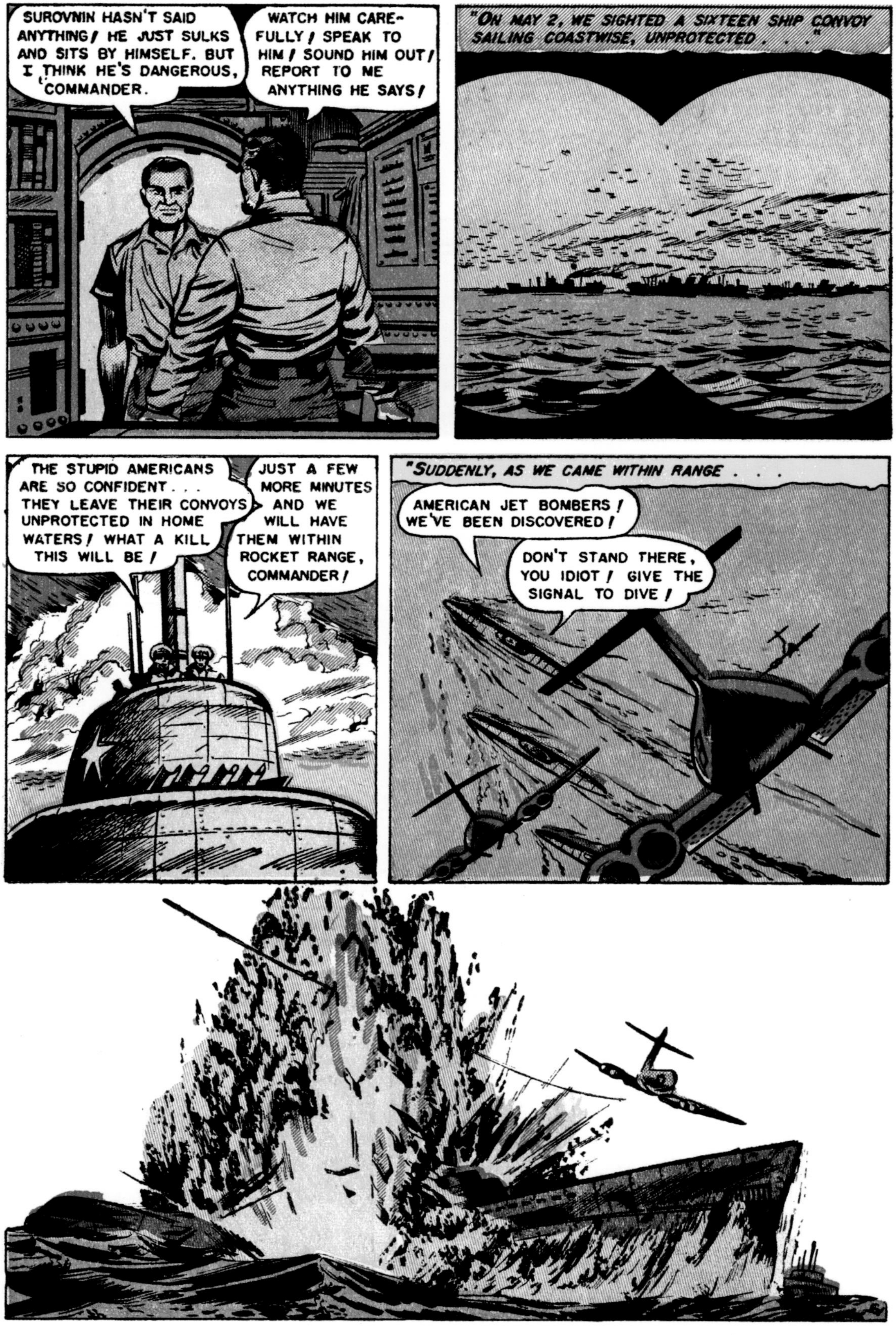
SUROVNIN HASN'T SAID ANYTHING! HE JUST SULKS AND SITS BY HIMSELF. BUT I THINK HE'S DANGEROUS, COMMANDER.
WATCH HIM CAREFULLY! SPEAK TO HIM! SOUND HIM OUT! REPORT TO ME ANYTHING HE SAYS!
"ON MAY 2, WE SIGHTED A SIXTEEN SHIP CONVOY SAILING COASTWISE, UNPROTECTED . . ."
THE STUPID AMERICANS ARE SO CONFIDENT . . . THEY LEAVE THEIR CONVOYS UNPROTECTED IN HOME WATERS! WHAT A KILL THIS WILL BE!
JUST A FEW MORE MINUTES AND WE WILL HAVE THEM WITHIN ROCKET RANGE, COMMANDER!
"SUDDENLY, AS WE CAME WITHIN RANGE . . .
AMERICAN JET BOMBERS! WE'VE BEEN DISCOVERED!
DON'T STAND THERE, YOU IDIOT! GIVE THE SIGNAL TO DIVE!

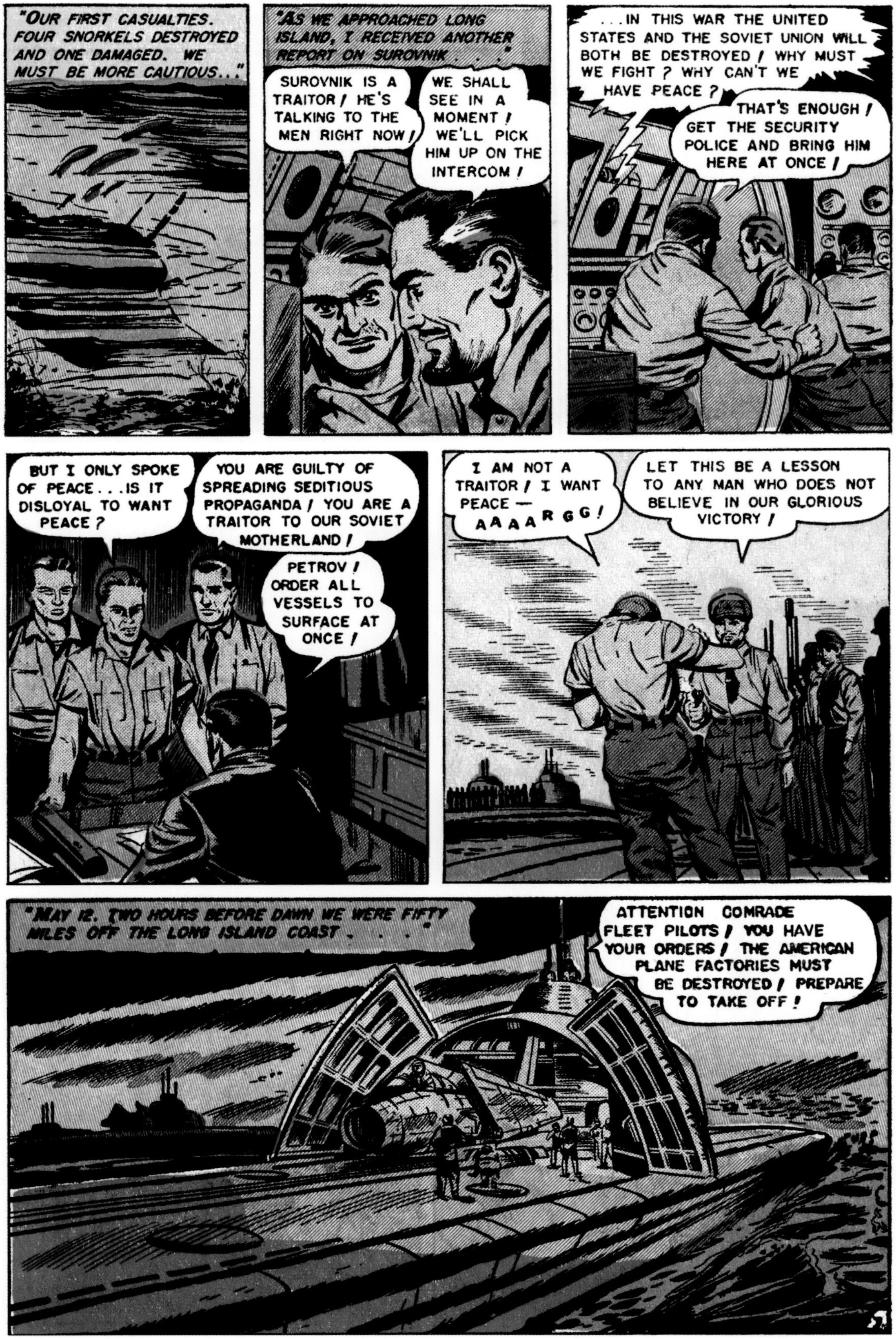
"OUR FIRST CASUALTIES. FOUR SNORKELS DESTROYED AND ONE DAMAGED. WE MUST BE MORE CAUTIOUS..."
"AS WE APPROACHED LONG ISLAND, I RECEIVED ANOTHER REPORT ON SUROVNIK . . ."
SUROVNIK IS A TRAITOR! HE'S TALKING TO THE MEN RIGHT NOW!
WE SHALL SEE IN A MOMENT! WE'LL PICK HIM UP ON THE INTERCOM!
...IN THIS WAR THE UNITED STATES AND THE SOVIET UNION WILL BOTH BE DESTROYED! WHY MUST WE FIGHT? WHY CAN'T WE HAVE PEACE?
THAT'S ENOUGH! GET THE SECURITY POLICE AND BRING HIM HERE AT ONCE!
BUT I ONLY SPOKE OF PEACE...IS IT DISLOYAL TO WANT PEACE?
YOU ARE GUILTY OF SPREADING SEDITIOUS PROPAGANDA! YOU ARE A TRAITOR TO OUR SOVIET MOTHERLAND!
PETROV! ORDER ALL VESSELS TO SURFACE AT ONCE!
I AM NOT A TRAITOR! I WANT PEACE — AAAARGG!
LET THIS BE A LESSON TO ANY MAN WHO DOES NOT BELIEVE IN OUR GLORIOUS VICTORY!
"MAY 12. TWO HOURS BEFORE DAWN WE WERE FIFTY MILES OFF THE LONG ISLAND COAST . . ."
ATTENTION COMRADE FLEET PILOTS! YOU HAVE YOUR ORDERS! THE AMERICAN PLANE FACTORIES MUST BE DESTROYED! PREPARE TO TAKE OFF!

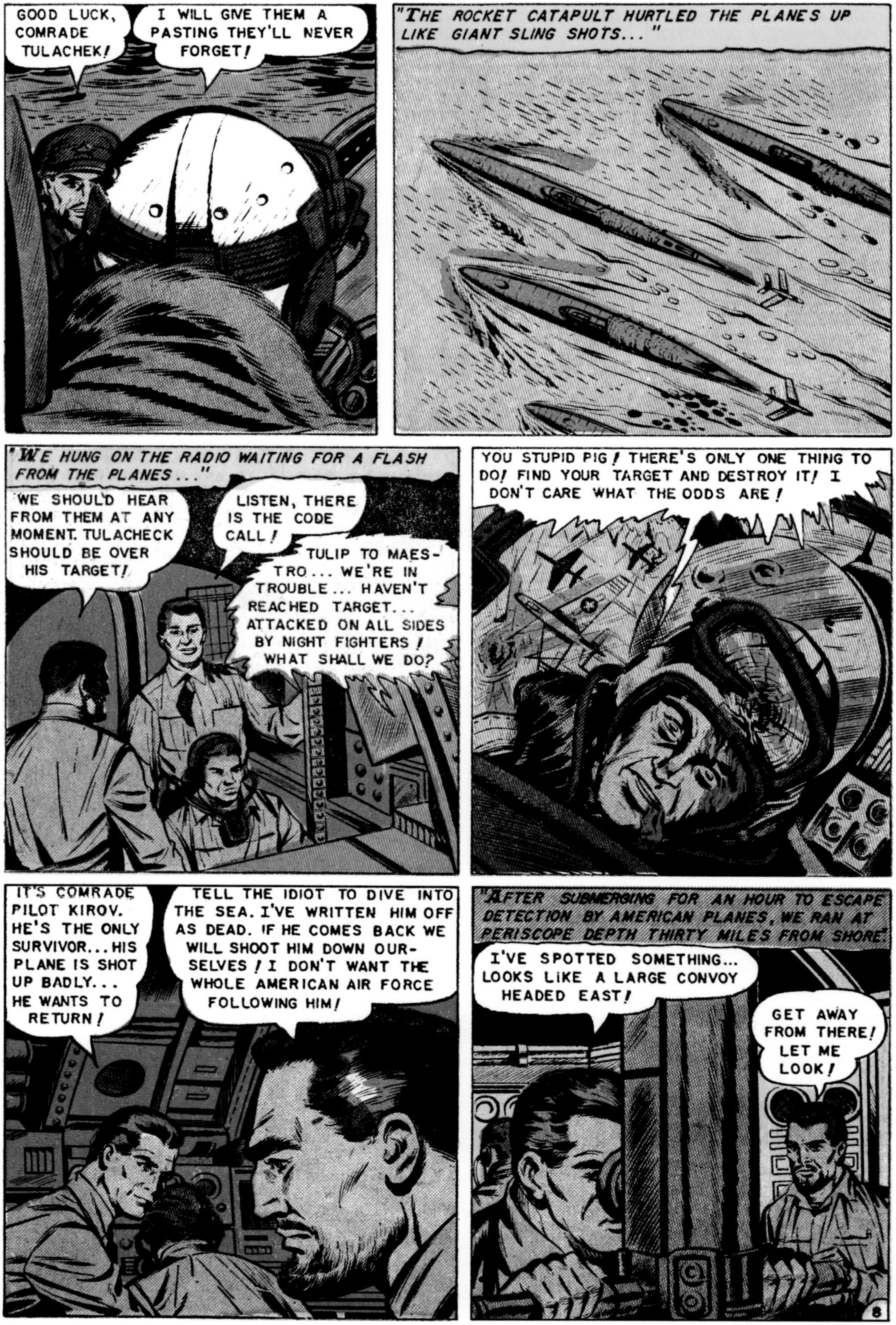
GOOD LUCK, COMRADE TULACHEK!
I WILL GIVE THEM A PASTING THEY'LL NEVER FORGET!
"THE ROCKET CATAPULT HURTLED THE PLANES UP LIKE GIANT SLING SHOTS..."
"WE HUNG ON THE RADIO WAITING FOR A FLASH FROM THE PLANES..."
WE SHOULD HEAR FROM THEM AT ANY MOMENT. TULACHECK SHOULD BE OVER HIS TARGET!
LISTEN, THERE IS THE CODE CALL!
TULIP TO MAESTRO... WE'RE IN TROUBLE... HAVEN'T REACHED TARGET... ATTACKED ON ALL SIDES BY NIGHT FIGHTERS! WHAT SHALL WE DO?
YOU STUPID PIG! THERE'S ONLY ONE THING TO DO! FIND YOUR TARGET AND DESTROY IT! I DON'T CARE WHAT THE ODDS ARE!
IT'S COMRADE PILOT KIROV. HE'S THE ONLY SURVIVOR... HIS PLANE IS SHOT UP BADLY... HE WANTS TO RETURN!
TELL THE IDIOT TO DIVE INTO THE SEA. I'VE WRITTEN HIM OFF AS DEAD. IF HE COMES BACK WE WILL SHOOT HIM DOWN OURSELVES! I DON'T WANT THE WHOLE AMERICAN AIR FORCE FOLLOWING HIM!
"AFTER SUBMERGING FOR AN HOUR TO ESCAPE DETECTION BY AMERICAN PLANES, WE RAN AT PERISCOPE DEPTH THIRTY MILES FROM SHORE."
I'VE SPOTTED SOMETHING... LOOKS LIKE A LARGE CONVOY HEADED EAST!
GET AWAY FROM THERE! LET ME LOOK!
8

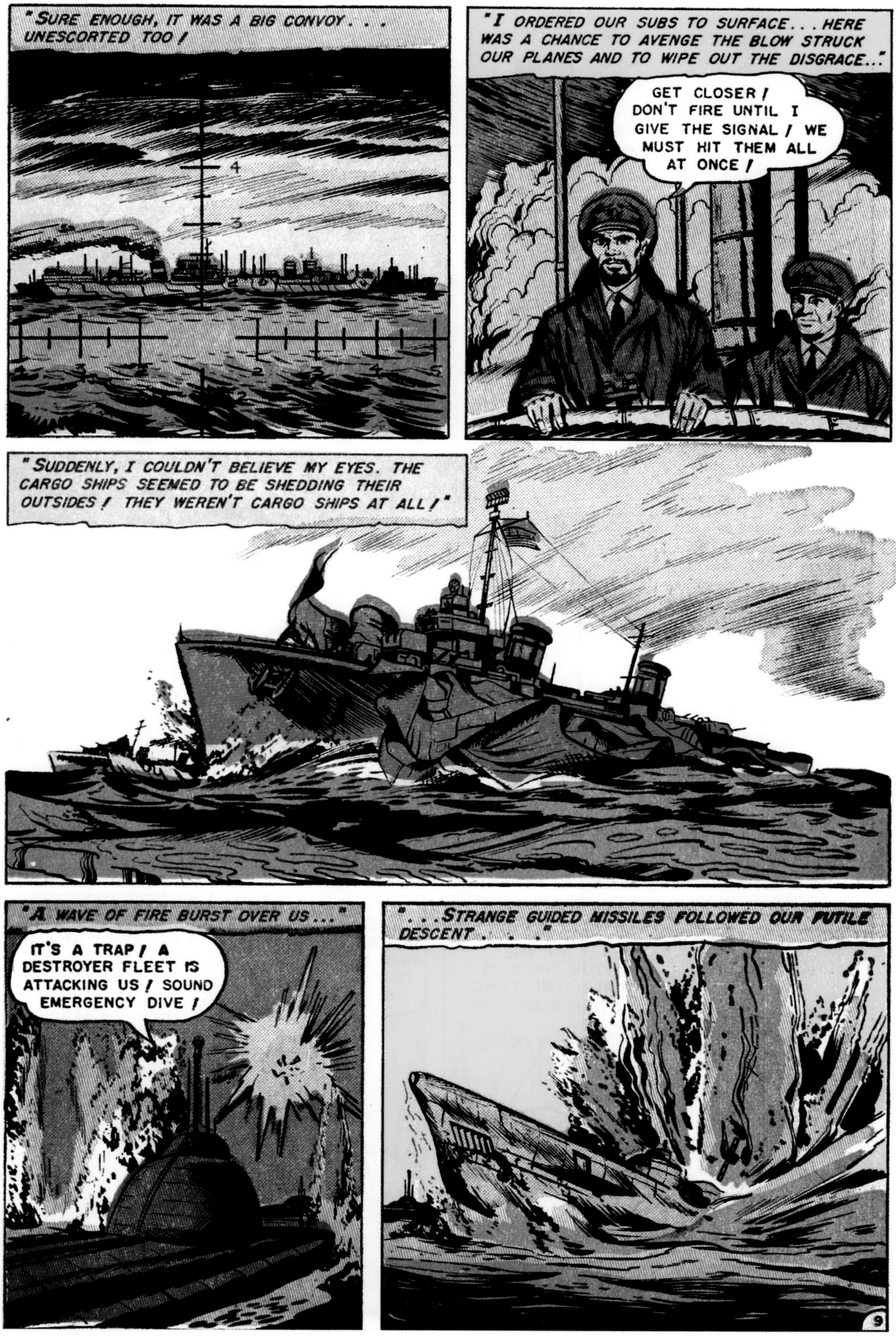
"SURE ENOUGH, IT WAS A BIG CONVOY . . . UNESCORTED TOO!
"I ORDERED OUR SUBS TO SURFACE . . . HERE WAS A CHANCE TO AVENGE THE BLOW STRUCK OUR PLANES AND TO WIPE OUT THE DISGRACE..."
GET CLOSER! DON'T FIRE UNTIL I GIVE THE SIGNAL! WE MUST HIT THEM ALL AT ONCE!
"SUDDENLY, I COULDN'T BELIEVE MY EYES. THE CARGO SHIPS SEEMED TO BE SHEDDING THEIR OUTSIDES! THEY WEREN'T CARGO SHIPS AT ALL!"
"A WAVE OF FIRE BURST OVER US..."
IT'S A TRAP! A DESTROYER FLEET IS ATTACKING US! SOUND EMERGENCY DIVE!
". . .STRANGE GUIDED MISSILES FOLLOWED OUR FUTILE DESCENT . . ."
9

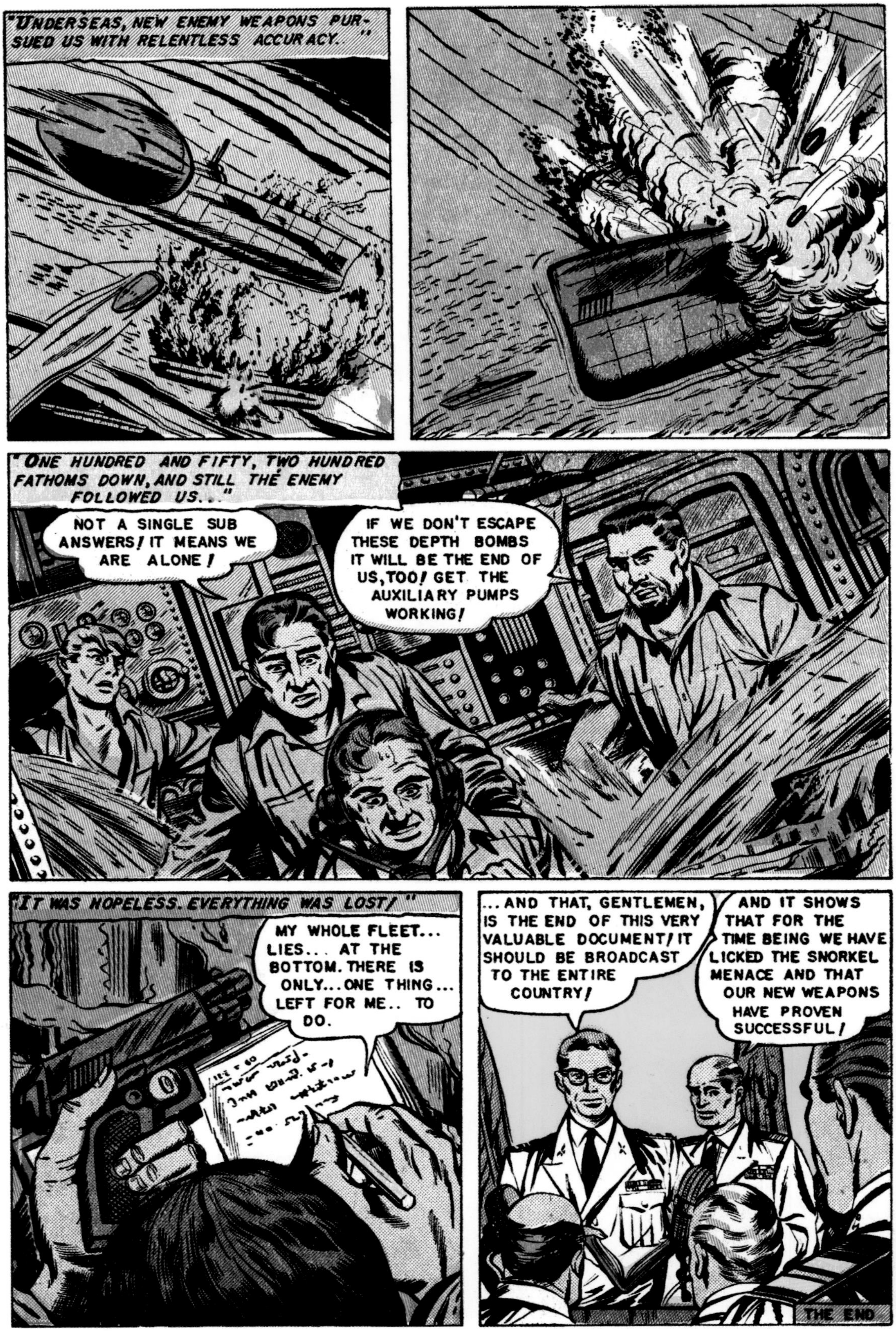
"UNDERSEAS, NEW ENEMY WEAPONS PURSUED US WITH RELENTLESS ACCURACY."
"ONE HUNDRED AND FIFTY, TWO HUNDRED FATHOMS DOWN, AND STILL THE ENEMY FOLLOWED US..."
NOT A SINGLE SUB ANSWERS! IT MEANS WE ARE ALONE!
IF WE DON'T ESCAPE THESE DEPTH BOMBS IT WILL BE THE END OF US, TOO! GET THE AUXILIARY PUMPS WORKING!
"IT WAS HOPELESS. EVERYTHING WAS LOST!"
MY WHOLE FLEET... LIES... AT THE BOTTOM. THERE IS ONLY... ONE THING... LEFT FOR ME.. TO DO.
...AND THAT, GENTLEMEN, IS THE END OF THIS VERY VALUABLE DOCUMENT! IT SHOULD BE BROADCAST TO THE ENTIRE COUNTRY!
AND IT SHOWS THAT FOR THE TIME BEING WE HAVE LICKED THE SNORKEL MENACE AND THAT OUR NEW WEAPONS HAVE PROVEN SUCCESSFUL!
THE END

THE INVADERS

The young Navy lieutenant hunched his shoulders, and bent lower over the wheel of his car, as he careened along the narrow, slippery road. The heavy slanting rain beat against his cracked windshield—rain that had been falling ever since the hydrogen bomb fell on the Naval shipyards at Newport News, Virginia.

The raid had not resulted in as many deaths as others the Russians had made on the continental United States, but it had done the most damage. The entire shipyard was out of action—no one knew for how long—and almost one third of the Atlantic fleet had been destroyed. Panic had somehow been averted; perhaps because those closest to the blast had been killed, and the others were still suffering from shock and disbelief. They had read about the great raids on New York, Philadelphia and Washington—had even seen them on their television screens—but they could not feel the full impact of a hydrogen bomb blast until it had happened to them.

The lieutenant had been sent down from the Pentagon—or, what was left of it—to work with the Naval personnel in salvaging what they could from the ruins of Newport News. His main job, however, was in line with his training as an intelligence officer. The Navy had top secret codes, plans, blueprints, and other valuable papers somewhere in the rubble, and it was vital to the nation's security that this material not fall into the wrong hands. His job was to find it.

He had finished for the day, and was heading for the place where he was staying—a small beach house outside the blast area, located on the back road leading to Cape Henry. He had worked late, as his orders were to finish the job as soon as possible. It was fortunate that he drove out when he did, for if he had been earlier, he would not have seen the submarine. The stretch of road he was on led steadily upwards toward the edge of a cliff, and then turned sharply to the right. At the turn, there was another road leading down to a small coastal station, set in the side of

the cliff, facing the ocean. As he slowed the car, preparing to make the turn, he saw something that made him instinctively cut off his lights and stop the car. About a quarter of a mile out to sea, illuminated briefly by his headlights, was a Russian submarine!

He had recognized it instantly. Long hours of studying all types of enemy craft had stamped their images firmly on his mind, and he could not be mistaken. The squat, broad hull; the high, narrow periscope, equipped with the German-designed snorkel; the thick, ugly atomic tubes . . . he could not be in error. But what were they doing out there? He had to find out! As he sat there, trying to collect his senses, a light opened up and started systematically sweeping the shore. He instinctively dropped down on the seat, grabbed his Navy .45 from the glove compartment, and slithered out onto the ground. As he started easing away from the tell-tale car, the light caught it. After a few seconds, apparently satisfied that the car was empty, the spotlight continued along the shore for a few hundred yards, and snapped off. The lieutenant realized that he had not breathed since he had first seen the submarine.

Still carrying the pistol, he crawled to the edge of the cliff and looked down. Heavy drops of rain cut into his face, driven hard by the off-ocean wind. He could see nothing. He had to get down. He eased over the edge, cutting his hand on a sharp rock, and started down. His foot dislodged a rock, and he heard it rattle down the hill below him. Once again the spotlight came on, and stabbed points of light over the face of the cliff. It did not pick up his huddled form. He thought the light was nearer the shore, but he could not be sure.

Slowly and painfully, favoring his injured hand, the lieutenant worked his way down until he stood on the sandy beach. He thought he heard something, but the heavy waves pounding on the beach drowned out everything. He moved closer, and then he knew he heard it—a command, hissed in a gutteral voice—in Russian! The lieutenant dropped to the sand straining his eyes, seeing nothing but white spray and rain. He rubbed his eyes, trying to clear them. He was soaked now, and cold.

Suddenly, a small rubber boat came tumbling over the surf, and bounced onto the beach. Three men picked themselves up from the sand, and one of them flashed a red light toward the ocean. An answering light came from the submarine. As the lieutenant watched, the men deflated the rubber boat, folded it carefully, and buried it in the sand. He could hear them talking quietly, one in Russian, and the others in English. Within a few seconds, the lieutenant learned that they were coming to do the same job to which he had been assigned—to get the secret records!

Their conversation revealed that they expected to find a deserted base and no opposition. The lieutenant gritted his teeth. He would give them some opposition—more than they bargained for, at any rate. The three men moved quickly across the beach toward the coastal station. It was too late for a warning, and the lieutenant heard the crack of several shots, as the guards were disposed of.

As he watched, the Russians blasted open the heavy door and went inside, leaving one man by the door. The lieutenant pulled himself to his feet, and ran low across the sand toward the station. He came up by one side and stood erect, watching the thickset guard as he looked warily toward the land, expecting any opposition to come from that direction. The lieutenant inched around the corner of the building, his body stiff, hardly breathing, moving toward the Russian. Within a few feet of his victim, the Russian suddenly turned, saw the American, and let out a hoarse cry. The lieutenant bounded forward, and struck him heavily on the head with his pistol butt. The guard fell silently.

The door burst open and a man ran out, carrying a sub-machine gun. He saw the lieutenant, and began firing, and the lieutenant felt a hot, searing pain in his left arm, but he fired rapidly—three times —at the man before him. The gun's clatter ceased abruptly, and the man dropped. Two down, and one to go. The lieutenant knew that if he stopped now, if he let the pain overwhelm him, he was finished.

With his arm dangling limply at his side, he pushed the front door open, and eased into the station. As he did so, he heard glass shatter on the land side, and rushed back to see a heavy figure climbing through the window. He fired once but the figure dropped from his sight. He ran to the window, and saw him running up the cliff toward the car. He started to fire again, and checked himself. There were only two shots left, and he had not brought another clip.

He ran quickly out the front door, and started pulling himself up the cliff. As he neared the top, he heard his engine roar into life, and he hurtled himself the rest of the way—in time to see the car start down the road toward the Naval base. He fired once at the left rear tire, and the car slewed sharply, wobbled crazily down the steep hill, and crashed at the bottom. No one moved. I've done it, he thought, when the bullet him him in the back.

He whirled around to see the third Russian, having regained consciousness, facing him. A flash of light, and another shot ripped into the lieutenant's shoulder, and he cursed himself for a fool, knowing he should have done better, and fired his last shot. The Russian straightened up, hesitated a moment, and then fell backwards over the hill.

The lieutenant dragged himself down to the coastal station again, and pulled a phone from its hook. After what seemed like hours, a voice called out, and the lieutenant stumbled out his story. The voice went away, and another voice came on, but the lieutenant could not hear it. The Tele-Screen was switched on at headquarters, and the astonished commander saw the lieutenant's body slumped on the floor, near one of the dead Russians.

Men were sent out; the area was searched; and the boat was found. Based on the few words they had heard from the lieutenant, plus what they could figure out, the night's events were reconstructed. A Sonar search was made for the submarine, and it was found and destroyed

Unfortunately, the lieutenant was not able to hear the speech made by the President, when he was awarded his posthumous Congressional Medal of Honor.

The End

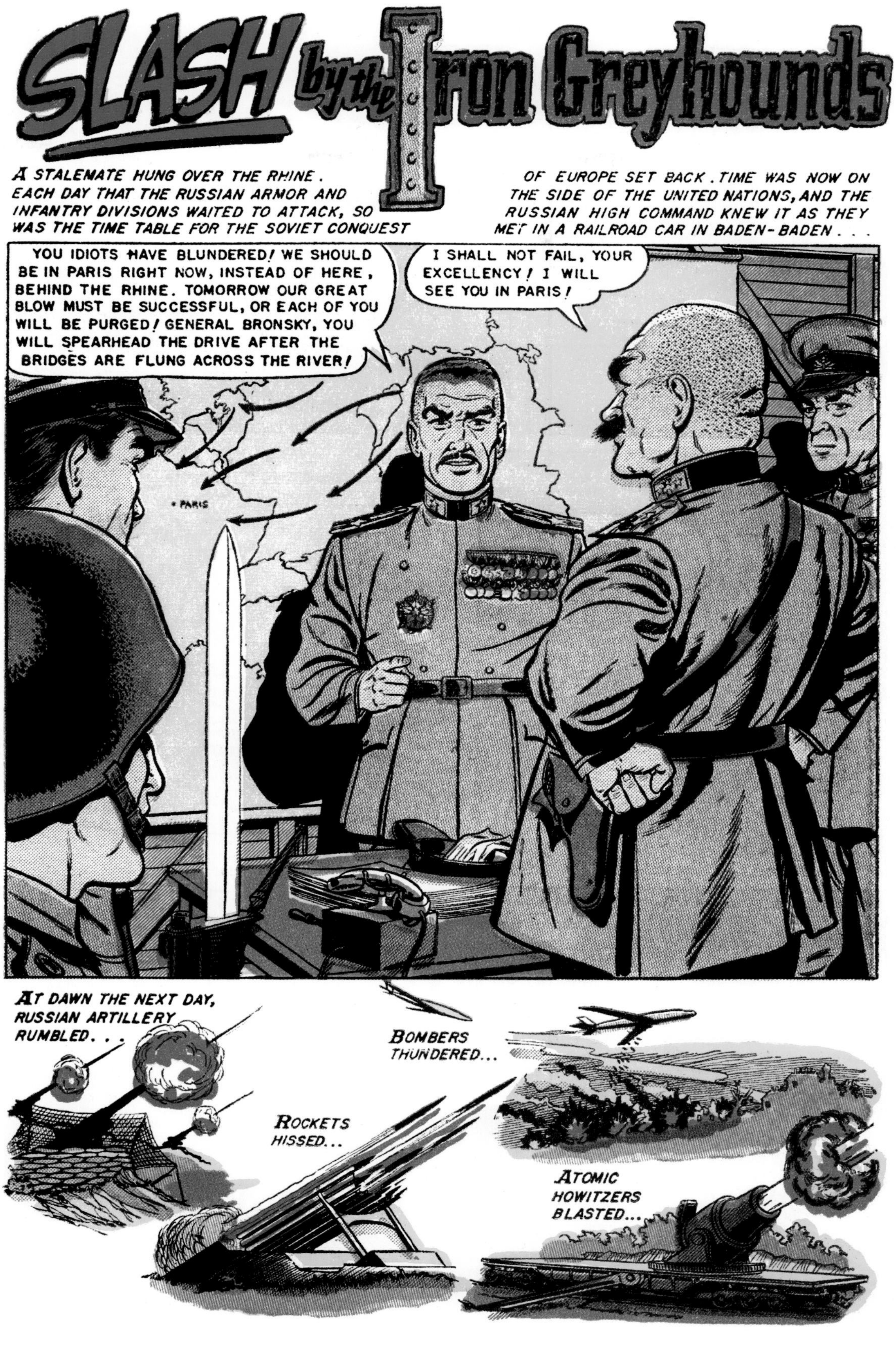
SLASH by the Iron Greyhounds
A STALEMATE HUNG OVER THE RHINE. EACH DAY THAT THE RUSSIAN ARMOR AND INFANTRY DIVISIONS WAITED TO ATTACK, SO WAS THE TIME TABLE FOR THE SOVIET CONQUEST OF EUROPE SET BACK. TIME WAS NOW ON THE SIDE OF THE UNITED NATIONS, AND THE RUSSIAN HIGH COMMAND KNEW IT AS THEY MET IN A RAILROAD CAR IN BADEN-BADEN . . .
YOU IDIOTS HAVE BLUNDERED! WE SHOULD BE IN PARIS RIGHT NOW, INSTEAD OF HERE, BEHIND THE RHINE. TOMORROW OUR GREAT BLOW MUST BE SUCCESSFUL, OR EACH OF YOU WILL BE PURGED! GENERAL BRONSKY, YOU WILL SPEARHEAD THE DRIVE AFTER THE BRIDGES ARE FLUNG ACROSS THE RIVER!
I SHALL NOT FAIL, YOUR EXCELLENCY! I WILL SEE YOU IN PARIS!
PARIS
AT DAWN THE NEXT DAY, RUSSIAN ARTILLERY RUMBLED. . .
BOMBERS THUNDERED...
ROCKETS HISSED...
ATOMIC HOWITZERS BLASTED...

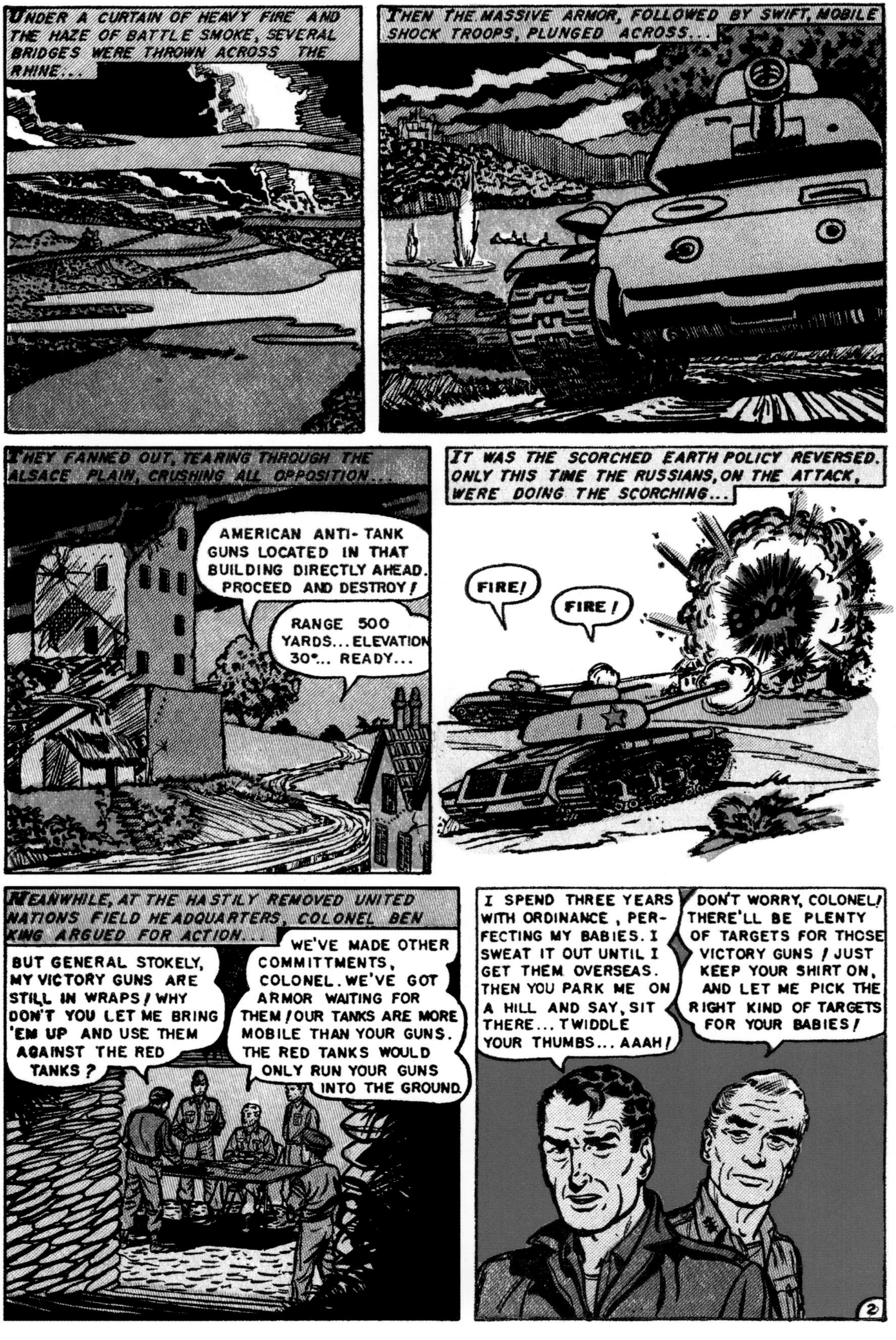

UNDER A CURTAIN OF HEAVY FIRE AND THE HAZE OF BATTLE SMOKE, SEVERAL BRIDGES WERE THROWN ACROSS THE RHINE...
THEN THE MASSIVE ARMOR, FOLLOWED BY SWIFT, MOBILE SHOCK TROOPS, PLUNGED ACROSS...
THEY FANNED OUT, TEARING THROUGH THE ALSACE PLAIN, CRUSHING ALL OPPOSITION...
AMERICAN ANTI- TANK GUNS LOCATED IN THAT BUILDING DIRECTLY AHEAD. PROCEED AND DESTROY!
RANGE 500 YARDS... ELEVATION 30°... READY...
IT WAS THE SCORCHED EARTH POLICY REVERSED. ONLY THIS TIME THE RUSSIANS, ON THE ATTACK, WERE DOING THE SCORCHING...
FIRE!
FIRE!
MEANWHILE, AT THE HASTILY REMOVED UNITED NATIONS FIELD HEADQUARTERS, COLONEL BEN KING ARGUED FOR ACTION...
BUT GENERAL STOKELY, MY VICTORY GUNS ARE STILL IN WRAPS! WHY DON'T YOU LET ME BRING 'EM UP AND USE THEM AGAINST THE RED TANKS?
WE'VE MADE OTHER COMMITTMENTS, COLONEL. WE'VE GOT ARMOR WAITING FOR THEM! OUR TANKS ARE MORE MOBILE THAN YOUR GUNS. THE RED TANKS WOULD ONLY RUN YOUR GUNS INTO THE GROUND.
I SPEND THREE YEARS WITH ORDINANCE, PERFECTING MY BABIES. I SWEAT IT OUT UNTIL I GET THEM OVERSEAS. THEN YOU PARK ME ON A HILL AND SAY, SIT THERE... TWIDDLE YOUR THUMBS... AAAH!
DON'T WORRY, COLONEL! THERE'LL BE PLENTY OF TARGETS FOR THOSE VICTORY GUNS! JUST KEEP YOUR SHIRT ON, AND LET ME PICK THE RIGHT KIND OF TARGETS FOR YOUR BABIES!
2

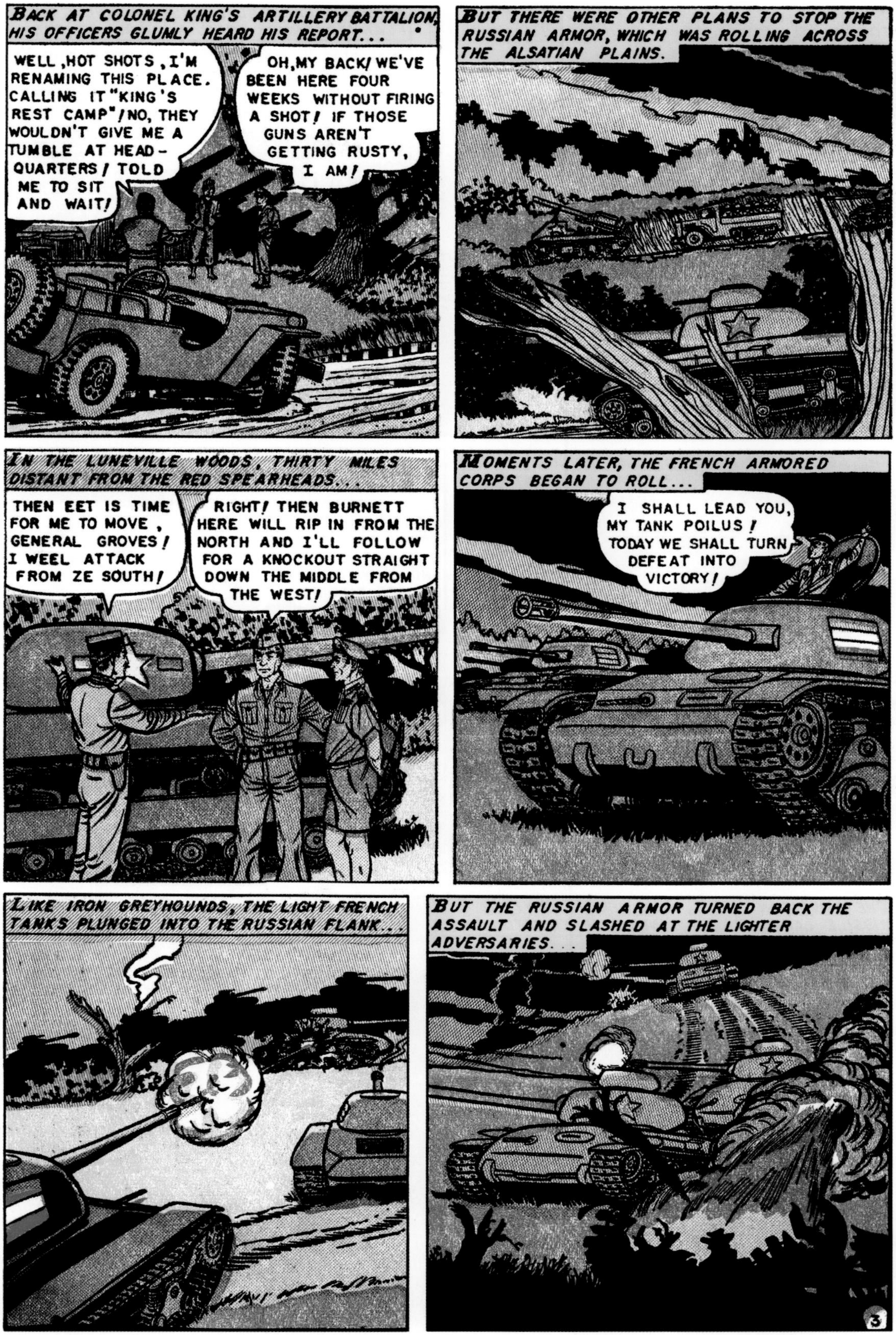

BACK AT COLONEL KING'S ARTILLERY BATTALION, HIS OFFICERS GLUMLY HEARD HIS REPORT...
WELL, HOT SHOTS, I'M RENAMING THIS PLACE. CALLING IT "KING'S REST CAMP"! NO, THEY WOULDN'T GIVE ME A TUMBLE AT HEAD-QUARTERS! TOLD ME TO SIT AND WAIT!
OH, MY BACK! WE'VE BEEN HERE FOUR WEEKS WITHOUT FIRING A SHOT! IF THOSE GUNS AREN'T GETTING RUSTY, I AM!
BUT THERE WERE OTHER PLANS TO STOP THE RUSSIAN ARMOR, WHICH WAS ROLLING ACROSS THE ALSATIAN PLAINS.
IN THE LUNEVILLE WOODS, THIRTY MILES DISTANT FROM THE RED SPEARHEADS...
THEN EET IS TIME FOR ME TO MOVE, GENERAL GROVES! I WEEL ATTACK FROM ZE SOUTH!
RIGHT! THEN BURNETT HERE WILL RIP IN FROM THE NORTH AND I'LL FOLLOW FOR A KNOCKOUT STRAIGHT DOWN THE MIDDLE FROM THE WEST!
MOMENTS LATER, THE FRENCH ARMORED CORPS BEGAN TO ROLL...
I SHALL LEAD YOU, MY TANK POILUS! TODAY WE SHALL TURN DEFEAT INTO VICTORY!
LIKE IRON GREYHOUNDS, THE LIGHT FRENCH TANKS PLUNGED INTO THE RUSSIAN FLANK...
BUT THE RUSSIAN ARMOR TURNED BACK THE ASSAULT AND SLASHED AT THE LIGHTER ADVERSARIES...
3

PRECISELY AT THE MOMENT THE REDS TURNED SOUTH, THE BRITISH ARMOR PLUNGED INTO THEIR REAR FROM THE NORTH...

GOOD WORK, LADDIES! HIGHLAND BATTALION... MOVE UP ON MY LEFT FLANK! LET THEM HAVE THOSE HOWITZERS!

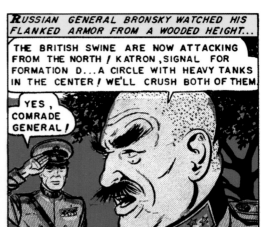

RUSSIAN GENERAL BRONSKY WATCHED HIS FLANKED ARMOR FROM A WOODED HEIGHT...

THE BRITISH SWINE ARE NOW ATTACKING FROM THE NORTH! KATRON, SIGNAL FOR FORMATION D...A CIRCLE WITH HEAVY TANKS IN THE CENTER! WE'LL CRUSH BOTH OF THEM.

YES, COMRADE GENERAL!

THE RED ARMOR CIRCLED, BEATING BACK BOTH FLANK ATTACKS WITH SUPERIOR FIRE POWER...

AT THIS MOMENT, GENERAL GROVES ISSUED HIS BATTLE ORDERS...

THIS IS IT, GANG! LET'S GO! RIGHT DOWN THE MIDDLE FOR A STRIKE! WE'LL TEAR THAT RED CIRCLE APART AND CHEW UP THOSE HEAVIES SITTING INSIDE!

THE AMERICAN TANKS, WITH REMOTE CONTROL MISSILE LAUNCHERS LEADING, CHURNED INTO THE HARRIED RUSSIAN LINES...

WHOOOOSH!

SWOOOOSH!

FIRE!

FIRE!

IVAN, LOOK OUT! AAAAAIIIEEE!

BLAM!

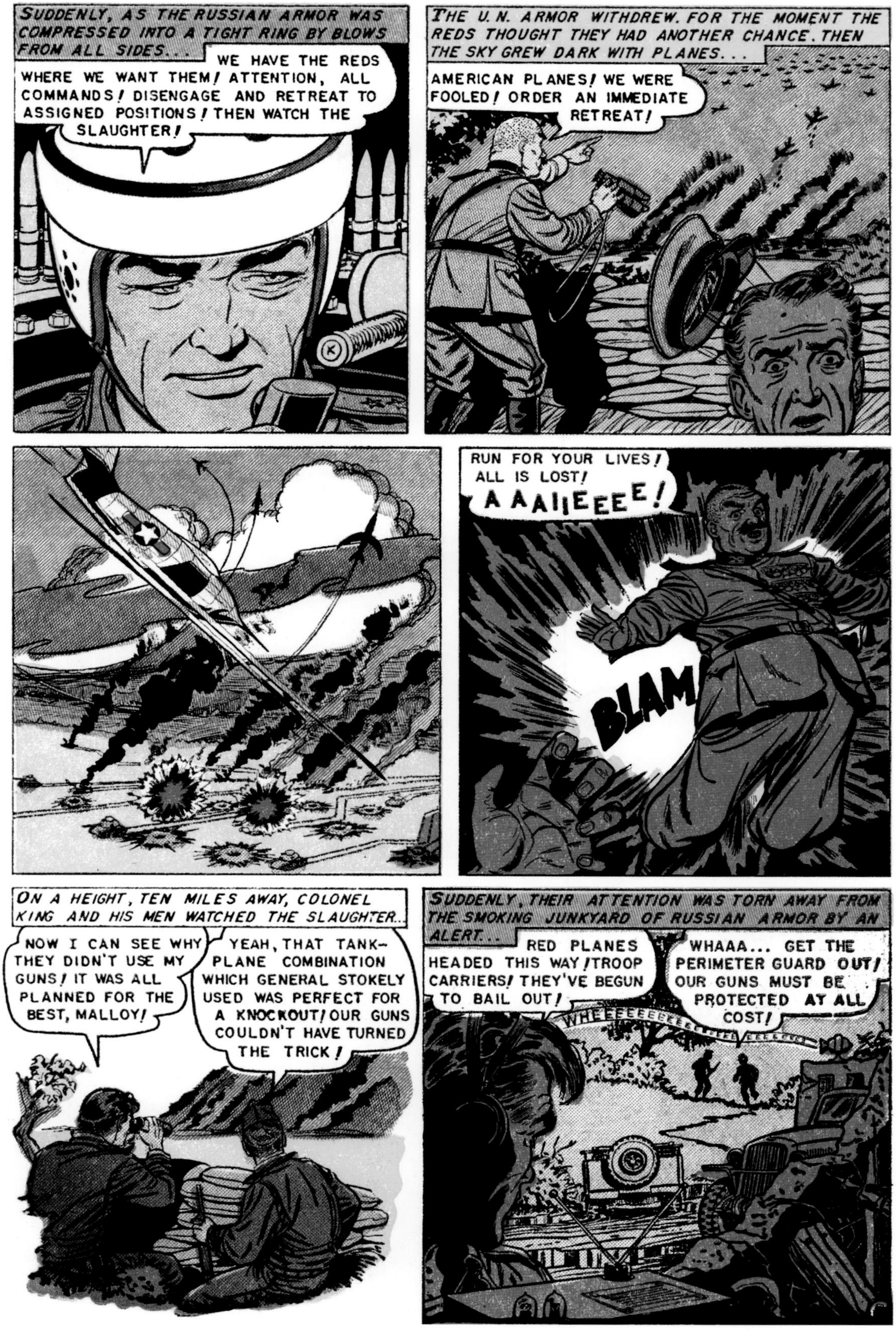
SUDDENLY, AS THE RUSSIAN ARMOR WAS COMPRESSED INTO A TIGHT RING BY BLOWS FROM ALL SIDES...
WE HAVE THE REDS WHERE WE WANT THEM! ATTENTION, ALL COMMANDS! DISENGAGE AND RETREAT TO ASSIGNED POSITIONS! THEN WATCH THE SLAUGHTER!
THE U.N. ARMOR WITHDREW. FOR THE MOMENT THE REDS THOUGHT THEY HAD ANOTHER CHANCE. THEN THE SKY GREW DARK WITH PLANES...
AMERICAN PLANES! WE WERE FOOLED! ORDER AN IMMEDIATE RETREAT!
RUN FOR YOUR LIVES! ALL IS LOST! AAAIIEEEE!
BLAM
ON A HEIGHT, TEN MILES AWAY, COLONEL KING AND HIS MEN WATCHED THE SLAUGHTER...
NOW I CAN SEE WHY THEY DIDN'T USE MY GUNS! IT WAS ALL PLANNED FOR THE BEST, MALLOY!
YEAH, THAT TANK-PLANE COMBINATION WHICH GENERAL STOKELY USED WAS PERFECT FOR A KNOCKOUT! OUR GUNS COULDN'T HAVE TURNED THE TRICK!
SUDDENLY, THEIR ATTENTION WAS TORN AWAY FROM THE SMOKING JUNKYARD OF RUSSIAN ARMOR BY AN ALERT...
RED PLANES HEADED THIS WAY! TROOP CARRIERS! THEY'VE BEGUN TO BAIL OUT!
WHAAA... GET THE PERIMETER GUARD OUT! OUR GUNS MUST BE PROTECTED AT ALL COST!
WHEEEEEEEEEEEEEEEEEEEE

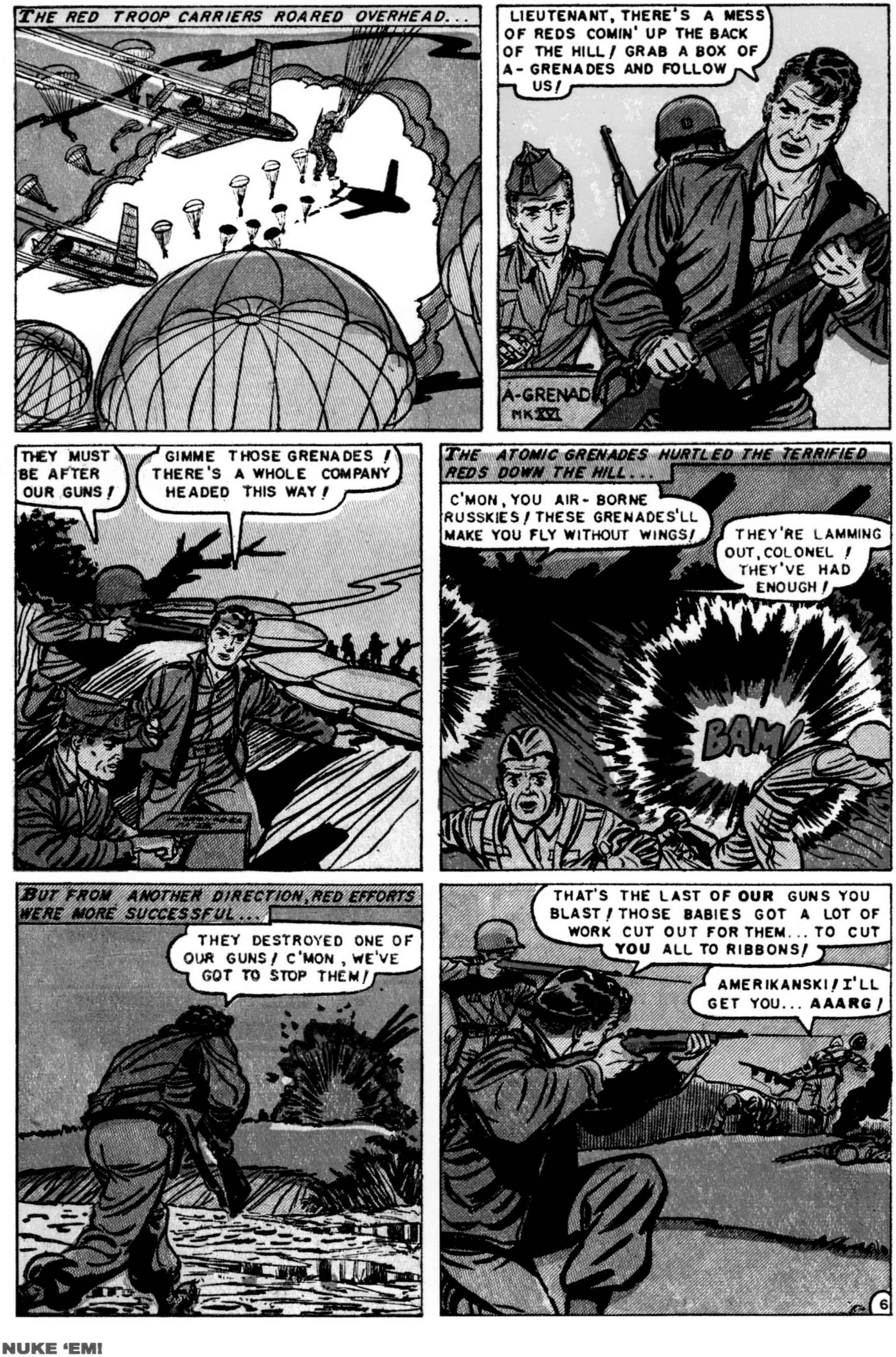
THE RED TROOP CARRIERS ROARED OVERHEAD...
LIEUTENANT, THERE'S A MESS OF REDS COMIN' UP THE BACK OF THE HILL! GRAB A BOX OF A-GRENADES AND FOLLOW US!
A-GRENAD MK XVI
THEY MUST BE AFTER OUR GUNS!
GIMME THOSE GRENADES! THERE'S A WHOLE COMPANY HEADED THIS WAY!
THE ATOMIC GRENADES HURTLED THE TERRIFIED REDS DOWN THE HILL...
C'MON, YOU AIR-BORNE RUSSKIES! THESE GRENADES'LL MAKE YOU FLY WITHOUT WINGS!
THEY'RE LAMMING OUT, COLONEL! THEY'VE HAD ENOUGH!
BAM!
BUT FROM ANOTHER DIRECTION, RED EFFORTS WERE MORE SUCCESSFUL...
THEY DESTROYED ONE OF OUR GUNS! C'MON, WE'VE GOT TO STOP THEM!
THAT'S THE LAST OF OUR GUNS YOU BLAST! THOSE BABIES GOT A LOT OF WORK CUT OUT FOR THEM... TO CUT YOU ALL TO RIBBONS!
AMERIKANSKI! I'LL GET YOU... AAARG!
6

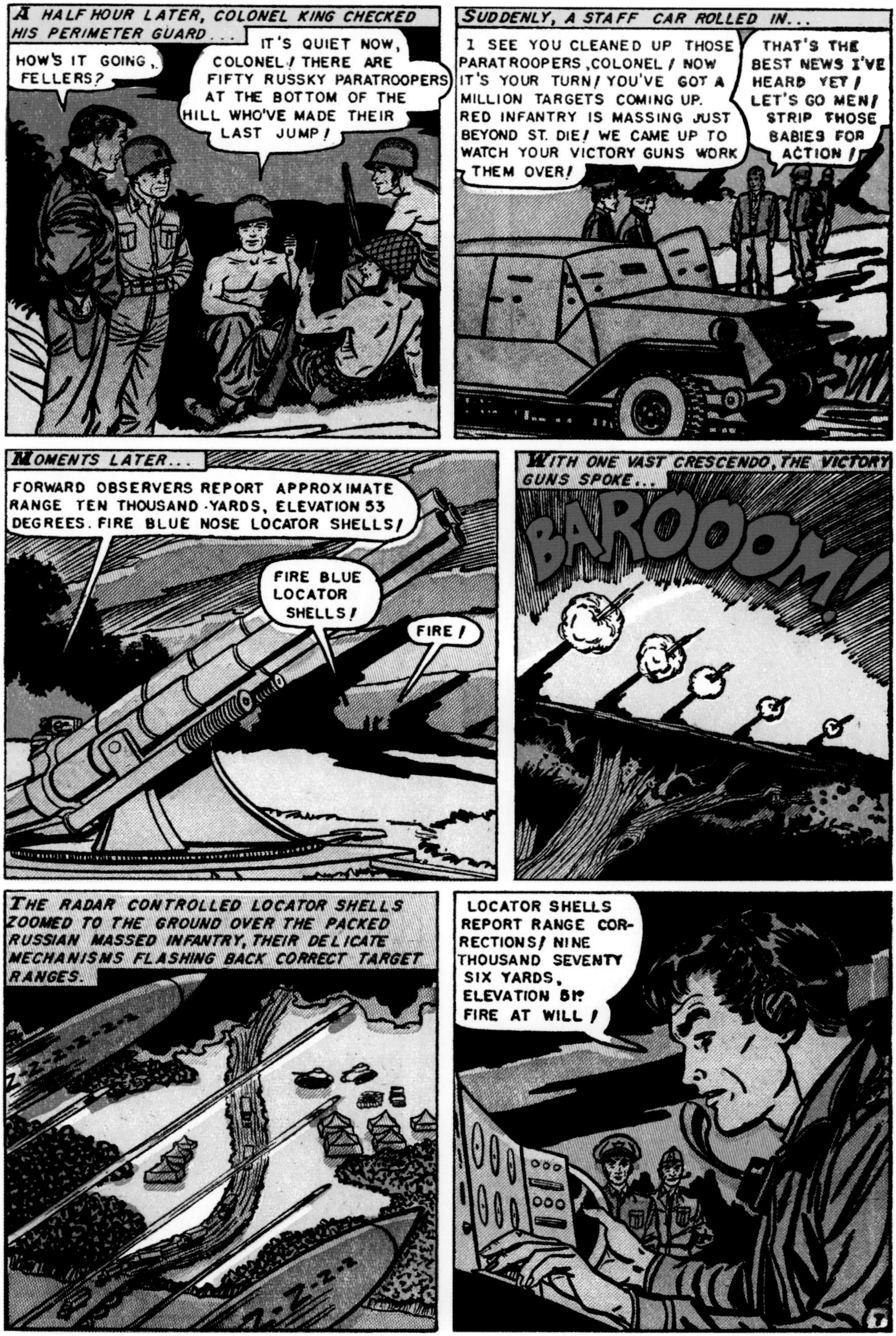
A HALF HOUR LATER, COLONEL KING CHECKED HIS PERIMETER GUARD...
HOW'S IT GOING, FELLERS?
IT'S QUIET NOW, COLONEL! THERE ARE FIFTY RUSSKY PARATROOPERS AT THE BOTTOM OF THE HILL WHO'VE MADE THEIR LAST JUMP!
SUDDENLY, A STAFF CAR ROLLED IN...
I SEE YOU CLEANED UP THOSE PARATROOPERS, COLONEL! NOW IT'S YOUR TURN! YOU'VE GOT A MILLION TARGETS COMING UP. RED INFANTRY IS MASSING JUST BEYOND ST. DIE! WE CAME UP TO WATCH YOUR VICTORY GUNS WORK THEM OVER!
THAT'S THE BEST NEWS I'VE HEARD YET! LET'S GO MEN! STRIP THOSE BABIES FOR ACTION!
MOMENTS LATER...
FORWARD OBSERVERS REPORT APPROXIMATE RANGE TEN THOUSAND YARDS, ELEVATION 53 DEGREES. FIRE BLUE NOSE LOCATOR SHELLS!
FIRE BLUE LOCATOR SHELLS!
FIRE!
WITH ONE VAST CRESCENDO, THE VICTORY GUNS SPOKE...
BAROOOM!
THE RADAR CONTROLLED LOCATOR SHELLS ZOOMED TO THE GROUND OVER THE PACKED RUSSIAN MASSED INFANTRY, THEIR DELICATE MECHANISMS FLASHING BACK CORRECT TARGET RANGES.
LOCATOR SHELLS REPORT RANGE CORRECTIONS! NINE THOUSAND SEVENTY SIX YARDS, ELEVATION 51°. FIRE AT WILL!

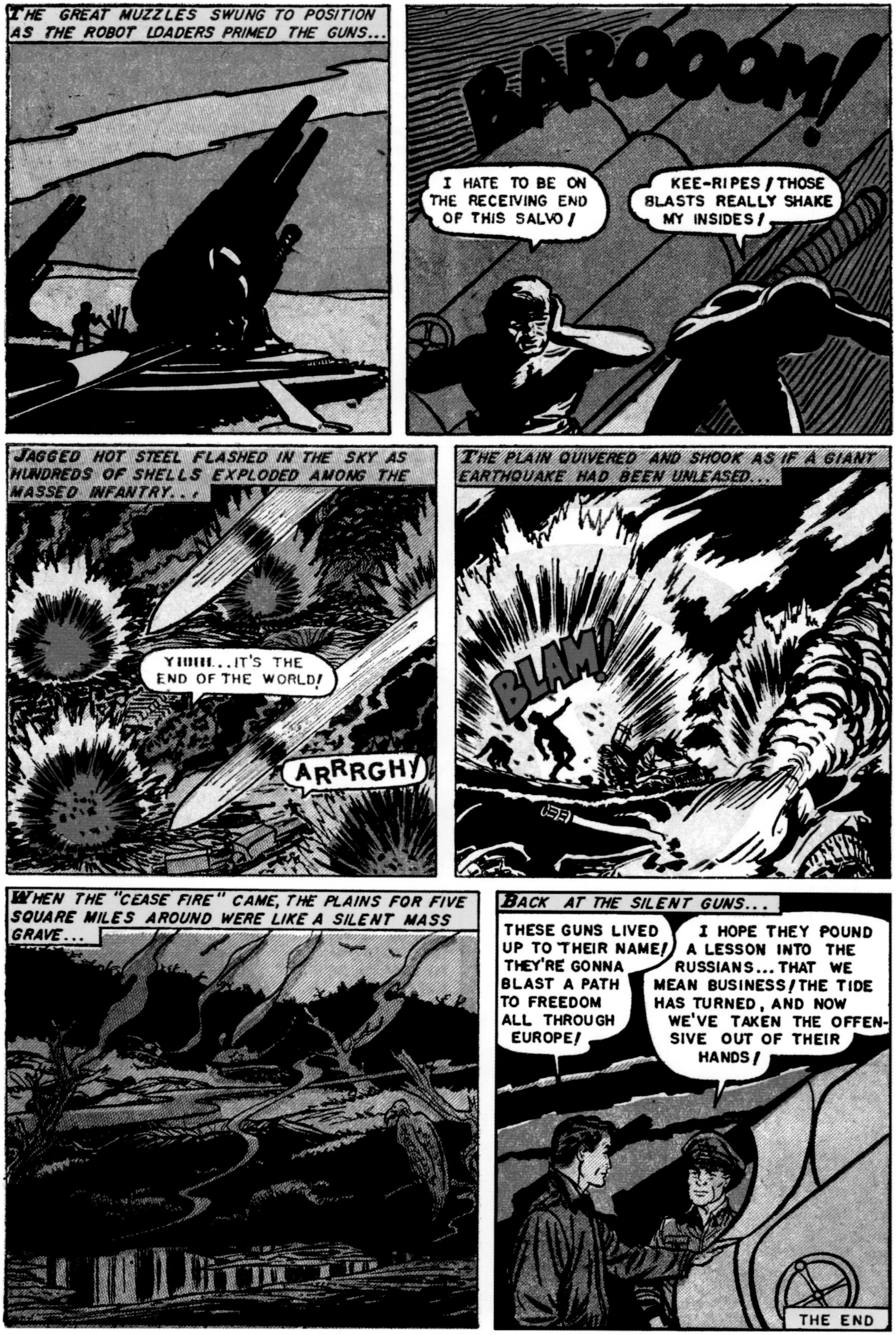
THE GREAT MUZZLES SWUNG TO POSITION AS THE ROBOT LOADERS PRIMED THE GUNS...
BAROOOOM!
I HATE TO BE ON THE RECEIVING END OF THIS SALVO!
KEE-RIPES! THOSE BLASTS REALLY SHAKE MY INSIDES!
JAGGED HOT STEEL FLASHED IN THE SKY AS HUNDREDS OF SHELLS EXPLODED AMONG THE MASSED INFANTRY...
YIIIIII...IT'S THE END OF THE WORLD!
ARRRGH!
THE PLAIN QUIVERED AND SHOOK AS IF A GIANT EARTHQUAKE HAD BEEN UNLEASED...
BLAM!
WHEN THE "CEASE FIRE" CAME, THE PLAINS FOR FIVE SQUARE MILES AROUND WERE LIKE A SILENT MASS GRAVE...
BACK AT THE SILENT GUNS...
THESE GUNS LIVED UP TO THEIR NAME! THEY'RE GONNA BLAST A PATH TO FREEDOM ALL THROUGH EUROPE!
I HOPE THEY POUND A LESSON INTO THE RUSSIANS...THAT WE MEAN BUSINESS! THE TIDE HAS TURNED, AND NOW WE'VE TAKEN THE OFFENSIVE OUT OF THEIR HANDS!
THE END

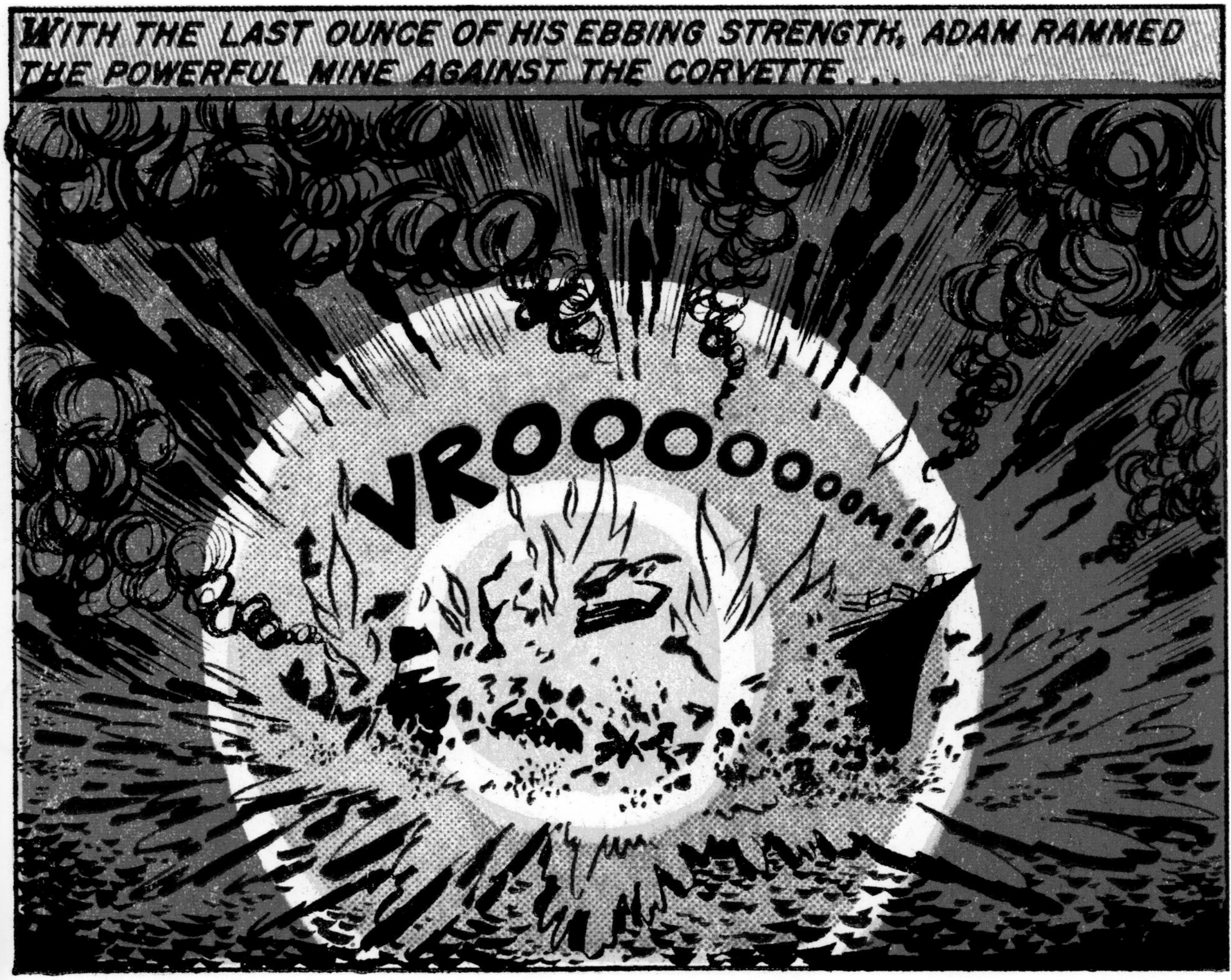
WITH THE LAST OUNCE OF HIS EBBING STRENGTH, ADAM RAMMED THE POWERFUL MINE AGAINST THE CORVETTE...
VROOOOOOoom!!

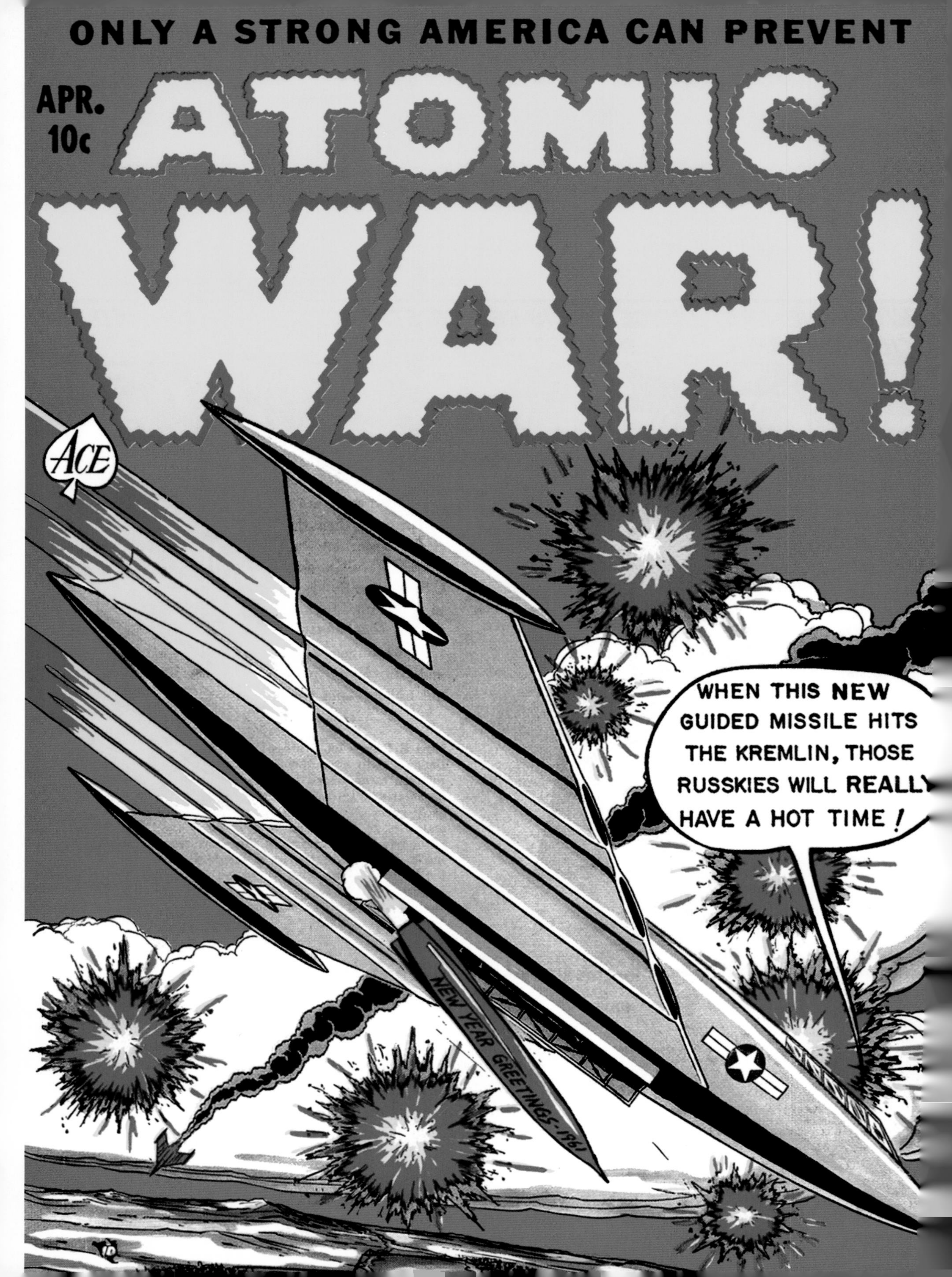
ONLY A STRONG AMERICA CAN PREVENT
ATOMIC WAR!
APR.
10c
ACE
WHEN THIS NEW GUIDED MISSILE HITS THE KREMLIN, THOSE RUSSKIES WILL REALLY HAVE A HOT TIME!
NEW YEAR GREETINGS-1961

This book is designed to shock America into vigilance---and to help keep the horrors of atomic war from our shores. It CAN happen here, unless friend and foe alike can be made to realize the awful devastation that another war will bring to all. So as you read these pages, pray that what you see here will never happen. And it won't---if we keep America strong!

ARCTIC ASSAULT

WHEN THE FIRST ATOMIC BOMBS FELL UPON AMERICAN CITIES EARLY IN 1960, RETALIATION AGAINST THE COMMUNIST AGGRESSORS WAS SWIFT AND TERRIBLE. BUT A-BOMBS ALONE COULD NOT DECIDE THIS TITANIC CONFLICT BETWEEN EAST AND WEST---AND SO NOW BOTH SIDES ARE ENGAGED IN A LONG-RANGE, GLOBAL SLUGGING MATCH, WITH NO PLACE TO HIDE . . . ON ONE OF THESE MANY SCATTERED FRONTS . . .

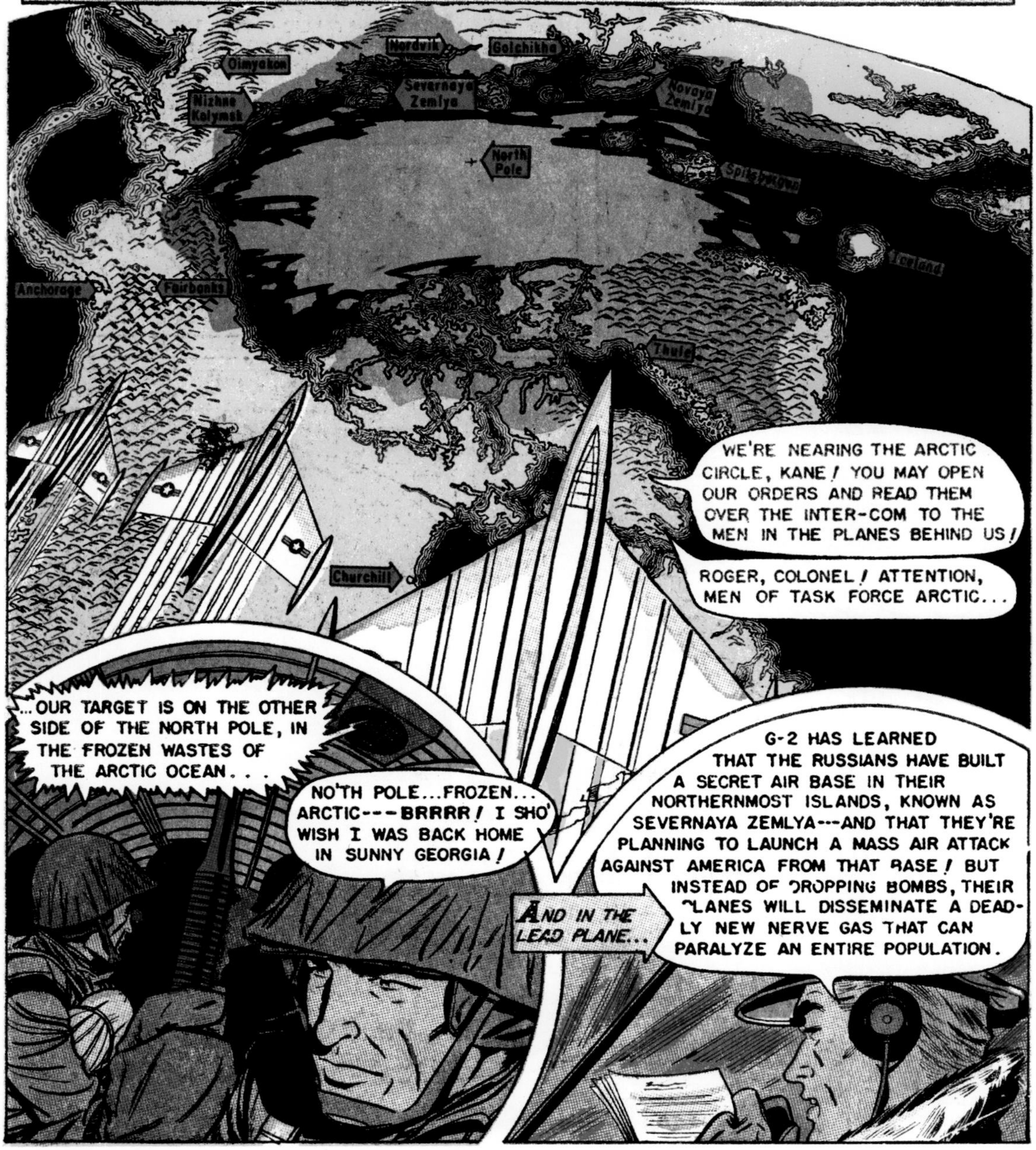

Nordvik
Golchikha
Oimyakon
Severnaya Zemlya
Nizhne Kolymsk
Novaya Zemlya
North Pole
Anchorage
Fairbanks
Thule
Churchill
WE'RE NEARING THE ARCTIC CIRCLE, KANE! YOU MAY OPEN OUR ORDERS AND READ THEM OVER THE INTER-COM TO THE MEN IN THE PLANES BEHIND US!
ROGER, COLONEL! ATTENTION, MEN OF TASK FORCE ARCTIC...
...OUR TARGET IS ON THE OTHER SIDE OF THE NORTH POLE, IN THE FROZEN WASTES OF THE ARCTIC OCEAN...
NO'TH POLE...FROZEN... ARCTIC---BRRRR! I SHO' WISH I WAS BACK HOME IN SUNNY GEORGIA!
AND IN THE LEAD PLANE...
G-2 HAS LEARNED THAT THE RUSSIANS HAVE BUILT A SECRET AIR BASE IN THEIR NORTHERNMOST ISLANDS, KNOWN AS SEVERNAYA ZEMLYA---AND THAT THEY'RE PLANNING TO LAUNCH A MASS AIR ATTACK AGAINST AMERICA FROM THAT BASE! BUT INSTEAD OF DROPPING BOMBS, THEIR PLANES WILL DISSEMINATE A DEADLY NEW NERVE GAS THAT CAN PARALYZE AN ENTIRE POPULATION.

AS YOU ALL KNOW, THE SHORTEST AIR DISTANCE BETWEEN AMERICA AND RUSSIA IS OVER THE NORTH POLE! THAT'S THE ROUTE THEY'RE PLANNING TO TAKE -- AND THAT'S THE ROUTE WE'RE TAKING NOW! WE'RE GOING TO DESTROY THAT RED AIR BASE -- OR DIE TRYING!

I KNOW HOW I'M GONNA DIE -- OF THE COLD! GEORGIA WAS NEVER LIKE THIS!

CHEER UP, GEORGIA! AS SOON AS WE FLY OVER THE NORTH POLE, WE'LL BE HEADING SOUTH!

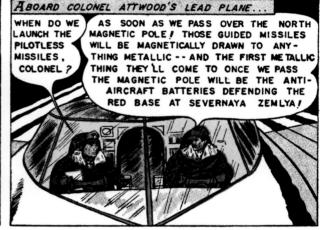

ABOARD COLONEL ATTWOOD'S LEAD PLANE...

WHEN DO WE LAUNCH THE PILOTLESS MISSILES, COLONEL?

AS SOON AS WE PASS OVER THE NORTH MAGNETIC POLE! THOSE GUIDED MISSILES WILL BE MAGNETICALLY DRAWN TO ANY- THING METALLIC -- AND THE FIRST METALLIC THING THEY'LL COME TO ONCE WE PASS THE MAGNETIC POLE WILL BE THE ANTI- AIRCRAFT BATTERIES DEFENDING THE RED BASE AT SEVERNAYA ZEMLYA!

BEYOND THE MAGNETIC POLE, MISSILE-LAUNCHING STUDS ARE PRESSED -- AND JET-PROPELLED PILOT- LESS CRAFT TAKE OFF FROM THE WINGS OF THEIR MOTHER PLANES!

ZOOM!

WHOOSH!

HIGH ABOVE THE FRIGID POLAR WASTES, THE MISSILES HURTLE ONWARD AT SUPER- SONIC SPEEDS!

SOON, AT THE RED BASE IN SEVERNAYA ZEMLYA...

CAPTAIN -- UNIDENTIFIED OBJECTS ARE COMING OUR WAY FROM THE NORTH AT 65,000 FEET!

IT MUST BE AN AMERICAN ATTACK! ORDER THE CAMOUFLAGE SHROUDS TAKEN OFF THE ANTI- AIRCRAFT GUNS!

2

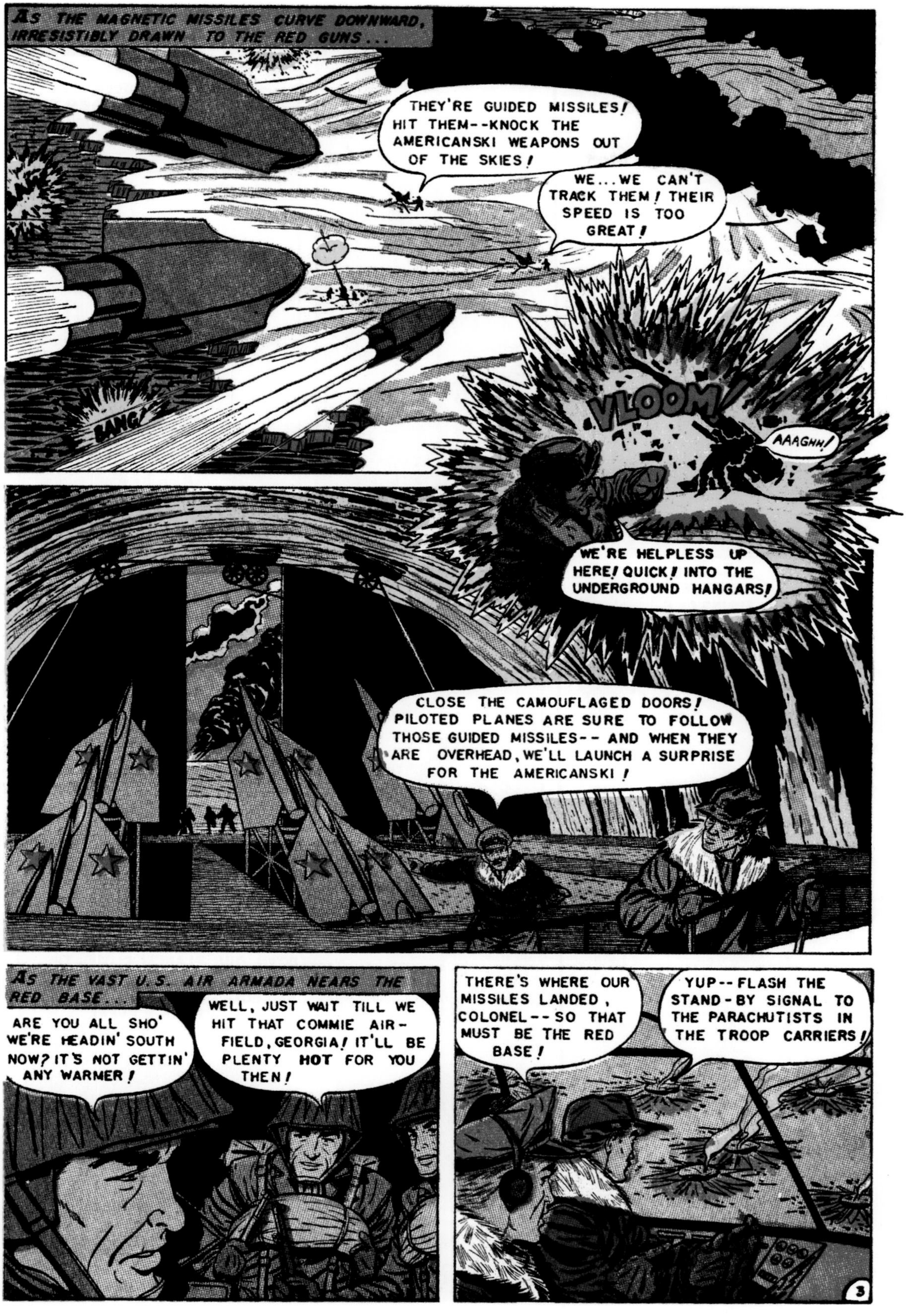
AS THE MAGNETIC MISSILES CURVE DOWNWARD, IRRESISTIBLY DRAWN TO THE RED GUNS...
THEY'RE GUIDED MISSILES! HIT THEM--KNOCK THE AMERICANSKI WEAPONS OUT OF THE SKIES!
WE...WE CAN'T TRACK THEM! THEIR SPEED IS TOO GREAT!
BANG!
VLOOM!
AAAGHH!
WE'RE HELPLESS UP HERE! QUICK! INTO THE UNDERGROUND HANGARS!
CLOSE THE CAMOUFLAGED DOORS! PILOTED PLANES ARE SURE TO FOLLOW THOSE GUIDED MISSILES-- AND WHEN THEY ARE OVERHEAD, WE'LL LAUNCH A SURPRISE FOR THE AMERICANSKI!
AS THE VAST U.S. AIR ARMADA NEARS THE RED BASE...
ARE YOU ALL SHO' WE'RE HEADIN' SOUTH NOW? IT'S NOT GETTIN' ANY WARMER!
WELL, JUST WAIT TILL WE HIT THAT COMMIE AIR-FIELD, GEORGIA! IT'LL BE PLENTY HOT FOR YOU THEN!
THERE'S WHERE OUR MISSILES LANDED, COLONEL--SO THAT MUST BE THE RED BASE!
YUP--FLASH THE STAND-BY SIGNAL TO THE PARACHUTISTS IN THE TROOP CARRIERS!
3

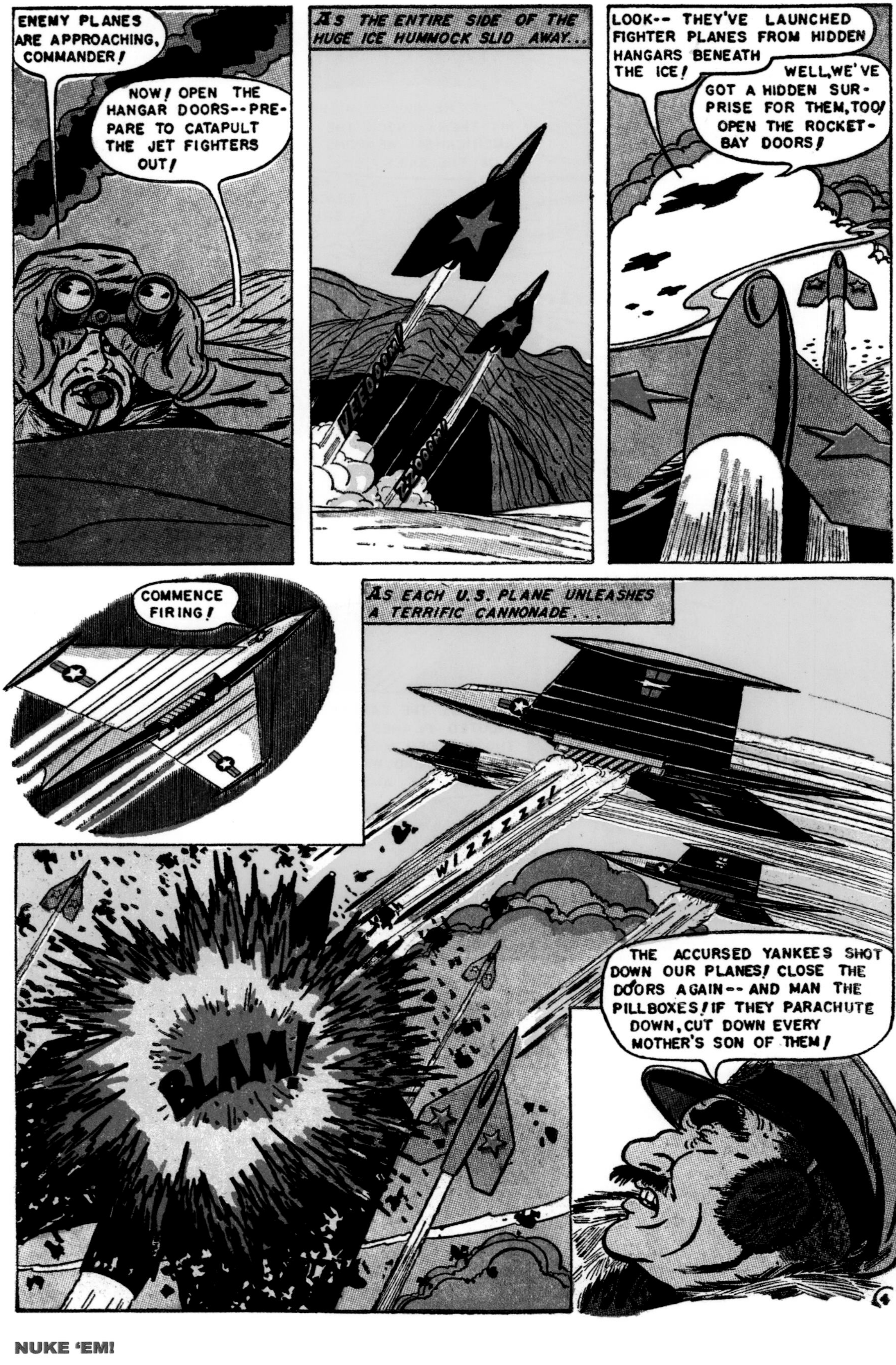
ENEMY PLANES ARE APPROACHING, COMMANDER!
NOW! OPEN THE HANGAR DOORS--PREPARE TO CATAPULT THE JET FIGHTERS OUT!
AS THE ENTIRE SIDE OF THE HUGE ICE HUMMOCK SLID AWAY...
LOOK-- THEY'VE LAUNCHED FIGHTER PLANES FROM HIDDEN HANGARS BENEATH THE ICE!
WELL, WE'VE GOT A HIDDEN SURPRISE FOR THEM, TOO! OPEN THE ROCKET-BAY DOORS!
COMMENCE FIRING!
AS EACH U.S. PLANE UNLEASHES A TERRIFIC CANNONADE...
BLAM!
THE ACCURSED YANKEES SHOT DOWN OUR PLANES! CLOSE THE DOORS AGAIN-- AND MAN THE PILLBOXES! IF THEY PARACHUTE DOWN, CUT DOWN EVERY MOTHER'S SON OF THEM!
4

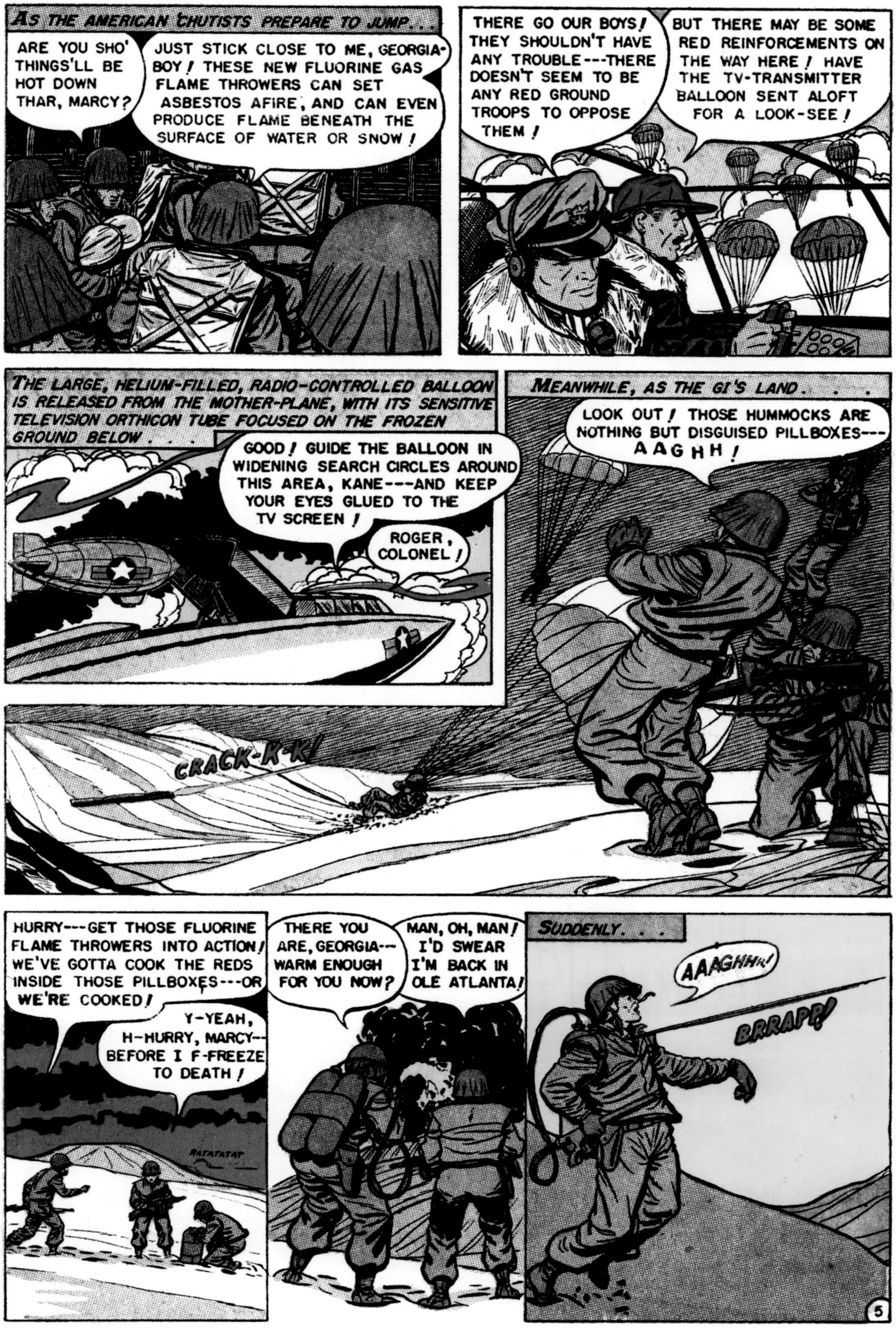

AS THE AMERICAN 'CHUTISTS PREPARE TO JUMP . . .
ARE YOU SHO' THINGS'LL BE HOT DOWN THAR, MARCY?
JUST STICK CLOSE TO ME, GEORGIA-BOY! THESE NEW FLUORINE GAS FLAME THROWERS CAN SET ASBESTOS AFIRE, AND CAN EVEN PRODUCE FLAME BENEATH THE SURFACE OF WATER OR SNOW!
THERE GO OUR BOYS! THEY SHOULDN'T HAVE ANY TROUBLE---THERE DOESN'T SEEM TO BE ANY RED GROUND TROOPS TO OPPOSE THEM!
BUT THERE MAY BE SOME RED REINFORCEMENTS ON THE WAY HERE! HAVE THE TV-TRANSMITTER BALLOON SENT ALOFT FOR A LOOK-SEE!
THE LARGE, HELIUM-FILLED, RADIO-CONTROLLED BALLOON IS RELEASED FROM THE MOTHER-PLANE, WITH ITS SENSITIVE TELEVISION ORTHICON TUBE FOCUSED ON THE FROZEN GROUND BELOW . . .
GOOD! GUIDE THE BALLOON IN WIDENING SEARCH CIRCLES AROUND THIS AREA, KANE---AND KEEP YOUR EYES GLUED TO THE TV SCREEN!
ROGER, COLONEL!
MEANWHILE, AS THE GI'S LAND . . .
LOOK OUT! THOSE HUMMOCKS ARE NOTHING BUT DISGUISED PILLBOXES--- AAGHH!
CRACK-K-K!
HURRY---GET THOSE FLUORINE FLAME THROWERS INTO ACTION! WE'VE GOTTA COOK THE REDS INSIDE THOSE PILLBOXES---OR WE'RE COOKED!
Y-YEAH, H-HURRY, MARCY-- BEFORE I F-FREEZE TO DEATH!
RATATATAT
THERE YOU ARE, GEORGIA-- WARM ENOUGH FOR YOU NOW?
MAN, OH, MAN! I'D SWEAR I'M BACK IN OLE ATLANTA!
SUDDENLY . . .
AAAGHHH!
BRRAPP!
5

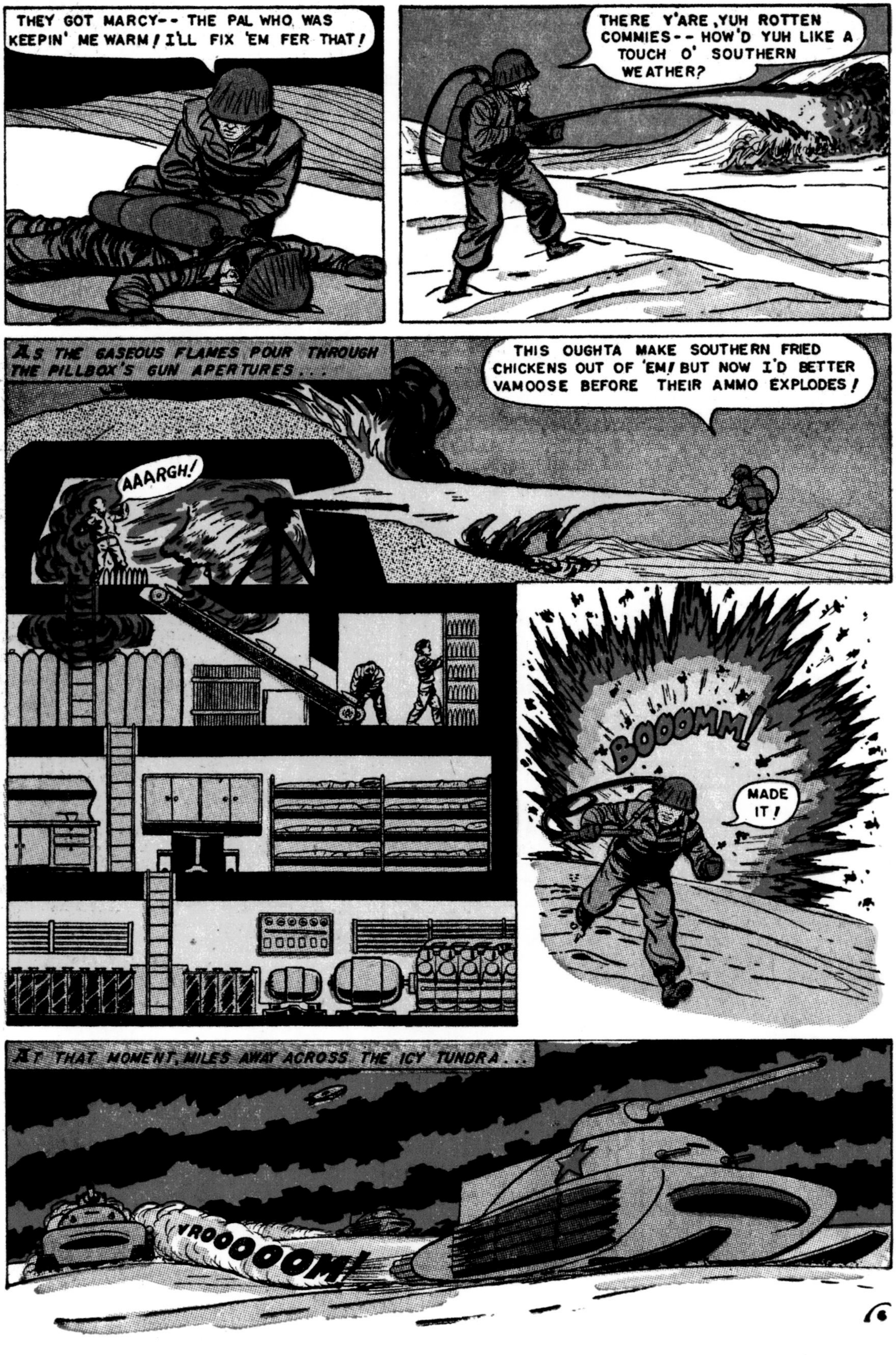

THEY GOT MARCY-- THE PAL WHO WAS KEEPIN' ME WARM! I'LL FIX 'EM FER THAT!
THERE Y'ARE, YUH ROTTEN COMMIES-- HOW'D YUH LIKE A TOUCH O' SOUTHERN WEATHER?
AS THE GASEOUS FLAMES POUR THROUGH THE PILLBOX'S GUN APERTURES...
THIS OUGHTA MAKE SOUTHERN FRIED CHICKENS OUT OF 'EM! BUT NOW I'D BETTER VAMOOSE BEFORE THEIR AMMO EXPLODES!
AAARGH!
BOOOMM!
MADE IT!
AT THAT MOMENT, MILES AWAY ACROSS THE ICY TUNDRA...
VROOOOOOM!

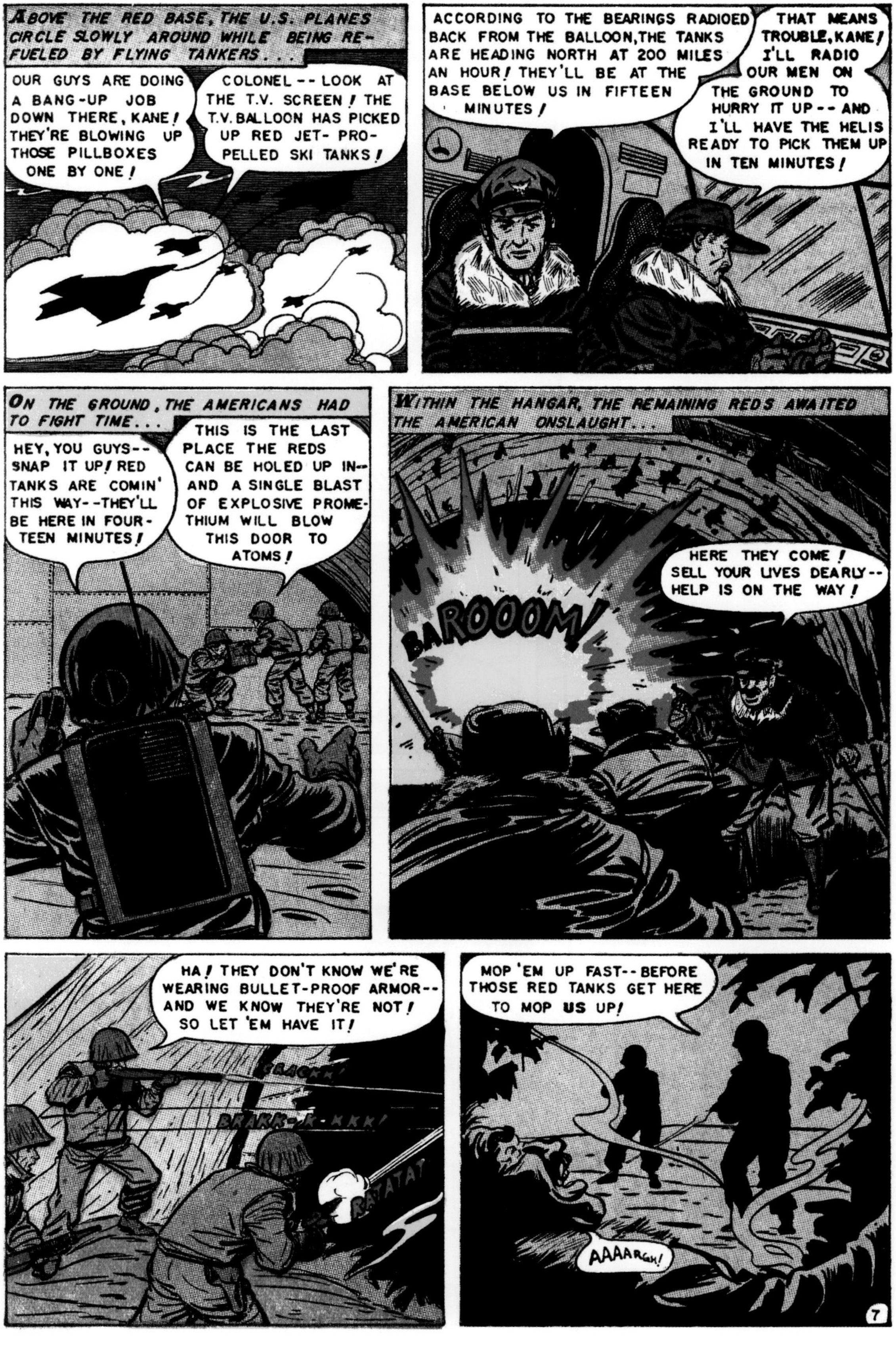
ABOVE THE RED BASE, THE U.S. PLANES CIRCLE SLOWLY AROUND WHILE BEING RE-FUELED BY FLYING TANKERS...
OUR GUYS ARE DOING A BANG-UP JOB DOWN THERE, KANE! THEY'RE BLOWING UP THOSE PILLBOXES ONE BY ONE!
COLONEL -- LOOK AT THE T.V. SCREEN! THE T.V. BALLOON HAS PICKED UP RED JET-PRO-PELLED SKI TANKS!
ACCORDING TO THE BEARINGS RADIOED BACK FROM THE BALLOON, THE TANKS ARE HEADING NORTH AT 200 MILES AN HOUR! THEY'LL BE AT THE BASE BELOW US IN FIFTEEN MINUTES!
THAT MEANS TROUBLE, KANE! I'LL RADIO OUR MEN ON THE GROUND TO HURRY IT UP -- AND I'LL HAVE THE HELIS READY TO PICK THEM UP IN TEN MINUTES!
ON THE GROUND, THE AMERICANS HAD TO FIGHT TIME...
HEY, YOU GUYS-- SNAP IT UP! RED TANKS ARE COMIN' THIS WAY--THEY'LL BE HERE IN FOUR-TEEN MINUTES!
THIS IS THE LAST PLACE THE REDS CAN BE HOLED UP IN-- AND A SINGLE BLAST OF EXPLOSIVE PROME-THIUM WILL BLOW THIS DOOR TO ATOMS!
WITHIN THE HANGAR, THE REMAINING REDS AWAITED THE AMERICAN ONSLAUGHT...
BAROOOM!
HERE THEY COME! SELL YOUR LIVES DEARLY-- HELP IS ON THE WAY!
HA! THEY DON'T KNOW WE'RE WEARING BULLET-PROOF ARMOR-- AND WE KNOW THEY'RE NOT! SO LET 'EM HAVE IT!
BRAKK-K-KKK!
RATATAT
MOP 'EM UP FAST--BEFORE THOSE RED TANKS GET HERE TO MOP US UP!
AAAARGH!
7

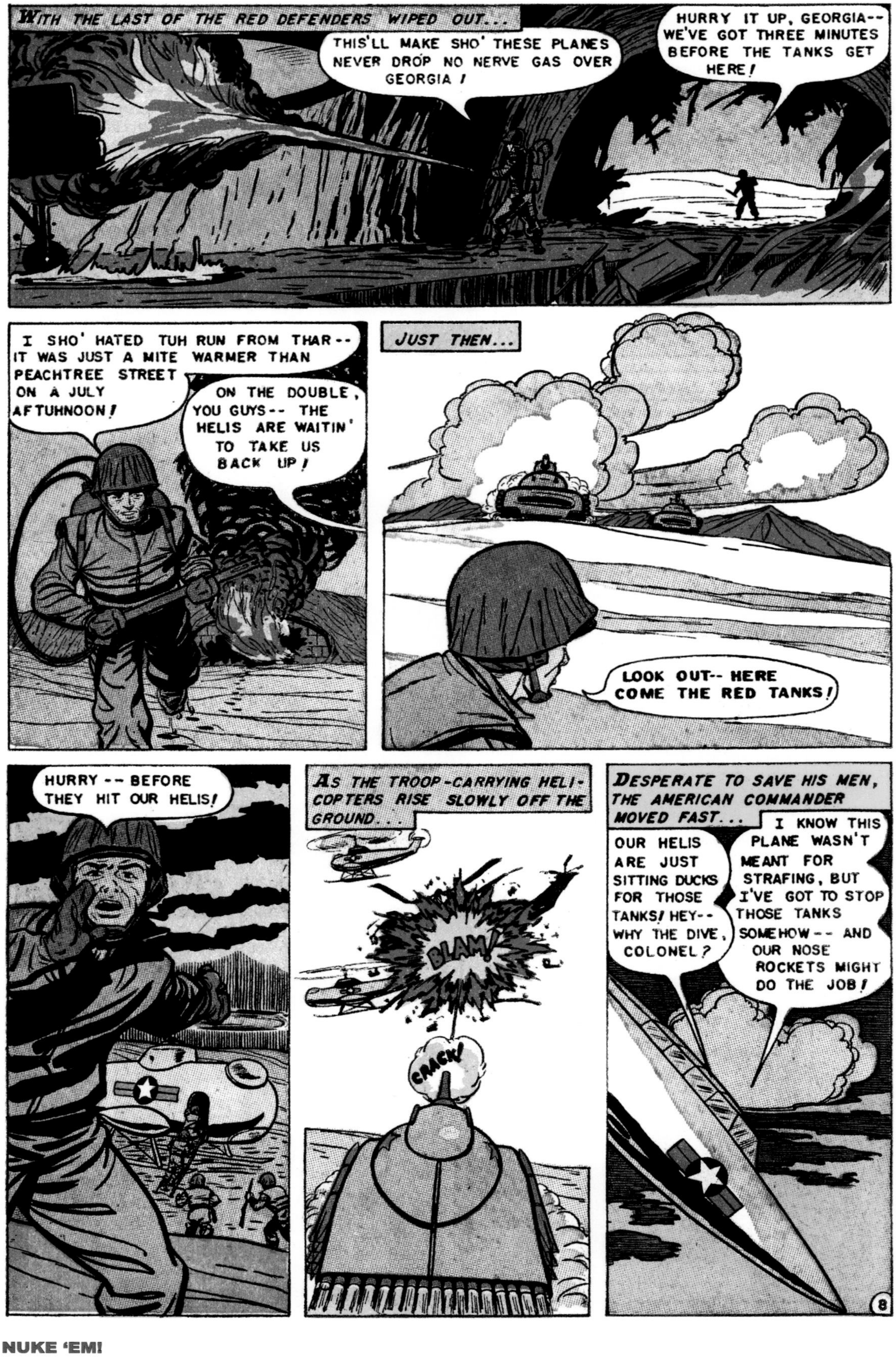
WITH THE LAST OF THE RED DEFENDERS WIPED OUT...
THIS'LL MAKE SHO' THESE PLANES NEVER DROP NO NERVE GAS OVER GEORGIA!
HURRY IT UP, GEORGIA-- WE'VE GOT THREE MINUTES BEFORE THE TANKS GET HERE!
I SHO' HATED TUH RUN FROM THAR-- IT WAS JUST A MITE WARMER THAN PEACHTREE STREET ON A JULY AFTUHNOON!
ON THE DOUBLE, YOU GUYS-- THE HELIS ARE WAITIN' TO TAKE US BACK UP!
JUST THEN...
LOOK OUT-- HERE COME THE RED TANKS!
HURRY -- BEFORE THEY HIT OUR HELIS!
AS THE TROOP-CARRYING HELICOPTERS RISE SLOWLY OFF THE GROUND...
BLAM!
CRACK!
DESPERATE TO SAVE HIS MEN, THE AMERICAN COMMANDER MOVED FAST...
OUR HELIS ARE JUST SITTING DUCKS FOR THOSE TANKS! HEY-- WHY THE DIVE, COLONEL?
I KNOW THIS PLANE WASN'T MEANT FOR STRAFING, BUT I'VE GOT TO STOP THOSE TANKS SOMEHOW-- AND OUR NOSE ROCKETS MIGHT DO THE JOB!
8

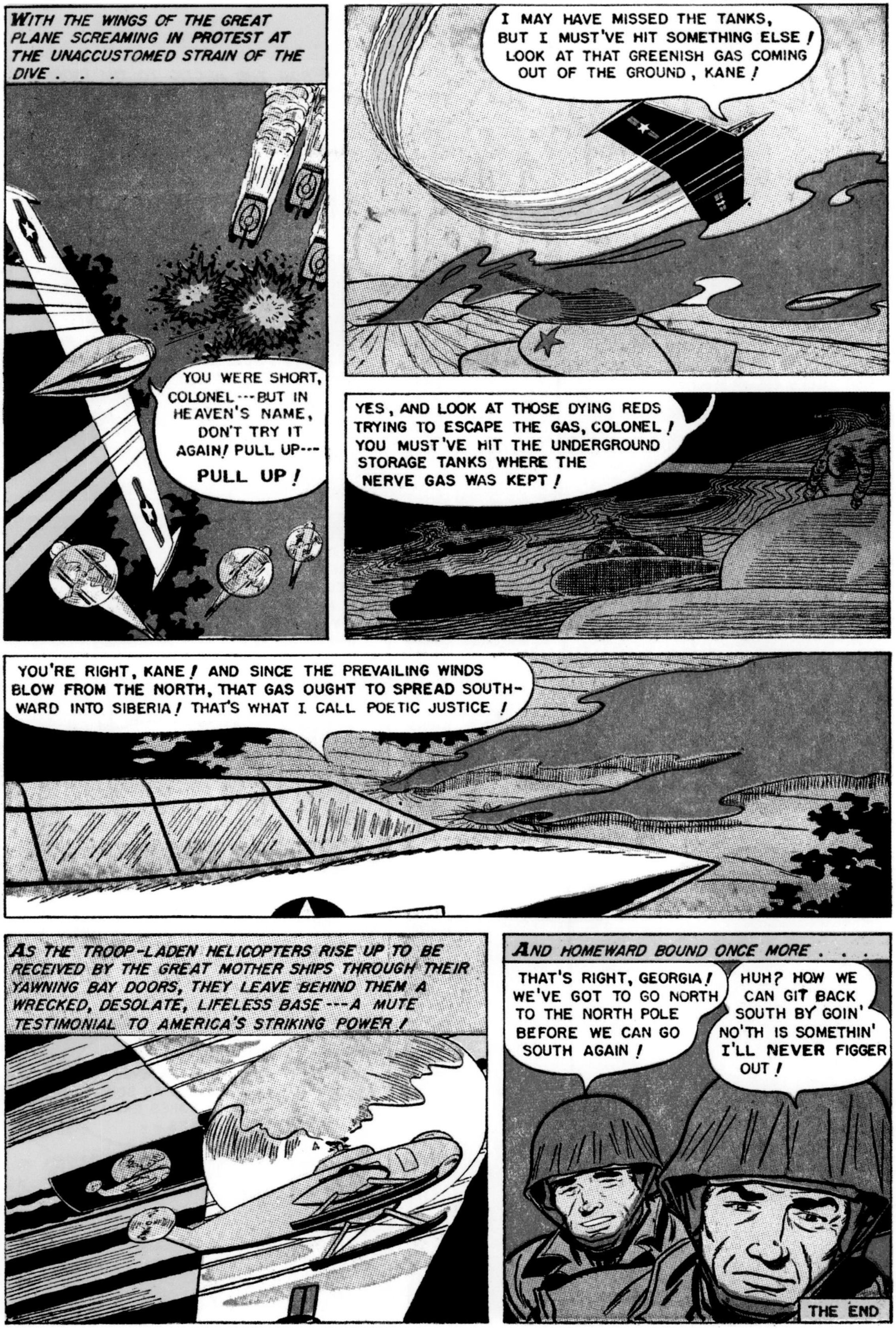
WITH THE WINGS OF THE GREAT PLANE SCREAMING IN PROTEST AT THE UNACCUSTOMED STRAIN OF THE DIVE . . .
YOU WERE SHORT, COLONEL---BUT IN HEAVEN'S NAME, DON'T TRY IT AGAIN! PULL UP--- PULL UP!
I MAY HAVE MISSED THE TANKS, BUT I MUST'VE HIT SOMETHING ELSE! LOOK AT THAT GREENISH GAS COMING OUT OF THE GROUND, KANE!
YES, AND LOOK AT THOSE DYING REDS TRYING TO ESCAPE THE GAS, COLONEL! YOU MUST'VE HIT THE UNDERGROUND STORAGE TANKS WHERE THE NERVE GAS WAS KEPT!
YOU'RE RIGHT, KANE! AND SINCE THE PREVAILING WINDS BLOW FROM THE NORTH, THAT GAS OUGHT TO SPREAD SOUTHWARD INTO SIBERIA! THAT'S WHAT I CALL POETIC JUSTICE!
AS THE TROOP-LADEN HELICOPTERS RISE UP TO BE RECEIVED BY THE GREAT MOTHER SHIPS THROUGH THEIR YAWNING BAY DOORS, THEY LEAVE BEHIND THEM A WRECKED, DESOLATE, LIFELESS BASE---A MUTE TESTIMONIAL TO AMERICA'S STRIKING POWER!
AND HOMEWARD BOUND ONCE MORE . . .
THAT'S RIGHT, GEORGIA! WE'VE GOT TO GO NORTH TO THE NORTH POLE BEFORE WE CAN GO SOUTH AGAIN!
HUH? HOW WE CAN GIT BACK SOUTH BY GOIN' NO'TH IS SOMETHIN' I'LL NEVER FIGGER OUT!
THE END

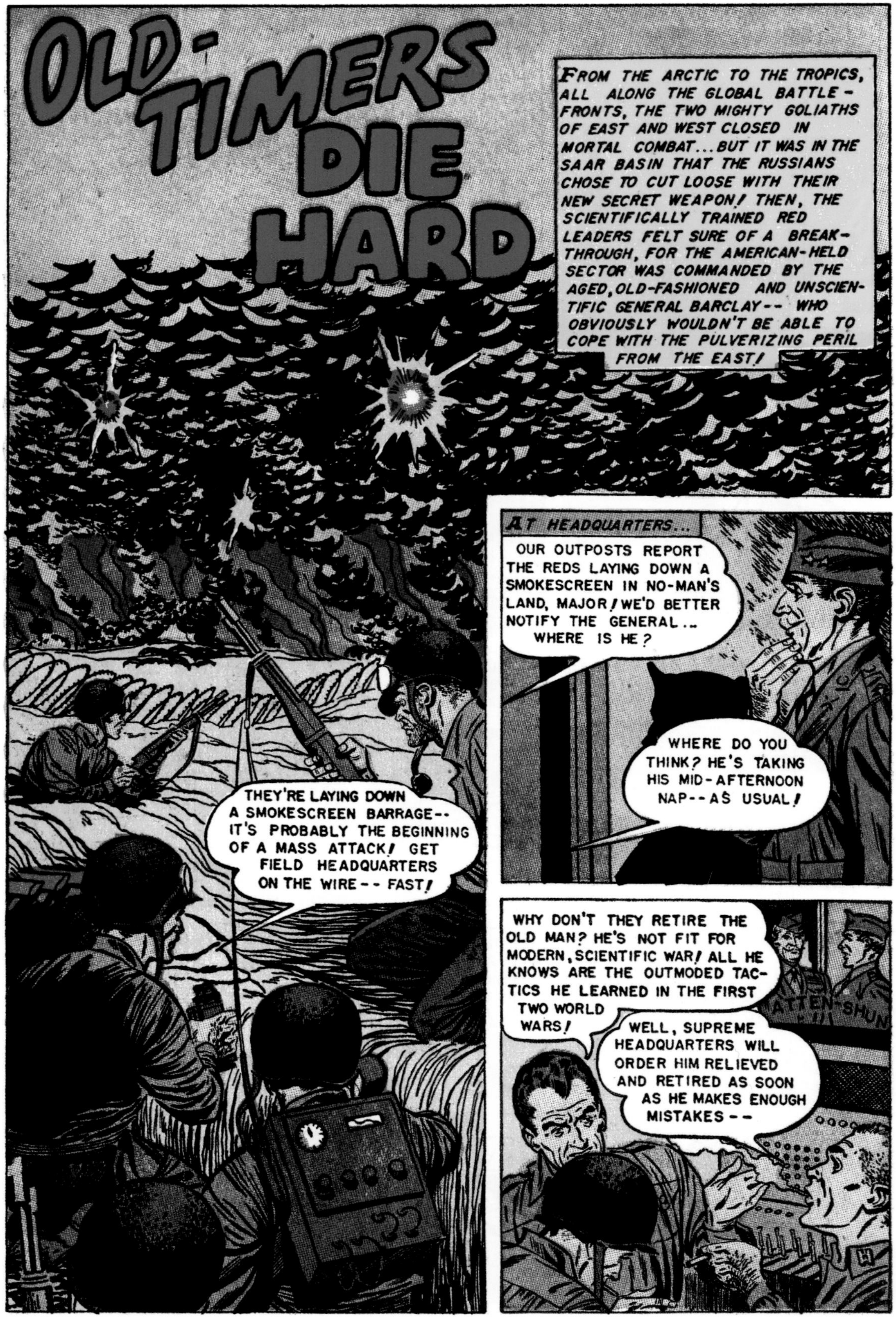
OLD-TIMERS DIE HARD
FROM THE ARCTIC TO THE TROPICS, ALL ALONG THE GLOBAL BATTLE-FRONTS, THE TWO MIGHTY GOLIATHS OF EAST AND WEST CLOSED IN MORTAL COMBAT... BUT IT WAS IN THE SAAR BASIN THAT THE RUSSIANS CHOSE TO CUT LOOSE WITH THEIR NEW SECRET WEAPON! THEN, THE SCIENTIFICALLY TRAINED RED LEADERS FELT SURE OF A BREAK-THROUGH, FOR THE AMERICAN-HELD SECTOR WAS COMMANDED BY THE AGED, OLD-FASHIONED AND UNSCIENTIFIC GENERAL BARCLAY -- WHO OBVIOUSLY WOULDN'T BE ABLE TO COPE WITH THE PULVERIZING PERIL FROM THE EAST!
THEY'RE LAYING DOWN A SMOKESCREEN BARRAGE-- IT'S PROBABLY THE BEGINNING OF A MASS ATTACK! GET FIELD HEADQUARTERS ON THE WIRE -- FAST!
AT HEADQUARTERS...
OUR OUTPOSTS REPORT THE REDS LAYING DOWN A SMOKESCREEN IN NO-MAN'S LAND, MAJOR! WE'D BETTER NOTIFY THE GENERAL.. WHERE IS HE?
WHERE DO YOU THINK? HE'S TAKING HIS MID-AFTERNOON NAP -- AS USUAL!
WHY DON'T THEY RETIRE THE OLD MAN? HE'S NOT FIT FOR MODERN, SCIENTIFIC WAR! ALL HE KNOWS ARE THE OUTMODED TACTICS HE LEARNED IN THE FIRST TWO WORLD WARS!
ATTEN-SHUN
WELL, SUPREME HEADQUARTERS WILL ORDER HIM RELIEVED AND RETIRED AS SOON AS HE MAKES ENOUGH MISTAKES --

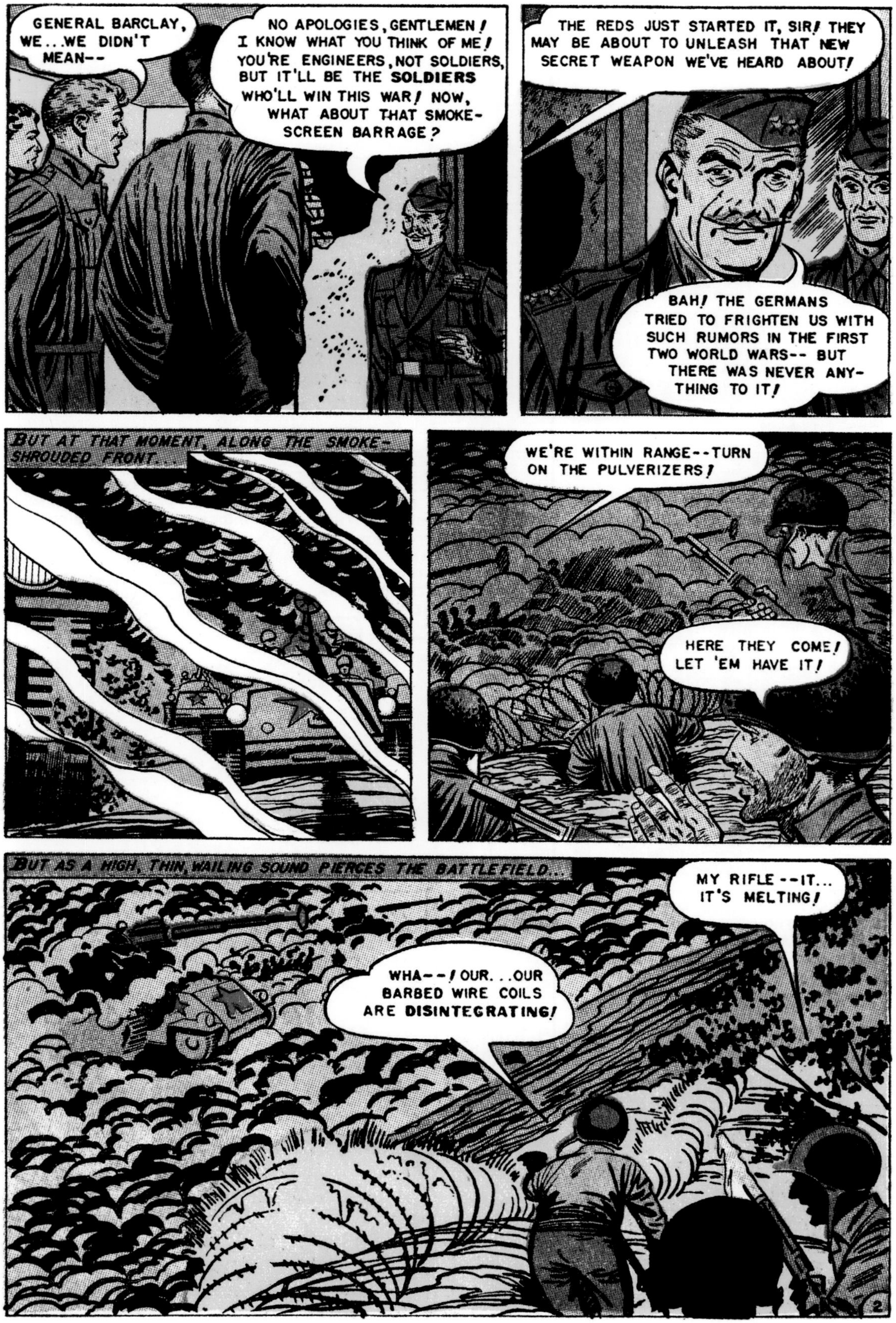
GENERAL BARCLAY, WE... WE DIDN'T MEAN--
NO APOLOGIES, GENTLEMEN! I KNOW WHAT YOU THINK OF ME! YOU'RE ENGINEERS, NOT SOLDIERS, BUT IT'LL BE THE SOLDIERS WHO'LL WIN THIS WAR! NOW, WHAT ABOUT THAT SMOKE-SCREEN BARRAGE?
THE REDS JUST STARTED IT, SIR! THEY MAY BE ABOUT TO UNLEASH THAT NEW SECRET WEAPON WE'VE HEARD ABOUT!
BAH! THE GERMANS TRIED TO FRIGHTEN US WITH SUCH RUMORS IN THE FIRST TWO WORLD WARS-- BUT THERE WAS NEVER ANY-THING TO IT!
BUT AT THAT MOMENT, ALONG THE SMOKE-SHROUDED FRONT...
WE'RE WITHIN RANGE--TURN ON THE PULVERIZERS!
HERE THEY COME! LET 'EM HAVE IT!
BUT AS A HIGH, THIN, WAILING SOUND PIERCES THE BATTLEFIELD...
MY RIFLE--IT... IT'S MELTING!
WHA--! OUR... OUR BARBED WIRE COILS ARE DISINTEGRATING!
2

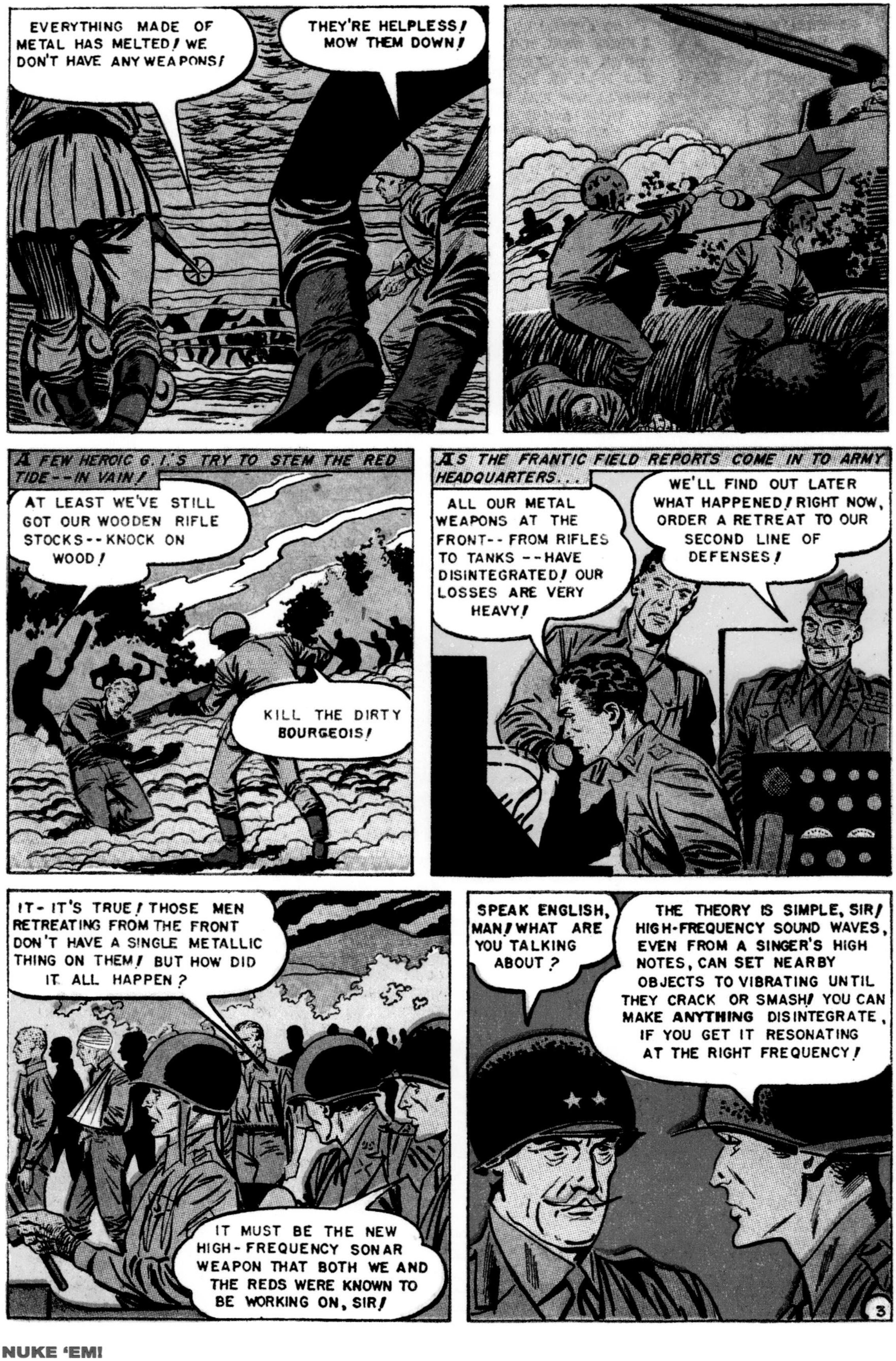
EVERYTHING MADE OF METAL HAS MELTED! WE DON'T HAVE ANY WEAPONS!
THEY'RE HELPLESS! MOW THEM DOWN!
A FEW HEROIC G.I.'S TRY TO STEM THE RED TIDE--IN VAIN!
AT LEAST WE'VE STILL GOT OUR WOODEN RIFLE STOCKS--KNOCK ON WOOD!
KILL THE DIRTY BOURGEOIS!
AS THE FRANTIC FIELD REPORTS COME IN TO ARMY HEADQUARTERS...
ALL OUR METAL WEAPONS AT THE FRONT--FROM RIFLES TO TANKS--HAVE DISINTEGRATED! OUR LOSSES ARE VERY HEAVY!
WE'LL FIND OUT LATER WHAT HAPPENED! RIGHT NOW, ORDER A RETREAT TO OUR SECOND LINE OF DEFENSES!
IT-IT'S TRUE! THOSE MEN RETREATING FROM THE FRONT DON'T HAVE A SINGLE METALLIC THING ON THEM! BUT HOW DID IT ALL HAPPEN?
IT MUST BE THE NEW HIGH-FREQUENCY SONAR WEAPON THAT BOTH WE AND THE REDS WERE KNOWN TO BE WORKING ON, SIR!
SPEAK ENGLISH, MAN! WHAT ARE YOU TALKING ABOUT?
THE THEORY IS SIMPLE, SIR! HIGH-FREQUENCY SOUND WAVES, EVEN FROM A SINGER'S HIGH NOTES, CAN SET NEARBY OBJECTS TO VIBRATING UNTIL THEY CRACK OR SMASH! YOU CAN MAKE ANYTHING DISINTEGRATE, IF YOU GET IT RESONATING AT THE RIGHT FREQUENCY!
3

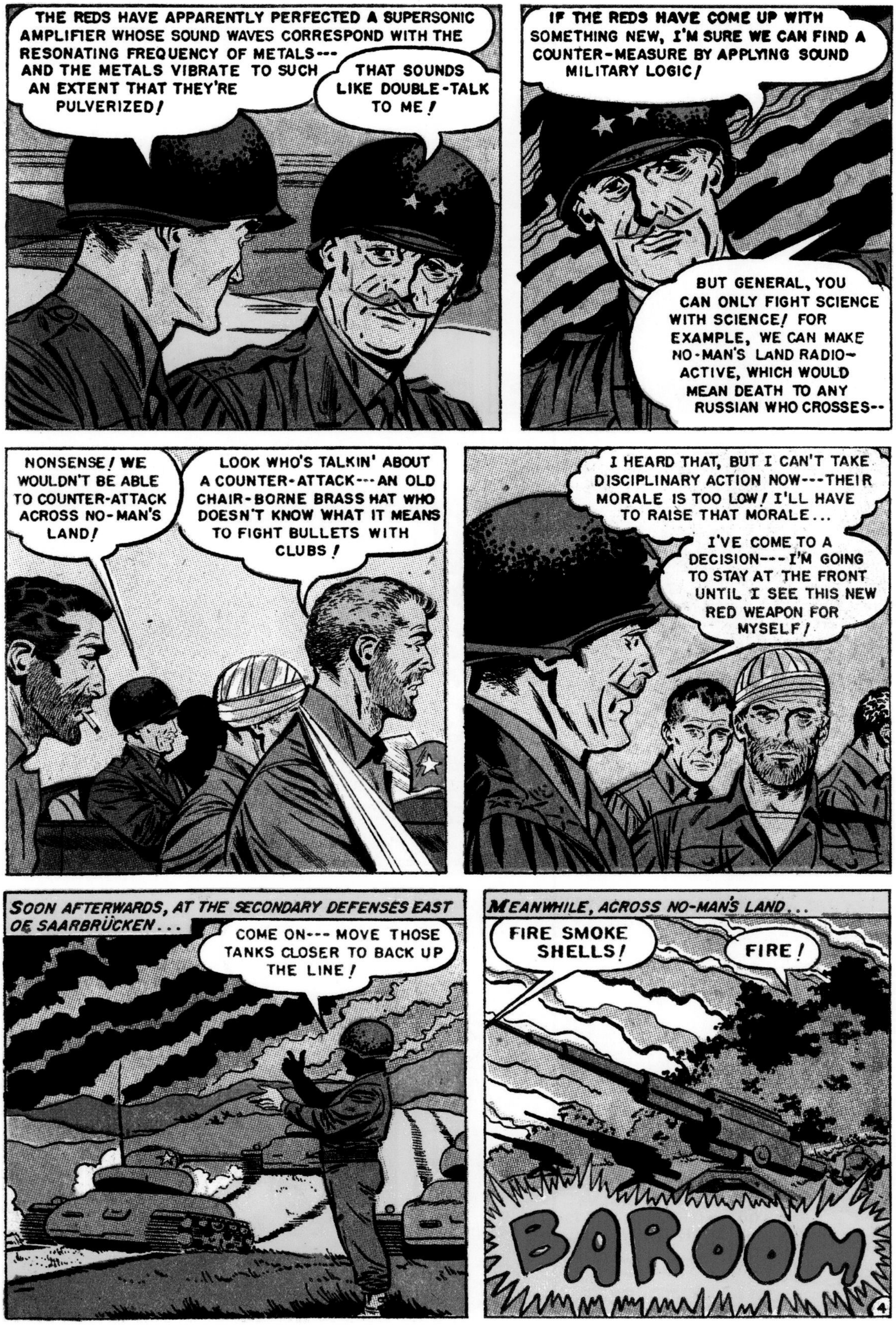
THE REDS HAVE APPARENTLY PERFECTED A SUPERSONIC AMPLIFIER WHOSE SOUND WAVES CORRESPOND WITH THE RESONATING FREQUENCY OF METALS--- AND THE METALS VIBRATE TO SUCH AN EXTENT THAT THEY'RE PULVERIZED!
THAT SOUNDS LIKE DOUBLE-TALK TO ME!
IF THE REDS HAVE COME UP WITH SOMETHING NEW, I'M SURE WE CAN FIND A COUNTER-MEASURE BY APPLYING SOUND MILITARY LOGIC!
BUT GENERAL, YOU CAN ONLY FIGHT SCIENCE WITH SCIENCE! FOR EXAMPLE, WE CAN MAKE NO-MAN'S LAND RADIO-ACTIVE, WHICH WOULD MEAN DEATH TO ANY RUSSIAN WHO CROSSES--
NONSENSE! WE WOULDN'T BE ABLE TO COUNTER-ATTACK ACROSS NO-MAN'S LAND!
LOOK WHO'S TALKIN' ABOUT A COUNTER-ATTACK--- AN OLD CHAIR-BORNE BRASS HAT WHO DOESN'T KNOW WHAT IT MEANS TO FIGHT BULLETS WITH CLUBS!
I HEARD THAT, BUT I CAN'T TAKE DISCIPLINARY ACTION NOW---THEIR MORALE IS TOO LOW! I'LL HAVE TO RAISE THAT MORALE...
I'VE COME TO A DECISION--- I'M GOING TO STAY AT THE FRONT UNTIL I SEE THIS NEW RED WEAPON FOR MYSELF!
SOON AFTERWARDS, AT THE SECONDARY DEFENSES EAST OF SAARBRÜCKEN...
COME ON--- MOVE THOSE TANKS CLOSER TO BACK UP THE LINE!
MEANWHILE, ACROSS NO-MAN'S LAND...
FIRE SMOKE SHELLS!
FIRE!
BAROOM
4

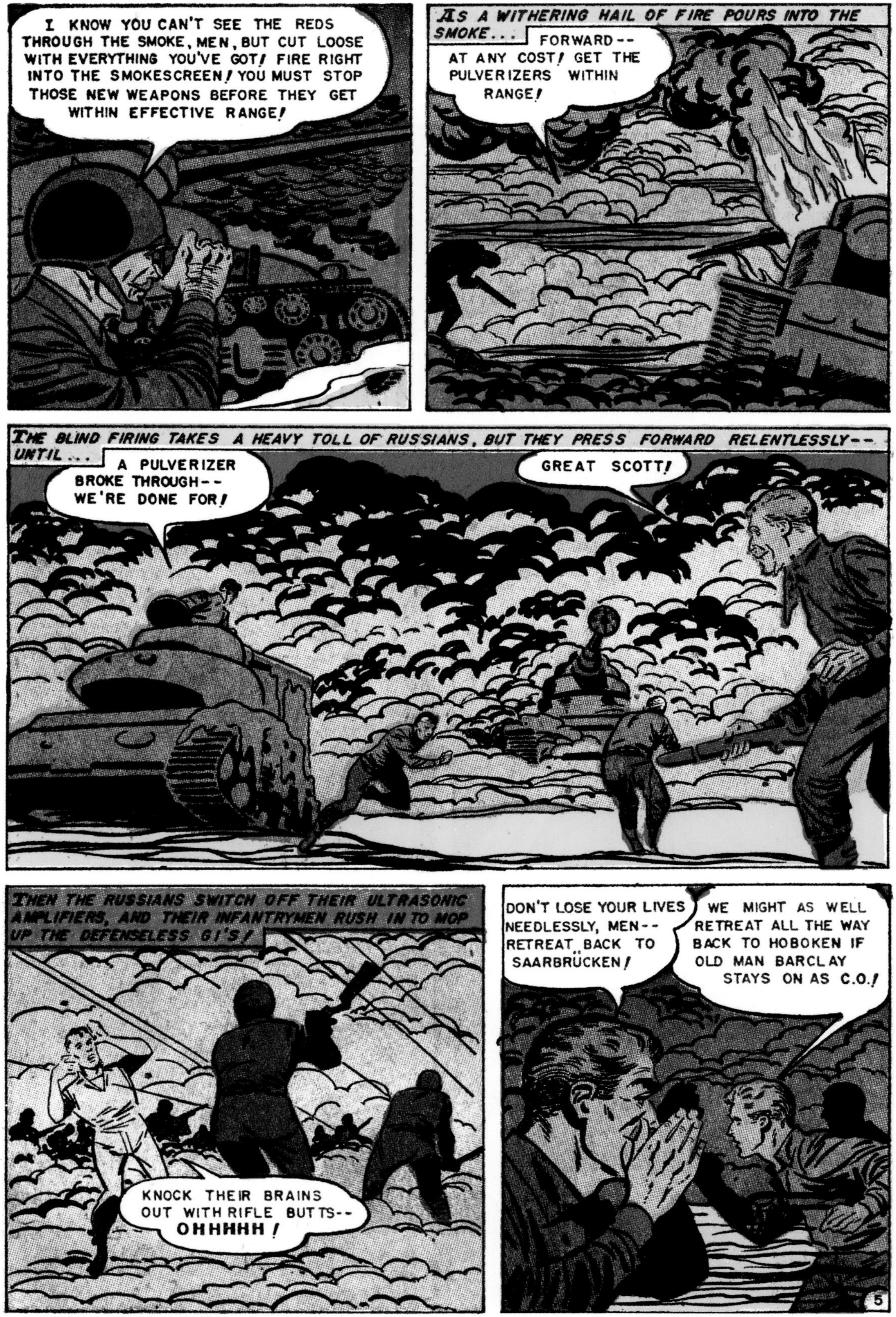
I KNOW YOU CAN'T SEE THE REDS THROUGH THE SMOKE, MEN, BUT CUT LOOSE WITH EVERYTHING YOU'VE GOT! FIRE RIGHT INTO THE SMOKESCREEN! YOU MUST STOP THOSE NEW WEAPONS BEFORE THEY GET WITHIN EFFECTIVE RANGE!
AS A WITHERING HAIL OF FIRE POURS INTO THE SMOKE...
FORWARD-- AT ANY COST! GET THE PULVERIZERS WITHIN RANGE!
THE BLIND FIRING TAKES A HEAVY TOLL OF RUSSIANS, BUT THEY PRESS FORWARD RELENTLESSLY-- UNTIL...
A PULVERIZER BROKE THROUGH-- WE'RE DONE FOR!
GREAT SCOTT!
THEN THE RUSSIANS SWITCH OFF THEIR ULTRASONIC AMPLIFIERS, AND THEIR INFANTRYMEN RUSH IN TO MOP UP THE DEFENSELESS GI'S!
KNOCK THEIR BRAINS OUT WITH RIFLE BUTTS-- OHHHHH!
DON'T LOSE YOUR LIVES NEEDLESSLY, MEN-- RETREAT BACK TO SAARBRÜCKEN!
WE MIGHT AS WELL RETREAT ALL THE WAY BACK TO HOBOKEN IF OLD MAN BARCLAY STAYS ON AS C.O.!
5

ONCE AGAIN THE ROUTED, WEAPONLESS DOUGHFEET PLOD SULLENLY WESTWARD IN DEFEAT...

OUR REAR GUARDS REPORT THAT THE REDS STOPPED AT THE FRINGES OF THEIR SMOKESCREEN AGAIN, GENERAL!

YES, BUT WE'LL HAVE TO FALL BACK TO SAARBRÜCKEN ---WHERE WE'LL REARM OUR TROOPS AND MAKE ANOTHER STAND!

REARM! WHAT GOOD IS THAT—THE WEAPONS WILL JUST BE PULVERIZED AGAIN! WHAT WE NEED IS A NEW GENERAL!

YEAH, SOMEONE YOUNG AND SCIENTIFIC, WHO'LL KNOW HOW TO STOP THOSE PULVERIZERS!

AT THE HASTILY SET-UP HEADQUARTERS IN THE RUINED FACTORY TOWN OF SAARBRÜCKEN...

WOW, SUPREME HEADQUARTERS IS SURE BURNING UP THE ETHER! THEY'RE ORDERING GENERAL BARCLAY TO HOLD THE REDS --- OR THEY'LL PUT A YOUNGER MAN IN CHARGE!

THIS IS IT! THE OLD MAN'S FINISHED!

MAYBE I'VE BEEN ATTACKING THE PROBLEM FROM THE WRONG ANGLE! LET'S SEE, THE REDS ALWAYS START OFF WITH A SMOKESCREEN--- SO IF I CAN GET RID OF THAT SCREEN---! WAIT--- THAT CHIMNEY! I'VE GOT IT!

EXCITEDLY, THE GENERAL CALLS A MEETING OF HIS STAFF...

GENTLEMEN, YOU ALL KNOW THAT BY 1959 ALL FACTORY CHIMNEYS IN EUROPE WERE EQUIPPED WITH PRECIPITRONS---THOSE LARGE MAZES OF ELECTRIFIED COPPER WIRE WHICH PRECIPITATE AND COLLECT THE MILLIONS OF PARTICLES OF CHIMNEY SMOKE...

YES, THAT'S COMMON KNOWLEDGE, SIR--- BUT WHAT ABOUT IT?

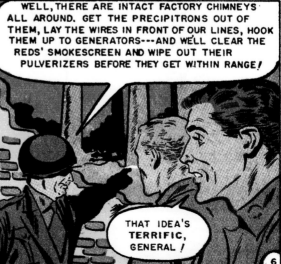

WELL, THERE ARE INTACT FACTORY CHIMNEYS ALL AROUND. GET THE PRECIPITRONS OUT OF THEM, LAY THE WIRES IN FRONT OF OUR LINES, HOOK THEM UP TO GENERATORS---AND WE'LL CLEAR THE REDS' SMOKESCREEN AND WIPE OUT THEIR PULVERIZERS BEFORE THEY GET WITHIN RANGE!

THAT IDEA'S TERRIFIC, GENERAL!

6

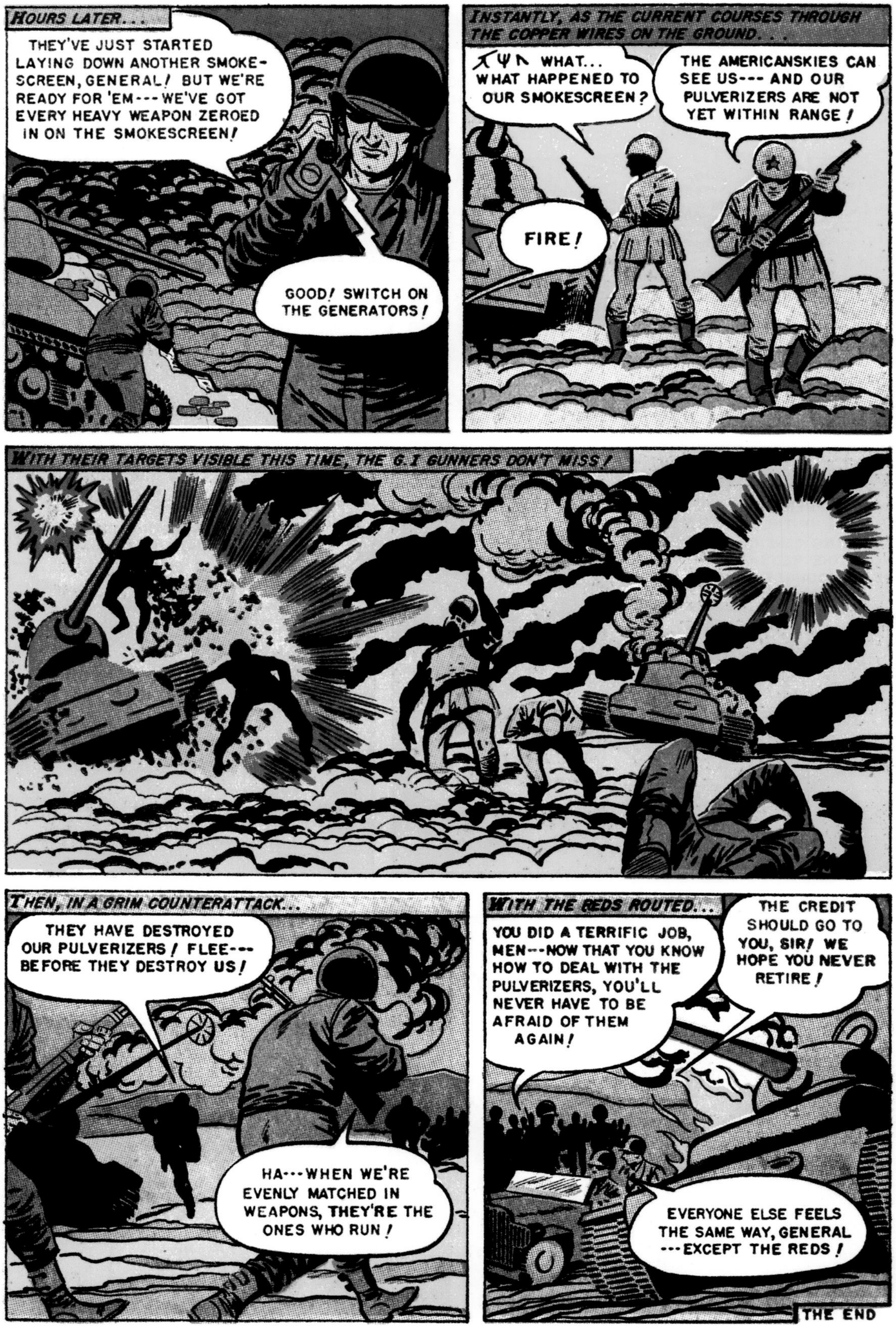
HOURS LATER...
THEY'VE JUST STARTED LAYING DOWN ANOTHER SMOKE-SCREEN, GENERAL! BUT WE'RE READY FOR 'EM---WE'VE GOT EVERY HEAVY WEAPON ZEROED IN ON THE SMOKESCREEN!
GOOD! SWITCH ON THE GENERATORS!
INSTANTLY, AS THE CURRENT COURSES THROUGH THE COPPER WIRES ON THE GROUND...
WHAT... WHAT HAPPENED TO OUR SMOKESCREEN?
THE AMERICANSKIES CAN SEE US--- AND OUR PULVERIZERS ARE NOT YET WITHIN RANGE!
FIRE!
WITH THEIR TARGETS VISIBLE THIS TIME, THE G.I GUNNERS DON'T MISS!
THEN, IN A GRIM COUNTERATTACK...
THEY HAVE DESTROYED OUR PULVERIZERS! FLEE--- BEFORE THEY DESTROY US!
HA---WHEN WE'RE EVENLY MATCHED IN WEAPONS, THEY'RE THE ONES WHO RUN!
WITH THE REDS ROUTED...
YOU DID A TERRIFIC JOB, MEN---NOW THAT YOU KNOW HOW TO DEAL WITH THE PULVERIZERS, YOU'LL NEVER HAVE TO BE AFRAID OF THEM AGAIN!
THE CREDIT SHOULD GO TO YOU, SIR! WE HOPE YOU NEVER RETIRE!
EVERYONE ELSE FEELS THE SAME WAY, GENERAL ---EXCEPT THE REDS!
THE END

WEAPON OF HORROR!

"We know the Americans are building an atomic guided missile weapon that will put all others to shame...and us out of power!" The speaker was a grim, roly-poly figure with a bullet head and pig-like eyes that flashed fire. He was dressed in a gaudy uniform, covered with decorations. His arms were short, his legs stumpy, his belly a barrel. But his importance was second to none in the land, for Dmitri Sorokov was Chief of Red Intelligence. His audience were the wisest, most ruthless operatives in the world. They were a bitter, determined group. They knew what was coming next from Sorokov's lips. — For they had failed in their assignment! Failed utterly and Sorokov *knew* it! They also knew the *penalty* for failure!

"In two years what has my spy apparatus achieved?" Sorokov sneered. He gestured briefly at a large table in one corner of the room. The heads of his listeners turned. They all flinched at the sight of a meaningless jumble of items on the table. "*That*, comrades ....that *mess* you see...is the accumulated evidence you have unearthed in two whole years! But are we any closer to an understanding of this weird inside bomb? I'll give you the answer!!" Witheringly, coldly, with his pig eyes glinting like bayonet steel, his gaze passed contemptuously over the group. "No!" he thundered "NO!! NO!! Nothing have you found! NOTHING! You are like idiots! Babies! TRAITORS! Yes—" Here Sorokov paused dramatically to let the word sink in. "*Traitors*, comrades. Not to discover how this baffling accretion of junk *works*, is *treachery* against the state! And Communists punish treachery as it deserves!" Here Sorokov made his fingers assume the shape of a revolver as he pressed an index finger against his temple. "With a BULLET!" He watched the men in front of him quiver, so realistic was Sorokov's image!

Then he curled his lips in an unearthly snarl. He balled his pudgy fist and shook it in front of their noses. "I want the last pieces which make this weapon comprehensible! I want these pieces in a *week*! *Die* to get them, comrades, because if you return here next week without them, I *myself* shall pull the triggers of the revolvers that will blow your stupid, bungling brains out!! Now *get out*! *Get out* and don't come back empty-handed, I, Sorokov, *warn* you!"

Sorokov dropped into his red leather chair, exhausted. His brass-button eyes followed the whipped, terrified group of men. "Imbeciles!" he shrieked after them. "*Imbeciles!* Don't dare to return without

the secret! Don't dare!" The door shut and he reached for a phone. He barked a number into the receiver. Then his face softened. His eyes smiled. He licked his lips eagerly. His raspy voice became a purr. He wiggled his fat rear in the plush, leathery seat.

"Yes, your excellency! I conveyed to them your explicit commands! Yes—they understand the weapon is to be assembled in a week—or else! What, your Excellency? Of course, Your Excellency! They will not fail! You will see. Next week, this dread American weapon of war will be in our hands! I *myself* will assemble it in this room!"

Outside the Chief's office the small group of agents puffed cigarettes and rubbed their chins unhappily.— All except one man...Rudetski by name. Rudetski was smiling to himself, as if enjoying some secret thought. They noticed Rudetski's unseemly glee and turned on him scoldingly, annoyed in the extreme.

"Shame, Rudetski! Shame! Our lives hang in the balance and you grin like a Cheshire cat! This is *idiocy*!"

Rudetski grinned and shook his head. "On the contrary, Comrades. It is the SAVING of your lives that I smile about!" He chuckled to himself and dug into a crumpled pack of cigarettes. They stared at him bewilderedly as he deliberately lighted a cigarette and puffed a thin curl of smoke heavenwards. "Yes, Comrades. I have the answer. The solution. You shall yet live to receive another decoration from the Highest Himself."

The men gasped. Rudetski grinned again. "*Out* with it, you devil!" they howled at him. "OUT WITH IT!" Rudetski shook off their clawing hands and laughed. "Take your time, pigs! Everything in good time!" he mocked them.

"*Time?!*" they screamed. "There IS no time! We have only till next week! MINUTES are precious! Out with it, Rudetski! OUT WITH IT!"

Rudetski smiled. It was an eloquent smile. A smile with triumph lurking in it. "I know where to get the last two pieces. I also know *how*. It may cost me my life—but what of that? The cause is everything!" Shadows, grim and ferocious darkened the gleam in Rudetski's eyes. "The world is torn by war...a war to the death. A war between Communism and the democracies! Every day a new bomb is dropped. An atomic bomb. A hydrogen bomb. Millions die. But this NEW weapon. It is the answer to *everything!* By merely pushing buttons these new missiles go ANYWHERE in the world, unpiloted, at incredible speed! The Americans have only to make this weapon in quantity and we are doomed! They will blanket our vast territory with a rain of horror! At one stroke —in one rainstorm of death, we shall be brought to our knees! The thought is too horrible to contemplate! Naturally, against these millions of deaths— against our inevitable surrender—my own life is absolutely nothing! Nothing at all!"

Rudetski smiled. "As you know," he continued. "I have been advanced in the American Department of Strategic Weapons! It just occurred to me that I will be permitted to learn all there is to know of this new guided missile! *More* than this—I can get my hands on the missing pieces!"

A gasp of delight shot through his friends. Rudetski smiled a wistful smile. "Yes. Some day, little school children will read about me in their history books. Rudetski—the savior of Communism!

Rudetski's comrades were only *too* eager to agree. Briefly, Rudetski told him where he would rendezvous with them in a few days—at which time, the missing pieces would be delivered to them. "But where will *you* be?" one of them asked curiously.

Rudetski shrugged. "Dead, probably" he answered. "No sooner will the theft be found out than I will be seized. I couldn't sneak the stuff out myself. It will have to be *smuggled* out somehow through some unsuspecting fool or in some mechanical manner."

One of the spies frowned. "That is all very well, Rudetski, but how will *we* know how to assemble the thing? You've GOT to come through *alive*. Without a knowledge of how to put the blasted weapon together, the pieces are useless!"

Rudetski paled slightly, then he recovered. "Y-You're quite right," he muttered. "Somehow I've got to deliver the pieces myself. So be it. I must survive, that's all!" And so the meeting broke up, each spy going his separate way, to his far-flung post in the democratic world! And as they parted they all looked at tight-lipped Rudetski and each murmured some word of pity. The responsibility was all his. The cause lived or died depending on Rudetski's heroism and self-sacrifice.

Four days later, Rudetski parachuted out of the sky from a cargo plane. His comrades strained their eyes!! Sure enough, Rudetski was clutching a bulky package! They squealed with delight! Rudetski had MADE it! He had gotten the missing pieces! America's super-weapon secret was now in the hands of the *Reds!* As Rudetski floated down he saw figures below shouting with joy and dancing like savages gone wild! Rudetski smiled. A long, slow smile.

Three hours later, Rudetski and his comrades walked into Comrade Sorokov's room. Sorokov rose from his leathern seat, his mouth agape . . . his eyes little round buttons of astonishment. "Y-You HAVE it??" he gasped. Rudetski smiled. Sorokov dove for

his battery of telephones. He called number after number, chattering hysterically into the wires. When he had finished, and sunk exhaustedly into his seat, he turned to Rudetski with a grin. "Rudetski, I have called every important political figure in the land, every general, every key scientist! They will be here in a few hours! They all want to share in that historic moment when you put the missing pieces together!"

Rudetski smiled and nodded and went over to the gigantic table. "May I begin to assemble the weapon now?" he asked. "By all means!" shouted Sorokov with a flourish. "Everything but the last piece! I want everybody present at that triumphal second!"

Rudetski smiled and went to work. The others watched him fascinated. Rudetski's fingers flew. He drew equations. He muttered to himself. He frowned. But bit by bit the thing took shape. One by one, the biggest dignitaries in the Red Empire arrived and were seated. Rudetski worked on. Sweat poured from his brow. Finally the room was jammed to the rafters with Communist powers-that-were. All eyes were glued on Rudetski as he held the last piece in his hand. Slowly he turned to his solemn audience. A slow smile broke over his face.

"The last piece, comrades. The last step in the conquest of Communism!" Sorokov frowned deeply. "The conquest of *Democracy!*" he snapped. "No," replied Rudetski with his slow, bright smile. "The conquest of *Communism!*" he repeated. "The Americans have tricked you, Sorokov, with my help," he went on. "There is no such weapon as has been described to you by me! You have wasted two years cracking a secret that wasn't even *there!*" He grinned as he fastened the last piece quickly in its place. "This, gentlemen, is a HYDROGEN BOMB! It was all my idea! The quickest way to end this war was to knock out the top Communist brains at one stroke —by gathering them together in one place to be killed!"

A horrified gasp broke from the lips of the assemblage. But shock froze them to their seats! A sweet smile spread across Rudetski's lips as he gave the last piece a final twist. "By the way," he said— "my real name is not Rudetski—but ROBERTS— Captain Roberts of the *American Espionage Service!* I thought you'd like to know why I'm smiling!"

A shriek burst from the lips of everybody in the room. But it was too late. A green glow shot from the machine. A white seering light burst forth—a light as bright as a thousand suns. Everything disappeared. The highest echelon of the Russian Bureaucracy was destroyed. The buildings. One mighty flash.

"Comrade Rudetski" was smiling when he was swept into nothingness. And he had *cause* to smile. The Red tyranny had been stopped for a little while.

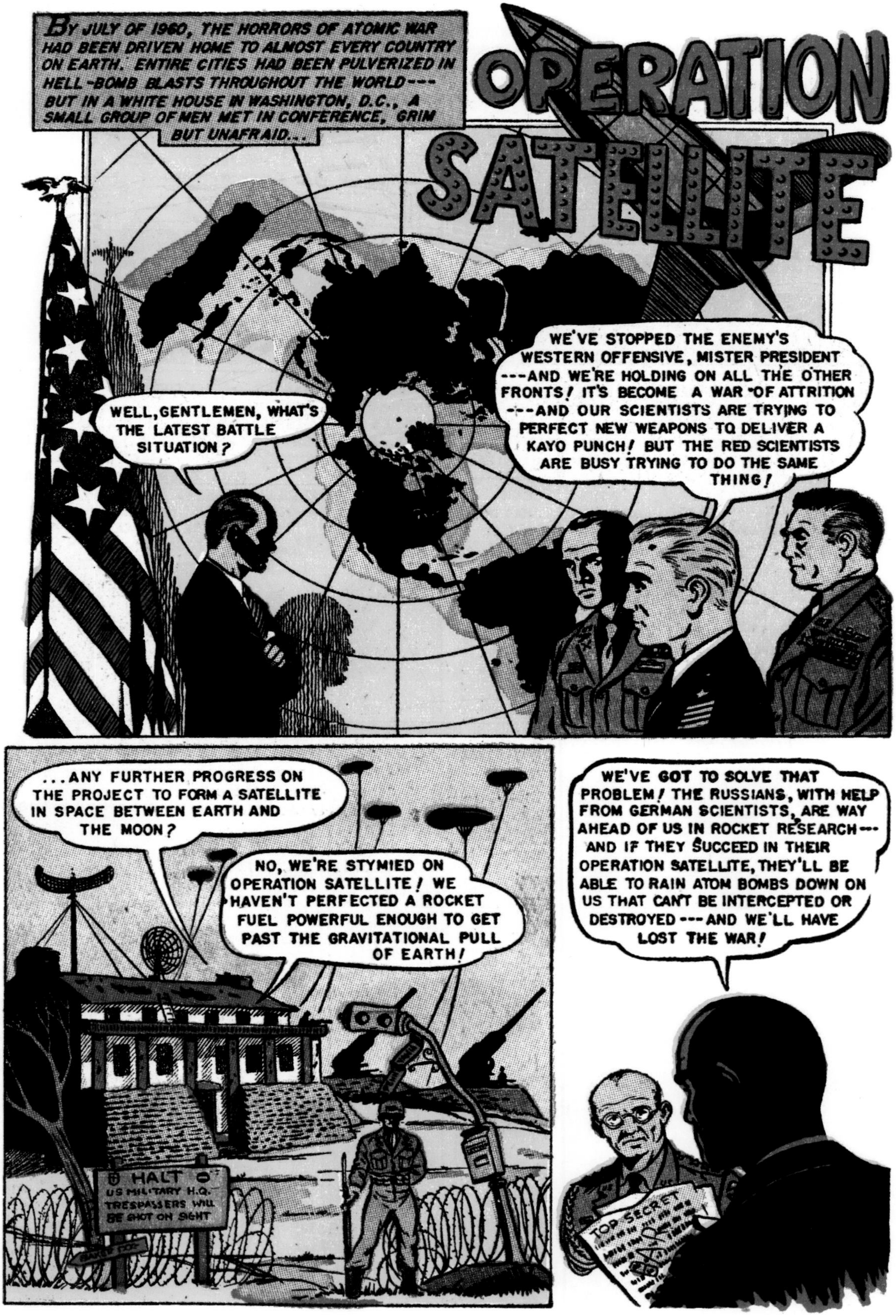
OPERATION SATELLITE
BY JULY OF 1960, THE HORRORS OF ATOMIC WAR HAD BEEN DRIVEN HOME TO ALMOST EVERY COUNTRY ON EARTH. ENTIRE CITIES HAD BEEN PULVERIZED IN HELL-BOMB BLASTS THROUGHOUT THE WORLD--- BUT IN A WHITE HOUSE IN WASHINGTON, D.C., A SMALL GROUP OF MEN MET IN CONFERENCE, GRIM BUT UNAFRAID...
WELL, GENTLEMEN, WHAT'S THE LATEST BATTLE SITUATION?
WE'VE STOPPED THE ENEMY'S WESTERN OFFENSIVE, MISTER PRESIDENT ---AND WE'RE HOLDING ON ALL THE OTHER FRONTS! IT'S BECOME A WAR OF ATTRITION ---AND OUR SCIENTISTS ARE TRYING TO PERFECT NEW WEAPONS TO DELIVER A KAYO PUNCH! BUT THE RED SCIENTISTS ARE BUSY TRYING TO DO THE SAME THING!
...ANY FURTHER PROGRESS ON THE PROJECT TO FORM A SATELLITE IN SPACE BETWEEN EARTH AND THE MOON?
NO, WE'RE STYMIED ON OPERATION SATELLITE! WE HAVEN'T PERFECTED A ROCKET FUEL POWERFUL ENOUGH TO GET PAST THE GRAVITATIONAL PULL OF EARTH!
HALT
US MILITARY H.Q. TRESPASSERS WILL BE SHOT ON SIGHT
WE'VE GOT TO SOLVE THAT PROBLEM! THE RUSSIANS, WITH HELP FROM GERMAN SCIENTISTS, ARE WAY AHEAD OF US IN ROCKET RESEARCH--- AND IF THEY SUCCEED IN THEIR OPERATION SATELLITE, THEY'LL BE ABLE TO RAIN ATOM BOMBS DOWN ON US THAT CAN'T BE INTERCEPTED OR DESTROYED---AND WE'LL HAVE LOST THE WAR!
TOP SECRET

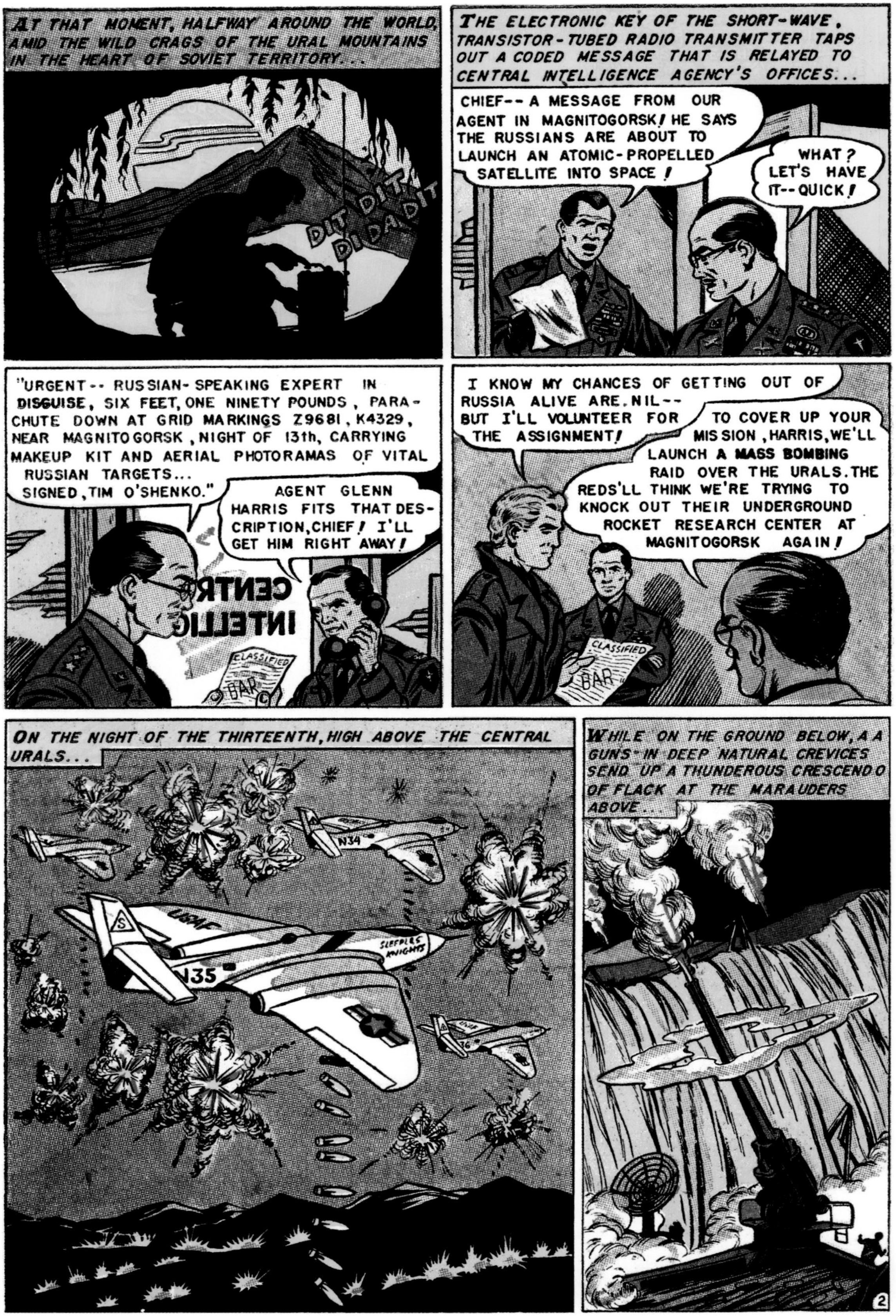
AT THAT MOMENT, HALFWAY AROUND THE WORLD, AMID THE WILD CRAGS OF THE URAL MOUNTAINS IN THE HEART OF SOVIET TERRITORY...
DIT DIT DI DA DIT
THE ELECTRONIC KEY OF THE SHORT-WAVE, TRANSISTOR-TUBED RADIO TRANSMITTER TAPS OUT A CODED MESSAGE THAT IS RELAYED TO CENTRAL INTELLIGENCE AGENCY'S OFFICES...
CHIEF-- A MESSAGE FROM OUR AGENT IN MAGNITOGORSK! HE SAYS THE RUSSIANS ARE ABOUT TO LAUNCH AN ATOMIC-PROPELLED SATELLITE INTO SPACE!
WHAT? LET'S HAVE IT--QUICK!
"URGENT-- RUSSIAN-SPEAKING EXPERT IN DISGUISE, SIX FEET, ONE NINETY POUNDS, PARACHUTE DOWN AT GRID MARKINGS Z9681, K4329, NEAR MAGNITOGORSK, NIGHT OF 13th, CARRYING MAKEUP KIT AND AERIAL PHOTORAMAS OF VITAL RUSSIAN TARGETS... SIGNED, TIM O'SHENKO."
AGENT GLENN HARRIS FITS THAT DESCRIPTION, CHIEF! I'LL GET HIM RIGHT AWAY!
CLASSIFIED
I KNOW MY CHANCES OF GETTING OUT OF RUSSIA ALIVE ARE NIL-- BUT I'LL VOLUNTEER FOR THE ASSIGNMENT!
TO COVER UP YOUR MISSION, HARRIS, WE'LL LAUNCH A MASS BOMBING RAID OVER THE URALS. THE REDS'LL THINK WE'RE TRYING TO KNOCK OUT THEIR UNDERGROUND ROCKET RESEARCH CENTER AT MAGNITOGORSK AGAIN!
CLASSIFIED
ON THE NIGHT OF THE THIRTEENTH, HIGH ABOVE THE CENTRAL URALS...
N34
USAF
135
SLEEPLESS KNIGHTS
WHILE ON THE GROUND BELOW, A A GUNS-IN DEEP NATURAL CREVICES SEND UP A THUNDEROUS CRESCENDO OF FLACK AT THE MARAUDERS ABOVE.
2

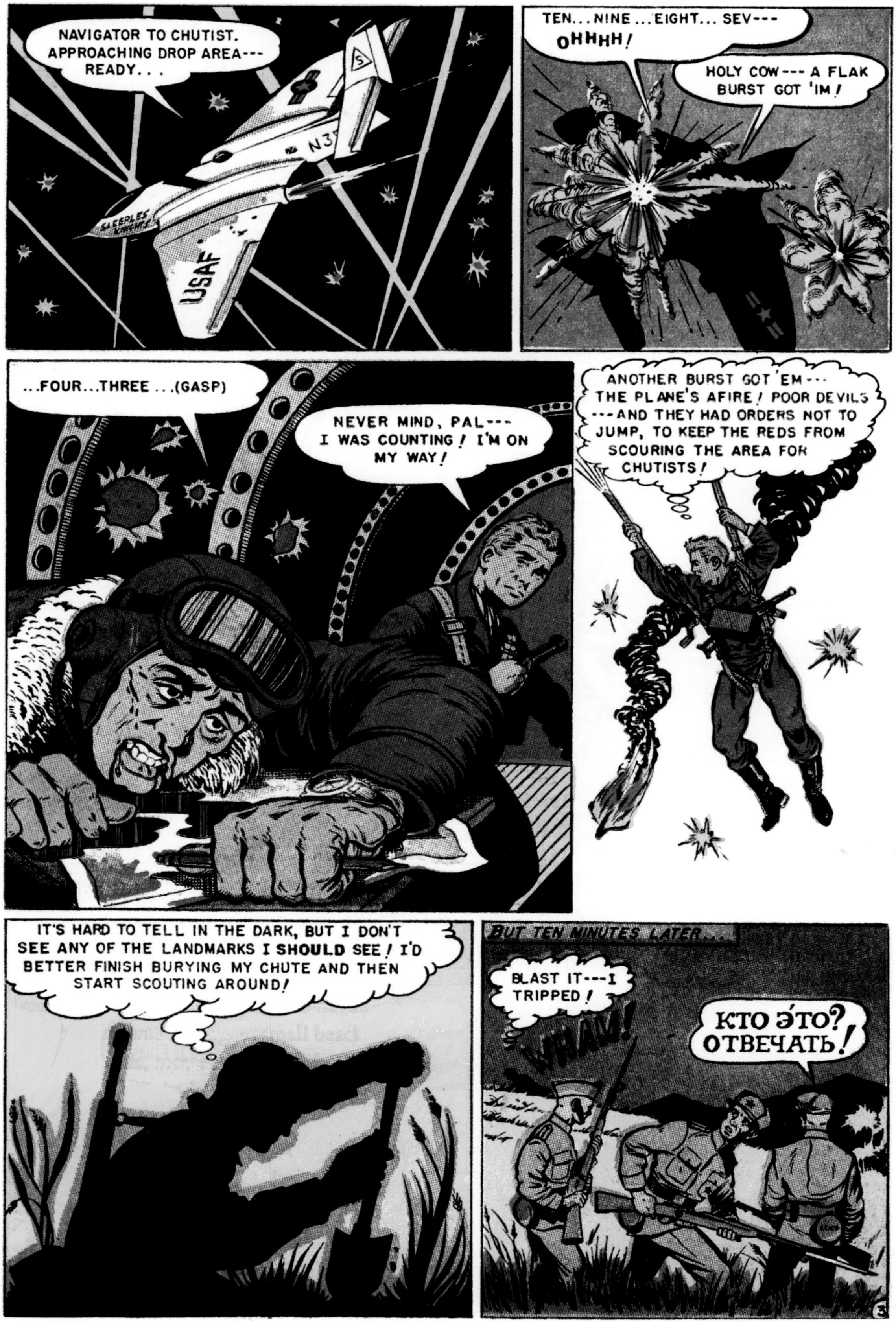

NAVIGATOR TO CHUTIST. APPROACHING DROP AREA--- READY...
SLEEPLESS KNIGHT
USAF
TEN...NINE...EIGHT... SEV--- OHHHH!
HOLY COW--- A FLAK BURST GOT 'IM!
...FOUR...THREE...(GASP)
NEVER MIND, PAL--- I WAS COUNTING! I'M ON MY WAY!
ANOTHER BURST GOT 'EM--- THE PLANE'S AFIRE! POOR DEVILS ---AND THEY HAD ORDERS NOT TO JUMP, TO KEEP THE REDS FROM SCOURING THE AREA FOR CHUTISTS!
IT'S HARD TO TELL IN THE DARK, BUT I DON'T SEE ANY OF THE LANDMARKS I SHOULD SEE! I'D BETTER FINISH BURYING MY CHUTE AND THEN START SCOUTING AROUND!
BUT TEN MINUTES LATER...
BLAST IT---I TRIPPED!
WHAM!
КТО ЭТО? ОТВЕЧАТЬ!
3

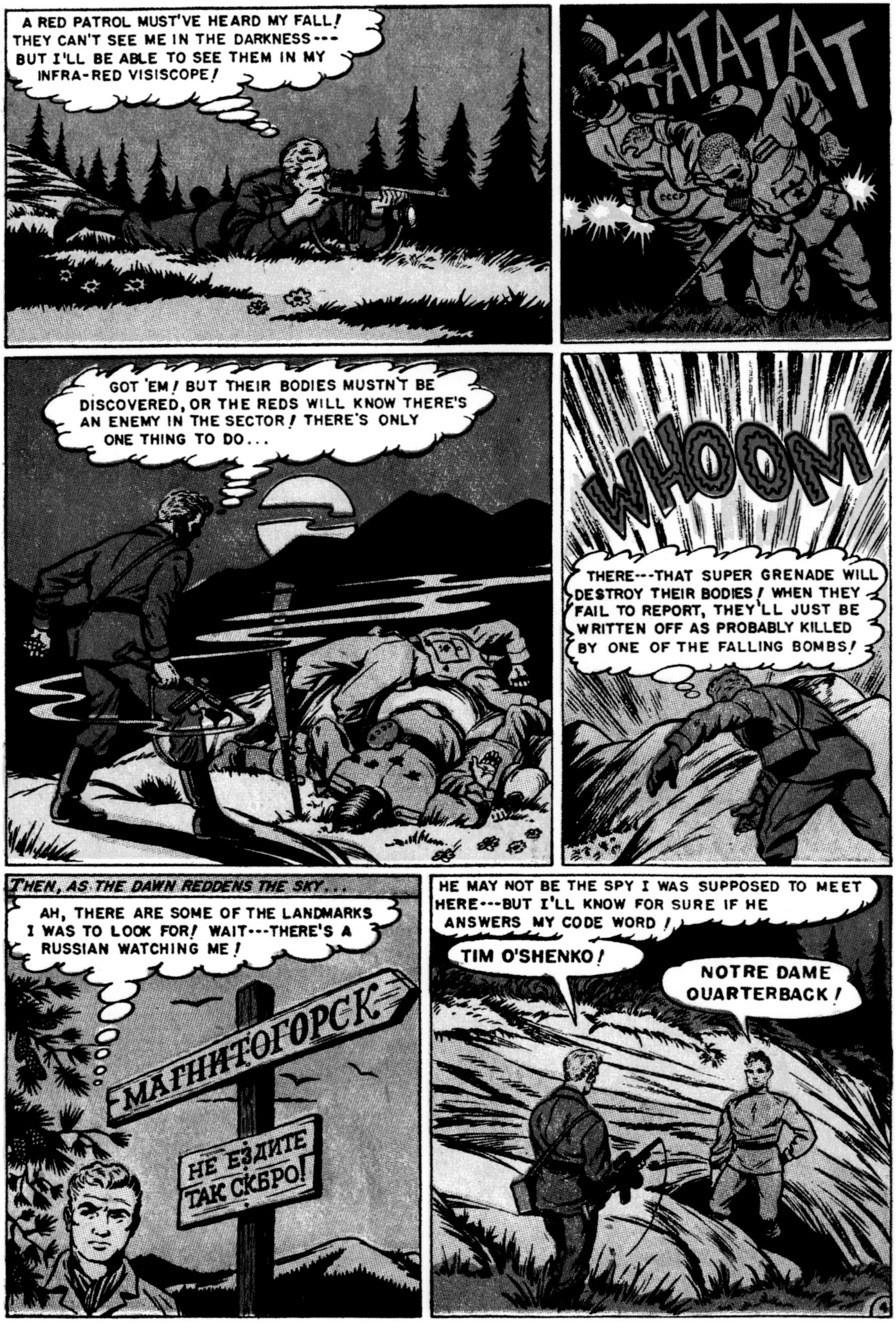
A RED PATROL MUST'VE HEARD MY FALL! THEY CAN'T SEE ME IN THE DARKNESS--- BUT I'LL BE ABLE TO SEE THEM IN MY INFRA-RED VISISCOPE!
TATATAT
GOT 'EM! BUT THEIR BODIES MUSTN'T BE DISCOVERED, OR THE REDS WILL KNOW THERE'S AN ENEMY IN THE SECTOR! THERE'S ONLY ONE THING TO DO...
WHOOM
THERE---THAT SUPER GRENADE WILL DESTROY THEIR BODIES! WHEN THEY FAIL TO REPORT, THEY'LL JUST BE WRITTEN OFF AS PROBABLY KILLED BY ONE OF THE FALLING BOMBS!
THEN, AS THE DAWN REDDENS THE SKY...
AH, THERE ARE SOME OF THE LANDMARKS I WAS TO LOOK FOR! WAIT---THERE'S A RUSSIAN WATCHING ME!
МАГНИТОГОРСК
НЕ ЕЗДИТЕ ТАК СКБРО!
HE MAY NOT BE THE SPY I WAS SUPPOSED TO MEET HERE---BUT I'LL KNOW FOR SURE IF HE ANSWERS MY CODE WORD!
TIM O'SHENKO!
NOTRE DAME QUARTERBACK!

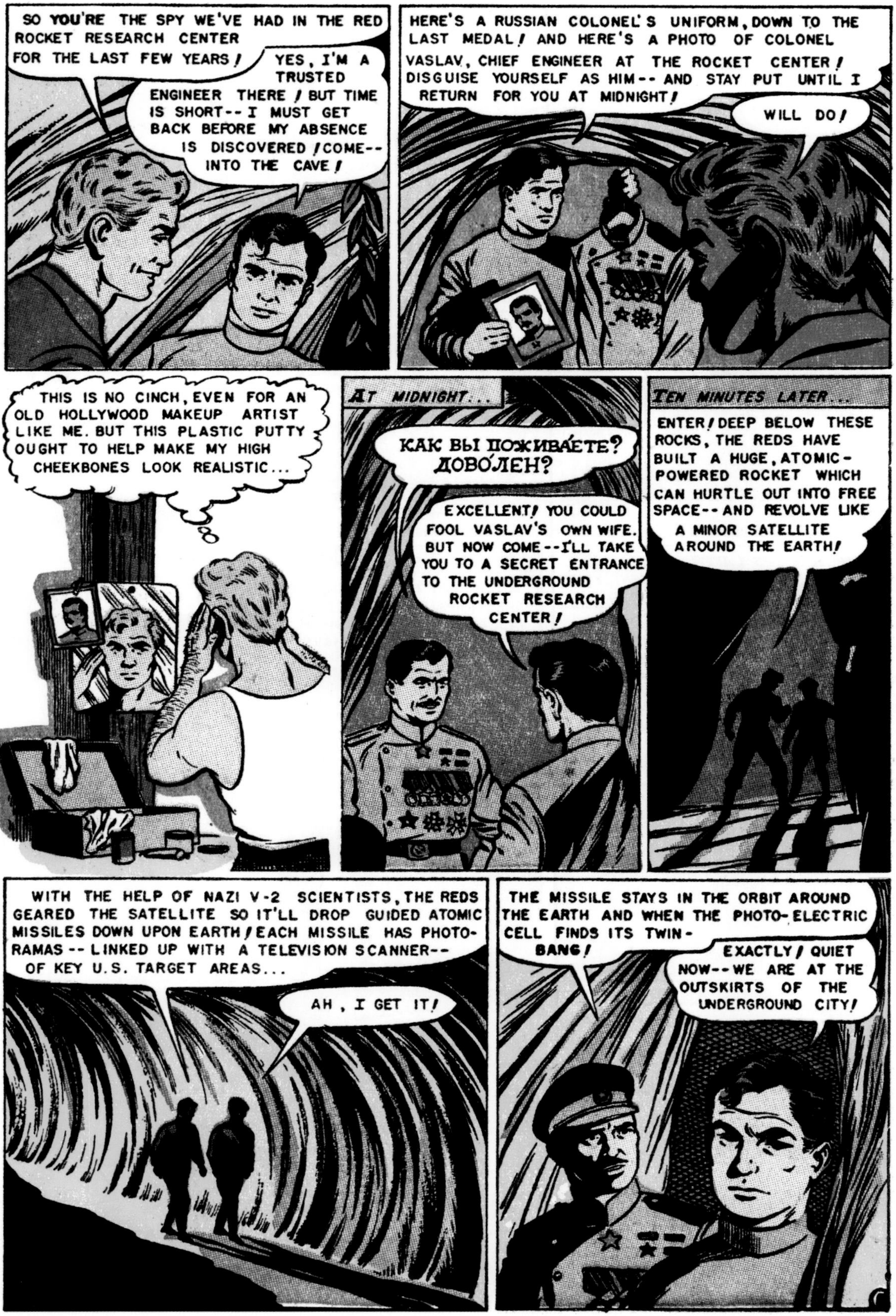
SO YOU'RE THE SPY WE'VE HAD IN THE RED ROCKET RESEARCH CENTER FOR THE LAST FEW YEARS!
YES, I'M A TRUSTED ENGINEER THERE! BUT TIME IS SHORT-- I MUST GET BACK BEFORE MY ABSENCE IS DISCOVERED! COME-- INTO THE CAVE!
HERE'S A RUSSIAN COLONEL'S UNIFORM, DOWN TO THE LAST MEDAL! AND HERE'S A PHOTO OF COLONEL VASLAV, CHIEF ENGINEER AT THE ROCKET CENTER! DISGUISE YOURSELF AS HIM-- AND STAY PUT UNTIL I RETURN FOR YOU AT MIDNIGHT!
WILL DO!
THIS IS NO CINCH, EVEN FOR AN OLD HOLLYWOOD MAKEUP ARTIST LIKE ME. BUT THIS PLASTIC PUTTY OUGHT TO HELP MAKE MY HIGH CHEEKBONES LOOK REALISTIC...
AT MIDNIGHT...
КАК ВЫ ПОЖИВАЕТЕ? ДОВОЛЕН?
EXCELLENT! YOU COULD FOOL VASLAV'S OWN WIFE. BUT NOW COME--I'LL TAKE YOU TO A SECRET ENTRANCE TO THE UNDERGROUND ROCKET RESEARCH CENTER!
TEN MINUTES LATER...
ENTER! DEEP BELOW THESE ROCKS, THE REDS HAVE BUILT A HUGE, ATOMIC-POWERED ROCKET WHICH CAN HURTLE OUT INTO FREE SPACE-- AND REVOLVE LIKE A MINOR SATELLITE AROUND THE EARTH!
WITH THE HELP OF NAZI V-2 SCIENTISTS, THE REDS GEARED THE SATELLITE SO IT'LL DROP GUIDED ATOMIC MISSILES DOWN UPON EARTH! EACH MISSILE HAS PHOTO-RAMAS -- LINKED UP WITH A TELEVISION SCANNER-- OF KEY U.S. TARGET AREAS...
AH, I GET IT!
THE MISSILE STAYS IN THE ORBIT AROUND THE EARTH AND WHEN THE PHOTO-ELECTRIC CELL FINDS ITS TWIN-BANG!
EXACTLY! QUIET NOW--WE ARE AT THE OUTSKIRTS OF THE UNDERGROUND CITY!

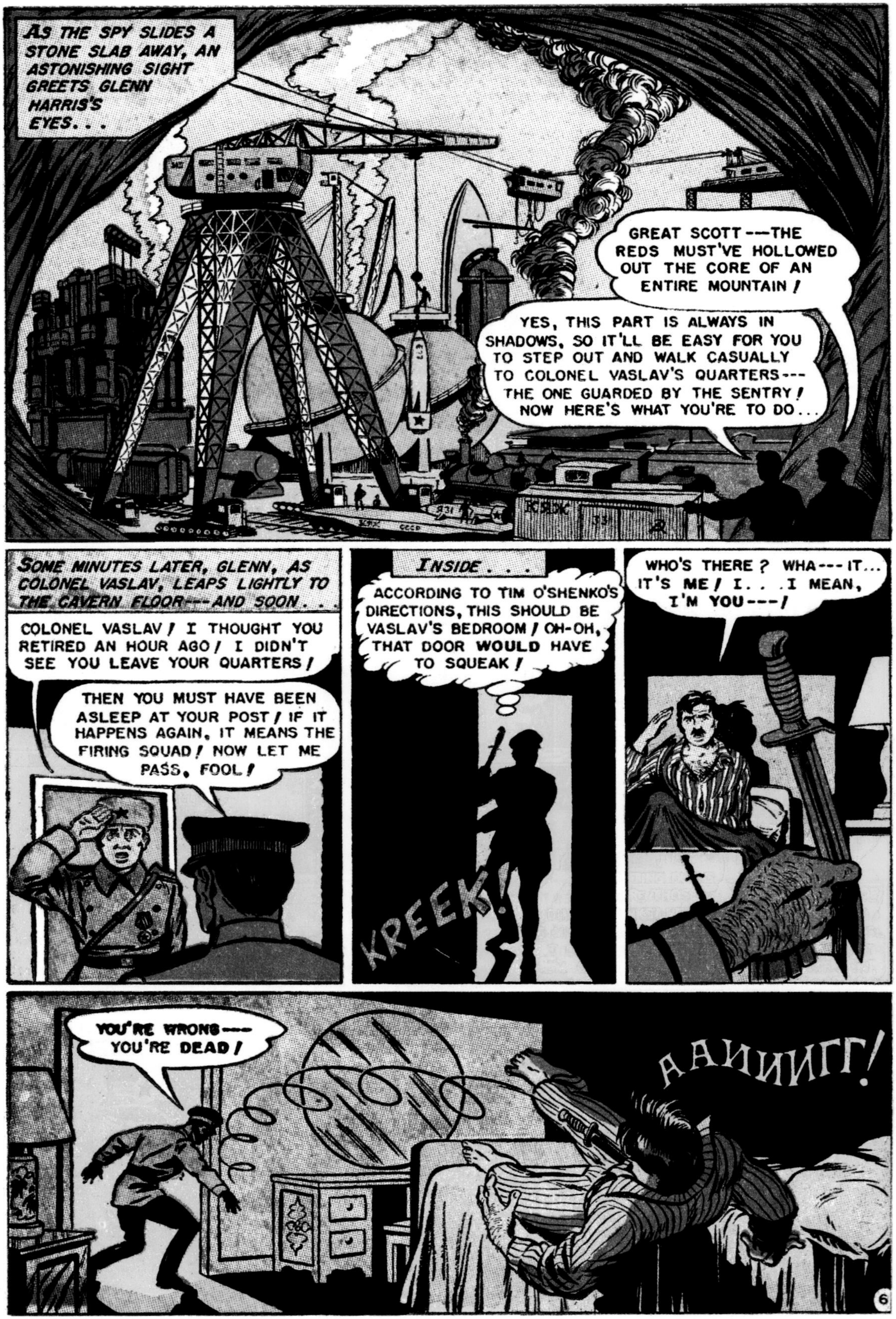
AS THE SPY SLIDES A STONE SLAB AWAY, AN ASTONISHING SIGHT GREETS GLENN HARRIS'S EYES. . .
GREAT SCOTT---THE REDS MUST'VE HOLLOWED OUT THE CORE OF AN ENTIRE MOUNTAIN!
YES, THIS PART IS ALWAYS IN SHADOWS, SO IT'LL BE EASY FOR YOU TO STEP OUT AND WALK CASUALLY TO COLONEL VASLAV'S QUARTERS--- THE ONE GUARDED BY THE SENTRY! NOW HERE'S WHAT YOU'RE TO DO...
SOME MINUTES LATER, GLENN, AS COLONEL VASLAV, LEAPS LIGHTLY TO THE CAVERN FLOOR---AND SOON. . .
COLONEL VASLAV! I THOUGHT YOU RETIRED AN HOUR AGO! I DIDN'T SEE YOU LEAVE YOUR QUARTERS!
THEN YOU MUST HAVE BEEN ASLEEP AT YOUR POST! IF IT HAPPENS AGAIN, IT MEANS THE FIRING SQUAD! NOW LET ME PASS, FOOL!
INSIDE . . .
ACCORDING TO TIM O'SHENKO'S DIRECTIONS, THIS SHOULD BE VASLAV'S BEDROOM! OH-OH, THAT DOOR WOULD HAVE TO SQUEAK!
KREEK!
WHO'S THERE? WHA--- IT... IT'S ME! I. . .I MEAN, I'M YOU---!
YOU'RE WRONG--- YOU'RE DEAD!
AAИИИГГ!
6

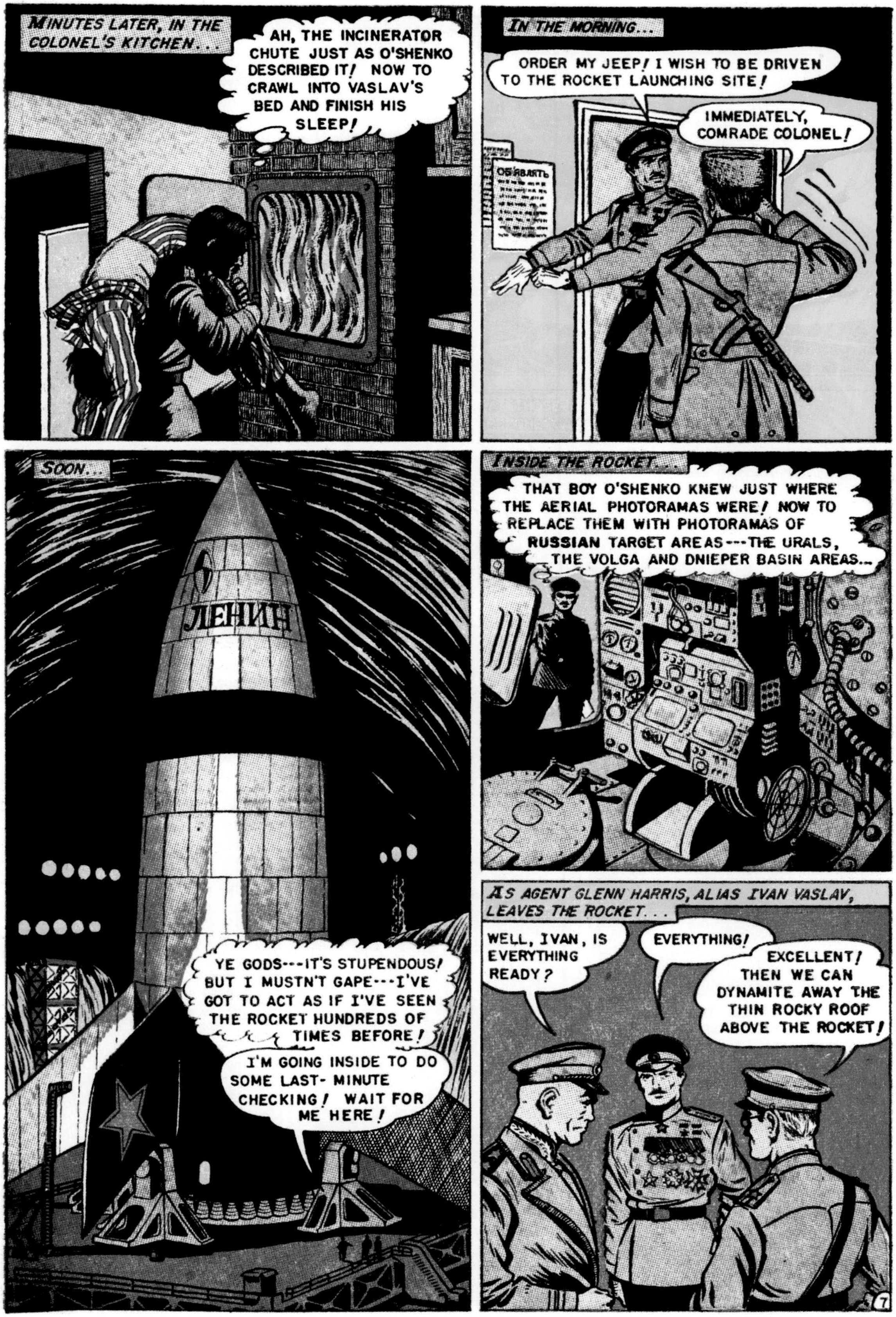
MINUTES LATER, IN THE COLONEL'S KITCHEN...
AH, THE INCINERATOR CHUTE JUST AS O'SHENKO DESCRIBED IT! NOW TO CRAWL INTO VASLAV'S BED AND FINISH HIS SLEEP!
IN THE MORNING...
ORDER MY JEEP! I WISH TO BE DRIVEN TO THE ROCKET LAUNCHING SITE!
IMMEDIATELY, COMRADE COLONEL!
SOON...
ЛЕНИН
YE GODS---IT'S STUPENDOUS! BUT I MUSTN'T GAPE---I'VE GOT TO ACT AS IF I'VE SEEN THE ROCKET HUNDREDS OF TIMES BEFORE!
I'M GOING INSIDE TO DO SOME LAST- MINUTE CHECKING! WAIT FOR ME HERE!
INSIDE THE ROCKET...
THAT BOY O'SHENKO KNEW JUST WHERE THE AERIAL PHOTORAMAS WERE! NOW TO REPLACE THEM WITH PHOTORAMAS OF RUSSIAN TARGET AREAS---THE URALS, THE VOLGA AND DNIEPER BASIN AREAS...
AS AGENT GLENN HARRIS, ALIAS IVAN VASLAV, LEAVES THE ROCKET...
WELL, IVAN, IS EVERYTHING READY?
EVERYTHING!
EXCELLENT! THEN WE CAN DYNAMITE AWAY THE THIN ROCKY ROOF ABOVE THE ROCKET!
7

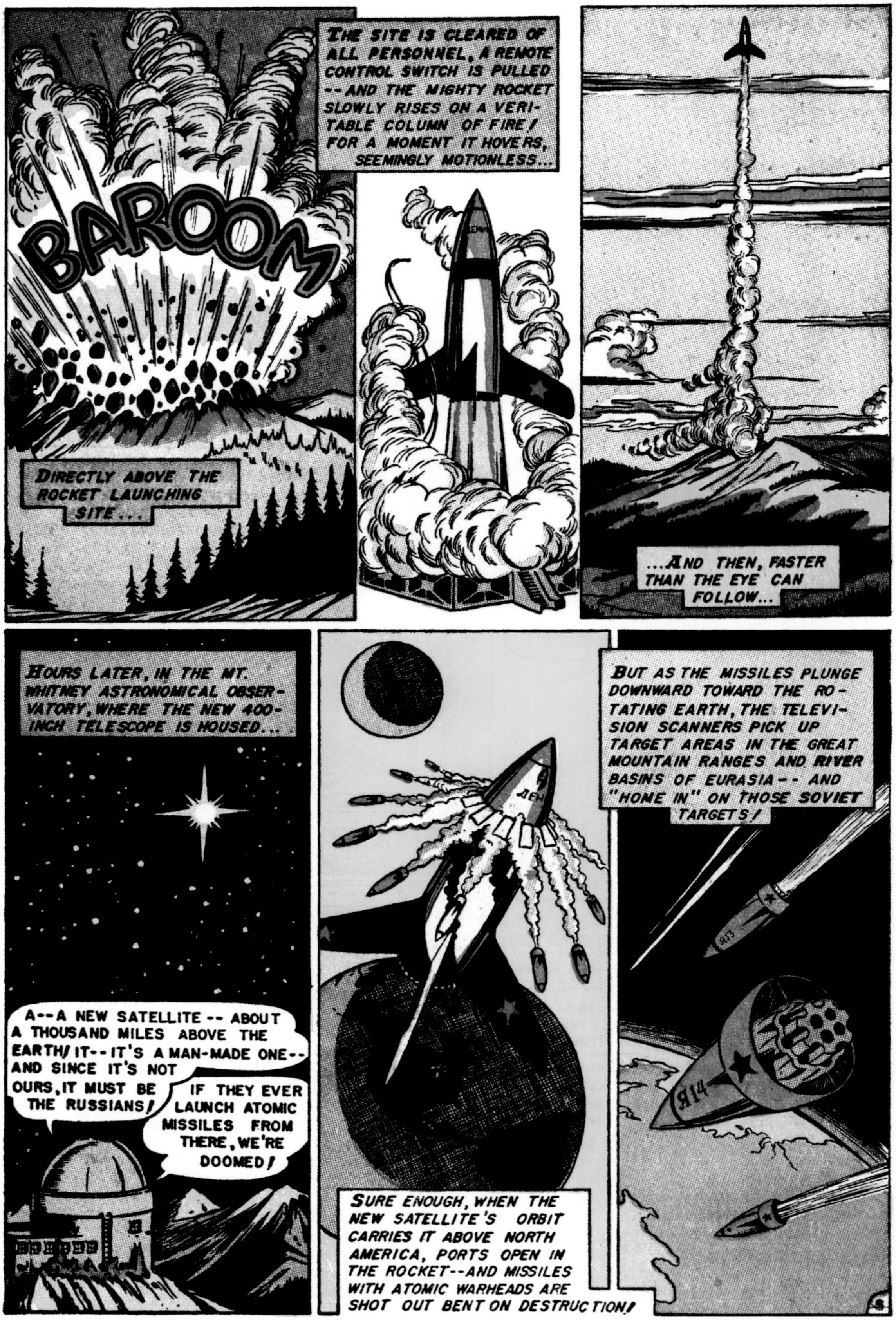
BAROOM
DIRECTLY ABOVE THE ROCKET LAUNCHING SITE...
THE SITE IS CLEARED OF ALL PERSONNEL, A REMOTE CONTROL SWITCH IS PULLED --AND THE MIGHTY ROCKET SLOWLY RISES ON A VERITABLE COLUMN OF FIRE! FOR A MOMENT IT HOVERS, SEEMINGLY MOTIONLESS...
...AND THEN, FASTER THAN THE EYE CAN FOLLOW...
HOURS LATER, IN THE MT. WHITNEY ASTRONOMICAL OBSERVATORY, WHERE THE NEW 400-INCH TELESCOPE IS HOUSED...
A--A NEW SATELLITE -- ABOUT A THOUSAND MILES ABOVE THE EARTH! IT--IT'S A MAN-MADE ONE--AND SINCE IT'S NOT OURS, IT MUST BE THE RUSSIANS!
IF THEY EVER LAUNCH ATOMIC MISSILES FROM THERE, WE'RE DOOMED!
SURE ENOUGH, WHEN THE NEW SATELLITE'S ORBIT CARRIES IT ABOVE NORTH AMERICA, PORTS OPEN IN THE ROCKET--AND MISSILES WITH ATOMIC WARHEADS ARE SHOT OUT BENT ON DESTRUCTION!
BUT AS THE MISSILES PLUNGE DOWNWARD TOWARD THE ROTATING EARTH, THE TELEVISION SCANNERS PICK UP TARGET AREAS IN THE GREAT MOUNTAIN RANGES AND RIVER BASINS OF EURASIA-- AND "HOME IN" ON THOSE SOVIET TARGETS!
Я14

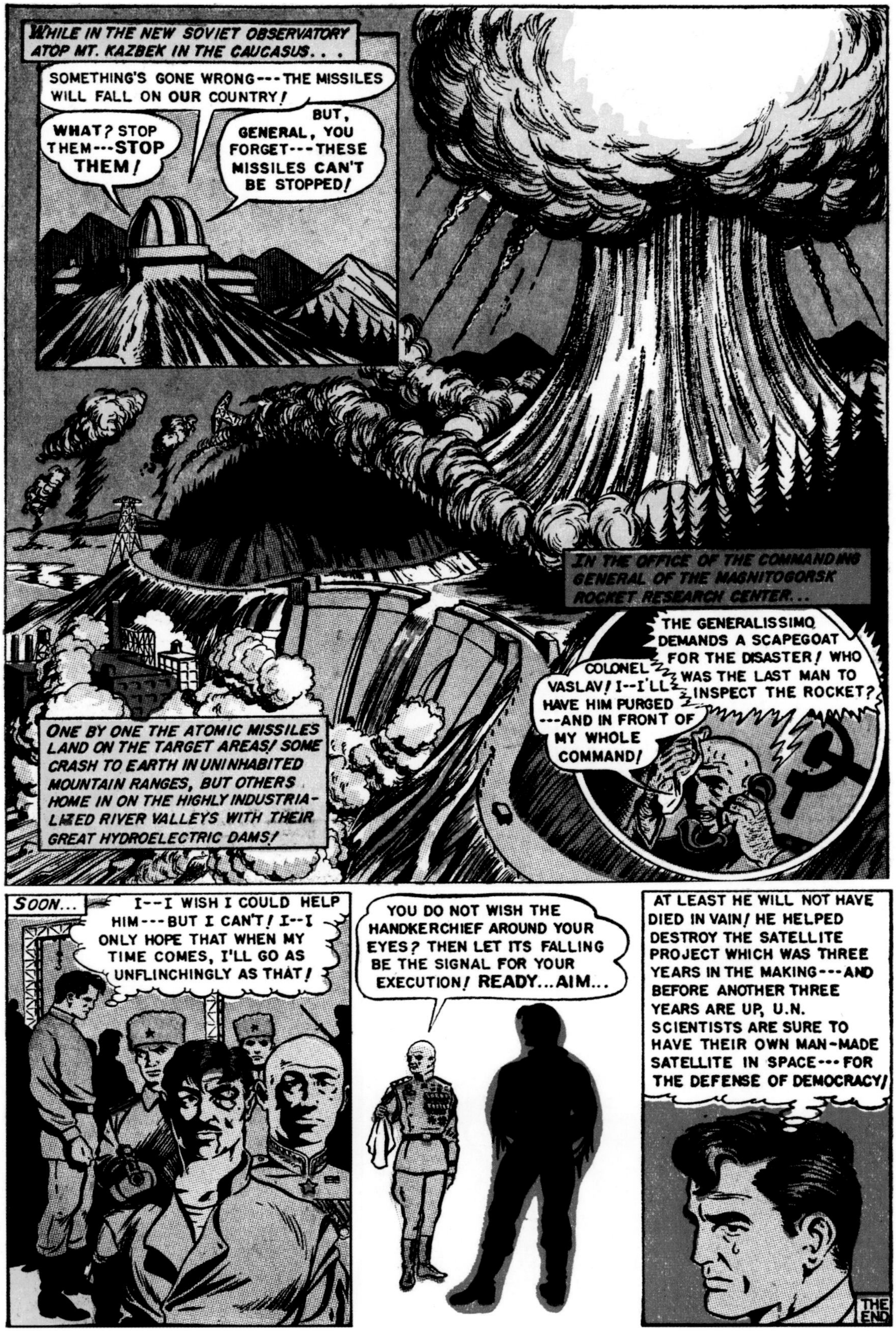
WHILE IN THE NEW SOVIET OBSERVATORY ATOP MT. KAZBEK IN THE CAUCASUS . . .
SOMETHING'S GONE WRONG---THE MISSILES WILL FALL ON OUR COUNTRY!
WHAT? STOP THEM---STOP THEM!
BUT, GENERAL, YOU FORGET---THESE MISSILES CAN'T BE STOPPED!
ONE BY ONE THE ATOMIC MISSILES LAND ON THE TARGET AREAS! SOME CRASH TO EARTH IN UNINHABITED MOUNTAIN RANGES, BUT OTHERS HOME IN ON THE HIGHLY INDUSTRIA-LIZED RIVER VALLEYS WITH THEIR GREAT HYDROELECTRIC DAMS!
IN THE OFFICE OF THE COMMANDING GENERAL OF THE MAGNITOGORSK ROCKET RESEARCH CENTER...
THE GENERALISSIMO DEMANDS A SCAPEGOAT FOR THE DISASTER! WHO WAS THE LAST MAN TO INSPECT THE ROCKET?
COLONEL VASLAV! I--I'LL HAVE HIM PURGED ---AND IN FRONT OF MY WHOLE COMMAND!
SOON...
I--I WISH I COULD HELP HIM---BUT I CAN'T! I--I ONLY HOPE THAT WHEN MY TIME COMES, I'LL GO AS UNFLINCHINGLY AS THAT!
YOU DO NOT WISH THE HANDKERCHIEF AROUND YOUR EYES? THEN LET ITS FALLING BE THE SIGNAL FOR YOUR EXECUTION! READY...AIM...
AT LEAST HE WILL NOT HAVE DIED IN VAIN! HE HELPED DESTROY THE SATELLITE PROJECT WHICH WAS THREE YEARS IN THE MAKING---AND BEFORE ANOTHER THREE YEARS ARE UP, U.N. SCIENTISTS ARE SURE TO HAVE THEIR OWN MAN-MADE SATELLITE IN SPACE---FOR THE DEFENSE OF DEMOCRACY!
THE END

PERIL at Ploesti

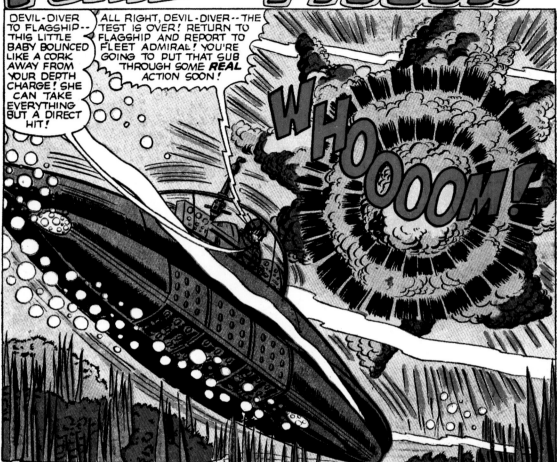

DEVIL-DIVER TO FLAGSHIP-- THIS LITTLE BABY BOUNCED LIKE A CORK AWAY FROM YOUR DEPTH CHARGE! SHE CAN TAKE EVERYTHING BUT A DIRECT HIT!

ALL RIGHT, DEVIL-DIVER-- THE TEST IS OVER! RETURN TO FLAGSHIP AND REPORT TO FLEET ADMIRAL! YOU'RE GOING TO PUT THAT SUB THROUGH SOME **REAL** ACTION SOON!

WHOOOOM!

AMERICA WAS NOT ALONE IN ITS BATTLE AGAINST THE COMMUNIST AGGRESSORS. FOR MORE THAN FIFTY UNITED NATIONS HAD JOINED THE WAR TO ERASE RED TYRANNY FROM THE FACE OF THE EARTH! BUT THERE WERE SOME AMERICANS WHO THOUGHT THEY COULD CLEAN UP THE WAR SINGLE-HANDEDLY IF LEFT ALONE -- AND ONE OF THOSE WAS CHIEF BO'SUN DON WALKER, NOW TESTING A NEW ONE-MAN SUBMARINE BENEATH THE WATERS OF THE TURKISH SEA OF MARMARA ...

SOON AFTERWARDS, IN THE ADMIRAL'S QUARTERS...

WE'VE BEEN TRYING TO KNOCK OUT THE PLOESTI OIL FIELDS IN RUMANIA WITH OUR CARRIER-BASED PLANES, BUT WE'VE LOST TOO MANY TO RED ANTI-AIRCRAFT! SO **YOU'RE** GOING TO MAKE A COMMANDO RAID AGAINST THOSE OIL FIELDS!

SOUNDS LIKE A GREAT MISSION, SIR!

YOU'LL TAKE ORDERS FROM A SEAMAN SECOND CLASS IN THE TURKISH NAVY, WHO'S BEEN TESTING OUR ONLY OTHER ONE-MAN SUBMERSIBLE! HE'S FAMILIAR WITH ALL THE NAVIGATION PROBLEMS IN THE BLACK SEA AND DANUBE RIVER!

BUT, SIR! HOW CAN I TAKE ORDERS FROM AN ORDINARY SEAMAN-- AND A FOREIGNER AT THAT?

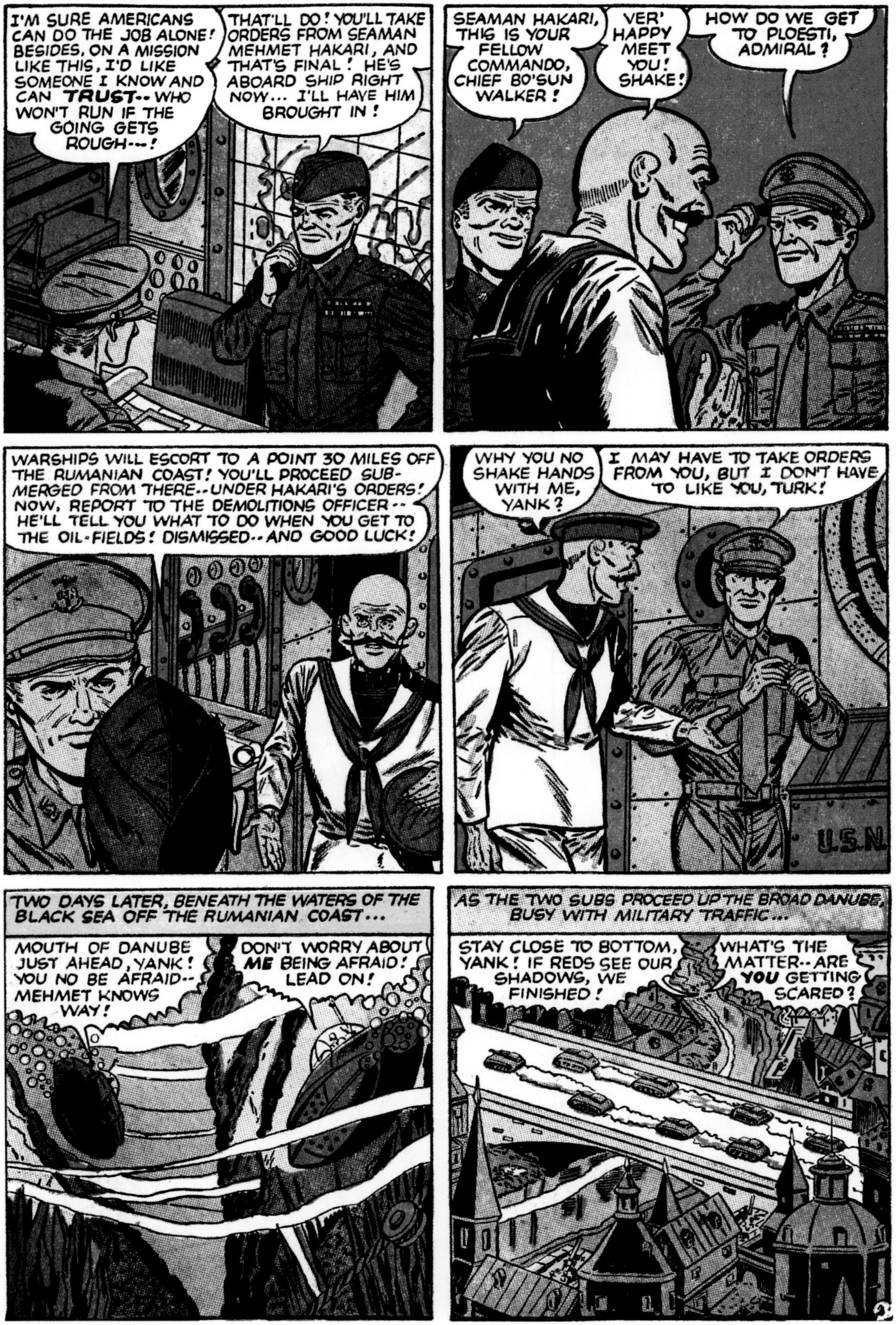

I'M SURE AMERICANS CAN DO THE JOB ALONE! BESIDES, ON A MISSION LIKE THIS, I'D LIKE SOMEONE I KNOW AND CAN TRUST-- WHO WON'T RUN IF THE GOING GETS ROUGH--!
THAT'LL DO! YOU'LL TAKE ORDERS FROM SEAMAN MEHMET HAKARI, AND THAT'S FINAL! HE'S ABOARD SHIP RIGHT NOW... I'LL HAVE HIM BROUGHT IN!
SEAMAN HAKARI, THIS IS YOUR FELLOW COMMANDO, CHIEF BO'SUN WALKER!
VER' HAPPY MEET YOU! SHAKE!
HOW DO WE GET TO PLOESTI, ADMIRAL?
WARSHIPS WILL ESCORT TO A POINT 30 MILES OFF THE RUMANIAN COAST! YOU'LL PROCEED SUB-MERGED FROM THERE--UNDER HAKARI'S ORDERS! NOW, REPORT TO THE DEMOLITIONS OFFICER-- HE'LL TELL YOU WHAT TO DO WHEN YOU GET TO THE OIL-FIELDS! DISMISSED--AND GOOD LUCK!
WHY YOU NO SHAKE HANDS WITH ME, YANK?
I MAY HAVE TO TAKE ORDERS FROM YOU, BUT I DON'T HAVE TO LIKE YOU, TURK!
U.S.N.
TWO DAYS LATER, BENEATH THE WATERS OF THE BLACK SEA OFF THE RUMANIAN COAST...
MOUTH OF DANUBE JUST AHEAD, YANK! YOU NO BE AFRAID-- MEHMET KNOWS WAY!
DON'T WORRY ABOUT ME BEING AFRAID! LEAD ON!
AS THE TWO SUBS PROCEED UP THE BROAD DANUBE, BUSY WITH MILITARY TRAFFIC...
STAY CLOSE TO BOTTOM, YANK! IF REDS SEE OUR SHADOWS, WE FINISHED!
WHAT'S THE MATTER--ARE YOU GETTING SCARED?

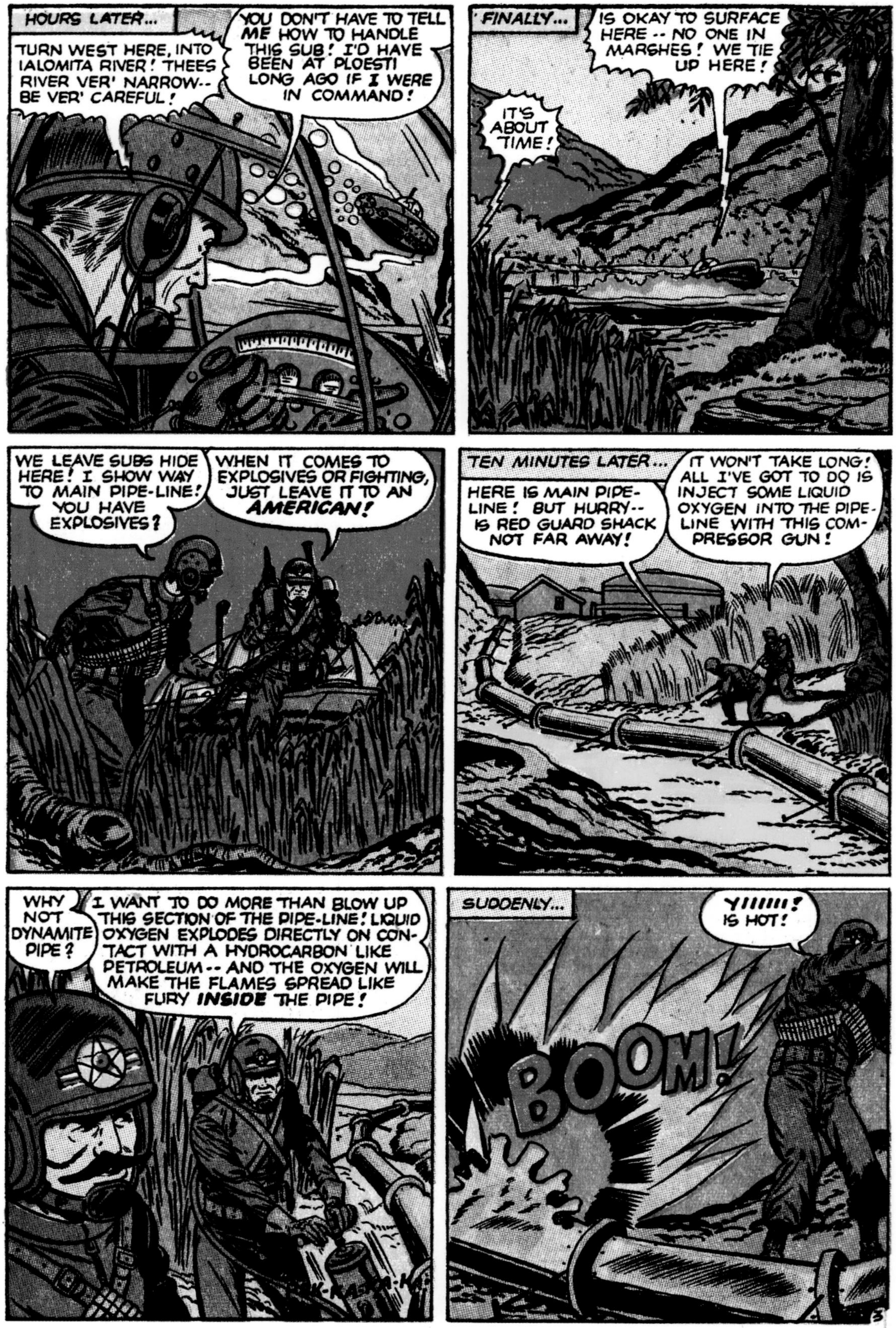
HOURS LATER...
TURN WEST HERE, INTO IALOMITA RIVER! THEES RIVER VER' NARROW-- BE VER' CAREFUL!
YOU DON'T HAVE TO TELL ME HOW TO HANDLE THIS SUB! I'D HAVE BEEN AT PLOESTI LONG AGO IF I WERE IN COMMAND!
FINALLY...
IS OKAY TO SURFACE HERE -- NO ONE IN MARSHES! WE TIE UP HERE!
IT'S ABOUT TIME!
WE LEAVE SUBS HIDE HERE! I SHOW WAY TO MAIN PIPE-LINE! YOU HAVE EXPLOSIVES?
WHEN IT COMES TO EXPLOSIVES OR FIGHTING, JUST LEAVE IT TO AN AMERICAN!
TEN MINUTES LATER...
HERE IS MAIN PIPE-LINE! BUT HURRY-- IS RED GUARD SHACK NOT FAR AWAY!
IT WON'T TAKE LONG! ALL I'VE GOT TO DO IS INJECT SOME LIQUID OXYGEN INTO THE PIPE-LINE WITH THIS COMPRESSOR GUN!
WHY NOT DYNAMITE PIPE?
I WANT TO DO MORE THAN BLOW UP THIS SECTION OF THE PIPE-LINE! LIQUID OXYGEN EXPLODES DIRECTLY ON CONTACT WITH A HYDROCARBON LIKE PETROLEUM -- AND THE OXYGEN WILL MAKE THE FLAMES SPREAD LIKE FURY INSIDE THE PIPE!
SUDDENLY...
YIIIIII! IS HOT!
BOOM!

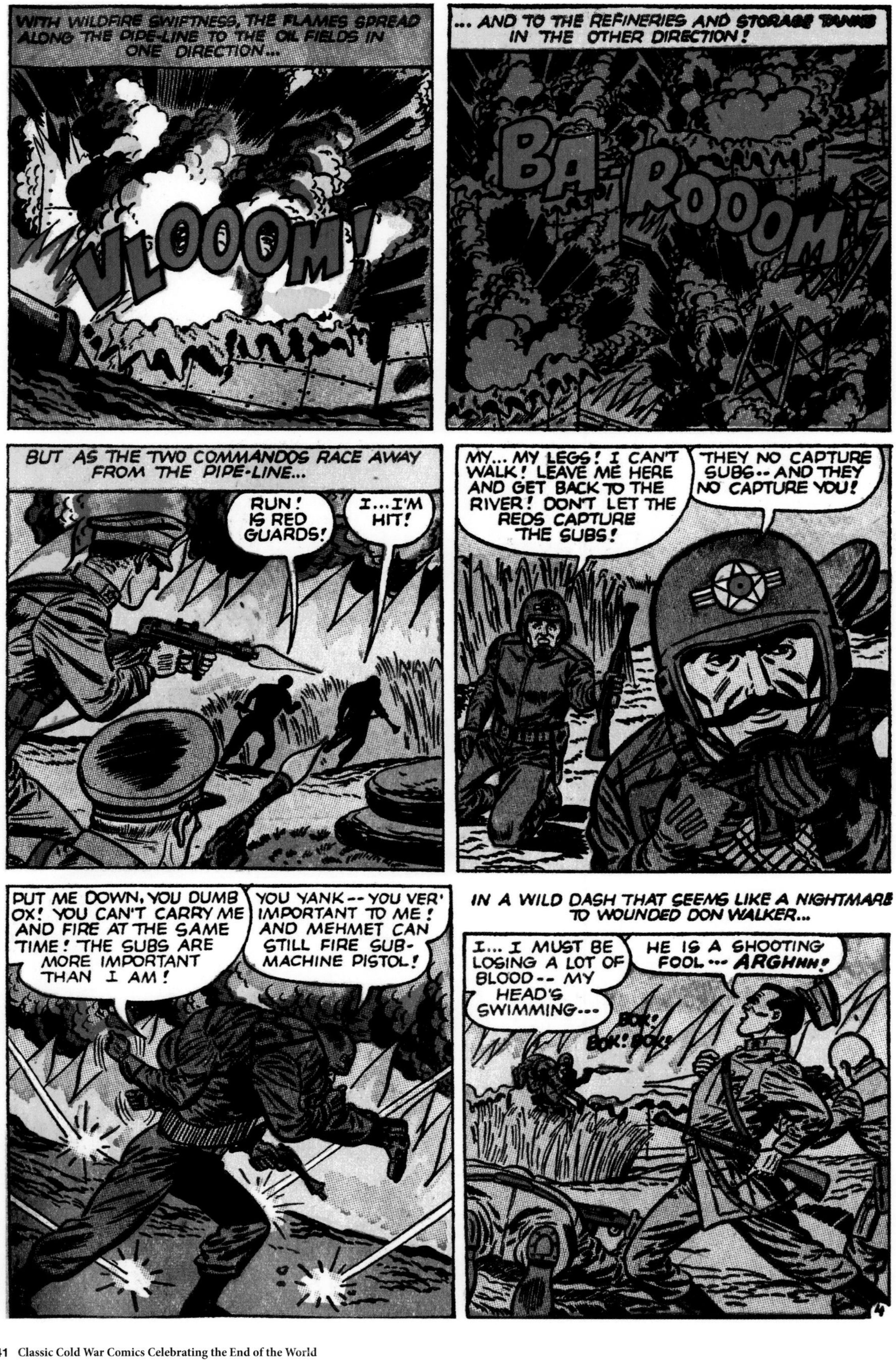
WITH WILDFIRE SWIFTNESS, THE FLAMES SPREAD ALONG THE PIPE-LINE TO THE OIL FIELDS IN ONE DIRECTION...
VLOOOM!
... AND TO THE REFINERIES AND STORAGE TANKS IN THE OTHER DIRECTION!
BA-ROOOM!
BUT AS THE TWO COMMANDOS RACE AWAY FROM THE PIPE-LINE...
RUN! IS RED GUARDS!
I...I'M HIT!
MY... MY LEGS! I CAN'T WALK! LEAVE ME HERE AND GET BACK TO THE RIVER! DON'T LET THE REDS CAPTURE THE SUBS!
THEY NO CAPTURE SUBS-- AND THEY NO CAPTURE YOU!
PUT ME DOWN, YOU DUMB OX! YOU CAN'T CARRY ME AND FIRE AT THE SAME TIME! THE SUBS ARE MORE IMPORTANT THAN I AM!
YOU YANK-- YOU VER' IMPORTANT TO ME! AND MEHMET CAN STILL FIRE SUB-MACHINE PISTOL!
IN A WILD DASH THAT SEEMS LIKE A NIGHTMARE TO WOUNDED DON WALKER...
I... I MUST BE LOSING A LOT OF BLOOD-- MY HEAD'S SWIMMING---
HE IS A SHOOTING FOOL--- ARGHNH!
BOK! BOK! BOK!
4

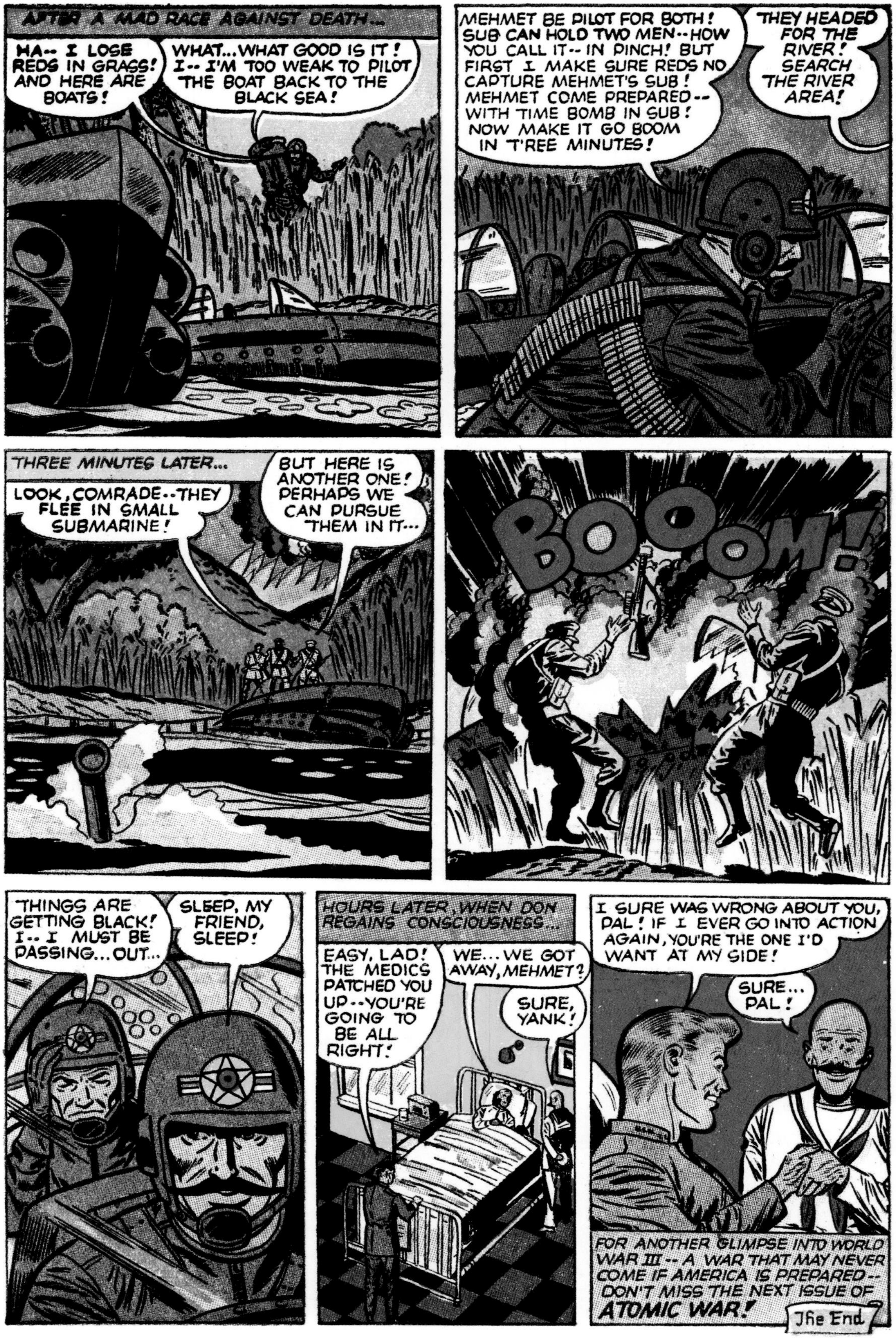
AFTER A MAD RACE AGAINST DEATH...
HA-- I LOSE REDS IN GRASS! AND HERE ARE BOATS!
WHAT...WHAT GOOD IS IT! I-- I'M TOO WEAK TO PILOT THE BOAT BACK TO THE BLACK SEA!
MEHMET BE PILOT FOR BOTH! SUB CAN HOLD TWO MEN--HOW YOU CALL IT-- IN PINCH! BUT FIRST I MAKE SURE REDS NO CAPTURE MEHMET'S SUB! MEHMET COME PREPARED-- WITH TIME BOMB IN SUB! NOW MAKE IT GO BOOM IN T'REE MINUTES!
THEY HEADED FOR THE RIVER! SEARCH THE RIVER AREA!
THREE MINUTES LATER...
LOOK, COMRADE--THEY FLEE IN SMALL SUBMARINE!
BUT HERE IS ANOTHER ONE! PERHAPS WE CAN PURSUE THEM IN IT...
BOOOOM!
THINGS ARE GETTING BLACK! I-- I MUST BE PASSING...OUT...
SLEEP, MY FRIEND, SLEEP!
HOURS LATER, WHEN DON REGAINS CONSCIOUSNESS...
EASY, LAD! THE MEDICS PATCHED YOU UP--YOU'RE GOING TO BE ALL RIGHT!
WE... WE GOT AWAY, MEHMET?
SURE, YANK!
I SURE WAS WRONG ABOUT YOU, PAL! IF I EVER GO INTO ACTION AGAIN, YOU'RE THE ONE I'D WANT AT MY SIDE!
SURE... PAL!
FOR ANOTHER GLIMPSE INTO WORLD WAR III -- A WAR THAT MAY NEVER COME IF AMERICA IS PREPARED-- DON'T MISS THE NEXT ISSUE OF ATOMIC WAR!
The End

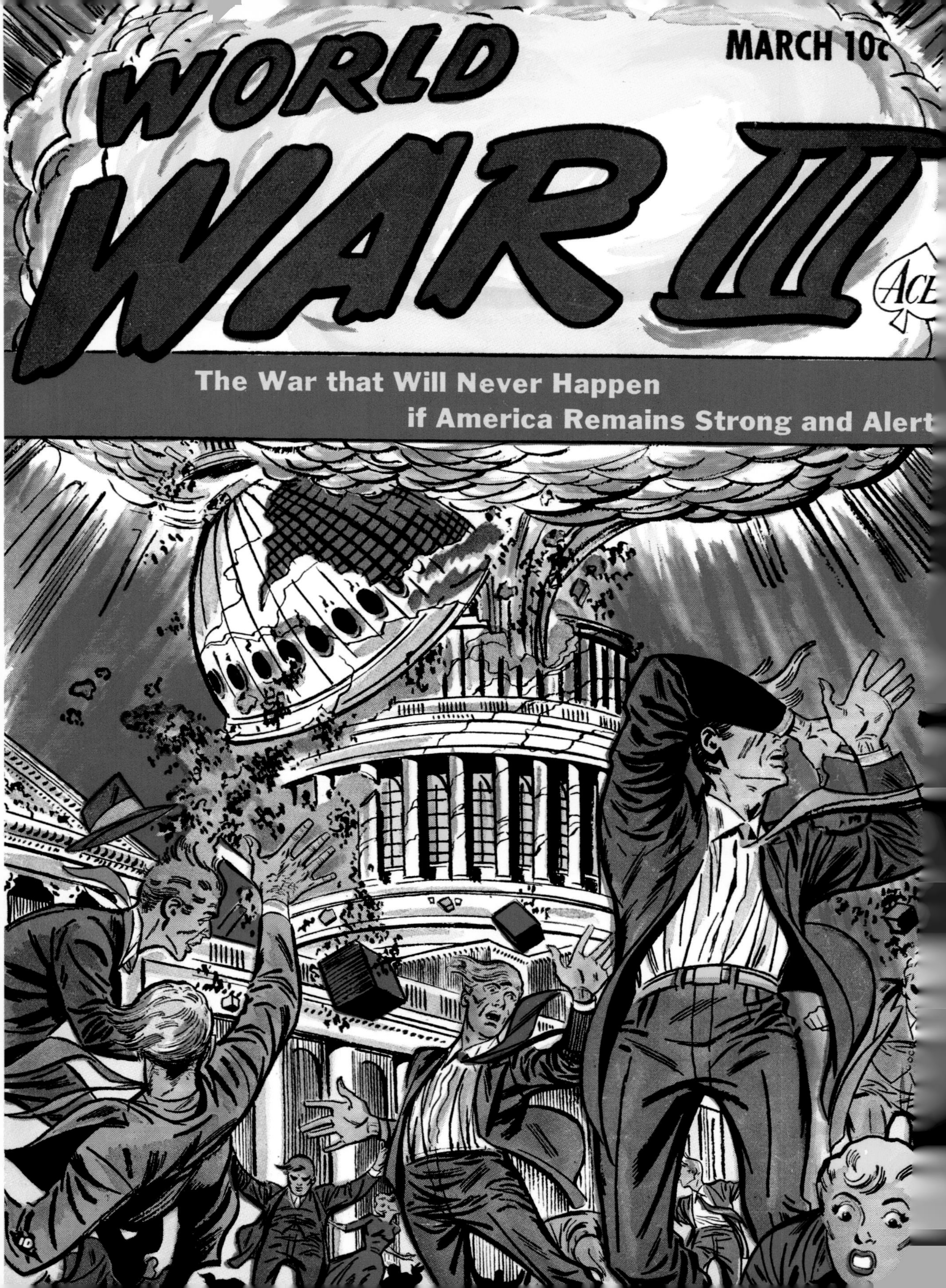
WORLD WAR III
MARCH 10¢
ACE
The War that Will Never Happen
if America Remains Strong and Alert

Let the reason for publishing this shocking account of World War III be completely clear. We want only to awaken America... and the world... to grim facts. The one way to prevent this mass destruction of humanity is to prepare *NOW*. Only a super-strong and fully enlightened America can stop this onrushing horror of the future!

THE EDITORS

WORLD WAR III Unleashed

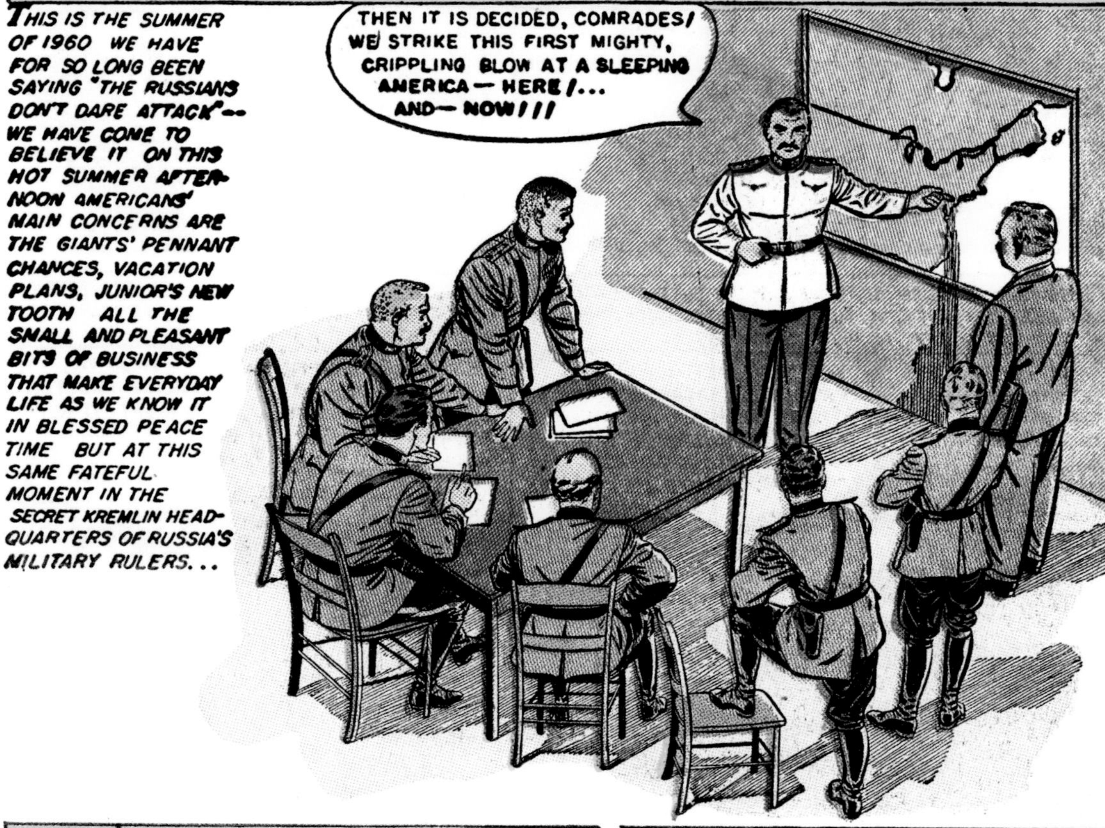
THIS IS THE SUMMER OF 1960 WE HAVE FOR SO LONG BEEN SAYING "THE RUSSIANS DON'T DARE ATTACK"-- WE HAVE COME TO BELIEVE IT ON THIS HOT SUMMER AFTERNOON AMERICANS' MAIN CONCERNS ARE THE GIANTS' PENNANT CHANCES, VACATION PLANS, JUNIOR'S NEW TOOTH ALL THE SMALL AND PLEASANT BITS OF BUSINESS THAT MAKE EVERYDAY LIFE AS WE KNOW IT IN BLESSED PEACE TIME BUT AT THIS SAME FATEFUL MOMENT IN THE SECRET KREMLIN HEADQUARTERS OF RUSSIA'S MILITARY RULERS...
THEN IT IS DECIDED, COMRADES! WE STRIKE THIS FIRST MIGHTY, CRIPPLING BLOW AT A SLEEPING AMERICA — HERE!... AND— NOW!!!

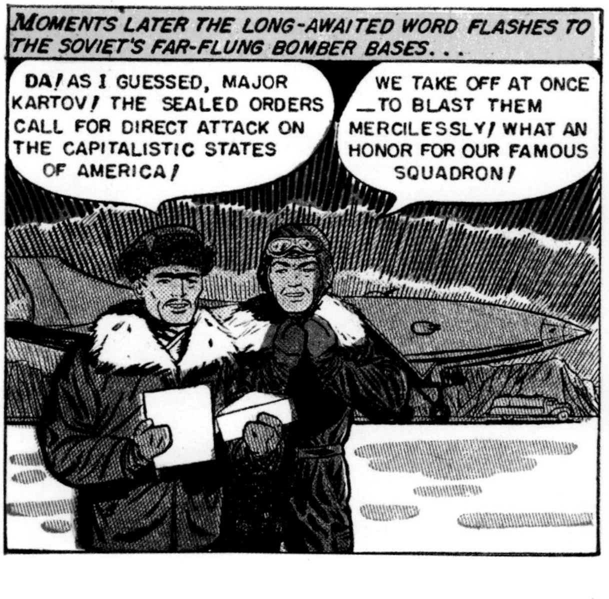
MOMENTS LATER THE LONG-AWAITED WORD FLASHES TO THE SOVIET'S FAR-FLUNG BOMBER BASES...
DA! AS I GUESSED, MAJOR KARTOV! THE SEALED ORDERS CALL FOR DIRECT ATTACK ON THE CAPITALISTIC STATES OF AMERICA!
WE TAKE OFF AT ONCE —TO BLAST THEM MERCILESSLY! WHAT AN HONOR FOR OUR FAMOUS SQUADRON!

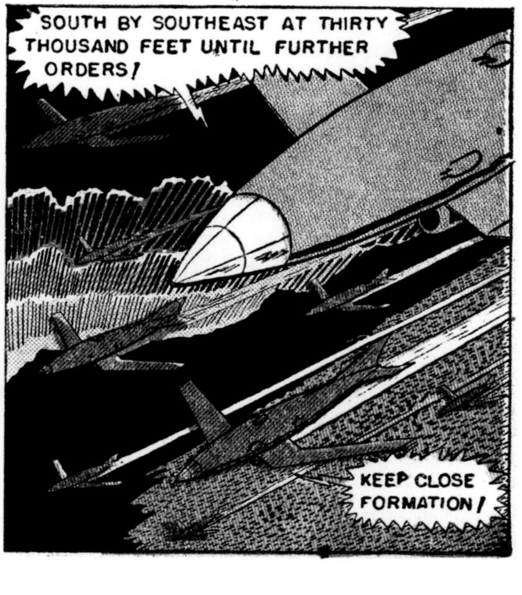
SOUTH BY SOUTHEAST AT THIRTY THOUSAND FEET UNTIL FURTHER ORDERS!
KEEP CLOSE FORMATION!

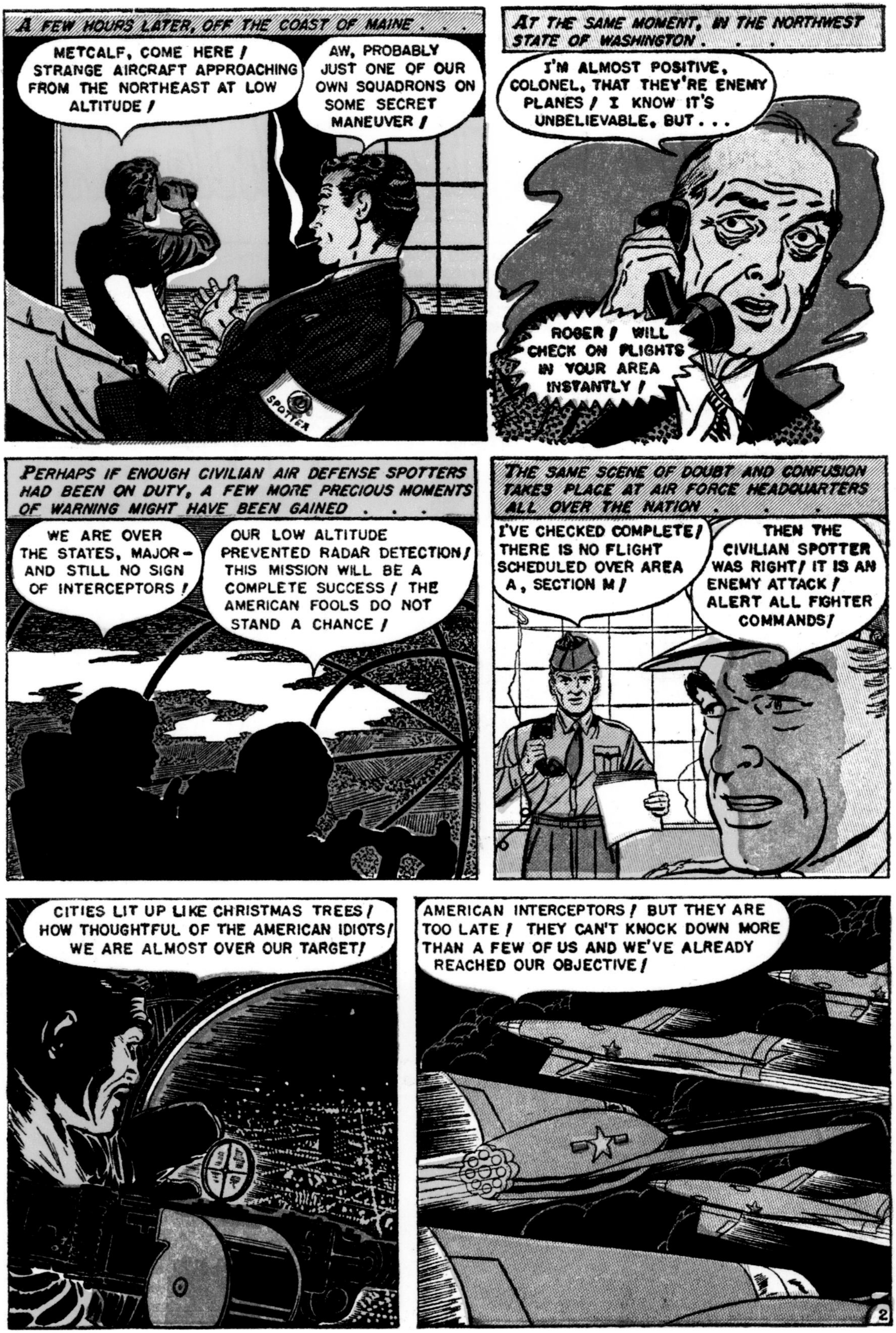
A FEW HOURS LATER, OFF THE COAST OF MAINE . . .
METCALF, COME HERE! STRANGE AIRCRAFT APPROACHING FROM THE NORTHEAST AT LOW ALTITUDE!
AW, PROBABLY JUST ONE OF OUR OWN SQUADRONS ON SOME SECRET MANEUVER!
SPOTTER
AT THE SAME MOMENT, IN THE NORTHWEST STATE OF WASHINGTON . . .
I'M ALMOST POSITIVE, COLONEL, THAT THEY'RE ENEMY PLANES! I KNOW IT'S UNBELIEVABLE, BUT . . .
ROGER! WILL CHECK ON FLIGHTS IN YOUR AREA INSTANTLY!
PERHAPS IF ENOUGH CIVILIAN AIR DEFENSE SPOTTERS HAD BEEN ON DUTY, A FEW MORE PRECIOUS MOMENTS OF WARNING MIGHT HAVE BEEN GAINED . . .
WE ARE OVER THE STATES, MAJOR— AND STILL NO SIGN OF INTERCEPTORS!
OUR LOW ALTITUDE PREVENTED RADAR DETECTION! THIS MISSION WILL BE A COMPLETE SUCCESS! THE AMERICAN FOOLS DO NOT STAND A CHANCE!
THE SAME SCENE OF DOUBT AND CONFUSION TAKES PLACE AT AIR FORCE HEADQUARTERS ALL OVER THE NATION . . .
I'VE CHECKED COMPLETE! THERE IS NO FLIGHT SCHEDULED OVER AREA A, SECTION M!
THEN THE CIVILIAN SPOTTER WAS RIGHT! IT IS AN ENEMY ATTACK! ALERT ALL FIGHTER COMMANDS!
CITIES LIT UP LIKE CHRISTMAS TREES! HOW THOUGHTFUL OF THE AMERICAN IDIOTS! WE ARE ALMOST OVER OUR TARGET!
AMERICAN INTERCEPTORS! BUT THEY ARE TOO LATE! THEY CAN'T KNOCK DOWN MORE THAN A FEW OF US AND WE'VE ALREADY REACHED OUR OBJECTIVE!
2

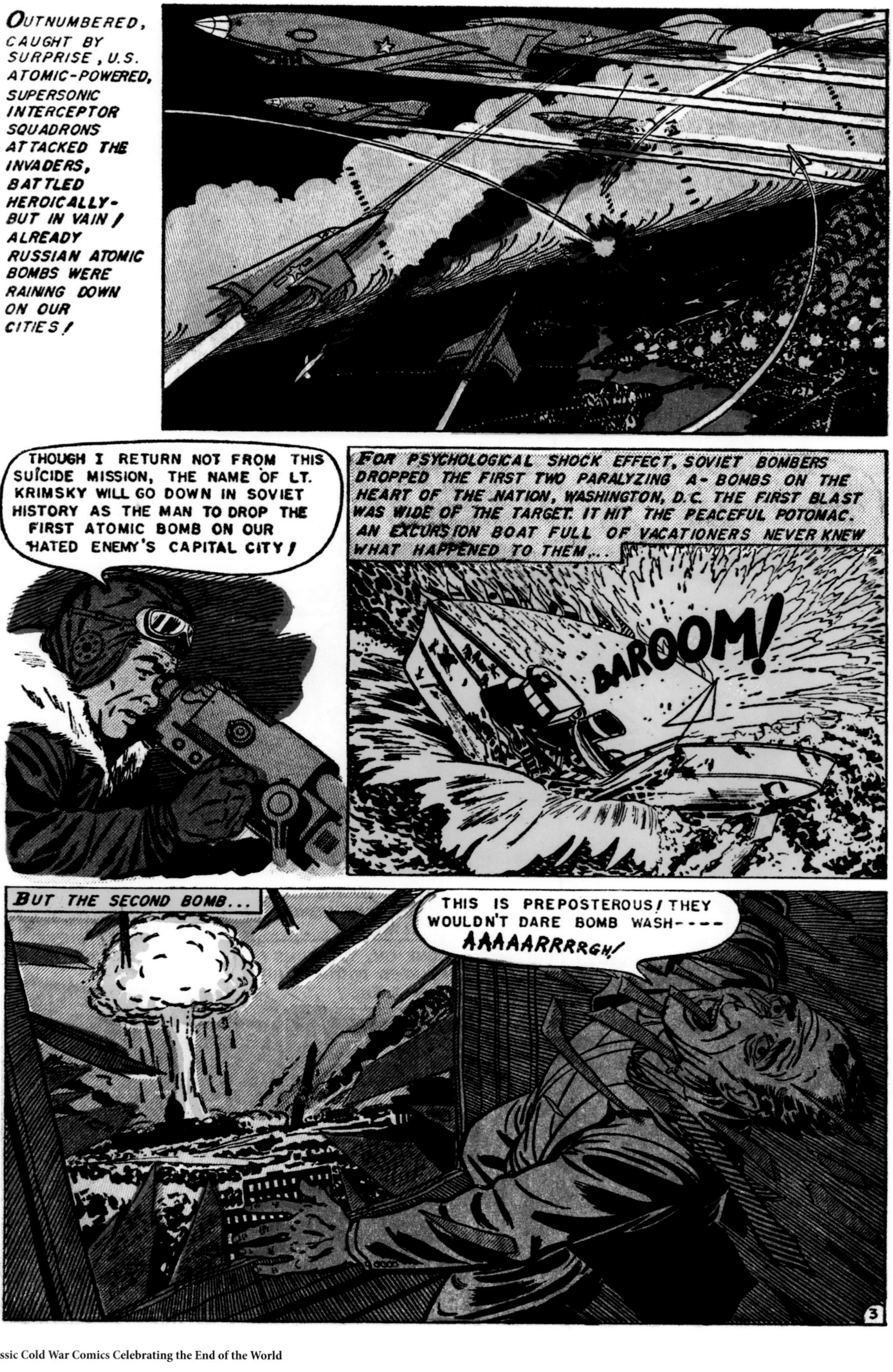
OUTNUMBERED, CAUGHT BY SURPRISE, U.S. ATOMIC-POWERED, SUPERSONIC INTERCEPTOR SQUADRONS ATTACKED THE INVADERS, BATTLED HEROICALLY- BUT IN VAIN! ALREADY RUSSIAN ATOMIC BOMBS WERE RAINING DOWN ON OUR CITIES!
THOUGH I RETURN NOT FROM THIS SUICIDE MISSION, THE NAME OF LT. KRIMSKY WILL GO DOWN IN SOVIET HISTORY AS THE MAN TO DROP THE FIRST ATOMIC BOMB ON OUR HATED ENEMY'S CAPITAL CITY!
FOR PSYCHOLOGICAL SHOCK EFFECT, SOVIET BOMBERS DROPPED THE FIRST TWO PARALYZING A-BOMBS ON THE HEART OF THE NATION, WASHINGTON, D.C. THE FIRST BLAST WAS WIDE OF THE TARGET. IT HIT THE PEACEFUL POTOMAC. AN EXCURSION BOAT FULL OF VACATIONERS NEVER KNEW WHAT HAPPENED TO THEM...
BAROOM!
BUT THE SECOND BOMB...
THIS IS PREPOSTEROUS! THEY WOULDN'T DARE BOMB WASH---- AAAAARRRRGH!
3

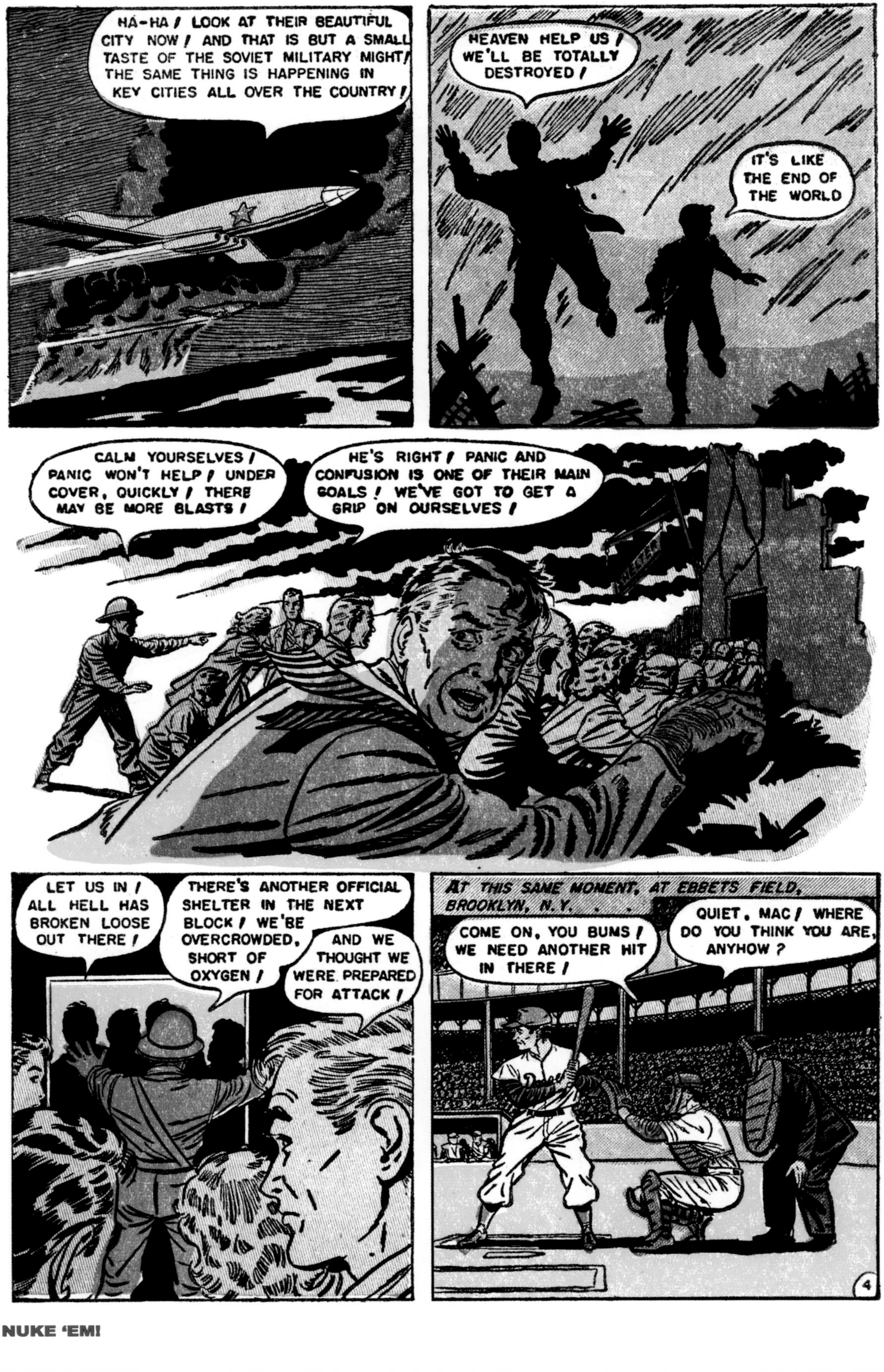
HA-HA! LOOK AT THEIR BEAUTIFUL CITY NOW! AND THAT IS BUT A SMALL TASTE OF THE SOVIET MILITARY MIGHT! THE SAME THING IS HAPPENING IN KEY CITIES ALL OVER THE COUNTRY!
HEAVEN HELP US! WE'LL BE TOTALLY DESTROYED!
IT'S LIKE THE END OF THE WORLD
CALM YOURSELVES! PANIC WON'T HELP! UNDER COVER, QUICKLY! THERE MAY BE MORE BLASTS!
HE'S RIGHT! PANIC AND CONFUSION IS ONE OF THEIR MAIN GOALS! WE'VE GOT TO GET A GRIP ON OURSELVES!
LET US IN! ALL HELL HAS BROKEN LOOSE OUT THERE!
THERE'S ANOTHER OFFICIAL SHELTER IN THE NEXT BLOCK! WE'BE OVERCROWDED, SHORT OF OXYGEN!
AND WE THOUGHT WE WERE PREPARED FOR ATTACK!
AT THIS SAME MOMENT, AT EBBETS FIELD, BROOKLYN, N.Y. . . .
COME ON, YOU BUMS! WE NEED ANOTHER HIT IN THERE!
QUIET, MAC! WHERE DO YOU THINK YOU ARE, ANYHOW?
4

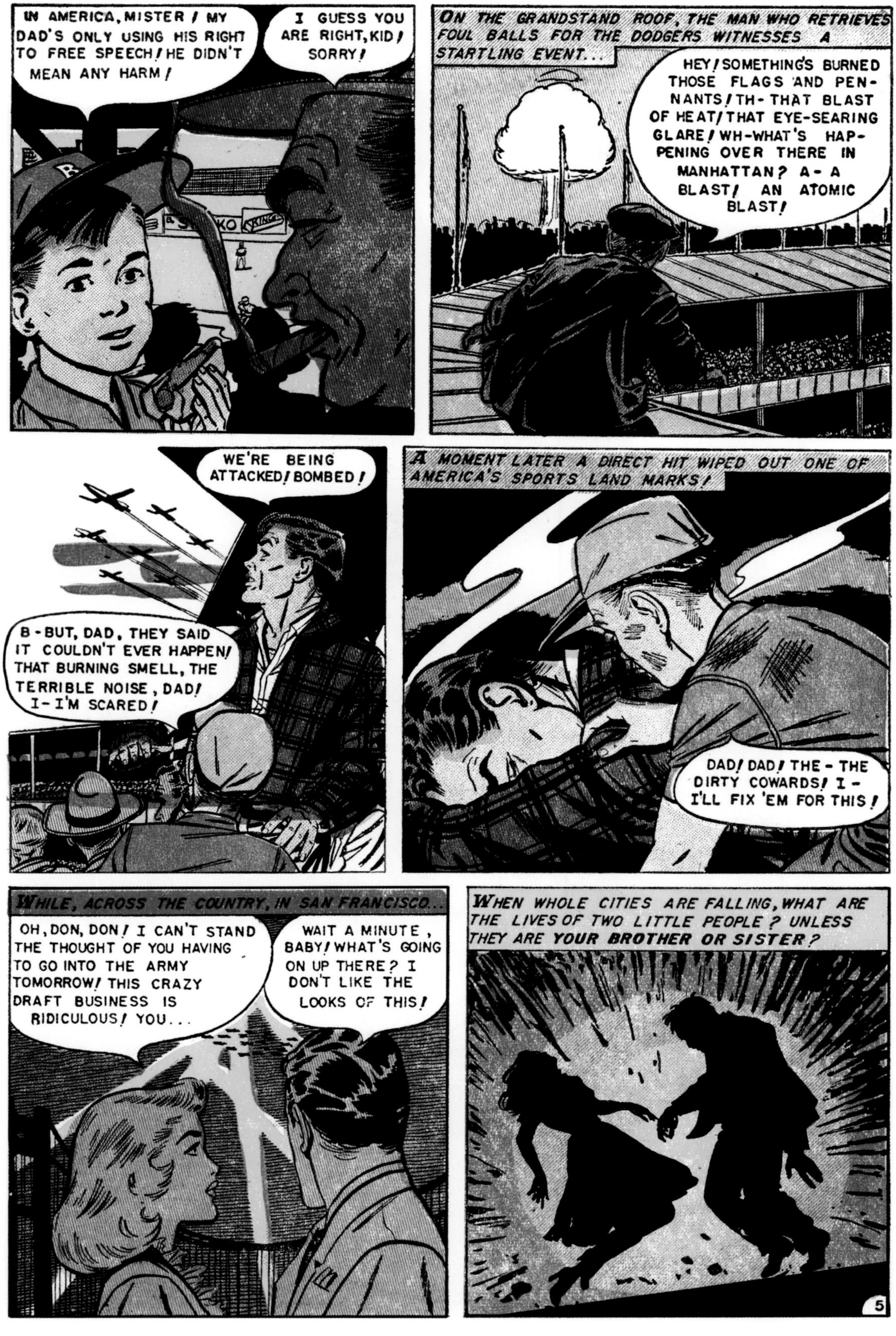
IN AMERICA, MISTER! MY DAD'S ONLY USING HIS RIGHT TO FREE SPEECH! HE DIDN'T MEAN ANY HARM!
I GUESS YOU ARE RIGHT, KID! SORRY!
ON THE GRANDSTAND ROOF, THE MAN WHO RETRIEVES FOUL BALLS FOR THE DODGERS WITNESSES A STARTLING EVENT...
HEY! SOMETHING'S BURNED THOSE FLAGS AND PENNANTS! TH-THAT BLAST OF HEAT! THAT EYE-SEARING GLARE! WH-WHAT'S HAPPENING OVER THERE IN MANHATTAN? A-A BLAST! AN ATOMIC BLAST!
WE'RE BEING ATTACKED! BOMBED!
B-BUT, DAD, THEY SAID IT COULDN'T EVER HAPPEN! THAT BURNING SMELL, THE TERRIBLE NOISE, DAD! I-I'M SCARED!
A MOMENT LATER A DIRECT HIT WIPED OUT ONE OF AMERICA'S SPORTS LAND MARKS!
DAD! DAD! THE-THE DIRTY COWARDS! I-I'LL FIX 'EM FOR THIS!
WHILE, ACROSS THE COUNTRY, IN SAN FRANCISCO...
OH, DON, DON! I CAN'T STAND THE THOUGHT OF YOU HAVING TO GO INTO THE ARMY TOMORROW! THIS CRAZY DRAFT BUSINESS IS RIDICULOUS! YOU...
WAIT A MINUTE, BABY! WHAT'S GOING ON UP THERE? I DON'T LIKE THE LOOKS OF THIS!
WHEN WHOLE CITIES ARE FALLING, WHAT ARE THE LIVES OF TWO LITTLE PEOPLE? UNLESS THEY ARE YOUR BROTHER OR SISTER?
5

NOT ONLY PEOPLE WERE VICTIMS OF THIS SAVAGE ALL-OUT ATTEMPT TO CRIPPLE AND ENSLAVE AMERICA IN ONE SMASH PUNCH! IN ADDITION TO SMALLER MILITARY AND PRODUCTION OBJECTIVES, THE VITAL NORFOLK-NEWPORT NEWS NAVAL BASE AND ENVIRONS, UNDER CONCENTRATED ATTACK BY SOVIET Z-M 49 SUPER HEAVY BOMBERS, BECAME ANOTHER PEARL HARBOR! AND WE SAID IT WOULD NEVER HAPPEN AGAIN! . . . .

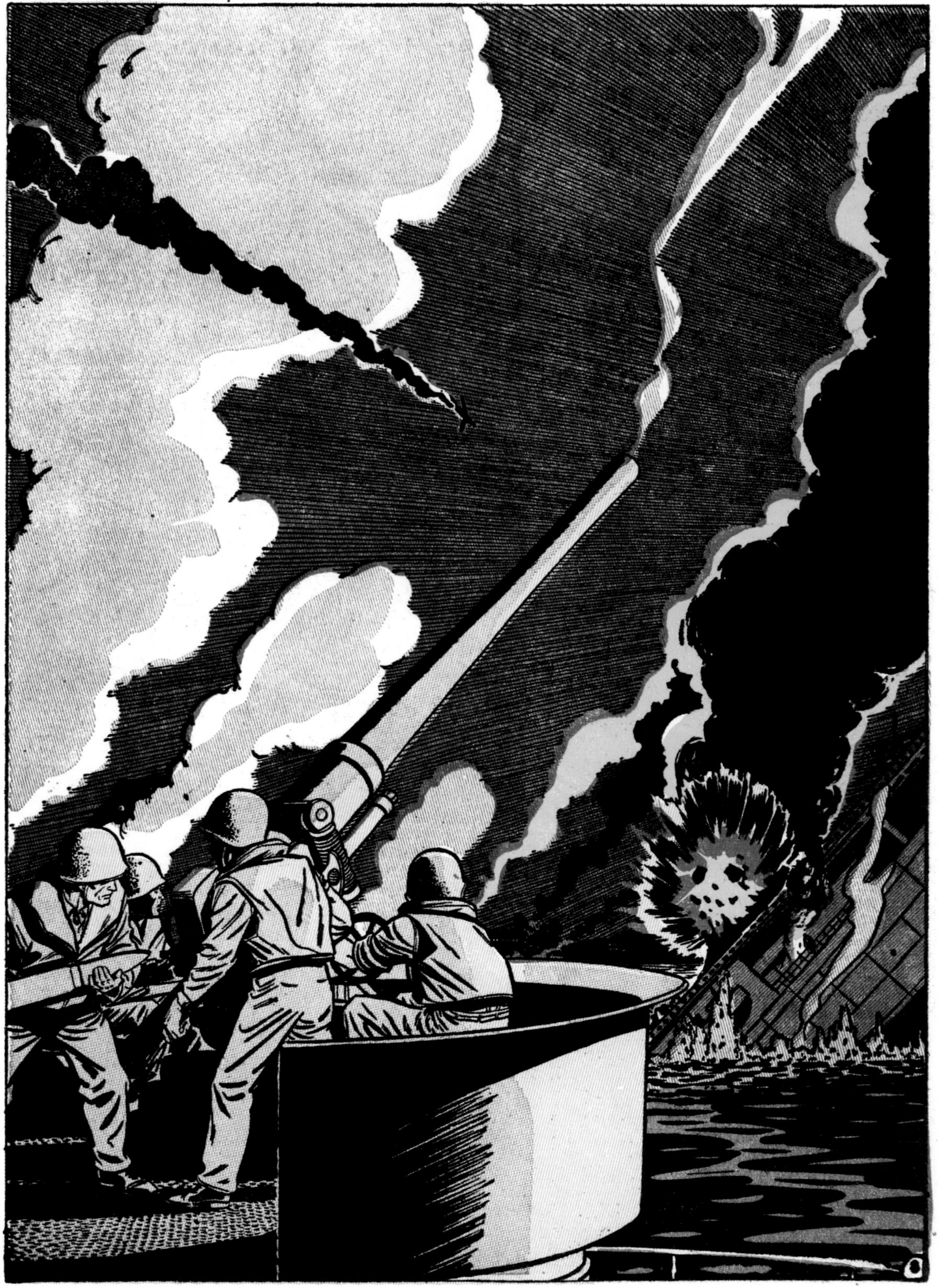

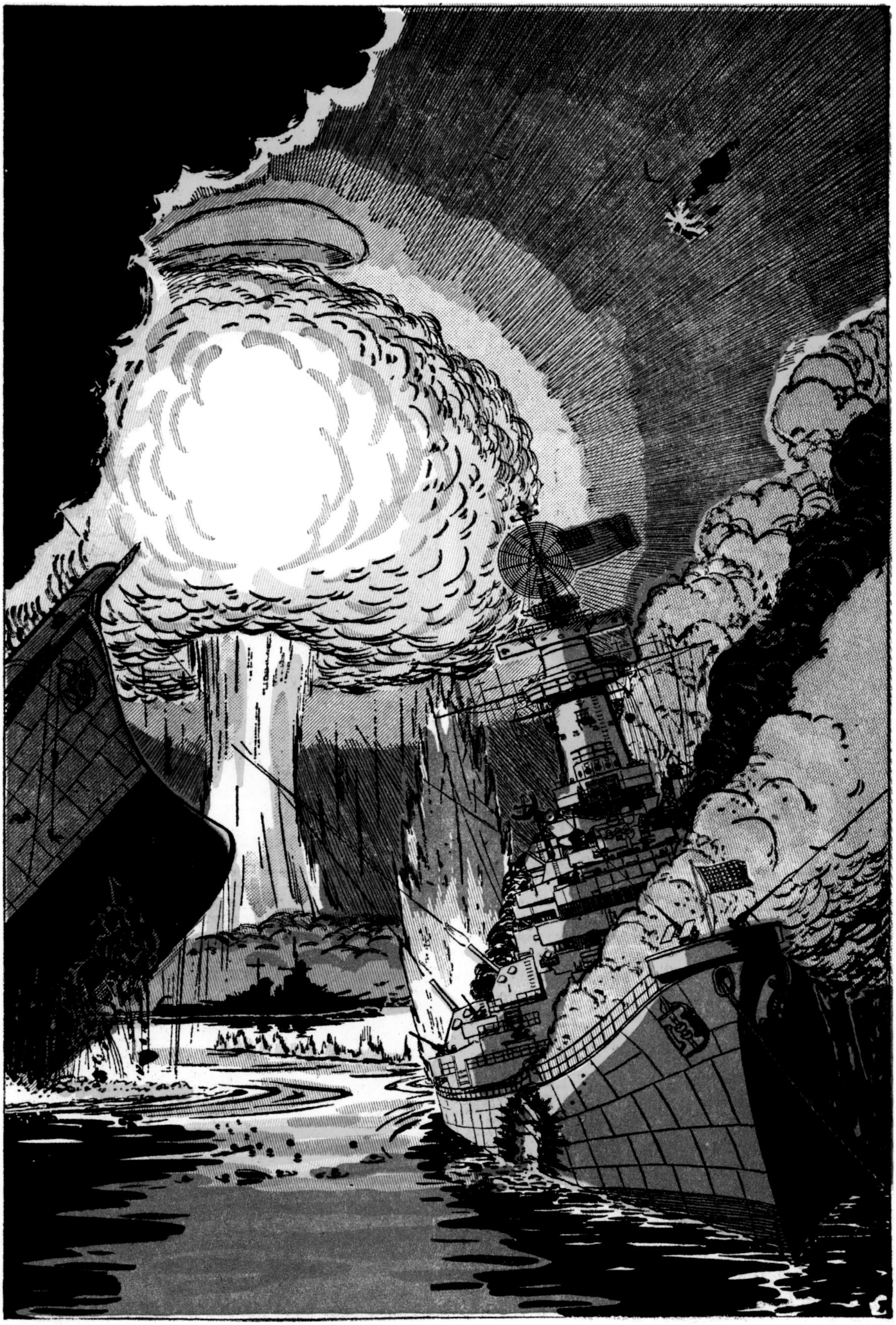

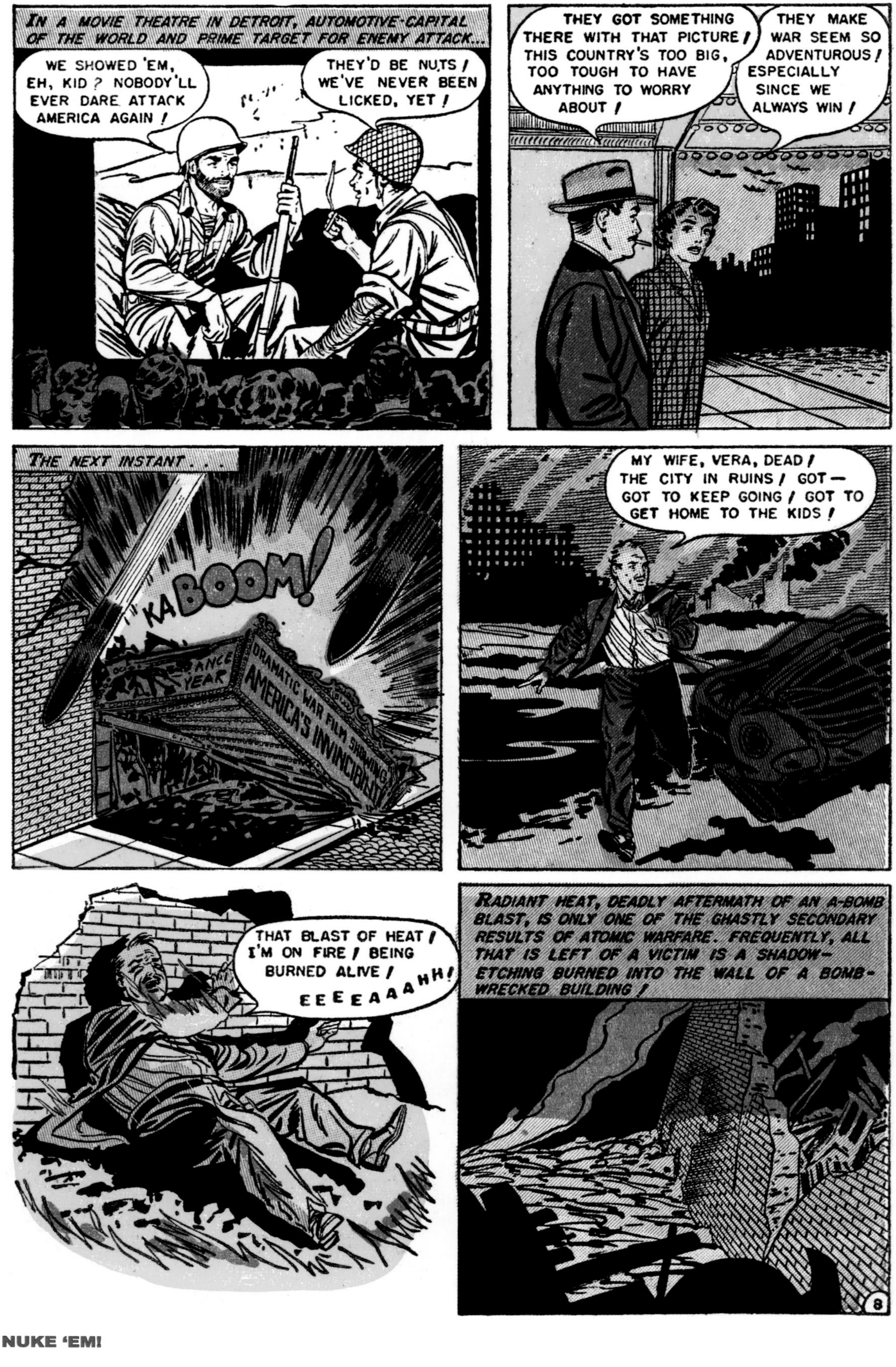
IN A MOVIE THEATRE IN DETROIT, AUTOMOTIVE-CAPITAL OF THE WORLD AND PRIME TARGET FOR ENEMY ATTACK...
WE SHOWED 'EM, EH, KID? NOBODY'LL EVER DARE ATTACK AMERICA AGAIN!
THEY'D BE NUTS! WE'VE NEVER BEEN LICKED, YET!
THEY GOT SOMETHING THERE WITH THAT PICTURE! THIS COUNTRY'S TOO BIG, TOO TOUGH TO HAVE ANYTHING TO WORRY ABOUT!
THEY MAKE WAR SEEM SO ADVENTUROUS! ESPECIALLY SINCE WE ALWAYS WIN!
THE NEXT INSTANT...
KA BOOM!
DRAMATIC WAR FILM SHOWING
AMERICA'S INVINCIBILITY
MY WIFE, VERA, DEAD! THE CITY IN RUINS! GOT— GOT TO KEEP GOING! GOT TO GET HOME TO THE KIDS!
THAT BLAST OF HEAT! I'M ON FIRE! BEING BURNED ALIVE! EEEEAAAAHH!
RADIANT HEAT, DEADLY AFTERMATH OF AN A-BOMB BLAST, IS ONLY ONE OF THE GHASTLY SECONDARY RESULTS OF ATOMIC WARFARE. FREQUENTLY, ALL THAT IS LEFT OF A VICTIM IS A SHADOW-ETCHING BURNED INTO THE WALL OF A BOMB-WRECKED BUILDING!
8

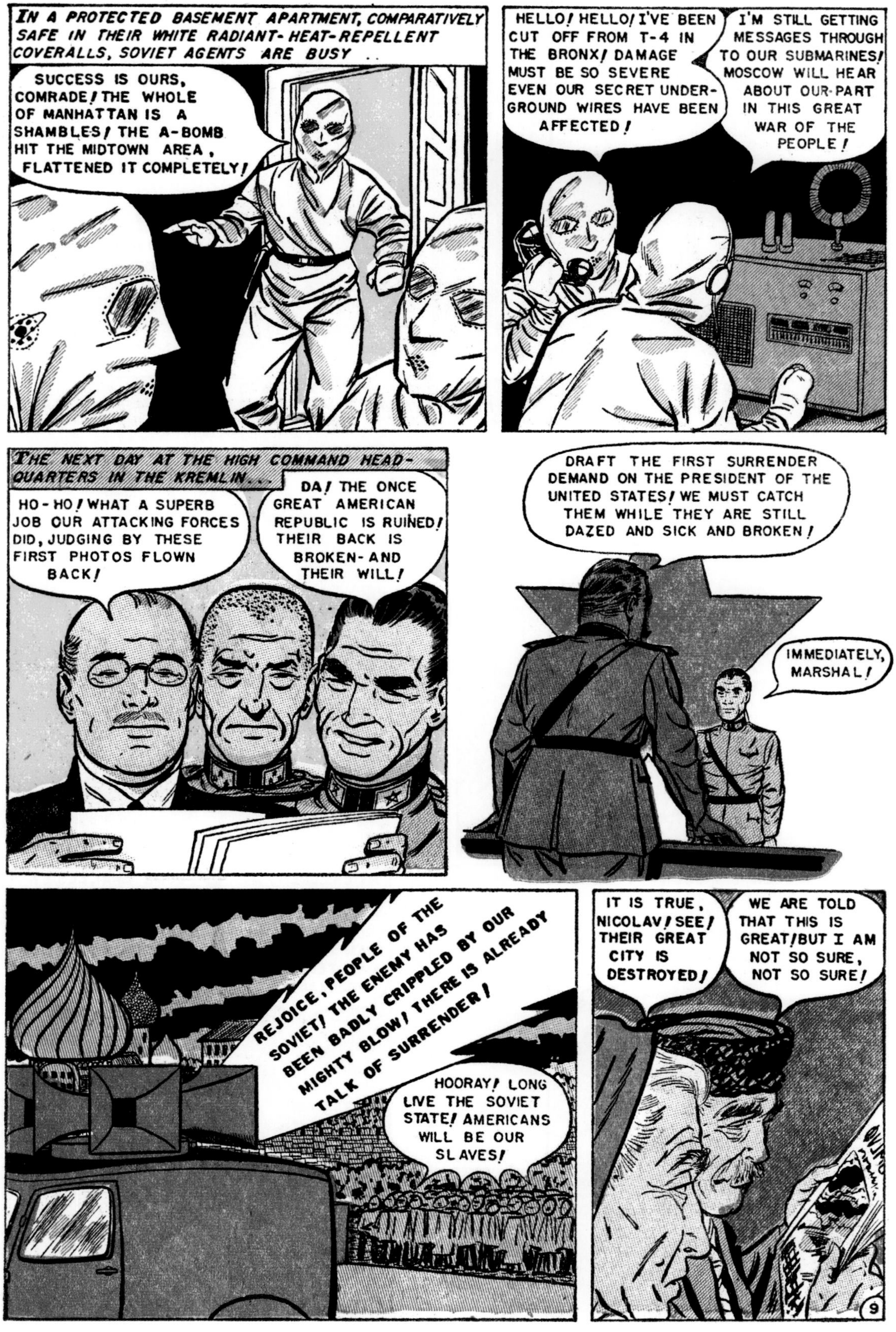
IN A PROTECTED BASEMENT APARTMENT, COMPARATIVELY SAFE IN THEIR WHITE RADIANT-HEAT-REPELLENT COVERALLS, SOVIET AGENTS ARE BUSY ..
SUCCESS IS OURS, COMRADE! THE WHOLE OF MANHATTAN IS A SHAMBLES! THE A-BOMB HIT THE MIDTOWN AREA, FLATTENED IT COMPLETELY!
HELLO! HELLO! I'VE BEEN CUT OFF FROM T-4 IN THE BRONX! DAMAGE MUST BE SO SEVERE EVEN OUR SECRET UNDER-GROUND WIRES HAVE BEEN AFFECTED!
I'M STILL GETTING MESSAGES THROUGH TO OUR SUBMARINES! MOSCOW WILL HEAR ABOUT OUR PART IN THIS GREAT WAR OF THE PEOPLE!
THE NEXT DAY AT THE HIGH COMMAND HEAD-QUARTERS IN THE KREMLIN...
HO-HO! WHAT A SUPERB JOB OUR ATTACKING FORCES DID, JUDGING BY THESE FIRST PHOTOS FLOWN BACK!
DA! THE ONCE GREAT AMERICAN REPUBLIC IS RUINED! THEIR BACK IS BROKEN- AND THEIR WILL!
DRAFT THE FIRST SURRENDER DEMAND ON THE PRESIDENT OF THE UNITED STATES! WE MUST CATCH THEM WHILE THEY ARE STILL DAZED AND SICK AND BROKEN!
IMMEDIATELY, MARSHAL!
REJOICE, PEOPLE OF THE SOVIET! THE ENEMY HAS BEEN BADLY CRIPPLED BY OUR MIGHTY BLOW! THERE IS ALREADY TALK OF SURRENDER!
HOORAY! LONG LIVE THE SOVIET STATE! AMERICANS WILL BE OUR SLAVES!
IT IS TRUE, NICOLAV! SEE! THEIR GREAT CITY IS DESTROYED!
WE ARE TOLD THAT THIS IS GREAT! BUT I AM NOT SO SURE, NOT SO SURE!
9

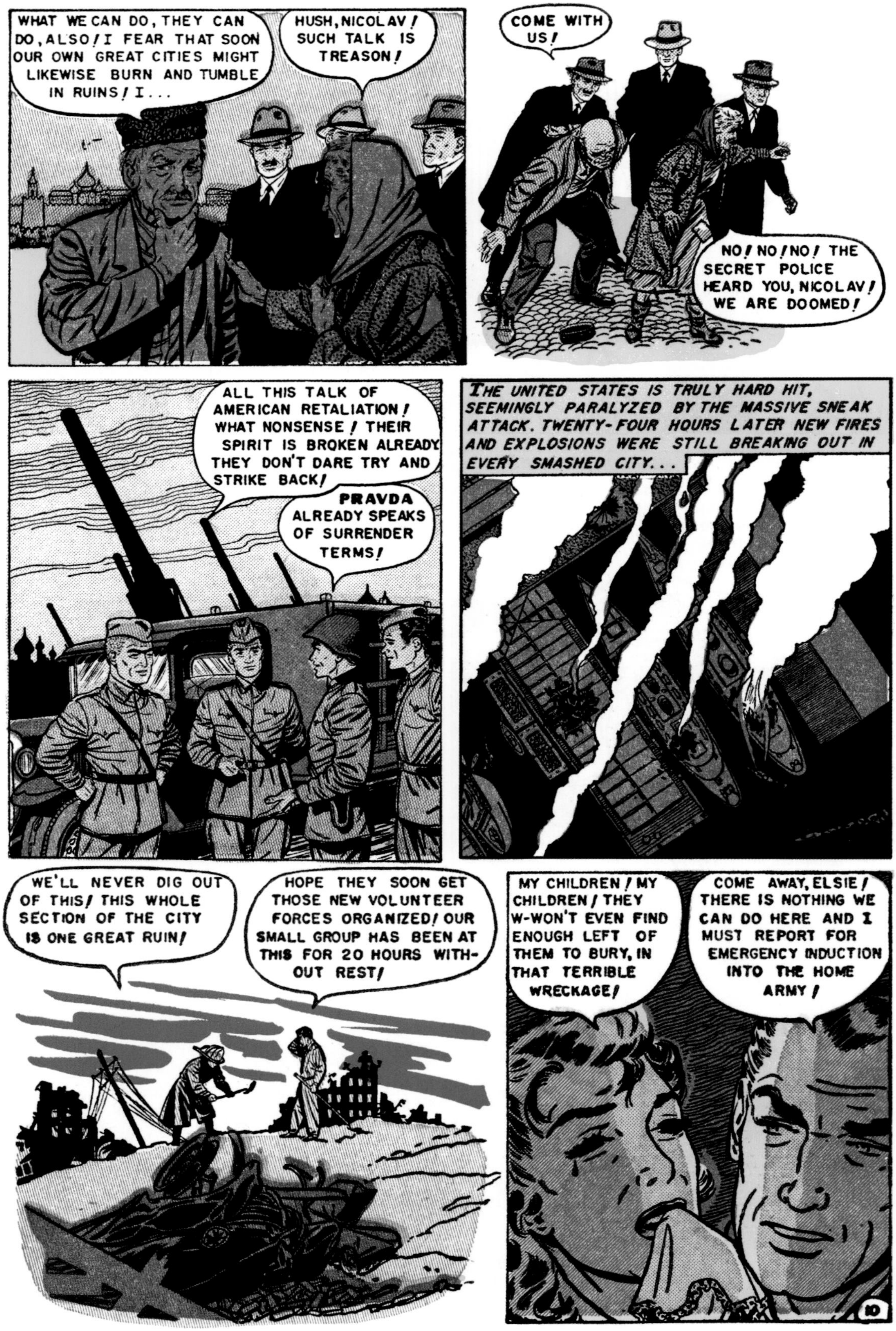
WHAT WE CAN DO, THEY CAN DO, ALSO! I FEAR THAT SOON OUR OWN GREAT CITIES MIGHT LIKEWISE BURN AND TUMBLE IN RUINS! I...
HUSH, NICOLAV! SUCH TALK IS TREASON!
COME WITH US!
NO! NO! NO! THE SECRET POLICE HEARD YOU, NICOLAV! WE ARE DOOMED!
ALL THIS TALK OF AMERICAN RETALIATION! WHAT NONSENSE! THEIR SPIRIT IS BROKEN ALREADY THEY DON'T DARE TRY AND STRIKE BACK!
PRAVDA ALREADY SPEAKS OF SURRENDER TERMS!
THE UNITED STATES IS TRULY HARD HIT, SEEMINGLY PARALYZED BY THE MASSIVE SNEAK ATTACK. TWENTY-FOUR HOURS LATER NEW FIRES AND EXPLOSIONS WERE STILL BREAKING OUT IN EVERY SMASHED CITY...
WE'LL NEVER DIG OUT OF THIS! THIS WHOLE SECTION OF THE CITY IS ONE GREAT RUIN!
HOPE THEY SOON GET THOSE NEW VOLUNTEER FORCES ORGANIZED! OUR SMALL GROUP HAS BEEN AT THIS FOR 20 HOURS WITHOUT REST!
MY CHILDREN! MY CHILDREN! THEY W-WON'T EVEN FIND ENOUGH LEFT OF THEM TO BURY, IN THAT TERRIBLE WRECKAGE!
COME AWAY, ELSIE! THERE IS NOTHING WE CAN DO HERE AND I MUST REPORT FOR EMERGENCY INDUCTION INTO THE HOME ARMY!
10

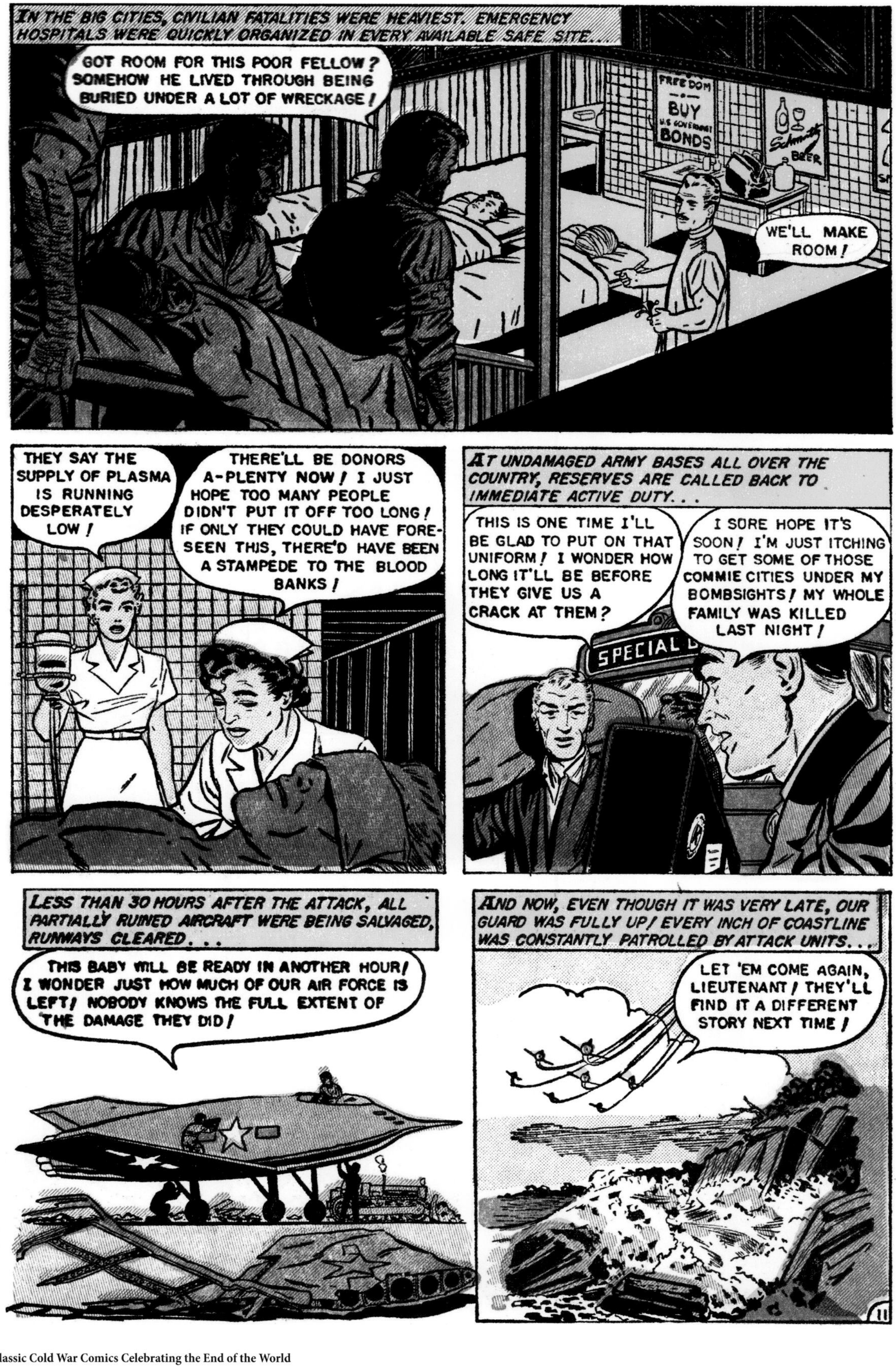

IN THE BIG CITIES, CIVILIAN FATALITIES WERE HEAVIEST. EMERGENCY HOSPITALS WERE QUICKLY ORGANIZED IN EVERY AVAILABLE SAFE SITE...
GOT ROOM FOR THIS POOR FELLOW? SOMEHOW HE LIVED THROUGH BEING BURIED UNDER A LOT OF WRECKAGE!
FREEDOM
BUY
U.S. GOVERNMENT
BONDS
BEER
WE'LL MAKE ROOM!
THEY SAY THE SUPPLY OF PLASMA IS RUNNING DESPERATELY LOW!
THERE'LL BE DONORS A-PLENTY NOW! I JUST HOPE TOO MANY PEOPLE DIDN'T PUT IT OFF TOO LONG! IF ONLY THEY COULD HAVE FORESEEN THIS, THERE'D HAVE BEEN A STAMPEDE TO THE BLOOD BANKS!
AT UNDAMAGED ARMY BASES ALL OVER THE COUNTRY, RESERVES ARE CALLED BACK TO IMMEDIATE ACTIVE DUTY...
THIS IS ONE TIME I'LL BE GLAD TO PUT ON THAT UNIFORM! I WONDER HOW LONG IT'LL BE BEFORE THEY GIVE US A CRACK AT THEM?
I SURE HOPE IT'S SOON! I'M JUST ITCHING TO GET SOME OF THOSE COMMIE CITIES UNDER MY BOMBSIGHTS! MY WHOLE FAMILY WAS KILLED LAST NIGHT!
SPECIAL
LESS THAN 30 HOURS AFTER THE ATTACK, ALL PARTIALLY RUINED AIRCRAFT WERE BEING SALVAGED, RUNWAYS CLEARED...
THIS BABY WILL BE READY IN ANOTHER HOUR! I WONDER JUST HOW MUCH OF OUR AIR FORCE IS LEFT! NOBODY KNOWS THE FULL EXTENT OF THE DAMAGE THEY DID!
AND NOW, EVEN THOUGH IT WAS VERY LATE, OUR GUARD WAS FULLY UP! EVERY INCH OF COASTLINE WAS CONSTANTLY PATROLLED BY ATTACK UNITS...
LET 'EM COME AGAIN, LIEUTENANT! THEY'LL FIND IT A DIFFERENT STORY NEXT TIME!
11

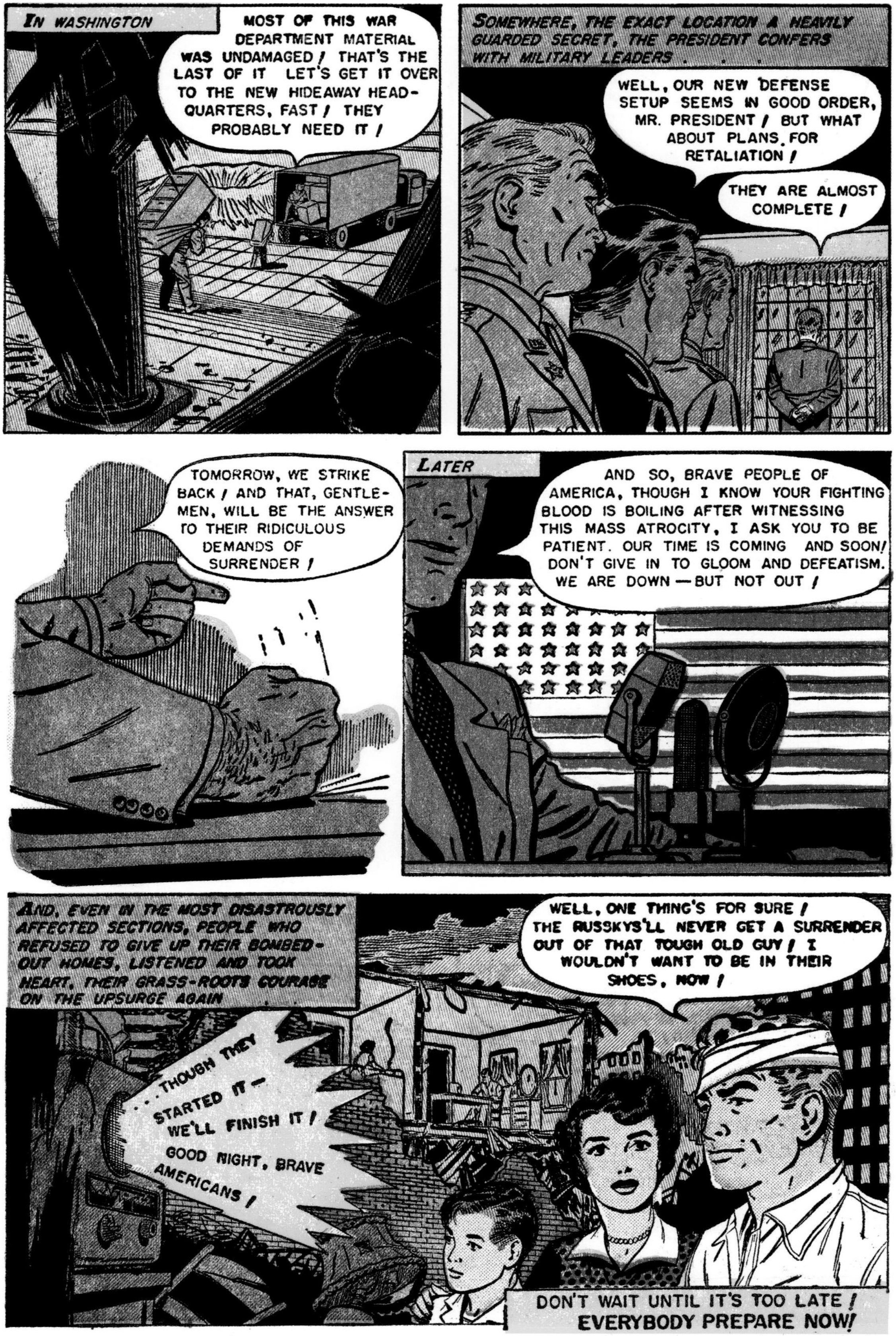
IN WASHINGTON
MOST OF THIS WAR DEPARTMENT MATERIAL WAS UNDAMAGED! THAT'S THE LAST OF IT LET'S GET IT OVER TO THE NEW HIDEAWAY HEAD-QUARTERS, FAST! THEY PROBABLY NEED IT!
SOMEWHERE, THE EXACT LOCATION A HEAVILY GUARDED SECRET, THE PRESIDENT CONFERS WITH MILITARY LEADERS . . .
WELL, OUR NEW DEFENSE SETUP SEEMS IN GOOD ORDER, MR. PRESIDENT! BUT WHAT ABOUT PLANS FOR RETALIATION!
THEY ARE ALMOST COMPLETE!
TOMORROW, WE STRIKE BACK! AND THAT, GENTLE-MEN, WILL BE THE ANSWER TO THEIR RIDICULOUS DEMANDS OF SURRENDER!
LATER
AND SO, BRAVE PEOPLE OF AMERICA, THOUGH I KNOW YOUR FIGHTING BLOOD IS BOILING AFTER WITNESSING THIS MASS ATROCITY, I ASK YOU TO BE PATIENT. OUR TIME IS COMING AND SOON! DON'T GIVE IN TO GLOOM AND DEFEATISM. WE ARE DOWN — BUT NOT OUT!
AND, EVEN IN THE MOST DISASTROUSLY AFFECTED SECTIONS, PEOPLE WHO REFUSED TO GIVE UP THEIR BOMBED-OUT HOMES, LISTENED AND TOOK HEART. THEIR GRASS-ROOTS COURAGE ON THE UPSURGE AGAIN
. . . THOUGH THEY STARTED IT — WE'LL FINISH IT! GOOD NIGHT, BRAVE AMERICANS!
WELL, ONE THING'S FOR SURE! THE RUSSKYS'LL NEVER GET A SURRENDER OUT OF THAT TOUGH OLD GUY! I WOULDN'T WANT TO BE IN THEIR SHOES, NOW!
DON'T WAIT UNTIL IT'S TOO LATE!
EVERYBODY PREPARE NOW!

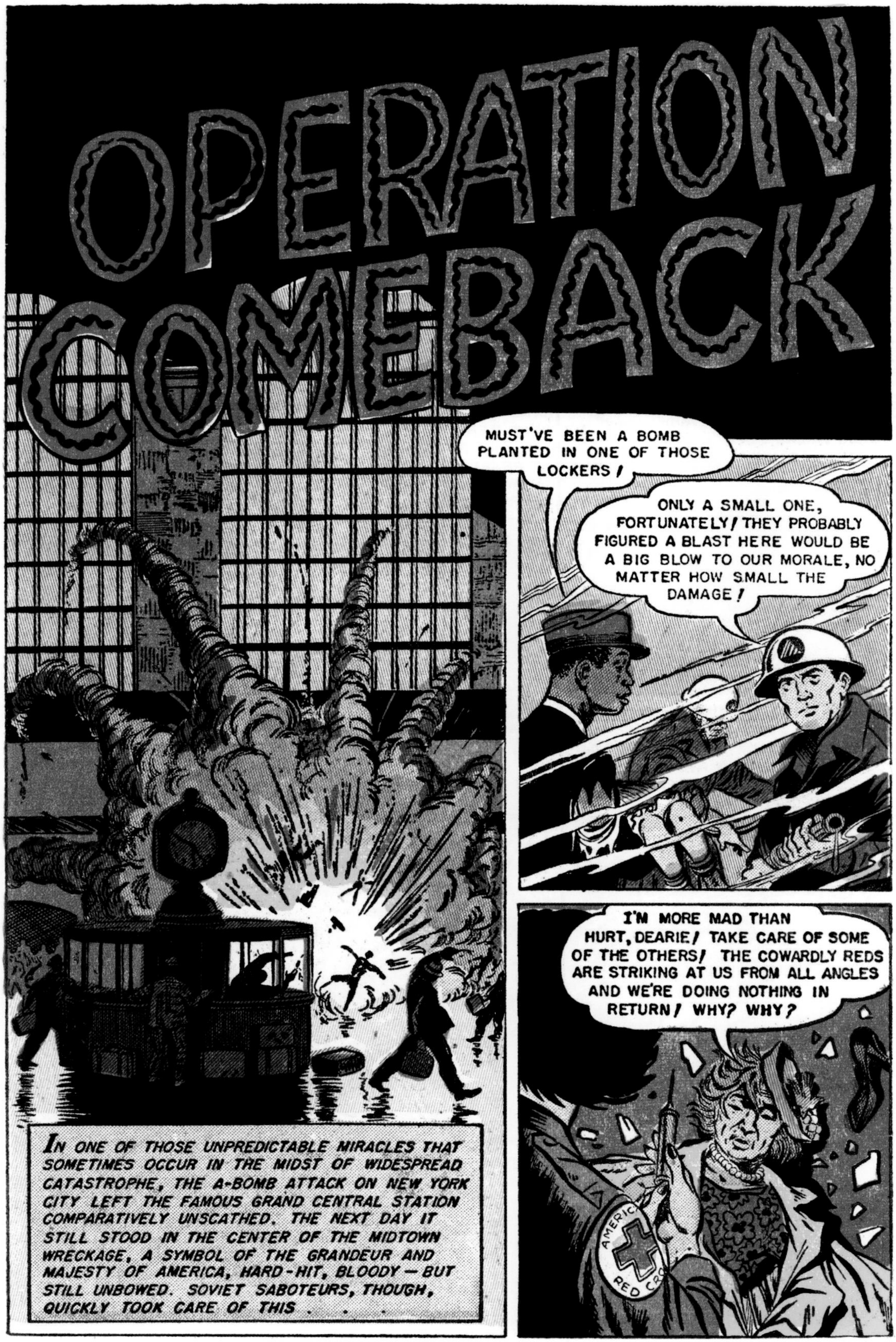
OPERATION COMEBACK
MUST'VE BEEN A BOMB PLANTED IN ONE OF THOSE LOCKERS!
ONLY A SMALL ONE, FORTUNATELY! THEY PROBABLY FIGURED A BLAST HERE WOULD BE A BIG BLOW TO OUR MORALE, NO MATTER HOW SMALL THE DAMAGE!
IN ONE OF THOSE UNPREDICTABLE MIRACLES THAT SOMETIMES OCCUR IN THE MIDST OF WIDESPREAD CATASTROPHE, THE A-BOMB ATTACK ON NEW YORK CITY LEFT THE FAMOUS GRAND CENTRAL STATION COMPARATIVELY UNSCATHED. THE NEXT DAY IT STILL STOOD IN THE CENTER OF THE MIDTOWN WRECKAGE, A SYMBOL OF THE GRANDEUR AND MAJESTY OF AMERICA, HARD-HIT, BLOODY — BUT STILL UNBOWED. SOVIET SABOTEURS, THOUGH, QUICKLY TOOK CARE OF THIS . . .
I'M MORE MAD THAN HURT, DEARIE! TAKE CARE OF SOME OF THE OTHERS! THE COWARDLY REDS ARE STRIKING AT US FROM ALL ANGLES AND WE'RE DOING NOTHING IN RETURN! WHY? WHY?

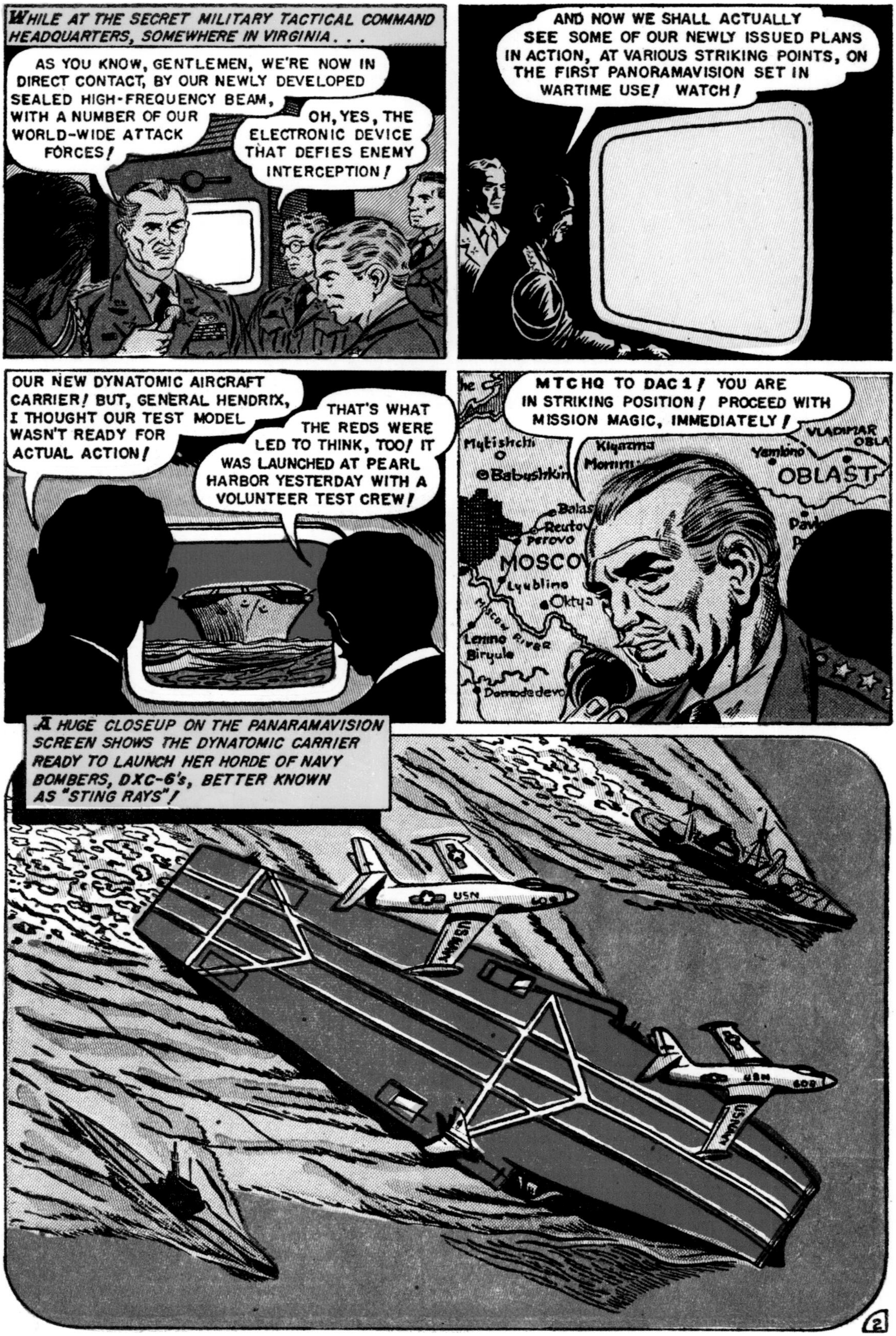

WHILE AT THE SECRET MILITARY TACTICAL COMMAND HEADQUARTERS, SOMEWHERE IN VIRGINIA . . .
AS YOU KNOW, GENTLEMEN, WE'RE NOW IN DIRECT CONTACT, BY OUR NEWLY DEVELOPED SEALED HIGH-FREQUENCY BEAM, WITH A NUMBER OF OUR WORLD-WIDE ATTACK FORCES!
OH, YES, THE ELECTRONIC DEVICE THAT DEFIES ENEMY INTERCEPTION!
AND NOW WE SHALL ACTUALLY SEE SOME OF OUR NEWLY ISSUED PLANS IN ACTION, AT VARIOUS STRIKING POINTS, ON THE FIRST PANORAMAVISION SET IN WARTIME USE! WATCH!
OUR NEW DYNATOMIC AIRCRAFT CARRIER! BUT, GENERAL HENDRIX, I THOUGHT OUR TEST MODEL WASN'T READY FOR ACTUAL ACTION!
THAT'S WHAT THE REDS WERE LED TO THINK, TOO! IT WAS LAUNCHED AT PEARL HARBOR YESTERDAY WITH A VOLUNTEER TEST CREW!
MTCHQ TO DAC 1! YOU ARE IN STRIKING POSITION! PROCEED WITH MISSION MAGIC, IMMEDIATELY!
Mytishchi
Babushkin
Balas
Reutov
Perovo
MOSCOW
Lyublino
Oktya
Moscow River
Lenino
Biryule
Domodedevo
OBLAST
Yambino
VLADIMIR OBLA
A HUGE CLOSEUP ON THE PANARAMAVISION SCREEN SHOWS THE DYNATOMIC CARRIER READY TO LAUNCH HER HORDE OF NAVY BOMBERS, DXC-6's, BETTER KNOWN AS "STING RAYS"!
USN
USN
2

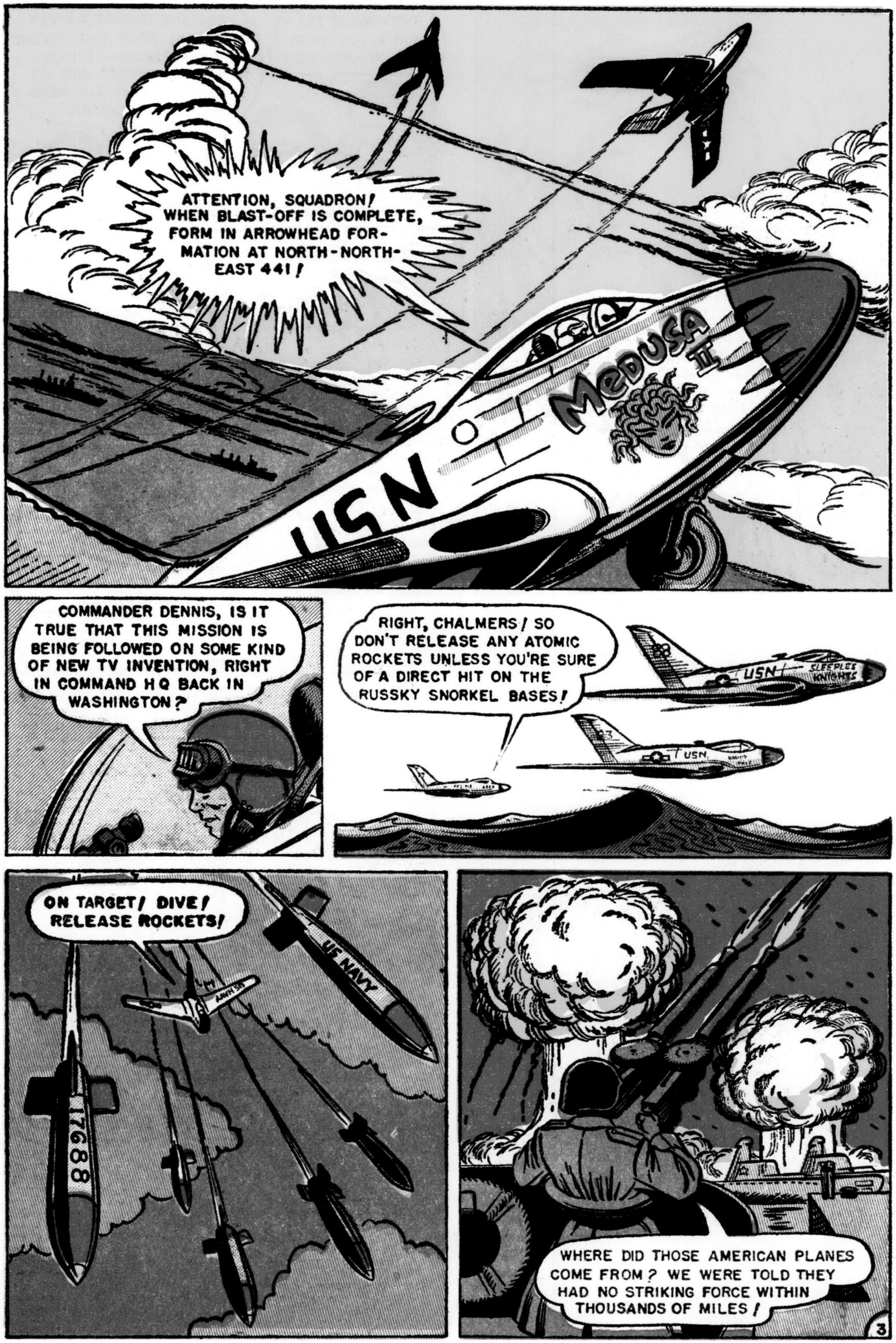

ATTENTION, SQUADRON! WHEN BLAST-OFF IS COMPLETE, FORM IN ARROWHEAD FORMATION AT NORTH-NORTH-EAST 441!
MEDUSA II
USN
COMMANDER DENNIS, IS IT TRUE THAT THIS MISSION IS BEING FOLLOWED ON SOME KIND OF NEW TV INVENTION, RIGHT IN COMMAND H Q BACK IN WASHINGTON?
RIGHT, CHALMERS! SO DON'T RELEASE ANY ATOMIC ROCKETS UNLESS YOU'RE SURE OF A DIRECT HIT ON THE RUSSKY SNORKEL BASES!
ON TARGET! DIVE! RELEASE ROCKETS!
US NAVY
17688
WHERE DID THOSE AMERICAN PLANES COME FROM? WE WERE TOLD THEY HAD NO STRIKING FORCE WITHIN THOUSANDS OF MILES!
3

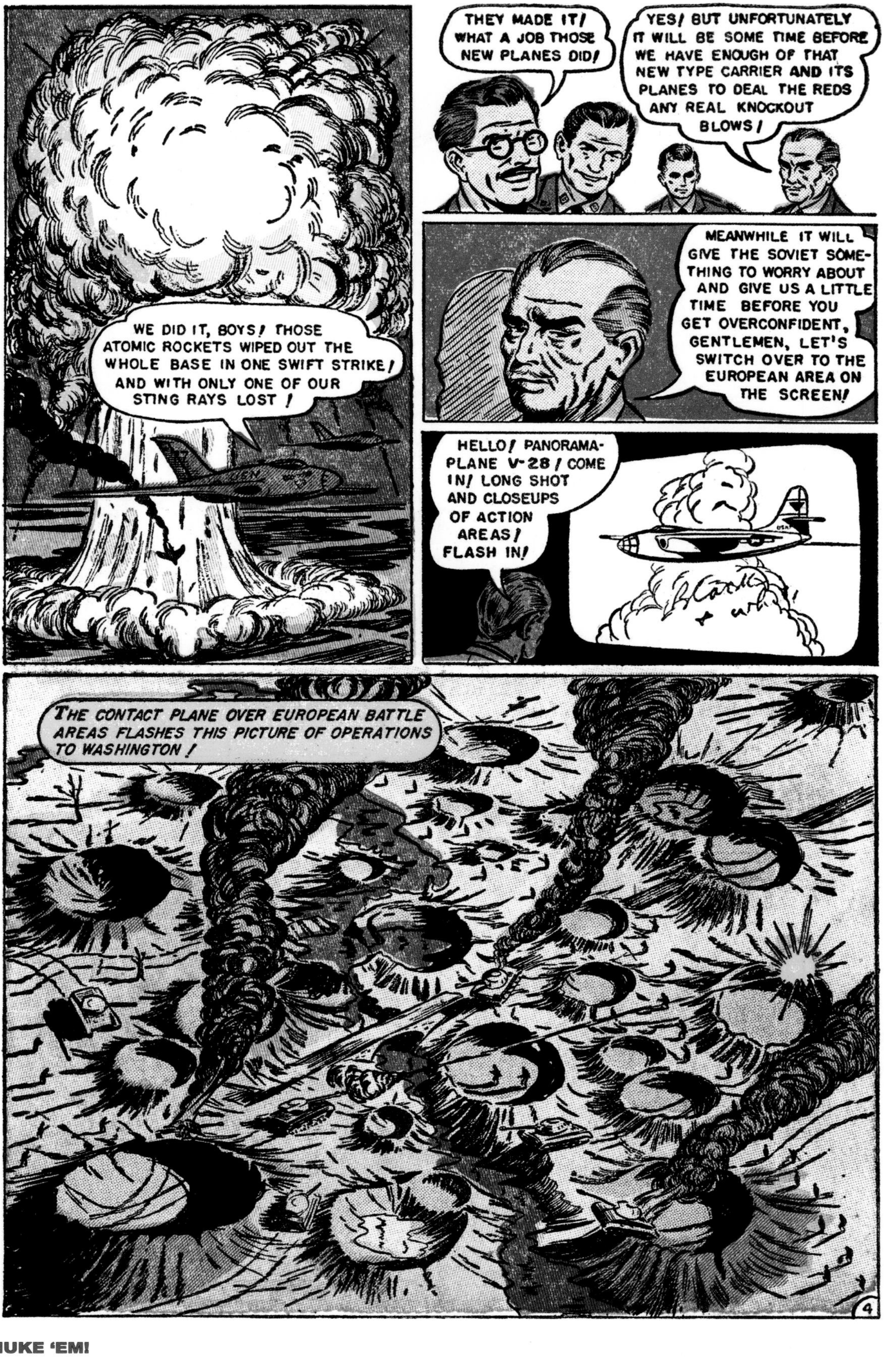
WE DID IT, BOYS! THOSE ATOMIC ROCKETS WIPED OUT THE WHOLE BASE IN ONE SWIFT STRIKE! AND WITH ONLY ONE OF OUR STING RAYS LOST!
THEY MADE IT! WHAT A JOB THOSE NEW PLANES DID!
YES! BUT UNFORTUNATELY IT WILL BE SOME TIME BEFORE WE HAVE ENOUGH OF THAT NEW TYPE CARRIER AND ITS PLANES TO DEAL THE REDS ANY REAL KNOCKOUT BLOWS!
MEANWHILE IT WILL GIVE THE SOVIET SOMETHING TO WORRY ABOUT AND GIVE US A LITTLE TIME BEFORE YOU GET OVERCONFIDENT, GENTLEMEN, LET'S SWITCH OVER TO THE EUROPEAN AREA ON THE SCREEN!
HELLO! PANORAMA-PLANE V-28! COME IN! LONG SHOT AND CLOSEUPS OF ACTION AREAS! FLASH IN!
THE CONTACT PLANE OVER EUROPEAN BATTLE AREAS FLASHES THIS PICTURE OF OPERATIONS TO WASHINGTON!
4

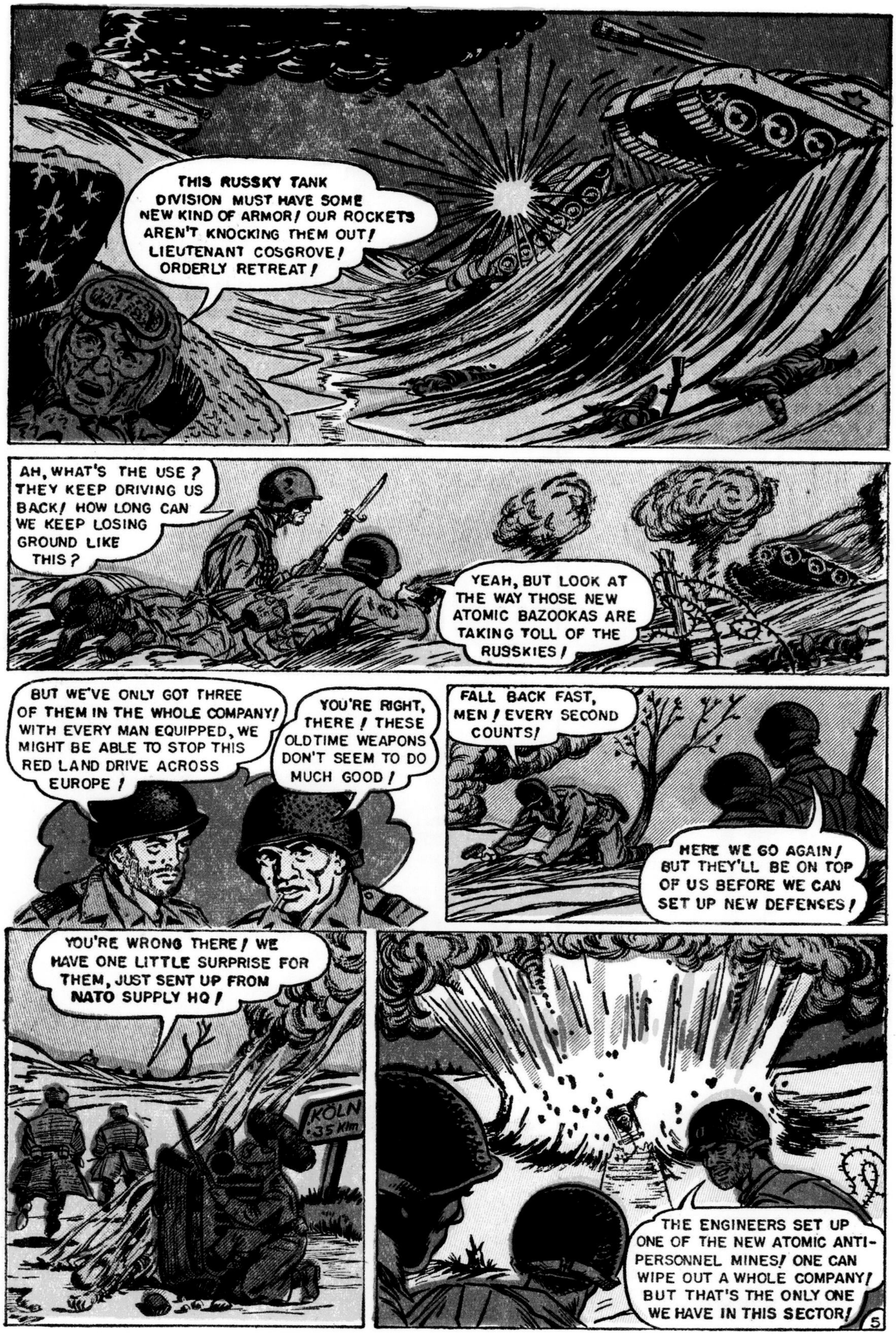
THIS RUSSKY TANK DIVISION MUST HAVE SOME NEW KIND OF ARMOR! OUR ROCKETS AREN'T KNOCKING THEM OUT! LIEUTENANT COSGROVE! ORDERLY RETREAT!
AH, WHAT'S THE USE? THEY KEEP DRIVING US BACK! HOW LONG CAN WE KEEP LOSING GROUND LIKE THIS?
YEAH, BUT LOOK AT THE WAY THOSE NEW ATOMIC BAZOOKAS ARE TAKING TOLL OF THE RUSSKIES!
BUT WE'VE ONLY GOT THREE OF THEM IN THE WHOLE COMPANY! WITH EVERY MAN EQUIPPED, WE MIGHT BE ABLE TO STOP THIS RED LAND DRIVE ACROSS EUROPE!
YOU'RE RIGHT, THERE! THESE OLDTIME WEAPONS DON'T SEEM TO DO MUCH GOOD!
FALL BACK FAST, MEN! EVERY SECOND COUNTS!
HERE WE GO AGAIN! BUT THEY'LL BE ON TOP OF US BEFORE WE CAN SET UP NEW DEFENSES!
YOU'RE WRONG THERE! WE HAVE ONE LITTLE SURPRISE FOR THEM, JUST SENT UP FROM NATO SUPPLY HQ!
KÖLN 35 Klm
THE ENGINEERS SET UP ONE OF THE NEW ATOMIC ANTI-PERSONNEL MINES! ONE CAN WIPE OUT A WHOLE COMPANY! BUT THAT'S THE ONLY ONE WE HAVE IN THIS SECTOR!
5

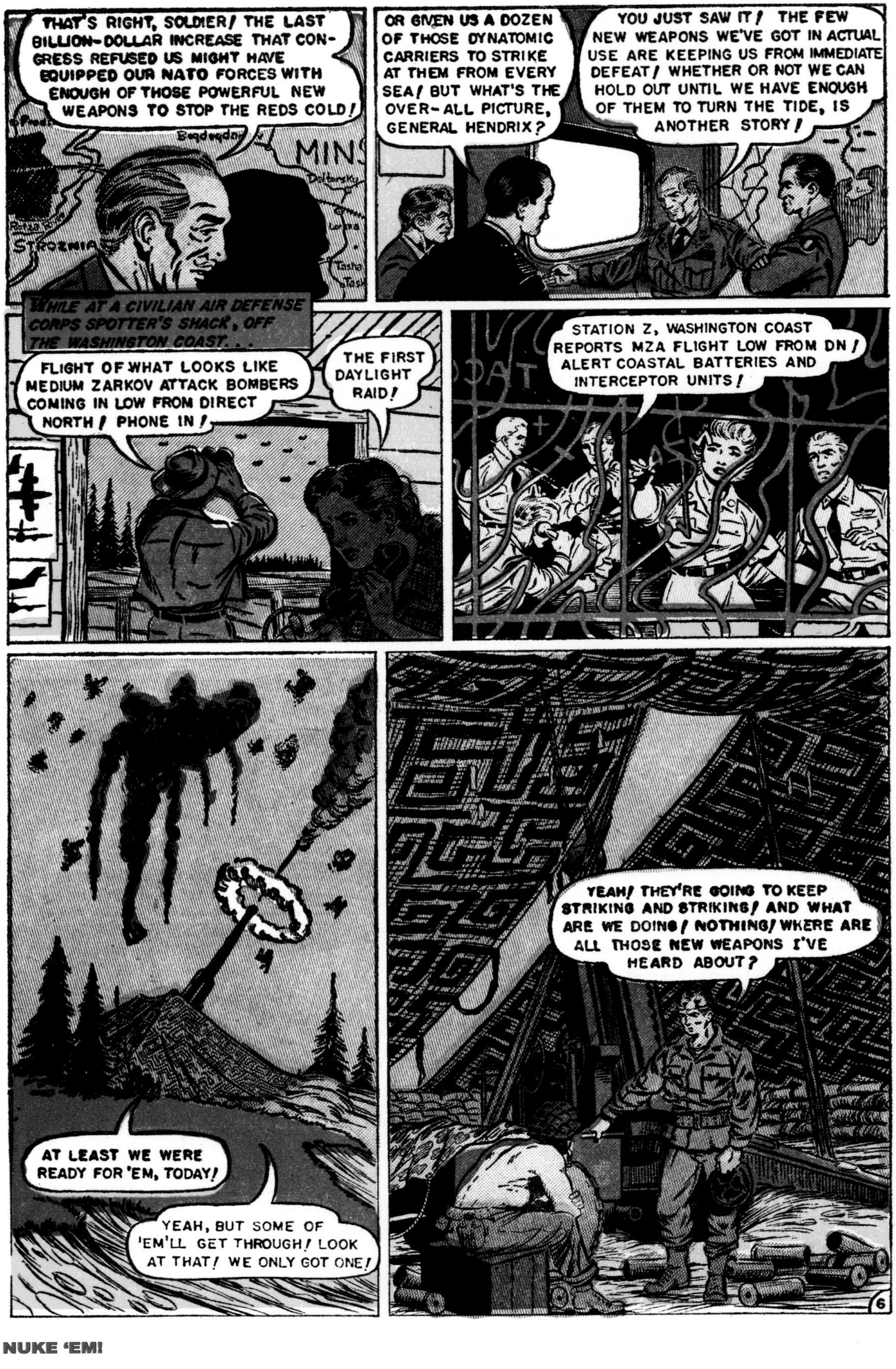
THAT'S RIGHT, SOLDIER! THE LAST BILLION-DOLLAR INCREASE THAT CONGRESS REFUSED US MIGHT HAVE EQUIPPED OUR NATO FORCES WITH ENOUGH OF THOSE POWERFUL NEW WEAPONS TO STOP THE REDS COLD!
MINS
STROZNIA
OR GIVEN US A DOZEN OF THOSE DYNATOMIC CARRIERS TO STRIKE AT THEM FROM EVERY SEA! BUT WHAT'S THE OVER-ALL PICTURE, GENERAL HENDRIX?
YOU JUST SAW IT! THE FEW NEW WEAPONS WE'VE GOT IN ACTUAL USE ARE KEEPING US FROM IMMEDIATE DEFEAT! WHETHER OR NOT WE CAN HOLD OUT UNTIL WE HAVE ENOUGH OF THEM TO TURN THE TIDE, IS ANOTHER STORY!
WHILE AT A CIVILIAN AIR DEFENSE CORPS SPOTTER'S SHACK, OFF THE WASHINGTON COAST...
FLIGHT OF WHAT LOOKS LIKE MEDIUM ZARKOV ATTACK BOMBERS COMING IN LOW FROM DIRECT NORTH! PHONE IN!
THE FIRST DAYLIGHT RAID!
STATION Z, WASHINGTON COAST REPORTS MZA FLIGHT LOW FROM DN! ALERT COASTAL BATTERIES AND INTERCEPTOR UNITS!
AT LEAST WE WERE READY FOR 'EM, TODAY!
YEAH, BUT SOME OF 'EM'LL GET THROUGH! LOOK AT THAT! WE ONLY GOT ONE!
YEAH! THEY'RE GOING TO KEEP STRIKING AND STRIKING! AND WHAT ARE WE DOING! NOTHING! WHERE ARE ALL THOSE NEW WEAPONS I'VE HEARD ABOUT?
6

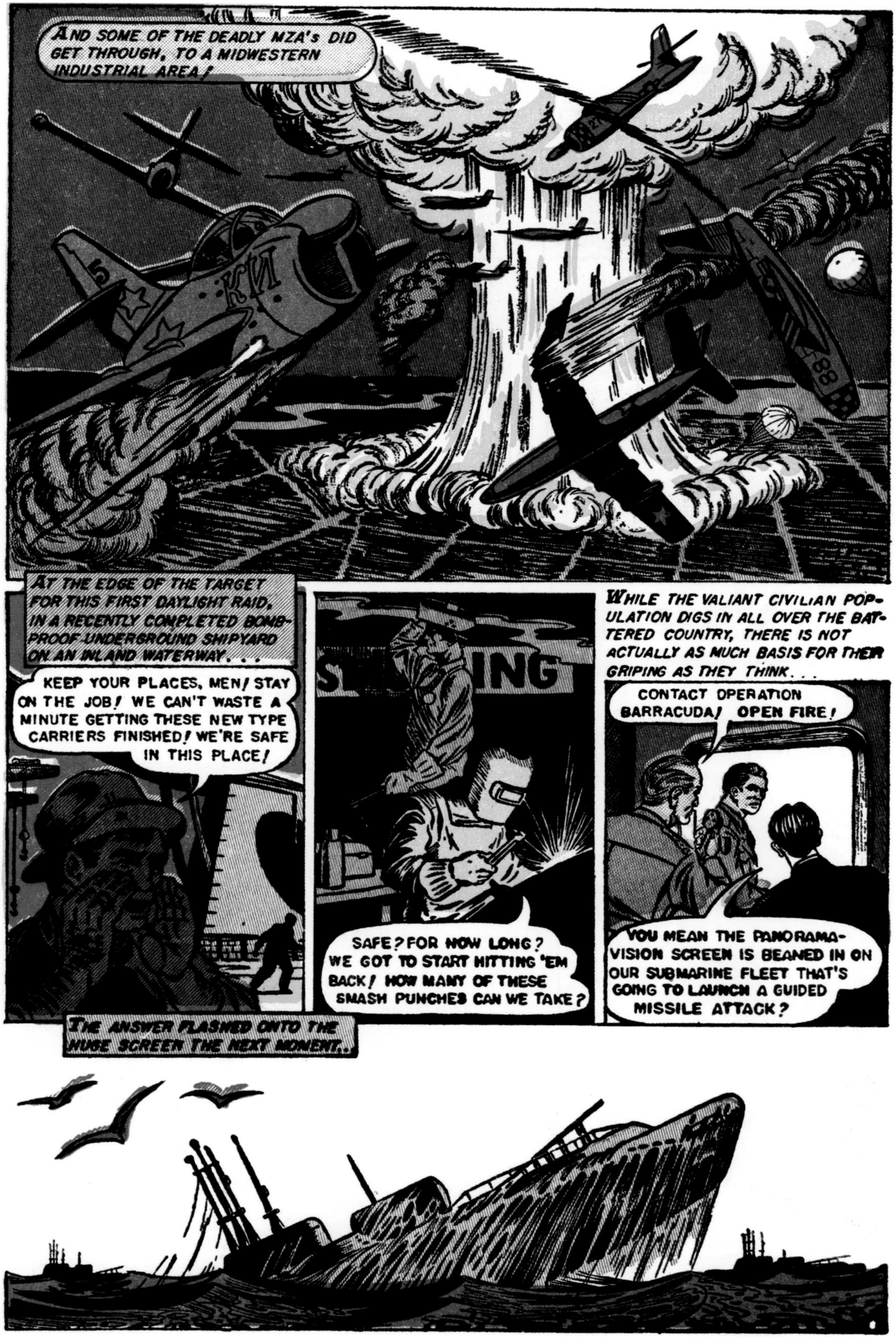
AND SOME OF THE DEADLY MZA's DID GET THROUGH, TO A MIDWESTERN INDUSTRIAL AREA!
AT THE EDGE OF THE TARGET FOR THIS FIRST DAYLIGHT RAID, IN A RECENTLY COMPLETED BOMB-PROOF UNDERGROUND SHIPYARD ON AN INLAND WATERWAY. . .
KEEP YOUR PLACES, MEN! STAY ON THE JOB! WE CAN'T WASTE A MINUTE GETTING THESE NEW TYPE CARRIERS FINISHED! WE'RE SAFE IN THIS PLACE!
SAFE? FOR HOW LONG? WE GOT TO START HITTING 'EM BACK! HOW MANY OF THESE SMASH PUNCHES CAN WE TAKE?
WHILE THE VALIANT CIVILIAN POP-ULATION DIGS IN ALL OVER THE BAT-TERED COUNTRY, THERE IS NOT ACTUALLY AS MUCH BASIS FOR THEIR GRIPING AS THEY THINK. . .
CONTACT OPERATION BARRACUDA! OPEN FIRE!
YOU MEAN THE PANORAMA-VISION SCREEN IS BEAMED IN ON OUR SUBMARINE FLEET THAT'S GOING TO LAUNCH A GUIDED MISSILE ATTACK?
THE ANSWER FLASHED ONTO THE HUGE SCREEN THE NEXT MOMENT..

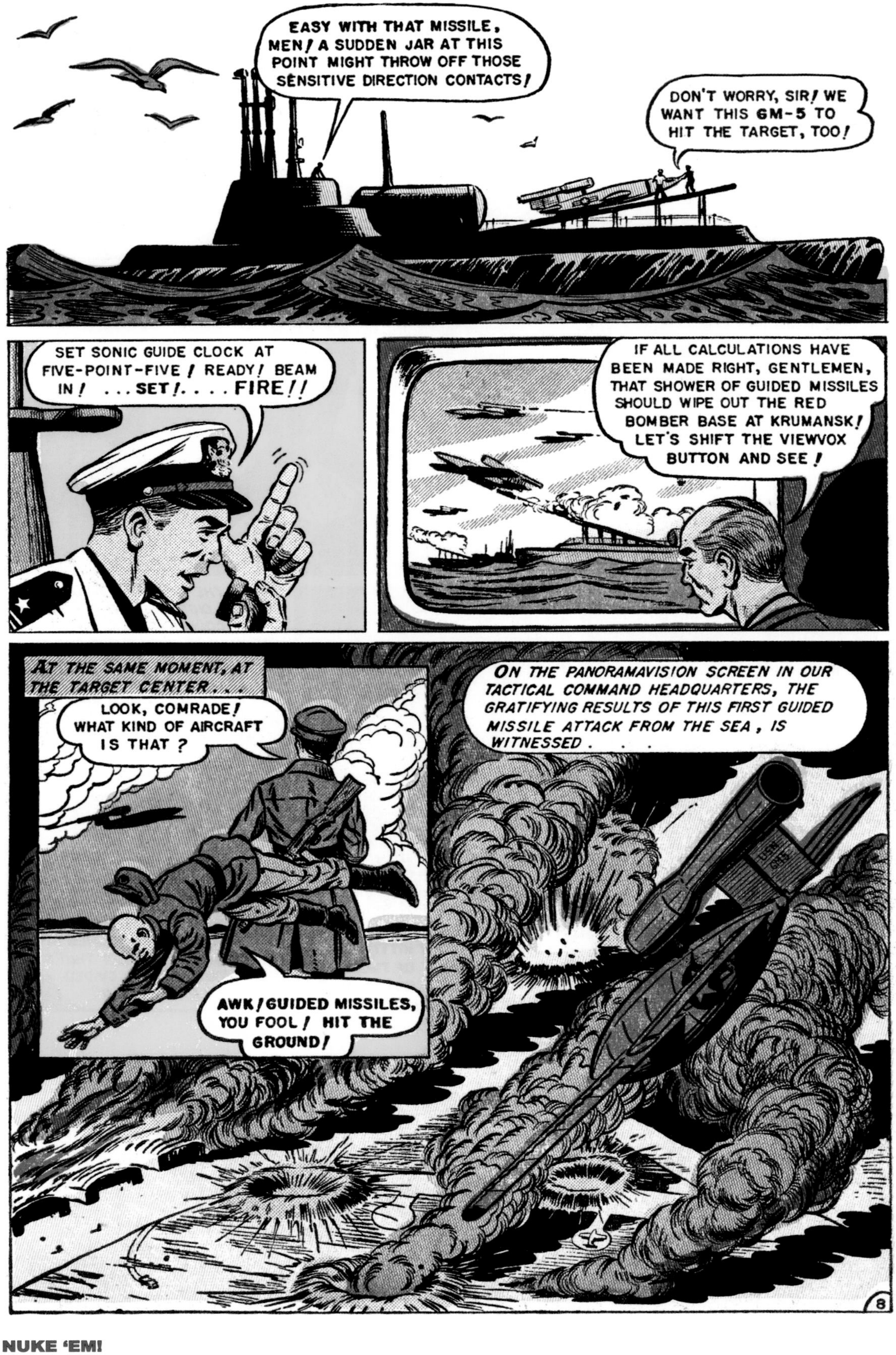
EASY WITH THAT MISSILE, MEN! A SUDDEN JAR AT THIS POINT MIGHT THROW OFF THOSE SENSITIVE DIRECTION CONTACTS!
DON'T WORRY, SIR! WE WANT THIS GM-5 TO HIT THE TARGET, TOO!
SET SONIC GUIDE CLOCK AT FIVE-POINT-FIVE! READY! BEAM IN! ...SET!...FIRE!!
IF ALL CALCULATIONS HAVE BEEN MADE RIGHT, GENTLEMEN, THAT SHOWER OF GUIDED MISSILES SHOULD WIPE OUT THE RED BOMBER BASE AT KRUMANSK! LET'S SHIFT THE VIEWVOX BUTTON AND SEE!
AT THE SAME MOMENT, AT THE TARGET CENTER...
LOOK, COMRADE! WHAT KIND OF AIRCRAFT IS THAT?
AWK! GUIDED MISSILES, YOU FOOL! HIT THE GROUND!
ON THE PANORAMAVISION SCREEN IN OUR TACTICAL COMMAND HEADQUARTERS, THE GRATIFYING RESULTS OF THIS FIRST GUIDED MISSILE ATTACK FROM THE SEA, IS WITNESSED...
8

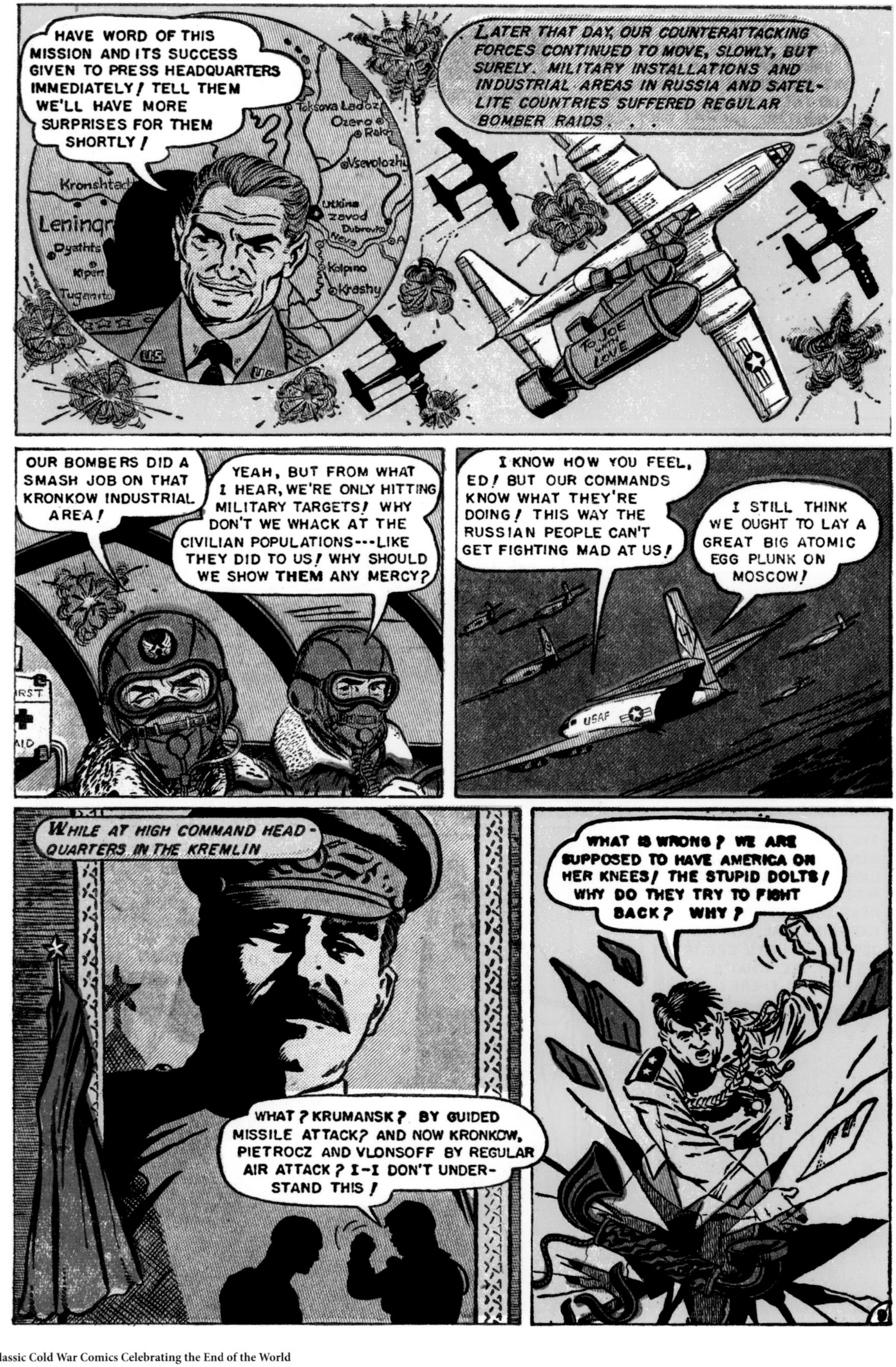
HAVE WORD OF THIS MISSION AND ITS SUCCESS GIVEN TO PRESS HEADQUARTERS IMMEDIATELY! TELL THEM WE'LL HAVE MORE SURPRISES FOR THEM SHORTLY!
LATER THAT DAY, OUR COUNTERATTACKING FORCES CONTINUED TO MOVE, SLOWLY, BUT SURELY. MILITARY INSTALLATIONS AND INDUSTRIAL AREAS IN RUSSIA AND SATEL-LITE COUNTRIES SUFFERED REGULAR BOMBER RAIDS . . .
TO JOE WITH LOVE
OUR BOMBERS DID A SMASH JOB ON THAT KRONKOW INDUSTRIAL AREA!
YEAH, BUT FROM WHAT I HEAR, WE'RE ONLY HITTING MILITARY TARGETS! WHY DON'T WE WHACK AT THE CIVILIAN POPULATIONS---LIKE THEY DID TO US! WHY SHOULD WE SHOW THEM ANY MERCY?
I KNOW HOW YOU FEEL, ED! BUT OUR COMMANDS KNOW WHAT THEY'RE DOING! THIS WAY THE RUSSIAN PEOPLE CAN'T GET FIGHTING MAD AT US!
I STILL THINK WE OUGHT TO LAY A GREAT BIG ATOMIC EGG PLUNK ON MOSCOW!
USAF
WHILE AT HIGH COMMAND HEAD-QUARTERS IN THE KREMLIN
WHAT? KRUMANSK? BY GUIDED MISSILE ATTACK? AND NOW KRONKOW, PIETROCZ AND VLONSOFF BY REGULAR AIR ATTACK? I-I DON'T UNDER-STAND THIS!
WHAT IS WRONG? WE ARE SUPPOSED TO HAVE AMERICA ON HER KNEES! THE STUPID DOLTS! WHY DO THEY TRY TO FIGHT BACK? WHY?

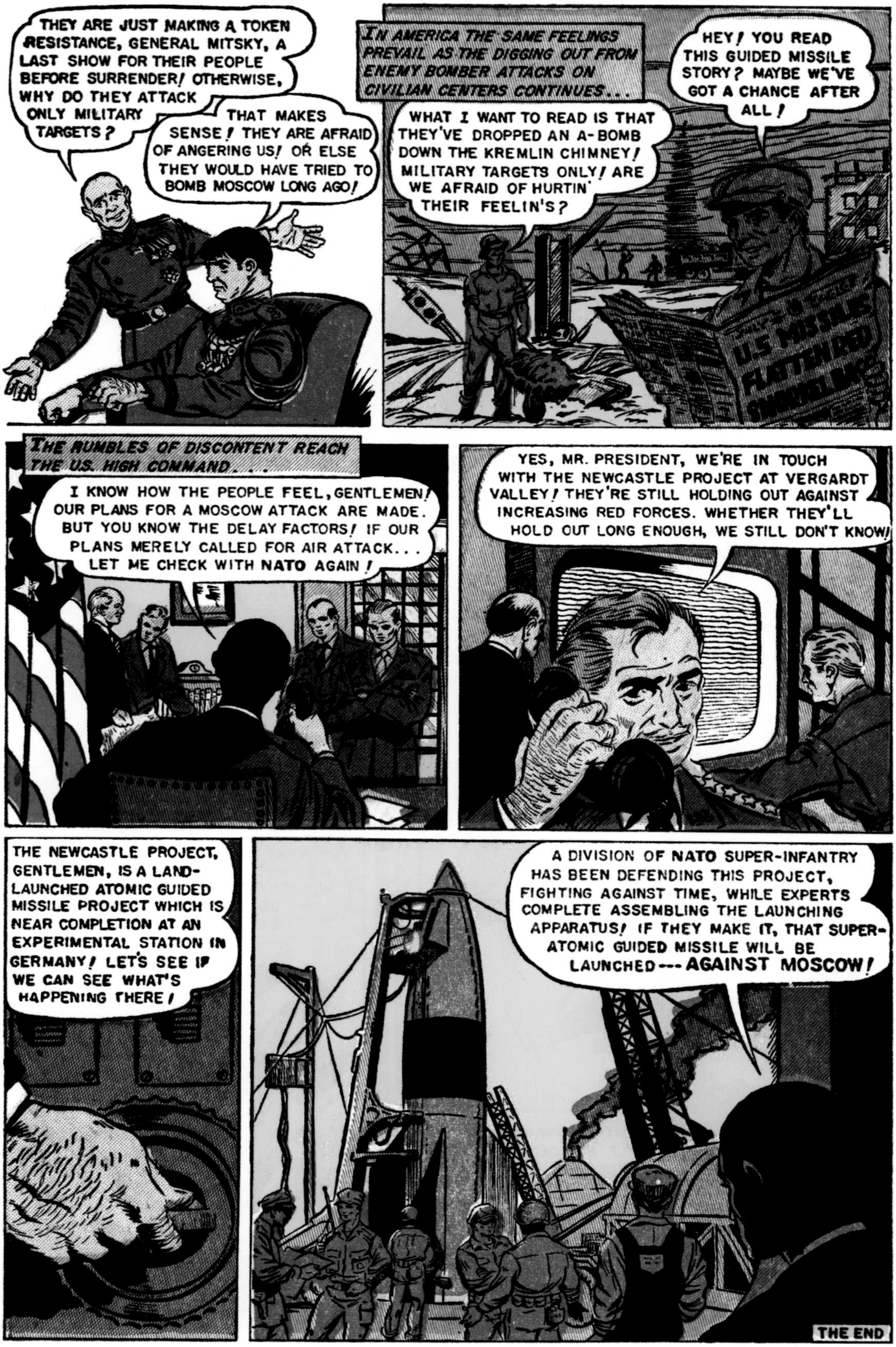
THEY ARE JUST MAKING A TOKEN RESISTANCE, GENERAL MITSKY, A LAST SHOW FOR THEIR PEOPLE BEFORE SURRENDER! OTHERWISE, WHY DO THEY ATTACK ONLY MILITARY TARGETS?
THAT MAKES SENSE! THEY ARE AFRAID OF ANGERING US! OR ELSE THEY WOULD HAVE TRIED TO BOMB MOSCOW LONG AGO!
IN AMERICA THE SAME FEELINGS PREVAIL AS THE DIGGING OUT FROM ENEMY BOMBER ATTACKS ON CIVILIAN CENTERS CONTINUES...
HEY! YOU READ THIS GUIDED MISSILE STORY? MAYBE WE'VE GOT A CHANCE AFTER ALL!
WHAT I WANT TO READ IS THAT THEY'VE DROPPED AN A-BOMB DOWN THE KREMLIN CHIMNEY! MILITARY TARGETS ONLY! ARE WE AFRAID OF HURTIN' THEIR FEELIN'S?
U.S. MISSILES FLATTEN RED
THE RUMBLES OF DISCONTENT REACH THE U.S. HIGH COMMAND...
I KNOW HOW THE PEOPLE FEEL, GENTLEMEN! OUR PLANS FOR A MOSCOW ATTACK ARE MADE. BUT YOU KNOW THE DELAY FACTORS! IF OUR PLANS MERELY CALLED FOR AIR ATTACK... LET ME CHECK WITH NATO AGAIN!
YES, MR. PRESIDENT, WE'RE IN TOUCH WITH THE NEWCASTLE PROJECT AT VERGARDT VALLEY! THEY'RE STILL HOLDING OUT AGAINST INCREASING RED FORCES. WHETHER THEY'LL HOLD OUT LONG ENOUGH, WE STILL DON'T KNOW!
THE NEWCASTLE PROJECT, GENTLEMEN, IS A LAND-LAUNCHED ATOMIC GUIDED MISSILE PROJECT WHICH IS NEAR COMPLETION AT AN EXPERIMENTAL STATION IN GERMANY! LET'S SEE IF WE CAN SEE WHAT'S HAPPENING THERE!
A DIVISION OF NATO SUPER-INFANTRY HAS BEEN DEFENDING THIS PROJECT, FIGHTING AGAINST TIME, WHILE EXPERTS COMPLETE ASSEMBLING THE LAUNCHING APPARATUS! IF THEY MAKE IT, THAT SUPER-ATOMIC GUIDED MISSILE WILL BE LAUNCHED --- AGAINST MOSCOW!
THE END

G. I. SHOWDOWN

Private Stan Bowes stood up slowly. His eyes were sharply hostile. "But I tell you, Captain—it ain't as if I'm making it up. My—"

Captain Rodgers, Medical Officer of the 662nd Combat Engineer Battalion, ruffled the papers impatiently. "Private," he interrupted in his staccato voice, "every test known to medical science shows there's nothing wrong. There's no disc in your spine, no sign of fracture, no muscle torn, no tumor. The X-ray—"

"Blast the X-rays!" Bowes snapped, and turning on his heel stomped out of the Aid Station. A couple of medics lounging near the entrance eyed him smirking, but Bowes stared them down and spat at their feet.

Let 'em call me names, he told himself. He was calling the shots now.

He looked out into the distance and he could see them still coming, the trucks that had been moving into the Division for days. New equipment. The engineers must have had all their equipment already, because the vehicles were beginning to turn off in the direction of the infantry regiments and artillery batteries. Bowes watched them a moment, tilted his cap and marched away whistling.

"This man's army is for the birds," he said to Franisek later, blowing smoke rings smoothly. "Kid, I can't miss. I been playing that doc like he was fish coming up for bait. Give me another two weeks—and if I ain't out of this army altogether I'll get myself transferred to Limited Service. Then it's Paris for me. Paris and a bed and good times—"

Franisek's eyes mocked him. "Man, you talk big. Just because they took your stripes away, you're— Hell, man, you found a home in this army."

"Nuts! I don't need them, they don't need me. Here it is 1960 and we're still playing soldier here.

... I tell you, Franny, this back business can't miss. All their tests and X-rays—they can't prove your back ain't ailing." He waved a kiss at the sky. "Paris, here I come."

"You been smokin' the wrong weed," Franisek said.

Bowes chuckled. "Two weeks," he chortled. "I'm laying ten to one."

That was on the 3rd, a Tuesday, and all night long the trucks kept rumbling by. At 0400 on the morning of the 4th—a gray, sullen morning marked on the calendar in the devil's own ink—a different rumble, a louder, growling rumble boomed apart the dark sky.

A hand grabbed at Bowes' shoulder.

"Franny," Bowes said, opening a bleary eye, "don't you ever learn? First, they send up samples of the new weapons, so we can study 'em. Then they equip the whole division with 'em. So now somebody's gotta play with 'em. ... Kid, it's too bad I'm leaving you. I coulda shaped you up good."

But then whistles blew, voices rang out sharply, the pound of feet and stirring of bodies filled the area. "Get the lead out, you men!" "Drag your tails, you guys!" "First platoon—fall in here! Combat packs!"

There was a scramble toward the voice in front, quick-moving shadows darting, the short breath and tight lips and gimlet eyes stabbing into the dark.

• A sharp whisper. "Bowes! Stan!"

"Here, kid!"

A shadow slithering in the lightless night. A hand groping. "Okay, kid. ... Take it easy, kid." And then Bowes started cursing, and as they mounted the trucks he cursed louder, and he cursed still while the vehicles rolled east, their glass eyes hooded in complete blackout.

"A fine time," Bowes growled, "to pull a night problem! Why don't they wait for maneuvers—when I won't be here!"

"This ain't no night problem," Kirk, the squad leader, said. "And it don't look like we'll have maneuvers.... And *you're* here!"

After that the men didn't talk, and when the trucks pulled to a halt the sky was turning a leaden gray and the rumbling was growing louder. *At least,* Kirk thought, *they're not throwing in the real heavy stuff. They don't want to chop up this land. They want to take it over.*

"This is the way it is," Kirk said. "Second platoon is setting up a field with the new anti-personnel and power mines. We're covering. Third platoon laying back in reserve."

And then there was a huddle between the platoon sergeant and the lieutenant and then the squad leaders posted their men. A Hq platoon truck carried all new equipment.

"Baby," said Bowes, patting his new M-5 bazooka as he and Franisek trudged off to their post, "take care of me this day, baby, and my first drink in Paris will be a toast to you."

He could make out the terrain now. He and Franisek had drawn the hot spot, where the first Red tanks would hit, to flank the division. If the tanks got through before the mine field was laid it would be the same old story—the old Belgian breakthrough.

"After this day," Bowes growled, "come hell or high water, I'm telling the doc I can't straighten my back enough to hoist a canteen."

And then they fell silent because they could see the saplings flatten before them and the heavy snouts of the Russian Skfar-17's poking up, the deadly 90mm. guns thrusting evilly. Behind the tanks came Russian infantrymen, or maybe they were engineers, to open a gap if the tanks hit a mine field.

"Cover me," Bowes said. "With this tripod and side-feed, I can handle this model bazooka alone."

Franisek said nothing. He was pumping his automatic rifle, trying to pick off a few infantrymen. Bowes cursed. Now the kid, firing too soon, had given the position away. If the Reds lobbed in a good one, there'd be nothing to hold the lead tanks and they'd be on the mine field before it was set.

He rushed his shot. The bazooka shell glanced off the rounded armor. The tank kept coming, and behind it another. The tanks had to converge now. If he could stop three, maybe two, they'd block the others long enough. His next shot was good. It had to be. The tank was forty yards away. It stopped short. The shell had burned through the armor and was shuttling around inside, cutting everything in it to ribbons.

"Hey, kid!" Exultation was in his voice. "I got—" And then he stopped. Franisek was no longer pumping lead. He'd stopped a rifle bullet in his right shoulder. The kid smiled wanly, and when Bowes looked away he saw the second Red tank had circled the first and he knew in two seconds the 90mm. would spout death.

In a blur of motion his arm fed the shell and his finger pressed the trigger. He didn't know if he'd sighted true because in that instant it was as if a million leopards had pounced on his back and their claws shredded his consciousness. . . .

The face of Captain Rodgers, the Medical O, grinned down at him. "We'll need X-rays," Rodgers said. "The tank fired high . . . chopped apart a tree. A branch got you. But those two tanks you got blocked the others long enough—"

"The kid . . . Franisek?"

"A flesh wound. But your back—on top of what you had before, I guess you're a cinch to go home and—"

"Doc," Bowes snapped, "cut the clowning. Stick on a Band-Aid and lemme outta here. . . . I gotta shape up that kid."

(end)

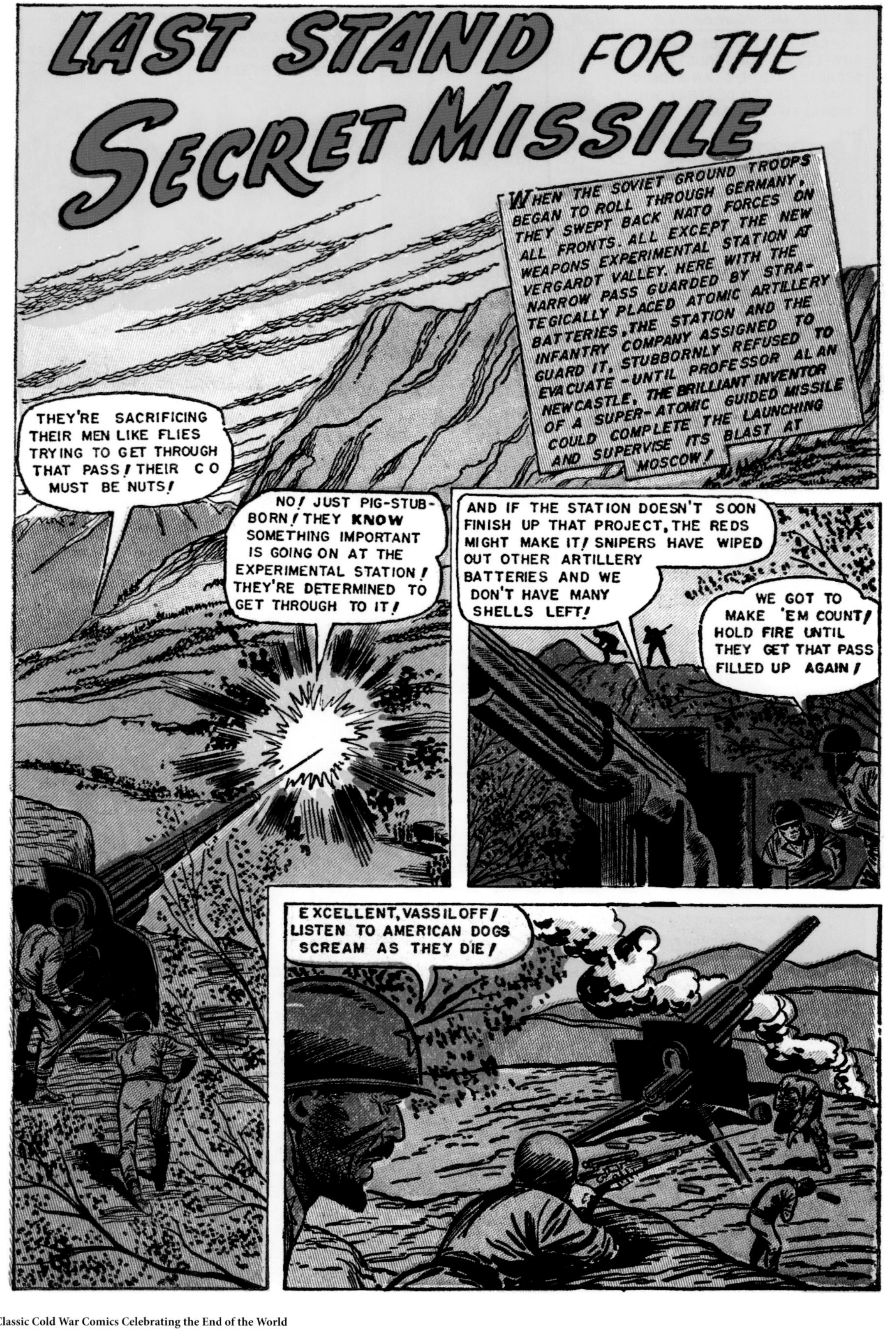
LAST STAND FOR THE SECRET MISSILE
WHEN THE SOVIET GROUND TROOPS BEGAN TO ROLL THROUGH GERMANY, THEY SWEPT BACK NATO FORCES ON ALL FRONTS. ALL EXCEPT THE NEW WEAPONS EXPERIMENTAL STATION AT VERGARDT VALLEY. HERE WITH THE NARROW PASS GUARDED BY STRA-TEGICALLY PLACED ATOMIC ARTILLERY BATTERIES, THE STATION AND THE INFANTRY COMPANY ASSIGNED TO GUARD IT, STUBBORNLY REFUSED TO EVACUATE -UNTIL PROFESSOR ALAN NEWCASTLE, THE BRILLIANT INVENTOR OF A SUPER-ATOMIC GUIDED MISSILE COULD COMPLETE THE LAUNCHING AND SUPERVISE ITS BLAST AT MOSCOW!
THEY'RE SACRIFICING THEIR MEN LIKE FLIES TRYING TO GET THROUGH THAT PASS! THEIR C O MUST BE NUTS!
NO! JUST PIG-STUBBORN! THEY KNOW SOMETHING IMPORTANT IS GOING ON AT THE EXPERIMENTAL STATION! THEY'RE DETERMINED TO GET THROUGH TO IT!
AND IF THE STATION DOESN'T SOON FINISH UP THAT PROJECT, THE REDS MIGHT MAKE IT! SNIPERS HAVE WIPED OUT OTHER ARTILLERY BATTERIES AND WE DON'T HAVE MANY SHELLS LEFT!
WE GOT TO MAKE 'EM COUNT! HOLD FIRE UNTIL THEY GET THAT PASS FILLED UP AGAIN!
EXCELLENT, VASSILOFF! LISTEN TO AMERICAN DOGS SCREAM AS THEY DIE!

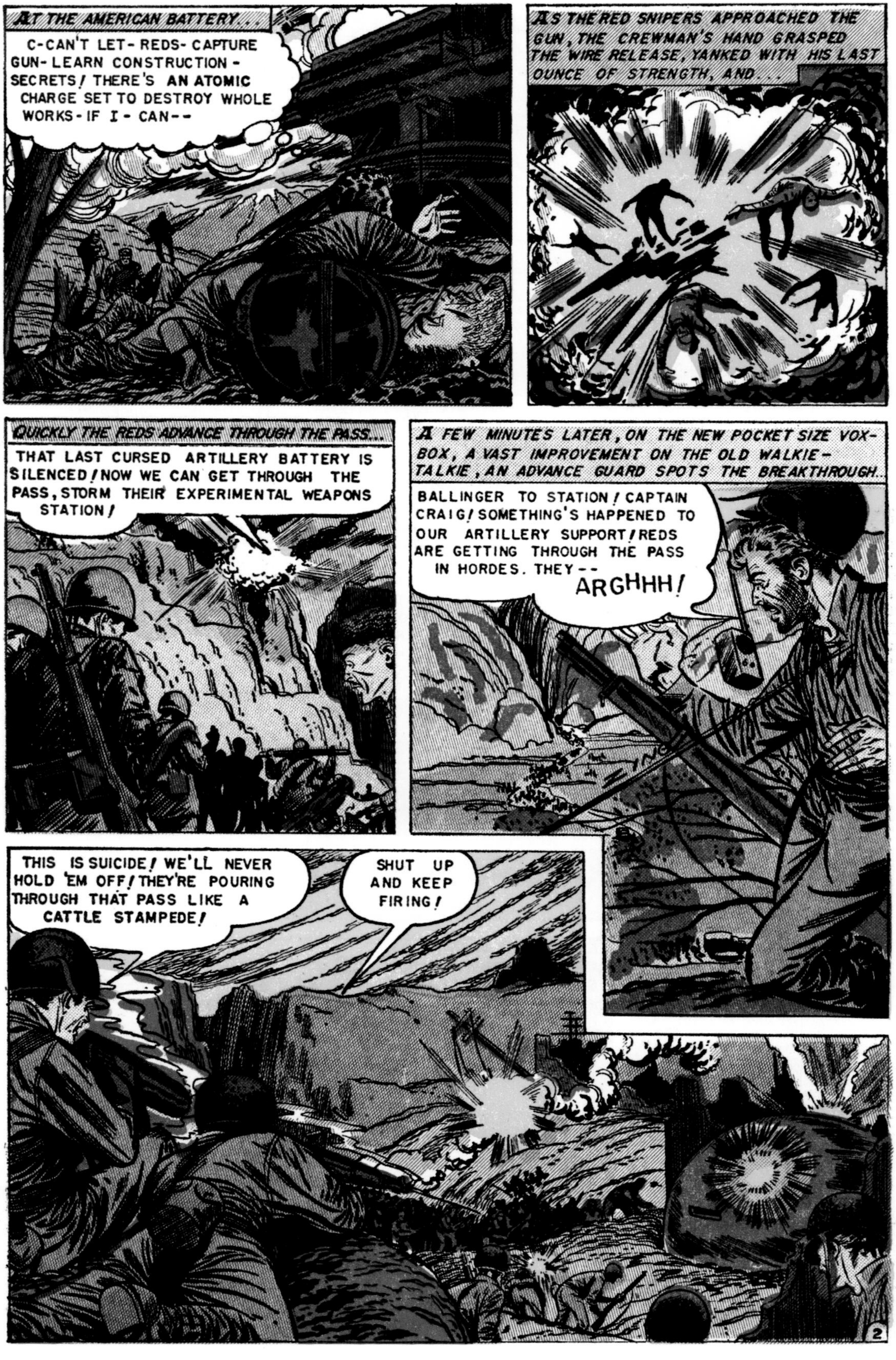
AT THE AMERICAN BATTERY...
C-CAN'T LET- REDS- CAPTURE GUN- LEARN CONSTRUCTION - SECRETS! THERE'S AN ATOMIC CHARGE SET TO DESTROY WHOLE WORKS - IF I - CAN--
AS THE RED SNIPERS APPROACHED THE GUN, THE CREWMAN'S HAND GRASPED THE WIRE RELEASE, YANKED WITH HIS LAST OUNCE OF STRENGTH, AND...
QUICKLY THE REDS ADVANCE THROUGH THE PASS...
THAT LAST CURSED ARTILLERY BATTERY IS SILENCED! NOW WE CAN GET THROUGH THE PASS, STORM THEIR EXPERIMENTAL WEAPONS STATION!
A FEW MINUTES LATER, ON THE NEW POCKET SIZE VOX-BOX, A VAST IMPROVEMENT ON THE OLD WALKIE-TALKIE, AN ADVANCE GUARD SPOTS THE BREAKTHROUGH...
BALLINGER TO STATION! CAPTAIN CRAIG! SOMETHING'S HAPPENED TO OUR ARTILLERY SUPPORT! REDS ARE GETTING THROUGH THE PASS IN HORDES. THEY-- ARGHHH!
THIS IS SUICIDE! WE'LL NEVER HOLD 'EM OFF! THEY'RE POURING THROUGH THAT PASS LIKE A CATTLE STAMPEDE!
SHUT UP AND KEEP FIRING!
2

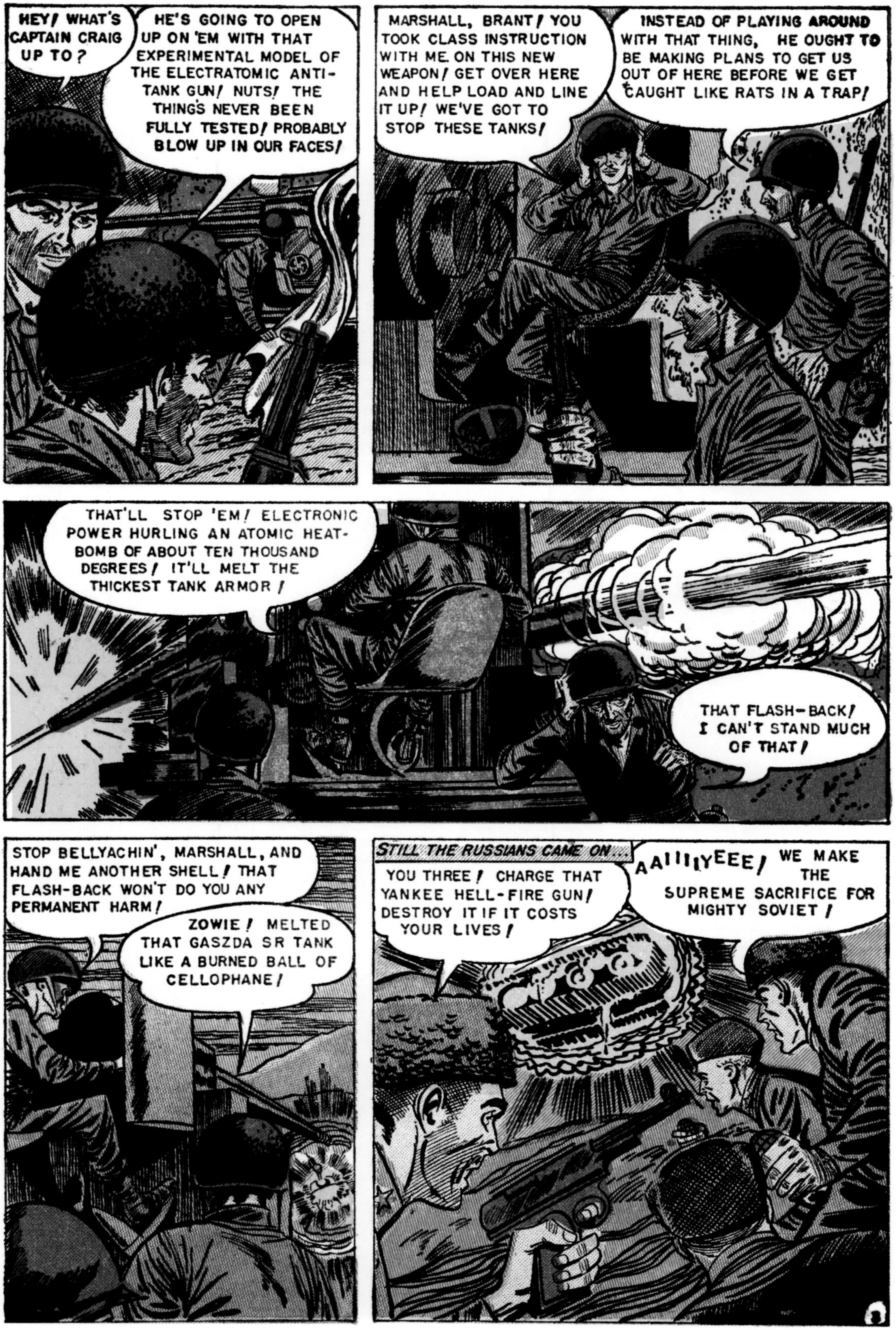
HEY! WHAT'S CAPTAIN CRAIG UP TO?
HE'S GOING TO OPEN UP ON 'EM WITH THAT EXPERIMENTAL MODEL OF THE ELECTRATOMIC ANTI-TANK GUN! NUTS! THE THING'S NEVER BEEN FULLY TESTED! PROBABLY BLOW UP IN OUR FACES!
MARSHALL, BRANT! YOU TOOK CLASS INSTRUCTION WITH ME ON THIS NEW WEAPON! GET OVER HERE AND HELP LOAD AND LINE IT UP! WE'VE GOT TO STOP THESE TANKS!
INSTEAD OF PLAYING AROUND WITH THAT THING, HE OUGHT TO BE MAKING PLANS TO GET US OUT OF HERE BEFORE WE GET CAUGHT LIKE RATS IN A TRAP!
THAT'LL STOP 'EM! ELECTRONIC POWER HURLING AN ATOMIC HEAT-BOMB OF ABOUT TEN THOUSAND DEGREES! IT'LL MELT THE THICKEST TANK ARMOR!
THAT FLASH-BACK! I CAN'T STAND MUCH OF THAT!
STOP BELLYACHIN', MARSHALL, AND HAND ME ANOTHER SHELL! THAT FLASH-BACK WON'T DO YOU ANY PERMANENT HARM!
ZOWIE! MELTED THAT GASZDA SR TANK LIKE A BURNED BALL OF CELLOPHANE!
STILL THE RUSSIANS CAME ON...
YOU THREE! CHARGE THAT YANKEE HELL-FIRE GUN! DESTROY IT IF IT COSTS YOUR LIVES!
AAIIIIYEEE! WE MAKE THE SUPREME SACRIFICE FOR MIGHTY SOVIET!
8

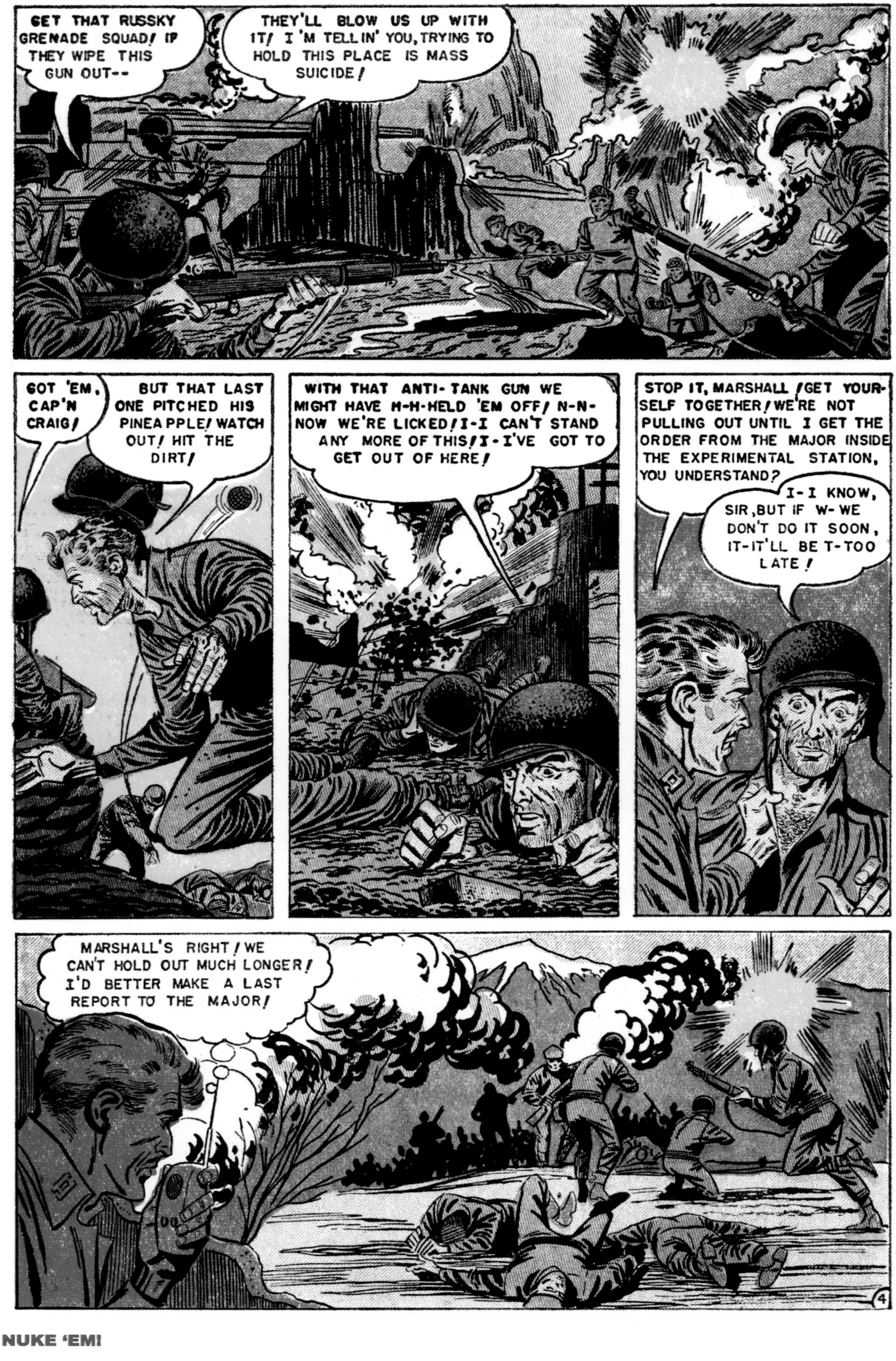
GET THAT RUSSKY GRENADE SQUAD! IF THEY WIPE THIS GUN OUT--
THEY'LL BLOW US UP WITH IT! I'M TELLIN' YOU, TRYING TO HOLD THIS PLACE IS MASS SUICIDE!
GOT 'EM, CAP'N CRAIG!
BUT THAT LAST ONE PITCHED HIS PINEAPPLE! WATCH OUT! HIT THE DIRT!
WITH THAT ANTI-TANK GUN WE MIGHT HAVE H-H-HELD 'EM OFF! N-N-NOW WE'RE LICKED! I-I CAN'T STAND ANY MORE OF THIS! I-I'VE GOT TO GET OUT OF HERE!
STOP IT, MARSHALL! GET YOURSELF TOGETHER! WE'RE NOT PULLING OUT UNTIL I GET THE ORDER FROM THE MAJOR INSIDE THE EXPERIMENTAL STATION, YOU UNDERSTAND?
I-I KNOW, SIR, BUT IF W-WE DON'T DO IT SOON, IT-IT'LL BE T-TOO LATE!
MARSHALL'S RIGHT! WE CAN'T HOLD OUT MUCH LONGER! I'D BETTER MAKE A LAST REPORT TO THE MAJOR!
4

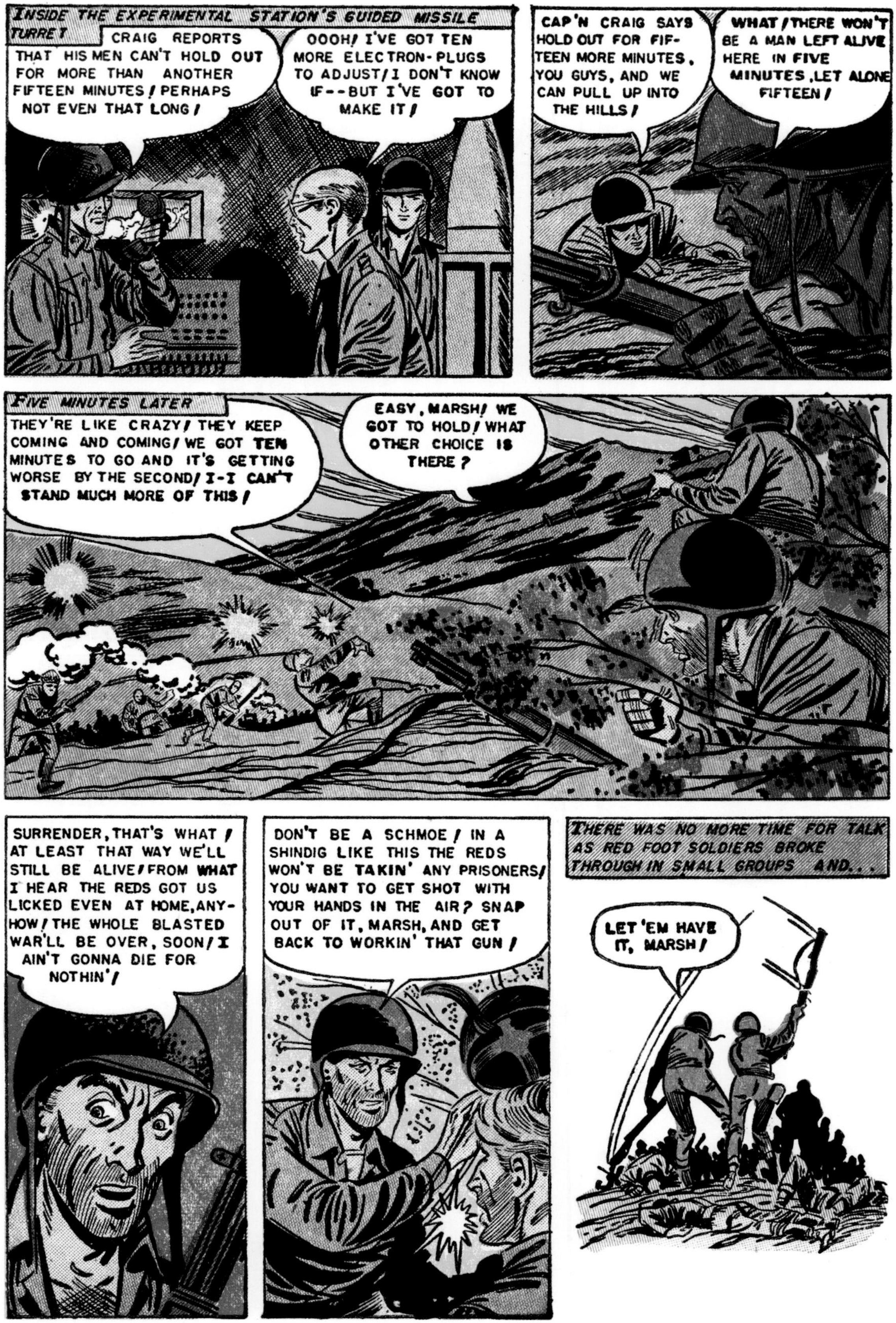
INSIDE THE EXPERIMENTAL STATION'S GUIDED MISSILE TURRET
CRAIG REPORTS THAT HIS MEN CAN'T HOLD OUT FOR MORE THAN ANOTHER FIFTEEN MINUTES! PERHAPS NOT EVEN THAT LONG!
OOOH! I'VE GOT TEN MORE ELECTRON-PLUGS TO ADJUST! I DON'T KNOW IF--BUT I'VE GOT TO MAKE IT!
CAP'N CRAIG SAYS HOLD OUT FOR FIFTEEN MORE MINUTES, YOU GUYS, AND WE CAN PULL UP INTO THE HILLS!
WHAT! THERE WON'T BE A MAN LEFT ALIVE HERE IN FIVE MINUTES, LET ALONE FIFTEEN!
FIVE MINUTES LATER
THEY'RE LIKE CRAZY! THEY KEEP COMING AND COMING! WE GOT TEN MINUTES TO GO AND IT'S GETTING WORSE BY THE SECOND! I-I CAN'T STAND MUCH MORE OF THIS!
EASY, MARSH! WE GOT TO HOLD! WHAT OTHER CHOICE IS THERE?
SURRENDER, THAT'S WHAT! AT LEAST THAT WAY WE'LL STILL BE ALIVE! FROM WHAT I HEAR THE REDS GOT US LICKED EVEN AT HOME, ANYHOW! THE WHOLE BLASTED WAR'LL BE OVER, SOON! I AIN'T GONNA DIE FOR NOTHIN'!
DON'T BE A SCHMOE! IN A SHINDIG LIKE THIS THE REDS WON'T BE TAKIN' ANY PRISONERS! YOU WANT TO GET SHOT WITH YOUR HANDS IN THE AIR? SNAP OUT OF IT, MARSH, AND GET BACK TO WORKIN' THAT GUN!
THERE WAS NO MORE TIME FOR TALK AS RED FOOT SOLDIERS BROKE THROUGH IN SMALL GROUPS AND...
LET 'EM HAVE IT, MARSH!

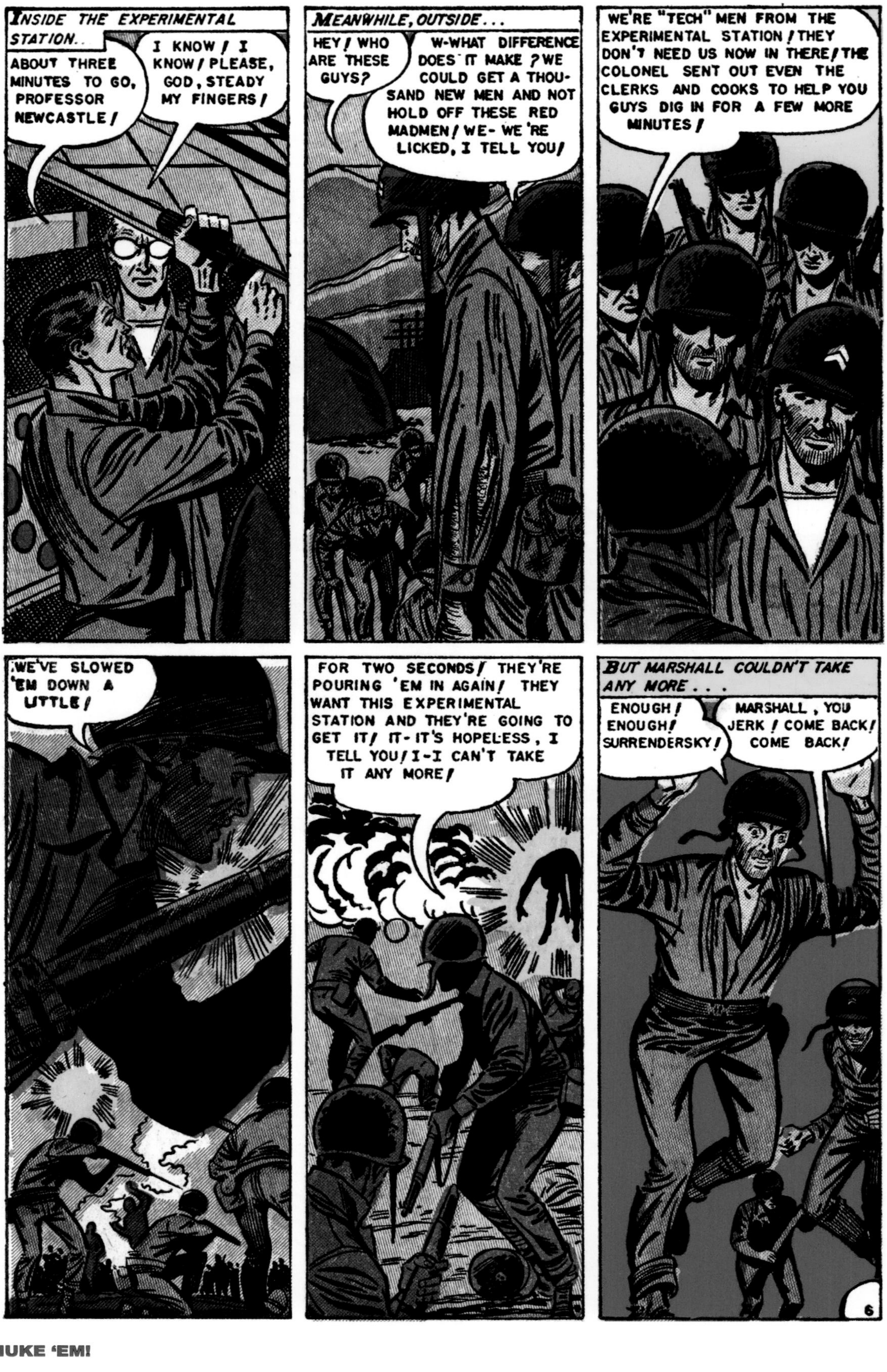
INSIDE THE EXPERIMENTAL STATION..
ABOUT THREE MINUTES TO GO, PROFESSOR NEWCASTLE!
I KNOW! I KNOW! PLEASE, GOD, STEADY MY FINGERS!
MEANWHILE, OUTSIDE...
HEY! WHO ARE THESE GUYS?
W-WHAT DIFFERENCE DOES IT MAKE? WE COULD GET A THOUSAND NEW MEN AND NOT HOLD OFF THESE RED MADMEN! WE- WE'RE LICKED, I TELL YOU!
WE'RE "TECH" MEN FROM THE EXPERIMENTAL STATION! THEY DON'T NEED US NOW IN THERE! THE COLONEL SENT OUT EVEN THE CLERKS AND COOKS TO HELP YOU GUYS DIG IN FOR A FEW MORE MINUTES!
WE'VE SLOWED 'EM DOWN A LITTLE!
FOR TWO SECONDS! THEY'RE POURING 'EM IN AGAIN! THEY WANT THIS EXPERIMENTAL STATION AND THEY'RE GOING TO GET IT! IT- IT'S HOPELESS, I TELL YOU! I-I CAN'T TAKE IT ANY MORE!
BUT MARSHALL COULDN'T TAKE ANY MORE . . .
ENOUGH! ENOUGH! SURRENDERSKY!
MARSHALL, YOU JERK! COME BACK! COME BACK!
6

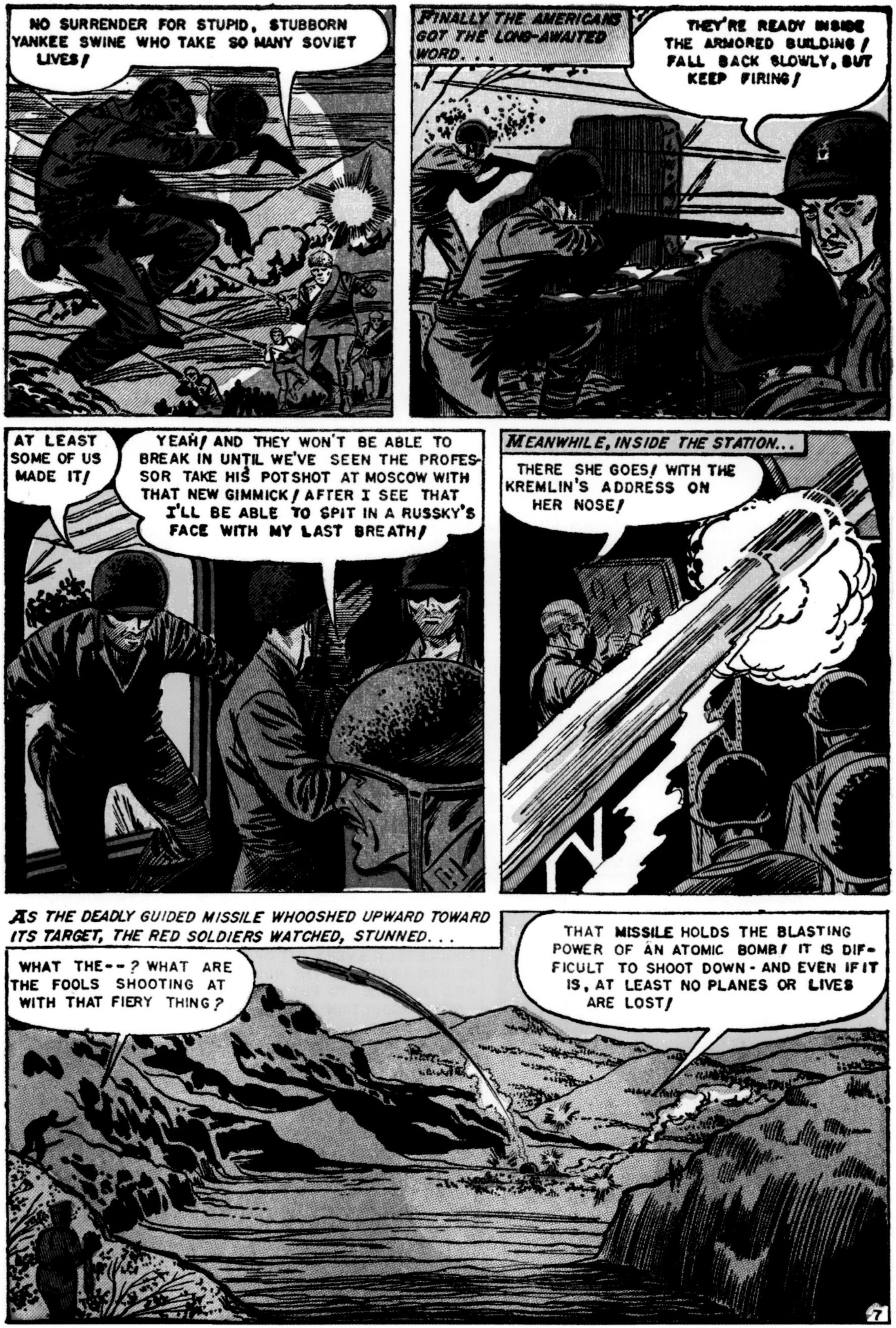
NO SURRENDER FOR STUPID, STUBBORN YANKEE SWINE WHO TAKE SO MANY SOVIET LIVES!
FINALLY THE AMERICANS GOT THE LONG-AWAITED WORD. . .
THEY'RE READY INSIDE THE ARMORED BUILDING! FALL BACK SLOWLY, BUT KEEP FIRING!
AT LEAST SOME OF US MADE IT!
YEAH! AND THEY WON'T BE ABLE TO BREAK IN UNTIL WE'VE SEEN THE PROFESSOR TAKE HIS POTSHOT AT MOSCOW WITH THAT NEW GIMMICK! AFTER I SEE THAT I'LL BE ABLE TO SPIT IN A RUSSKY'S FACE WITH MY LAST BREATH!
MEANWHILE, INSIDE THE STATION...
THERE SHE GOES! WITH THE KREMLIN'S ADDRESS ON HER NOSE!
AS THE DEADLY GUIDED MISSILE WHOOSHED UPWARD TOWARD ITS TARGET, THE RED SOLDIERS WATCHED, STUNNED. . .
WHAT THE--? WHAT ARE THE FOOLS SHOOTING AT WITH THAT FIERY THING?
THAT MISSILE HOLDS THE BLASTING POWER OF AN ATOMIC BOMB! IT IS DIFFICULT TO SHOOT DOWN - AND EVEN IF IT IS, AT LEAST NO PLANES OR LIVES ARE LOST!
7

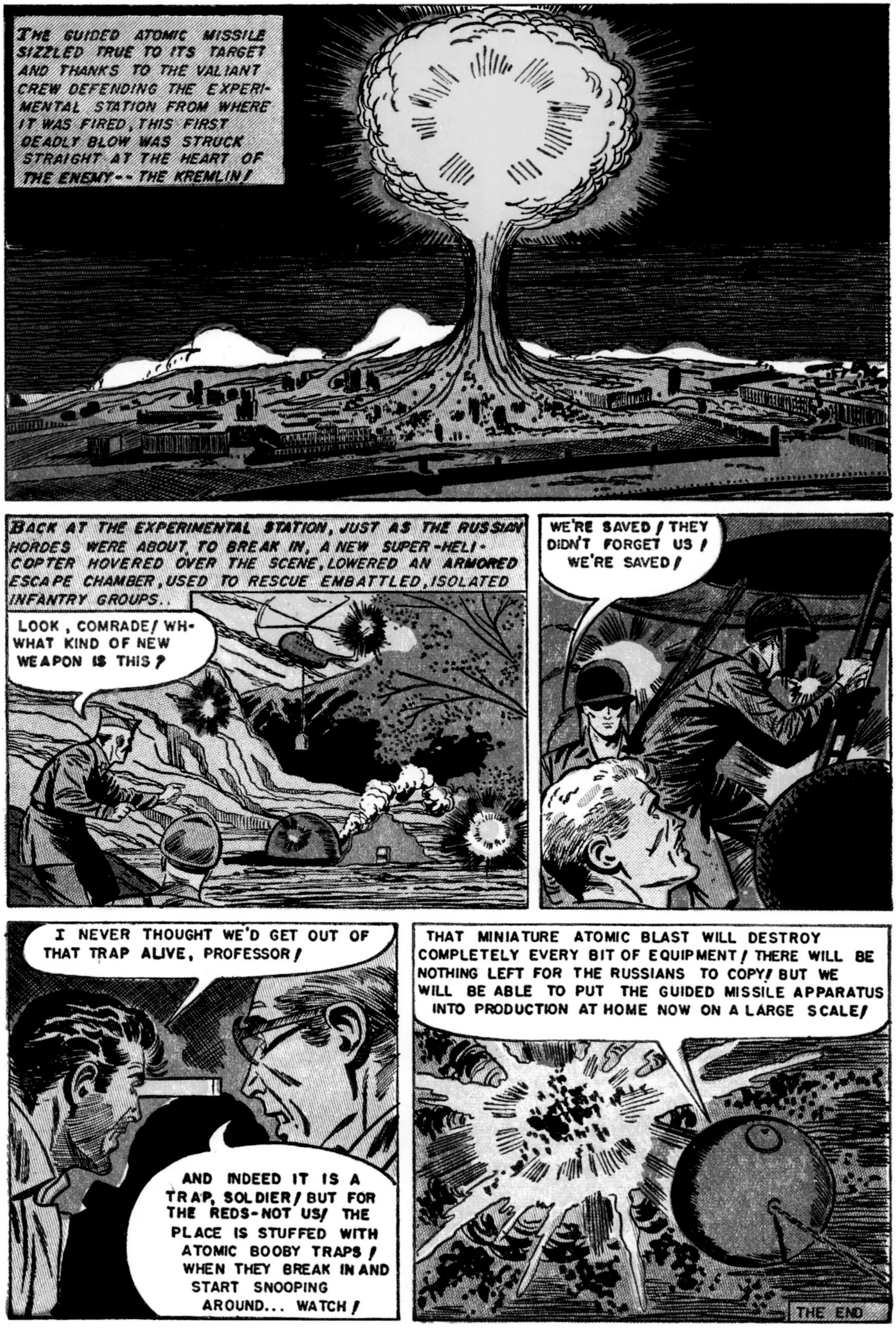
THE GUIDED ATOMIC MISSILE SIZZLED TRUE TO ITS TARGET AND THANKS TO THE VALIANT CREW DEFENDING THE EXPERIMENTAL STATION FROM WHERE IT WAS FIRED, THIS FIRST DEADLY BLOW WAS STRUCK STRAIGHT AT THE HEART OF THE ENEMY-- THE KREMLIN!
BACK AT THE EXPERIMENTAL STATION, JUST AS THE RUSSIAN HORDES WERE ABOUT TO BREAK IN, A NEW SUPER-HELICOPTER HOVERED OVER THE SCENE, LOWERED AN ARMORED ESCAPE CHAMBER, USED TO RESCUE EMBATTLED, ISOLATED INFANTRY GROUPS.
LOOK, COMRADE! WH- WHAT KIND OF NEW WEAPON IS THIS?
WE'RE SAVED! THEY DIDN'T FORGET US! WE'RE SAVED!
I NEVER THOUGHT WE'D GET OUT OF THAT TRAP ALIVE, PROFESSOR!
AND INDEED IT IS A TRAP, SOLDIER! BUT FOR THE REDS-NOT US! THE PLACE IS STUFFED WITH ATOMIC BOOBY TRAPS! WHEN THEY BREAK IN AND START SNOOPING AROUND... WATCH!
THAT MINIATURE ATOMIC BLAST WILL DESTROY COMPLETELY EVERY BIT OF EQUIPMENT! THERE WILL BE NOTHING LEFT FOR THE RUSSIANS TO COPY! BUT WE WILL BE ABLE TO PUT THE GUIDED MISSILE APPARATUS INTO PRODUCTION AT HOME NOW ON A LARGE SCALE!
THE END

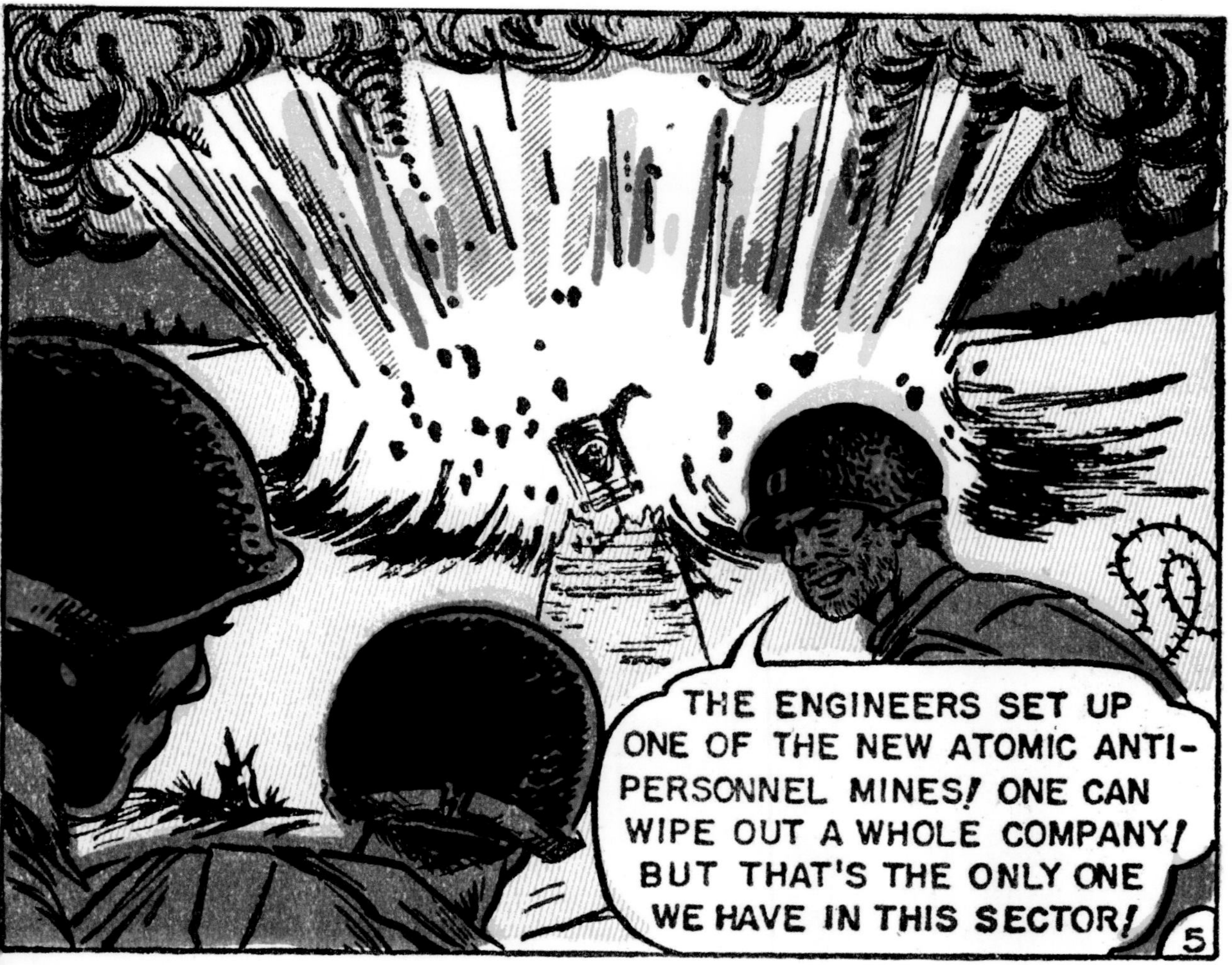
THE ENGINEERS SET UP ONE OF THE NEW ATOMIC ANTI-PERSONNEL MINES! ONE CAN WIPE OUT A WHOLE COMPANY! BUT THAT'S THE ONLY ONE WE HAVE IN THIS SECTOR!
5

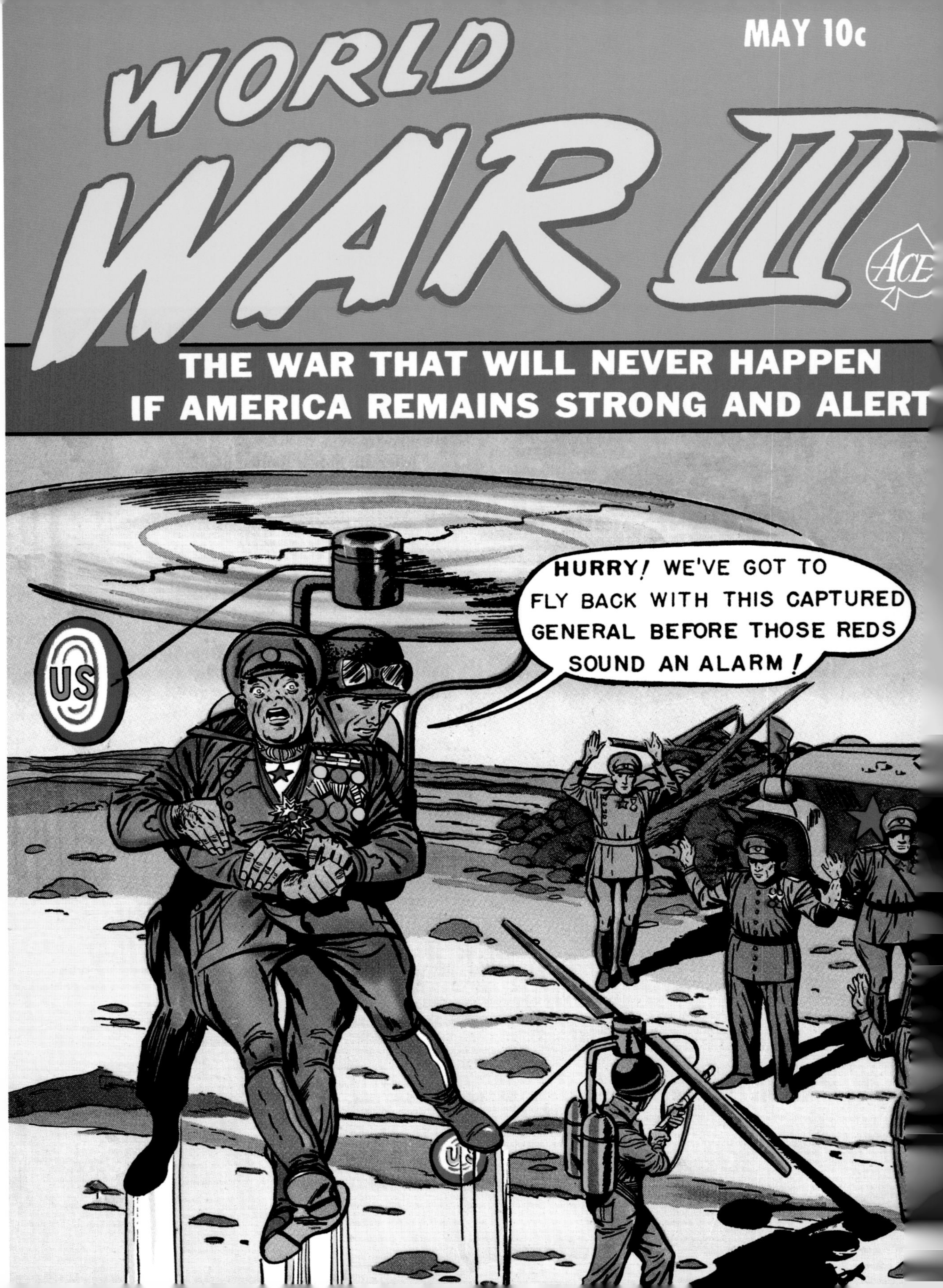
MAY 10c
WORLD WAR III
ACE
THE WAR THAT WILL NEVER HAPPEN
IF AMERICA REMAINS STRONG AND ALERT
HURRY! WE'VE GOT TO FLY BACK WITH THIS CAPTURED GENERAL BEFORE THOSE REDS SOUND AN ALARM!
US
US

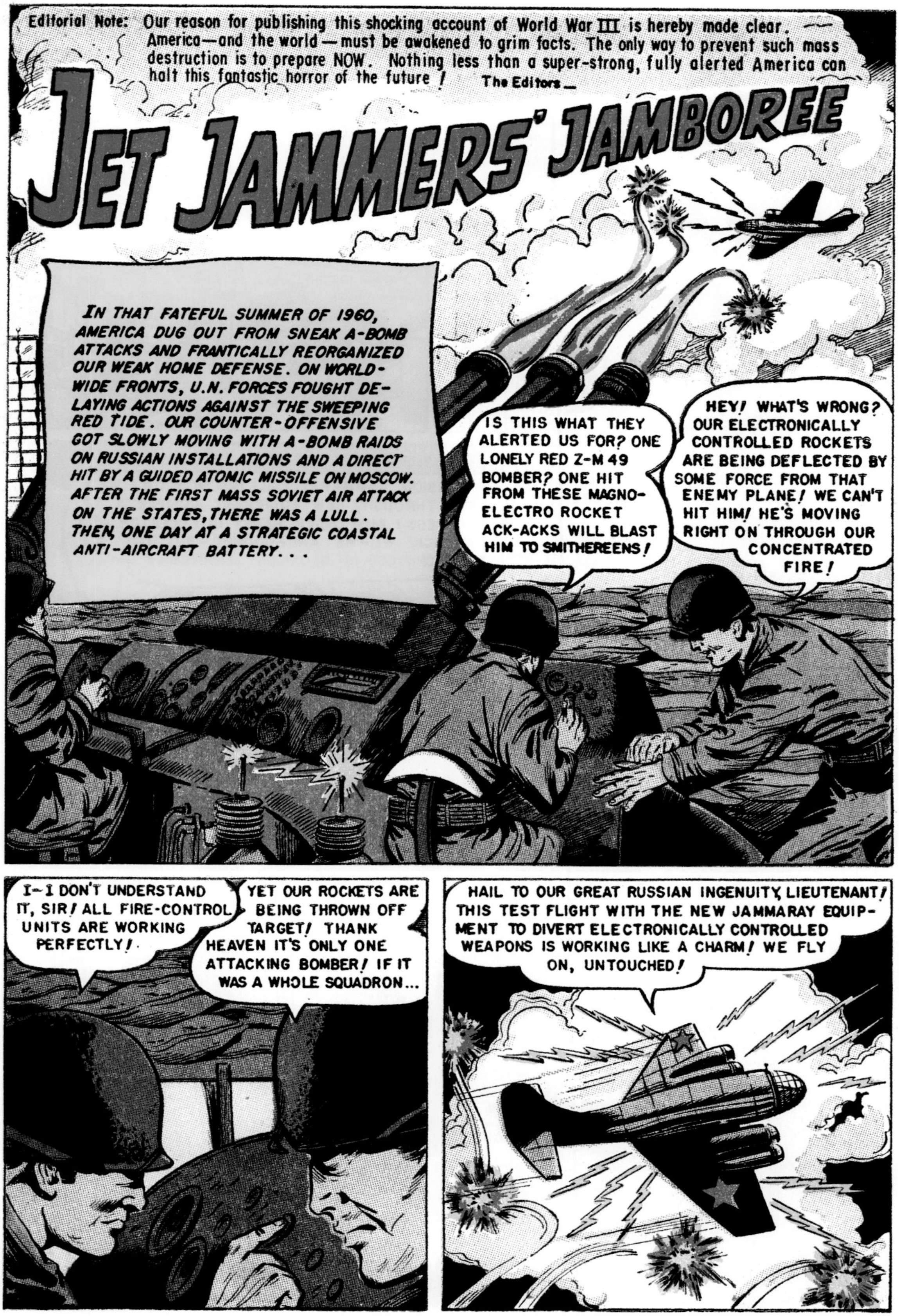
Editorial Note: Our reason for publishing this shocking account of World War III is hereby made clear. — America—and the world—must be awakened to grim facts. The only way to prevent such mass destruction is to prepare NOW. Nothing less than a super-strong, fully alerted America can halt this fantastic horror of the future! The Editors—
JET JAMMERS' JAMBOREE
IN THAT FATEFUL SUMMER OF 1960, AMERICA DUG OUT FROM SNEAK A-BOMB ATTACKS AND FRANTICALLY REORGANIZED OUR WEAK HOME DEFENSE. ON WORLD-WIDE FRONTS, U.N. FORCES FOUGHT DELAYING ACTIONS AGAINST THE SWEEPING RED TIDE. OUR COUNTER-OFFENSIVE GOT SLOWLY MOVING WITH A-BOMB RAIDS ON RUSSIAN INSTALLATIONS AND A DIRECT HIT BY A GUIDED ATOMIC MISSILE ON MOSCOW. AFTER THE FIRST MASS SOVIET AIR ATTACK ON THE STATES, THERE WAS A LULL. THEN, ONE DAY AT A STRATEGIC COASTAL ANTI-AIRCRAFT BATTERY...
IS THIS WHAT THEY ALERTED US FOR? ONE LONELY RED Z-M 49 BOMBER? ONE HIT FROM THESE MAGNO-ELECTRO ROCKET ACK-ACKS WILL BLAST HIM TO SMITHEREENS!
HEY! WHAT'S WRONG? OUR ELECTRONICALLY CONTROLLED ROCKETS ARE BEING DEFLECTED BY SOME FORCE FROM THAT ENEMY PLANE! WE CAN'T HIT HIM! HE'S MOVING RIGHT ON THROUGH OUR CONCENTRATED FIRE!
I-I DON'T UNDERSTAND IT, SIR! ALL FIRE-CONTROL UNITS ARE WORKING PERFECTLY!
YET OUR ROCKETS ARE BEING THROWN OFF TARGET! THANK HEAVEN IT'S ONLY ONE ATTACKING BOMBER! IF IT WAS A WHOLE SQUADRON...
HAIL TO OUR GREAT RUSSIAN INGENUITY, LIEUTENANT! THIS TEST FLIGHT WITH THE NEW JAMMARAY EQUIPMENT TO DIVERT ELECTRONICALLY CONTROLLED WEAPONS IS WORKING LIKE A CHARM! WE FLY ON, UNTOUCHED!

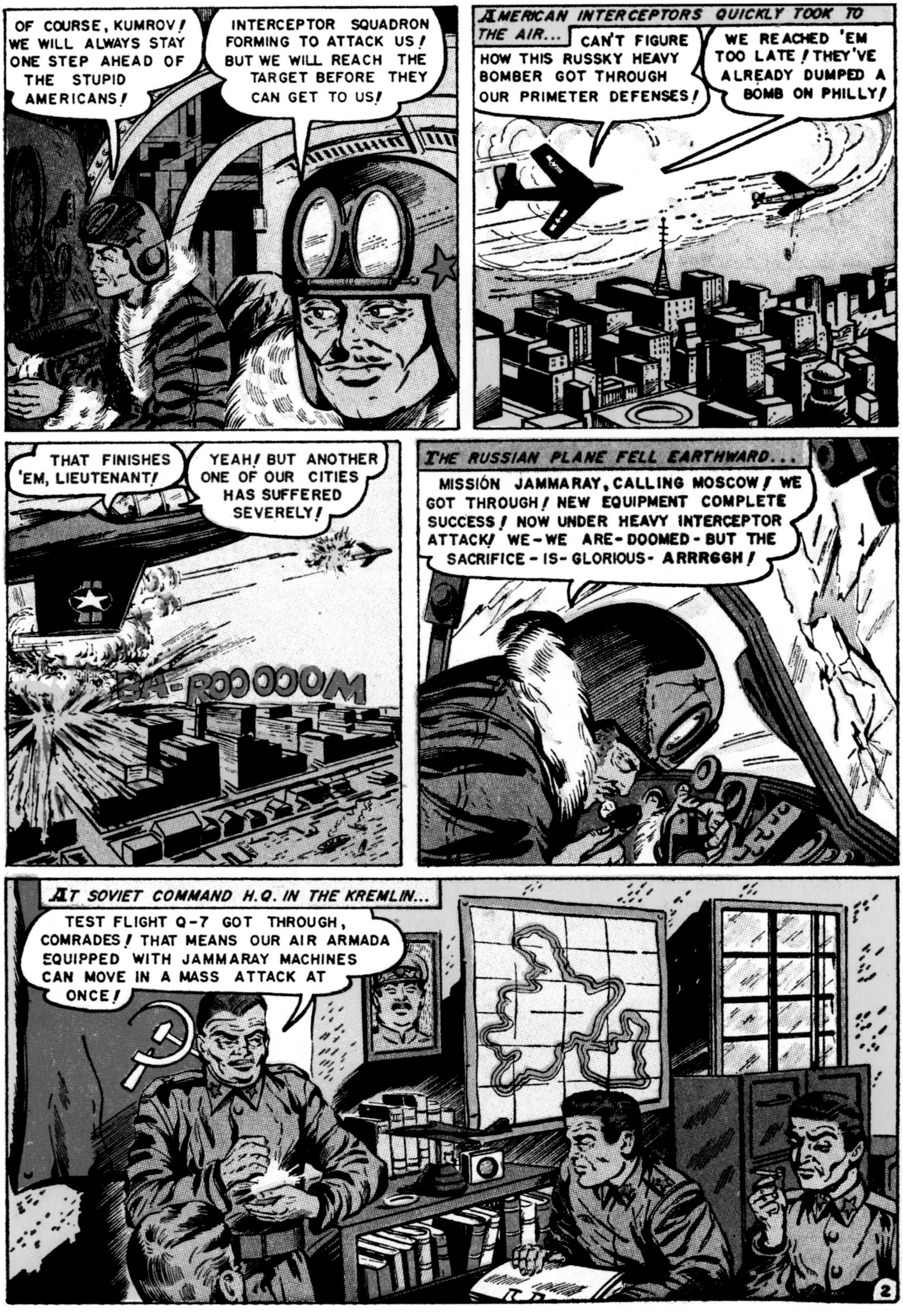
OF COURSE, KUMROV! WE WILL ALWAYS STAY ONE STEP AHEAD OF THE STUPID AMERICANS!
INTERCEPTOR SQUADRON FORMING TO ATTACK US! BUT WE WILL REACH THE TARGET BEFORE THEY CAN GET TO US!
AMERICAN INTERCEPTORS QUICKLY TOOK TO THE AIR...
CAN'T FIGURE HOW THIS RUSSKY HEAVY BOMBER GOT THROUGH OUR PRIMETER DEFENSES!
WE REACHED 'EM TOO LATE! THEY'VE ALREADY DUMPED A BOMB ON PHILLY!
THAT FINISHES 'EM, LIEUTENANT!
YEAH! BUT ANOTHER ONE OF OUR CITIES HAS SUFFERED SEVERELY!
BA-ROOOOOM
THE RUSSIAN PLANE FELL EARTHWARD...
MISSIÓN JAMMARAY, CALLING MOSCOW! WE GOT THROUGH! NEW EQUIPMENT COMPLETE SUCCESS! NOW UNDER HEAVY INTERCEPTOR ATTACK! WE-WE ARE-DOOMED-BUT THE SACRIFICE-IS-GLORIOUS- ARRRGGH!
AT SOVIET COMMAND H.Q. IN THE KREMLIN...
TEST FLIGHT Q-7 GOT THROUGH, COMRADES! THAT MEANS OUR AIR ARMADA EQUIPPED WITH JAMMARAY MACHINES CAN MOVE IN A MASS ATTACK AT ONCE!
2

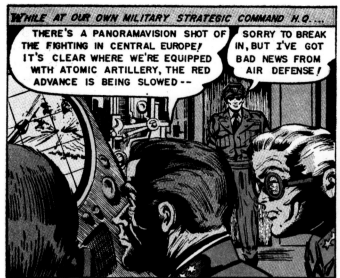

WHILE AT OUR OWN MILITARY STRATEGIC COMMAND H.Q. ...

THERE'S A PANORAMAVISION SHOT OF THE FIGHTING IN CENTRAL EUROPE! IT'S CLEAR WHERE WE'RE EQUIPPED WITH ATOMIC ARTILLERY, THE RED ADVANCE IS BEING SLOWED --

SORRY TO BREAK IN, BUT I'VE GOT BAD NEWS FROM AIR DEFENSE!

THE NEWS OF THE LONE RUSSIAN BOMBER IS RECEIVED WITH GRIM ALARM ...

WHAT HAPPENED IS OBVIOUS. THE REDS HAVE A MACHINE THAT JAMS THE DIRECTION-BEAMS OF OUR ELECTRONICALLY CONTROLLED MISSILES - THE ONE WEAPON WE WERE COUNTING ON TO REPEL NEW RAIDS!

AND - AND NOW IT'S USELESS!

NOW THAT THEIR TEST FLIGHT WAS A SUCCESS, WE CAN EXPECT A MASS RAID. WITH OUR COASTAL DEFENSES PRACTICALLY HELP-LESS, ENOUGH RED RAIDERS WILL EVADE OUR INTERCEPTORS, REACH THEIR TARGETS, TO MAKE THEIR FIRST ATOMIC STRIKES SEEM LIKE A PICNIC!

BUT THE COUNTRY CAN'T STAND MUCH MORE SUCH DE-VESTATING A-BOMB ATTACKS!

WE HAVE ONE LAST-DITCH AERIAL DEFENSE WEAPON, THE OPERATION OF WHICH CANNOT BE FOULED UP BY ANY RUSSIAN DEVICE - BECAUSE IT IS HUMANLY OPERATED! HAVE YOU FORGOTTEN COLONEL JEFFERS? HIS UNIT CAN BE READIED FOR ACTION, AT ONCE!

AN HOUR LATER, AT A MIDWEST JET INTERCEPTOR AIR FORCE BASE ...

HI, COLONEL JEEFERS, OLD BOY! HAVEN'T THEY YET GOTTEN AROUND TO RETIRING YOU OLD WAR DOGS FROM THE LAST WAR?

LISTEN, HAL! YOU AND YOUR JET-JOCKEYS HAVE BEEN GOING TOO FAR, RIDING MY BOYS! IT'S GOT TO STOP! UNDERSTAND?

YES, SIR, COLONEL! IS THAT AN ORDER, COLONEL, SIR! GUESS YOU OLD HAS-BEENS JUST CAN'T TAKE A LITTLE KIDDING!

I SAID CUT IT, HAL! I HATE TO PULL RANK ON MY OWN BROTHER, BUT...

③

SKIP THE APOLOGIES! IT'S BAD ENOUGH YOU OLD GOATS HAVE TO LOUSE UP THE AIRWAYS WITH YOUR SILLY RAMMER PLANES, WITHOUT GETTING SORE ABOUT IT, IN THE BARGAIN!

LISTEN TO ME, YOU YOUNG PUNK!

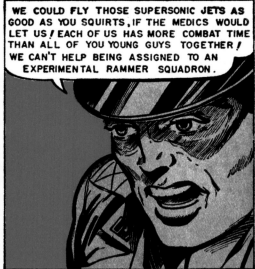

WE COULD FLY THOSE SUPERSONIC JETS AS GOOD AS YOU SQUIRTS, IF THE MEDICS WOULD LET US! EACH OF US HAS MORE COMBAT TIME THAN ALL OF YOU YOUNG GUYS TOGETHER! WE CAN'T HELP BEING ASSIGNED TO AN EXPERIMENTAL RAMMER SQUADRON.

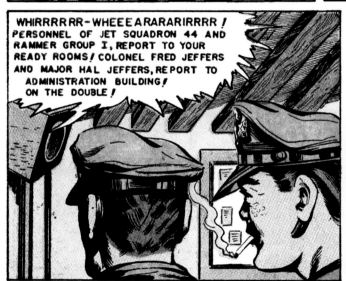

WHIRRRRRR-WHEEEARARARIRRRR! PERSONNEL OF JET SQUADRON 44 AND RAMMER GROUP I, REPORT TO YOUR READY ROOMS! COLONEL FRED JEFFERS AND MAJOR HAL JEFFERS, REPORT TO ADMINISTRATION BUILDING! ON THE DOUBLE!

AN ALERT FOR BOTH OUR OUTFITS! I DON'T GET IT! IF IT'S AN ENEMY ATTACK, WHAT DO THEY NEED YOUR RAMMER PLANES FOR? OUR INTERCEPTORS CAN HANDLE ANY COMMY CRATES!

WE'LL SOON SEE!

AT THIS MOMENT, FAR OUT AT SEA...

ATTENTION, MSGHQ! PANORAMA CONTACT SUB, X-9, FOCUSED ON FLIGHT ENEMY HEAVY BOMBERS, Z-M 49'S, HEADING EAST SOUTH EAST!

GENERAL COMMAND HEADQUARTERS GETS THE FLASH.

THAT'S THEM, ALL RIGHT! AND THE WAY THE MAGNO-ELECTRO ROCKETS FROM THE SUB ARE BEING DEFLATED, THAT WHOLE RED SQUADRON MUST BE EQUIPPED WITH THEIR NEW JAMMING DEVICE!

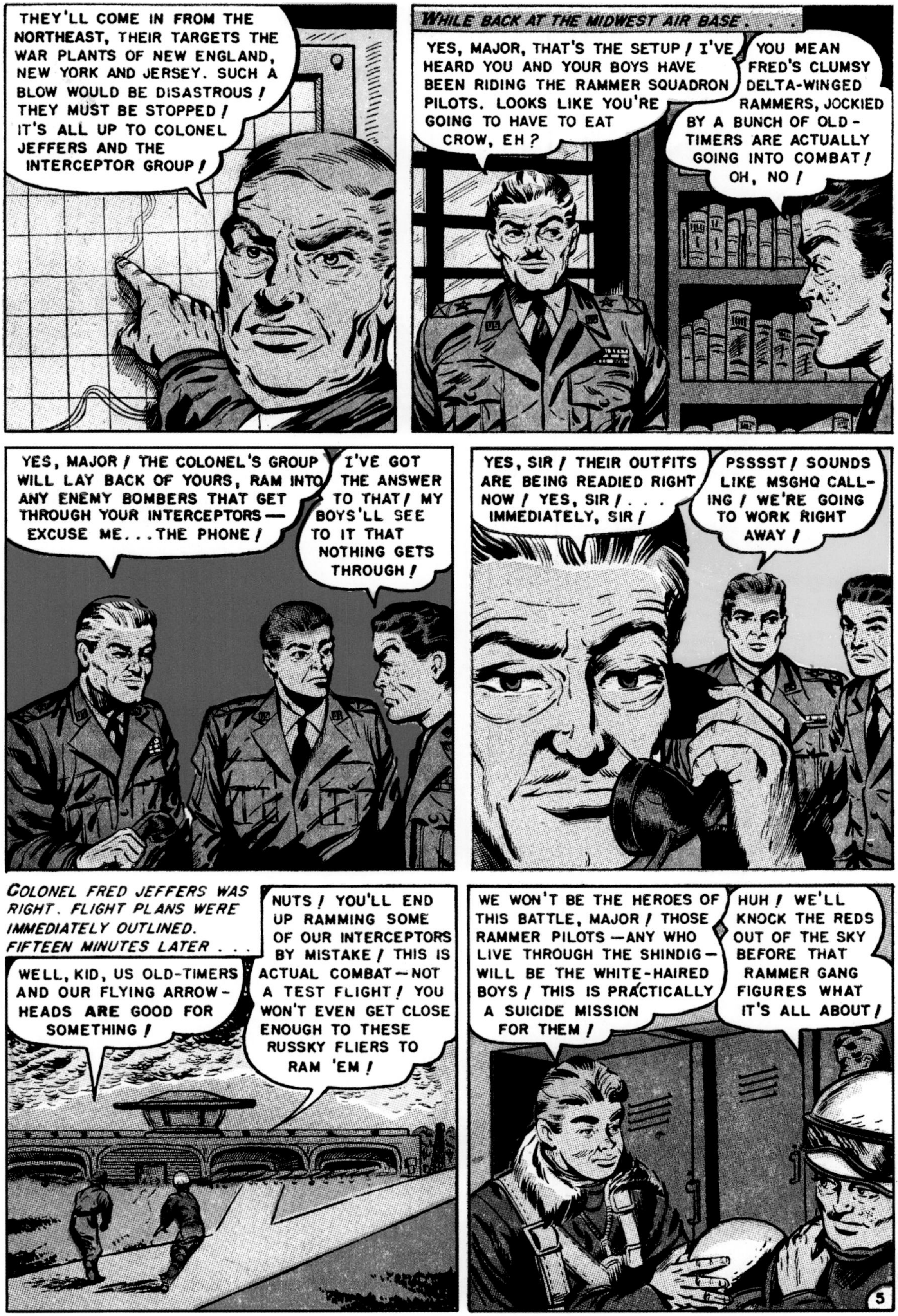
THEY'LL COME IN FROM THE NORTHEAST, THEIR TARGETS THE WAR PLANTS OF NEW ENGLAND, NEW YORK AND JERSEY. SUCH A BLOW WOULD BE DISASTROUS! THEY MUST BE STOPPED! IT'S ALL UP TO COLONEL JEFFERS AND THE INTERCEPTOR GROUP!
WHILE BACK AT THE MIDWEST AIR BASE . . .
YES, MAJOR, THAT'S THE SETUP! I'VE HEARD YOU AND YOUR BOYS HAVE BEEN RIDING THE RAMMER SQUADRON PILOTS. LOOKS LIKE YOU'RE GOING TO HAVE TO EAT CROW, EH?
YOU MEAN FRED'S CLUMSY DELTA-WINGED RAMMERS, JOCKIED BY A BUNCH OF OLD-TIMERS ARE ACTUALLY GOING INTO COMBAT! OH, NO!
YES, MAJOR! THE COLONEL'S GROUP WILL LAY BACK OF YOURS, RAM INTO ANY ENEMY BOMBERS THAT GET THROUGH YOUR INTERCEPTORS— EXCUSE ME. . .THE PHONE!
I'VE GOT THE ANSWER TO THAT! MY BOYS'LL SEE TO IT THAT NOTHING GETS THROUGH!
YES, SIR! THEIR OUTFITS ARE BEING READIED RIGHT NOW! YES, SIR! . . . IMMEDIATELY, SIR!
PSSSST! SOUNDS LIKE MSGHQ CALLING! WE'RE GOING TO WORK RIGHT AWAY!
COLONEL FRED JEFFERS WAS RIGHT. FLIGHT PLANS WERE IMMEDIATELY OUTLINED. FIFTEEN MINUTES LATER . . .
WELL, KID, US OLD-TIMERS AND OUR FLYING ARROWHEADS ARE GOOD FOR SOMETHING!
NUTS! YOU'LL END UP RAMMING SOME OF OUR INTERCEPTORS BY MISTAKE! THIS IS ACTUAL COMBAT—NOT A TEST FLIGHT! YOU WON'T EVEN GET CLOSE ENOUGH TO THESE RUSSKY FLIERS TO RAM 'EM!
WE WON'T BE THE HEROES OF THIS BATTLE, MAJOR! THOSE RAMMER PILOTS—ANY WHO LIVE THROUGH THE SHINDIG—WILL BE THE WHITE-HAIRED BOYS! THIS IS PRACTICALLY A SUICIDE MISSION FOR THEM!
HUH! WE'LL KNOCK THE REDS OUT OF THE SKY BEFORE THAT RAMMER GANG FIGURES WHAT IT'S ALL ABOUT!
5

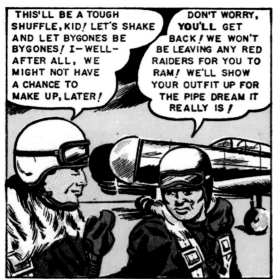

THIS'LL BE A TOUGH SHUFFLE, KID! LET'S SHAKE AND LET BYGONES BE BYGONES! I—WELL—AFTER ALL, WE MIGHT NOT HAVE A CHANCE TO MAKE UP, LATER!

DON'T WORRY, **YOU'LL** GET BACK! WE WON'T BE LEAVING ANY RED RAIDERS FOR YOU TO RAM! WE'LL SHOW YOUR OUTFIT UP FOR THE PIPE DREAM IT REALLY IS!

WITH THOSE JET-INTERCEPTORS DOING SUCH A BANG-UP JOB, HAL'S GOTTEN TOO BIG FOR HIS BRITCHES! HE'S RIDIN' FOR A FALL!

EVERYTHING CHECKED, SIR— AIR BRAKES, DRAG CHUTE, EJECTOR SEAT— ALL OKAY! GOOD LUCK, COLONEL!

COLONEL JEFFERS TO RAMMER SQUADRON! WE TAKE OFF WHEN THE JETS CIRCLE THE FIELD! WAIT FOR SIGNAL!

OPEN TURBO-JETS FULL SPEED! STRIKE OUT NORTH-NORTH-EAST, CLIMBING. LEVEL OFF AT 20,000!

IN THE LEAD JET PLANE, MAJOR HAL JEFFERS TO INTERCEPTOR SQUADRON...

WE'RE GOING TO CIRCLE WIDE, IN FORMATION, GIVE THOSE SLOWPOKE RAMMER CRATES A CHANCE TO CATCH UP! THEY'RE ALREADY SO FAR BEHIND, THEY'LL NEVER---

BUT BEFORE THE MAJOR'S EYES...

HAL! THIS IS FRED! LET'S GET GOING! WHAT'RE WE WAITING FOR? WE'VE GOT A DATE WITH THE COMMIES OFF THE MAINE COAST!

WHAT THE---? WHERE DID THEY COME FROM? HOW--?

6

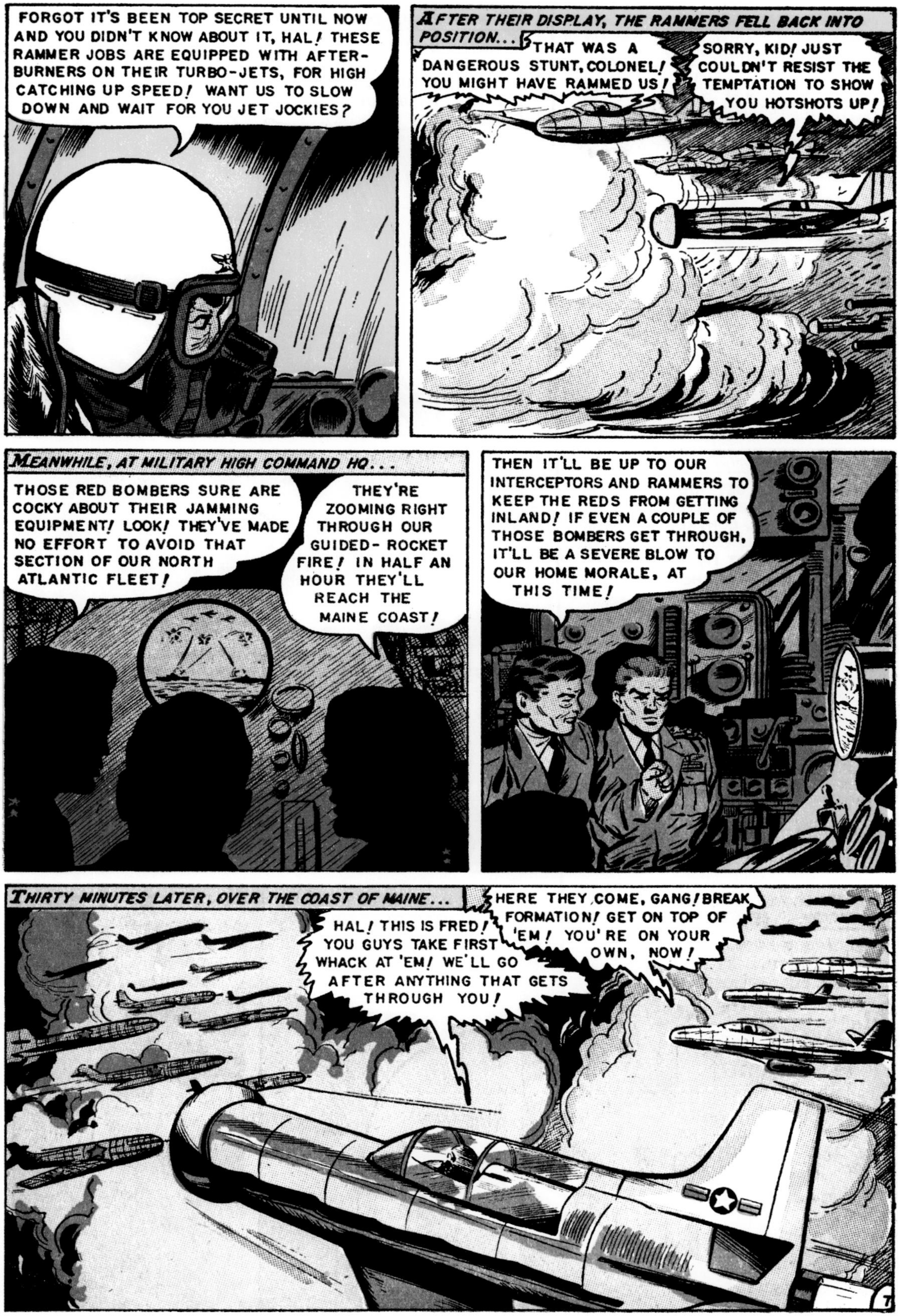
FORGOT IT'S BEEN TOP SECRET UNTIL NOW AND YOU DIDN'T KNOW ABOUT IT, HAL! THESE RAMMER JOBS ARE EQUIPPED WITH AFTER-BURNERS ON THEIR TURBO-JETS, FOR HIGH CATCHING UP SPEED! WANT US TO SLOW DOWN AND WAIT FOR YOU JET JOCKIES?
AFTER THEIR DISPLAY, THE RAMMERS FELL BACK INTO POSITION...
THAT WAS A DANGEROUS STUNT, COLONEL! YOU MIGHT HAVE RAMMED US!
SORRY, KID! JUST COULDN'T RESIST THE TEMPTATION TO SHOW YOU HOTSHOTS UP!
MEANWHILE, AT MILITARY HIGH COMMAND HQ...
THOSE RED BOMBERS SURE ARE COCKY ABOUT THEIR JAMMING EQUIPMENT! LOOK! THEY'VE MADE NO EFFORT TO AVOID THAT SECTION OF OUR NORTH ATLANTIC FLEET!
THEY'RE ZOOMING RIGHT THROUGH OUR GUIDED-ROCKET FIRE! IN HALF AN HOUR THEY'LL REACH THE MAINE COAST!
THEN IT'LL BE UP TO OUR INTERCEPTORS AND RAMMERS TO KEEP THE REDS FROM GETTING INLAND! IF EVEN A COUPLE OF THOSE BOMBERS GET THROUGH, IT'LL BE A SEVERE BLOW TO OUR HOME MORALE, AT THIS TIME!
THIRTY MINUTES LATER, OVER THE COAST OF MAINE...
HAL! THIS IS FRED! YOU GUYS TAKE FIRST WHACK AT 'EM! WE'LL GO AFTER ANYTHING THAT GETS THROUGH YOU!
HERE THEY COME, GANG! BREAK FORMATION! GET ON TOP OF 'EM! YOU'RE ON YOUR OWN, NOW!
7

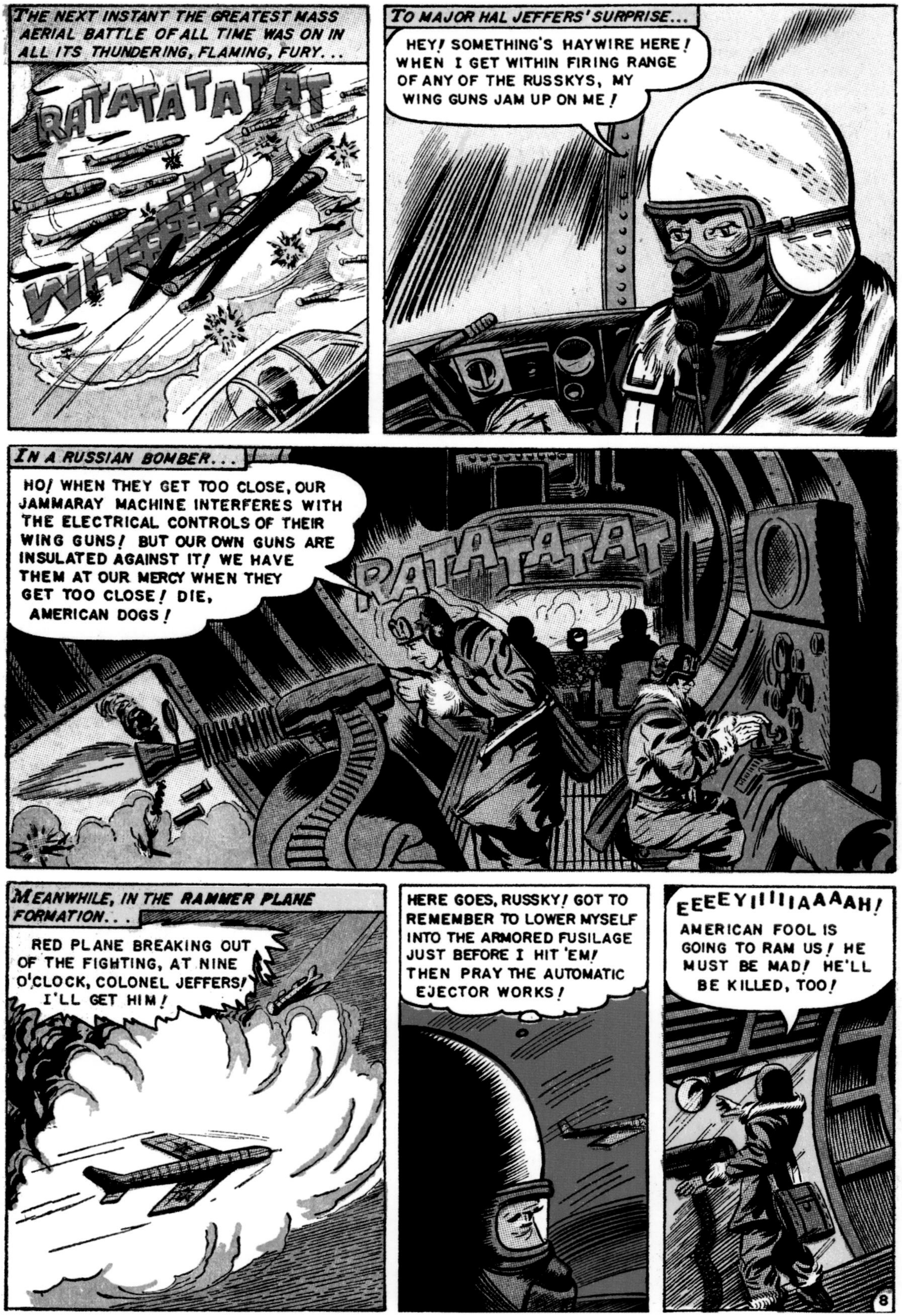
THE NEXT INSTANT THE GREATEST MASS AERIAL BATTLE OF ALL TIME WAS ON IN ALL ITS THUNDERING, FLAMING, FURY...
RATATATATAT
WHEEEEE
TO MAJOR HAL JEFFERS' SURPRISE...
HEY! SOMETHING'S HAYWIRE HERE! WHEN I GET WITHIN FIRING RANGE OF ANY OF THE RUSSKYS, MY WING GUNS JAM UP ON ME!
IN A RUSSIAN BOMBER...
HO! WHEN THEY GET TOO CLOSE, OUR JAMMARAY MACHINE INTERFERES WITH THE ELECTRICAL CONTROLS OF THEIR WING GUNS! BUT OUR OWN GUNS ARE INSULATED AGAINST IT! WE HAVE THEM AT OUR MERCY WHEN THEY GET TOO CLOSE! DIE, AMERICAN DOGS!
RATATATATAT
MEANWHILE, IN THE RAMMER PLANE FORMATION...
RED PLANE BREAKING OUT OF THE FIGHTING, AT NINE O'CLOCK, COLONEL JEFFERS! I'LL GET HIM!
HERE GOES, RUSSKY! GOT TO REMEMBER TO LOWER MYSELF INTO THE ARMORED FUSILAGE JUST BEFORE I HIT 'EM! THEN PRAY THE AUTOMATIC EJECTOR WORKS!
EEEEYIIIIIAAAAH!
AMERICAN FOOL IS GOING TO RAM US! HE MUST BE MAD! HE'LL BE KILLED, TOO!
8

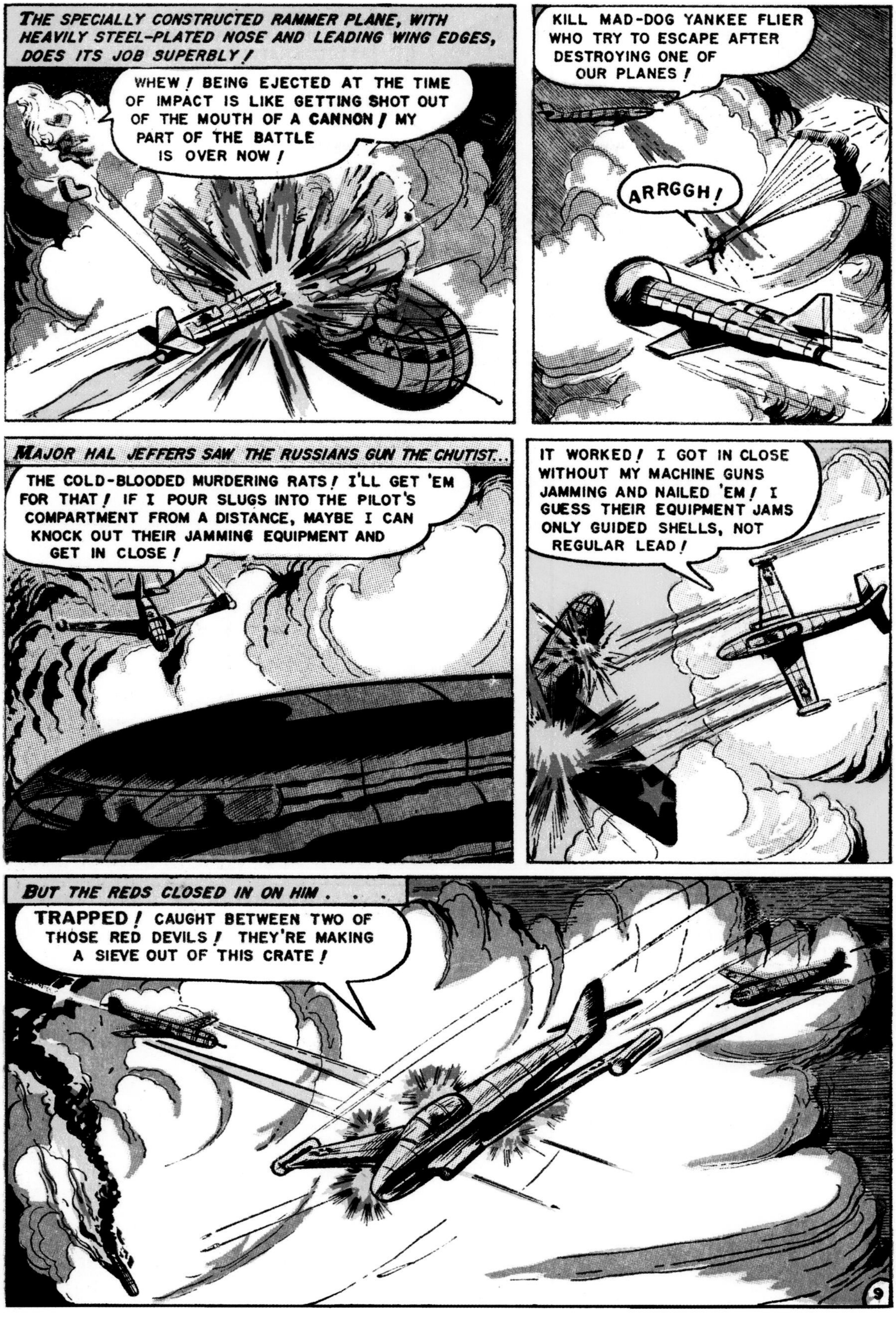
THE SPECIALLY CONSTRUCTED RAMMER PLANE, WITH HEAVILY STEEL-PLATED NOSE AND LEADING WING EDGES, DOES ITS JOB SUPERBLY!
WHEW! BEING EJECTED AT THE TIME OF IMPACT IS LIKE GETTING SHOT OUT OF THE MOUTH OF A CANNON! MY PART OF THE BATTLE IS OVER NOW!
KILL MAD-DOG YANKEE FLIER WHO TRY TO ESCAPE AFTER DESTROYING ONE OF OUR PLANES!
ARRGGH!
MAJOR HAL JEFFERS SAW THE RUSSIANS GUN THE CHUTIST...
THE COLD-BLOODED MURDERING RATS! I'LL GET 'EM FOR THAT! IF I POUR SLUGS INTO THE PILOT'S COMPARTMENT FROM A DISTANCE, MAYBE I CAN KNOCK OUT THEIR JAMMING EQUIPMENT AND GET IN CLOSE!
IT WORKED! I GOT IN CLOSE WITHOUT MY MACHINE GUNS JAMMING AND NAILED 'EM! I GUESS THEIR EQUIPMENT JAMS ONLY GUIDED SHELLS, NOT REGULAR LEAD!
BUT THE REDS CLOSED IN ON HIM . . .
TRAPPED! CAUGHT BETWEEN TWO OF THOSE RED DEVILS! THEY'RE MAKING A SIEVE OUT OF THIS CRATE!
9

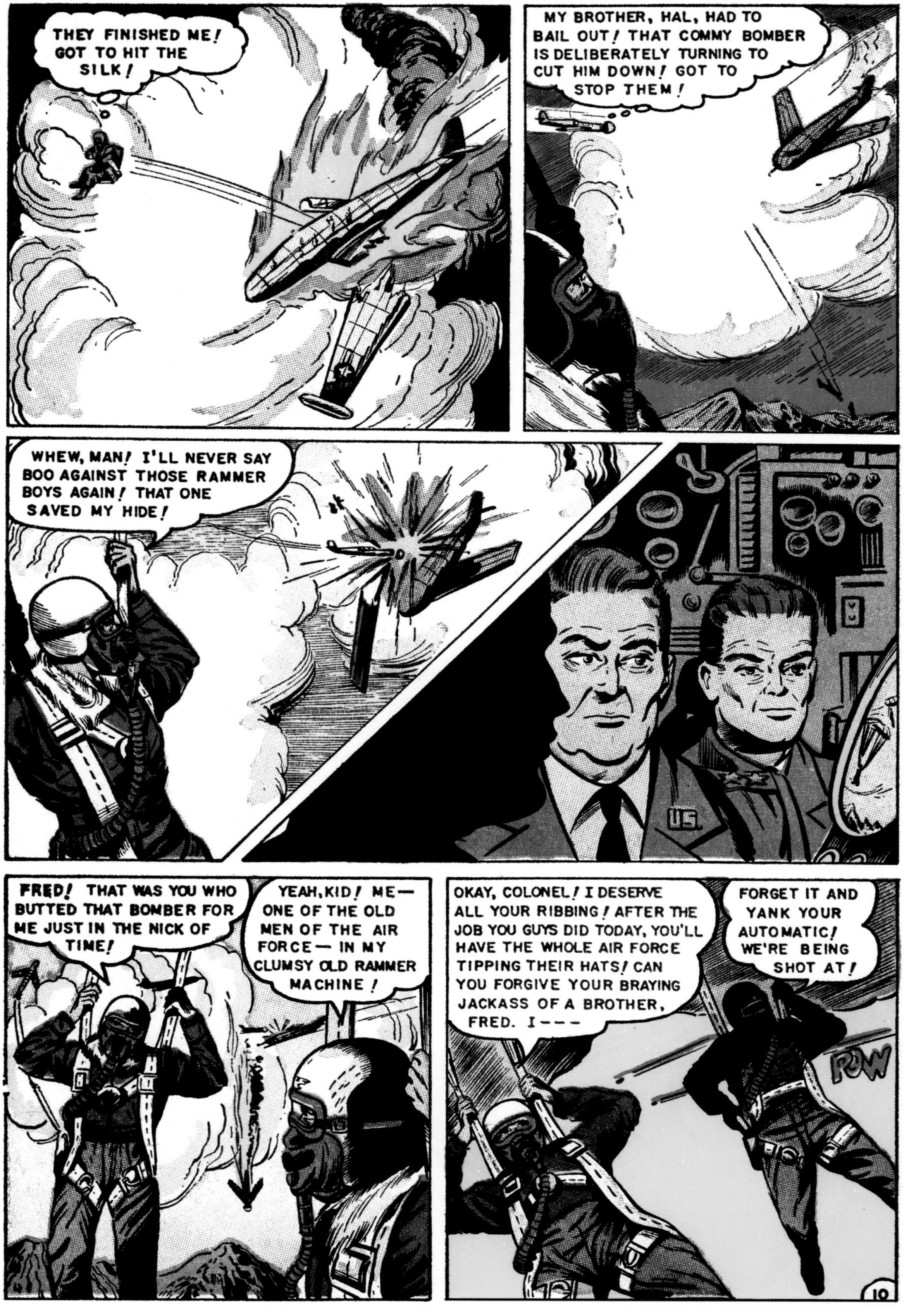
THEY FINISHED ME! GOT TO HIT THE SILK!
MY BROTHER, HAL, HAD TO BAIL OUT! THAT COMMY BOMBER IS DELIBERATELY TURNING TO CUT HIM DOWN! GOT TO STOP THEM!
WHEW, MAN! I'LL NEVER SAY BOO AGAINST THOSE RAMMER BOYS AGAIN! THAT ONE SAVED MY HIDE!
U.S.
FRED! THAT WAS YOU WHO BUTTED THAT BOMBER FOR ME JUST IN THE NICK OF TIME!
YEAH, KID! ME— ONE OF THE OLD MEN OF THE AIR FORCE— IN MY CLUMSY OLD RAMMER MACHINE!
OKAY, COLONEL! I DESERVE ALL YOUR RIBBING! AFTER THE JOB YOU GUYS DID TODAY, YOU'LL HAVE THE WHOLE AIR FORCE TIPPING THEIR HATS! CAN YOU FORGIVE YOUR BRAYING JACKASS OF A BROTHER, FRED. I---
FORGET IT AND YANK YOUR AUTOMATIC! WE'RE BEING SHOT AT!
POW
10

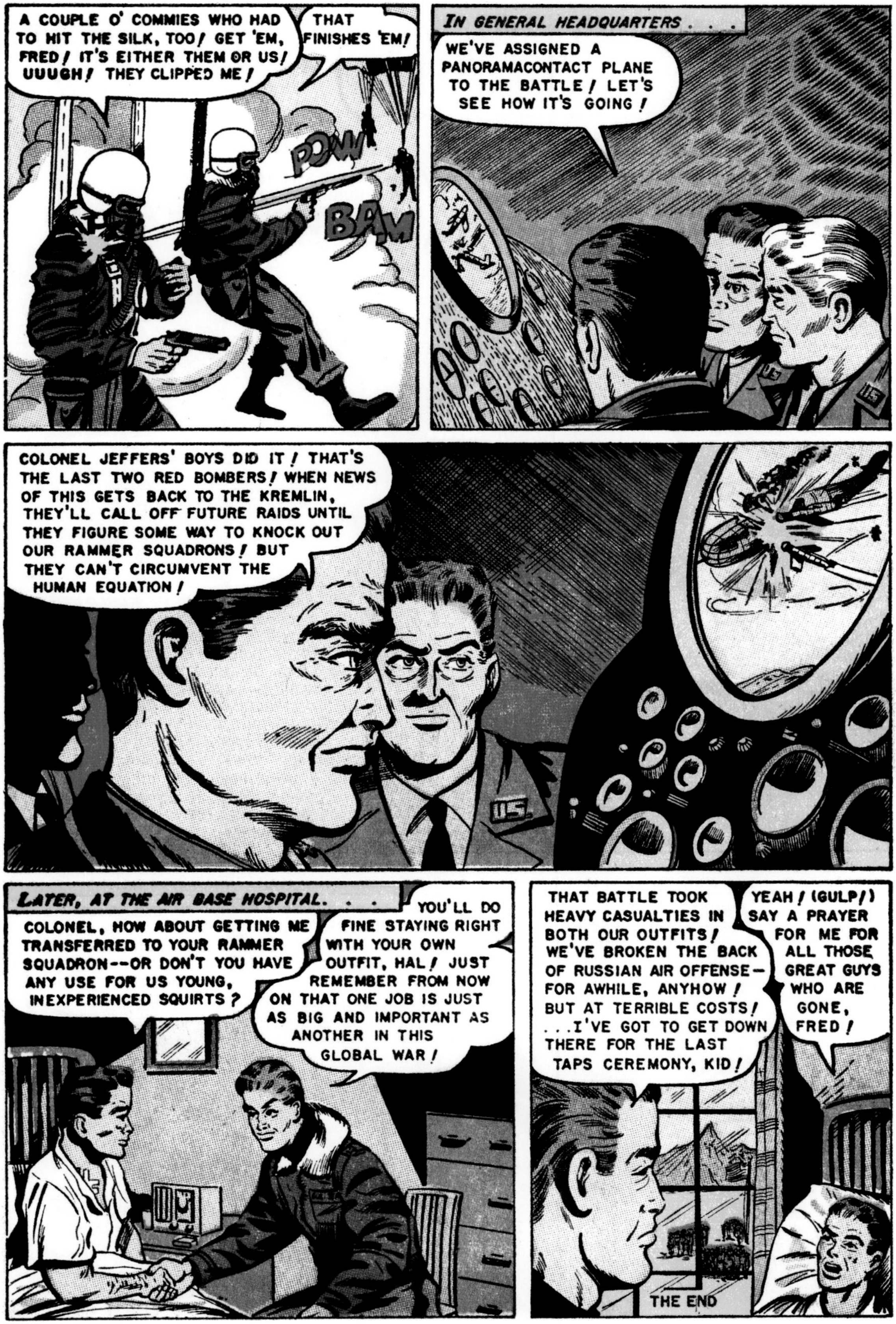
A COUPLE O' COMMIES WHO HAD TO HIT THE SILK, TOO! GET 'EM, FRED! IT'S EITHER THEM OR US! UUUGH! THEY CLIPPED ME!
THAT FINISHES 'EM!
POW
BAM
IN GENERAL HEADQUARTERS . . .
WE'VE ASSIGNED A PANORAMACONTACT PLANE TO THE BATTLE! LET'S SEE HOW IT'S GOING!
COLONEL JEFFERS' BOYS DID IT! THAT'S THE LAST TWO RED BOMBERS! WHEN NEWS OF THIS GETS BACK TO THE KREMLIN, THEY'LL CALL OFF FUTURE RAIDS UNTIL THEY FIGURE SOME WAY TO KNOCK OUT OUR RAMMER SQUADRONS! BUT THEY CAN'T CIRCUMVENT THE HUMAN EQUATION!
LATER, AT THE AIR BASE HOSPITAL. . .
COLONEL, HOW ABOUT GETTING ME TRANSFERRED TO YOUR RAMMER SQUADRON--OR DON'T YOU HAVE ANY USE FOR US YOUNG, INEXPERIENCED SQUIRTS?
YOU'LL DO FINE STAYING RIGHT WITH YOUR OWN OUTFIT, HAL! JUST REMEMBER FROM NOW ON THAT ONE JOB IS JUST AS BIG AND IMPORTANT AS ANOTHER IN THIS GLOBAL WAR!
THAT BATTLE TOOK HEAVY CASUALTIES IN BOTH OUR OUTFITS! WE'VE BROKEN THE BACK OF RUSSIAN AIR OFFENSE--FOR AWHILE, ANYHOW! BUT AT TERRIBLE COSTS! . . .I'VE GOT TO GET DOWN THERE FOR THE LAST TAPS CEREMONY, KID!
YEAH! (GULP!) SAY A PRAYER FOR ME FOR ALL THOSE GREAT GUYS WHO ARE GONE, FRED!
THE END

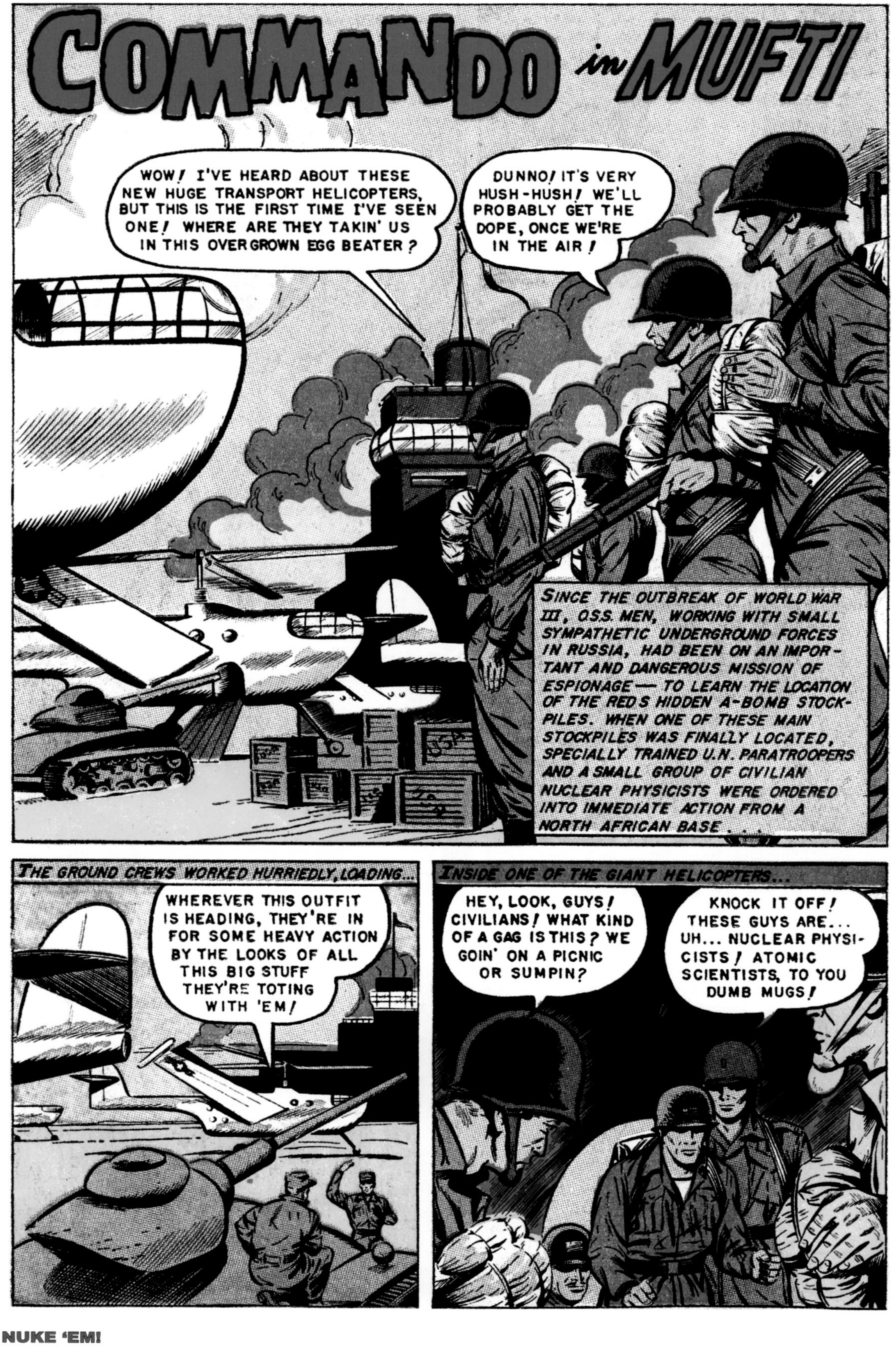
COMMANDO in MUFTI
WOW! I'VE HEARD ABOUT THESE NEW HUGE TRANSPORT HELICOPTERS, BUT THIS IS THE FIRST TIME I'VE SEEN ONE! WHERE ARE THEY TAKIN' US IN THIS OVERGROWN EGG BEATER?
DUNNO! IT'S VERY HUSH-HUSH! WE'LL PROBABLY GET THE DOPE, ONCE WE'RE IN THE AIR!
SINCE THE OUTBREAK OF WORLD WAR III, O.S.S. MEN, WORKING WITH SMALL SYMPATHETIC UNDERGROUND FORCES IN RUSSIA, HAD BEEN ON AN IMPORTANT AND DANGEROUS MISSION OF ESPIONAGE— TO LEARN THE LOCATION OF THE RED'S HIDDEN A-BOMB STOCKPILES. WHEN ONE OF THESE MAIN STOCKPILES WAS FINALLY LOCATED, SPECIALLY TRAINED U.N. PARATROOPERS AND A SMALL GROUP OF CIVILIAN NUCLEAR PHYSICISTS WERE ORDERED INTO IMMEDIATE ACTION FROM A NORTH AFRICAN BASE . . . .
THE GROUND CREWS WORKED HURRIEDLY, LOADING...
WHEREVER THIS OUTFIT IS HEADING, THEY'RE IN FOR SOME HEAVY ACTION BY THE LOOKS OF ALL THIS BIG STUFF THEY'RE TOTING WITH 'EM!
INSIDE ONE OF THE GIANT HELICOPTERS...
HEY, LOOK, GUYS! CIVILIANS! WHAT KIND OF A GAG IS THIS? WE GOIN' ON A PICNIC OR SUMPIN?
KNOCK IT OFF! THESE GUYS ARE... UH... NUCLEAR PHYSICISTS! ATOMIC SCIENTISTS, TO YOU DUMB MUGS!

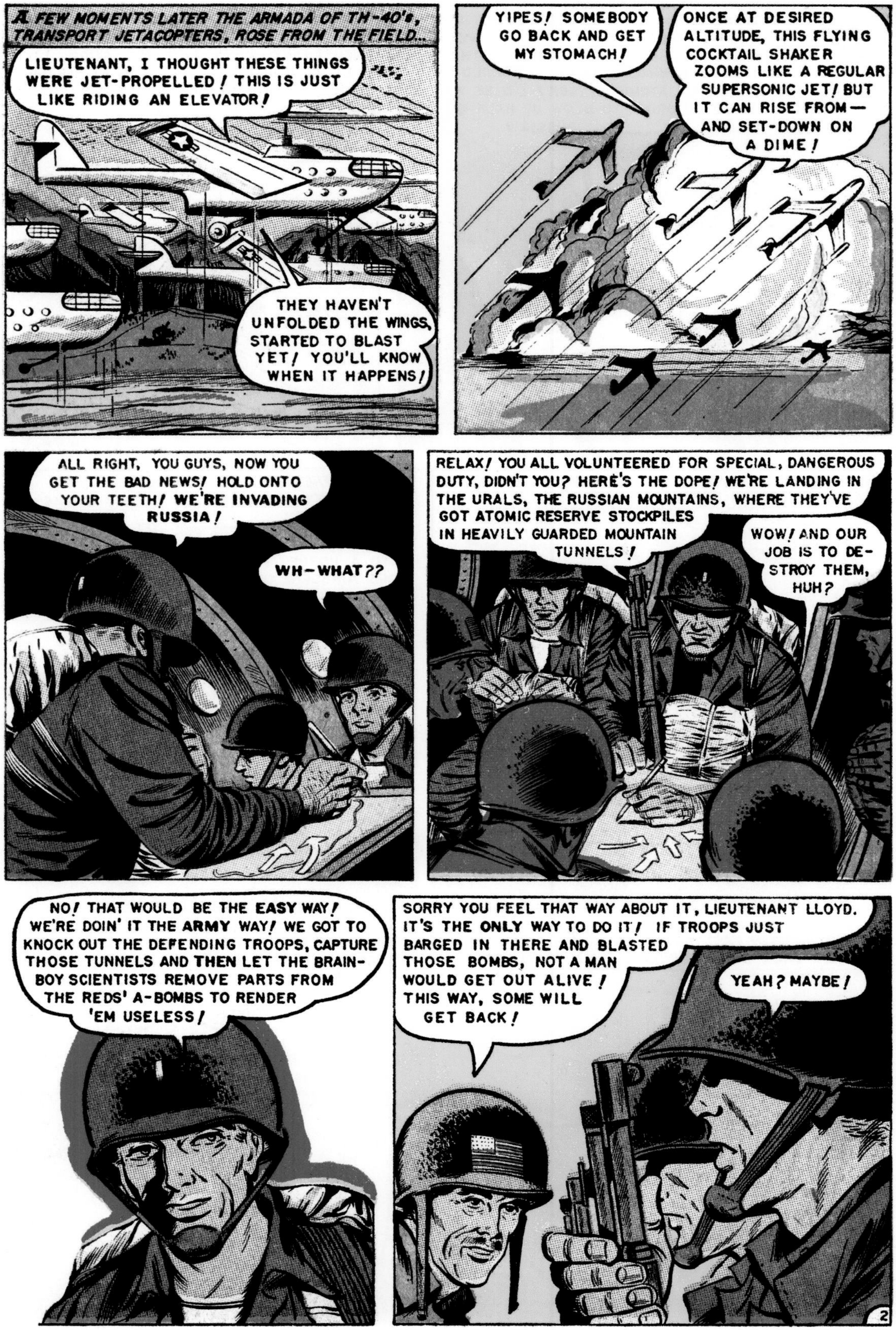
A FEW MOMENTS LATER THE ARMADA OF TH-40's, TRANSPORT JETACOPTERS, ROSE FROM THE FIELD...
LIEUTENANT, I THOUGHT THESE THINGS WERE JET-PROPELLED! THIS IS JUST LIKE RIDING AN ELEVATOR!
THEY HAVEN'T UNFOLDED THE WINGS, STARTED TO BLAST YET! YOU'LL KNOW WHEN IT HAPPENS!
YIPES! SOMEBODY GO BACK AND GET MY STOMACH!
ONCE AT DESIRED ALTITUDE, THIS FLYING COCKTAIL SHAKER ZOOMS LIKE A REGULAR SUPERSONIC JET! BUT IT CAN RISE FROM— AND SET-DOWN ON A DIME!
ALL RIGHT, YOU GUYS, NOW YOU GET THE BAD NEWS! HOLD ONTO YOUR TEETH! WE'RE INVADING RUSSIA!
WH-WHAT??
RELAX! YOU ALL VOLUNTEERED FOR SPECIAL, DANGEROUS DUTY, DIDN'T YOU? HERE'S THE DOPE! WE'RE LANDING IN THE URALS, THE RUSSIAN MOUNTAINS, WHERE THEY'VE GOT ATOMIC RESERVE STOCKPILES IN HEAVILY GUARDED MOUNTAIN TUNNELS!
WOW! AND OUR JOB IS TO DESTROY THEM, HUH?
NO! THAT WOULD BE THE EASY WAY! WE'RE DOIN' IT THE ARMY WAY! WE GOT TO KNOCK OUT THE DEFENDING TROOPS, CAPTURE THOSE TUNNELS AND THEN LET THE BRAIN-BOY SCIENTISTS REMOVE PARTS FROM THE REDS' A-BOMBS TO RENDER 'EM USELESS!
SORRY YOU FEEL THAT WAY ABOUT IT, LIEUTENANT LLOYD. IT'S THE ONLY WAY TO DO IT! IF TROOPS JUST BARGED IN THERE AND BLASTED THOSE BOMBS, NOT A MAN WOULD GET OUT ALIVE! THIS WAY, SOME WILL GET BACK!
YEAH? MAYBE!
2

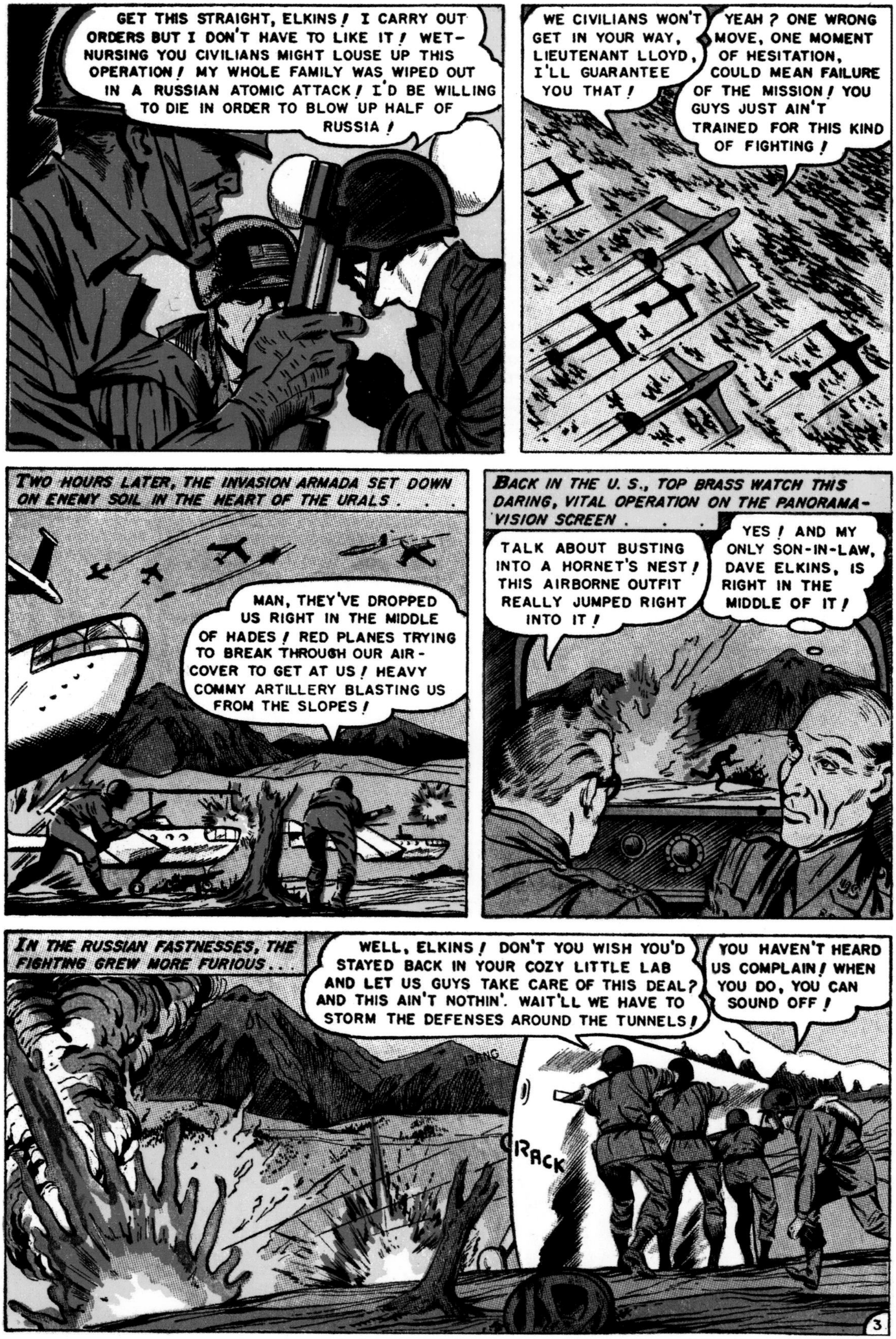
GET THIS STRAIGHT, ELKINS! I CARRY OUT ORDERS BUT I DON'T HAVE TO LIKE IT! WET-NURSING YOU CIVILIANS MIGHT LOUSE UP THIS OPERATION! MY WHOLE FAMILY WAS WIPED OUT IN A RUSSIAN ATOMIC ATTACK! I'D BE WILLING TO DIE IN ORDER TO BLOW UP HALF OF RUSSIA!
WE CIVILIANS WON'T GET IN YOUR WAY, LIEUTENANT LLOYD, I'LL GUARANTEE YOU THAT!
YEAH? ONE WRONG MOVE, ONE MOMENT OF HESITATION, COULD MEAN FAILURE OF THE MISSION! YOU GUYS JUST AIN'T TRAINED FOR THIS KIND OF FIGHTING!
TWO HOURS LATER, THE INVASION ARMADA SET DOWN ON ENEMY SOIL IN THE HEART OF THE URALS . . .
MAN, THEY'VE DROPPED US RIGHT IN THE MIDDLE OF HADES! RED PLANES TRYING TO BREAK THROUGH OUR AIR-COVER TO GET AT US! HEAVY COMMY ARTILLERY BLASTING US FROM THE SLOPES!
BACK IN THE U. S., TOP BRASS WATCH THIS DARING, VITAL OPERATION ON THE PANORAMA-VISION SCREEN . . .
TALK ABOUT BUSTING INTO A HORNET'S NEST! THIS AIRBORNE OUTFIT REALLY JUMPED RIGHT INTO IT!
YES! AND MY ONLY SON-IN-LAW, DAVE ELKINS, IS RIGHT IN THE MIDDLE OF IT!
IN THE RUSSIAN FASTNESSES, THE FIGHTING GREW MORE FURIOUS...
WELL, ELKINS! DON'T YOU WISH YOU'D STAYED BACK IN YOUR COZY LITTLE LAB AND LET US GUYS TAKE CARE OF THIS DEAL? AND THIS AIN'T NOTHIN'. WAIT'LL WE HAVE TO STORM THE DEFENSES AROUND THE TUNNELS!
YOU HAVEN'T HEARD US COMPLAIN! WHEN YOU DO, YOU CAN SOUND OFF!
CRACK
3

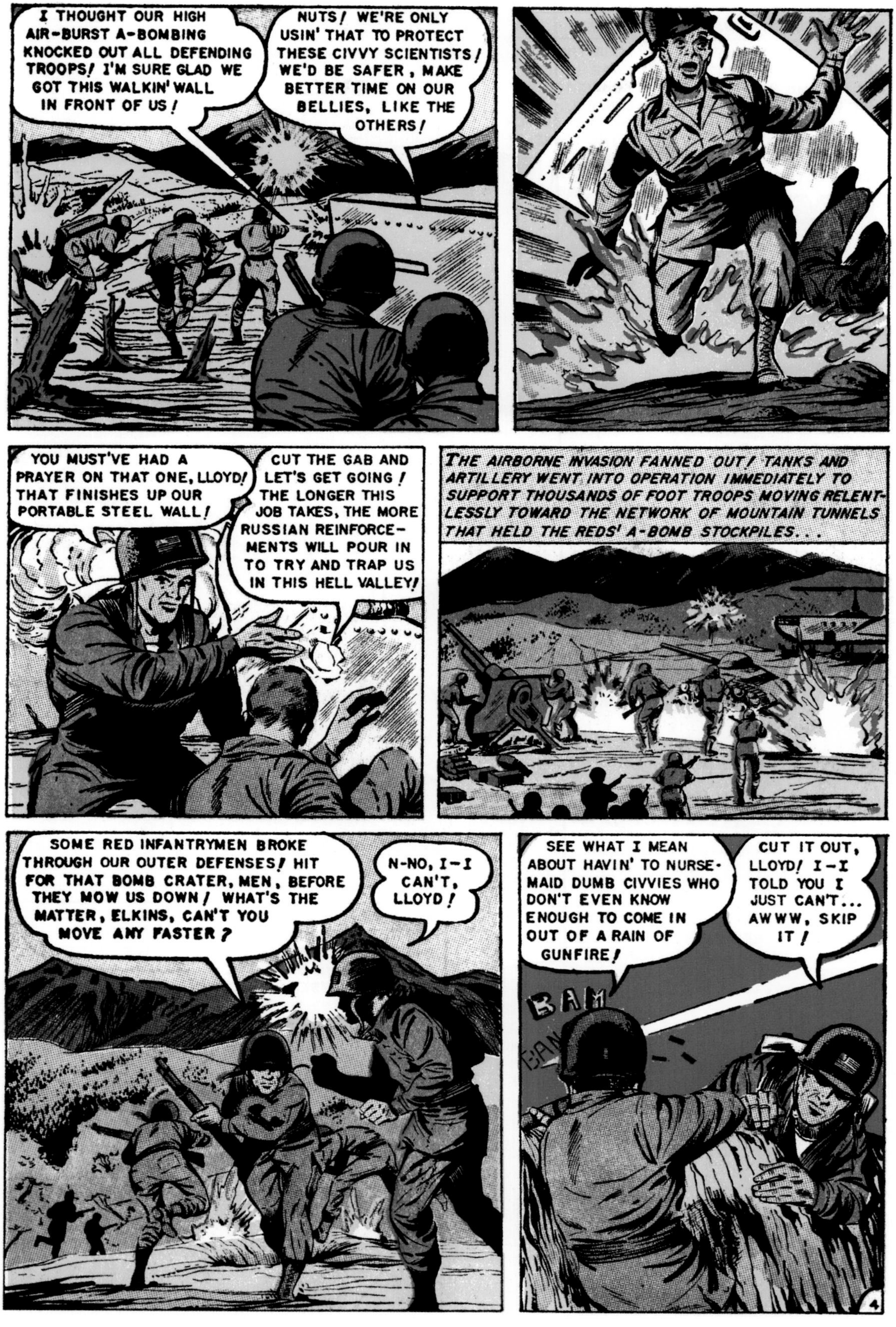
I THOUGHT OUR HIGH AIR-BURST A-BOMBING KNOCKED OUT ALL DEFENDING TROOPS! I'M SURE GLAD WE GOT THIS WALKIN' WALL IN FRONT OF US!
NUTS! WE'RE ONLY USIN' THAT TO PROTECT THESE CIVVY SCIENTISTS! WE'D BE SAFER, MAKE BETTER TIME ON OUR BELLIES, LIKE THE OTHERS!
YOU MUST'VE HAD A PRAYER ON THAT ONE, LLOYD! THAT FINISHES UP OUR PORTABLE STEEL WALL!
CUT THE GAB AND LET'S GET GOING! THE LONGER THIS JOB TAKES, THE MORE RUSSIAN REINFORCEMENTS WILL POUR IN TO TRY AND TRAP US IN THIS HELL VALLEY!
THE AIRBORNE INVASION FANNED OUT! TANKS AND ARTILLERY WENT INTO OPERATION IMMEDIATELY TO SUPPORT THOUSANDS OF FOOT TROOPS MOVING RELENTLESSLY TOWARD THE NETWORK OF MOUNTAIN TUNNELS THAT HELD THE REDS' A-BOMB STOCKPILES...
SOME RED INFANTRYMEN BROKE THROUGH OUR OUTER DEFENSES! HIT FOR THAT BOMB CRATER, MEN, BEFORE THEY MOW US DOWN! WHAT'S THE MATTER, ELKINS, CAN'T YOU MOVE ANY FASTER?
N-NO, I-I CAN'T, LLOYD!
SEE WHAT I MEAN ABOUT HAVIN' TO NURSEMAID DUMB CIVVIES WHO DON'T EVEN KNOW ENOUGH TO COME IN OUT OF A RAIN OF GUNFIRE!
CUT IT OUT, LLOYD! I-I TOLD YOU I JUST CAN'T... AWWW, SKIP IT!
BAM
4

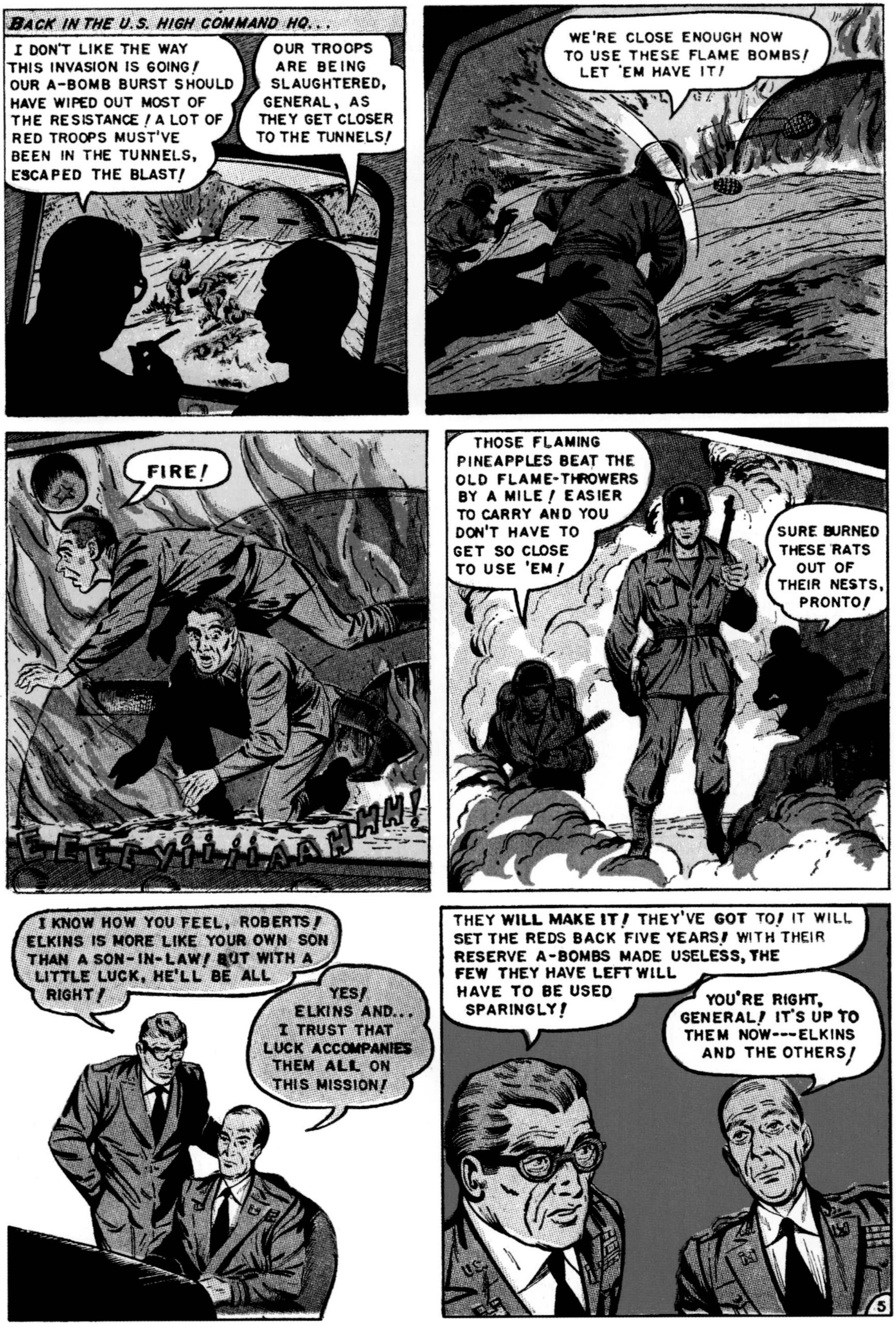
BACK IN THE U.S. HIGH COMMAND HQ...
I DON'T LIKE THE WAY THIS INVASION IS GOING! OUR A-BOMB BURST SHOULD HAVE WIPED OUT MOST OF THE RESISTANCE! A LOT OF RED TROOPS MUST'VE BEEN IN THE TUNNELS, ESCAPED THE BLAST!
OUR TROOPS ARE BEING SLAUGHTERED, GENERAL, AS THEY GET CLOSER TO THE TUNNELS!
WE'RE CLOSE ENOUGH NOW TO USE THESE FLAME BOMBS! LET 'EM HAVE IT!
FIRE!
EEEEYIIIIAAHHHH!
THOSE FLAMING PINEAPPLES BEAT THE OLD FLAME-THROWERS BY A MILE! EASIER TO CARRY AND YOU DON'T HAVE TO GET SO CLOSE TO USE 'EM!
SURE BURNED THESE RATS OUT OF THEIR NESTS, PRONTO!
I KNOW HOW YOU FEEL, ROBERTS! ELKINS IS MORE LIKE YOUR OWN SON THAN A SON-IN-LAW! BUT WITH A LITTLE LUCK, HE'LL BE ALL RIGHT!
YES! ELKINS AND... I TRUST THAT LUCK ACCOMPANIES THEM ALL ON THIS MISSION!
THEY WILL MAKE IT! THEY'VE GOT TO! IT WILL SET THE REDS BACK FIVE YEARS! WITH THEIR RESERVE A-BOMBS MADE USELESS, THE FEW THEY HAVE LEFT WILL HAVE TO BE USED SPARINGLY!
YOU'RE RIGHT, GENERAL! IT'S UP TO THEM NOW---ELKINS AND THE OTHERS!
5

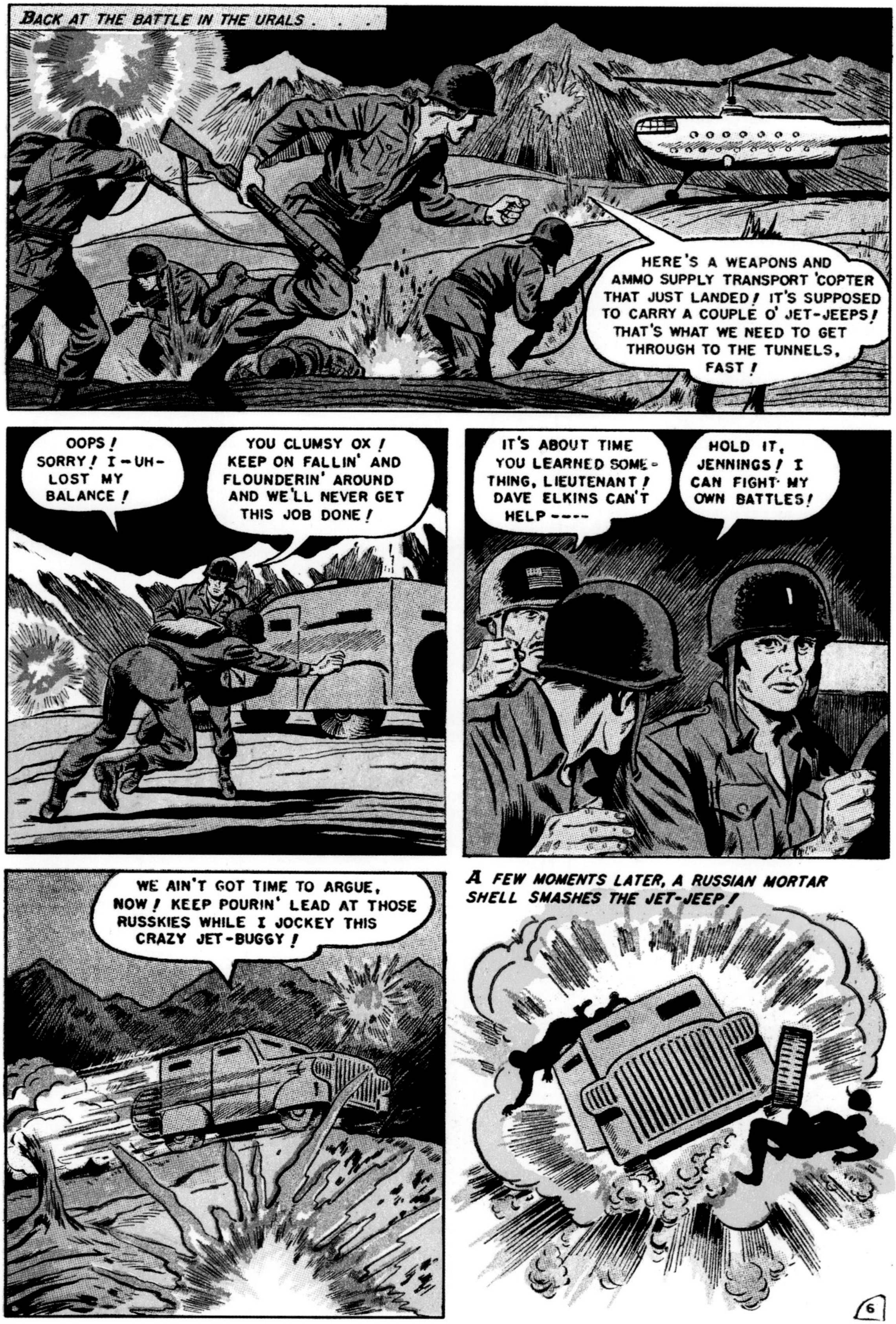
BACK AT THE BATTLE IN THE URALS . . .
HERE'S A WEAPONS AND AMMO SUPPLY TRANSPORT 'COPTER THAT JUST LANDED! IT'S SUPPOSED TO CARRY A COUPLE O' JET-JEEPS! THAT'S WHAT WE NEED TO GET THROUGH TO THE TUNNELS, FAST!
OOPS! SORRY! I-UH- LOST MY BALANCE!
YOU CLUMSY OX! KEEP ON FALLIN' AND FLOUNDERIN' AROUND AND WE'LL NEVER GET THIS JOB DONE!
IT'S ABOUT TIME YOU LEARNED SOME-THING, LIEUTENANT! DAVE ELKINS CAN'T HELP ----
HOLD IT, JENNINGS! I CAN FIGHT MY OWN BATTLES!
WE AIN'T GOT TIME TO ARGUE, NOW! KEEP POURIN' LEAD AT THOSE RUSSKIES WHILE I JOCKEY THIS CRAZY JET-BUGGY!
A FEW MOMENTS LATER, A RUSSIAN MORTAR SHELL SMASHES THE JET-JEEP!
6

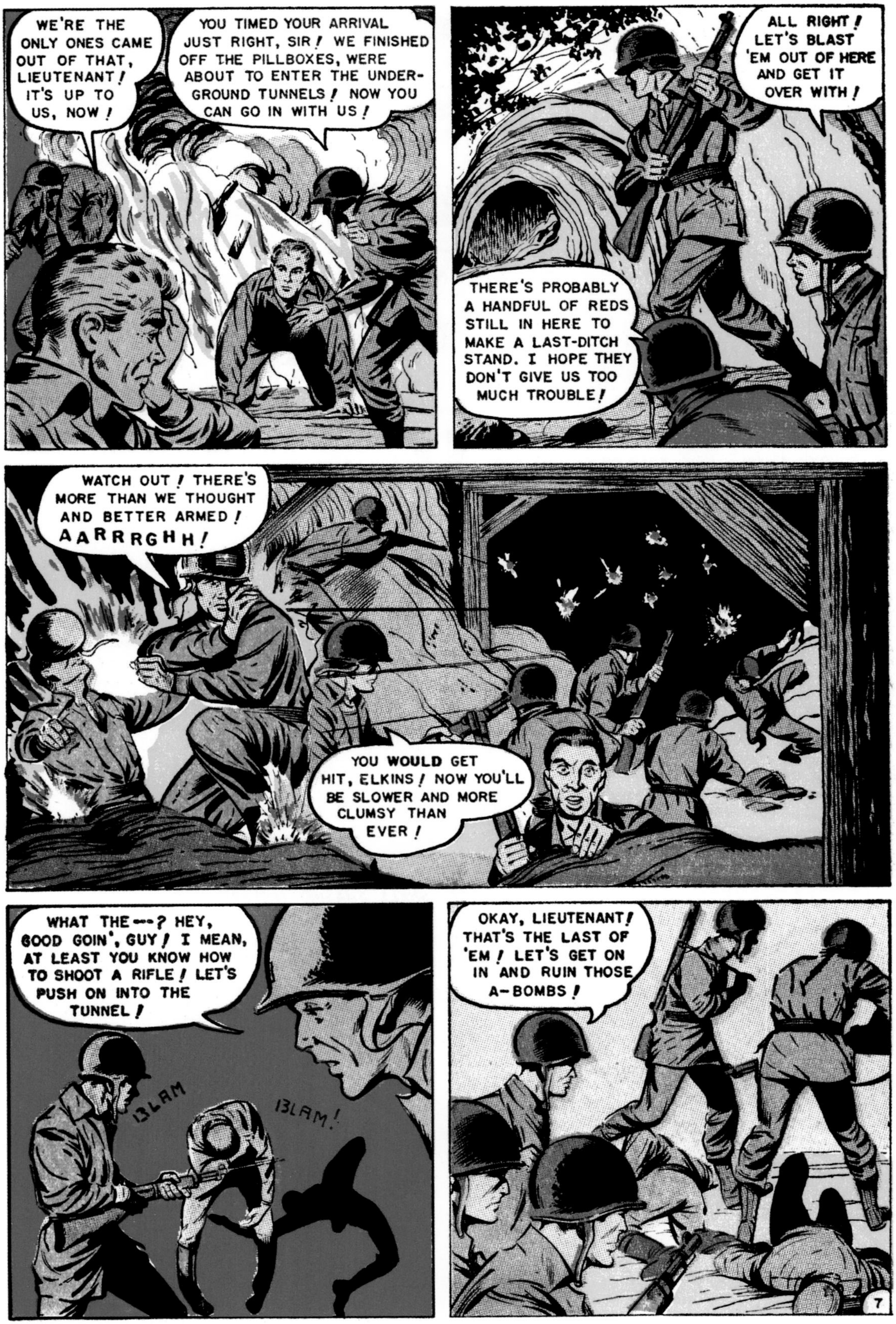
WE'RE THE ONLY ONES CAME OUT OF THAT, LIEUTENANT! IT'S UP TO US, NOW!
YOU TIMED YOUR ARRIVAL JUST RIGHT, SIR! WE FINISHED OFF THE PILLBOXES, WERE ABOUT TO ENTER THE UNDER-GROUND TUNNELS! NOW YOU CAN GO IN WITH US!
ALL RIGHT! LET'S BLAST 'EM OUT OF HERE AND GET IT OVER WITH!
THERE'S PROBABLY A HANDFUL OF REDS STILL IN HERE TO MAKE A LAST-DITCH STAND. I HOPE THEY DON'T GIVE US TOO MUCH TROUBLE!
WATCH OUT! THERE'S MORE THAN WE THOUGHT AND BETTER ARMED! AARRRGHH!
YOU WOULD GET HIT, ELKINS! NOW YOU'LL BE SLOWER AND MORE CLUMSY THAN EVER!
WHAT THE---? HEY, GOOD GOIN', GUY! I MEAN, AT LEAST YOU KNOW HOW TO SHOOT A RIFLE! LET'S PUSH ON INTO THE TUNNEL!
BLAM
BLAM!
OKAY, LIEUTENANT! THAT'S THE LAST OF 'EM! LET'S GET ON IN AND RUIN THOSE A-BOMBS!
7

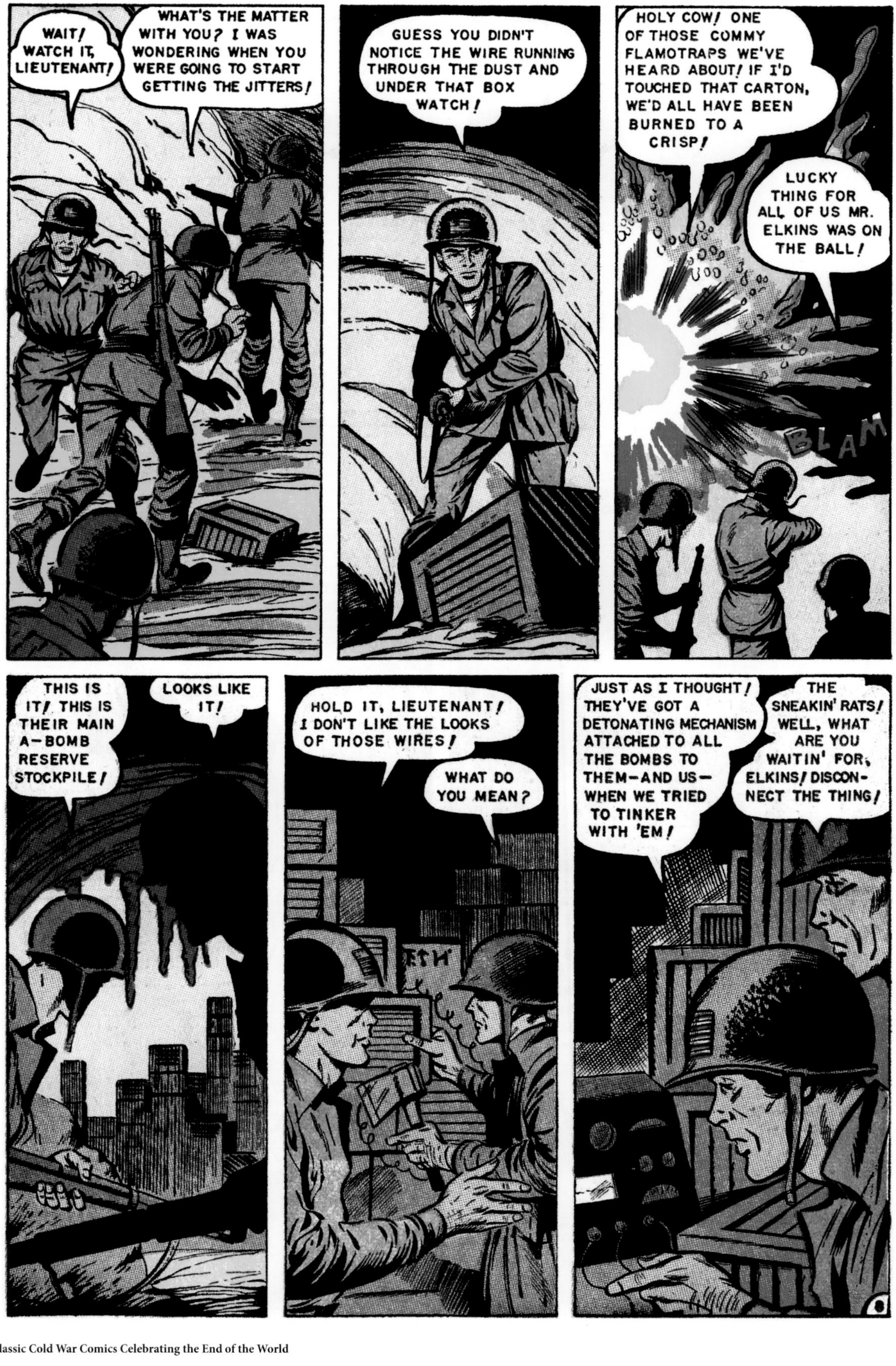

WAIT! WATCH IT, LIEUTENANT!
WHAT'S THE MATTER WITH YOU? I WAS WONDERING WHEN YOU WERE GOING TO START GETTING THE JITTERS!
GUESS YOU DIDN'T NOTICE THE WIRE RUNNING THROUGH THE DUST AND UNDER THAT BOX WATCH!
HOLY COW! ONE OF THOSE COMMY FLAMOTRAPS WE'VE HEARD ABOUT! IF I'D TOUCHED THAT CARTON, WE'D ALL HAVE BEEN BURNED TO A CRISP!
LUCKY THING FOR ALL OF US MR. ELKINS WAS ON THE BALL!
BLAM
THIS IS IT! THIS IS THEIR MAIN A-BOMB RESERVE STOCKPILE!
LOOKS LIKE IT!
HOLD IT, LIEUTENANT! I DON'T LIKE THE LOOKS OF THOSE WIRES!
WHAT DO YOU MEAN?
JUST AS I THOUGHT! THEY'VE GOT A DETONATING MECHANISM ATTACHED TO ALL THE BOMBS TO THEM—AND US—WHEN WE TRIED TO TINKER WITH 'EM!
THE SNEAKIN' RATS! WELL, WHAT ARE YOU WAITIN' FOR, ELKINS! DISCON-NECT THE THING!

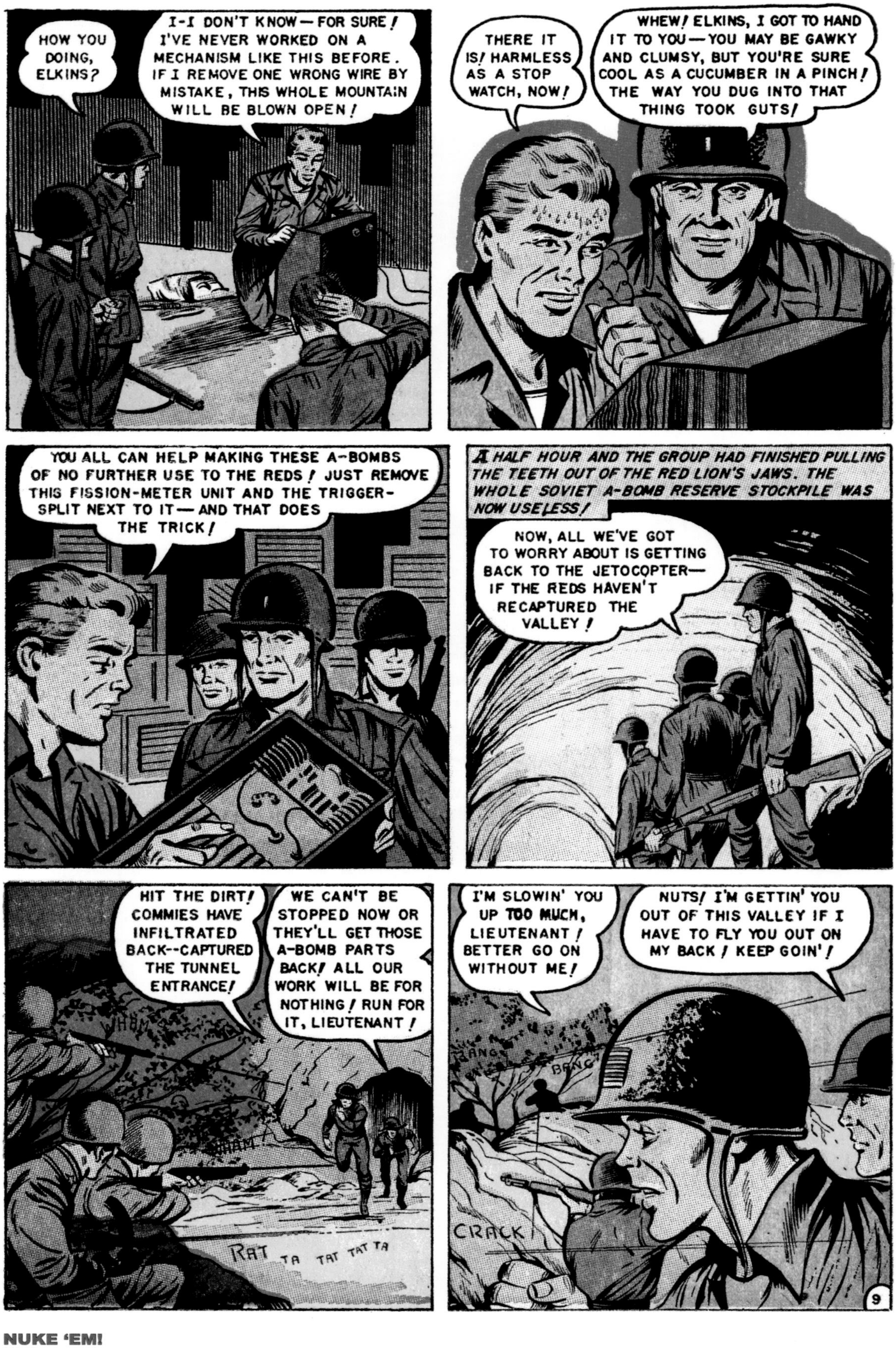
HOW YOU DOING, ELKINS?
I-I DON'T KNOW — FOR SURE! I'VE NEVER WORKED ON A MECHANISM LIKE THIS BEFORE. IF I REMOVE ONE WRONG WIRE BY MISTAKE, THIS WHOLE MOUNTAIN WILL BE BLOWN OPEN!
THERE IT IS! HARMLESS AS A STOP WATCH, NOW!
WHEW! ELKINS, I GOT TO HAND IT TO YOU — YOU MAY BE GAWKY AND CLUMSY, BUT YOU'RE SURE COOL AS A CUCUMBER IN A PINCH! THE WAY YOU DUG INTO THAT THING TOOK GUTS!
YOU ALL CAN HELP MAKING THESE A-BOMBS OF NO FURTHER USE TO THE REDS! JUST REMOVE THIS FISSION-METER UNIT AND THE TRIGGER-SPLIT NEXT TO IT — AND THAT DOES THE TRICK!
A HALF HOUR AND THE GROUP HAD FINISHED PULLING THE TEETH OUT OF THE RED LION'S JAWS. THE WHOLE SOVIET A-BOMB RESERVE STOCKPILE WAS NOW USELESS!
NOW, ALL WE'VE GOT TO WORRY ABOUT IS GETTING BACK TO THE JETOCOPTER— IF THE REDS HAVEN'T RECAPTURED THE VALLEY!
HIT THE DIRT! COMMIES HAVE INFILTRATED BACK--CAPTURED THE TUNNEL ENTRANCE!
WE CAN'T BE STOPPED NOW OR THEY'LL GET THOSE A-BOMB PARTS BACK! ALL OUR WORK WILL BE FOR NOTHING! RUN FOR IT, LIEUTENANT!
WHAM
WHAM
RAT TA TAT TAT TA
I'M SLOWIN' YOU UP TOO MUCH, LIEUTENANT! BETTER GO ON WITHOUT ME!
NUTS! I'M GETTIN' YOU OUT OF THIS VALLEY IF I HAVE TO FLY YOU OUT ON MY BACK! KEEP GOIN'!
BANG
BANG
CRACK
9

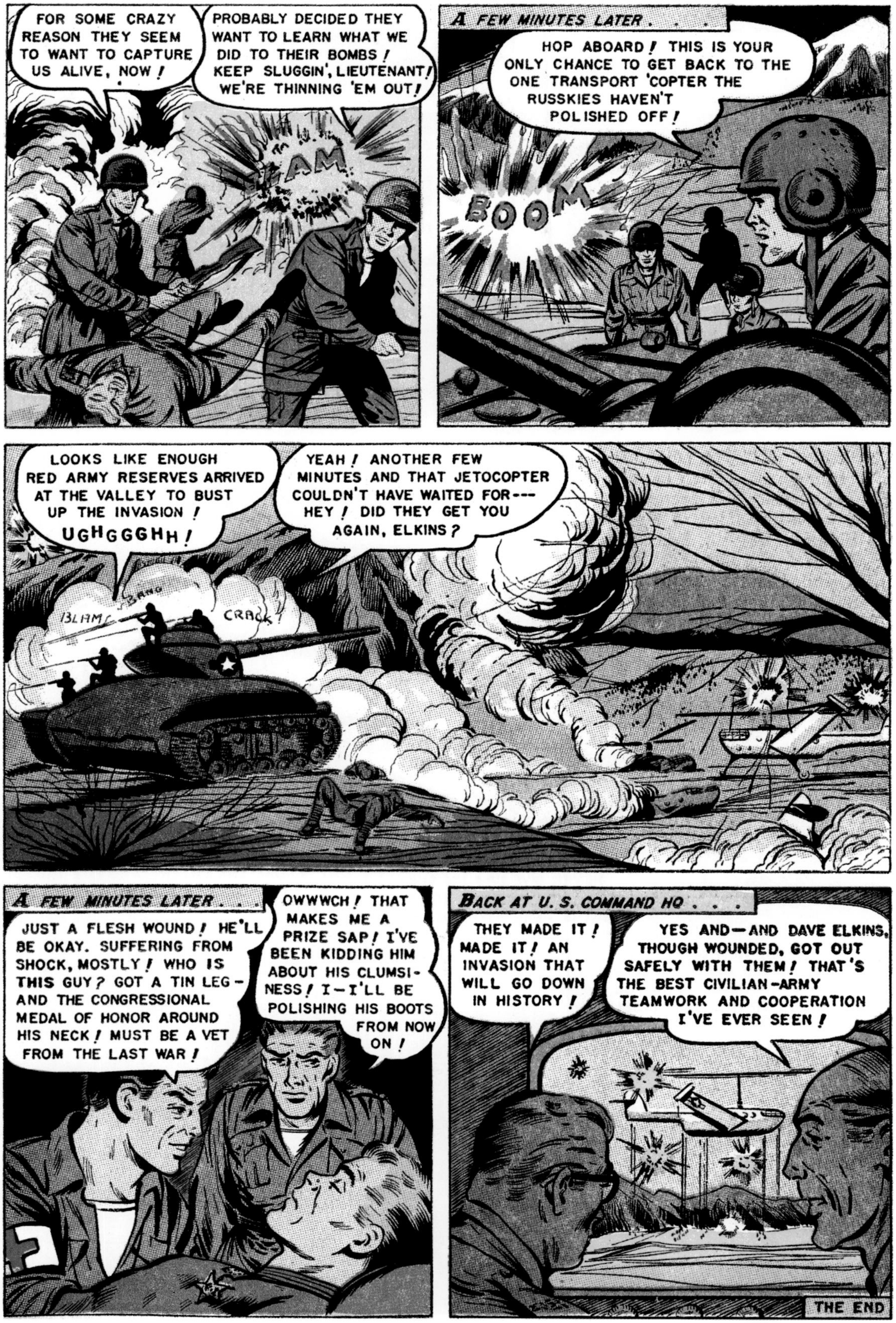
FOR SOME CRAZY REASON THEY SEEM TO WANT TO CAPTURE US ALIVE, NOW!
PROBABLY DECIDED THEY WANT TO LEARN WHAT WE DID TO THEIR BOMBS! KEEP SLUGGIN', LIEUTENANT! WE'RE THINNING 'EM OUT!
A FEW MINUTES LATER . . .
HOP ABOARD! THIS IS YOUR ONLY CHANCE TO GET BACK TO THE ONE TRANSPORT 'COPTER THE RUSSKIES HAVEN'T POLISHED OFF!
BOOM
LOOKS LIKE ENOUGH RED ARMY RESERVES ARRIVED AT THE VALLEY TO BUST UP THE INVASION! UGHGGGHH!
YEAH! ANOTHER FEW MINUTES AND THAT JETOCOPTER COULDN'T HAVE WAITED FOR--- HEY! DID THEY GET YOU AGAIN, ELKINS?
BLAM
BANG
CRACK!
A FEW MINUTES LATER . . .
JUST A FLESH WOUND! HE'LL BE OKAY. SUFFERING FROM SHOCK, MOSTLY! WHO IS THIS GUY? GOT A TIN LEG- AND THE CONGRESSIONAL MEDAL OF HONOR AROUND HIS NECK! MUST BE A VET FROM THE LAST WAR!
OWWWCH! THAT MAKES ME A PRIZE SAP! I'VE BEEN KIDDING HIM ABOUT HIS CLUMSI-NESS! I-I'LL BE POLISHING HIS BOOTS FROM NOW ON!
BACK AT U. S. COMMAND HQ . . .
THEY MADE IT! MADE IT! AN INVASION THAT WILL GO DOWN IN HISTORY!
YES AND—AND DAVE ELKINS, THOUGH WOUNDED, GOT OUT SAFELY WITH THEM! THAT'S THE BEST CIVILIAN-ARMY TEAMWORK AND COOPERATION I'VE EVER SEEN!
THE END

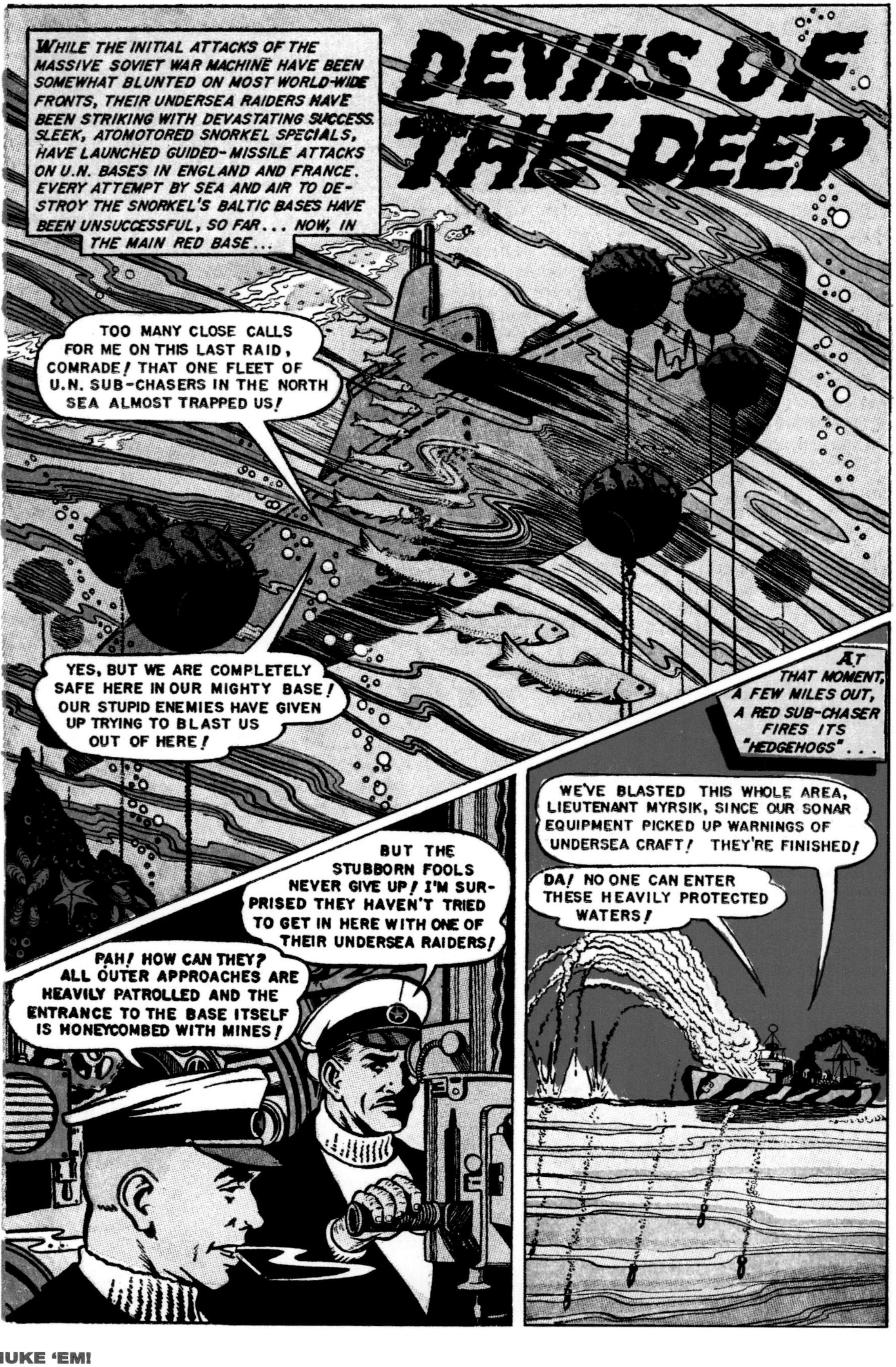
WHILE THE INITIAL ATTACKS OF THE MASSIVE SOVIET WAR MACHINE HAVE BEEN SOMEWHAT BLUNTED ON MOST WORLD-WIDE FRONTS, THEIR UNDERSEA RAIDERS HAVE BEEN STRIKING WITH DEVASTATING SUCCESS. SLEEK, ATOMOTORED SNORKEL SPECIALS, HAVE LAUNCHED GUIDED-MISSILE ATTACKS ON U.N. BASES IN ENGLAND AND FRANCE. EVERY ATTEMPT BY SEA AND AIR TO DESTROY THE SNORKEL'S BALTIC BASES HAVE BEEN UNSUCCESSFUL, SO FAR... NOW, IN THE MAIN RED BASE...
DEVILS OF THE DEEP
TOO MANY CLOSE CALLS FOR ME ON THIS LAST RAID, COMRADE! THAT ONE FLEET OF U.N. SUB-CHASERS IN THE NORTH SEA ALMOST TRAPPED US!
YES, BUT WE ARE COMPLETELY SAFE HERE IN OUR MIGHTY BASE! OUR STUPID ENEMIES HAVE GIVEN UP TRYING TO BLAST US OUT OF HERE!
BUT THE STUBBORN FOOLS NEVER GIVE UP! I'M SURPRISED THEY HAVEN'T TRIED TO GET IN HERE WITH ONE OF THEIR UNDERSEA RAIDERS!
PAH! HOW CAN THEY? ALL OUTER APPROACHES ARE HEAVILY PATROLLED AND THE ENTRANCE TO THE BASE ITSELF IS HONEYCOMBED WITH MINES!
AT THAT MOMENT, A FEW MILES OUT, A RED SUB-CHASER FIRES ITS "HEDGEHOGS"...
WE'VE BLASTED THIS WHOLE AREA, LIEUTENANT MYRSIK, SINCE OUR SONAR EQUIPMENT PICKED UP WARNINGS OF UNDERSEA CRAFT! THEY'RE FINISHED!
DA! NO ONE CAN ENTER THESE HEAVILY PROTECTED WATERS!

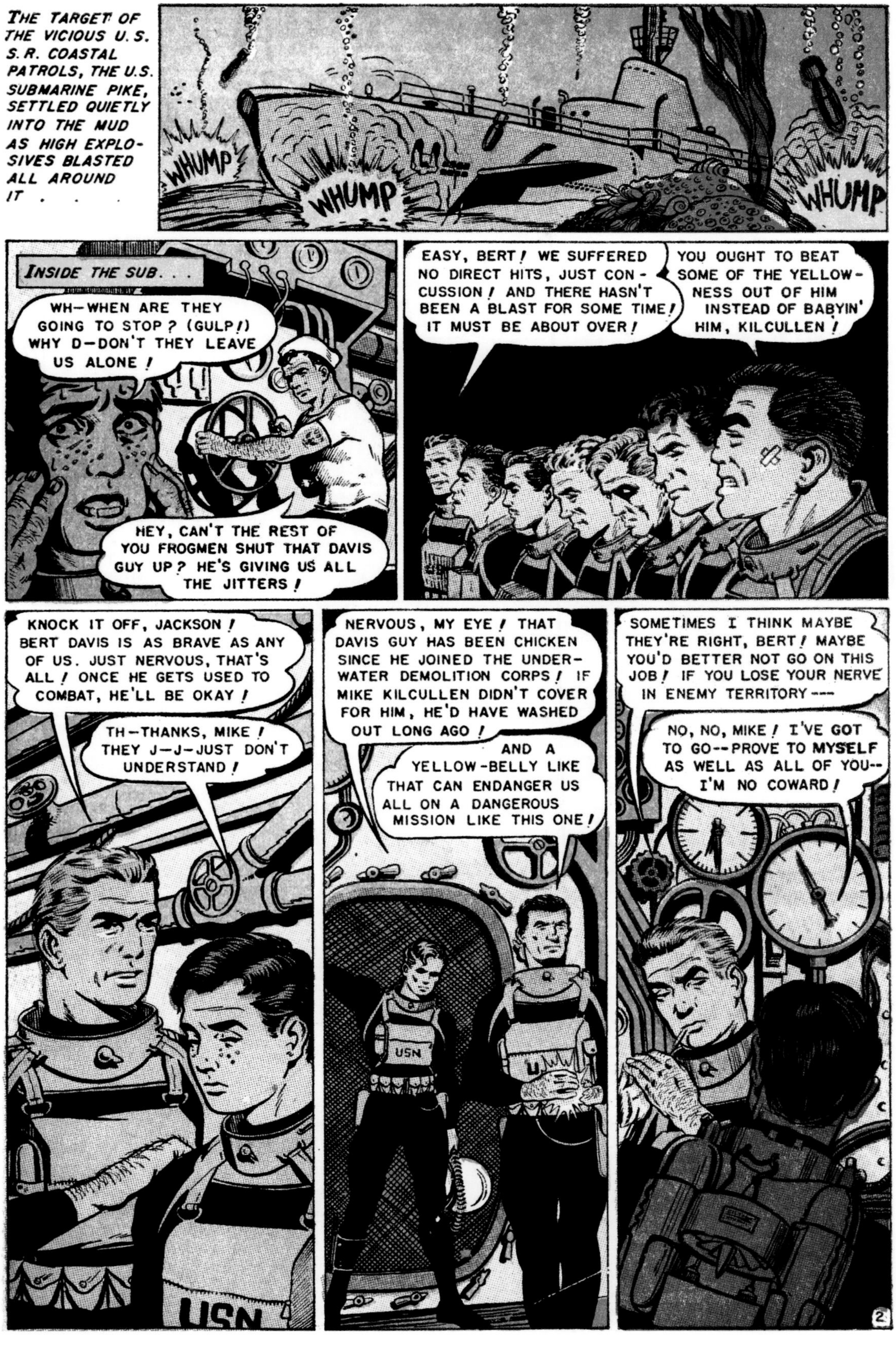
THE TARGET OF THE VICIOUS U.S.S.R. COASTAL PATROLS, THE U.S. SUBMARINE PIKE, SETTLED QUIETLY INTO THE MUD AS HIGH EXPLOSIVES BLASTED ALL AROUND IT . . .
WHUMP
WHUMP
WHUMP
INSIDE THE SUB...
WH-WHEN ARE THEY GOING TO STOP? (GULP!) WHY D-DON'T THEY LEAVE US ALONE!
HEY, CAN'T THE REST OF YOU FROGMEN SHUT THAT DAVIS GUY UP? HE'S GIVING US ALL THE JITTERS!
EASY, BERT! WE SUFFERED NO DIRECT HITS, JUST CONCUSSION! AND THERE HASN'T BEEN A BLAST FOR SOME TIME! IT MUST BE ABOUT OVER!
YOU OUGHT TO BEAT SOME OF THE YELLOWNESS OUT OF HIM INSTEAD OF BABYIN' HIM, KILCULLEN!
KNOCK IT OFF, JACKSON! BERT DAVIS IS AS BRAVE AS ANY OF US. JUST NERVOUS, THAT'S ALL! ONCE HE GETS USED TO COMBAT, HE'LL BE OKAY!
TH-THANKS, MIKE! THEY J-J-JUST DON'T UNDERSTAND!
USN
NERVOUS, MY EYE! THAT DAVIS GUY HAS BEEN CHICKEN SINCE HE JOINED THE UNDERWATER DEMOLITION CORPS! IF MIKE KILCULLEN DIDN'T COVER FOR HIM, HE'D HAVE WASHED OUT LONG AGO!
AND A YELLOW-BELLY LIKE THAT CAN ENDANGER US ALL ON A DANGEROUS MISSION LIKE THIS ONE!
USN
SOMETIMES I THINK MAYBE THEY'RE RIGHT, BERT! MAYBE YOU'D BETTER NOT GO ON THIS JOB! IF YOU LOSE YOUR NERVE IN ENEMY TERRITORY---
NO, NO, MIKE! I'VE GOT TO GO--PROVE TO MYSELF AS WELL AS ALL OF YOU--I'M NO COWARD!
2

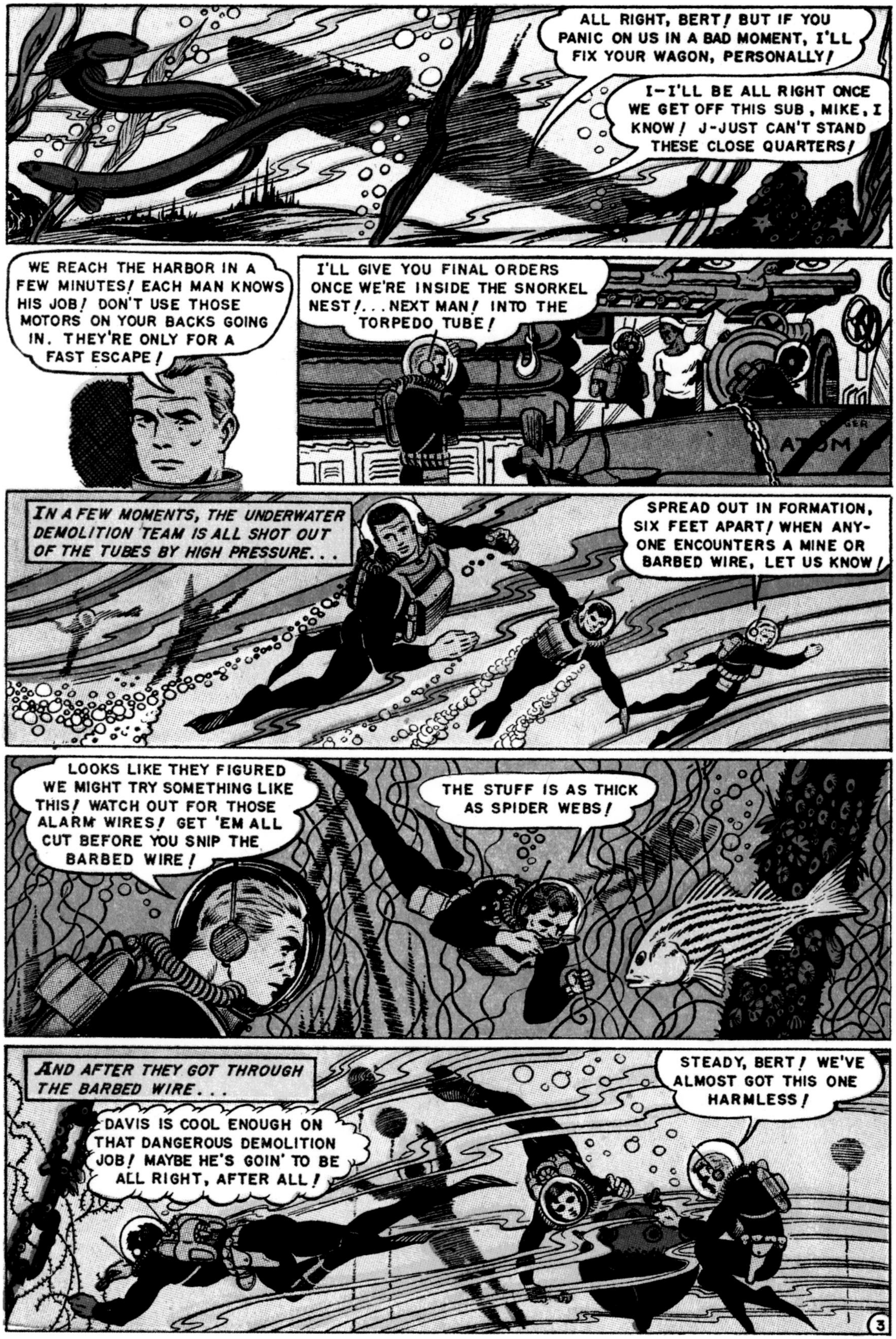
ALL RIGHT, BERT! BUT IF YOU PANIC ON US IN A BAD MOMENT, I'LL FIX YOUR WAGON, PERSONALLY!
I-I'LL BE ALL RIGHT ONCE WE GET OFF THIS SUB, MIKE, I KNOW! J-JUST CAN'T STAND THESE CLOSE QUARTERS!
WE REACH THE HARBOR IN A FEW MINUTES! EACH MAN KNOWS HIS JOB! DON'T USE THOSE MOTORS ON YOUR BACKS GOING IN. THEY'RE ONLY FOR A FAST ESCAPE!
I'LL GIVE YOU FINAL ORDERS ONCE WE'RE INSIDE THE SNORKEL NEST!... NEXT MAN! INTO THE TORPEDO TUBE!
IN A FEW MOMENTS, THE UNDERWATER DEMOLITION TEAM IS ALL SHOT OUT OF THE TUBES BY HIGH PRESSURE...
SPREAD OUT IN FORMATION, SIX FEET APART! WHEN ANYONE ENCOUNTERS A MINE OR BARBED WIRE, LET US KNOW!
LOOKS LIKE THEY FIGURED WE MIGHT TRY SOMETHING LIKE THIS! WATCH OUT FOR THOSE ALARM WIRES! GET 'EM ALL CUT BEFORE YOU SNIP THE BARBED WIRE!
THE STUFF IS AS THICK AS SPIDER WEBS!
AND AFTER THEY GOT THROUGH THE BARBED WIRE...
STEADY, BERT! WE'VE ALMOST GOT THIS ONE HARMLESS!
DAVIS IS COOL ENOUGH ON THAT DANGEROUS DEMOLITION JOB! MAYBE HE'S GOIN' TO BE ALL RIGHT, AFTER ALL!
3

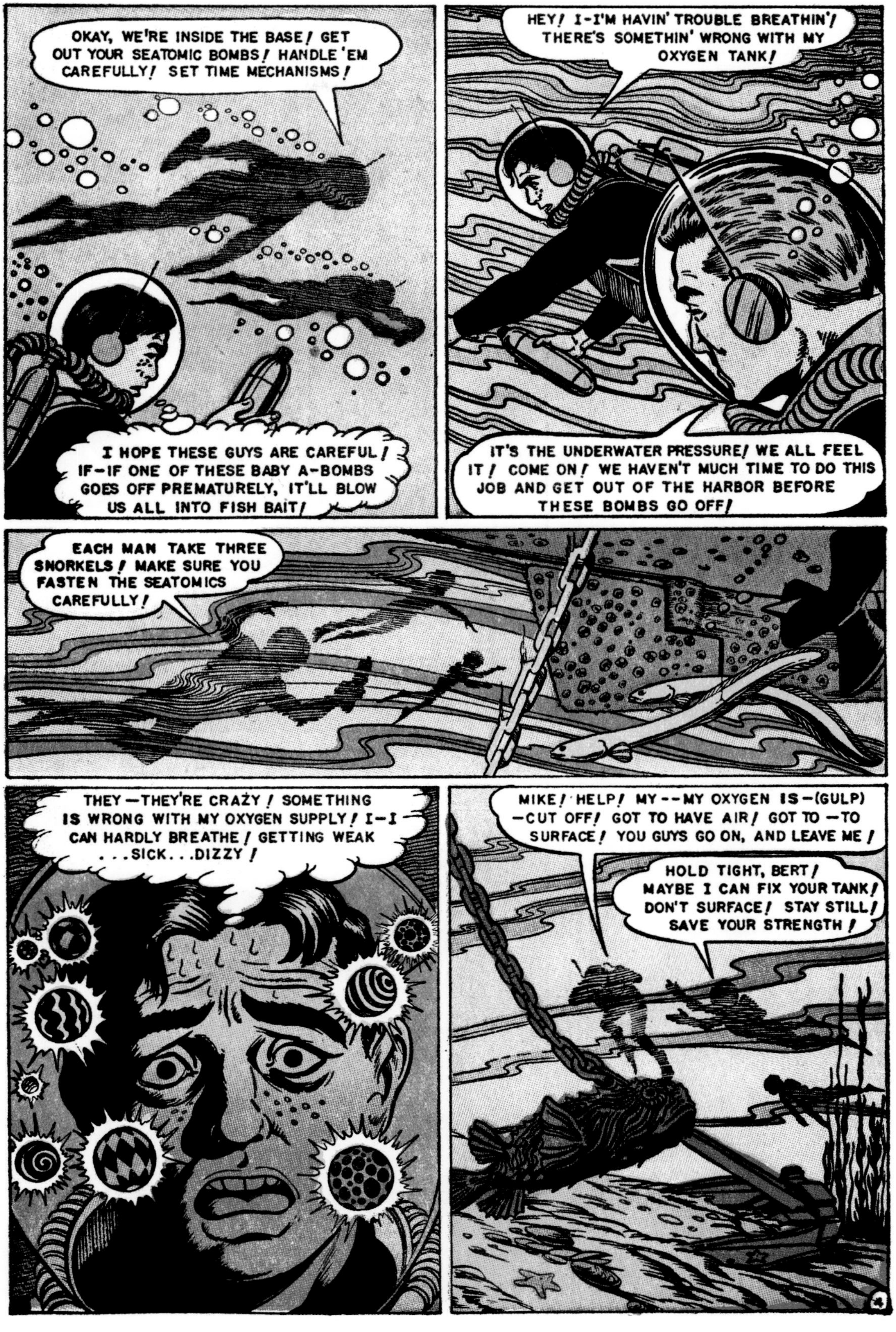
OKAY, WE'RE INSIDE THE BASE! GET OUT YOUR SEATOMIC BOMBS! HANDLE 'EM CAREFULLY! SET TIME MECHANISMS!
I HOPE THESE GUYS ARE CAREFUL! IF—IF ONE OF THESE BABY A-BOMBS GOES OFF PREMATURELY, IT'LL BLOW US ALL INTO FISH BAIT!
HEY! I-I'M HAVIN' TROUBLE BREATHIN'! THERE'S SOMETHIN' WRONG WITH MY OXYGEN TANK!
IT'S THE UNDERWATER PRESSURE! WE ALL FEEL IT! COME ON! WE HAVEN'T MUCH TIME TO DO THIS JOB AND GET OUT OF THE HARBOR BEFORE THESE BOMBS GO OFF!
EACH MAN TAKE THREE SNORKELS! MAKE SURE YOU FASTEN THE SEATOMICS CAREFULLY!
THEY—THEY'RE CRAZY! SOMETHING IS WRONG WITH MY OXYGEN SUPPLY! I-I CAN HARDLY BREATHE! GETTING WEAK ...SICK...DIZZY!
MIKE! HELP! MY--MY OXYGEN IS—(GULP) —CUT OFF! GOT TO HAVE AIR! GOT TO —TO SURFACE! YOU GUYS GO ON, AND LEAVE ME!
HOLD TIGHT, BERT! MAYBE I CAN FIX YOUR TANK! DON'T SURFACE! STAY STILL! SAVE YOUR STRENGTH!
4

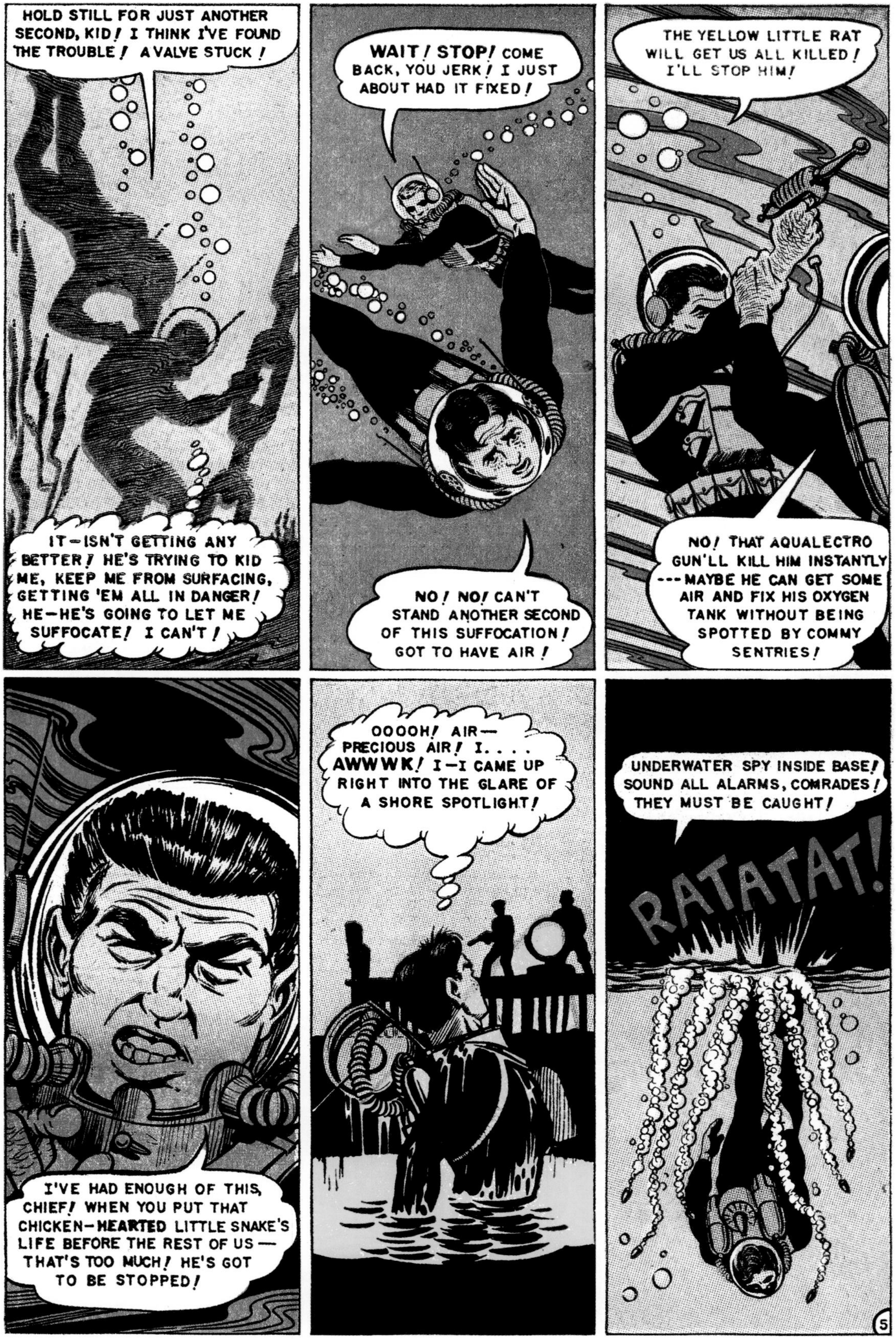
HOLD STILL FOR JUST ANOTHER SECOND, KID! I THINK I'VE FOUND THE TROUBLE! A VALVE STUCK!
IT—ISN'T GETTING ANY BETTER! HE'S TRYING TO KID ME, KEEP ME FROM SURFACING, GETTING 'EM ALL IN DANGER! HE—HE'S GOING TO LET ME SUFFOCATE! I CAN'T!
WAIT! STOP! COME BACK, YOU JERK! I JUST ABOUT HAD IT FIXED!
NO! NO! CAN'T STAND ANOTHER SECOND OF THIS SUFFOCATION! GOT TO HAVE AIR!
THE YELLOW LITTLE RAT WILL GET US ALL KILLED! I'LL STOP HIM!
NO! THAT AQUALECTRO GUN'LL KILL HIM INSTANTLY---MAYBE HE CAN GET SOME AIR AND FIX HIS OXYGEN TANK WITHOUT BEING SPOTTED BY COMMY SENTRIES!
I'VE HAD ENOUGH OF THIS, CHIEF! WHEN YOU PUT THAT CHICKEN-HEARTED LITTLE SNAKE'S LIFE BEFORE THE REST OF US— THAT'S TOO MUCH! HE'S GOT TO BE STOPPED!
OOOOH! AIR— PRECIOUS AIR! I. . . . AWWWK! I—I CAME UP RIGHT INTO THE GLARE OF A SHORE SPOTLIGHT!
UNDERWATER SPY INSIDE BASE! SOUND ALL ALARMS, COMRADES! THEY MUST BE CAUGHT!
RATATAT!
5

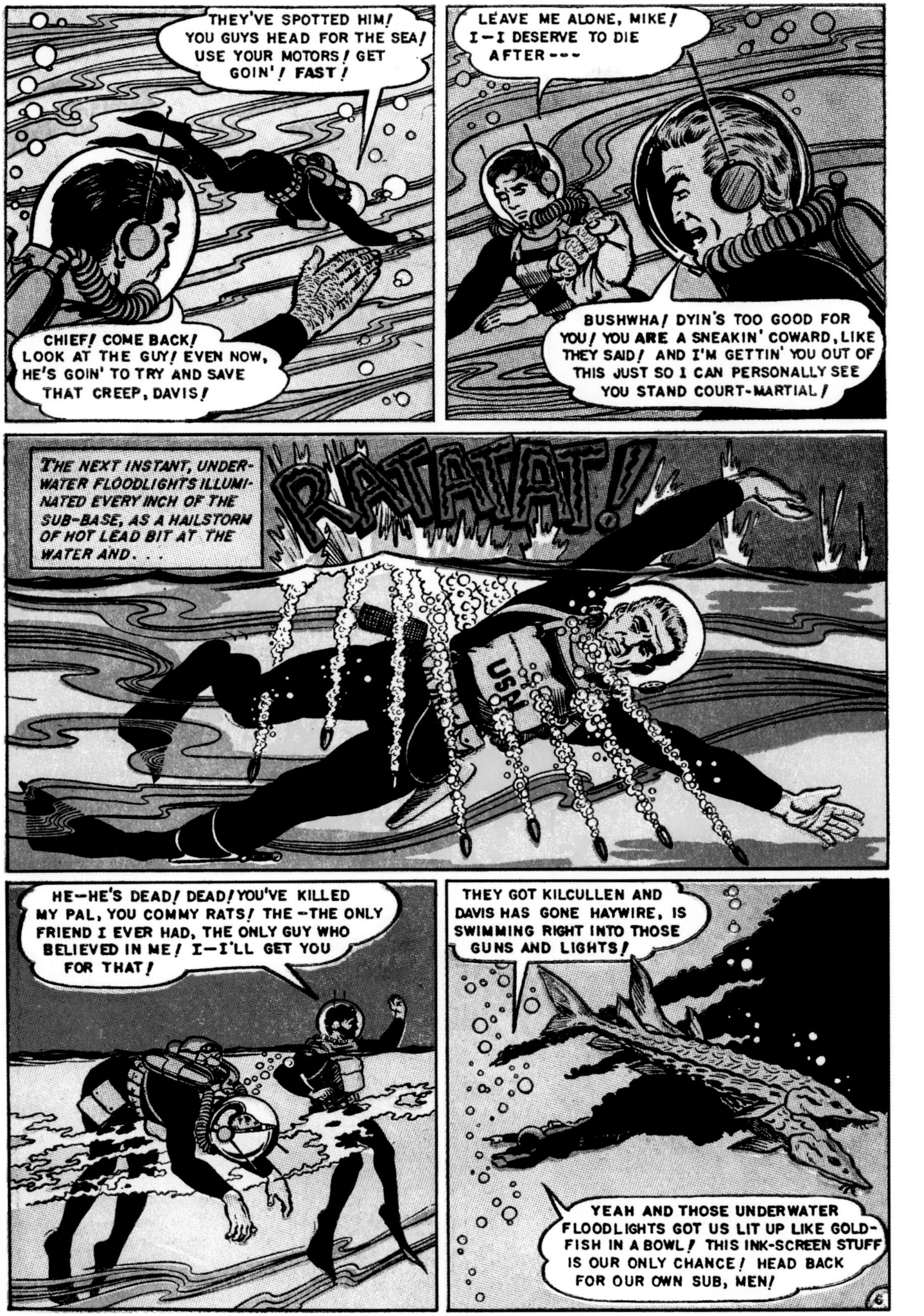
THEY'VE SPOTTED HIM! YOU GUYS HEAD FOR THE SEA! USE YOUR MOTORS! GET GOIN'! FAST!
CHIEF! COME BACK! LOOK AT THE GUY! EVEN NOW, HE'S GOIN' TO TRY AND SAVE THAT CREEP, DAVIS!
LEAVE ME ALONE, MIKE! I—I DESERVE TO DIE AFTER---
BUSHWHA! DYIN'S TOO GOOD FOR YOU! YOU ARE A SNEAKIN' COWARD, LIKE THEY SAID! AND I'M GETTIN' YOU OUT OF THIS JUST SO I CAN PERSONALLY SEE YOU STAND COURT-MARTIAL!
THE NEXT INSTANT, UNDERWATER FLOODLIGHTS ILLUMINATED EVERY INCH OF THE SUB-BASE, AS A HAILSTORM OF HOT LEAD BIT AT THE WATER AND...
RATATAT!
USN
HE—HE'S DEAD! DEAD! YOU'VE KILLED MY PAL, YOU COMMY RATS! THE—THE ONLY FRIEND I EVER HAD, THE ONLY GUY WHO BELIEVED IN ME! I—I'LL GET YOU FOR THAT!
THEY GOT KILCULLEN AND DAVIS HAS GONE HAYWIRE, IS SWIMMING RIGHT INTO THOSE GUNS AND LIGHTS!
YEAH AND THOSE UNDERWATER FLOODLIGHTS GOT US LIT UP LIKE GOLDFISH IN A BOWL! THIS INK-SCREEN STUFF IS OUR ONLY CHANCE! HEAD BACK FOR OUR OWN SUB, MEN!

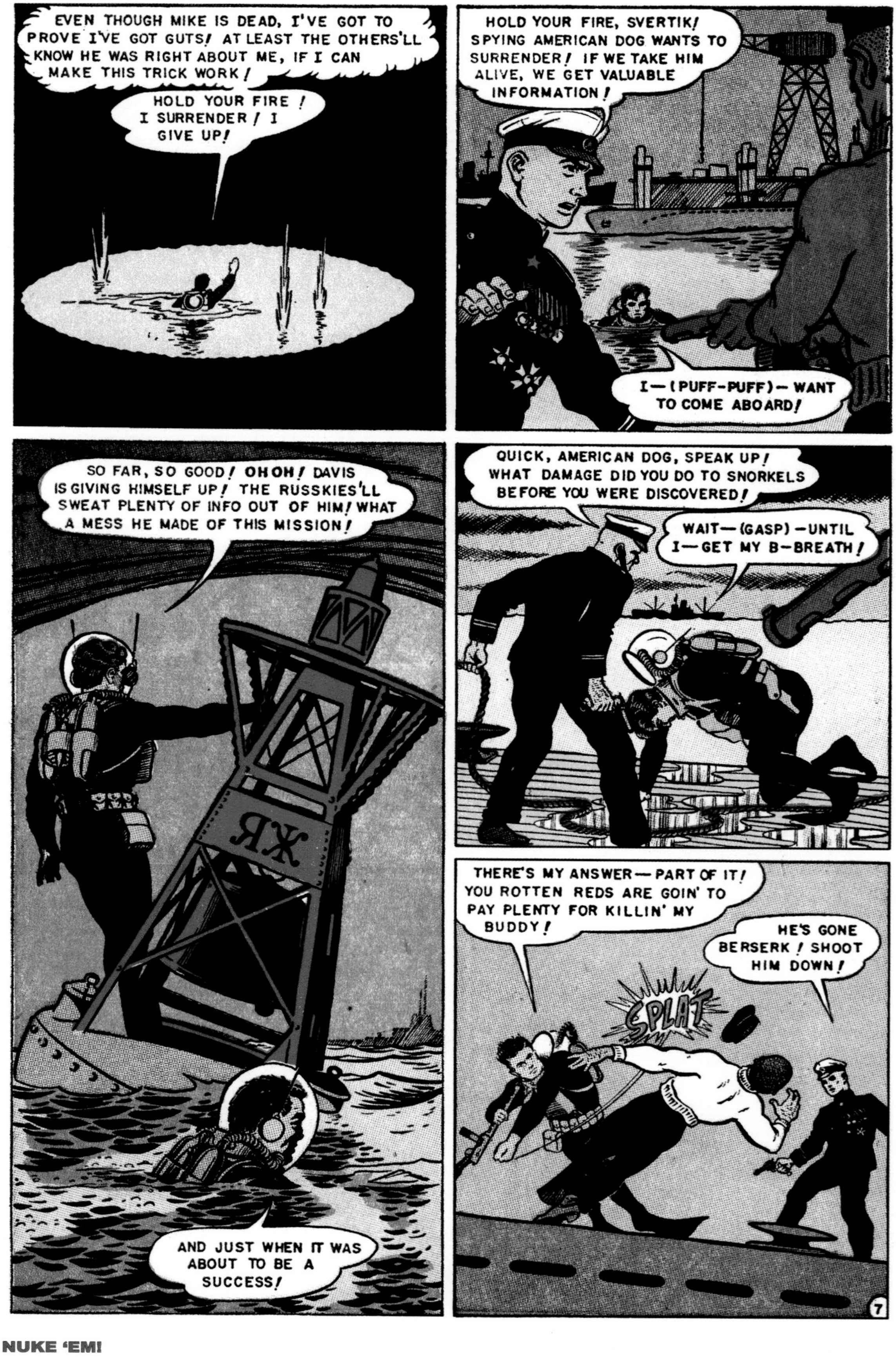
EVEN THOUGH MIKE IS DEAD, I'VE GOT TO PROVE I'VE GOT GUTS! AT LEAST THE OTHERS'LL KNOW HE WAS RIGHT ABOUT ME, IF I CAN MAKE THIS TRICK WORK!
HOLD YOUR FIRE! I SURRENDER! I GIVE UP!
HOLD YOUR FIRE, SVERTIK! SPYING AMERICAN DOG WANTS TO SURRENDER! IF WE TAKE HIM ALIVE, WE GET VALUABLE INFORMATION!
I—(PUFF-PUFF)—WANT TO COME ABOARD!
SO FAR, SO GOOD! OHOH! DAVIS IS GIVING HIMSELF UP! THE RUSSKIES'LL SWEAT PLENTY OF INFO OUT OF HIM! WHAT A MESS HE MADE OF THIS MISSION!
ЯЖ
AND JUST WHEN IT WAS ABOUT TO BE A SUCCESS!
QUICK, AMERICAN DOG, SPEAK UP! WHAT DAMAGE DID YOU DO TO SNORKELS BEFORE YOU WERE DISCOVERED!
WAIT—(GASP)—UNTIL I—GET MY B-BREATH!
THERE'S MY ANSWER—PART OF IT! YOU ROTTEN REDS ARE GOIN' TO PAY PLENTY FOR KILLIN' MY BUDDY!
HE'S GONE BERSERK! SHOOT HIM DOWN!
SPLAT
7

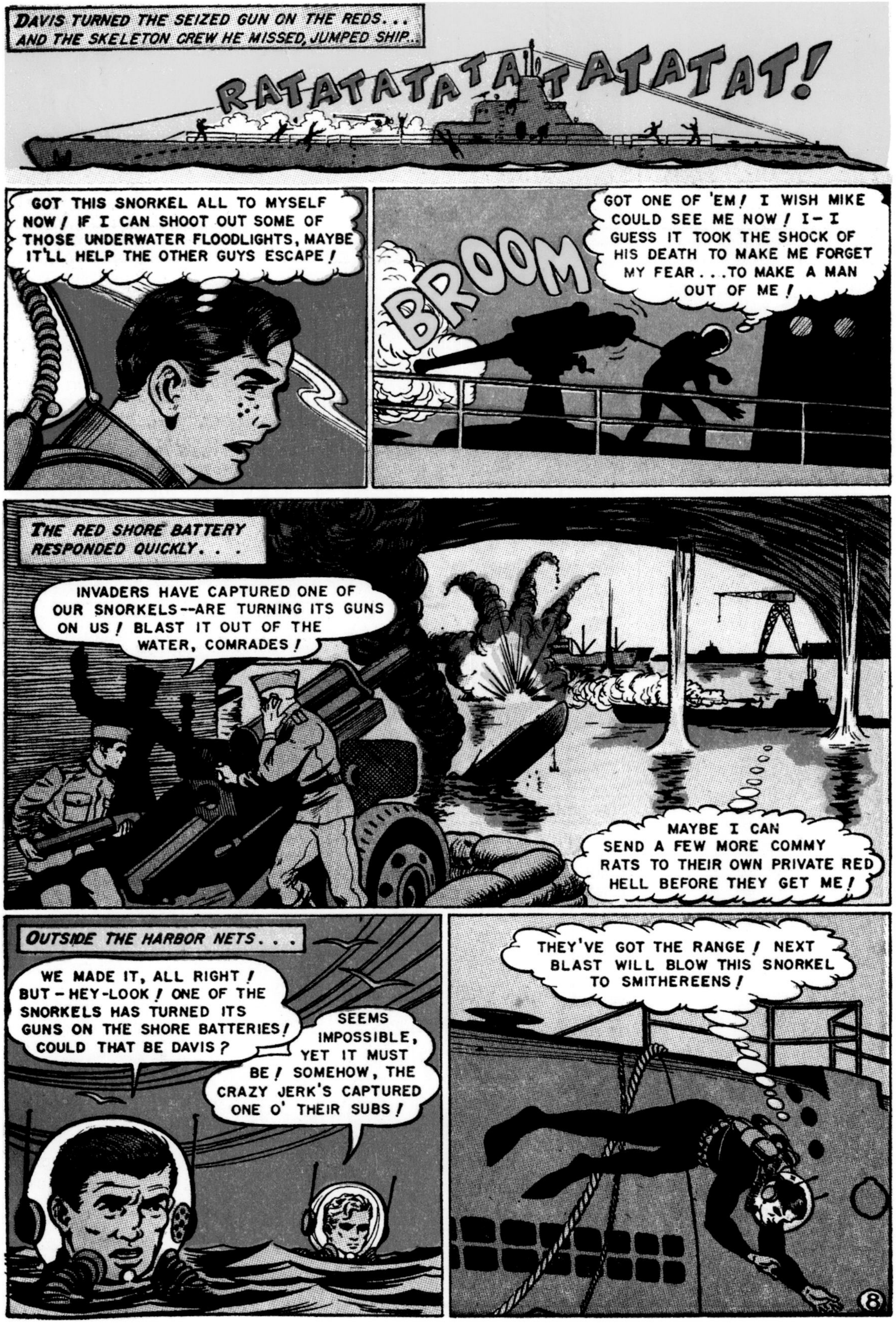

DAVIS TURNED THE SEIZED GUN ON THE REDS... AND THE SKELETON CREW HE MISSED, JUMPED SHIP..
RATATATATATATATAT!
GOT THIS SNORKEL ALL TO MYSELF NOW! IF I CAN SHOOT OUT SOME OF THOSE UNDERWATER FLOODLIGHTS, MAYBE IT'LL HELP THE OTHER GUYS ESCAPE!
GOT ONE OF 'EM! I WISH MIKE COULD SEE ME NOW! I-I GUESS IT TOOK THE SHOCK OF HIS DEATH TO MAKE ME FORGET MY FEAR...TO MAKE A MAN OUT OF ME!
BROOM
THE RED SHORE BATTERY RESPONDED QUICKLY. . .
INVADERS HAVE CAPTURED ONE OF OUR SNORKELS--ARE TURNING ITS GUNS ON US! BLAST IT OUT OF THE WATER, COMRADES!
MAYBE I CAN SEND A FEW MORE COMMY RATS TO THEIR OWN PRIVATE RED HELL BEFORE THEY GET ME!
OUTSIDE THE HARBOR NETS. . .
WE MADE IT, ALL RIGHT! BUT-HEY-LOOK! ONE OF THE SNORKELS HAS TURNED ITS GUNS ON THE SHORE BATTERIES! COULD THAT BE DAVIS?
SEEMS IMPOSSIBLE, YET IT MUST BE! SOMEHOW, THE CRAZY JERK'S CAPTURED ONE O' THEIR SUBS!
THEY'VE GOT THE RANGE! NEXT BLAST WILL BLOW THIS SNORKEL TO SMITHEREENS!
8

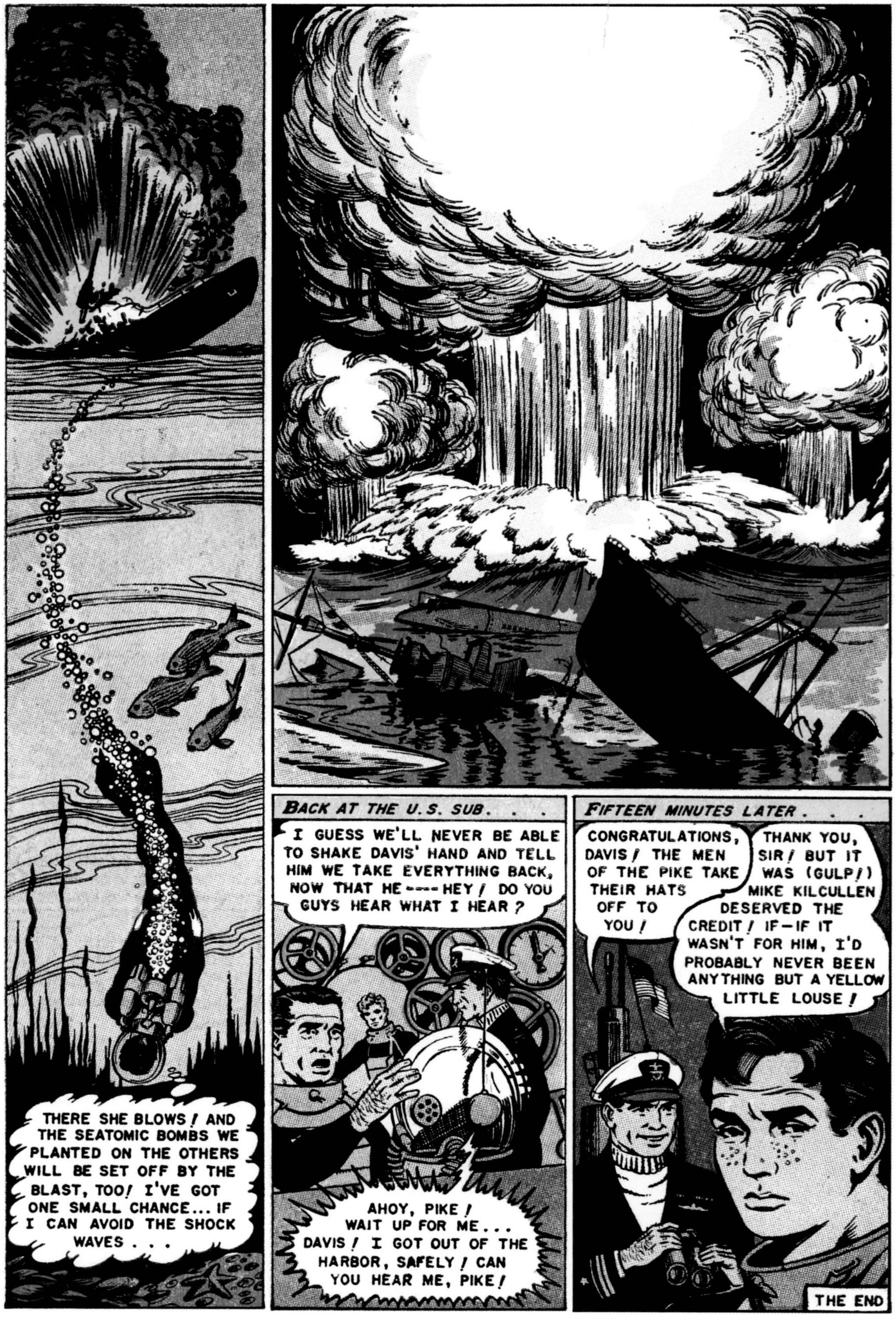
THERE SHE BLOWS! AND THE SEATOMIC BOMBS WE PLANTED ON THE OTHERS WILL BE SET OFF BY THE BLAST, TOO! I'VE GOT ONE SMALL CHANCE... IF I CAN AVOID THE SHOCK WAVES . . .
BACK AT THE U.S. SUB. . .
I GUESS WE'LL NEVER BE ABLE TO SHAKE DAVIS' HAND AND TELL HIM WE TAKE EVERYTHING BACK, NOW THAT HE---- HEY! DO YOU GUYS HEAR WHAT I HEAR?
AHOY, PIKE! WAIT UP FOR ME... DAVIS! I GOT OUT OF THE HARBOR, SAFELY! CAN YOU HEAR ME, PIKE!
FIFTEEN MINUTES LATER . . .
CONGRATULATIONS, DAVIS! THE MEN OF THE PIKE TAKE THEIR HATS OFF TO YOU!
THANK YOU, SIR! BUT IT WAS (GULP!) MIKE KILCULLEN DESERVED THE CREDIT! IF—IF IT WASN'T FOR HIM, I'D PROBABLY NEVER BEEN ANYTHING BUT A YELLOW LITTLE LOUSE!
THE END